Using Your *Texas Write Source* Book

Your *Texas Write Source* book is loaded with information to help you learn about writing. One section that will be especially helpful is the "Proofreader's Guide" at the back of the book. This section covers all of the rules for language and grammar.

The book also includes three main units covering the types of writing that you may have to complete on district or state writing tests. At the end of each unit, there are samples and tips for writing in science, social studies, and math.

The *Texas Write Source* book will help you with other learning skills, too—test taking, note taking, listening, and speaking. This help makes the *Texas Write Source* book a valuable writing and learning guide in all of your classes.

Your *Texas Write Source* guides . . .

With practice, you will be able to use the guides explained below to quickly find information in this book.

The **CONTENTS** lists the major sections of the book and the chapters found in these sections.

The **INDEX** (starting on page 793) lists the topics covered in the book in alphabetical order. Use the index when you are interested in a specific topic.

The **COLOR CODING** used for "Basic Grammar and Writing," "A Writer's Resource," and the "Proofreader's Guide" make these important sections easy to find.

The **SPECIAL PAGE REFERENCES** in the book tell you where to turn for additional information about a specific topic.

If at first you're not sure how to find something in the *Texas Write Source* book, ask your teacher for help. With a little practice, you will find everything quickly and easily.

TEXAS
WRITE
SOURCE

Authors
Dave Kemper, Patrick Sebranek, and Verne Meyer

Consulting Author
Gretchen Bernabei

Illustrator
Chris Krenzke

GREAT
SOURCE®

HOUGHTON MIFFLIN HARCOURT

TEXAS
WRITE
SOURCE
Online

www.hmheducation.com/tx/writesource

Copyright © 2012 by Houghton Mifflin Harcourt Publishing Company

Printed in the U.S.A.

ISBN-13 978-0-547-39478-7

1 2 3 4 5 6 7 8 9 10 0914 19 18 17 16 15 14 13 12 11 10

Quick Guide

Texts Write Source

Texas Write Source

The Forms of Writing

DESCRIPTIVE WRITING

NARRATIVE WRITING

EXPOSITORY WRITING

PERSUASIVE WRITING

RESPONDING TO TEXTS

CREATIVE WRITING

RESEARCH WRITING

The Tools of Language

process
forms
SPEAK resource
proofreader's guide
xiii

Contents

Basic Grammar and Writing

WORKING WITH WORDS

BUILDING EFFECTIVE SENTENCES

CONSTRUCTING STRONG PARAGRAPHS

A Writer's Resource

Proofreader's Guide

Why Write?

This story by a middle school student will help answer this question.

Mr. Gibson made Randy my lab partner. I thought, "Great! I have to work with one of the biggest goof-offs in school."

One day my "partner" was absent. Mr. Gibson said that Randy and his older brother were beekeepers, and they were getting in a new shipment of bees. Randy, a beekeeper? I couldn't believe it.

That night I wrote about Randy in my journal. The more that I wrote, the more I began to understand him. He may not have liked school very much, but he still was learning a lot. He just did some of it in his own way.

Writing will do that. It can help you understand the people and the experiences in your life. What could be more important than that?

Maybe that's why you should write!

What's Ahead

- Reasons to Write
- Starting Points for Writing

Reasons to Write

Good things will happen if you write for the four reasons listed below. You will learn a lot about yourself and become a better writer.

1. To Explore Your Life

Writing in a personal journal helps you learn about yourself. All you have to do is set aside 10 or 15 minutes every day and write about people, places, and events in your life.

 Writing in a personal journal is great practice. You might already set aside time to practice a musical instrument or an athletic skill. Do the same with your writing.

2. To Understand New Ideas

Writing in a learning log helps you become a better student. In a learning log, you write about new ideas presented in your classes and in your reading assignments. Think of a learning log as your all-purpose study helper.

3. To Show Learning

Your teachers assign paragraphs, essays, and reports to see how well you are learning. To do well on these assignments, you must (1) understand the subjects you are studying and (2) use your best writing skills.

4. To Share Ideas

Write personal narratives (true stories), made-up stories, and poems. These genres of writing are meant to be shared with your classmates.

 Write to explore. Write nonstop for 5 to 8 minutes about something that happened to you yesterday or today. Write for the entire time. If you get stuck, write "I'm stuck" until something comes to mind. When you finish, you will have written a lot and learned something about yourself. Congratulations!

Starting Points for Writing

If you want to write, but you can't think of a good topic, review the ideas listed on this page. You're sure to find plenty of good starting points. (See pages **592–595** for more topics.)

Sample Topics

Describing   *(telling what a topic looks like, sounds like, and so on)*

People: a neighbor, a friend, someone you wish you were like, a movie character

Places: an attic, an alley, the gym, a river, a church, a hideaway

Objects or things: a poster, a photograph, a stuffed animal, a hat

Narrating   *(telling about something that happened)*

having a great day, making a mistake, showing friendship, moving, learning to _____ , getting hurt, doing something funny, learning a lesson

Explaining   *(sharing information)*

How to . . . make your favorite food, make a friend, earn extra money, play a game, dress in style, fix something, clean a bedroom

The causes of . . . thunderstorms, earthquakes, erosion, the flu, baldness

Kinds of . . . music, friends, heroes, exercise, snack foods, diets, TV shows

Definition of . . . courage, faith, school, teamwork, love

Persuading   *(expressing your opinion about a topic)*

dieting, dress codes, bicycle helmets, security officers in schools, curfews, recycling programs, movie or music reviews

Find a topic. Write "Starting Points for Writing" at the top of a piece of paper. Then list these headings—Describing, Narrating, Explaining, and Persuading—down the left-hand margin. Leave space between each heading. Write two new writing ideas under each heading. Add other ideas throughout the school year.

publish
draft
EDIT

ELPS 2C, 2G, 2H, 2I, 3E, 4G

The Writing Process

Writing Focus

Learning Language

Work with a partner. Read the meanings and share answers to the questions.

1. To assess something is to determine its quality or value.
   Assess a popular song that is familiar to you.

2. A logical plan is orderly and makes sense.
   What is a logical way for you to get to school?

3. A peer is someone equal to you in age or grade.
   Name a peer in your classroom.

prewrite.
revise

Understanding the Writing Process

You may already know about the writing process from experience. Just think of your best stories, reports, and essays. You probably worked very hard on each one, making many changes from one draft to the next. To do your best work, you must take your writing through a series of steps before sharing it. That is why writing is called a *process*.

The writing process is the key to unlocking your true writing potential. By taking a little time at each step along the way, you can become a stronger writer. You'll be amazed at the doors that writing can open for you.

This chapter will help you understand the writing process and build good writing habits along the way.

What's Ahead

- **Developing Good Writing Habits**
- **The Writing Process**
- **The Process in Action**
- **Getting the Big Picture**

ELPS 2G, 2H, 2I, 3E, 3G, 3H

Developing Good Writing Habits

To become a good writer, you must act like one. Following the tips listed on this page will help you do that.

Make reading part of your life.

Read lots of books, magazines, and newspapers. This will help you acquire an ear for good writing.

> Reading is to the mind what exercise is to the body.
>
> —Sir Richard Steele

Make writing part of your life.

Write as often as you can. Write early in the morning, late at night, or anytime in between. Just keep writing!

> Writing is not apart from living. Writing is a kind of double living.
>
> —Catherine Drinker Bowen

Write about topics that are important to you.

It's important for you to write about things you're interested in. Otherwise, it's like going out for softball when your favorite sport is track.

> When I speak to students about writing, I tell them to write about what they know.
>
> —Robert Cormier

 Write about a quotation. Write nonstop for 3–5 minutes about one of the quotations on this page. Discuss your thoughts with your partner.

The Writing Process

Experienced writers use the writing process to help them do their best work. The steps in the process are described below.

The Steps in the Writing Process

Prewriting At the start of an assignment, a writer explores possible topics. The writer also thinks about the purpose and audience, and decides on a genre. Then the writer collects details about the topic and plans how to use them when writing.

Drafting During this step, a writer completes a first draft, using the plan as a guide. This draft is a writer's *first* chance to get everything down on paper.

Revising After reviewing the draft, a writer changes any ideas that are not clear or complete. The writer also rethinks questions of purpose, audience, and genre. A wise writer will ask at least one other person to review the draft, as well.

Editing A writer then checks his or her revised writing for correctness before preparing a neat final copy. The writer proofreads the final copy for errors before sharing or publishing it.

Publishing This is the final step in the writing process. Publishing is to a writer what an exhibit is to an artist— an opportunity to share his or her work with others.

Assess your process. On your own paper, explain the process you used to complete your best piece of writing—what you did first, second, third, and so on. How similar was your process to the one described above?

 TEKS 6.14A, 6.14B, 6.14C

The Process in Action

The next two pages show you the writing process in action. Use this information as a general guide for each of your writing assignments.

Prewriting Selecting a Topic

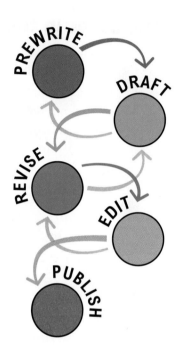

- Think about the writing assignment: What is your purpose (to share, to inform, to persuade, to entertain)? Who is your audience? What genre of writing should you use? These are your questions of purpose, audience, and genre.
- Search for possible writing topics that meet the requirements of the assignment.
- Select a specific topic that really interests you.

Gathering Details

- Learn as much as you can about the topic before you start writing.
- Consider what to emphasize in the writing—either an interesting part of the topic or your personal feelings about it. This will be the focus, or thesis, of your writing.
- Decide which details you want to include in your writing. Also decide on the best strategy to organize the details.

Drafting Developing the First Draft

- Concentrate on getting your ideas on paper, not on being perfect.
- Use the details you collected and your prewriting plan as a general guide but feel free to add points that relate to your main idea.
- Make sure your writing has a beginning, a middle, and an ending.
- Think about your purpose, audience, and genre as you write.

Revising **Improving Your Writing**

- Review your first draft, but only after setting it aside for a while.
- Think about how well you addressed the questions of purpose, audience, and genre.
- Use these questions as a general revising guide:
  - **Are the ideas clear and in the right order?**
  - **Does the beginning draw the reader into the writing?**
  - **Does the ending say something important about the topic?**
  - **Are the sentences varied? Do they read smoothly?**
- Have at least one other person review your work and offer feedback.
- Add, cut, or rewrite parts based on feedback.

Editing **Checking for Conventions**

- Edit for correctness by checking for grammar, mechanics, sentence structure, and spelling errors. Also ask someone else to check your writing for errors.
- Then prepare a neat final copy of your writing. Proofread this copy for errors before sharing it.

Publishing **Sharing Your Writing**

- Share your finished work with your classmates, teacher, friends, and family members.
- Decide whether you will include the writing in your portfolio.
- Consider submitting your writing to your school newspaper or some other publication.

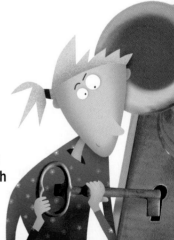

 Consider the steps. On your own paper, list one new thing that you learned on pages 8–9 about each step in the writing process.

Getting the Big Picture

At this point, you may be wondering why writing has to be this involved. "Why can't I just sit down, write, and be done?" Well, you can, but your work won't be as good as it would have been if you had used the writing process.

Writers can't think of everything at once. First, they choose a focus and make a plan for organizing their ideas. Then, they develop those ideas by writing paragraphs and sentences. They use a voice that engages the reader. Last, they correct and sharpen what they have written by looking at conventions, such as sentence structure and spelling. These five qualities of writing are often called the five traits.

- ☐ **Focus and Coherence**

- ☐ **Organization**

- ☐ **Development of** Ideas

- ☐ **Voice**

- ☐ **Conventions**

Focus on the process. Imagine that you will be writing an essay describing a spring day. On your own paper, match each activity on the left to its proper place in the writing process on the right.

___ 1. Edit my writing for correct grammar, mechanics, sentence structure, and spelling.

___ 2. Decide on an audience for my essay.

___ 3. Move paragraphs so ideas are in the right order.

___ 4. Illustrate my description and share it with others.

___ 5. Write a strong beginning, middle, and ending.

A. Prewriting
B. Drafting
C. Revising
D. Editing
E. Publishing

One Writer's Process

Whether you want to tell a funny story, describe a roaring waterfall, or complain about something unfair, you have many things to write about. The challenge is writing down exactly what you want to say. The best way to express yourself is to use the writing process.

This chapter shows you how sixth-grader Reece King used the writing process to tell the story of meeting his closest friend. From the start, it was obvious how meaningful this event was to him. As he moved through the stages of the writing process, his story got better and better.

What's Ahead

- Previewing the Goals
- Prewriting
- Drafting
- Revising
- Editing
- Publishing
- Evaluating and Reflecting on the Final Copy
- Evaluating and Reflecting on Your Writing

★ **ELPS** 2G, 2I, 3D, 3E, 3G, 3H, 4C, 4I, 4K

Previewing the Goals

Before Reece began writing, he looked at the goals for his narrative assignment, which are shown below. These goals helped him get started. He also previewed the rubric for narrative writing on page 130–135.

Goals of Narrative Writing

Focus and Coherence

Make sure your narrative has one main idea and that all your sentences help readers understand that idea.

Organization

Write an engaging beginning. Then present events in the correct order. Check that transitions are used to take readers from one idea to the next.

Development of Ideas

Use details and dialogue to enhance events, people, and places in your narrative. Make sure each sentence leads to the next one.

Voice

Your essay should sound natural and as if only you could have written it. Choose words and details that show your personality.

Conventions

Be sure that your grammar, mechanics (punctuation and capitalization), sentence structure, and spelling are correct.

 To understand the important goals for Reece's assignment, answer the following questions:

1. What types of ideas should he use to tell his story?

2. How should he organize his ideas?

3. How should his narrative sound?

Discuss your answers with a partner. Be sure to share your opinions, ideas, and feelings.

 **TEKS** 6.14A, 6.14B

Prewriting **Selecting a Topic**

Reece was asked to write a personal narrative about meeting a special friend for the first time. He used an organizational strategy called a cluster (or web) to determine which friend to write about. Reece chose to write about meeting his dog, Russet.

Cluster

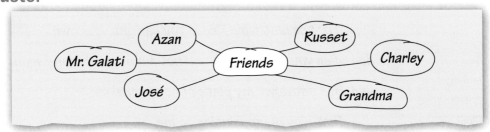

 Have you ever used a cluster? Try one now by clustering the names of your own friends. Could you write a story about a first meeting with one of the friends that you identified?

Gathering and Organizing Details

Reece used a time chart to order the events he wants to cover in his narrative. He lists ideas for each event. He builds on those ideas and adds details that clearly relate to the focus of his essay.

Time Chart

First ➡	Next ➡	Last
Mom said, "No pets until you're 12 years old." My Birthday. Waiting outside the animal shelter. Excited. Knew just what my dog would be like.	Looked for a golden retriever. Saw white terrier. Snarled. Old basset hound. Lots of mutts. Lots of barking. Didn't see what I was looking for!	Headache from all the barking. I tell Mom "HE'S NOT HERE!" I can see Russet in my mind. Then I saw him! His eyes were right! My dog at last.

 Have you ever used a time chart or time line to gather details? (See page **596**.) Use a graphic organizer to gather as many details as possible about a first meeting with one of your friends.

Drafting **Developing Your First Draft**

Reece sat down to write his story. He used the ideas he had gathered and organized in his chart. His head was full of thoughts, and he wanted to get them all down on paper. (There are errors in Reece's first draft.)

The introduction presents the main idea.

"For the last time Reece you can get your own dog when you turn twelve, and not a moment before" mom said. She set down my plate of hot pancakes.

That was disappointing to me.

A week later, my moment arrived. In exactly thirty seconds, the animal shelter would open.

Details create a clear picture.

"I hope they have the one I want," I said. I even knew his name: Russet. I had imagined the perfect dog. He'd be a retreiver puppy with a tale that wouldn't quit wagging. He'd be standing up at the gate of his cage, yipping. We'd know we were meant for each other. "Come on its a minute past!"

"Reece!"

Dialogue moves the story forward.

The door was unlocked by a nice lady who came up to the other side of the door. I waited, and then I opened the door. I said "Good morning. We need a dog."

She said, "Why don't you go have a look."

PROCESS

Time order is used to organize events.

"Thanks!" I moved around the lady. I went to the door. The room beyond had cages. The moment my foot hit the cement, barking filled the air. There must have been thirty dogs in there. But which one was Russet?

The first dog was little. His cage was on the left. He growled at me. "I don't want you, either," I said and moved on. Next was a cute mutt. I kept going. Another dog and another, but where was my retriever?

I wandered the whole place twice. There wasn't a single retriever. I couldn't believe it. Maybe I missed it. After all, a puppy would be pretty small. While the dogs yapped, I searched their eyes. None of them was right.

Words sound natural and real.

"Have you decided?" Mom asked.

"He's not here, Mom!" I said. "I can't believe it. After all this waiting." Then I saw him! His outside was wrong, but his eyes were right. . . .

 On page 13, Reece used a time chart to plan what he would say first, next, and last. Does his first draft follow his plan? Does he add any new details or leave any out? Explain to a partner.

TEKS 6.19A(vii)
ELPS 2C, 2G, 2H, 2I, 3D, 3E, 3G, 4G, 4C, 4G, 4I, 4K

Revising **Focusing on the Big Picture**

After Reece finished his first draft, he looked again at the goals on page 12 and used them as a revising guide. His thoughts tell you what changes he plans to make.

Focus and Coherence

Make sure your narrative has one main idea and that all your sentences help readers understand that idea.

"My overall focus is good, but I included some sentences that don't help to tell the story. I'll delete those sentences."

Organization

Organize the story so that one event leads to another. Transitional words and phrases can help move the story forward.

"I want my writing to flow smoothly. Adding transitional phrases before some sentences will help."

 Team up with a partner to reread and review Reece's first draft. Write down at least two things that you like about the draft and one or two things that could be improved. Discuss your ideas with a partner.

TEKS 6.14C
ELPS 2C, 2G, 3E, 3D, 2I,
4C, 4I, 4G, 4K

Reviewing Reece's First Revision

After Reece reviewed his first draft, he made the following revisions, or changes.

PROCESS

Reece adds text to develop the main idea in the introduction.

> "For the last time Reece you can get your own
>
> dog when you turn twelve, and not a moment before"
>
> She repeated, "Not a moment before!"
> mom said. She set down my plate of hot pancakes.
>
> "And not a moment after."
> ~~That was disappointing to me.~~
>
> At last I was twelve years old.
> A week later, my moment arrived. In exactly
>
> thirty seconds, the animal shelter would open.
>
> "I hope they have the one I want," I said to my mom.

Reece deleted a sentence that does not help to advance the story.

> I even knew his name: Russet. I had imagined the perfect
>
> dog. He'd be a retreiver puppy with a tale that wouldn't
>
> quit wagging. ~~A dog that wags its tail is friendly.~~ He'd be
>
> standing up at the gate of his cage, yipping. We'd know we
>
> were meant for each other. "Come on its a minute past!"

Logic is improved by rearranging sentences.

> "Reece!"
>
> Finally,
> ~~The door was unlocked by~~ a nice lady who came
> unlocked
> ~~up to the other side of~~ the door. I waited . . .

 Review Reece's changes. Find one idea or a detail in a sentence that he added, cut, moved, and rewrote.

TEKS 6.14C
ELPS 2C, 2G, 2I, 3D, 3E, 3G, 3H, 4C, 4G, 4I, 4K

Revising Using a Peer Response Sheet

One of Reece's classmates read his story. She spotted more places that could use improvement. Reece's classmate wrote her comments on a "Peer Response Sheet."

Peer Response Sheet

Writer: *Reece King*   Responder: *Chiara Davidson*

Title: *"Looking at the Inside"*

What I liked about your writing:

  * *Your beginning made me want to read more.*

  * *Your word choices showed that you sure wanted a dog.*

  * *You used dialogue that sounded like real people.*

Changes I would suggest:

  * *Sometimes, could you tell what the speakers are doing when*

  they say something?

  * *Could you add a few sentences with details in the beginning?*

  * *What kind of retriever did you want?*

With a partner, review the classmate's list of suggestions. Which one do you think is the most important? Discuss your ideas with your partner. Then add one suggestion of your own.

TEKS 6.14C, 6.14E
ELPS 2G, 2H, 2I, 3D, 3E, 3G, 3H

PROCESS

Revising with a Peer Response Sheet

Using the comments made by his classmate, Reece revised his story again. The new details and quotations he used filled out his narrative.

Add sentences or text to tell what you were doing.

You forgot to say your mom was with you.

Tell what kind of retriever.

Tell what people were doing.

"For the last time Reece you can get your own

dog when you turn twelve, and not a moment before"

mom said. She set down my plate of hot pancakes. She

repeated, "Not a moment before!"
  I started to spread the butter.
  ∧*"And not a moment after."*
          It was Saturday, April 24 2011.
      A week later, my moment arrived.∧*At last I*

was twelve years old. In exactly thirty seconds, the
                  her hand on my shoulder,
animal shelter would open. Mom stood beside me,∧

"Just hold on."

    "I hope they have the one I want," I said. I had
              golden
imagined the perfect dog. He'd be a∧*retreiver puppy*

with a tale that wouldn't quit wagging. He'd be

standing up at the gate of his cage, yipping. We'd

know we were meant for each other. I even knew his
              I said, knocking on the door.
name: Russet. "Come on its a minute past!"∧
        Mom pulled me back.
  "Reece!" . . .∧

 Have you ever used peer responding during a writing assignment? Discuss the experience with your classmates. Consider why peer responding is (or could be) helpful.

 **TEKS** 6.14C
ELPS 2G, 2I, 3E, 3G

Revising After Peer Revision

After Reece had revised his first draft to improve focus and coherence, and organization, he used his peer response sheet and then decided to check for development of ideas and voice. Reece wanted to be sure that his ideas painted a picture and his own style came through.

Development of Ideas

Think carefully about the details that will enhance your story. Add, delete, and combine sentences to tell your story clearly and in your own way.

> *"Some of my sentences are not very interesting. I'll find ways to add more variety."*

Voice

Write your story using language that expresses your personality and individuality. Choose colorful words to enhance your writing style make your story come alive.

> *" I need to make sure this story sounds like me. I think I'll add words that express my feelings."*

 Team up with a partner to review Reece's revised writing on page 19 for style. Find one or two places where he could change sentences to develop his ideas or show his style more clearly. Discuss your choices with your partner.

TEKS 6.14C, 6.19A
ELPS 2I, 3G, 4I, 4K

PROCESS

Checking Reece's Improvements in Style

Reece combined sentences and added transitions to improve his narrative. He kept his purpose and audience in mind as he made changes.

Combining these two sentences helps to keep the style natural.

"For the last time Reece you can get your

own dog when you turn twelve, and not a moment

before" mom~~said~~ snapped *She set down my plate of hot*

pancakes, ~~She~~ and *repeated, "Not a moment before!"*

I started to spread the butter. "And not

a moment after."

A week later, my moment arrived. It was

Saturday, April 24, 2011, and *At last I was twelve years*

old. In exactly thirty seconds, the animal shelter

would open, its doors. *Mom stood beside me, her hand on my*

shoulder, "Just hold on."

Over the last five months,
"I hope they have the one I want," I said. I had

Adding transitional phrases helps the writing flow.

imagined the perfect dog. He'd be a golden retreiver

puppy with a tale that wouldn't quit wagging. He'd

be standing up at the gate of his cage, yipping.
The moment our eyes would meet,
We'd know we were meant for each other. . . .

 With your partner, compare Reece's comments about the style and flow of his writing (page 20) with the changes he actually made. How are they alike or different? Would you change anything?

 **TEKS** 6.14D
ELPS 2I, 3D, 3G, 4I

Editing Checking for Conventions

Once Reece was pleased with the style of his story, he checked his work for conventions. Conventions deal with grammar, mechanics (punctuation and capitalization), sentence structure, and spelling.

Conventions

Be sure that your punctuation, capitalization, spelling, and grammar are correct.

"Spelling and punctuation are tough. I'll ask a classmate to help me catch everything."

For help with writing rules, Reece turned to the "Proofreader's Guide" in the back of his *Write Source* book. He also used a checklist to help him look for errors.

Editing Checklist

GRAMMAR

_____ **1.** Do my subjects and verbs agree in number?

_____ **2.** Do I use the right word *(to, too, two)*?

MECHANICS (Punctuation and Capitalization)

_____ **3.** Do I use end punctuation after all my sentences?

_____ **4.** Do I use commas correctly?

_____ **5.** Do I use apostrophes to show possession *(boy's bike)*?

_____ **6.** Do I start all my sentences with capital letters?

_____ **7.** Do I capitalize all proper names of people and places?

SENTENCE STRUCTURE

_____ **8.** Do I use complete sentences throughout?

_____ **9.** Do I avoid rambling, or run-on, sentences?

SPELLING

_____ **10.** Have I spelled all my words correctly?

 Work with a partner. Using the checklist, find two or three errors in Reece's revised draft on page 21 to discuss.

TEKS 6.14D
ELPS 2I, 3G, 4I

PROCESS

Checking Reece's Editing for Conventions

Before writing a final draft, Reece checked his narrative for grammar, mechanics, sentence structure, and spelling errors. (See the inside back cover of this book for a list of common editing and proofreading marks.)

Punctuation mistakes are fixed.

Capitalization errors are corrected.

Error in sentence structure is addressed.

Spelling and usage errors are corrected.

"For the last time Reece you can get your

own dog when you turn ~~twelve,~~ and not a moment
                        12,

before" mom snapped. She set down my plate of
         =

hot pancakes and repeated, "Not a moment before!"

   I started to spread the butter. "And not a

moment after."

   A week later, my moment arrived. It was

Saturday, April 24, 2011, and at last I was ~~twelve~~
                                          12

years old. In exactly ~~thirty~~ seconds, the animal
                       30

shelter would open its doors. Mom stood beside

me, her hand on my shoulder "Just hold on."

   "I hope they have the one I want," I said. Over

the last five months, I had imagined the perfect
                    retriever   tail
dog. He'd be a golden ~~retreiver~~ puppy with a ~~tale~~

that wouldn't quit wagging. He'd be standing . . .

Review the editing changes Reece made. Find a place where he added a period to help his audience understand. Find a place where he changed a comma to a period to fix a run-on sentence. Read the edited sentences aloud.

Publishing Sharing Your Writing

Reece used the tips below to help him write the final copy of his story. (See pages 25–26.)

Focus on Presentation

Tips for Handwritten Copies

- Use blue or black ink and write neatly.
- Write your name following your teacher's instructions.
- Skip a line and center your title; skip another line and start your writing.
- Indent every paragraph and leave a one-inch margin on all four sides.
- Write your last name and page number on every page after page 1.

Reece King

Looking at the Inside

"For the last time, Reece, you can get your own dog when you turn 12, and not a moment before," Mom snapped. She set down my plate of hot pancakes and repeated, "Not a moment before!"

I started to spread the butter. "And not a moment after."

A week later, my moment arrived. It was Saturday, April 24, 2011, and at last I was 12 years old. In exactly 30 seconds, the animal shelter would open its doors. Mom stood beside me, her hand on my shoulder. "Just hold on."

"I hope they have the one I want," I said. Over the last five months, I'd imagined the perfect dog. He'd be a golden retriever puppy with a tail that wouldn't quit wagging. He'd be standing up at the gate of his cage, yipping. The moment our eyes would meet, we'd know we were meant for each other. I even knew his name: Russet. "Come on! It's a minute past!" I said, knocking on the door.

"Reece!" Mom pulled me back.

Finally, a nice lady unlocked the door and opened it.

I said, "Good morning. We need a dog."

She replied, "Why don't you go have a look?"

"Thanks!" I dodged around the lady and rushed to the door marked "Kennel." The room beyond was lined with cages. The moment my foot hit the cement, barking filled the air. There must have been 30 dogs in there, and all of them were shouting, "Me! Me! Pick me!" But which one was Russet?

King 2

moment my foot hit the cement, barking filled the air. There must ha Pi

yo A re

r I p s

King 2

Reece King

Looking at the Inside

"For the last time, Reece, you can get your own dog when you turn 12, and not a moment before," Mom snapped. She set down my plate of hot pancakes and repeated, "Not a moment before!"

I started to spread the butter. "And not a moment after."

A week later, my moment arrived. It was Saturday, April 24, 2011, and at last I was 12 years old. In exactly 30 seconds, the animal shelter would open its doors. Mom stood beside me, her hand on my shoulder. "Just hold on."

"I hope they have the one I want," I said. Over the last five months, I'd imagined the perfect dog. He'd be a golden retriever puppy with a tail that wouldn't quit wagging. He'd be standing up at the gate of his cage, yipping. The moment our eyes would meet, we'd know we were meant for each other. I even knew his name: Russet. "Come on! It's a minute past!" I said, knocking on the door.

"Reece!" Mom pulled me back.

Finally, a nice lady unlocked the door and opened it.

I said, "Good morning. We need a dog."

She replied, "Why don't you go have a look?"

"Thanks!" I dodged around the lady and rushed to the door marked "Kennel." The room beyond was lined with cages. The

Tips for Computer Copies

- Use an easy-to-read font and a 12-point type size.
- Double-space and leave a one-inch margin around each page.

Reece's Final Draft

Reece felt great about his final story. It really captured the exciting day when he met his closest "friend."

Reece King

Looking at the Inside

"For the last time, Reece, you can get your own dog when you turn 12, and not a moment before," Mom snapped. She set down my plate of hot pancakes and repeated, "Not a moment before!"

I started to spread the butter. "And not a moment after."

A week later, my moment arrived. It was Saturday, April 24, 2011, and at last I was 12 years old. In exactly 30 seconds, the animal shelter would open its doors. Mom stood beside me, her hand on my shoulder. "Just hold on."

"I hope they have the one I want," I said. Over the last five months, I'd imagined the perfect dog. He'd be a golden retriever puppy with a tail that wouldn't quit wagging. He'd be standing up at the gate of his cage, yipping. The moment our eyes would meet, we'd know we were meant for each other. I even knew his name: Russet. "Come on! It's a minute past!" I said, knocking on the door.

"Reece!" Mom pulled me back.

Finally, a nice lady unlocked the door and opened it.

I said, "Good morning. We need a dog."

She replied, "Why don't you go have a look?"

"Thanks!" I dodged around the lady and rushed to the door marked "Kennel." The room beyond was lined with cages. The moment my foot hit the cement, barking filled the air. There must have been 30 dogs in there, and all of them were shouting, "Me! Me! Pick me!" But which one was Russet?

The first dog was a little terrier that growled at me. "I don't want you, either," I said and moved on. Next was a cute mutt. I kept going. A shepherd, a bulldog, a hound—but where was my golden retriever?

I wandered the whole place twice. There wasn't a single retriever. I couldn't believe it. Maybe I missed it. After all, a puppy would be pretty small. While the dogs leaped at their gates and yapped, I searched their eyes. None of them was right.

"Have you decided?" Mom asked, coming up behind me.

"He's not here, Mom!" I said. "I can't believe it. After all this waiting." Suddenly, I saw him. His outside was wrong, but his eyes were right. "Here! This is the one. This is Russet!"

Mom blinked at the puppy. "He's a beagle."

"You're looking at the outside," I said. I stuck my fingers in the cage. Russet bounced up to lick my hand. "You've got to look at his inside. He's the one."

That was the day I met my best friend. On that day, I learned that sometimes you need to look at the inside and not the outside. That beagle mutt sure turned out to be my Russet. I wouldn't trade him for any other dog in the world. And I doubt Russet would trade me for any other kid, either.

Evaluating and Reflecting on the Final Copy

Reece's teacher used a rubric like the one that appears on pages 130–135 to evaluate the final draft of his narrative. The very best score that a writer can receive is a 4. The teacher also wrote comments about his writing.

4 Score

Your narrative is very effective. It was a creative twist to choose your dog for the topic of meeting your best friend. You stay focused on this main idea, and your story follows a clear time organization. Your dialogue, sentences, and word choices do a good job of developing your ideas. They also give your story a strong voice. I could hear you speaking to me in every line. Your first page is very smooth, but the second page feels choppy in places. A few more transitions could help next time. Your story has no grammar, mechanics, or spelling errors. Good work!

Discuss the assessment. Do you agree with the score and comments made by Reece's teacher? Why or why not? Explain your thinking to a partner.

Evaluating and Reflecting on Your Writing

After the whole process was finished, Reece filled out a reflection sheet.

Reece King

My Personal Narrative

1. The best score for my personal essay is . . .
   4

2. It's the best score because . . .
   the writing was very strong.

3. The best part of my narrative is . . .
   the voice. Even Mrs. Wilson says so. She said she can hear my voice in every line. That means my personality comes through in the writing.

4. The part that still needs work is . . .
   using a few more transitions to strengthen organization.

5. The main thing I learned about writing a personal narrative is . . .
   it's a process. If I had given up after the first draft, my story would never have turned out this good.

6. In my next narrative, I would like to . . .
   write about people instead of dogs.

Peer Responding

Dancers practice in front of mirrors to see how well they are dancing. Writers don't have mirrors to tell them how well they are writing. To see their work from another angle, writers need the opinions of readers.

Your peers can give you feedback. They can use a response sheet to organize their comments, or simply talk about the writing in a group. Writers can then revise their work in response to the feedback they receive from their peers.

In this chapter, you will learn how to share your writing—and how to respond to the work of others. A careful peer response can be just what a writer needs to improve a piece of writing.

Learning Language

Work with a partner. Read the meanings and share your answers.

1. A **response** is a thought or reaction to something.
   What was your response to the last movie you watched?

2. When you think **overall** about something, you think of it as a whole.
   What is your overall feeling about math?

3. When you give **constructive criticism**, you give helpful comments.
   What is an example of constructive criticism?
   Have you received criticism that was not constructive? Explain.

What's Ahead

- **Basic Rules of Peer Responding**
- **Writing-Group Guidelines**

Basic Rules of Peer Responding

Learning how to respond thoughtfully to another person's writing can take some practice. Whether you're reading or listening to a piece of writing, alone or in a group, follow these rules:

- **Be prepared.** Know the assignment. Read the final draft all the way through once to get familiar with it. Then read it again critically.

- **Listen carefully.** If you are listening to a peer's draft, be attentive. Make brief notes about what you notice as you listen.

- **Give constructive feedback.** Tell the writer about both strengths and weaknesses. Word all your comments in a way that respects the writer's efforts. Use constructive criticism.

Using a Response Sheet

One of the best ways to react to someone else's writing is to complete a response sheet.

 As you read the following paragraphs about a special childhood object, focus on the writer's strengths and weaknesses. Then read the sample response sheet shown on the next page.

My Best Friend

Gizmo is not a fancy guy, but he would definitely stand out in a crowd. His whole body is blue, except for an orange, bulb-shaped nose and a pair of golf-ball-shaped eyes with black pupils. His hands have a few gigantic fingers, his feet have two toes, and his mouth spreads across his face in a huge smile. Staying in fashion has never been a problem for Gizmo, because he doesn't wear clothes.

His voice sounds something like mine, but it's higher. It really gets shrill when he laughs. He can even sing, and his favorite tune is the "A, B, C" song. These days, he talks and sings less than he used to. Gizmo doesn't have ears.

PROCESS

Peer Response Sheet

A classmate responded to the writing on the previous page using the following plan.

1 First he read the writing to get the overall picture.

2 Next he read the piece again, focusing on its strengths and weaknesses.

3 Then he filled out a response sheet for his peer, or classmate.

Peer Response Sheet

Writer: *Lien*   Responder: *Dean*

Title: *"My Best Friend"*

What I liked about your writing:

* *You were brave to write about the toy, Gizmo. Lots of us liked him when we were little, but we don't admit it now.*

* *You have lots of details telling how Gizmo looks, sounds, and feels. Nice job!*

* *Your voice is friendly and funny. It fits the subject.*

Changes I would suggest:

* *Is the fact that Gizmo doesn't have ears out of place?*

* *The assignment asked you to tell why the object was important to you. Why do you care about Gizmo?*

Practice. Exchange a recent piece of writing with a classmate.

1 Read the writing once to get an overall feel for it.

2 Then read it again, focusing on what you like and what you think needs improving.

3 Fill out a peer response sheet. Discuss your feedback with the author.

★ ELPS 2I, 3G, 3H, 4G

Writing-Group Guidelines

You can read your writing out loud to a partner or a group and get immediate feedback. If you've never been in a writing group before, it might be helpful to work with a classmate first. You can take turns practicing the author's and the responder's roles. As a responder, take notes and be ready to ask questions and give feedback to the author. In the author's role, answer questions and respond to the feedback.

The Author's Role

As the author, you need to choose a piece of writing that you want someone to review. The writing can be at any stage in the process. If possible, make a copy for each member of the group. Then follow these guidelines.

- **Introduce your writing** but don't say too much.
- **Read your writing out loud** or have people read it silently.
- **Ask others for comments** and listen to what they say.
- **Take notes** to help you remember what was said.
- **Be open and polite** when you explain your writing.
- **Answer questions** that readers ask about your writing.
- **Ask your group for help** with any writing problems.

The Responder's Role

As the responder, you need to show interest and respect. Follow these guidelines.

- **Review the goals** for the genre of writing you are responding to so that you will know what to listen for.
- **Listen carefully and take notes** to help you remember what you want to say.
- **Ask questions** if you are confused about something or want to know more.
- **Tell what works well** in the writing.
- **Tell what needs to be improved** by politely making specific suggestions.

Remember, don't just say, "Everything is great."

Understanding the Traits of Writing

How can you tell if a piece of writing is good? One way is very easy: Writing is good when it keeps you reading from paragraph to paragraph. It's that simple. The best stories and essays hold your interest from start to finish. However, explaining *why* something keeps you reading is not as easy. You need to know what to look for.

This chapter identifies the traits, or qualities, found in all good writing. Once you understand these traits, you can apply them to everything you write.

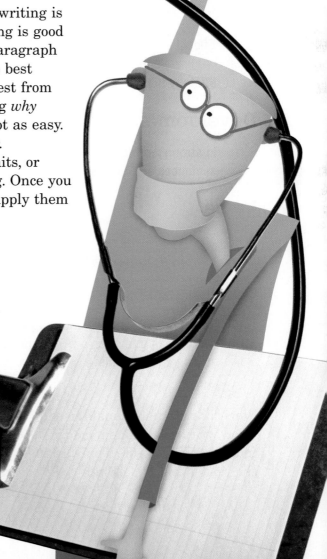

What's Ahead

- **Introducing the Texas Traits**
- **Understanding Focus and Coherence**
- **Understanding Organization**
- **Understanding Development of Ideas**
- **Understanding Voice**
- **Understanding Conventions**

Introducing the Texas Traits

There are five main traits, or qualities, to any piece of writing. You will do your best work if you keep these traits in mind as you write. The list below introduces the traits. The next 10 pages provide a closer look at each one.

Focus and Coherence

An excellent piece of writing has one main idea, and everything in the composition relates to that idea.

Organization

Effective writing moves smoothly from sentence to sentence and paragraph to paragraph. An organizational strategy helps present ideas.

Development of Ideas

In strong writing, each idea is developed in depth. Chains of sentences add details and meanings that build on each other.

Voice

The best writing is original. The writer says things in a way that shows his or her individuality or personal viewpoint.

Conventions

Good writing is polished through careful editing. Every sentence is free of errors in grammar, mechanics, sentence structure, and spelling.

You should also consider the presentation of your writing. Good writing looks neat and follows guidelines for margins, spacing, indenting, and so on. The way the writing looks on the page attracts the reader and makes him or her *want* to read on.

Understanding Focus and Coherence

Effective writing begins with a clear focus. This is the main idea about a topic that you want to get across to your readers. When all parts of an essay relate to this main idea, the essay has coherence.

PROCESS

What makes a writing topic good?

The topic is what your essay is about. For example, you might write about snails, car racing, a lake vacation, or the fairness of a new rule at school. The key is to choose a topic that interests you, that you know about (or can learn about), and that fits your assignment.

Sample Assignment: Write about a time when you learned something.

Possible Topics
- *Too Broad*   Things I've learned from Great-grandma
- *Too Narrow* Last night's e-mail message from Great-grandma
- *Just Right*   A memorable afternoon with Great-grandma

How do I decide on a focus for my writing?

A well-chosen topic and main idea will allow you to produce an essay of the right depth and length for your assignment. Remember that a topic and main idea are two different things. The topic is the subject. The main idea narrows down the topic by focusing on one aspect of it.

> **Focus statement:** *A memorable afternoon with Great-grandma* (topic) *taught me about her experiences in school* (a certain part).

Practice choosing a good topic and a clear focus by following these directions: *Recall the hardest thing you have ever done. Then write a focus statement about this topic.* (Use the information on this page as a guide for your work.)

How do I keep my essay focused?

In a well-written essay, every part is clearly connected to the main idea about your topic. The chart on the next page shows a plan for a story about a personal experience. Notice that all three parts include words that refer to the topic (getting braces) and the main idea (worry about how braces make the writer look).

Creating a plan for your essay like the one shown can help you stay focused on your main idea as your write.

How do I show coherence when I write paragraphs?

Like your essay as a whole, each paragraph within it should show focus and coherence. A well-focused paragraph has a main idea, and all the details in the paragraph support that idea. The paragraph feels complete. Nothing unrelated is included.

Focused

> On my birthday, I and six of my friends had a blast at the water park. First, we rode the waves on our rafts. Then, we went down the giant water slide over and over. It was the most fun, even though we had to stand in line each time. After that, we did cannonballs off the low diving board. I made the biggest splash!

Unfocused

> We had a blast at the water park and ate pizza. It reminds me of one I used to visit where I used to live. First, we rode the waves on our rafts. Then, we went down the giant water slide and did cannonballs off the low diving board. There was a long line at the slide. Later, we got pizza.

 Reread the *Focused* paragraph above. State the main idea or focus in a phrase. Then reread the *Unfocused* paragraph. Discuss with a partner what makes this paragraph unfocused.

conventions development of ideas
VOICE organization focus & coherence 37
 ELPS 3D, 4C
Traits of Writing

Texas Traits Understanding Organization

The organization of an essay includes a clear beginning, middle, and ending. This is the basic structure. A specific organizational strategy gives the middle part of your essay structure.

PROCESS

How should I organize my writing assignment?

The best essays have a clearly defined beginning, middle, and ending. The chart below shows this basic plan of organization.

Beginning

Engage readers with a question, striking statement, or brief story. Then establish your focus.

There was my face in the mirror: brown hair, green eyes, freckled cheeks—and silver teeth! Well, that's how my shiny new braces looked. I didn't like having crooked teeth, but now I had a new reason to hide my smile.

Middle

Present and develop the main ideas related to your focus.

Getting the braces put on my teeth was uncomfortable.

My brothers teased me about my braces.

I got used to seeing my face with braces, and so did others.

After the braces, my teeth were nice and straight.

Ending

Offer an interesting final thought that underscores your focus.

Now when I look in the mirror, I'm glad I had braces. I flash my smile every day. Having braces was hard at first, but it all paid off in the end.

 Share with the class a strong beginning or ending from something you have written or read. Explain why it is effective.

What organizational strategy should I use in the middle part?

The middle part of your essay presents your main ideas with supporting details. How you organize these details depends on the form of writing.

Descriptive

Organize details by *location.*

At the top of my closet, you will find boxes of shoes and sweaters lining the shelf. Below the shelf is the clothes bar. Clothes are crammed together in this space. On the floor, there are piles of shoes and games that I just toss in.

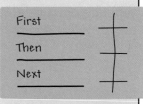

Narrative

Organize details *chronologically* (in time order).

First the orthodontist jammed metal bands around my molars. Then he glued sharp little squares of steel to all of my front teeth. Next he attached little wires to the squares.

Expository

Organize details by *logical order* or *categories.*

What can we do to save our environment? First of all, we must stop littering. In addition, we must promote recycling. Equally important, we must reuse materials whenever possible.

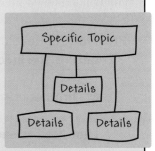

Persuasive

Organize details by *order of importance.*

First of all, letting students wear regular clothes saves money. Second, it sends the proper message. Third, and most importantly, it helps students become more responsible.

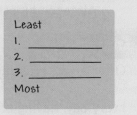

 Complete a graphic organizer and write a short passage following one of the methods of organization above. Your writing should include at least three or four sentences.

Texas Traits
Understanding Development of Ideas

When you develop an idea, you think about it deeply. You discover the details that will make the idea interesting, meaningful, and understandable to your readers. When you write, you connect the details to the idea in a logical way.

What are the most important details to include?

Certain kinds of details are needed in almost every kind of essay. You can remember these details as the 5 W's: who, what, when, where, and why. This paragraph includes all of the 5 W's.

> This morning at 7:00 I took my dog Barney on a walk. It was my job to give Barney some exercise each day before I left for school. We were strolling along our usual route: down the block to the park. As we paused by a tree, we heard a loud "Caw! Caw!" from the branch above us. We looked up and saw a giant crow.

- **Who** Barney (a dog), Barney's owner
- **What** walking the dog; hearing and seeing a crow
- **Where** down the block to the park (city sidewalk)
- **When** 7:00 in the morning
- **Why** exercise

How do I recognize if writing has depth or not?

When ideas are well-developed, details help explain the writer's ideas and unique point of view. Writing that is shallow is boring to read. **Here are some things to avoid:**

- **Telling people things they already know.** *In many places, winter is a time for playing in the snow.*
- **Describing things briefly and flatly.** *The game was fun.*
- **Using formulas to say things.** *Practice makes perfect.*
- **Repeating the same basic thought.** *I knew I was right. I was positive I was right.*

 Choose an essay or paragraph you have written. List your 5 W's. If one is missing, add it to your paragraph. Share your results with a partner.

What kind of details hold the reader's interest?

Details add depth by supporting and clarifying your ideas. They also keep your reader engaged. The type of details you include will depend on your focus and the form of the writing. For example, details about feelings are appropriate in a narrative, while a report has many factual details. Here are some examples of different types of details.

Facts and Statistics
A fact is a detail that can be proved. A statistic is a fact that uses numbers.

> **Great-grandma went to an all-girl school in England.**
> **In her class, 60 percent of the girls went on to college.**

Examples
An example is a detail that illustrates or shows an idea.

> **Sports were encouraged at her school. Great-grandma played field hockey and tennis.**

Thoughts and Feelings
These are the writer's own ideas or attitude about a topic.

> **I was impressed by Great-grandma's tennis trophy.**

Sensory Details
Sensory details appeal to one or more of the five senses: sight, hearing, touch, smell, and taste.

> **Great-grandma's wire-rimmed glasses glinted in the sunlight.**

 Choose one of your own narratives or find a news story to review for details. Label any facts, statistics, examples, thoughts, or feelings that you find.

PROCESS

Understanding Voice

Author Ralph Fletcher says, "Writing that has voice is writing that breathes." Voice is what makes your writing sound fresh and original. When you write in your own natural voice, your readers can sense you as a real person.

How can I put a "face" on my writing?

To make sure your writing reflects who you are, show that you are truly interested in your topic. If you are interested, your readers will be, too.

Faceless Writing (uninterested)

One of my ancestors was born in Rhode Island a long time ago. She was unusual because she became a soldier. That's about all I know.

Writing with a Face (interested)

My ancestor Delia Coffin was born in Rhode Island a long time ago. I think of her as Daring Delia because she had a thirst for great adventure. She dressed up like a soldier and went off to war.

How can my writing voice sound more natural?

The three tips below will help you write more naturally.

- Keep a personal journal.
- "Talk" to friends and relatives in friendly letters and e-mail messages.
- Begin writing assignments by freely recording your thoughts about your topic.

This writing sounds natural

When we were walking, I looked up and saw the moon was out. It made the fog seem to glow. Off in the distance, I heard a dog bark and then a chorus of barks. I felt a shiver crawl up my spine. It was probably just the cold.

 Write freely for 5 to 10 minutes about your day so far: *What has happened? How do you feel about what's happened?* Check your writing for voice by underlining words and phrases that sound like the real you.

Understanding Conventions

In good writing, one sentence flows smoothly to the next. Each sentence moves the essay forward and deepens the reader's understanding. One way to achieve fluent writing is to think about sentence structure. This is one of the conventions of writing.

How does sentence structure contribute to fluent writing?

Here are some things to keep in mind about sentences as you strive for a natural flow to your writing.

- Every sentence is important.
- Using a variety of sentences adds interest to your writing.
- Short, choppy sentences can be combined to improve flow.
- Transition words help to combine sentences and paragraphs.

How can I combine sentences?

Here are a few ways you can combine short, choppy sentences into a longer, more fluent sentence.

Combine Using a Key Word

Chinwe plans to go hiking. She will go hiking tomorrow.
Chinwe plans to go hiking tomorrow.

Combining Using a Prepositional Phrase

My lazy cat takes long naps. It naps on top of the TV.
My lazy cat takes long naps on top of the TV.

Combine Using a Compound Verb

Parnell picked up the flat stone. He examined its strange markings.
Parnell picked up the flat stone and examined its strange markings.

Combine Using a Transition Word

Ada went to the library. She wanted a book about the planets.
Ada went to the library because she wanted a book about the planets.

conventions development of ideas

VOICE organization focus & coherence

43

TEKS 6.14C
ELPS 4K

Traits of Writing

PROCESS

How can I combine larger units of text to make my writing clearer?

A paragraph is a group of sentences that relate to one idea. In the examples below, notice how combining larger units of text into one paragraph improves the flow and clarity of the writing.

Combining Related Sentences

Before

Soccer is becoming more popular in the United States. Many schools have started soccer programs so more students are now able to play on organized teams.

Most schools have separate teams for boys and girls. Boys and girls could play together on the same teams.

After

Soccer is becoming more popular in the United States. Since many schools have started soccer programs, more students are now able to play on organized teams. Most schools have separate teams for boys and girls. However, boys and girls could easily play together on the same teams.

Combining Related Sentences and Adding a Transition

Before

William looked at his science project. He picked it up and glued one more piece in place.

He set it down. He thought, "Now, I am ready for the science fair."

After

William looked at his science project. He picked it up and glued one more piece in place. After setting it down, he thought, "Now, I am ready for the science fair."

Choose one of your own narratives or essays to review. Look for a place where you could combine sentences or larger units of text to improve the flow and achieve your purpose in writing.

TEKS 6.14D
ELPS 5E

Conventions are simply the rules of language. Grammar, mechanics (punctuation and capitalization), sentence structure, and spelling all have special rules. When you follow these rules, the reader can focus on your ideas instead of being distracted by mistakes.

How can I make sure my writing follows the rules?

A conventions checklist like the one below can guide you as you edit and proofread your writing. When you are not sure about a certain rule, refer to the "Proofreader's Guide." (See pages **626–781**.)

Conventions

GRAMMAR

_____ **1.** Do my subjects and verbs agree in number?

_____ **2.** Do I use the right word *(to, too, two)*?

MECHANICS (Punctuation and Capitalization)

_____ **3.** Do I use end punctuation after all my sentences?

_____ **4.** Do I use commas correctly?

_____ **5.** Do I start all my sentences with capital letters?

_____ **6.** Do I capitalize all proper names of people and places?

SENTENCE STRUCTURE

_____ **7.** Do I use complete sentences throughout?

_____ **8.** Do I avoid rambling, or run-on, sentences?

SPELLING

_____ **9.** Have I spelled all my words correctly?

Evaluating Your Writing

How do you become a good athlete? First, you learn the necessary skills. Then you compete as much as you can and evaluate each performance. In many ways, that's how you become a good writer, too. You learn the important skills, practice different types of writing, and evaluate each finished product.

This chapter explains a basic skill—using a rubric. **Rubrics** are charts that help you measure or evaluate your writing.

What's Ahead

- **Understanding Holistic Scoring**
- **Reading a Rubric**
- **The *Write Source* Scoring Rubric**
- **Model Essays**
- **Evaluating a Narrative**

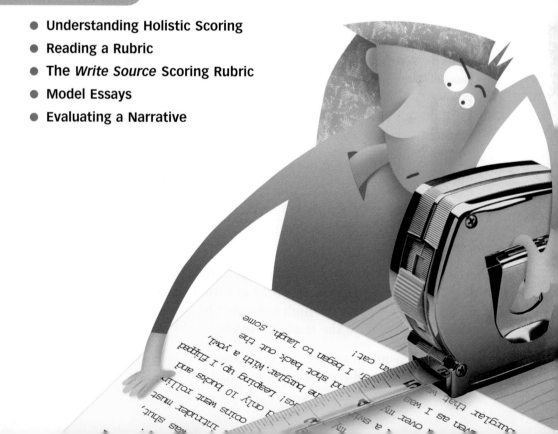

ELPS 4C, 4K

Understanding Holistic Scoring

"The whole is greater than the sum of its parts."

Do you know what this expression means? Think about looking at a face. When you respond to a face, you don't tend to think separately about its shape, features, color, and expression. You think of the face as a whole and the overall impression it makes on you.

The same is true for a piece of writing. You can evaluate it as a whole, or holistically. With holistic evaluation you follow these steps:

- Think about how well the essay addresses the five traits of writing.
- Ask: What is the total impression the essay makes on the reader?
- Assign a score of 1, 2, 3, or 4 that stands for the overall quality of the writing.

How do I know what score to give an essay?

With holistic scoring, you do not give a separate score for each trait. You give a single score, using these guidelines.

 A **4** means that the writing is strong in **all** of the traits.

 A **3** means that the writing is strong in **most** of the traits.

 A **2** means that the writing is strong in **some** of the traits.

 A **1** means that the writing is weak in **most** of the traits.

With holistic scoring, no single trait determines the score. For example, an essay does not get a low score just because it has many mechanical errors. An essay also does not get a high score just because it is well organized. You must think about all of the traits together.

 Reread an essay you have written. When you think about it as a whole, should it receive a score of 1, 2, 3, or 4?

Reading a Rubric

For the rubrics in this book, the four score points are color coded. There is a description for each rating to help you evaluate your writing.

The *Write Source* Scoring Rubric

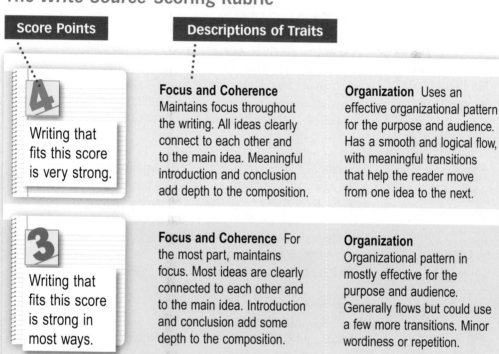

Score Points	Descriptions of Traits	
4 Writing that fits this score is very strong.	**Focus and Coherence** Maintains focus throughout the writing. All ideas clearly connect to each other and to the main idea. Meaningful introduction and conclusion add depth to the composition.	**Organization** Uses an effective organizational pattern for the purpose and audience. Has a smooth and logical flow, with meaningful transitions that help the reader move from one idea to the next.
3 Writing that fits this score is strong in most ways.	**Focus and Coherence** For the most part, maintains focus. Most ideas are clearly connected to each other and to the main idea. Introduction and conclusion add some depth to the composition.	**Organization** Organizational pattern in mostly effective for the purpose and audience. Generally flows but could use a few more transitions. Minor wordiness or repetition.

Guiding Your Writing

Learning how to use a rubric helps you . . .

- think like a writer—understanding your goal,
- make meaningful changes in your writing—using the traits of writing, and
- assess your final copies—rating their strengths and weaknesses.

Review the complete rubric. Review the scoring rubric on pages 48–49 and list one thing that you learned from reviewing it and one question that you have about it. Share this information with your class.

The *Write Source* Scoring Rubric

Use the descriptions for each score to holistically evaluate your writing or that of your peers.

Writing that fits this score is very strong.

Focus and Coherence
Maintains focus throughout the writing. All ideas clearly connect to each other and to the main idea. Meaningful introduction and conclusion add depth to the composition.

Organization Uses an effective organizational pattern for the purpose and audience. Has a smooth and logical flow, with meaningful transitions that help the reader move from one idea to the next.

Writing that fits this score is strong in most ways.

Focus and Coherence For the most part, maintains focus. Most ideas are clearly connected to each other and to the main idea. Introduction and conclusion add some depth to the composition.

Organization
Organizational pattern is mostly effective for the purpose and audience. Generally flows but could use a few more transitions. Minor wordiness or repetition.

Writing that fits this score is strong in a few ways.

Focus and Coherence Is somewhat focused. May suddenly shift from one idea to another, but the ideas are related. Some ideas do not add to the writing. Introduction and conclusion do not add depth.

Organization
Organizational pattern may not suit the purpose and audience. Thoughts do not always flow clearly or logically. Wordiness or repetition may interfere with ideas.

Writing that fits this score is weak.

Focus and Coherence Lacks focus. Includes a large amount of information not connected to the main idea. Is missing an introduction and/or conclusion.

Organization Has no clear organizational pattern or logical flow of ideas. Has no transitions or uses ones that do not make sense. Wordiness and repetition interfere with ideas.

Development of Ideas
Supports all ideas thoroughly and with specific detail. Shows deep or creative thinking that adds to the overall quality of the writing.

Voice Engages the reader throughout the writing. Sounds authentic and original; expresses the writer's personality or unique viewpoint.

Conventions Shows a strong command of grammar, sentence structure, mechanics, and spelling.

Development of Ideas
Supports all ideas, but some need to be developed more thoroughly. Development may be thoughtful but may not show creative thinking.

Voice Engages the reader for most of the writing. Sounds authentic and original and expresses the writer's unique viewpoint.

Conventions Includes only minor errors in grammar, sentence structure, capitalization, punctuation, and spelling.

Development of Ideas
Support is general or shows little depth of thinking. Support may be only a list. Information may be missing. The message may be unclear.

Voice Engages the reader in some parts of the writing. Sounds authentic and original in only a few places. Does not express a unique viewpoint.

Conventions Several errors in grammar, sentence structure, mechanics, and spelling. Errors may interfere with the reader's understanding.

Development of Ideas
Does not support ideas or provides only general and unclear support. Important information may be left out. The message is unclear.

Voice Does not engage the reader. Does not sound authentic and original. Does not express a unique viewpoint.

Conventions Major errors in grammar, sentence structure, mechanics, and spelling. These problems interfere with the reader's understanding.

Model Essays

To learn how to evaluate a essay, you'll use the scoring rubric on pages 48–49 and the narratives that follow. These stories are examples of writing for each score on the rubric.

Notice that this first narrative received a score of 4. Read the description for a score of 4 on page 48. Then read the narrative. Use the same steps to study the other examples. Always remember to think about the overall quality of the writing.

Writing that fits a score of 4 is very strong.

Essay focuses on one experience—visiting GG.

Realistic dialogue and concrete words engage the reader.

A Visit with GG

I don't get to visit my great-grandmother very often, but each time I do, I learn something new about her. It happened again last Saturday, when I spent the afternoon at her house. This time I learned that GG (that's the nickname she lets me use) went to school in England when she was a girl. Even more interesting is that it was an all-girl school.

How did I discover this? It started with an old photograph I noticed over the fireplace. It showed a little girl in braids and a crisp white shirt, holding a field hockey stick. The girl looked about my age. "Is that really you, GG?" I asked. "I didn't know you used to play sports."

GG was sitting on the couch. Her wire-rimmed glasses glinted in the sunlight. "Oh, yes, dear." she said. "I played field hockey at school. Our school was quite forward-thinking when it came to girls and sports."

Few errors in conventions.

"That's so cool," I said.

When I asked GG if she had other pictures from her school days, she brought out an old photo album. We sat on the couch together, turning the pages and looking at the small black-and-white photographs that were pasted on large black-paper pages.

Paragraphs form a logical chain of ideas and events.

Some of the pictures showed an ivy-covered building with wide stone steps. Others showed groups of girls wearing the same uniform. Each girl was wearing a plaid skirt and a little cap. GG explained that she attended a boarding school just for girls. That means the students live at the school, like in a college. The school was in England because that's where GG's dad worked when she was growing up.

"I don't know if I'd like an all-girl school," I said.

"There are some advantages," GG said. "Sometimes boys and girls can distract each other." I had to agree.

We turned another page in the album, and there was GG, a few years older, standing with a row of girls holding hockey sticks. They were arranged around a big shiny trophy. "That was the year we took the championship," GG said.

Ending completes by telling the effect of the experience.

Before I knew it, two hours had passed, and it was time to say good-bye. "You rock, GG," I said. "Next time, will you tell me the rules for field hockey?" She smiled and gave me a kiss.

Writing that fits a score of 3 is strong in most ways.

How I Learned to Rollerblade

"Okay, now take a step forward." It was my sister Esme talking to me as I was standing in front of her. I was teetering on my new rollerblades and felt frozen. "Come on, you're on carpet. Just take a few steps!" I felt like a stiff giant as I put one foot in front of the other and progressed from the chair to the couch. "You go, boy!" Yeah, right, I thought. I knew that when I asked Esme to teach me how to rollerblade I would be in for some teasing. She had already started. To be frank, I was worried if I could get the hang of it.

After I could walk around on the blades pretty good, we went to the garage. The cars were gone, but there was lots of stuff along the walls—bikes, tools, cardboard boxes full of rags and who knows what. Now I had on all my equipment—knee pads, elbow pads, wrist guards, and a helmet.

At first I put my hands on Esme's arm and kind of scooted along beside her while she walked. When she let go, both feet were together and I was rolling straight toward a stack of cardboard boxes and held out my arms to stop. At least I didn't fall. Then I turned around and tried again and after a while, Esme said I was ready to hit the bike path.

Beginning makes focus of essay clear.

Transitions link paragraphs.

Writer tends to use run-on sentences.

Its important to remember that gravel and rocks and sand are bad news for rollerbladers. They can make you fall down. You need a smooth surface.

So now Esme was on her own blades beside me and talking to me. "Okay, little bro," she said, "let's see what you can do." Being on the pavement with nothing to hold onto made me nervous again. I took a few short strides. "Try to feel the rhythm," she said. "Your pushing on the wheels too hard." I tried to lengthen my stride but going slowly.

"If you shift your weight to each foot, you'll have a longer glide," Esme said. Glide, glide, glide, I thought to myself. I was concentrating so hard on how I was moving that I didn't see a small rock that was right in my path, and one of my skates hit it, and I was back to making windmills. "Whoooooa!" I said as I veered off the bike path into the weeds. I fell forward on my knees onto the soft ground. "Good job!" Esme said. At first I thought she was teasing me again, but she meant that if you fall you should fall forward, on your padding, and not backward, so I did the right thing

The funny thing was that after my fall, I didn't feel so nervous. Now I knew what to do if it happened again. Back on my feet, I started gliding—left, right, left, right. My strides were getting smoother. I was starting to feel the rhythm.

Generally good control of conventions.

Dialogue and word choices sound natural.

Writing that fits a score of 2 is strong in some ways.

One main idea controls all parts of the writing.

Frequent errors in conventions.

To improve flow, transitions are needed.

Voice is not strong.

Heading for Middle School

How did you feel when it was time to start Middle School? I was looking forwerd to it but I was also worried some. The orientasion really helped. It happened on a Saturday morning in August before school was going to start.

the principal and all the teachers were there. They shook our hand when we arrived to welcom us. They also wore sines that said "Ask me." They seemed really friendly.

I was worried about the large number of students at the school. A lot of my old friends would not be there, I thought. Would I make new friends? Plus there would be more homework, and I heared it would be harder and take longer. So thats another reason I was worried.

They showed us lots of things at orientasion. Like where all the rooms in the school are and how to use our lockers. I will have a different teacher for every class.

They showed us how to use an agenda to plan our homework assinements each week and be able to turn them in on time. You have to set sevral dedlines to get it done.

After the orientasion I felt much better. I think I will do fine in Middle School.

PROCESS

Writing that fits a score of 1 is weak.

Focus is not clear.

Repetition slows flow of essay.

To improve flow, transitions are needed.

The Sheep Ranch

I really liked the sheep ranch which was in the panhandel. The ranch has 5000 sheep so it was one of the largest. There are cowboys on horsback who check the sheep when nessessary and each cowboy had two or three sheepdogs. I think it would be fun to have a sheepdog but then you would need some sheep to keep him happy!

I never went to a sheep ranch before. This one was called Willow Bar. I have seen sheep before at a fair but not a whole sheep ranch.

The man in charge of the ranch showed us some sheep in a pen that we could pet. Sometimes they were noisy. When they speak "Baaaaa!" you can see their tongues. I was pretty good at immatating them.

We also watched a sheep get sheared. The sheep sheer uses electric clippers and the sheep just sits there quitely. They gave us small peeces of fluffy white wool to take home.

the best part was when we watched three sheepdogs work with the sheep. There were some sheep just eating here and there in the field far away. The cowboy gave some special whistles that the dogs under stand. Then the dogs make a circle to bring the sheep together. Then they brought the sheep in closer.

ELPS 3E, 3G, 4G, 4I, 4K

Evaluating a Narrative

As you read through the personal narrative below, pay attention to the strengths and weaknesses in the writing. Then follow the directions at the bottom of the page. **(The essay contains some errors.)**

Squealer

I was so excited when I got first-chair trumpet in our middle school band. I even beat out Chuck, an eighth grader. That made him jealous, since I'd be playing all the trumpet solos.

For the spring concert, Mr. Moore handed out sheet music for "Summertime." It had a great trumpet solo, but it was really high. Chuck loaned me a "squealer" mouthpiece—extra small for playing really high notes. I learned the solo, and it worked great.

At dress rehearsal, the band played "Summertime," and I blew everyone away. Even Chuck said I rocked. I was so excited, I forgot to switch from the squealer to my regular mouthpiece for the next song, "I Love You, Porgy." It started with a real low solo. I tried to play it, but the squealer made every note blat and wobble. It was torture. Mr. Moore stared at me, pleading for just one good note, but I couldn't give it to him. Afterward, Chuck said I sounded like a bike tire losing air!

Well, I was embarrassed, but some good came of it. I asked Mr. Moore if Chuck could play the second solo. He said yes, and at the concert, we both sounded great.

Use the scoring rubric. Assess the narrative you have just read using the rubric on pages 48–49 as a guide. Remember to leave room after each trait for comments. When you are done, compare and discuss your comments with a partner.

Publishing Your Writing

To publish or share your writing, you need an audience. Your writing is ready for publication when it says exactly what you want it to say and is as close to error free as you can make it. In other words, you've given it your best effort.

In this chapter, you will find information on a variety of ways to publish your work.

Learning Language

Work with a partner. Read the meanings and share answers to the questions.

1. A **portfolio** is a collection of a person's artistic work, such as pieces of writing or art.
   What types of things would you include in a portfolio of your work?

2. To **carry out** a plan means it has been completed.
   What is a plan or goal that you will carry out today?

3. **Typography** is the way words look and are arranged on a page.
   Describe the typography of this page.

What's Ahead

- **Sharing Your Writing**
- **Preparing to Publish**
- **Designing Your Writing**
- **Making Your Own Web Site**
- **Publishing Online**

Sharing Your Writing

Some publishing ideas are easy to carry out, like sharing your writing with your classmates. Others take more time and effort, like entering a writing contest. Try a number of these publishing ideas during the school year. All of them will help you grow as a writer.

Performing

- Sharing with Classmates
- Reading to an Audience
- Preparing a Multimedia Presentation
- Presenting a Storyboard
- Videotaping for Special Audiences
- Performing Onstage

In School

- School Newspapers
- Classroom Collections
- School Handbooks
- Writing Portfolios

Self-Publishing

- Family Newsletters
- Greeting Cards
- Bound Writings
- Online Publications

Posting

- Classroom Bulletin Boards
- School or Public Libraries
- Hallway Display Cases
- Business Windows
- Clinic Waiting Rooms

Sending It Out

- Local Newspapers
- Young Writers' Conferences
- Magazines and Contests
- Various Web Sites

Chart your publishing history. List the headings above on a piece of paper: *Performing, Posting, In School, Self-Publishing, Sending It Out.* Leave two or three lines between each heading. Under each heading, identify the publishing ideas that you have already tried. Then list and highlight those you would like to try. Discuss your list with a partner.

TEKS 6.14E

Preparing to Publish

Your writing is ready to publish when it is clear, complete, and correct. Getting your writing to this point requires careful revising and editing. Follow the tips below to help you prepare your writing for publication.

Publishing Tips

- **Work with your writing.**
  Continue working until you feel good about your writing from beginning to end.

- **Ask for advice during the writing process.**
  Be sure your writing answers any questions your readers may have about your topic.

- **Revise the focus, organization, ideas, and voice.**
  Every part of your writing should be clear and complete, and your voice appropriate to your audience. Revise your writing based on feedback given by a teacher or classmate.

- **Check grammar, mechanics, sentences, and spelling.**
  Ask at least one classmate to check your work for conventions.

- **Prepare a neat finished piece.**
  Use a pen (blue or black ink) and one side of the paper if you are writing by hand. If you are writing with a computer, use a font that is easy to read. Double-space your writing.

- **Know your options.**
  Explore the many different ways to publish your writing.

- **Follow all publication guidelines.**
  Just as your teacher wants assignments presented in a certain way, so do the newspapers, magazines, or Web sites that review the writing you submit.

  Save all drafts for each writing project. This will help you keep track of the changes you have made. If you are preparing a portfolio, you may be required to include early drafts as well as finished pieces.

 TEKS 6.17D
ELPS 3E, 3H

Designing Your Writing

Whenever you write, always focus on content *first*. Then think about how you want your paper to look. You can follow the guidelines below.

Typography

- Use an easy-to-read font for both the body and headings.
- Use an appropriate title and headings. A title sets the tone for your writing, and headings break the writing into smaller pieces.

Spacing and Margins

- Double-space your writing and leave one-inch margins on all four sides of your paper.
- Indent the first line of every paragraph.
- Use one space after every period.
- Avoid awkward breaks between pages. For example, don't leave a heading or the first line of a paragraph at the bottom of a page.

Graphic Devices

- Use text and graphics available through your technology, including bulleted or numbered lists.
- Include a table, a chart, or an illustration if it can help make a point clearer. (See pages **622–623** for examples.)
- Keep each graphic small enough so that it doesn't dominate the page. A larger graphic can be put by itself on a separate page.

 Share effective design. Find an article in a magazine, newspaper, or book that is well designed. Share the article with the class and identify and describe the design features.

Computer Design in Action

The following two pages show a well-designed student essay. The side notes explain all of the design features.

The title is 18-point and boldfaced.

The main text is 12-point type.

Headings are 14-point.

Margins are at least one inch all around.

Will Lee

Wake Up the Wild Side!

"In each of you, there is a wild creature screaming to get out," Ms. Hillary tells the drama club at the start of each meeting. "It's the part of you that can be a star on this stage." Then she begins our warm-ups, which really get our bodies and minds in gear. They also help the group start working together. Some warm-ups are for individuals, and some are for partners. Ms. Hillary uses both types at every meeting.

Individual Warm-Ups

Every meeting begins with warm-ups to help individuals find their "centers." One is "Shake It Out," and the other is "Greet the Sun."

- **Shake It Out:** In this warm-up, people stand on tiptoes with their hands stretched over their heads and shake out all the tension from their bodies. Everyone ends up completely loose and relaxed.
- **Greet the Sun:** Then everyone lies on the floor and rises like a plant, growing toward the sun. Everyone ends up with faces lifted and hands out like leaves.

ELPS 3E

Lee 2

Partner Warm-Ups

After "Shake It Out" and "Greet the Sun," everyone gets a partner. Ms. Hillary then leads one of the following warm-ups:

> **A bulleted list helps organize the essay.**

- **Setting:** She shouts out a setting—optometrist's office, Niagara Falls, detention room, whatever— and the pairs must act out a scene in that location.
- **Character:** She names two characters—a pizza cook and a superhero, a dog and a salesperson, a genius and a child—and each partner must play one role and create a scene between the characters.
- **Conflict:** She calls out a conflict—an argument over a goat, a staring contest, two couch potatoes with two TV remotes—and partners have to act out a scene that shows that conflict.

Ready to Act

Once the individual and partner warm-ups are completed, the whole group is ready to act together. With everyone's wild side fully awake, it's time to hit the stage.

Design a page. Using the guidelines on page 60, create an effective design for an essay you've already written. Share your design with a classmate to get some feedback: Does your design help make your writing clear and easy to follow? Will any of it distract the reader?

PROCESS

Making Your Own Web Site

You can make your own Web site for a multimedia presentation if your family has an Internet account. Ask your provider how to get started. If you are using a school account, ask your teacher for help. Then start designing your site. Use the questions and answers below as a starting point.

How do I plan my site?

Think about how many pages you want on your Web site. Should you put everything on one page, or would you like to have several pages? Check out other sites for ideas. Then plan your pages by sketching them out.

How do I make the pages?

Start each page as a text file using your computer. Use the text styles and graphics that are available through the technology you have. Many new word-processing programs let you save a file as a Web page. If yours doesn't, you will have to use Web page editing software or add HTML (Hypertext Markup Language) codes to format the text and make links to graphics and other pages. Look for instructions about HTML on the Net or at the library.

How do I know whether my pages work?

Test your pages. Using a browser, open your first page. Then follow the links to make sure they work correctly and that all the pages look right.

How do I get my pages on the Net?

You must upload your finished pages to the Internet. (Ask your Internet provider how to do this.) After the upload, visit your site to make sure it still works. Also check it on other computers if possible. Ask friends to visit the site and give you feedback. Use their comments to revise your site.

How do I let people know about my site?

Once your site is up, e-mail your friends and tell them to visit it!

 Keep a journal of Web pages that impress you. Ask questions about each one: What is unique about this page? What isn't? When designing your own pages, refer to your answers.

 **TEKS** 6.14E, 6.17D
ELPS 4G

Publishing Online

The Internet offers many publishing opportunities, including online magazines and writing contests. The information below will help you submit your writing on the Net. (Always get a parent's approval first.)

How should I get started?

Check with your teacher to see if your school has its own Internet site where you can post your work. Also ask your teacher about other Web sites. There are a number of online magazines that accept student writing.

How do I search for possible sites?

Use a search engine to find places to publish. Some search engines also offer their own student links.

How do I submit my work?

Before you do anything, make sure that you understand the publishing guidelines for each site. Be sure to share this information with your teacher and your parents. Then follow these steps:

- **Send your writing in the correct form.**
  Some sites have online forms. Others will ask you to send it by mail or e-mail. Always explain why you are sending your writing.

- **Give the publisher information for contacting you.**
  However, only give personal information if your parents approve.

- **Be patient.**
  It may be several weeks before you hear if your writing will be used or not. Some sites will give you feedback. Compare the site's comments with feedback you received from a classmate or teacher. Revise your work based on all of the responses.

 Search for Web sites. Use the guidelines above to search the Internet for sites that publish student work. Create a list of sites to share with the class. When you complete writing assignments, consider submitting your work for publication using one of the Web sites from your class list.

ELPS 2C, 3E, 4G

Creating a Portfolio

A portfolio is a collection of your best writing completed during a semester or a grading period. With a portfolio, you can compare different pieces of writing to see how you have improved over time.

Think of a portfolio as a form of publishing your writing. Instead of sharing just one piece, a portfolio lets you share an entire "writing album." A portfolio presents a clear picture of you as a writer.

Learning Language

Work with a partner. Read the meanings and answer the questions.

1. A cover sheet is a top page that tells about pages following it.
   What would you write on a cover sheet for your portfolio?

2. A dog-eared page has the top corner folded down.
   Why would you make a dog-eared page?

3. People who reflect on something think about it.
   Reflect on your family. What do you think about them?

What's Ahead

- **Types of Portfolios**
- **Parts of a Portfolio**
- **Planning Ideas**
- **Sample Portfolio Reflections**

 TEKS 6.14E
ELPS 3H

Types of Portfolios

There are four types of portfolios for different audiences: a showcase portfolio, a growth portfolio, a personal portfolio, and an electronic portfolio. Decide which portfolio would be appropriate for your audience.

Showcase Portfolio

A showcase portfolio presents the best writing you have done in school. A showcase is the most common type of portfolio and is usually put together for evaluation at the end of a grading period.

Growth Portfolio

A growth portfolio shows your progress as a writer. It contains writing assignments that show how your writing skills are developing:

- writing beginnings and endings,
- writing with voice, and
- using specific details.

Personal Portfolio

In a personal portfolio, you save writing that you want to keep and share with others. Many professional people—including writers, artists, and musicians—keep personal portfolios. You can arrange this type of portfolio according to different types of writing, different themes, and so on.

Electronic Portfolio

An electronic portfolio is any type of portfolio (showcase, growth, or personal) available on a CD or a Web site. Besides your writing, you can include graphics, video, and sound with this type of portfolio. Now your writing can be available to friends and family members no matter where they are!

 Select your best writing. Let's say you were going to create a portfolio showcasing your last two or three years in school. On your own paper, list four pieces of writing that you would include in this portfolio. Explain your choices to a partner.

PROCESS

Parts of a Portfolio

A showcase portfolio is one of the most common types of portfolios used in schools. It may contain the parts listed below, but always check with your teacher to be sure.

- A **table of contents** lists the writing samples you have included in your portfolio.
- A **brief essay** or **letter** introduces your portfolio—telling how you put it together, how you feel about it, and what it means to you.
- A **collection of writing samples** presents your best work. Your teacher may require that you include all of your planning, drafting, and revising for one or more of your writings.
- A **cover sheet for each sample** explains why you selected it.
- **Evaluations, reflections,** or **checklists** identify the basic skills you have mastered and those skills that you still need to work on.

Gathering Tips

- **Keep track of all your work,** including prewriting notes, first drafts, and revisions for each writing assignment. Then, when you put together a portfolio, you will have everything that you need.
- **Store all of your writing in a pocket folder.** This will help you avoid dog-eared or ripped pages.
- **Set a schedule for working on your portfolio.** You can't put together a good portfolio by waiting until the last minute.
- **Take pride in your work.** Make sure your portfolio shows you at your best.

Reflect on your writing progress. Imagine that your teacher wants you to put together a portfolio, including a paragraph about your writing progress. Write such a paragraph, identifying your strengths and weaknesses as a writer. Also tell what types of writing you like to do best, what your favorite piece of writing is, and so on.

ELPS 3E

Planning Ideas

The following tips will help you choose your best pieces of writing to include in your portfolio.

1 Be patient.

Don't make quick decisions about which pieces of writing to include in your portfolio. Just keep gathering everything—including all your drafts—until you are ready to review all of your writing assignments.

2 Make good decisions.

When it's time to choose writing for your portfolio, review each piece. Remember the feelings you had during each assignment. Which one makes you feel the best? Which one did your readers like the best? Which one taught you the most?

3 Reflect on your choices.

Read the sample reflections on page 69. Then answer these questions about your writing:

- Why did I choose this piece?
- Why did I write this piece? (What was my purpose?)
- How did I write it? (What was my process?)
- What does it show about my writing abilities?
- What can I do differently next time?
- What have I learned that will make me a better writer?

4 Set future writing goals.

After putting together your portfolio, set some goals for the future. Here are some of the goals that other students have set:

I will write about topics that really interest me.

I will spend more time on my beginnings and endings.

I will make sure that my sentences read smoothly.

Plan a portfolio cover. On a piece of plain paper, design a creative cover for a portfolio folder. Include your name and an interesting title. Add sketches or photos related to your writing, your classes, your favorite pastime, and so on. Present your portfolio to a partner.

Sample Portfolio Reflections

When you take time to reflect on your writing assignments, think about the process that you used to develop each one. Also think about what you might do differently next time. The following samples will help you with your own reflections.

Student Reflections

The story about my ancestor in New York is my most interesting piece of writing, ever. I couldn't believe how much I learned about this person. All of my research was actually fun. Ms. Peña always tells us to write about topics that really interest us. Now I know just what she means.

—DeAndra Barker

One of our first assignments this year was to write about a life-changing experience. My narrative about playing in a basketball tournament turned out to be the best thing that I wrote all year. Instead of telling everything about the tournament, I focused on one important part. I wrote about my friend becoming ill and how his illness changed me. I like just about everything about this story, except that it could use more dialogue.

—Todd Ryan

Professional Reflections

I wrote *Mad Merlin* by combining legends of Camelot with histories and myths. As I look back at the novel, though, I see it is mostly about my own life. Good fiction is that way—creative in the details but otherwise full of truth.

—J. Robert King

With each book I write, I become more and more convinced that the books have a life of their own, quite apart from me.

—Madeleine L'Engle

SPECIFY

picture

TEXAS
WRITE
SOURCE
Online
www.hmheducation.com/tx/writesource

Descriptive Writing

Writing Focus

- Descriptive Paragraph
- Descriptive Essay

Learning Language

Learning these words and expressions will help you understand this unit. Work with a partner to read the meanings and answer the prompts.

1. A description tells more about something.
   Give a description of your favorite animal.

2. To capture something means to catch it.
   Name an animal that you could capture.

3. A movie that gives facts about a topic is called a documentary.
   Name a documentary that you have seen.

4. Getting big air means to make a big jump off the ground.
   In what sports might you say that you are getting big air?

express
describe
portray

Descriptive Writing

Descriptive Paragraph

What animal has two points on the top of its head, big bright eyes, sharp claws, and an appetite for rodents? You might have said, "A cat, of course!" but what about an owl—or even the double-crested dinosaur called a Dilophosaurus? All three of these animals could easily fit the description.

When you write a description, you want to make sure your reader knows exactly what you are talking about. Your writing should create a mental picture in your reader's mind by using sensory details. In this chapter, you will write a paragraph describing an interesting animal. Your goal is to tell about the creature's shape, size, and color, as well as the sounds it makes and the way it moves. With words alone, you can capture a wild animal!

Writing Guidelines

Subject: An animal you have seen

Purpose: To describe an animal

Form: Descriptive paragraph

Audience: Classmates

ELPS 2C, 2G, 2H, 3D, 3E, 3G, 4G, 4I, 4J

Descriptive Paragraph

A **descriptive paragraph** gives a detailed picture of a person, a place, a thing, or an event. It begins with a **topic sentence** that tells what the paragraph is about. The sentences in the **body** give all of the descriptive details about the topic. The **closing sentence** wraps up the paragraph. The paragraph below uses colorful details to describe a special bird of prey.

Night Visitor

Topic Sentence

In the glowing sunset, the great horned owl sat straight and still on top of the fence post. With pointed ears and a thick, long body, its shadow looked like a cat. The owl's head swiveled slowly from side to side

Body

like a security camera. Its ears listened for the softest sound. Its round, lemon-colored eyes looked for even the slightest movement. The owl's deep, sad voice haunted the

Closing Sentence

darkness with *who-who-whooooooo.* Then the owl was ready to move on. It spread its wide, powerful wings, lifted from its perch, and glided away into the darkness.

Respond to the reading. On your own paper, answer the following questions. Discuss your answers with a partner.

- ☐ Focus and Coherence **(1) How is the focus introduced?**
- ☐ Organization **(2) What method of organization (time order, order of location, order of importance) did the writer use? Explain.**
- ☐ Development of Ideas **(3) What ideas make the animal seem real to the reader?**

DESCRIPTIVE

Prewriting Selecting a Topic

To get started, you need to plan your draft by choosing a topic. Choose an animal that you've seen either in real life or in pictures. The animal should interest you. The writer of the paragraph on page 72 made the following list of possible topics using sentence starters.

List

> ### Animals I Have Seen
>
> The most beautiful animal is . . . a toucan.
>
> The most mysterious is . . . a great horned owl.
>
> The ugliest animal is . . . an armadillo.
>
> The smallest animal is . . . a mouse.
>
> The scariest animal is . . . a black bear.
>
> The funniest animal is . . . a flying squirrel.

Select a topic. Create your own list of possible animal topics by completing the sentence starters above. Then choose one that really interests you to describe in a paragraph.

Gathering Details—Show, Don't Tell

In a descriptive paragraph, the goal is to *show* using sensory details instead of *telling* about it. Details that show are specific and colorful.

Collect your details. Answer the following questions to help you gather specific details about your animal.

- What does your animal's head look like?
- What does its body look like?
- What color and texture are its fur, feathers, or skin?
- What does it sound like?
- Where do you usually find it?
- What unusual or interesting things does it do?
- What can you compare this animal to?

 **TEKS** 6.14D
ELPS 3H

Drafting **Creating Your First Draft**

The goal of a first draft is to get all of your ideas and details down on paper. Follow the guidelines below.

- Start with a topic sentence that catches your reader's interest.
- Arrange the descriptive sentences in the body according to location. Include the details that you gathered on page 73.
- End with a sentence that keeps the reader thinking about the topic.

 Write your first draft. Get your best ideas and details down on paper. Describe the animal from top to bottom or from left to right. Then give your paragraph a title.

Revising **Improving Your Paragraph**

When you revise, consider how well you've used focus and coherence, organization, ideas, and voice in your first draft.

1 Is my topic sentence clear? Do I stay focused on the topic throughout the paragraph?

2 Have I organized the details in my paragraph using order of location?

3 Do I use specific nouns, verbs, and adjectives?

4 Do I sound interested in my topic?

 Revise your paragraph. Use the questions above as a guide when you revise your paragraph.

Editing **Checking for Conventions**

Carefully edit your revised paragraph for grammar, punctuation, capitalization, and spelling. Then write a neat final copy.

 Edit and proofread your work. Use the following questions to check your paragraph for errors. Then write a neat final copy.

1 Do the verbs in each sentence agree with the subjects that I used?

2 Do I use correct punctuation, capitalization, and spelling?

Descriptive Writing

Describing an Event

Describing an event is sort of like filming a documentary. Your job is to capture the moment so people anywhere in the world can experience it for themselves. In order to give your reader a clear picture of what you are describing, you should use sensory details. You need to convey what you see, hear, taste, touch, and smell.

In this chapter, you will write about an animal—and take your readers on an animal safari!

Writing Guidelines

Subject: **An event**

Purpose: **To inform by clearly describing an animal**

Form: **Descriptive essay**

Audience: **Classmates**

 TEKS 6.14B
ELPS 4I

Descriptive Essay

In this sample essay, the writer describes an encounter with a bullfrog. As you read, notice how the writer develops a focused and coherent description. The notes in the margin will explain the important parts of the writing.

The Watcher in the Water

Beginning

The beginning introduces the animal being described to show the focus of the essay.

Eyes! I saw eyes staring back at me from the murky, muddy edge of the river. Those were definitely eyes. I immediately recognized the watcher in the water to be a big, olive green bullfrog.

The eyes barely broke the surface. The bullfrog blended perfectly into the slimy, yellow brown water that lapped against the river's edge. With all the sticks and dead leaves floating around it, this bullfrog had found the perfect place to hide.

Middle

The middle uses sensory words and phrases. Each description focuses the reader on the bullfrog and its surroundings.

I stood completely still on the sticky riverbank and listened to the "rom-rom-rom" call from the bullfrog. The noise echoed through the dark woods that surrounded me. The bullfrog was small, but its call was loud and deep. It sounded like it should be coming from a larger animal. If I hadn't been staring at the frog, I would have thought the call belonged to a cow!

TEKS 6.14B
ELPS 2G, 2H, 3D, 3G, 4I

DESCRIPTIVE

I watched the frog watching me. It looked like a statue that someone had tossed into the river. Still, I could see a slight movement in its throat as it continued to entertain me with its slow rhythmic song.

One of the frog's powerful hind legs twitched. The water circled out in tiny ripples that grew larger as they neared me. The frog twitched again and then leapt from its rocky perch. Like an acrobat, it twisted in the air and pushed itself forward toward the center of the river. The splash it made left me wiping water drops from my legs. As the water settled again, I listened carefully. In the distance, I heard another smaller splash followed by the deep drumming of the bullfrog's lullaby.

Ending
....
The ending tells how the writer's encounter with the bullfrog concludes.

Respond to the reading. Answer the following questions about the essay.

☐ **Focus and Coherence** (1) What experience does the writer share? (2) What details focus the reader on the bullfrog and its surroundings?

☐ **Organization** (3) How is the essay organized—by order of importance, by location, or by both order of importance and location?

☐ **Voice** (4) What words show that the writer is interested in the subject?

 **TEKS** 6.14A
ELPS 3H, 5G

Prewriting **Selecting a Topic**

The general topic for your essay is an animal. To plan your first draft, you will need to determine specific details that create a mental picture of your animal. A chart like the one below is a good strategy for brainstorming ideas about animals and what they do.

Topic Chart

Animal	Descriptive Action
tiger	stalks prey
salmon	swims upstream to spawn
peacock	roams around the zoo
blue jay	watches over a bird feeder
hunting dog	retrieves a duck
house cat	curls up to sleep

Create a topic chart. In the first column, list different animals that you would like to write about. In the second column, list an action or event related to each animal. When you complete your chart, select one animal for your essay. Pick one whose actions you can describe effectively.

Gathering Details

As you plan your draft, you will need to gather details that develop your thesis, or main idea, and keep you focused on your topic throughout the essay. One way to do this is to analyze, or think carefully about your topic.

Gather details. Answer the following questions to analyze your topic.

1 What does the animal look like? (Describe it from top to bottom or from front to back.)

2 What do I see, hear, smell, or feel when I see or think about this animal in action?

3 What is the animal similar to and different from?

4 What are its strengths and weaknesses?

TEKS 6.14B
ELPS 3H, 5G

Organizing Your Details

When writing about an animal, you may use two different organizational strategies in your essay—order of importance and order of location.

- **Order of importance** *(least important to most important; most important to least important)*: You will use this method of organization to describe an event. The writer of the essay told about the bullfrog using order of importance. (See list below.)

- **Order of location** *(top to bottom, front to back)*: You may also use this method if part of your essay describes the animal in detail.

List

1. See the enormous peacock
2. Roamed around the entrance
3. Spread its huge tail feathers
4. Peacocks dance around each other
5. Tail feathers look like eyes

Prewrite

Organize your details. Imagine you are a filmmaker creating a movie that shows an animal in its habitat. Decide which organizational strategy is best. Use the strategy to list details of scenes you will show your audience.

Using Figures of Speech

You can use figures of speech to make your descriptive writing clearer and more creative. Two common figures of speech are similes and metaphors. They both create special word pictures.

- A **simile** compares two different things using *like* or *as*.
  The owl swiveled its head from side to side like a security camera.

- A **metaphor** compares two different things without using *like* or *as*.
  The bullfrog was a stone, sitting completely still.

Try It

Write a simile and metaphor about your animal in action. If you like how either one turns out, include it in your essay.

TEKS 6.14B
ELPS 3H, 5G

Drafting **Starting Your Descriptive Essay**

The beginning paragraph should introduce the topic in a focused way. This tells your reader what your essay is about and keeps it organized. Here are two approaches to writing a focused and exciting beginning paragraph.

Beginning Paragraph

■ **Put yourself in the description.** Tell where you were, what you were doing, or how you felt.

The writer makes a personal connection.

When I was younger, we visited the zoo on Sunday afternoons. An enormous, mean peacock always roamed around near the main entrance. I imagined that it was a multicolored, screaming monster waiting to attack. It terrified me.

■ **Observe the scene.** Focus your description on the animal, and not on your personal connection with it. Be sure that all of your details relate to the topic to keep the paragraph coherent.

The writer focuses on the animal.

The peacock at the local zoo was enormous and mean. It always roamed around near the main entrance. To some of the younger kids, it wasn't just a bird, it was a multicolored, screaming monster.

Using an Engaging Voice

Voice is the special way that a writer expresses his or her ideas. A writer's voice engages the reader and keeps this connection throughout the essay. Keep the following tips about voice in mind as you write.

● Use a natural, sincere voice and show your enthusiasm.
● Share descriptive details as if you were having a conversation.

Write your beginning paragraph. Choose one of the approaches above to draft a focused, organized, and coherent beginning paragraph. Try different strategies until you are pleased with your result.

TEKS 6.14B
ELPS 3H, 5G

Developing the Middle Part

In the middle paragraphs of your essay, you should build on ideas to create a clear, focused mental picture of your animal. By using sensory details and sharing feelings, you show the reader what happened in a creative way. Use the organization list strategies from page 79 to help you.

Middle Paragraphs

Review these sample middle paragraphs for focus, organization, and coherence.

The paragraph describes one scene.

I remember the peacock jumping in front of me as I walked with my father. My first impression was that it was taller than I was. A flurry of blue and green swam in front of me as it bobbed back and forth. I thought it had a hundred little eyes on is back but later realized it was just a pattern on its brightly colored tail feathers. The peacock opened its tiny, pointy beak. I expected a sweet little chirp. Instead I was shocked by its high-pitched scream. I was definitely afraid, but something made me want to get a closer look.

The paragraph describes a second scene with the peacock.

When my class visited the zoo a few weeks later, I set out to find the peacock again. I hid a safe distance away. I could clearly see those eye-shaped marks on is feathers. They were surrounded by what looked like grass. The colors of green, blue, orange, and gold were so bright they almost sparkled. I noticed that the peacock had feathers standing on top of its head. It seemed to be wearing a fancy hat. Those little feathers bounced as it danced and bobbed at anyone who dared to walk too close. I spent the whole field trip watching the peacock and hoping it would not see me.

Draft

Write your middle paragraphs. Use sensory details and feelings to create a focused, well-organized, coherent picture for your reader. Try to describe one main scene in each paragraph.

 **TEKS** 6.14B, 6.14D
ELPS 3H, 5G

Ending Your Essay

Your ending paragraph should bring your essay to a close and give your reader a sense of completeness. Try to say something to keep the reader thinking about your animal.

Ending Paragraph

The writer makes a final personal connection.	*Most people think that peacocks are beautiful, gentle birds. I agree that they are beautiful, but peacocks don't seem so gentle to me. I have heard their awful, screechy cries. I have seen those spooky tail feather eyes that appear to follow my every move. That why I chose to watch the peacock from a distance!*

 Write your ending paragraph. When you write your ending, be sure to stay focused on your topic. Make a final comment or tell about an event to help the readers remember the animal.

Revising and Editing

A first draft can always be improved. You may need to make a detail clearer and more focused or reorganize ideas to ensure coherence.

☐ **Focus and Coherence** Do I have a clear topic? Do I stay focused and coherent throughout the whole essay?

☐ **Organization** Do I organize the details in the order of their importance? Do I tell about my animal using order of location?

☐ **Development of Ideas** Do I use sensory words and feelings to tell about my animal and its environment?

☐ **Voice** Do I sound interested in my topic?

 Revise your first draft. Revise your essay, using the questions above as a guide.

 Edit your description. Use the checklist on page 128 to help you edit for grammar, mechanics (punctuation and capitalization), sentence structure, and spelling. Then write and proofread your final copy.

Descriptive Writing
Across the Curriculum

Descriptive writing is often assigned in other classes. For example, in social studies, you may be asked to describe life in a different time. In math, you may be asked to describe a geometric shape. In science class, you may be asked to describe a common—or not so common—natural event.

To write strong descriptions, you need to know lots about your topic: what it looks like, how it works, where it occurs, what makes it special, and so on. You will need to use sensory details in your description to help your reader see a clear picture. If your description is a success, a reader will be able to picture the topic in his or her mind.

What's Ahead

- **Social Studies:** Describing a Scene in a Different Time
- **Math:** Describing Geometric Terms
- **Science:** Describing a Natural Event
- **Practical Writing:** Creating a Thank-You Note

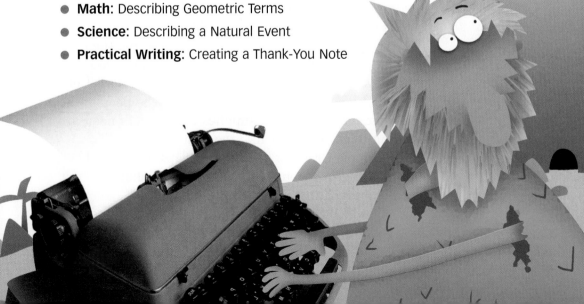

Social Studies:
Describing a Scene in a Different Time

Descriptive writing is one way to share information about a different time and place. The student writer of the following essay puts herself back in time to bring to life a Colorado town during the gold rush.

Gold Rush Days

The **beginning** sets the scene.

  It's 1891. The town of Cripple Creek, Colorado, has appeared almost overnight since gold was discovered nearby. Hundreds of people arrive by crowded trains and by dusty stagecoaches. Others also come on foot or by horseback to make their fortunes.

The **middle** helps the reader create a mental image by using sensory details.

  Towering snowcapped mountains surround the town. Pikes Peak, one of the highest points in the Rocky Mountains, can be seen to the east. A muddy stagecoach trail follows the shoulders of the big peak and winds down toward the wild new town. The land all around Cripple Creek is full of tree stumps. The wood from these trees was used to build houses and mining tunnels. Hills above the town are dotted with piles of dirt from all the new mines.

  Hotels, cafes, churches, and saloons line the dirt streets of Cripple Creek. People hurry along wood-plank sidewalks. Because of the gold, there's a lot of money here, but prices are very high. The people who sell the tools, food, and supplies that miners need are trying to get rich just like the miners.

The **ending** offers a final thought.

  Cripple Creek is growing by leaps and bounds, but its future depends on the miners. If they strike it rich, who knows how big the town will get!

Writing Tips

Before you write . . .

- **Choose a different time and place that interests you.**
  Select a topic related to the subjects you are studying.
- **Do your research.**
  Learn as much as you can about your topic. Make sure to study any pictures that you can find.
- **Take notes.**
  Write down important details that will help you with your description.

Cluster

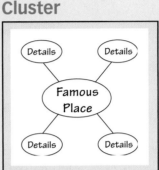

During your writing . . .

- **Write a clear beginning, middle, and ending.**
  In the beginning, set the scene. In the middle part, describe the place. End with a final thought about it.
- **Organize your thoughts.**
  When you describe a place, you may describe it from top to bottom, from left to right, or from far to near.
- **Use an engaging voice.**
  Your voice should sound as though you know a lot about your topic and are really interested in it.

After you've written a first draft . . .

- **Check for completeness.**
  Make sure that you have included enough information so that the reader can see your topic in his or her mind.
- **Check for correctness.**
  Proofread your essay to make sure there are no mistakes in punctuation, capitalization, spelling, or grammar.

DESCRIPTIVE

 Choose a time and place that interests you. Then write a creative and complete description about it to share with your classmates.

Math: Describing Geometric Terms

Descriptive writing can be used to write about geometric terms. In each paragraph below, notice how the student describes a geometric term.

The writer uses math words a reader should understand.

A Straight Angle

A line is just a straight mark until a person learns more about it in a math class. A line is really a set of points in a straight row. It goes on forever, but as soon as two end points are put on it, a line segment is formed. A line segment measured with a protractor measures 180 degrees. A line segment is also called a straight angle. There's more to a straight line than a person might think.

180°

Line Segment/Straight Angle

An illustration helps describe the term.

A Right Angle

It takes three things to form a right angle. It starts with two rays. A ray begins at a point and goes on forever in a straight line. Second, each of the rays must share one endpoint, or vertex. Third, the angle between the two rays must measure 90 degrees. It's as simple as that!

90°

Vertex

TEKS 6.14A, 6.14B, 6.14D

ELPS 3E

Writing Tips

Before you write . . .

- **Review the geometric term** you plan to describe.
- **Be sure you understand all of the vocabulary** that is needed to describe the term.
- **Make a plan,** starting with the simplest part of your description.
- **Organize the details** that will help you write a clear and interesting description.

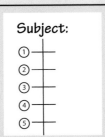

Time line

Subject:
①
②
③
④
⑤

During your writing . . .

- **Study your basic plan and make it coherent.**
- **Describe everything very carefully** and be sure each sentence is clear and leads logically to the next sentence.
- **Use math words your reader will understand** and explain any words that may be confusing.
- **Add details** in a logical order.
- **Include an illustration** if it helps describe the term.

After you've written a first draft . . .

- **Check for completeness.**
  Be sure that you used the correct vocabulary to describe your term.
- **Check for order and coherence.**
  Read through your description to make sure it is organized in a logical way and coherent. Revise sentences as needed.
- **Check for correctness.**
  Are the words spelled correctly? Are the sentences capitalized and punctuated correctly?

DESCRIPTIVE

 Write your own description of a geometric term—possibly one of the polygons or triangles. Use the tips listed above. Share your description with your classmates.

Science: Describing a Natural Event

The world is filled with fascinating subjects to describe. Plants, landforms, animals, and weather all offer many excellent topics. In the following essay, a student describes what it is like to observe the fog.

The beginning gets the reader's attention.

The middle describes the topic using specific details.

The ending offers a final thought.

Fog

Yesterday morning, I sat on the porch waiting for the school bus to arrive. The world looked very different. Overnight a strange mist had silently crept across the valley and surrounded my house in a thick, dense fog.

From the porch, I could taste the wetness in the air. My cheeks and hands were damp. There was no wind. Even the sounds of morning were quiet in the haze. No birds sang out today.

Just down the steps, my mother's bright flowers looked pale and dull. The usually green grass was faded and wet with drops of water left over from last night's rain. Looking to the edge of the yard, the fog was even thicker. The leaves on the bushes melted together making it look like a shadowy lump.

I peeked down the road. I could not see the intersection at the end of the street. The big tree on the corner was just a pencil sketch against a pure white background. I heard the bus before I could see it. Maybe the fog had swallowed it up. Slowly it came into focus, escaping the mist and reaching my house. The world may have looked very different, but the school bus looked the same.

★ **TEKS** 6.14A, 6.14B, 6.14D

Writing Tips

Before you write . . .

- **Choose a topic that interests you.**
  If possible, select a natural event that you have seen or experienced yourself.

- **Research your topic.**
  Think about your experience with the topic and read about it. Take notes and organize your research.

During your writing . . .

- **Write a clear beginning, middle, and ending.**
  Grab your reader's interest in the beginning part. In the middle, describe your topic in the most interesting way you can. Close with a final thought about it.

- **Organize your thoughts.**
  Think about the organization of your description. The one on page 88 is organized from far away to very close. If there is a lot of action, you should probably organize your description according to time.

- **Use specific words.**
  A strong description contains specific nouns, vivid verbs, and modifiers (adjectives and adverbs).

After you've written a first draft . . .

- **Check for completeness.**
  Make sure that you have included all the details that the reader needs to understand your description. Revise as needed.

- **Check for correctness.**
  Proofread your description for punctuation, capitalization, spelling, and grammar.

 Select a natural event to describe. Gather plenty of details about your topic. Then describe it in an essay using the tips above.

TEKS 6.17B

Practical Writing:
Creating a Thank-You Note

Descriptive writing appears in almost any form. Descriptions add life to letters, e-mail messages, notes, and greeting cards. The writer of this thank-you note describes a snowboard to his aunt.

❖ ❖ ❖ ❖ ❖ ❖ *Thank You* ❖ ❖ ❖ ❖ ❖ ❖

Dear Aunt Gloria,

The **beginning** identifies the reason for the note.

Thanks for the gift certificate you sent me for my birthday. I used it to buy what every kid here in Duluth wants, a freestyle snowboard!

The **middle** describes the topic and gives information.

The board I bought is called the Atomic Storm. If you stood it up next to me, you would see that it is almost as tall as I am. It is about 10 inches wide, which makes it a lot wider than an old-fashioned ski. The front is called the nose, and it is rounded, like the end of a paper clip. The design on it is awesome. Bright orange rows of flames spill all the way down the shiny black center. When you get to the back, or the tail, of the board, you find out that the fire is coming from a slick red race car. The tail of the board is rounded, just like the nose.

The **ending** gives some final thoughts.

I love my new board. It's perfect for getting big air at the snowboard park and doing spins and tricks like a pro. I'll send you some pictures of me using it.

Love,

Jy

TEKS 6.17B

Writing Tips

Before you write . . .

- **Select a topic.**
  Choose a topic for your thank-you note: a special gift that you received from a family member or friend.
- **List main ideas you want to include.**
  Since you are thanking someone for a gift, consider what it looks like, why you like it, and how you are using it.
- **Gather specific details.**
  List details to describe the gift.
- **Consider your feelings.**
  Ask yourself how you feel about the gift.

During your writing . . .

- **Organize your thoughts.**
  State the reason for the note in the beginning. Give the descriptive details in the middle part. Offer a final thought in the ending part.
- **Use colorful words.**
  Use specific nouns, strong action verbs, and colorful adjectives to describe the gift.

After you've written a first draft . . .

- **Check for completeness.**
  Keep your paragraphs fairly short. Are there enough details to make your description clear and fun to read? Do your sentences flow smoothly?
- **Check for correctness.**
  Proofread your note to make sure there are no mistakes in punctuation, capitalization, spelling, or grammar.

Create a thank-you note for a family member or friend. Describe a special gift in your note. Use the tips above and the sample note on page **90**.

relate *tell*

ELPS 2C, 2G, 2H, 2I, 3D, 3E, 3G, 3H, 4C, 4G

TEXAS
WRITE
SOURCE
Online

www.hmheducation.com/tx/writesource

Narrative Writing

Writing Focus

- Narrative Paragraph
- Personal Narrative
- Biographical Narrative

Grammar Focus

- Reflexive Pronouns

Learning Language

Learning these words and expressions will help you understand this unit. Work with a partner to read the meanings and answer the prompts.

1. Something that is narrative tells a story.
   Describe a narrative you have written recently.
2. You can't forget something that is unforgettable.
   What has been unforgettable about this year so far?
3. Transition words help you change from idea to idea.
   Name one transition word you know.
4. To shed light on something is to give information about it.
   What is one topic you could shed light on?

narrate remember share

Narrative Writing

Narrative Paragraph

The next time you're with a friend, pay attention to what you say to each other. Maybe you talk about what happened on your walk to school, about a movie you saw last night, about the time Grandpa won the karate championship. . . . You and your friends tell all kinds of stories!

You can capture your storytelling talents on paper by writing a narrative. The following pages will help you write a narrative paragraph about a pleasant surprise.

Writing Guidelines

Subject: A pleasant surprise that you experienced

Purpose: To entertain

Form: Narrative paragraph

Audience: Classmates

ELPS 2H, 2I, 3D, 3E, 3G, 3H, 4C, 4G, 4I, 4K

Narrative Paragraph

Some of the most entertaining stories contain surprises. Perhaps your hamster escaped from his cage, but at school you opened up your backpack and discovered him chewing on your math assignment. Maybe you spiked your hair, thinking it was "Crazy Hair Day," when it was actually "Picture Day." These kinds of surprises make entertaining narrative paragraphs. The following narrative paragraph tells about a nighttime surprise.

Topic Sentence

Body

Closing Sentence

Things That Go Bump

One night last week, I was surprised by a thing that went "bump!" I was just drifting off to sleep when I heard a footstep in my dark bedroom. I gasped and sat up. Somebody was in the room with me. My door was shut, but the window was open. That's how the intruder must have gotten in. Something crashed, and coins went rolling all over the floor. My bank! Sure, I had only 10 bucks and some change, but it was my 10 bucks! Leaping up, I flipped on the light and took a swing at the burglar. With a yowl, Whiskers jumped over my fist and shot back out the window. Even as I was shaking, I began to laugh. Some cat burglar that was—my own cat!

Respond to the reading. Respond to the following questions on your own paper.

☐ **Focus and Coherence** (1) What is the topic of the paragraph?

☐ **Organization** (2) How does the writer organize the events in the paragraph?

☐ **Voice** (3) What words or phrases show you that the writer enjoys this topic?

TEKS 6.14A
ELPS 3H, 5G

Prewriting **Selecting a Topic**

Plan your draft by first deciding on a topic. The writer of "Things That Go Bump" used a cluster to write down some of his surprising experiences.

Cluster

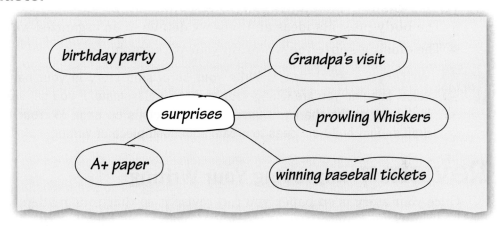

Prewrite

Create a cluster. In the middle of your paper, write the word "surprises" and circle it. Then create a cluster of four or five of your own surprising experiences. Choose one of these experiences as your topic.

Gathering Details

To gather details, the writer of the sample paragraph on page 94 listed what happened first, what he expected to happen next, and what surprise actually happened.

Chart

What Happened First	What I Expected to Happen Next	What Surprise Actually Happened
heard a sound in my room at night	to see a burglar	saw my cat Whiskers

Prewrite

Chart your surprise. Make a chart like the one above. Write what happened first, what you expected to happen next, and what surprise happened.

NARRATIVE

 **TEKS** 6.14B, 6.14C
ELPS 3H, 5G

Drafting Developing the First Draft

A narrative paragraph has a topic sentence, a body, and a closing sentence. Each part serves a different purpose. All parts build on ideas to create a focused piece of writing.

- The **topic sentence** introduces the focus of your story.
- The **body** presents ideas and sensory details in an organized way.
- The **closing sentence** wraps up your paragraph.

 Write your first draft. Write your surprising story in your natural voice. Imagine you are telling your story to a classmate. If you get stuck, look back at the chart you used to gather details on page 95. Your first draft should build on ideas to create a focused piece of writing.

Revising Improving Your Writing

Once your story is on paper, you can revise it so that your readers will feel like they experienced it right along with you. Here are a few tips.

- **Keep your focus.** Make sure you focus on one experience and include details about only that experience.
- **Check the order.** Tell events in the order they happened.
- **Clarify meaning.** Add sentences or larger units of text if needed to make things clear.
- **Develop ideas.** Use colorful language and sensory details that help readers understand and appreciate your experience.

 Revise your paragraph. Check your focus, organization, development of ideas, and voice as you revise your narrative paragraph. Look for ways to improve your opening and closing sentences.

Editing Checking for Conventions

Carefully edit your revised paragraph by checking for grammar, punctuation, capitalization, and spelling errors.

 Proofread and edit your work. Use the following questions to check for errors. Then write a final copy.

1 Do I use correct grammar, punctuation, capitalization, and spelling?

2 Do I use transition words to tie my sentences together?

Narrative Writing

Personal Narrative

Like everyone else, you have stories to tell. Think about how many times you have said, "Guess what happened to me!" or "Do you know what I did?" Your life is full of stories. You took a trip, broke your arm, or finally got your own pet. Writing a personal narrative is a way to share one of your important stories. Personal narratives have a clear focus and communicate reasons for actions or consequences. Writing narratives is also a way for you to learn about yourself and your special place in the world.

Think about personal experiences that you could share with your classmates. You could write about something that happened to you, something you did, or someone you have a special relationship with. Here are some guidelines to help you get started.

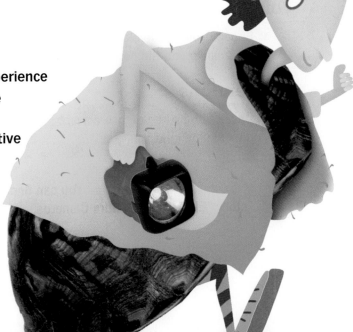

Writing Guidelines

Subject:	**A personal experience**
Purpose:	**To share a true experience**
Form:	**Personal narrative**
Audience:	**Classmates**

Understanding Your Goal

Your goal in this chapter is to write an essay about an interesting personal experience. The traits listed in the chart below will help you plan and write your personal narrative. The scoring rubric on pages 48 and 49 will also help you. Refer to it often to improve your writing.

Traits of Narrative Writing

Focus and Coherence

Write about a time that sticks out in your mind. To help readers appreciate the story, use details and dialogue that make readers feel that they are with you.

Organization

Arrange the events in time order. Use transitions to help readers understand the order of events.

Development of Ideas

Make the experience come alive for your readers. Use specific nouns and action verbs that create details that bring events to life.

Voice

Engage your readers and keep them interested by making your personality and the personalities of others come through.

Conventions

Check to be sure you use correct grammar, capitalization, punctuation, and spelling.

Literature Connection: You can find a personal narrative in the short story "Eleven," by Sandra Cisneros.

TEKS 6.16A

ELPS 4I

Personal Narrative

In this personal narrative, the student author writes about a special group that taught her about turtles. The side notes point out important parts of the narrative.

Turtle Rescue

Beginning

The beginning has a clearly defined focus. It tells what the story is about.

When we first moved to Texas, Dad and I went to the ocean every week and enjoyed just taking walks on the beach. The beach was usually deserted, except for some seagulls and a few sand crabs. However, one night, we spotted a campfire way down the beach. We went to check it out. As we got closer, we saw dark forms sitting in the sand near the dying flames. The glow of the fire revealed University of Texas sweatshirts.

"Stop right there! Don't move," a student wearing a red bandanna whispered loudly. Not far from where I stood, I made out the shape of a huge turtle digging in the sand. "That turtle needs her space right now."

"Why, what's wrong?" I whispered back.

Middle

The middle develops the narrative in greater detail. The voice of the writer reveals his or her personality and keeps readers interested.

"She's digging out a nest, and she'll lay her eggs there tonight. When she's done, she'll go back to the sea."

"Who are you?" I whispered.

The student came closer. "We're students that come from Austin on spring break. We clean up the beach so it's safe for the turtles. If you two want to listen, we'd love to tell you more about Kemp's ridley sea turtles."

Every day my Dad and I hiked up the beach to help the students, and every day we learned more about Kemp's ridleys and other sea turtles. We'd sit around the campfire. Some nights other volunteers would join us. They spoke of the many turtles they had seen over the years.

TEKS 6.16A
ELPS 2G, 3D, 3G,
4G, 4I, 4J, 4K

Middle
The events are arranged in time order so readers can understand and appreciate the experience.

Ending
. . . .

The ending wraps up the experience and shows readers its importance.

Soon, the college students left. After a couple of months, an amazing thing happened. The sand near that first nest began to ripple and shake. A couple days later, dozens of little turtles tunneled their way out from under the sand and scrambled toward the sea. The waves tossed some of them back onto the shore. That's when my Dad, other volunteers, and I grabbed the baby turtles that landed upside down and couldn't get up. We quickly rescued them and gently placed them back in the ocean. If we had not been there, the hatchlings would have died, or they might have become some seagull's supper.

Rescuing those turtles was the coolest thing I've ever done. As quickly as the turtle rescue had begun, it was over. The turtles no longer needed us.

As the last turtle disappeared into the ocean, I turned to my Dad and asked, "Can we come back again next year?"

"Definitely," he said. "I wouldn't miss this for the world." Rescuing the turtles meant a lot to both of us.

Respond to the reading. Why is "Turtle Rescue" such a good personal narrative? To find out, answer the following questions.

☐ **Focus and Coherence** (1) What unforgettable experience does the writer share?

☐ **Organization** (2) How does the writer organize the events in the story?

☐ **Voice** (3) Which expressions and details show the writer's personality?

Go Online!

Prewriting

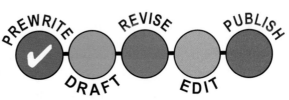

PREWRITE ✓ REVISE PUBLISH
DRAFT EDIT

Before you are ready to write your narrative, you need to choose a personal experience to write about. After selecting a topic, you will continue prewriting by gathering and organizing details.

Keys to Effective Prewriting

1. Select an experience that you know well and would like to share.

2. Make sure you can answer the 5 W questions about the experience.

3. Think about and describe the people in your narrative.

4. Put the events in order by using a quick list or a time line.

5. Gather sensory details to make the experience come alive to the reader.

NARRATIVE

PROD. NO.
SCENE
TAKE
ROLL
SOUND

TEKS 6.14A

Prewriting Selecting a Topic

The key to a good personal narrative is finding an interesting topic—one that both you and the reader will enjoy. The chart below is a strategy that shows how one writer plans a first draft by brainstorming appropriate and interesting topics around people, places, and other experiences.

Brainstorm Chart

People I Know	Places I've Been	Animals I Remember	Things I've Done
My brother Sam	The Alamo	B. J., the dog	Marched in a parade
My friend Kenny	Mexico	Big raccoon	Met the governor
Tyisha, the dancer	My uncle's wedding	Snake at the campground	Explored a cave

Prewrite

Brainstorm for topics. On your own paper, draw a chart like the one above. Use the same four headings for your categories. Then use your personal experiences to choose an interesting topic and develop a focus for your narrative.

1 Brainstorm at least three ideas under each heading.

2 Now go over your ideas. Think carefully about each one. How much can you say about the topic? Will readers enjoy reading about it?

3 Circle the topic that you think would make the best story.

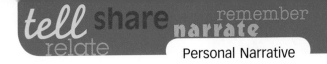

TEKS 6.14A, 6.16A
ELPS 3H, 5G

Sizing Up Your Idea

Your narrative should have a clearly defined focus about an experience you had at a specific time and place. It should communicate the importance of the experience or the reasons for your specific actions or responses. You can use the 5 W's to find out if your story idea has all of these details.

1. **Who** are the people in my story?
2. **What** main experience will I write about?
3. **When** and **where** did the experience take place?
4. **Why** did the experience change me?

Prewrite

Size up your story idea. Write your answers to the 5 W questions above. Review your answers. Do you have a clear focus for your story? Do you have enough details to develop your idea? If not, choose another topic from your chart (page 102).

Gathering Details About People

A personal narrative tells about your experiences, so you will be in your story as well as any other people or animals. A personality web is a strategy that can help you develop ideas or details about the people in your story.

Personality Web

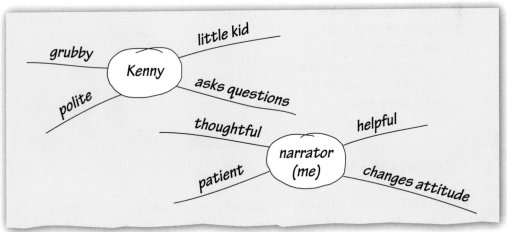

NARRATIVE

Prewrite

Make personality webs. Create a personality web for each important person in your story. Write each person's name in a circle and include details about the person on the lines. Study your web and determine if your topic is appropriate and can be developed.

 **TEKS** 6.19A(viii)
ELPS 3H, 5G

Prewriting Putting Events in Order

Once you've decided your topic, list the events in your story. Most narratives are organized in chronological (time) order. That means events appear in the order in which they happened. To help you organize your narrative, write a quick list using transitional words and phrases.

Quick List

> *My Friend Kenny*
>
> – *I thought little kids were a pain.*
> – *Then Uncle Eddie asked me to volunteer at bike camp.*
> – *There were tons of little kids at the camp.*
> – *So I thought bike camp would be a drag.*
> – *Then I made friends with a neat little kid named Kenny.*
> – *As a result, I learned to like little kids.*

Prewrite

Create your quick list. Make a list like the one above. Write your story topic at the top. Then write the details of your story in the order in which they occurred. Use transitional words to develop and link your story ideas.

Texas Traits

★ Focus on the Texas Traits

Organization Once you have the main details of the story in time order, think of more transitional words and phrases that could help keep your ideas logically organized. (See pages 620–621.) Add these words to your list or change the ones you have.

Gathering Sensory Details

A good story has lots of colorful, specific details. Some of these details should relate to the senses. Then the reader is able to imagine not only what things look like but also how things sound, smell, taste, and feel.

Making a sensory chart, like the one below, is one way you can gather sensory details about your experience.

Sensory Chart

SENSORY DETAILS

I saw...	– little kids riding trikes – squirmy kids
I heard...	– Uncle Eddie – trike bells and bike horns
I smelled...	– chocolate on Kenny's clothes
I felt...	– Kenny's sticky little fingers – pain in my foot
I tasted...	– (could almost taste) the chocolate bar smeared on Kenny's face

Prewrite

Create a sensory chart. List the five senses with space after each one. Then recall your experience and fill in the chart as completely as you can. (It's all right to have many details for some senses and only a few or none for others.) You will use some of these details in your narrative.

Texas Traits

★ Focus on the Texas Traits

Voice The details and feelings you use in your writing are part of your individual voice. The words you choose to describe what you saw, heard, smelled, tasted, or touched are also part of your voice and express your personality.

TEKS 6.19A(viii)
ELPS 3H, 5G

Prewriting Reviewing Your Details

Before you begin writing your story, look over your prewriting quick list, personality web, and sensory chart. Be sure you've collected enough details to write a good personal narrative.

 Read the paragraph below. Then answer these questions about the details used in "A Hair-Raising Experience."

1. Are the 5 W's (*who, what, when, where,* and *why*) answered?

2. What transitional words show the time order of the paragraph?

3. What sensory details help create a clear picture?

A Hair-Raising Experience

1 One evening, my mom was downstairs doing the laundry.
2 As usual, she was trying to do 10 jobs at once when she grabbed
3 the wet clothes from the washer and tossed them into the dryer.
4 She slammed the dryer door, turned the timer, and started to
5 run upstairs. All of a sudden, a whining sound stopped her in her
6 tracks. The sound was coming from the dryer. She yelled for me.
7 As I raced downstairs, the sound grew louder and louder. I flung
8 open the dryer door. There to our surprise was Mica, our cat. He
9 looked like someone who had just gotten off a Tilt-A-Whirl ride. His
10 eyes bugged out, and his hair looked like a cartoon character with
11 a finger in an electric outlet. Mica darted out of the dryer and up
12 the stairs. After that, Mom always checked out the dryer before
13 slamming the door, and Mica stayed clear of the laundry room for
14 a long, long time.

 Examine your details. Review your prewriting activities before you begin to write your first draft. Use the following guidelines.

1 Be sure you can answer the 5 W's (*who, what, when, where,* and *why*) about your story.

2 Check your quick list to make sure you used the correct transitional words and the events are listed in the order that they happened.

3 Review the details in your sensory chart.

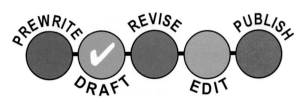

TEKS 6.14C

Go Online!

Drafting

PREWRITE   REVISE   PUBLISH
✓
DRAFT   EDIT

Now that you have gathered and organized your ideas, you are ready to write the first draft of your narrative. Focus on putting your ideas on paper in the best order. Use your own unique storytelling voice.

Keys to Effective Drafting

1. Write strong beginning and ending paragraphs.

2. Use time order to organize events.

3. Write with your purpose, form, and audience in mind. Ask yourself these questions as you write:
   • Do I share a true story about a time in my life?
   • Are my ideas clear? Do I need to explain anything?
   • Do I keep my classmates interested?

4. Show the reader the reason for and importance of actions and consequences.

5. Use sensory details to let the reader experience the event.

NARRATIVE

 TEKS 6.14B, 6.16A
ELPS 3H, 5G

Drafting Getting the Big Picture

The chart below shows how the parts of a personal narrative fit together. (The examples are from the narrative on pages 109–112.) You're ready to write your narrative once you . . .

- build on ideas to create a focused, organized piece of writing.
- give reasons for actions or consequences.

Beginning

Write a strong **beginning** to introduce the experience and make readers want to know what happens next. Introduce the focus of the piece.

Opening Sentences
Little kids are a pain—or so I thought. Then Uncle Eddie asked me to volunteer at bike camp . . .

Middle

The **middle** gives details about what happened first, second, third, and so on. It gives reasons for actions or consequences. It uses dialogue and sensory details to help readers appreciate the experience.

When I arrived at bike camp . . .

My first job was to teach . . .

Kenny and I saw a lot . . .

By the end of camp, I wished . . .

Ending

The **ending** tells *why* or *how* you were changed because of this experience.

Closing Sentences
Little kids just don't know much yet. They need a big kid, like me, to give them some attention and answer their questions. . . .

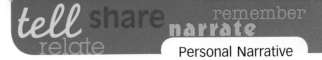

NARRATIVE

Starting Your Personal Narrative

Once you have a plan for your story, you are ready to write your first draft. Write as though you were telling a friend your story. The first paragraph should catch your friend's interest and introduce the focus of your story. Here are several ways to begin your narrative.

- **Place yourself in the middle of the action.**
  When Uncle Eddie asked me to volunteer at bike camp, I said, "Sure." Secretly, I didn't want to because I thought little kids were a pain.

- **Begin with a surprising statement or fact.**
  Little kids can be a real pain!

- **Start with someone speaking (dialogue).**
  "Get off the field!" my friends and I yelled.

Beginning Paragraph

The writer catches the reader's interest with dialogue. The writer introduces the focus of the story.	*"Get off the field!" That's what my friends and I are always yelling at the little kids who get in the way when we are trying to have a game of softball. Little kids are a pain—or so I thought. Then Uncle Eddie asked me to volunteer at bike camp. The camp is a special Saturday when kids learn safety rules for riding their trikes and bikes. I didn't want to, but my family always helps run the camp, so I politely told Uncle Eddie, "Sure."*

Write your beginning. On your own paper, write the beginning of your narrative. Try using one of the three ways suggested on this page to create a focused piece of writing.

TEKS 6.16A
ELPS 3G, 3H, 5G

Drafting **Developing the Middle Part**

Once you have your reader's attention, keep it by adding interesting details. Don't tell everything. Tell just enough to capture the experience and maintain focus. Remember:

- **Include a number of sensory details.**
- **Let the people in the narrative tell the story using their own words (dialogue).**
- **Share your feelings throughout the story.**
- **Show readers the reasons for the actions of the people in the narrative and why they are important.**

Middle Paragraphs

Strong sensory details let the reader "see and feel" the experience.

When I arrived at bike camp, I heard the ringing ting-a-ling of trike bells and the constant beep, beep, beeping of bike horns. The parking lot was a sea of little kids pedaling around and around and back and forth. They looked like a bunch of ants rushing around but going nowhere.

"Kyle," Uncle Eddie said, "it looks like we have our work cut out for us today."

Notice the words that show what the writer feels.

"Yeah," I mumbled. I wasn't looking forward to this at all.

My first job was to teach the squirmy little kids on trikes to watch out for hazards. One grubby little five-year-old rode over my foot.

"What's a haz—zard?" he asked. A chocolate bar was smeared in a brown mustache under his nose.

Action leads to a specific consequence.

Suddenly he put his trike in reverse and rolled back over my foot. A sharp pain shot up my leg.

TEKS 6.14B, 6.16A, 6.20B(ii)

ELPS 3H, 5G

NARRATIVE

The writer uses dialogue with correct punctuation and spacing.

"It is something dangerous," I said. I was talking very slowly so he couldn't tell how much my foot hurt. "A hazard is something that can hurt you or someone else," I answered. I was thinking to myself, "You are a hazard!"

"Boy, you sure are smart," said the little boy, whose name was Kenny.

Kenny and I saw a lot of each other all day. He was full of questions, and he looked up to me as if I had all the answers. He became my talking shadow.

Details show how the writer was changed by the experience with Kenny.

By the end of camp, I wished that I had a little brother just like Kenny. When he reached out to shake my hand, he said, "Thanks for helping me." I didn't even notice the chocolate on my hand until he was pedaling away to meet his dad.

Write your middle paragraphs. Build on ideas that stay focused on the single experience. Add sensory details that help readers experience it, too. Be sure to communicate the importance of or reasons for actions and consequences. Remember to use dialogue with proper punctuation and spacing to bring the experience to life.

 **TEKS** 6.14C, 6.16A
ELPS 3H, 4G, 5G

Drafting Ending Your Personal Narrative

After you share the most important moment, bring your story to a close. In the final paragraph, explain the importance of or reasons for actions and consequences. Explain how you changed as a result of the experience.

■ **Show or tell how the experience changed you.**

> By the end of bike camp, I decided that I was wrong about little kids. Kenny taught me that I should give them a break. The kids at camp learned a lot, but so did I. Now I can't wait for next year's camp.

■ **Tell why the experience was important.**

Ending Paragraph

The writer tells why the experience was important.	*Did I say that little kids are a real pain? Well, I was wrong. Little kids just don't know much yet. They need a big kid, like me, to give them some attention and answer their questions. And maybe someday, when they're bigger, they'll remember and be nice to little kids, too.*

 Write your ending. Communicate why the experience was important to you.

 Form a complete first draft. Before revising, evaluate your first draft by rethinking your questions of purpose, form, and audience: Have I developed an organized, focused, coherent piece of writing? Do all the ideas clarify and bring to life a single experience? Is my draft interesting to my audience? If you can answer "yes" to these questions, you are ready to revise and fine-tune your writing.

Go Online!

Revising

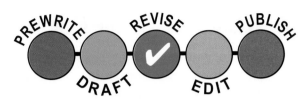

PREWRITE · REVISE · PUBLISH

DRAFT · EDIT

When you revise, you improve your first draft in many ways. You might spice up descriptions, add dialogue, or experiment with different beginnings and endings. Revision can make even a ho-hum draft into something special.

Keys to Effective Revising

1. Read your narrative to yourself to see how it works as a whole.

2. Check your beginning, middle, and ending to make sure each part works well.

3. Revise for focus and coherence, organization, development of ideas, and voice.

4. Mark anything you see that needs to be changed.

5. Use the editing and proofreading marks inside the back cover of this book.

NARRATIVE

 **TEKS** 6.14B, 6.14C
ELPS 3E, 3H, 5G

 Texas Traits

Revising **for** Focus and Coherence

When you revise for *focus* and *coherence,* you make sure you have written about only one thing. All events, details, and dialogue in your personal narrative should be about that one experience. Your narrative should have a strong beginning and ending. These help readers understand why your experience was so unforgettable.

Is my narrative focused?

You know you have focused on one experience if all your ideas in your narrative relate to that one experience. Make sure you take out any ideas that don't relate to the experience.

Try IT Read the narrative and identify the unforgettable experience. Decide which sentences should be deleted to make the narrative focused and coherent. Discuss with a partner.

> Every Saturday, we run a swim clinic for young children. One little boy would not get into the pool. One day I brought a raft with me. I put on sunglasses, then lay back on the raft. The little boy laughed. I pushed the raft to where he was. "Want a turn?" I asked. "You can wear my sunglasses." My sunglasses were new and trendy. I had just gotten them at the mall.
>
> The boy let me put him on the raft and push him around. Pretty soon he was on his stomach, using his arms to help steer the raft.
>
> "Good job, Captain," I said. "If you can steer this craft, you'll be a natural in the water."
>
> He just beamed at me. It felt good to help someone get over his fear of water.

 Revise

Check your focus. Read through your first draft. Be sure all ideas are connected to your unforgettable experience. Delete sentences or larger units of text that do not belong.

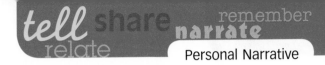

TEKS 6.14B, 6.14C
ELPS 3H, 5G

How do I know if my beginning is strong?

Your beginning works well if it introduces the problem or challenge and it interests the reader. Check your beginning by asking yourself these questions.

1. Does my beginning get the reader's attention?
2. What does my reader need to know to understand my experience?
3. What other way could I begin my narrative?

Reread your beginning. Look at each sentence in your narrative. Make a list of words that you feel are dull or overused. Replace them with synonyms.

How do I know if my ending is strong?

A strong ending leaves your reader with something to think about. It shows your reader why the experience was important to you. You know your ending is strong if it:

- gives the reader something to think about.
- explains how you feel about the experience.
- tells how the experience changed you.
- shares what you learned from the experience.

Check your ending. Does your ending stick to your purpose and present a focused, organized, and coherent piece of writing? Does it share what was important about the experience? Invite a partner to read it and tell how well it addresses the points listed above.

 TEKS 6.14B, 6.19A(viii)
ELPS 3H, 5F

Revising for Organization

When you revise for *organization*, check to be sure your narrative is easy to follow, the order of ideas makes sense, and it has a clear beginning, middle, and end.

Can readers follow the order of events?

Check your narrative to make sure you have arranged events in the order in which they happened. This is called chronological order, or time order. Transitional words and phrases can help you move the reader through your story. Here are some transitional words that show time.

first	while	meanwhile	now	then
second	then	today	soon	next
third	when	tomorrow	later	as soon as

Organization
The writer adds transitions so that ideas flow together.

      After   *Then*
  ⋀We did warm-ups, we jumped into the pool.⋀We did

model strokes to show the little kids how they looked.
Soon
⋀The children were eager to join us. They hit the water,

they tried to copy our strokes. They got tired, we worked

one-on-one with them to show them how to move their
          Finally
arms and legs.⋀It was time for "free swim." We all splashed

around until it was time to leave

Review your events. Look at your sentences and paragraphs. Be sure you have transitional words and phrases that will help readers understand the order of events.

TEKS 6.14C, 6.19A(viii)

How do I check the organization?

Most personal narratives are arranged in chronological or time order. When you revise your personal narrative for organization, you should make sure the events are arranged in the correct order that they happened. Sometimes you may need to rearrange a sentence or sentences so that they follow the order in which they happened.

Organization
The writer moves two sentences to put ideas in time order.

I worked with my little buddy every day. The little guy trusted me. He watched me in the water. He tried to copy everything I did. Every day he became less afraid of the water. I got him to put his head under water. I even got him to float upside down.

"You're going to be a strong swimmer someday," I told him. "Just keep practicing."

"I'm going to swim like you," he said. "Then I'll teach little kids how to swim."

NARRATIVE

Revise

Review for time order. Check the middle paragraphs of your narrative. Rearrange sentences or larger units of text as needed to make sure your events are in chronological order. Also make sure that you used transitional words and phrases to move your reader easily through your story.

Revising for Development of Ideas

When you revise for *development of ideas,* be sure you have focused on one experience. Check to see if you have answered the 5 W's and included sensory details. Sensory details help readers picture what the event looks, sounds, tastes, feels, and smells like.

Have I included the important ideas and details?

Readers will understand your narrative if you include details that answer the 5 W's.

1. Who are the people in my narrative?

2. What events are included in this experience?

3. When do the events happen?

4. Where does my narrative take place?

5. Why is this experience important?

 Read the following paragraph and answer the *who, what, when, where,* and *why* questions.

1   Every other weekend, Mom drives me out to the family farm
2   where my older cousin, Buster, teaches me all kinds of new things.
3   He has taught me how to shoot arrows, fix an engine, and bale hay.
4   Usually, we spend the evenings in his workshop. The last time we got
5   together, Buster taught me how to carve a piece of wood into a
6   simple whistle. I really enjoyed carving and can hardly wait to start my
7   next project. I'd like to carve a figure of a wolf, but that may be too
8   hard for now. No matter what Buster teaches me, we have a great time
9   together.

 Check your ideas. Read through your first draft. Be sure your narrative includes details that answer the 5 W's.

tell share remember

narrate

relate

119

ELPS 3H, 5G

Personal Narrative

Does my narrative seem real?

Your narrative will come to life if you have included enough sensory details. They help your readers use their imaginations—and their five senses—to connect with your experience.

 In the following paragraph, find and list at least five sensory details.

1 During the summer of 2005, my family lived on a busy street in
2 Cincinnati. During the daytime, buses rumbled and screeched right in
3 front of our second-floor apartment. The noise and oily exhaust from
4 these vehicles is something I will always remember. In the heat of
5 that summer, we passed the time playing hearts or rummy. My little
6 sister often sat in an old rocking chair and watched us. Mom always
7 made sure that there was a pitcher of sweet lemonade in the fridge.
8 Once in a while, she'd even surprise us with some fresh strawberries.
9 It may have been hot and noisy, but that summer was one of the best
10 ones ever.

NARRATIVE

 Check your ideas. Have you included a variety of sensory details in your narrative. Do your details bring your narrative to life for your readers?

Development of Ideas
A sensory detail and a detail that tells "where" are added.

When I arrived at bike camp, I heard the ringing ting-
and the constant beep, beep, beeping of bike horns
a-ling of trike bells. The parking lot was a sea of little kids
around and around and back and forth
pedaling. They looked like a bunch of ants rushing around

but going nowhere.

Revising **for** Voice

When you revise for *voice,* check to see if your writing sounds natural, as if you were talking to someone. Also make sure you have used dialogue.

Have I used a natural-sounding voice?

Your voice sounds natural if your reader can "hear" your personality in your narrative. Ask yourself: Does my writing sound like me? Can my readers tell that I am interested in telling my story? Am I expressing my unique personality and point of view?

> **Writer 1:**
>
> I flipped open my locker and jabbed my hand in. I got a fistful of fuzz. "Whoa. What's this critter doing in my locker!"
>
> **Writer 2:**
>
> I pulled open my locker and sighed. What a day! What could go wrong now? I reached in and felt something furry and alive. "Yikes! A rat!" I screamed.

 Write for 3 to 5 minutes about the experience below. Use your imagination to add lots of details. Your writing should sound like you're telling a story to a friend. When you finish, underline words and phrases that show your unique personality, or voice.

> While cleaning up after a parade, I found a $50 bill on a littered street.

 Check your voice. Read through your personal narrative. Underline two sentences that show your unique voice. Then check the rest of your narrative for places where the voice can be improved. Revise as needed.

How can dialogue improve my narrative?

Using dialogue in your writing helps you "show" instead of just "tell." Dialogue can make your narrative feel as if it is happening right now. When you write dialogue, make sure that it matches each person's personality. Here are some tips for writing dialogue.

- Think about the people in your story and choose words that each of them would use.
- Make the words sound like everyday conversation.
- Indent each time a different person speaks. Be sure to use quotations marks and proper punctuation.

 Write an exchange of dialogue between one of the pairs of people listed below.

- A coach and a player
- Two friends
- A clerk and a customer
- A brother and sister

 Read your narrative carefully. **Make changes if your voice or the dialogue doesn't sound right.**

NARRATIVE

Voice
Dialogue is changed to fit the little boy's age.

"A hazard is something that can hurt you or someone else," I answered. I was thinking to myself, "You are a hazard!"

"Boy, ~~I think~~ you sure are ~~intelligent~~ smart," said the little boy, whose name was Kenny.

 **TEKS** 6.14E
ELPS 3H, 5G

Texas
Traits

Revising Using a Checklist

Revise

Check your revising. On a piece of paper, write the numbers 1 to 10. If you can answer "yes" to a question, put a check mark after that number. If not, continue to work with that part of your essay.

Focus and Coherence

_____ **1.** Are all the events focused on a single experience?
_____ **2.** Are my beginning and ending effective?
_____ **3.** Do I include important events?

Organization

_____ **4.** Have I reorganized parts that were out of place?
_____ **5.** Have I used transitions to show the order of events?

Development of Ideas

_____ **6.** Do I include all the important details and answer the 5 W's?
_____ **7.** Do I include enough sensory details?

Voice

_____ **8.** Does my voice sound natural?
_____ **9.** Do I sound interested in my topic?
_____ **10.** Does the dialogue fit each person's personality?

Revise

Make a clean copy. Ask a classmate to read and respond to your narrative. Make any needed revisions. Create a clean copy for editing.

Editing

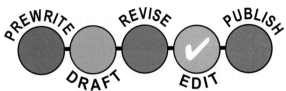

After you've finished revising your narrative, it's time to edit it for your use of conventions. Check to make sure you have followed the rules for grammar, sentence structure, punctuation, capitalization, and spelling. These rules are called the conventions of writing.

Keys to Effective Editing

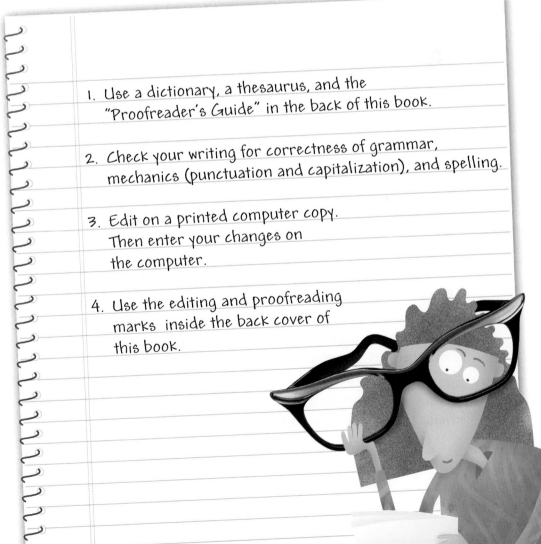

1. Use a dictionary, a thesaurus, and the "Proofreader's Guide" in the back of this book.

2. Check your writing for correctness of grammar, mechanics (punctuation and capitalization), and spelling.

3. Edit on a printed computer copy. Then enter your changes on the computer.

4. Use the editing and proofreading marks inside the back cover of this book.

NARRATIVE

Editing for **Conventions**

Grammar

When you edit for *grammar*, make sure you have used parts of speech correctly. Check to see if you used adjectives and adverbs to capture your experience. Also check to see if you have replaced overused words with synonyms.

Have I used adjectives and adverbs well?

You have used adjectives and adverbs well if they help create a clear and interesting picture. Adjectives describe nouns or pronouns. Adverbs add meaning to verbs, adjectives, and other adverbs. The example below shows how a writer improved a basic sentence by adding adjectives and adverbs.

> **The cafeteria served sandwiches.**
>
>   *adj.*   *adj. adj.*   *adv.*
> **The school cafeteria served spicy sub sandwiches yesterday.**

GRAMMAR Try It Copy this paragraph and fill in the missing adjectives and adverbs. Compare your paragraph with a classmate's.

> Our soccer team had practiced *(adverb)* to get ready for the championship game with our *(adjective)* rival. I arrived *(adverb)* on Saturday to find a flooded field, ruined by the *(adjective)* rain the night before. After running to the gym, I found our coach talking *(adverb)* to some other *(adjective)* players about postponing the game.

Edit for adjectives and adverbs. In your narrative, use adjectives and adverbs to help create a clear picture.

TEKS 6.19A(iv)
ELPS 2C, 3C, 3E

Do I use conjunctive adverbs well?

Conjunctive adverbs, such as *consequently, furthermore,* and *indeed* connect ideas and help move the story along. Conjunctive adverbs join clauses or sentences of equal importance. Here are some other examples of conjunctive adverbs.

however	moreover	nevertheless	therefore
thus	accordingly	besides	likewise

Provide a conjunctive adverb that fits each sentence below.

1. A great philosopher once said: I think, ____, I am.
2. My dog doesn't like peanuts; ____ he gobbles up peanut butter!
3. They left the cookie package open; ____ the cookies got hard as rocks.
4. Our team won the final game, ____, they went on to the regional playoffs.
5. I don't like team sports; ____ I enjoy swimming and skiing.

Edit for conjunctive adverbs. Make sure you have used conjunctive adverbs correctly in your narrative. For help, see pages 640–641.

Learning Language

Many adjectives can be changed into adverbs by adding *–ly* to the end. Adverbs sometimes answer the question "how." For example, *How did you finish your homework so fast? I worked quickly.*

loud/loudly	The students laughed loudly.
quick/quickly	I finished my homework quickly.
bright/brightly	The sun shone brightly.

Add *–ly* to the adjectives below to change them to adverbs. With a partner, alternate asking questions and then answering using these adverbs or other adverbs you can think of. For example, *How did your friend like the joke? She laughed loudly.*

beautiful____	quietly____	slow____

NARRATIVE

 **TEKS** 6.14C
ELPS 5F

Sentence Structure

When you revise for *sentence structure,* you need to check your writing for a variety of sentence lengths. You may need to combine sentences or larger units of text to have a smoother flow.

Are too many sentences of the same length?

You can check your sentence lengths by counting the number of words in each sentence. When you speak, you automatically use sentences of many different lengths. This gives a natural flow to your sentences. When you write, you want to do the same.

How do I combine sentences?

Two easy ways to combine short sentences are (1) creating compound sentences and (2) using a series of words.

Create Compound Sentences

I see the shoe-shine man each morning. He is always in the same spot.
I see the shoe-shine man each morning, and he is always in the same spot.
(Two sentences are combined using a comma and the conjunction and.)

Use a Series of Words

Each day he wears green pants. He has a red cap. He has a long leather vest.
Each day he wears green pants, a red cap, and a long leather vest.
(Three short sentences are combined into one using a series of words.)

 Combine these sets of sentences using the method given.

1. I've always enjoyed reading about dinosaurs.
   I didn't realize that they had once lived in my neighborhood.
   (Create a compound sentence using a comma and a conjunction.)

2. My grandmother has taught me how to sew.
   She also showed me how to crochet and quilt.
   (Combine sentences using a series of words.)

 Revise sentences. Use the rules and examples above to make sure you have a variety of sentence lengths. Combine sentences if needed.

⭐ **TEKS** 6.20B(ii)

Mechanics: Punctuation

Have I punctuated dialogue correctly?

To be sure you know how to correctly punctuate dialogue, review the following rules.

- Commas are used to set off the words of the speaker from the rest of the sentence.

    "A raccoon crawled down the chimney," Laura announced, "and I think it's still in there."

- Sometimes an exclamation point or a question mark separates the speaker's words from the rest of the sentence.

    "Are you sure it went down the chimney?" Regina asked.

- The speaker's exact words are placed within the quotation marks.

    "I'm positive!" Laura replied.

How do I know when to indent dialogue?

As you write your narrative, remember that you need to indent and begin a new paragraph each time a different person speaks.

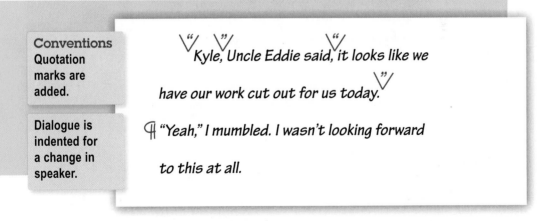

Conventions
Quotation marks are added.

Dialogue is indented for a change in speaker.

"Kyle, Uncle Eddie said, it looks like we

have our work cut out for us today."

¶ "Yeah," I mumbled. I wasn't looking forward

to this at all.

Edit **Check the dialogue in your narrative.** Have you started a new paragraph each time there's a new speaker? Does your dialogue have the correct spacing and punctuation?

NARRATIVE

TEKS 6.14d, 6.20B

Editing Using a Checklist

Check your editing. On a piece of paper, write the numbers 1 to 10. If you can answer "yes" to a question, put a check mark after that number. If not, continue to edit for that convention of writing.

Conventions

GRAMMAR

_____ **1.** Do I use adjectives to describe nouns?

_____ **2.** Do I use adverbs to help describe the action?

MECHANICS (Punctuation and Capitalization)

_____ **3.** Have I used correct punctuation in my sentences?

_____ **4.** Do I use commas after items in a series?

_____ **5.** Do I use commas in all my compound sentences?

_____ **6.** Do I use correct punctuation for dialogue?

SENTENCE STRUCTURE

_____ **7.** Do I have varied sentence lengths?

_____ **8.** Have I combined sentences using compound sentences?

_____ **9.** Have I combined sentences using series' of words?

SPELLING

_____ **10.** Have I spelled my words correctly?

Creating a Title

- Use strong, colorful words: **A Weird and Wonderful Artist**
- Give the words rhythm: **My Little Buddy Kenny**
- Be imaginative: **Turtle Lady**

Publishing

Sharing Your Narrative

After you have worked so hard to improve your story, make a neat final copy to share. You may also decide to present your story in the form of an illustration, a skit, or a recording. (See the suggestions below.)

Focus on Presentation

- Use blue or black ink and write neatly.
- Write your name in the upper left-hand corner of page 1.
- Skip a line and center your title; skip another line and start your writing.
- Indent every paragraph and leave a one-inch margin on all four sides.
- Write your last name and the page number in the upper right-hand corner of every page after the first one.

NARRATIVE

Illustrate Your Narrative

Pick an important part of your narrative and draw a picture of it. Post the picture and the story in your classroom.

Go Online
Upload your personal narrative for others to read.

Record Your Storytelling

Record yourself telling your narrative. Play the recording back and think of ways to improve your storytelling. Keep trying until you are satisfied. Share the final recording with friends or family.

Make a final copy. Follow your teacher's instructions or use the guidelines below to format your story. (If you are using a computer, see page 60.) Create a clean final copy of your narrative.

Evaluating a Narrative

To learn how to evaluate a narrative, you'll use the scoring rubric on pages 130–135 and the narratives that follow. These narratives are examples of writing for each score on the rubric.

Notice that this first personal narrative received a score of 4. Read the description for a score of 4 on pages 48–49. Then read the narrative. Use the same steps to study the other examples. Always remember to think about the overall quality of the writing.

Writing that fits a score of 4 is very strong.

Clearly defined focus grabs readers' attention

Dialogue gives characters their voice.

The New Texans

"The first sound I heard when my cousins, my aunt, and my uncle walked up the driveway was their Boston accents. "Should we pak the cah heah?" Uncle Paul asked. Laughing, I raced outside and gave everyone a hug. I was super-excited for the next three days because my cousins were visiting.

After we talked and drank some iced tea, it was time for dinner. We went to the greatest barbecue place. My cousins Jon and Stacy gaped with awe at the smoker barrels outside the building. A mouth-watering aroma of wood smoke rose up when the man showed us the sauce-covered ribs and briskets. Then we went inside to eat. Licking his fingers happily, Jon exclaimed, "I've never tasted anything like this before!".

The next morning, we drove to Hamilton Pool. Hamilton Pool is incredible. It's round, and it has a cliff that goes halfway around it. The bottom of the cliff is

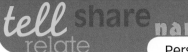

scooped-out from when the water was a lot higher. Not only that, there's a trail that goes around the whole pool so that you can walk under the cliff! A waterfall shoots down from the top of the cliff. That was only the first of part of the fun I had planned for them for their trip.

Back home that evening, we planned the next day's adventures. I wanted Jon and Stacy to love everything about being here. I wished they could live here near us.

The next day, we bought sundaes from our favorite ice cream place, went back to Hamilton Pool, and then went to see the bats at Congress Avenue bridge. Every evening, at sunset the bats that live there fly out from under the bridge and scatter in all directions. It is an amazing sight as the sky is filled with what look black missiles shooting out to hit their targets—insects.

After we got home that night, we sat on the deck. Unfortunately, bugs were swarming us.

"We need the bats to come here and get rid of these pests," Dad said, waving his hand rapidly in front of his face. He turned to my cousins and asked, "How's your visit going, kids?"

"Barbecue, yes," Stacy said. "Swimming hole, yes. Bats…yes! Mosqitos…" She made an "ewww" face.

"Well, that's how every true Texan feels about mosquitoes," Dad said. "So welcome home!" At that moment, I really wished Texas could be their home.

Transitional words and phrases show time order.

The only spelling error is in a difficult word.

The ending wraps up the narrative.

Writing that fits a score of 3 is strong in most ways.

Growing Wildflowers

Variety in sentence styles helps pull the reader in.

The narrative communicates the importance of or reasons for actions.

Repetition of details weakens the organization.

I grew wildflowers in our garden this year. It was my favorite thing that I have ever done, I think. Best of all, it was my idea all the way. One day in the spring we were driving on a hiway and there were lots of wildflowers growing by the side of the road. They looked like a box of crayons. "Wow, what if we could grow flowers like that?" I asked curiously.

I was surprised that my parents said I could. But that wasn't really the time to plant wildflower seeds. They would die once it got hot. so what we had to do was wait until the fall. In the fall we went to this farm where they grow wildflowers in big huge fields. That sounds funny to me, because if you are farming them are they still wild? But we bought a plastic bag full of all kinds of wildflower seeds. And then it was all up to me.

I read the directions carefully. What we had to do was wait till around Oct. and then we could plant the seeds. First you rake the part of the dirt that you're going to plant the wildflower seeds in. You only rake it a tiny bit, not deep. It's like you're drawing lines with the rake. Then you're ready to sew your seeds.

Basikly you just walk around in your garden in the bare dirt and sprinkle the seeds wherever you want them. Its even okay if you step on them with your foot by accident or even not by accident, because then you're pushing the seed lightly into the soil so it can take root.

tell share remember **narrate**
relate

133

ELPS 4I, 4K

Personal Narrative

NARRATIVE

I tried to throw the seeds over as much of the ground as I could, but I threw too many of them at first. I didnt have enough left for the left side of the garden. But that's okay, because I'm going to plant more next year and I will concentrate on those spots.

After you plant the seeds you water them, so that is what I did next. Don't soak them, just get them moist. The only trouble is you have to keep them moist all the time! until they get established, so you end up having to water them almost every day for months. But it's worth it because you get flowers.

I was so proud when the first flower popped up. It was near the end of Febuary, pretty early. Believe it or not, the next day there were three more, and every day after that there were more until after about two weeks the little red flowers were all over the garden. The next ones to appear were orange and yellow, then little white ones and a few of one purple kind. The whole garden looked like a painting.

I'm proud of my flowers and I'm proud of myself for growing them. Next year I will grow even more wildflowers!

Transitions clarify time order.

There are some errors in spelling, grammar, and mechanics.

Writing that fits a score of 2 is strong in some ways.

The narrative has a clearly defined focus on one event.

Errors in spelling, grammar, usage, and mechanics weaken the composition.

Development of the action lacks detail.

Voice sounds natural and real.

Splinter Man

I get splinters a lot! Its a pain. The worse one I got was two years ago on the boardwalk at the beach. I was just walking along minding my own bisiness, no I was running along not minding my own bisiness, ha ha ha. Me and my freinds were running down the boardwalk racing. It was crowded. I was barefoot. I was the only barefoot one because Josh Marco and Jeffry put their flipflops on at the sand. I thought I coud run better barefoot but--All of a sudden this huge sliver of wood goes into the bottom of my foot. I knew immediatly that it was trouble.

My freinds went with me to the first Aid staytion but there wasnt much the people their could, in fact nothing. My parents werent with me so they couldn't give permissin for the First aid staytion to do anything, so my freinds walked home with me and my parents took me to the ER at the hospital.

We waited a pretty long time but the people were all nice, and they kept coming around and telling me "The dr. will see you soon". The ones who took care of me were a nurse a nurses aid a younger doctor and an older doctor. They worked hard. They put a little licquid on my foot so I wouldn't feel nothing. Also they stuck a little needel there. The younger doctor did most of it, then the older doctor came and checked his work. It all worked out fine and the younger doctor shook my hand. I'm good patient. I just get so sick of getting splinters all the time.

Writing that fits a score of 1 is weak.

Hail Storm

Have you ever been in a hail storm. I have. It was great.

our whole famly went to a dude ranch for vacasion. It was fun. We where sittin at the pool when the hail storm begun. The pool had a roof that was green you could look up and see thru it.

We where sittin at the pool. I had swam but now I was out. I just learned to swim. Next thing we no, somthings makin a terrible loud sound? Where was it comin from? It was hittin off the roof like rocks. They bounsed off the roof and landed. The ones that mist the roof landed to.

It was the fist time I ever seen hail. Thay were big and white. About as big as a golf ball. Thay were bounsin like golf balls to. My dad pays golf but not a lot.

Why was the hail storm fun. It was fun because we wached it for a long time and we were rite out in it but under that roof so none of the hail din get on us. We just wached it bounsin. Would you believ the whole siment part around the pool was covered with hail?? It all came down in about ten minutes. That was one hard storm, dad says. But we wer safe. I wisht it woudn never stop haling. When it stopped we went to our cabin. I piked up a hail stone and held it was cold. Then all the hail melted. It din hail agen. I hope it does this summer? I think hail is beatyful do you?

Beginning doesn't grab reader's attention.

Lack of detail weakens the scene.

Lack of transitions makes the narrative hard to follow.

The writer's voice is not clear or individual.

NARRATIVE

Evaluating and Reflecting on Your Writing

You've put a lot of time and effort into your personal narrative. Now take some time to score and think about your writing. On your own paper, finish each sentence starter below. To score your writing, refer to the scoring rubric on pages 48–49 and the examples you just read.

My Narrative

1. The best score for my personal narrative is . . .

2. It's my best score because . . .

3. The best part of my narrative is . . .

4. The part that still needs work is . . .

5. The main thing I learned about writing a personal narrative is . . .

Narrative Writing

Biographical Narrative

"What happened when your friend got her new bike?" "What happened when your mother went to Puerto Rico?" "What happened when your older brother joined the soccer team?" If you sat down with a friend or family member and asked, "What happened when . . . ?" you would probably hear some great stories.

Writing a story about an important event in another person's life can help you and others understand that person. This type of writing is called a *biographical narrative,* and the next few pages will help you write one.

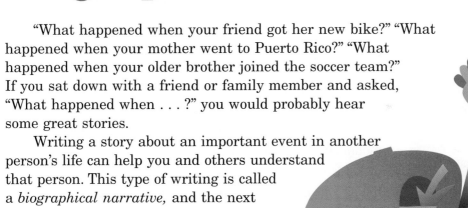

Writing Guidelines

Subject:	An event from someone else's life
Purpose:	To understand another person
Form:	Biographical narrative
Audience:	Classmates

 **TEKS** 6.16A

Biographical Narrative

A biographical narrative tells the story of a single event in a person's life. The event should reveal something interesting about the person. Sharese, the writer of the biographical narrative below, tells a story about her father.

The Last Reckless Ride

Beginning

The beginning introduces the event and states clearly that the focus is her Dad's extreme ride.

Dad used to be a thrill seeker. He enjoyed extreme sports like bungee jumping and rock climbing, and he took lots of careless risks. But one day, when he was riding his mountain bike, things got too extreme—even for him.

It was a perfect day for riding. The sun was shining, the air was brisk, and people weren't yet crowding the high trails. Dad pumped the pedals of his mountain bike and climbed the gravel path. Once he reached the high point of the trail, he shot downhill. The rear tire of his bike sprayed gravel, and the front tire bounced down the path. He picked up speed and whooped as he tore around a corner.

Middle

Specific details and actions move the story along.

Suddenly, something jumped up in the path ahead of him. It was a black bear!

Dad jammed on the brakes. He left a long skid on the path behind him and slid to within 10 feet of the bear.

It stared right at him and growled.

Rising Action

Showing consequences from actions moves the story along.

"Easy . . . easy," Dad said. There would be no way to ride past the bear. Dad glanced back over his shoulder. If he tried to turn around, the bear would just chase him down.

The bear stepped toward my dad.

That's when Dad got off the bike and lifted it like a shield. "Take it easy. We're both scared." He took a step back. "I'll go this way, and you go that way."

tell share remember
relate **narrate**

139

Biographical Narrative

TEKS 6.16A
ELPS 3E, 4G

The bear took another step forward.

Dad's heart pounded. He should have had a noisemaker on his bike to scare off bears. His life was on the line because of his own carelessness.

Lifting his bike overhead, Dad said in a deep voice, "Back, you! Back, bear!"

The bear stopped in its tracks and sniffed. Then it turned and ambled off into the woods.

Dad trembled as he lowered the mountain bike. His legs felt like jelly. He turned and walked his bike back up the trail. Just to make sure he scared off any other bears, he sang at the top of his lungs.

That close call got Dad's attention. From then on, he was less reckless in his extreme sports.

High Point
. . . .
At the high point, the importance of actions is evident.

Ending
. . . .
The ending tells how the consequences change the person.

NARRATIVE

Respond to the reading. Answer the following questions about the biographical narrative. Discuss with a partner.

☐ **Focus and Coherence** (1) What actions keep the story focused on the same topic?

☐ **Organization** (2) How does the writer begin the story? (3) In her ending, how does she show the importance of the consequences of her Dad's actions?

☐ **Voice** (4) What words or phrases show that the writer enjoys this story?

TEKS 6.14A
ELPS 3F, 3H, 5G

Prewriting **Selecting a Topic**

Think about your favorite people: family members, friends, teachers, or even famous people. What stories do you know about them? These stories are topic ideas. Now you must find a way to pick the best one.

Sharese, the writer of the sample biographical narrative, used a line diagram to list her favorite people and stories about their lives.

Line Diagram

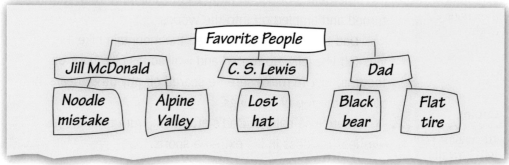

Choose your topic. Create your own line diagram. List favorite people and story ideas about their lives. Then decide which is the best topic.

Gathering Details

To write a biographical narrative, you must learn as much as you can about the person's experience. Sharese used questions based on the 5 W's and H to interview her father.

5 W's and H List

1. *Who was with you when you ran into the bear? no one*
2. *What did you do when you saw it? skidded to a stop and held up my bike like a shield*
3. *Where did this happen? on a bike trail in the mountains*
4. *When did it happen? on a cool spring morning five years ago*
5. *Why did it happen? because I didn't carry a noisemaker*
6. *How did the event change you? was less reckless after that*

Use the 5 W's and H questions. If possible, interview the person you are writing about. Base your interview questions on the 5 W's and H.

 **TEKS** 6.14B 6.16A
ELPS 3F, 3H, 5G

Organizing Details

Choosing an appropriate strategy is important in organizing details. To organize her details, Sharese chose to use a time line. Time is a basic organizational method for narratives. Above the time line, she identified the most important actions. Below, she wrote details related to each action.

Time Line

Rode down trail	Met the bear	Used bike as shield	Shouted at bear
spraying gravel	skidded to a stop	heart pounded	turned back

 Prewrite **Create a time line.** Using the model above, organize the details and order of events of your biographical narrative in a time line.

Texas Traits

Focus on the Texas Traits

Focus and Coherence The best narratives communicate the importance of or reasons for consequences. Each action in a story line has a consequence that moves the narrative forward to the next action.

Story Line

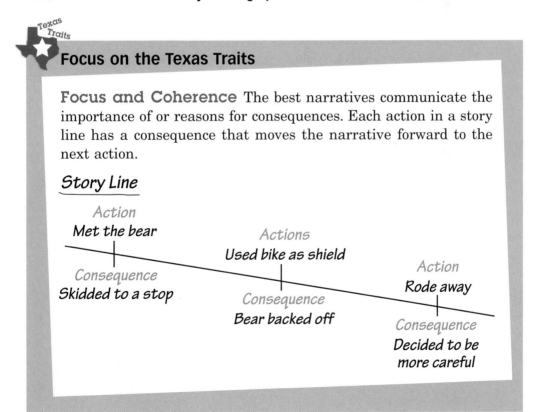

Action
Met the bear

Consequence
Skidded to a stop

Actions
Used bike as shield

Consequence
Bear backed off

Action
Rode away

Consequence
Decided to be more careful

NARRATIVE

TEKS 6.16A
ELPS 3H, 5G

Drafting **Developing Your First Draft**

Follow your time line as you write your first draft. Use the tips below to guide your writing.

Beginning Grab the reader's attention and start the story.

- **Begin with a clear focus on your topic.** *But one day, when he was riding his mountain bike, things got too extreme—even for him.*
- **Use a quotation.** *"I was careless the day I met a bear."*
- **Start in the middle of the action.** *My dad pumped the pedals of his mountain bike and climbed the gravel path.*

Middle Build the excitement in the narrative.

- **Be selective.** Tell only the important parts. Leave out anything that doesn't move the story along.
- **Use action and dialogue to show the importance of people's actions and the consequences.** Show what happened, why it is important, and use dialogue.
- **Use sensory details.** Include sights, sounds, smells, textures, and tastes so that the reader can experience the story.
- **Build to a high point.** Use the action, dialogue, and sensory details to build to the most exciting part of the story.

Ending Bring your story to a close.

- **Describe the final action.** Write what happens after the high point.
- **Tell why the event was important.**
- **Focus on how the consequences of actions changed the person.**

Write the first draft. When you are writing, remember to communicate the importance of actions and their consequences to your readers.

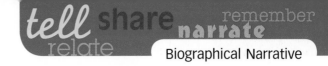

Revising **Improving Your Writing**

After you finish writing, set your narrative aside for a little while. When you are ready to revise, keep the following traits in mind.

☐ **Focus and Coherence** Make sure everything you have written contributes to the reader's understanding of the main idea or narrative. Combine sentences to tighten the focus.

> **FROM:**
>
> That's when Dad got off the bike. Dad lifted the bike like a shield. Dad said, "Take it easy. We're both scared."
>
> **TO:**
>
> That's when Dad got off the bike and lifted it like a shield. "Take it easy. We're both scared."

☐ **Organization** Each sentence should be logically linked to the next sentence, forming a kind of "chain," moving the narrative forward.

> Dad jammed on the brakes. He left a long skid on the path behind him and slid to within 10 feet of the bear.

☐ **Development of Ideas** Make sure you have brought the experience to life for your readers by including specific sensory details.

> The sun was shining, the air was brisk, and people weren't yet crowding the high trails.

☐ **Voice** Make sure your storytelling voice is authentic, original, and expresses the narrator's or character's personality and feelings in each part of the story.

> My dad trembled as he lowered the mountain bike. His legs felt like jelly.

Revise your narrative. Respond to your teacher's feedback when you revise. Combine sentences to tighten your narrative.

NARRATIVE

 **TEKS** 6.14D, 6.14E
ELPS 3E

Editing **Checking for Conventions**

Once you have completed your revising, it's time to focus on editing your narrative. Keep the following traits in mind.

Conventions

Once your story sounds the way you want it to, check your grammar, mechanics, sentence structure, and spelling. The following checklist can help you.

GRAMMAR

_____ **1.** Do I use correct verb forms *(things got, not things gotten)*?

_____ **2.** Do my subjects and verbs agree in number *(Dad and I were going, not Dad and I was going.)*?

_____ **3.** Do I use the right words *(for, four, fore)*?

MECHANICS (Punctuation & Capitalization)

_____ **4.** Do I use end punctuation after all my sentences?

_____ **5.** Do I use apostrophes to show possession *(Dad's heart)*?

_____ **6.** Do I start all my sentences with capital letters?

_____ **7.** Do I capitalize all proper nouns?

SENTENCE STRUCTURE

_____ **8.** Did I combine sentences to help focus?

SPELLING

_____ **9.** Have I spelled all my words correctly?

 Edit your biographical narrative. Edit your biographical narrative. Correct any errors you find in grammar, mechanics, sentence structure, and spelling.

Publishing **Sharing Your Writing**

Narratives are meant for sharing. They help us connect with people around us—friends, family members, and classmates.

 Share your biographical narrative. Share your biographical narrative. Develop a controlling idea or thesis that will reach as many people in your audience as possible.

Narrative Writing

Across the Curriculum

Writing narratives is a common activity in every one of your classes. For example, in social studies you may be asked to write journal entries or keep class minutes. In math, you may be asked to write story problems. In science class, you may be asked to connect a personal experience to a scientific concept.

To write strong narratives, no matter what the class, you must learn as much as you can about your topic and share the key details about it. If everything works out, your writing will help your readers understand as much as you do about your topic.

What's Ahead

- **Social Studies:**
  Writing Classroom Journals
- **Math:** Writing Story Problems
- **Science:** Writing an Anecdote
- **Practical Writing:**
  Recording Class Minutes

Social Studies: Writing Classroom Journals

Writing in a classroom journal can help you learn. When you write about what happens in class, you remember details better and gain a deeper understanding of the subject. The following journal entries are from a social studies class.

The date is given first.

The student reflects on events in class.

The student records details learned in class.

Monday, October 19: Today Mr. Henry showed us a video about Mexico City. It's huge! I thought New York City was big, but Mexico City has millions more people. It's the biggest city in the world.

The coolest part of the video showed the Plaza of the Three Cultures. It has ruins of an Aztec temple. Those ruins are 600 years old!

After the video, Mr. Henry told us what happened at the plaza. He said that on one day in 1521, the Aztecs and Cortez had a battle, and 40,000 Aztecs died. What a horrible day! Still, that was the beginning of Mexico.

Tuesday, October 20: Today Mr. Henry passed around postcards from his trip to Mexico. There sure are lots of beautiful places.

The most amazing pictures were from Chichen Itza. It's an ancient Mayan city. It has a gigantic pyramid called the Great Pyramid. The Mayans lived near it 1,300 years ago.

Writing Tips

Before you write . . .

- **Set up your journal.**
  Designate part of a notebook for your journal and also make sure to follow your teacher's guidelines.

During your writing . . .

- **Record the date.**
  Write the date of each journal entry.
- **React to what you are learning.**
  Record the most important facts. Also write your thoughts and any experiences that relate to the information you are studying.
- **Include sketches.**
  Make a sketch in your journal if your teacher shows you a picture of something interesting. Also copy and label any important diagrams. Pictures can help you remember as you look back at your journal.

The Great Pyramid

After you've written a first draft . . .

- **Reread your work.**
  Read the journal to help you remember what you're learning in class.
- **Review your journal for essay ideas.**
  Look through your journal whenever you need writing ideas.

Write a journal entry about something you learned in social studies class. Remember to record the facts but also include your thoughts and feelings about them.

 TEKS 6.17C

Math: Writing Story Problems

One way to create a story problem is to base it on a familiar fable, fairy tale, or nursery rhyme. When Alex read "The Ant and the Grasshopper," he wondered exactly how much work the ant has to do to prepare for winter. Later in math class, Alex wrote a story problem to figure out the answer.

The **beginning** summarizes the story.

The **middle** gives the variables, the problem to solve, and the story problem.

The **ending** shows the solution.

The Ant and the Grasshopper

One fine winter day, an ant was drying grain that he had collected in the summer. A hungry grasshopper came begging for food. The ant asked, "Why didn't you store food during the summer?" He replied, "I spent the summer singing." The ant said, "If you sing all summer, you go hungry in the winter."

Math Variables: Each day an ant

- gathers 6 grams of food, and
- eats 2 grams of food.

Problem to Solve: How many days must an ant work to gather enough food for a year?

Story Problem: An ant eats 2 grams of food every day of the year. He can gather 6 grams each day. How many days must he work to gather a year's supply of food?

1. First, find out how many grams of food the ant eats in a year. (365 x 2 = 730 grams of food eaten in one year)
2. Then find out how many days it will take to gather 730 grams of food. (730 ÷ 6 = 121.6 days needed to collect the food)

Solution: The ant needs to work 121.6 days to gather enough food for a year.

Writing Tips

Before you write . . .
- **Find a short fable, fairy tale, or nursery rhyme.**
- **Read the story and think of how you can include math variables.** For example, the rates of speed could be one variable in the fable of the tortoise and the hare.

During your writing . . .
- **Prepare a summary of the story.**
- **List the math variables.**
- **State the problem to be solved.**
- **Write the story problem.**
- **Explain each step that is used to solve the problem.**

After you've written a first draft . . .
- **Make sure your story summary and story problem are clear.**
- **Check your answer.**
- **Get a classmate to try to solve your problem.**
- **Check your writing for conventions.**

NARRATIVE

 Respond to the following story summary by writing a story problem. Use information from the text to identify the problem, the variables, and the solution. Check your answer. Then follow the writing tips above to create your own story problem for others to solve.

Summary of story:

The Crow and the Pitcher

A thirsty crow saw a pitcher of water and flew to it. The pitcher contained only 3 inches of water. How will he take a drink? This gave the crow an idea. He flew off, brought back a stone, and dropped it in. This raised the water 5/8 of an inch. One by one, the crow dropped stones to raise the water until he could finally take a drink.

Science: Writing an Anecdote

When you write an anecdote, you tell a brief story to help make an idea clearer. Your story should be imaginative, but it should also have a clear focus, plot, and point of view. This type of writing is helpful for learning scientific ideas. In the sample below, a student used a personal experience to help explain the concept of buoyancy.

The **beginning** paragraph tells the focus of the story and clarifies the point of view.

The **middle** explains the scientific concept and illustrates it, while also moving the plot along.

The **ending** reflects on the story.

Oh, Buoyancy!

When Ms. Allard started teaching us about buoyancy, everybody said, "Huh?" Well, I understood right away because of my adventure in a canoe.

My sister Sarah took me canoeing, and I accidentally tipped over the boat. We flipped into the water, but our life jackets popped us up. Unfortunately, the metal canoe sank.

"Oh no! The canoe!" I shouted.

Sarah just laughed. "It'll come back up."

Sure enough, even though it was full of water, that metal canoe rose to the surface. "How did it do that?"

"It has buoyancy material in each end," Sarah said. "It's foam, like our life jackets."

We dumped out as much water as we could. Then we started bailing.

"Each time we throw a gallon of water out of the boat, the boat rises by a gallon."

"I get it. As the canoe weighs less, it sits higher."

"Right. That's buoyancy."

After that day, I'll always understand buoyancy. It's just too bad we had to get all wet in the process.

TEKS 6.15A

Writing Tips

Before you write . . .

● **Select a story that illustrates an idea or a concept.**
Think about how the things you are learning in science relate to your everyday experiences. For example, when you're outside, have you ever noticed that frost sometimes remains in a shaded spot but has evaporated in the sunlit areas? That experience tells you something about freezing and evaporation.

● **Get your science facts correct.**
Check into the scientific facts behind your story.

During your writing . . .

● **Express your feelings and ideas.**
Have fun writing your story so the reader will have fun reading it. Keep it interesting by expressing your ideas and feelings.

● **Be clear and direct.**
Make your explanation of the idea or concept as simple and clear as possible. Also, keep the focus, plot, and point of view clearly defined.

After you've written a first draft . . .

● **Revise your first draft.**
Make sure that your story is complete, easy to follow, and interesting.

● **Check for accuracy.**
Double-check your facts and details.

● **Edit for correctness.**
Check for punctuation, spelling, capitalization, and grammar errors.

 Think of an experience you have had that illustrates a principle of science. Use that experience and imagination to write an anecdote to help your classmates understand the concept.

Practical Writing: Recording Class Minutes

Class minutes tell the story of what happened in class. They can remind you about important information and help an absent classmate catch up. The following minutes were taken in a social studies class.

The **beginning** states the class information.

Social Studies, Third Period
Tuesday, November 17, 2009

<u>Absent</u>: *Laura Parker and José Velasquez*

<u>Topic</u>: *Mississippi Mound Builders*

<u>Handout</u>: *Ms. Lindell handed out a fact sheet on mound builders (attached). She pointed out two things:*
1. *Mississippi Mound Builders built large mounds as temples, burial sites, and bases for government.*
2. *This culture lasted for 1,000 years, from 700 to 1700.*

The **middle** identifies each activity in the order it happened.

<u>Video</u>: *Ms. Lindell showed a video about Cahokia, IL.*
1. *Monk's Mound is 100 feet tall.*
2. *More than 100 other mounds are near Cahokia.*
3. *This was once a society of 40,000 people.*
4. *Builders hauled baskets of dirt on their backs.*

<u>Discussion</u>: *Ms. Lindell stressed two things:*
1. *The cities had complex government and trade.*
2. *Most mound builders died in the 1500s because of diseases from Europe.*

The **ending** lists the assignment.

<u>Assignment</u>: *Ms. Lindell had the class write journal entries about mound builders.*

Writing Tips

Before you write . . .

- **Check the format.**
  Follow your teacher's guidelines for class minutes or use the model on page 152 as a guide.

During your writing . . .

- **Record the basic class information.**
  Make sure you note the day's topic and the students who are absent.
- **Be brief.**
  Write your minutes so that a reader can quickly tell what happened in class.
- **Write down the key points.**
  Consider what an absent person needs to know to keep up. Don't write down everything, but listen carefully to find out what the teacher considers most important.
- **Write neatly.**
  Make sure everyone can read your writing.

After you've written a first draft . . .

- **Double-check activities and assignments.**
  Make sure your information is complete. Ask a classmate to review the minutes to see if you missed anything.
- **Edit and proofread the minutes.**
  Correct any errors in your minutes. Other students may depend on them for makeup work, so it's important to be accurate.

NARRATIVE

 For class minutes in any subject area, follow the writing tips above. Record only the most important facts and examples.

Narrative Writing
Writing for the Texas Assessment

When you take state tests in Texas, you often have to write. The prompt tells you what to write about and gives some things to remember. Read the following prompt:

Prompt

Write a personal narrative about a day that you would like to live over again.

Use the information below to help you write your personal narrative.

REMEMBER THAT YOU SHOULD—

☐ write about a day that you would like to live over again.

☐ make sure each sentence logically leads to the next sentence.

☐ include specific details about your ideas to make sure readers fully understand what you have to say.

☐ try to use correct sentences, grammar, punctuation, capitalization, and spelling.

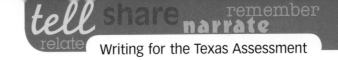
Prewriting **Selecting a Form**

The prompt doesn't tell you what form of writing to use. To decide which form to use, think about which best fits your composition.

Do you want to—
- describe a person or place?
- offer a solution to a problem?
- explain how something works?
- share a personal experience?
- give information?
- persuade your reader to take an action?

Answering these questions will help you to determine the best form for your writing.

Tony wanted to share a personal experience. He decided a narrative was the best form because it allowed him to tell a story of what he would do on a day he could live over again.

Putting Events in Order

Tony remembered how he felt the day he did not get up to go to school on time. He decided to write about reliving that experience.

To plan his draft, Tony used a time line. It helped him choose events and organize them.

Time Line

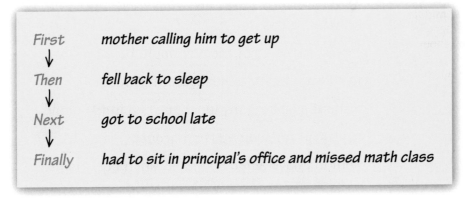

First → mother calling him to get up

Then → fell back to sleep

Next → got to school late

Finally → had to sit in principal's office and missed math class

NARRATIVE

Drafting **Writing the Narrative**

Next, Tony used his time line to write his personal narrative. Read Tony's narrative.

The **beginning** gives the focus of the response and uses key words from the prompt. (underlined).

> "Tony, this is the last time that I'm going to tell you to get up and get ready for school." I hardly heard my Mom's words before falling back to sleep. This was a big mistake. <u>If I could live yesterday over again, I would want it to be different, especially at the start.</u>
>
> Most importantly, I would get out of bed early enough to make it to school on time. Then I'd be there to hear my math teacher go over the assignment instead of sitting in the principal's office. You see, I need all the help I can get in math if I want to pass.

The **middle** paragraphs tell about the experience.

> The middle of the day would be different, too. I wouldn't have rushed out of the house without grabbing my lunch. Eating lunch would have kept me from getting grouchy. Then I wouldn't have acted so stupid when I got home.

ELPS 5G

NARRATIVE

The **middle** part is organized by time.

> After school, I wouldn't have slammed our front door and blamed my mother for my bad day. I wouldn't have been sent to my room for being snotty. Instead, I would have relaxed and watched TV for a while before supper.

The **ending** tells what the writer learned from the experience.

> Yesterday could have easily been a better day, but I can't live my life over. I was surprised how much better it felt to get up right away this morning, have a good breakfast, and leave for school on time with a lunch in my hand. My mother felt much better about everything, too.

Respond to the reading. Answer the following questions about the sample response.

☐ **Development of Ideas 1)** Does the writer expand on his ideas? Explain. (2) Do you think the writer's idea is fresh and original? Why?

☐ **Organization (3)** How is the response organized?

☐ **Voice (4)** Does the writing express the writer's personality and point of view? Give examples.

Literature Connection: You can find an example of a personal narrative by reading the short story "The Jacket" by Gary Soto.

Writing Tips

Before you write . . .

- **Understand the prompt.**
  Make sure you understand what you are being asked to write. Decide on a form for your writing.
- **Plan your narrative.**
  Select a topic from your life. Jot down a time line of events.

Time Line

Time Line
① ┼
② ┼
③ ┼
④ ┼
⑤ ┼

During your writing . . .

- **Decide on a focus.**
  Use key words from the prompt in your beginning paragraph.
- **Choose carefully.**
  Tell only the main events in your story.
  Use sensory details to make the story come alive.
- **End in a meaningful way.**
  Connect the experience to the prompt or tell why it was important.

After you've written a first draft . . .

- **Check the prompt and your narrative.**
  Make sure you have done what the prompt asks.
- **Check for conventions.**
  Correct any errors in mechanics, spelling, and grammar.

 Plan and write a response. Respond to the prompt on page 154 within the time frame your teacher gives you. Remember to select a form and to use the tips above.

tell share remember
narrate
relate
Writing for the Texas Assessment
159

Narrative Writing in Review

Purpose: In narrative writing, you *tell a story* about something that has happened.

Topics: An experience you have had
An event from someone else's life

Prewriting

Select a topic from your life experiences. (See page 102.)

Gather important details using a graphic organizer to list details for your narrative. (See page 103.)

Gather important details about the people involved and the order of events. List sensory details to use in the narrative. (See pages 103–106.)

Drafting

In the beginning, introduce the focus of your story and grab the reader's interest. (See page 109.)

In the middle, tell the events of the story in time order. Use your own words and express your feelings. Use sensory details and dialogue. (See pages 110–111.)

In the ending, tell why the experience was important and what you learned from it. (See page 112.)

Revising

First, review your focus and coherence, organization, and development of ideas. Then check your **voice.** (See pages 114–124.)

Editing

Check for conventions. Look for errors in mechanics, spelling, and grammar. Also ask a friend to edit your writing. (See pages 126–128.)

Make a final copy and proofread it before sharing it with other people. (See page 129.)

Assessing

Use the scoring rubric to assess your finished narrative. (See pages 130–131.)

NARRATIVE

describe
define

ELPS 3E, 3G, 4C, 4G

TEXAS
WRITE
SOURCE
Online

www.hmheducation.com/tx/writesource

Expository Writing

Writing Focus

- Expository Paragraph
- Explaining a Process
- Classification Essay

Grammar Focus

- Noncount Nouns
- Irregular Verbs

Learning Language

Work with a partner. Read the meanings and share answers to the questions.

1. A strategy is a plan that allows you to reach a goal.
   What is a good strategy for making friends?

2. Something is effective if it brings about a desired result.
   Is an umbrella effective for keeping you dry?

3. To get across means to make something understandable.
   How would you get across the idea of feeling sad?

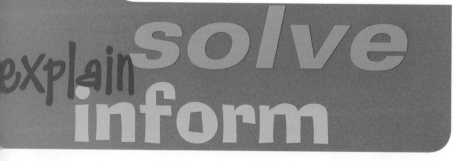

explain solve inform

Expository Writing

Expository Paragraph

What can you do really well? Can you shoot a free throw or kick a soccer ball? Do you know how to wash a dog, make an omelet, or calculate the lowest common denominator? Think about what you know how to do and how you could explain it to someone else.

Writing that explains things is called *expository* writing. Most essays, reports, and newspaper articles are examples of expository writing. In each case, the writer knows something that he or she wants to explain to the reader.

In this chapter, you will write an expository paragraph about something you know how to do. You will become the teacher, sharing your knowledge with your classmates.

Writing Guidelines

Subject: Something you know how to do
Purpose: To share knowledge
Form: Expository paragraph
Audience: Classmates

TEKS 6.17A(iii)
ELPS 2H, 3E, 4C, 4G

Expository Paragraph

The expository paragraph is a basic form of writing. It almost always begins with a **topic sentence**, which tells the reader what the paragraph is about. The sentences in the **body** explain or support the topic sentence, and the **closing sentence** wraps up the paragraph. The paragraph below was written by a student who likes to cook her own breakfast.

Topic Sentence

The body includes specific facts and details in an organized structure.

Closing Sentence

How to Make an Omelet

Anyone can make a delicious omelet, even if a person has never cooked before. For tools, all an omelet maker needs are a bowl, a hand beater, a frying pan, and a spatula. For ingredients, he or she needs two eggs, two tablespoons of milk, a quarter cup of grated cheese, a little salt and pepper, and a pat of butter. Then the person should follow these steps. First, break the eggs into a bowl and add the milk, salt, and pepper. Second, mix everything with the beater until it is foamy. Next, heat the frying pan and add the butter. Make sure the melted butter covers the whole bottom of the pan. When the butter begins to sizzle, pour the egg mixture into the pan and sprinkle the cheese over it. Let it cook until the eggs get firm around the edges. Then use the spatula to flip half of the omelet over the other half, like a taco. Give it another minute or so to melt the cheese and finish cooking the eggs. Finally, slide the omelet onto a plate to be enjoyed!

Respond to the reading. On your own paper, answer each of the following questions. Discuss your answers with a partner.

☐ **Focus and Coherence** **(1) What is the focus of the paragraph?**

☐ **Organization** **(2) How did the writer organize details in the paragraph (time order or order of importance)? Explain.**

☐ **Voice** **(3) What words or ideas show you that the writer is really interested in the topic?**

TEKS 6.14A2, 6.14A3
ELPS 5B

Prewriting Selecting a Topic

When it comes to planning a first draft, you should first determine an appropriate topic. Think of things you know how to do or want to learn. Can you bunt a baseball? Do you know how to draw cartoons or care for a pet? Have you ever set up a tent or built a fort?

The writer of the sample paragraph on page 162 brainstormed topics in a list of "Things I Know How to Do."

Brainstorm List

Things I Know How to Do

fix a flat tire	whistle	make balloon animals
make an omelet	knit	do a French braid
study for a test	juggle	play trombone

Brainstorm and select a topic. Using the list above as a guide, make your own list of things you know how to do. Then choose one that really interests you, one you could explain in a paragraph.

Writing a Topic Sentence

Write a sentence that tells what your how-to paragraph will be about. The topic sentence should guide the controlling idea of your paragraph. A good topic sentence names the topic and states your feelings about it. Here is a simple formula for writing good topic sentences:

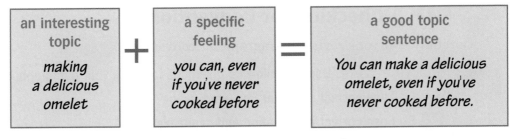

an interesting topic	a specific feeling	a good topic sentence
making a delicious omelet	you can, even if you've never cooked before	You can make a delicious omelet, even if you've never cooked before.

+ =

Write your topic sentence. Write a topic sentence for your paragraph. Use the basic formula shown above. Be sure it focuses on your controlling idea. You may have to try a couple of times before your sentence says exactly what you want it to say.

EXPOSITORY

 **TEKS** 6.14D, 6.14E
ELPS 5B, 5G

Drafting Creating Your First Draft

When you write a first draft, your goal is to get all your ideas and details down on paper. Follow the suggestions below.

- Start with your topic sentence.
- Arrange the how-to steps in the correct order.
- End with a closing sentence that wraps up the instructions and shows your enthusiasm for the topic.

 Write your first draft. Try to get all of the important information down on paper, including the materials needed and the steps to follow.

Revising Improving Your Paragraph

When you revise your first draft, look for ways to clarify your meaning and improve the organization of your paragraph.

 Review and revise your paragraph. Use the following questions as a guide. Ask your teacher for feedback. Revise as needed.

1 Is my topic sentence clear?

2 Have I clearly explained all the steps in the correct order?

3 Do I use specific nouns and action verbs?

4 Do I sound interested in the topic?

5 Do I write complete sentences that read smoothly?

Editing Checking for Conventions

Carefully edit your revised paragraph for conventions.

 Edit your work. Use the following questions to check your paragraph.

1 Do I use correct grammar and word usage?

2 Do I use correct punctuation and capitalization?

3 Have I checked the words my spell check may have missed?

 Proofread your paragraph. After making a final copy of your how-to paragraph, check it one more time for errors.

Expository Writing

Explaining a Process

How do you make spaghetti? How do you find the secret passage to the next level of your favorite video game? How do you skateboard or snowboard? The answers to questions like these may involve several steps. When you explain how to do or make something in an essay, you are doing expository writing.

In this chapter, you will write an expository essay. Your how-to essay should tell readers exactly what materials they will need and what steps they should follow. You will do your best writing if you choose a topic you care about—something you do well or enjoy doing.

Writing Guidelines

Subject: Something you know how to do or make

Purpose: To explain how to do or make something

Form: How-to essay

Audience: Classmates

Texas Traits Understanding Your Goal

Your goal in this chapter is to write a well-organized, interesting essay that explains how to do or make something. The traits listed in the chart below will help you plan and write your how-to essay. The scoring rubric on pages 48–49 will also help you. Refer to it often to improve your writing.

Traits of Expository Writing

Focus and Coherence

Make sure your essay has a clear statement of the controlling idea and clearly presents all the steps in the how-to-process you have selected.

Organization

Write an engaging introduction, a middle that informs and guides the reader, and an effective conclusion.

Development of Ideas

Use fact, details, and examples that support your ideas to help readers understand key ideas in each step.

Voice

Use an informative, confident voice that fits the audience.

Conventions

Check your essay for correct grammar, mechanics (punctuation and capitalization), and spelling.

Literature Connection: You can find a how-to essay in "How to Read a Road Map" in a major encyclopedia.

Expository Essay

In the following expository essay, Lamar explains how to give a dog a bath—step-by-step.

How to Give a Dog a Bath

Beginning

The beginning effectively introduces the topic by presenting the focus statement (**underlined**).

If you or any of your friends have a dog, you know how much fun a pet can be. You also know that a dog can be a lot of work, especially if he is very active. It doesn't take long for a high-energy dog to look a mess and smell even worse. When that happens, it's time to gather up the dog shampoo and conditioner and freshen up your dog. If you follow these steps, bathing your dog can be easy and enjoyable.

To begin, get the bath ready and gather what you need. Use a nylon collar and leash (leather gets ruined by water) to control your dog during the bath. Your dog also needs something to stand on so he won't slip. A bath mat or towel will make him feel secure. Make sure the water is warm. Water that is too hot can burn a dog's skin. Cold water—especially from an outside hose—may scare your dog and send him running. Next, you'll need a way to get water all over your dog. A shower hose is the easiest method, but a plastic bucket can work well, too. You'll also need a special dog shampoo and conditioner because human shampoo is too strong for dogs. Of course, you'll need some big towels for the end of the bath.

Middle

The middle paragraphs include materials needed and provide a step-by-step explanation. Transitions help the reader follow the steps (**underlined**).

To continue, begin bathing your dog. Get your dog nice and wet. Then use enough shampoo to make a foamy lather on his coat. Talk to your dog all the time to help him relax.

EXPOSITORY

 **TEKS** 6.17A1(ii),
6.17A4(ii)
ELPS 3E, 3G

Middle
The middle paragraphs also provide important supporting details. Transitions keep it organized (underlined).

Ending
The concluding paragraph is effective. It restates the reason for bathing your dog and stresses that it can be fun.

Try to keep soapy water out of his eyes and ears. Then rinse your dog with fresh, warm water until his coat is shiny and free of soap. After that, you can rub some conditioner into his coat.

To finish, dry your dog as completely as possible. Use big towels and give your dog a complete rubdown. Dogs love this part! However, watch out because wet dogs like to shake. If you choose to use a hair dryer to dry your dog, keep it moving because holding it over one area too long could burn his skin. If you are outside, you'll discover that dogs like to roll when they're wet. After your dog shakes himself, play tag with him or offer him a chew treat—anything to keep him from rolling in the dirt!

If you treat your dog calmly and gently, giving him a bath should be fun. Dogs that get used to taking baths learn to enjoy them. Remember, whenever your dog starts smelling too doggy, it's time to gather your supplies and wash him until he's clean and huggable again.

Respond to the reading. After reading the sample essay, answer the following questions to discover how to use four important traits in your writing. Discuss with a partner.

☐ **Focus and Coherence** (1) Which sentence states the controlling idea of the how-to essay?

☐ **Organization** (2) Does the writer clearly guide the reader from step to step? Give an example.

☐ **Voice** (3) List words and phrases that show the writer cares about the topic.

Prewriting

Prewriting is the first step in the writing process. It involves selecting a topic, gathering specific details, and organizing your ideas.

Keys to Effective Prewriting

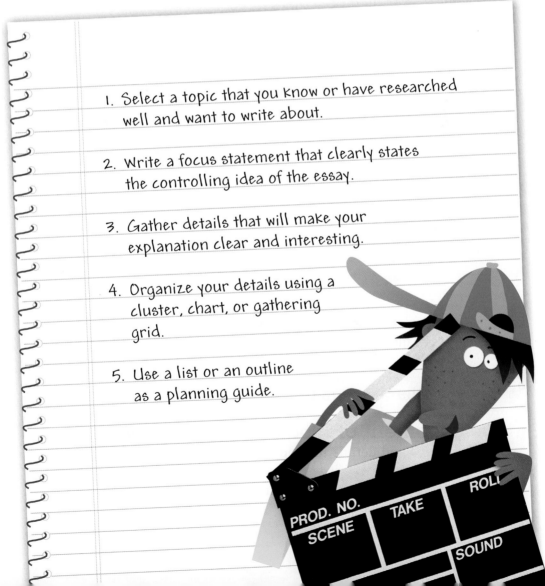

1. Select a topic that you know or have researched well and want to write about.

2. Write a focus statement that clearly states the controlling idea of the essay.

3. Gather details that will make your explanation clear and interesting.

4. Organize your details using a cluster, chart, or gathering grid.

5. Use a list or an outline as a planning guide.

EXPOSITORY

★ TEKS 6.14A, 6.17A(ii)

Prewriting **Selecting a Topic**

The purpose of your essay is to explain how to do or make something. However, your essay should be more than just a list of directions. You need to guide your readers so they can easily understand and follow each step. In the steps, you need to explain each key idea with evidence.

To select a topic, think about things you know how to do or make. Making a cluster or web diagram like Soledad's below is one strategy for gathering ideas for your how-to essay.

Cluster

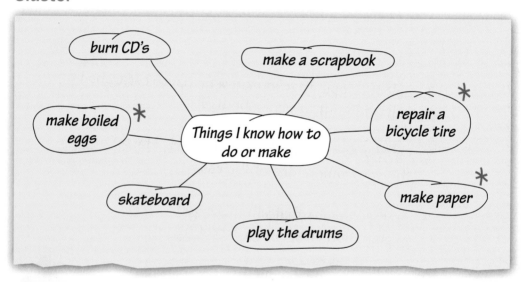

burn CD's

make a scrapbook

make boiled eggs ✶

repair a bicycle tire ✶

Things I know how to do or make

skateboard

make paper ✶

play the drums

Prewrite **Create your own cluster.** Start your cluster with "Things I know how to do or make." List as many ideas as you can. Then put a star (✶) next to two or three of your favorite topics.

Texas Traits

Focus on the Texas Traits

Development of Ideas Choose a process that has enough steps and details to keep your audience interested. The process should be also one that interests you and that you understand well. Consider a process that is especially fun, challenging, or unusual.

TEKS 6.14A
ELPS 3E

Sizing Up Your Topic

To make sure a topic is appropriate list the steps that are involved. Discuss the topics with a classmate to test if they will interest someone in your audience. These two strategies will help you size up the topic.

If you look at Soledad's lists below, you'll see that "Repairing a bicycle tire" may be too broad or complicated, while "Making boiled eggs" may be too narrow. "Making paper," however, has about the right number of steps.

Lists

Making boiled eggs
- *Put eggs in pot of water*
- *Bring to a boil*
- *Cover, shut off heat*
- *Let sit 15 minutes*

Making paper
- *Tear up newspaper*
- *Blend with water*
- *Pour pulp into a pan*
- *Strain pulp*
- *Tip onto felt*
- *Roll pulp between felt pieces*
- *Hang paper to dry*

Repairing a bicycle tire
- *Remove nails or glass*
- *Remove the wheel*
- *Push valve stem inside*
- *Pry tire edge over the rim*
- *Work the inner tube out*
- *Clean the puncture area*
- *Apply glue and let dry*
- *Press the patch over the puncture*
- *Pull the tube back into place*
- *Inflate the tube a little*
- *Work the tire into place*

EXPOSITORY

Prewrite

Size up your topic. Try the strategies above. Using your starred topics, list each of the necessary steps. Test them on a classmate. Then ask yourself these questions about each topic:

1 Did I include all the necessary steps?

2 Is this topic too narrow? Too broad? About right?

3 Is my topic appropriate for my audience?

Prewrite

Choose your topic. After evaluating your topics, choose the best one.

Prewriting Writing a Focus Statement

Your focus statement includes the topic and controlling idea you center your writing around. This formula will help you write a focus statement.

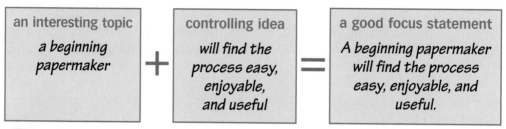

an interesting topic		controlling idea		a good focus statement
a beginning papermaker	**+**	*will find the process easy, enjoyable, and useful*	**=**	*A beginning papermaker will find the process easy, enjoyable, and useful.*

 Write your focus statement. Write the focus statement of your draft using the formula. Include your topic and controlling idea to help you.

Gathering and Sorting Details

Remember, the details you gather for your essay should relate to the controlling idea. A chart is one way to organize the details for your essay.

Chart

Topic	Materials Needed	Steps
How to make paper	*– old newspapers* *– blender and water* *– pan* *– piece of wire screen* *– two pieces of felt* *– rolling pin*	*To begin* *– Tear up newspaper* *– Mix with water* *To continue* *– Pour pulp into a pan* *– Strain pulp* *To finish* *– Tip onto piece of felt*

 Gather and sort your details. Choose an organizational strategy for your own topic. One strategy could be to chart the "steps" you will have under three headings: "To begin," "To continue," and "To finish."

Focus on the Texas Traits

Organization Graphic organizers like the one above can help you organize the steps in your process.

TEKS 6.14B, 6.17A(i), 6.17A(ii)
ELPS 5B

Planning Your Paragraphs

Your essay as a whole has a controlling idea that helps to focus your writing. To be effective, all the paragraphs in your essay will be linked by the one common controlling idea. Your essay needs a strong introduction (first paragraph) that gives the focus statement. The steps you listed in your planning chart will become the middle paragraphs of your essay. Your conclusion (last paragraph) should summarize important points that support your controlling idea.

Writing Topic Sentences

The main idea of a paragraph is usually stated in a topic sentence. The other sentences in the paragraph give evidence to support the main idea. Your goal for each paragraph is to guide and inform readers so they understand the key idea using your evidence.

Look again at the steps in your planning chart on page 172. In your middle paragraphs, each of your topic sentences can start with one of these phrases: to begin, to continue, to finish. Here are the topic sentences for the middle paragraphs in the essay on pages 167–168. Notice that each one covers a different part of the dog-washing process.

- ■ *To begin,* get the bath ready and gather what you need.
- ■ *To continue,* begin bathing your dog.
- ■ *To finish,* dry your dog as completely as possible.

Write your topic sentences. Use the steps you listed and the points below to help you write these sentences and key ideas. Consider what evidence will support those ideas.

1 What information is covered first?
Topic sentence: To begin,

2 What information is covered next?
Topic sentence: To continue,

3 What information is covered last?
Topic sentence: To finish,

EXPOSITORY

 **TEKS** 6.14B

Prewriting **Organizing Your Ideas**

You next need to put these pieces of your essay in the best order by choosing an appropriate organizational strategy. Below is an *organized list* for Soledad's essay. She used the directions to create her *organized list* of steps and topic sentences for her essay.

Directions

Write your focus statement.

Write your first topic sentence.

List any steps.

Write your second topic sentence.

List any steps.

Write your third topic sentence.

List any steps.

Organized List

A beginning papermaker will find the process easy, enjoyable, and useful.

1. *To begin, prepare the paper pulp.*
   - *Tear up paper*
   - *Put water in blender*
   - *Add shredded paper*
   - *Blend paper and water*

2. *To continue, work with the pulp.*
   - *Pour into pan with clean water*
   - *Stir gently and cover screen*
   - *Lift screen to drain*

3. *To finish, press the paper after it has drained.*
   - *Remove paper from screen*
   - *Squeeze out extra water*
   - *Hang to dry*

Prewrite **Organize ideas.** Choose a strategy to organize the steps and details you will put in your essay. A list like the one above works like an outline,

TEKS 6.14C

Go Online!

Drafting

PREWRITE · DRAFT ✓ · REVISE · EDIT · PUBLISH

Once you've finished your prewriting, it's time to write your first draft. You're ready to write a first draft when you know enough about your topic and have written a clear focus statement.

Keys to Effective Drafting

1. Use a clear topic sentence for each paragraph.

2. Add clear, step-by-step details.

3. Use transitions to tie everything together.

4. Write with your purpose, form, and audience in mind. Ask yourself these questions as you write:
   - Why am I writing this essay?
   - How can I most clearly explain my topic?
   - Who will be reading my essay?

EXPOSITORY

 **TEKS** 6.17A(i), 6.17A(ii), 6.17A(iii)
ELPS 5B, 5G

Drafting Getting the Big Picture

The chart below shows how the parts of a how-to essay fit together in an organized structure. (The examples are from the sample essay on pages 177–180.) You're ready to write your essay once you . . .

- know enough about the steps in the process.
- state your topic in a clear focus statement.
- plan your introductory, middle, and concluding paragraphs and write your topic sentences.

Beginning

The **beginning** introduces the topic and tells why the activity is important or interesting. It also gives the focus statement.

Focus Statement
A beginning papermaker will find the process easy, enjoyable, and useful if he or she follows these basic steps.

Middle

The **middle** gives all the how-to information and a step-by-step explanation. It presents facts, details, and examples in an organized way, which will inform the reader's understanding of the topic.

Three Topic Sentences
To begin, prepare the paper pulp.

To continue, work with the pulp.

To finish, press the paper after it has drained.

Ending

The **ending** may summarize the process and offer some final thoughts in the conclusion.

Closing Sentences
So have some fun, save a tree, and give papermaking a try!

TEKS 6.14A, 6.17A(i)
ELPS 3E, 5B, 5G

Starting Your Essay

In the first part of your expository essay you should present an effective introduction. State your topic and introduce the controlling idea in a focus statement.

You can also add voice to your essay if you begin with a personal story. An anecdote or point of interest will help develop your controlling idea.

Beginning
Middle
Ending

- **Share how you became interested in this process.**
- **Tell how you first learned this process.**
- **Show why the reader may like the activity.**

Beginning Paragraph

In the introductory paragraph below, Soledad uses a story to capture the reader's attention. The focus statement presents the controlling idea that she will develop in the essay—making paper is fun, easy, and useful.

The writer's interest is explained.

Materials are listed.

The controlling idea is given (underlined).

On a class trip to the Natural History Museum with Mr. Yu, I saw paper that had been made by ancient Egyptians. It was beautiful, and I wondered if I could make paper, too. I discovered at the HPM (Handmade Paper Makers) web site that if you want to make paper, you need the following items: old newspapers, a piece of wire screen, a bucket or pan, two pieces of felt, a rolling pin, a blender, and some water. After a few tries, I found that making paper is <u>*fun, easy, and useful.*</u>

EXPOSITORY

Draft

Write an effective introductory paragraph. Do the following three things when you write your beginning paragraph. Share it with a partner.

1 Introduce your topic in an interesting way.

2 Include a clear focus statement that presents your controlling idea.

3 Lead into your following paragraph to develop your controlling idea.

TEKS 6.17A(iii), 6.17A(iv)
ELPS 5B, 5G

Drafting **Developing the Middle Part**

In the middle paragraphs of your how-to essay, you provide facts, details, and examples to explain each step. Each paragraph should cover one main part of the process. Look at how the steps are handled in the middle paragraphs on these two pages.

Connecting Your Paragraphs

Transition words or phrases cue the reader that you are beginning a new step. Use transitions to vary your sentences and move your ideas from paragraph to paragraph. Here are some transitions you can use to connect paragraphs and show time order in a how-to essay:

First	One	First of all	One way	To begin
Second	Then	Next	Another way	To continue
Third	Another	Finally	A third way	To finish

Remember: The last sentence of each paragraph should get the reader ready to move on to the next part of the process.

Middle Paragraphs

In the three middle paragraphs that follow, transitions help guide the reader from one step to the next. Paragraphs are clearly focused with a clear topic sentence and precise details that expand the main idea.

The topic sentence conveys the key idea of the paragraph. Precise details help the reader understand exactly what to do (underlined).

First, you must prepare the paper pulp. You can make pulp from newspapers, brown paper bags, magazine pages, or just about any other kind of paper. First, tear the paper into small strips. Then, pour two cups of water into the blender. Next, sprinkle in a few handfuls of the shredded paper. Finally, cover the blender, press the medium-speed button, and blend for a few seconds. When the mixture in the blender looks like thick potato soup, your paper pulp is ready.

TEKS 6.14B2, 6.17A(iii),
6.17A(iv)
ELPS 5B, 5G

Transitional phrases help to connect paragraphs (underlined).

Last sentence of paragraph (underlined) cues reader that this stage of the process is complete.

<u>In the next step,</u> you work with the pulp. Pour it into a flat pan with clean water and a piece of wire screen in it. Now is the time to add fun things like grass, flower petals, or glitter. During this step, keep the pulp from settling on the bottom by stirring it gently. After that, move the screen around so that the paper pulp settles onto it. Cover the screen as evenly as possible. <u>Then, slowly lift it out of the water and let the water drain.</u>

<u>To finish,</u> press the paper after it has drained. Turn your paper-covered screen over onto one of the pieces of felt. The paper should fall off the screen easily. If it doesn't, just tap the back of the screen. Next, put the other piece of felt on top of the paper. Roll the rolling pin over the top layer of felt to squeeze out all the extra water. Finally, remove the damp paper from between the pieces of felt and hang it in a sunny place. In about three hours, you will have a sheet of paper.

EXPOSITORY

Draft

Write your middle paragraphs. Use your organized notes from your prewriting strategy to help you write the middle paragraphs. Remember to focus on your controlling idea. Follow the "Drafting Tips" below.

Drafting Tips

- **As you write,** use time order to organize each step. Use a variety of sentences and transitions to link your paragraphs.
- **If you get stuck,** jot down specific facts a person needs to know to do the step or give a helpful example. Refer to your notes to write sentences.

TEKS 6.14C, 6.17A(i), 6.17A(ii)
ELPS 3E, 3G, 3H, 5G

Drafting **Ending Your Essay**

After you've clearly explained all the steps, write an effective concluding paragraph. You might restate the controlling idea of your essay, make a final comment about the process, or invite the reader to try the activity.

Beginning

Middle

Ending

Ending Paragraph

End with an invitation to try the activity.

Papermaking is an easy, inexpensive hobby, and it is lots of fun. Your friends and family will love to get notes and cards on your homemade paper. You can also feel proud that you are helping to save trees by recycling paper. So have some fun, be creative, and save a tree. Give papermaking a try!

 Reread the concluding paragraph of the how-to essay on washing your dog (page 168). Discuss your answers with a partner.

1. What is the key idea in this paragraph?

2. What evidence helps the reader understand this idea?

3. Is this an effective conclusion for the essay? Why or why not?

 Write your ending. Now write an effective conclusion for your own how-to essay. Restate the controlling idea with evidence that supports your idea.

 Rethink purpose, audience, and genre. Review your entire how-to essay. Does it fully explain the process? Is it interesting and understandable to your audience? If you answered "no" to either question, think about what revisions you could make.

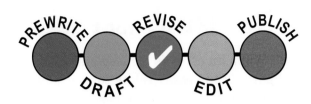

PREWRITE REVISE PUBLISH
DRAFT EDIT

Revising

A first draft never turns out just right. One part may need more details. Another part may not be clear enough. To fix or improve these parts, you need to revise your first draft.

Keys to Effective Revising

1. Read through your entire draft to get a feeling of how well your essay works.

2. Make sure your focus statement states your topic clearly.

3. Check your paragraphs to make sure the steps and details are clear and in the right order.

4. Use the editing and proofreading marks inside the back cover of this book.

EXPOSITORY

 **TEKS** 6.14B, 6.17A(i)
ELPS 3E, 3G, 4G, 4I

Revising for Focus and Coherence

When an essay is focused and coherent, it has one controlling idea and all parts of the essay relate to that idea. It seems whole and complete.

In a strong essay, the beginning and ending paragraphs contribute to this feeling of wholeness.

- The beginning introduces the topic in a focus statement and lets the reader know why it is interesting or important.
- The ending reinforces something important about the topic. It can also leave the reader with something to think about.

Is my writing focused on one idea?

To make sure your how-to essay is focused, look for any sentences that do not help readers understand the process or procedure.

 Read the paragraph below. What is the focus or controlling idea? What sentences make this paragraph less coherent? Discuss your thoughts with a partner.

> In summer, nothing is more refreshing than an icy glass of fresh lemonade. Making it is simple. All you need is lemons, water, and sugar. First, select six lemons. Sometimes lemons are very hard. Cut them in half. Then, using a glass or juicer, squeeze out the juice. Sometimes juicers are made of wood. I like to collect old juicers. You should get about 1 cup. In a large pitcher, mix the lemon juice with 6 cups of cold water and 1 cup of sugar. Stir well. Then pour into glasses over ice. Add a slice of lemon for decoration. Then sit back and enjoy the best hot-weather drink there is.

 Check your how-to essay. Read through your draft, or have a partner read it to check that all ideas are related to the controlling idea of your essay. Discuss your findings and make any revisions for focus and coherence.

TEKS 6.14B(i), 6.17A(i),
ELPS 3E, 4G, 4I, 4K

How do I know if my introduction is effective?

An effective introduction sets up your essay. Your introduction will be effective if:

- it introduces the topic or controlling idea in a focus statement
- it hooks the audience, making them interested to read more

 Ask a partner to read the beginning of your how-to essay and answer these questions. Decide if you should make revisions.

1. **What is this how-to essay about?**
2. **What details or ideas make me want to read further?**
3. **Which sentence presents the controlling idea of the essay?**

 Check your introduction. Reread your first paragraph. Does it clearly state your focus—your feeling or controlling idea about the topic? Does it include details or ideas that will make your audience want to learn more? If not, revise your beginning.

How do I create an effective conclusion?

An effective conclusion builds on the ideas that you presented in the beginning and middle of your essay and brings them to a close. An effective conclusion could:

- restate the controlling idea in a fresh way
- offer some final thoughts or summarize findings
- remind readers why the procedure is important, useful, or interesting
- suggest the reader try the activity

Review your conclusion. What strategy or strategies did you use in your final paragraph? Is the ending as strong as it can be? If not, revise the ending.

EXPOSITORY

Revising for Organization

When you revise for *organization,* check to see if your thoughts are organized into three main parts: a beginning, a middle, and an ending. Also check your transitions. Make sure each paragraph flows to the next.

How do I check my overall organization?

You can check the overall organization of your how-to essay by making sure the details in each paragraph are in the right place. Also make sure that each paragraph builds on the one before it to create an organized piece of writing. Use the chart below as a guide.

| **Beginning Paragraph** | The focus statement states your controlling idea. It belongs somewhere in the opening paragraph. |

| **Middle Paragraphs** | The first topic sentence begins the explanation of the process.
The second topic sentence continues the explanation, building on the ideas in the first sentence.
The third topic sentence finishes the explanation. It should logically lead to the next paragraph. |

| **Ending Paragraph** | The closing sentences summarize the process and encourage the reader to try it. |

Check your organization. Carefully check each part of your essay.

1 Underline the focus statement in your essay.

2 Place a **1** next to the first topic sentence, a **2** next to the second topic sentence, and a **3** next to the third topic sentence. Make sure each sentence logically leads to the next sentence.

3 Then place a star (✱) at the beginning of the ending paragraph. Check to see that all of the paragraphs build on ideas and move them forward to lead smoothly to the ending.

4 Revise anything that makes your essay unorganized.

TEKS 6.14C, 6.17A(iv)
6.19A(v)
ELPS 3E, 3G, 4K

How can I use transitions?

In a how-to essay, the steps of the process must be clear and in the correct order. That's why using transitions and sentence variety to link paragraphs is so important. Transitions help keep your writing organized, and they lead the reader step-by-step through your explanation.

You can also use prepositional phrases that make your sentence structure sound more interesting to show connections between the steps. Prepositions can be used to convey location, time, direction, and to provide details. The following prepositions can be used to help organize your essay. (Also see pages **540–541** and **774** for more information about using prepositions.)

Prepositions

about	before	during	in	through
after	below	for	near	until
along	between	from	off	with

Prepositional Phrases

Cover the bowl and let the mixture rest **for a while**. **After two hours**, add two teaspoons of salt and a little oil to the batter. **Along with the salt and oil**, add . . .

Revise

Review for transitions and sentence variety. Read your paper. Are the steps easy to follow? Are there a variety of sentences? If not, add transition words and prepositional phrases that will make your directions more clear. With a partner, discuss how the transitions and prepositions make your sentences better and help to link your paragraphs.

EXPOSITORY

Organization
Transition and prepositional phrases are added.

During this step,
Keep the pulp from settling on the bottom by
                    After that,
stirring it gently. Move the screen around so that the

paper pulp settles onto it. Cover the screen . . .

 Texas Traits

Revising **for** Development of Ideas

When you revise your essay for *ideas,* you check for these things: that your focus statement and controlling idea are clear, and your supporting details are specific. If not you may need to add text.

How can I add interest to my main points?

You can improve your how-to essay by adding sentences or larger units of text that tell personal details. Personal details will add interest to your essay and allow you to lead into the next idea smoothly. Below are three types of personal details and a chart prepared by the student who wrote the essay about making paper.

1. **Memory details** include personal memories about what happened as you learned to do or make something. The details might include how you became interested in the topic or the mistakes you made as you first learned the process.

2. **Reflective details** include personal thoughts about the process and why it is important to you.

3. **Sensory details** include descriptions of what the activity looks, feels, tastes, smells, or sounds like.

Memory details	Reflective details	Sensory details
I saw Egyptian paper in a museum. Once I added glitter.	I like recycling. People like notes on handmade paper.	Pulp looks like potato soup. It smells like a wet dog.

 Revise

Check your details. Make a chart like the one above for your topic.

1 Write the three types of details across the top.

2 Then list several specific details under each type.

3 Check the details that could make your essay interesting.

4 Revise your draft by adding sentences or larger units of text that offer the interesting details and improve the flow of your ideas.

TEKS 6.14C
ELPS 3E, 3G, 4K

Do I need to combine some groups of sentences?

When you revise, group related details into logical sentences or paragraphs. This helps your writing flow from one idea to the next.

In reviewing her essay, Soledad noticed that certain sentences add meaning to previous ones. She realized that all of the sentences below relate to working with the pulp. So she combined them into one paragraph.

> *In the next step, work with the pulp. Pour it into a flat pan with clean water and place a piece of wire screen in it. Now is the time to add fun things like grass, flower petals, or glitter.*
>
> *During this step, keep the pulp from settling by stirring it gently.*

 Read the sentences below with a partner. Explain why combining these groups of sentences in this way improves the writing.

> *Next, attach the dried leaves to the wreath. Select several attractive ones. You may wish to add glitter or paint to the tips.*
>
> *Take a 10-inch piece of wire and gently work the middle of wire through the leaves. Then position them on the wreath. Push the ends of the wires through the greenery to the back and twist them so the leaves are snug.*

 Review your writing. Look for places in your essay where combining sentences or units of text would improve the development of your ideas.

Development of Ideas
Specific details are added to add interest.

> *To begin, prepare the paper pulp. You can make newspapers, brown paper bags, magazine pages, or pulp from just about any other kind of paper. First, tear the paper into small strips. Then, pour two cups of water into the blender. Next, sprinkle in a few. . .*

 **TEKS** 6.14C
ELPS 3D, 3E, 3H, 4I

Texas Traits

Revising for Voice

When revising your essay for *voice*, check to see if you sound confident and enthusiastic. Make a connection to your audience using your authentic voice, but staying true to the form of the writing.

Does my voice fit my audience?

In writing, your voice should change depending on your audience and your topic. Your voice fits your audience when it matches the people—teachers, parents, or friends—you are talking to. To check your voice, answer three questions:

1. Who is my audience?
2. How should I speak to that audience?
3. How should I present my topic to that audience?

Audience	Teacher	Classmates	Friends
Voice	formal, polite	informal, but respectful	very informal

 Number your paper from 1 to 3. Write which of the audiences listed above in red would fit the voice in each of the following sentences.

1. Would you hand me that pencil?
2. May I please borrow a pencil?
3. Hey, got a pencil I could use?

 Think about your audience. Read your essay to a classmate. Think of how well you addressed your audience. Does your voice fit your audience? Discuss these questions with your partner. Revise if necessary.

Voice
A phrase is changed to fit the audience.

... *press the medium-speed button and blend for*

a few seconds. When the mixture in the blender

like thick potato soup
looks ~~really gross~~, your paper pulp is ready.

TEKS 6.14C2
ELPS 2I, 4I

Is my voice too informal?

Using the right voice for your purpose and audience will help you get across the ideas and information in your essay. Your purpose is to give clear instructions. Using a voice that is too informal can interfere with that goal.

Your voice also shows who you are as a person and your personal style. To gain your audience's attention and respect, use a somewhat formal but enthusiastic voice. Read the two explanations for the same process below. Notice that the voice in "just right" example is formal but still personal.

Voice 1: Too Informal

First, grab a couple of eggs and whack 'em against the side of the bowl. Dump them into the bowl. Next, throw in a little milk, a pinch of salt, and a drop of vanilla for extra oomph. Whip it all up with a fork and pour it into a hot pan. Keep pushing everything around until all the raw stuff is gone. When it looks ready to eat, chow down!

Voice 2: Just Right

Select two large eggs. Crack them one at a time into a bowl. Add one tablespoon of milk for each egg, a quarter teaspoon of salt, and a drop of yummy vanilla. Next, whisk everything together with a fork. Then, empty the bowl into a sizzling, buttered pan. Stir the eggs until they firm up into a hot, golden heap. You're now ready to eat and enjoy!

 Compare the two explanations shown above. List four words or phrases that make "Voice 1" too informal for an essay.

 Listen to your voice. Read your essay and listen to your voice. Do you sound knowledgeable, confident, and enthusiastic but still like you? Use the tips below to help you revise your draft so that your style come through.

1 Write down three words from your writing that fit your purpose and audience.

2 Then look for words from your writing that don't fit.

3 Replace the words that don't fit with ones that match the voice you want to create in your essay and that enhance your writing style.

EXPOSITORY

TEKS 6.14E
ELPS 4I

Revising **Using a Checklist**

Revise

Check your revising. On a piece of paper, write the numbers 1 to 9. If you can answer "yes" to a question, put a check mark after that number. If not, continue to work with that part of your essay.

Focus and Coherence

_____ **1.** Do I focus on an interesting controlling idea?

_____ **2.** Do the ideas fit together to form a whole?

_____ **3.** Are my introduction and conclusion effective?

Organization

_____ **4.** Have I presented all the steps in the correct order?

_____ **5.** Do I use transitions to guide the reader through the process?

Development of Ideas

_____ **6.** Do facts, details, and examples help the reader understand what to do?

_____ **7.** Have I removed details or ideas that do not relate to my focus?

Voice

_____ **8.** Does my voice engage readers and inspire their confidence?

_____ **9.** Do I show interest in—and knowledge of—my topic?

Revise

Make a clean copy. Ask a classmate and your teacher to read and respond to your essay. Make any needed revisions. Then create a clean copy for editing.

Go Online!

Editing

PREWRITE • • REVISE • ✓ • PUBLISH
DRAFT   EDIT

After you've finished revising your essay, it's time to edit your work for your use of grammar, mechanics, sentence structure, and spelling.

Keys to Effective Editing

1. Use a dictionary, a thesaurus, and the "Proofreader's Guide" in the back of this book.

2. Check for any words or phrases that may be confusing to the reader.

3. Check your writing for correctness of grammar, mechanics (punctuation and capitalization), sentence structure, and spelling.

4. Edit on a printed computer copy. Then enter your changes on the computer.

5. Use the editing and proofreading marks located inside the back cover of this book.

EXPOSITORY

 **TEKS** 6.19A(ii)
ELPS 3E, 4G, 4K

Texas
Traits
Editing **for Conventions**

Grammar

When you edit for *grammar*, you check to see that you have used nouns, verbs, and other parts of speech correctly. On this page and the next, you will edit for conventions in two ways: using noncount nouns correctly and using irregular verbs correctly.

*H*ave I used noncount nouns correctly?

Nouns can refer to things that are countable, such as pencils, forks, or hamburgers. They can also refer to things that cannot be counted, such as *rice* and *mustard*. Remember these points when you use noncount nouns.

- **Noncount nouns do not have a plural form.**
  There is *rice* on my plate. There is much *rice* on my plate.
- **Use *the* before a noncount noun or omit the article.**
  Rinse *the* rice. We enjoy rice.
- **Use a singular verb after the noun.**
  Rice *is* healthy.

GRAMMAR
Try IT

Look at the sentences below. With a partner, identify the noncount noun. Some sentences are incorrect. Work together to identify the sentences that are correct. Then rewrite the incorrect sentences using the tips above.

1. First, prepare the pulp.
2. Here is how to make a popcorn.
3. Water are essential for this process.
4. The grass needs to be cut.
5. Next, add a salt to the flour mixture.

Edit

Check your nouns. Review your essay and look at your nouns. Change general nouns to specific nouns where it will make your writing clearer. Check that you used noncount nouns correctly in sentences. Edit any errors.

TEKS 6.19A(i)
ELPS 2I, 2G, 4C, 5B

Do I use irregular verbs correctly?

Regular verbs in English form the past tense by adding *-d* or *-ed*. Some verbs have special forms in the past tense. They are called irregular verbs. (See examples on page **756**.)

Present tense	Past tense	Past participle
tear(s)	tore	(has, had, have) torn
fall(s)	fell	(has, had, have) fallen
make(s)	made	(has, had, have) made

The past participle is also used in sentences written in the passive voice, as in: *The call had been made earlier that morning.*

Rewrite the sentences, using the correct form of the past tense verb.

1. Brian had told me what to do.
2. The newspaper had been tore into narrow strips.
3. The soft, wet paper falled from the frame onto the felt.
4. Several students brung their supplies to the demonstration.

Edit for verb tenses. Have you used the correct past tense verbs and past participle verbs in your essay? Check your writing. Edit where needed.

Learning Language

Some irregular verbs follow a pattern in the way they form the past tense and past participle. With a partner, say the forms of each verb below. What pattern do you hear? Look for the spelling pattern of each verb.

Present tense	Past tense	Past participle
grow(s)	grew	(has, had, have) grown
know(s)	knew	(has, had, have) known
throw(s)	threw	(has, had, have) thrown

Discuss what you did last weekend with your partner. Practice using irregular verbs in your conversation. For help, see page **756** for a list of common irregular verbs.

EXPOSITORY

 TEKS 6.14C, 6.19C2(ii)

Sentence Structure

When you edit for *sentence structure*, you check that your sentences are put together correctly. Many times, you find places where combining shorter sentences would help improve the flow and sense of your essay.

How can I combine sentences?

To combine sentences, use a coordinating conjunction such as *and, or, but, for, so,* or *yet,* and insert a comma before the conjunction.

> **Poor flow**
>
> **I want to avoid drips. I wipe the paintbrush against the palette.**

> **Better flow and sense**
>
> **I want to avoid drips, so I wipe the paintbrush against the palette.**

Remember that when you combine two sentences by making a compound sentence, you must make sure the subject and verb in each clause still agree.

 Combine the sentences using the coordinating conjunction in parentheses. Correct subject-verb agreement as needed.

1. Jan have the wire screen. The boys have brought the other supplies. (and)
2. This room is for crafts. The room by the lockers are for music. (and)
3. The trip to the museum inspired us to make some paper. Jan and I am going to a workshop. (so)
4. Leo has a talent for making paper. He have studied the process before. (or)
5. I plan to make some note cards. Jeremy thinks I should make a book. (but)

 Expand your sentences. When you create compound sentences, add the conjunction and make sure the subject and verb in each clause agree. Check that you have improved the flow of your writing.

TEKS 6.20A(i), 6.20(ii)

Mechanics: Capitalization

When you edit for *mechanics*, you check for correct use of capitalization and punctuation. To edit for capitalization, look for words, abbreviations, initials, and acronyms that require capital letters. (See pages **664–671**.)

When do I capitalize letters?

A capital letter is used to begin the first word in a sentence and any word that is a proper noun. Capitals are also in:

> **abbreviations:** Mr. Nimms has a Ph.D. in biology.
> **initials:** I like the writer A. A. Milne.
> **acronyms:** MOMA is my favorite art museum.

An *acronym* is a kind of abbreviation formed from the first letters of each word in a term, such as CPU (computer processing unit) or FBI (Federal Bureau of Investigation). Each letter in the acronym is capitalized, and no periods are used. We usually speak acronyms as a word.

 Correct the use of capital letters in each sentence.

1. Nick went to see dr. Rustagi at his office.
2. The author's name is j. r. Mendoza.
3. Anna's mother works in the It (information technology) department of the bank.
4. My brother is a student at Osu (Oklahoma State University).
5. N.A.S.A. has sent many astronauts into space.

 Check your capitalization. Read your essay to be sure you have used capital letters correctly in any abbreviations, initials, or acronyms.

EXPOSITORY

Editing Using a Checklist

Check your editing. On a piece of paper, write the numbers 1 to 9. If you can answer "yes" to a question, put a check mark after that number. If not, continue to edit for that convention.

Conventions

GRAMMAR

_____ 1. Do I use noncount nouns correctly?

_____ 2. Do I use the correct past-tense forms of irregular verbs?

MECHANICS (Punctuation and Capitalization)

_____ 3. Do I start all sentences and proper nouns with a capital letter?

_____ 4. Have I used capitals correctly in abbreviations?

_____ 5. Have I capitalized all initials and acronyms?

SENTENCE STRUCTURE

_____ 6. Do my subjects and verbs agree in number?

_____ 7. Have I checked both parts of a compound sentence for subject-verb agreement?

SPELLING

_____ 8. Have I spelled all my words correctly?

_____ 9. Have I double-checked the words my spell-check may have missed?

Creating a Title

Write a title for your expository essay, using any one of the following suggestions.

■ Create a word picture: **Making Amazing Maps**

■ Repeat a sound: **From Pulp to Paper**

■ Use action words: **Print with Potatoes**

 **TEKS** 6.14E, 6.17D

Go Online!

Publishing

Sharing Your Essay

After you have worked so hard writing your essay, you'll want to proofread it and make a neat copy to share. You may also decide to present your essay as a video, poster, or Web page. (See the suggestions below.)

 Make a final copy. Follow your teacher's instructions or use the guidelines below to format your essay. (If you are using a computer, see page 60.) Create a clean final copy of your essay and carefully proofread it.

Focus on Presentation

- Use blue or black ink and write neatly.
- Write your name in the upper left corner of page 1.
- Skip a line and center your title; skip another line and start your writing.
- Indent every paragraph and leave a one-inch margin on all four sides.
- Write your last name and the page number in the upper right corner of every page after the first one.

EXPOSITORY

Create a Poster

Make a poster based on your essay. List the steps in the process. Make sure the instructions are clear; then decorate your poster in an eye-catching way.

Create a Video

Film a demonstration of the process you covered in your essay. Use text cards to sum up key points at each stage. Show credits at the end.

Go Online
Upload your how-to essay for others to read.

ELPS 4I, 4K

Evaluating an Expository Essay

To learn how to evaluate an expository essay, you'll use the scoring rubric on pages 48–49 and the expository essays that follow. These expository essays are examples of writing for each score on the rubric.

Notice that this first expository essay received a score of 4. Read the description for a score of 4 on pages 48–49. Then read the essay. Use the same steps to study the other examples. Always remember to think about the overall quality of the writing.

Writing that fits a score of 4 is very strong.

Strong focus statement in the beginning paragraph

Transitions help the paragraphs fit together and flow smoothly.

Making Amazing Maps

If you have an independent geography project and you're not sure what to do, why not make a plaster map? Most maps that we work with are printed on paper, but a plaster map is special and gives you a better idea of what the land looks like. To make this kind of map, all you need is a printed map, a pencil, a bag of plaster, some water, vinegar, and a board that's large enough for the map to fit on top. It's fun, it's easy, and it makes an impressive project for school.

The first thing to do is copy the outline of the printed map onto the board with a pencil. Just draw the outline, not the inner parts. The printed map needs to be the kind that shows land elevations, because you will shape the plaster to show where the land is high or low.

When your drawing is finished, mix your plaster. Put about two cups of dry plaster into a bowl. Add a little water at a time until the mixture is like thick oatmeal.

EXPOSITORY

Plaster dries very quickly, so add a few drops of vinegar to slow the drying process. That will let you shape the plaster before it dries. Rinse out the bowl as soon as you're finished.

Now it's time to shape your map by building up the plaster to show mountains, hills, and level places. Start by pouring some plaster onto your board. Build it up to match the elevations shown on the printed map. Use your fingers or a wooden stick to scoop out the shapes of lakes. Use a toothpick or the edge of a table knife to scrape the shapes of rivers through the wet plaster. As you work, keep checking your work to the printed map.

After your map dries, you're not finished! There's another fun part; in fact it's the part I like best. Here's where you get to plaint your plaster map. Use blue for bodies of water, green for grassland or farmland, and light brown for deserts. I used watercolor for my map, but some people use food coloring, which also produces an attractive look.

Making plaster maps is an enjoyable way to learn geography, and it's probably one you never thought of before. When you're done, you'll have a project that will make your class and teacher say, "Wow!". Later, when the class is done with it, you can take it home and keep it among your creative projects. You'll not only have a clearer view of the world, but you'll feel great knowing that you made an artistic object.

The writer's voice comes through and sounds authentic.

Very few errors in conventions

ELPS 4I, 4K

Writing that fits a score of 3 is strong in most ways.

Effective introductory paragraph

The writer keeps purpose and audience in mind.

Voice is confident and informative.

Take Care of Your Gecko!

You've been asking for a pet for months, but your mom is allergic to dogs and your dad is allergic to cats. What can you do? The answer is, get a smaller pet that you can keep in a cage at home. I chose a gecko. It's a perfect first pet for a middle-schooler like you or me. But before you run out and buy that gecko, you'll need to learn how to take care of it, so that when you take it home, you'll be ready. So in this essay I will tell you how to take care of a gecko.

The first thing you need to know is that during your gecko's first few weeks you'll have to handle it very carefully. It needs to become familiar with its new environment. It needs to feel safe! If you have other reptile pets you need to quarantine it, which means keep it in a separate cage for a while (but if this is your first pet, you don't have to know that). Anyway, when you first put the gecko into its cage, it will probably dig down into the bottom and hide for a couple of days. Don't handle much and if you handle it, don't squeeze it or you can hurt it.

You should have the cage ready before you bring your gecko home. A good home for a gecko means a glass tank. The tank should be big enough for it to move around in. The tank must have a substrate in it. A substrate is a material that goes on the bottom for the gecko to walk on safely. My gecko has a paper substrate; you can also use carpet. Don't use wood shavings or sand. Your gecko will be very happy if you provide places for it to hide and climb in its tank. You can bring in a small log that you find outdoors, or you can use a cardboard box or buy a plastic reptile cave.

Once your gecko is in it's cage, you need to feed and water it. Don't get scared if the gecko doesn't eat much the first couple of days. That's normal. Geckos eat insects. They like crickets best. Juvenile geckos eat every day, while adult geckos eat every two days. Water is also very important. Keep a little dish of water in the cage. Keep it clean. In additon, you can mist your gecko, which means spraying a fine mist of water on it. You can buy a mister at the pet store.

Raising geckos is one of the most fun things you can do in your home, and if you take proper care of your gecko it will live a long time, maybe even twenty years. You may want to raise a family of geckos, or get other lizards. Did you ever think that you would love lizards? And it's all because your parents wouldn't get you a dog or cat!

Topic sentences focus paragraphs.

Choppy sentences and spelling errors

EXPOSITORY

Writing that fits a score of 2 is strong in some ways.

Sentences are not fluent.

Includes facts and details.

Steps in the process are omitted.

Ineffective concluding paragraph

How to Build a Wooden Go Cart

Would you like to know how to build a wooden go cart? I will tell you. It is a fun thing to do and it is not too hard.

The first thing is to find a plan for a good go cart. Buy the plan at a hobby store. Your plan tells you what steps you need to do. First, make sure you have the rite tools and buy the materials you need. You have to buy wood. The usual wood is either pine or oak. You will need a saw to cut the wood to the right lengths and widths that you find in the plan. You also need wheeles. You could them get off an old wagon or buy new at the hobby store. For steering you could tie a rope to the axle to pull it to the right or left, or you could use a wooden bar like on an old-fashioned wagon. You can even steer by pushing the axle right or left with your feet.

For tools you will need a hammer, a saw, a drill, measuring tape, then you will need round nails to hammer the wooden parts together. The front and rear axles are metal rods with wooden supports.

There are many different plans for making gocarts so when you choose your own you will know exactly what the measurements of each part should be. But this tells you the basic idea of building a go cart. I hope it has been helpful to help you know how to build a go-cart.

Writing that fits a score of 1 is weak.

Pizza

One of the best times I ever had was making pizza with my mom, she got a crust at the store because its a lot harder if you make your own crust from scrach. But the crust at the store is good.

Theres many different things you can put on a pizza but the most basic thing is the cheese and the tomatoe sawse. You can just use sawse from a can, its no big deal. If you want something speshul you can get a can of tomatoes slice em and lay them on top of the sawse.

You put the sawse on first then you lay the cheese over. The cheese might come in shredded peaces or mite be a chunk that you cut.

You want some flavorings to like maybe olive oil black peper garlik. Then you put on your items!! I like peperony. I tried olives once I didnt like them. My mom likes mushrooms and green peper. I havnt tried them.

So you have all you're ingrediyents on top of the pizza – I forgot that you shud sprinkle on lots of parmejan cheese to, it gives it a real nice flavor.

Then you bake it. The packidge from the pizza crust will tell you how long and how hot. Pizza needs a pretty hot oven. I think ours was 400 for 20 mins. but yours might be different.

Then you're pizzas ready! Have fun eating!

The writer's words show she is interested.

Many errors in spelling, grammar, and usage.

Not specific, doesn't paint a clear picture.

Unnecessary details are included.

EXPOSITORY

Evaluating and Reflecting on Your Writing

You've put a lot of time and effort into your expository essay. Now take some time to think about and score your writing. On your own paper, finish each sentence starter below. To score your writing, refer to the scoring rubric on pages 48–49 and the examples you just read.

My Expository Essay

1. The best score for my expository essay is . . .

2. The best part of my essay is . . .

3. The part that still needs work is . . .

4. The main thing I learned about writing an expository essay is . . .

5. In my next piece of expository writing, I would like to . . .

6. Here is one question I still have about writing an expository essay:

⭐ **TEKS** 6.17A

Expository Writing

Classifi|ca|tion Essay

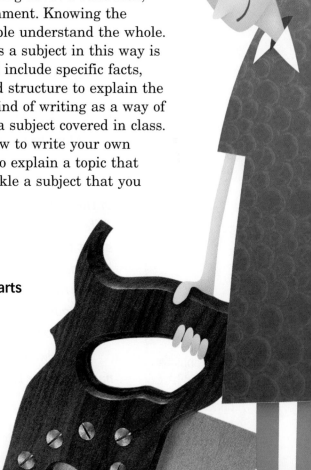

One way to explain a topic is to divide it into its parts. That's true whether you're talking about a sandwich, a bicycle, or the United States government. Knowing the different parts of a subject helps people understand the whole.

An expository essay that explains a subject in this way is called a classification essay. It should include specific facts, details, and examples in an organized structure to explain the subject. Often, teachers assign this kind of writing as a way of checking students' understanding of a subject covered in class.

In this chapter, you will learn how to write your own classification essay. You may choose to explain a topic that you know a lot about, or you may tackle a subject that you want to understand better.

Writing Guidelines

Subject: A topic with different parts
Purpose: To explain
Form: Classification essay
Audience: Classmates

Classification Essay

In the following student essay, Jana explains the main types of band instruments and tells why each type is different. She learned about the types of instruments by attending a band information night.

The focus statement introduces the controlling idea (underlined).

Specific facts, details, and examples add interest.

Strong details add to development.

Transitions between paragraphs guide the reader's understanding.

What Instrument Are You?

At the beginning of the school year, Riverview Middle School held a band information night. An incredible number of instruments were introduced, including four different sizes of saxophones. Some instruments have wooden reeds, and others have mouthpieces. There are even four different kinds of drums. It was hard to keep the instruments all straight. Then Mrs. Delgato clarified things. <u>Our band program uses just three types of instruments: brass, woodwinds, and percussion.</u>

Most brass instruments are made out of brass, of course, or some other kind of metal. They get their sound from blowing into the mouthpiece. The size of the mouthpiece and the length of tubing create different pitches. Cornets have small mouthpieces and short tubing, so they can play high notes. Trombones have medium mouthpieces and tubing, so they hit the middle range of notes. Tubas and sousaphones have huge mouthpieces and lots of tubing, which is why they sound so low.

Woodwinds, the next type of instrument, get their name because they used to be made of wood and the

TEKS 6.17A(iii)
ELPS 3E, 3G, 4K

sound comes from blowing into them. Some clarinets, oboes, and bassoons are still made of wood. Flutes and piccolos are metal. These two woodwinds make sound by having the player blow air over an opening. Other woodwinds create sound with a vibrating wooden reed.

Percussion instruments make noise when one thing hits another thing. A drumstick hits a drumhead or wood block, or a mallet hits a bar on a xylophone. Surprisingly, a piano is actually a percussion instrument, too. It makes sounds when hammers hit metal strings! Most percussion instruments, like cymbals or bass drums, don't have an exact pitch. Others, like chimes and kettledrums, do.

Once Mrs. Delgato explained the different kinds of instruments to us, no one felt so overwhelmed. Instead of walking out the door, most beginning band members checked out all the instruments and found the one that was just right for them. Now comes the real challenge, becoming a skilled trombonist or drummer.

Examples help readers understand each class of instruments.

The ending reflects on the ideas in the essay.

EXPOSITORY

Respond to the reading. On your own paper, answer the following questions about the sample essay. Discuss with a partner.

☐ **Focus and Coherence** (1) How do the beginning and ending help tie the essay together?

☐ **Organization** (2) How does the writer organize her description of band instruments?

☐ **Development of Ideas** (3) Without looking back at the essay, name several instruments that were mentioned. What details helped you remember these instruments?

 TEKS 6.14A2, 6.22A
ELPS 3E

Prewriting Selecting a Topic

To choose a topic for a classification essay, think of topics that can be divided into different types, or groups. Jana wrote a list of things she had learned about recently. Then she chose a topic from that list.

List

types of clouds	<u>types of band instruments</u>
branches of government	the food pyramid
the respiratory system	planets in the solar system

Choose your topic. Write a list of topics you find interesting. (Try to write at least five.) Underline the topic you would like for your own essay.

Asking Questions About Your Topic

A good way to begin exploring a topic is to talk to other people. First, come up with some questions about your topic. Most of them should be open-ended questions. For example, Jana listed these questions:

Questions

How many types of band instruments are there?
How are the types different from each other?
What does each type of instrument sound like?
What do the instruments look like?

Consult with others. Discuss your ideas and topic choices with classmates. Decide upon your topic and then formulate several open-ended questions to guide your research for what your essay will be about.

TEKS 6.17A(iii)

Organizing with a Line Diagram

To organize her facts, details, and examples, Jana made a line diagram. She divided her main topic—band instruments—into its three divisions: brass, woodwinds, and percussion. Next, she listed examples of each.

Line Diagram

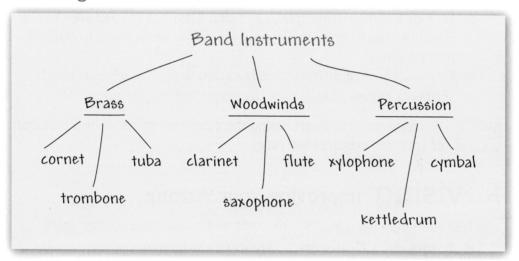

 Prewrite **Organize your thoughts.** Make your own line diagram to show examples, facts, or details about your topic.

Researching the Topic

Looking at her line diagram, Jana decided to gather more examples of instruments for her essay. She also wanted to include a few details about each one. She visited the band room again and jotted down notes.

> Sousaphone – brass, low pitch
> Trombone – slide is three feet long!
> Clarinet, oboe, bassoon – woodwinds made of wood
> Flute, piccolo – woodwinds made of metal

 Prewrite **Do your research.** What do you need to find out about your topic? Gather more facts, specific details, and examples. Take organized notes.

EXPOSITORY

 **TEKS** 6.14D, 6.14E, 6.17A(i), 6.17A(iii), 6.17A(iv)
ELPS 3E

Drafting Creating Your First Draft

Using your research questions, line diagram, and notes as a guide, write your first draft. Keep these points in mind.

- Your first paragraph should introduce your topic or controlling idea in an engaging way and clearly state your focus.
- In your middle paragraphs, use facts, details, and examples to clearly explain each part of your topic. Use transitions to connect paragraphs.
- Use sentences of different kinds as you develop each paragraph.
- Write an ending that makes the essay feel complete.

 Write your first draft. Using the guidelines above, write a first draft of your own classification essay.

Revising Improving Your Writing

Use the following questions to guide you as you revise your draft.

- **Focus and Coherence** Are my introduction and conclusion effective? Is controlling idea clear throughout my writing?
- **Organization** Do my transitions and sentences flow from paragraph to paragraph?
- **Development of Ideas** Do I need additional facts, details, or examples to fully explain my ideas?
- **Voice** Does my voice suit my purpose and audience?

 Revise your writing. Carefully consider the questions above. Then revise your writing as needed to make it clear and interesting.

Editing Checking for Conventions

When your revising is completed, edit your paper for conventions.

- **Conventions** Have I checked grammar, mechanics (punctuation and capitalization), sentence structure, and spelling?

 Edit your work. Edit your essay for the conventions. Have someone else check it over, too. Make needed corrections. Then make a final copy and proofread it.

Expository Writing

Across the Curriculum

Expository writing is used to share information, so you will find it in every school subject. In social studies, you may be asked to take a survey and present the results. In science, you may write up an explanation of how something works. In math, you may have to explain a concept. In any class, you may be asked to write directions. All are forms of expository writing.

On the following pages, you will work with four types of expository writing for other classes. You will learn the form needed for each, along with tips for using the writing process. At the end of the chapter, you will have the chance to practice writing for an assessment test.

What's Ahead

- **Social Studies**: Creating a Report
- **Math**: Explaining a Concept
- **Science**: Respond to an Article
- **Practical Writing**: Drafting Directions in an Informal Letter

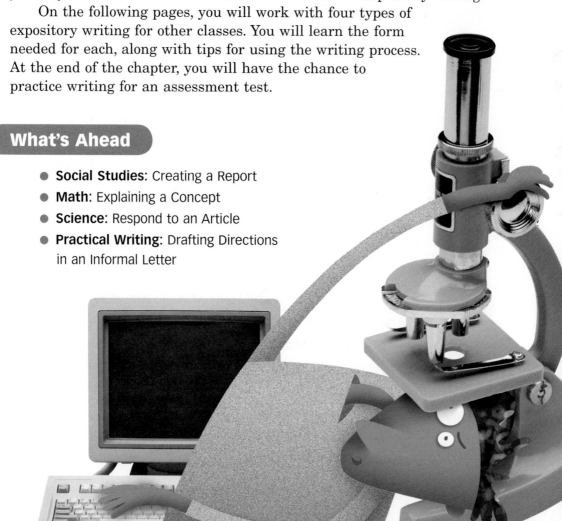

TEKS 6.17A(i), 6.25A(iii)

Social Studies: Creating a Report

In many of your classes you will have to explain ideas or facts in a report. Sometimes you will have to research the facts and ideas you explain. LaToya created a research plan, gathered sources, compiled information, and then created the following report on Robert Dennard.

The **beginning** introduces the controlling idea.

> Do you play games or check e-mail on a computer? If Robert Dennard had not been born in Terrell, Texas, in 1932, a computer in your home or classroom might not have been possible.
>
> In 1967, Robert Dennard invented a computer chip called dynamic random access memory, or DRAM. (Hicks 5) This little chip allowed computers to have more memory for less money. Before this invention, computers were too expensive. Most people and schools could not afford computers.

Ideas are presented in a consistent format.

> A large computer company started making computers using Dennard's chip and selling them to the public. This was the beginning of the computer industry. (Garza 7) Since then, more microchips have been developed, making computers faster and cheaper.
>
> Even though DRAM was invented over 40 years ago, Robert Dennard is still honored as an important person in the history of computers. In 1988, he was awarded the National Medal of Technology. Dennard was inducted into the National Inventors Hall of Fame in 1997.

The **ending** is effective and stays to the controlling idea.

> Next time you log on to simply send a quick e-mail, think about what your life would be like without computers. You can thank Mr. Robert Dennard for his contribution to something you use everyday!

describe solve.
define explain inform

213

Writing in Social Studies

TEKS 6.22A, 6.23A,
6.23D, 6.25A–C, 6.23E
ELPS 3E

Writing Tips

Before you write . . .

- **Select a topic.**
  Brainstorm ideas, talk with peers about possible topics and determine your topic.

- **Generate a research plan.**
  Gather relevant information to create effective questions.

- **Gather sources.**
  Follow your research plan. Use your questions as a guide to gather your research from a variety of sources.

- **Take notes.**
  Take thorough notes, documenting your sources.

During your writing . . .

- **Synthesize information.**
  Compile the information from your notes and summarize. Present your findings in a consistent style and format.

- **Keep it fair.**
  Paraphrase and quote your sources.

After you've written a first draft . . .

- **Check for completeness.**
  Make sure you have included all of the information needed to answer your research questions.

- **Check for correctness.**
  Proofread your report several times for punctuation, spelling, capitalization, and other conventions.

EXPOSITORY

Try It Follow the writing tips above to write a report on a social studies topic that you are interested in. Share your ideas with a classmate and get his or her feedback.

Math: Explaining a Concept

Josh was asked to write an explanation of an important topic in math. His goal was to help readers understand the key ideas and evidence about the topic. He chose "rates of speed." After writing, he found he understood the idea much better.

The **beginning** states the key idea.

The **middle** part presents evidence that helps the reader understand the key idea.

The **ending** identifies ways to apply or use the key idea.

Rates of Speed

In math, "rates of speed" are used to compare time to distance. For example, miles per hour (mph) is a very common way to describe the speed of cars, airplanes, and other machines.

Miles per hour is really just a ratio that tells how far something goes during a certain time. Other common rates of speed are feet per second (fps) and kilometers per hour (kph). A rate of speed used by scientists, especially astronomers, is the speed of light. It is 186,000 miles per second. It takes a ray of sunlight only about 8 minutes to travel the 93 million miles from the sun to the earth.

When figuring a rate of speed, ask these two questions: How far did it go? How long did it take? The first answer divided by the second is a rate of speed. So, if a train goes 120 miles in 2 hours, its rate of speed is 120 ÷ 2, or 60 miles per hour.

Rates of speed are easy to use. To find out how far something traveled, multiply the time it traveled by its rate of speed. For example, if it took 60 seconds to read this essay, the light first used would be 11,160,000 miles away by now (60 seconds × 186,000 miles per second).

TEKS 6.17A(ii)

Writing Tips

Before you write . . .

- **Select a topic.**
  If you have not been given a topic, use your math textbook or your notes to find a concept that you can write about.
- **Study your topic.**
  Pick a few examples that will help you make your writing clear. In the sample, the speed of light provides a clear and interesting example.

During your writing . . .

- **Organize your thoughts.**
  Decide on an order for the information. You could start with a definition and offer some examples. Then explain the concept and how it relates to the real world.
- **Use examples and comparisons to guide and inform.**
  Using clear examples helps guide and inform your reader's understanding of the ideas and evidence presented.
- **Think of some questions.**
  Include some questions in your essay. Choose questions that you can answer using the math concept.

After you've written a first draft . . .

- **Check your sources.**
  Make sure you have explained the concept correctly.
- **Keep it simple.**
  Look for places where your explanation may be unclear. Try to make your explanation as simple as possible.
- **Check for correctness.**
  Review facts and figures, as well as grammar, punctuation, spelling, and other conventions.

EXPOSITORY

Write an explanation to guide and inform the reader's understanding of a math concept that you learned. Define the concept and include examples, details, and comparisons to explain

TEKS 6.17C(ii)

Science: Respond to an Article

Scientists often use expository writing to share their knowledge with readers through articles and books. In his science class, Ravi wrote an expository response to an article he read about geysers.

How a Geyser Erupts

The **beginning** presents the controlling idea of the response.

"Letting Off Steam," an article in Science Seekers magazine by Bob Lester, is filled with fascinating facts about geysers. Geysers are awesome eruptions of water or steam from the earth. The power and beauty of geysers is amazing, but what makes them erupt? That is the part I found most interesting.

Geysers are often located near volcanoes. They are created when water seeps down through the ground and touches molten rock called magma. The heat turns the water to steam. The trapped steam builds up pressure under more water. Finally, the steam and hot

The **middle** provides evidence from the text to demonstrate understanding.

water blast up through a crack and out of the ground. The blast reduces the pressure, and then the geyser stops. The process is repeated, and when the pressure builds up, the geyser erupts again.

Different geysers act in different ways. Old Faithful in

The **ending** offers some interesting facts and restates the controlling idea.

Yellowstone Park erupts almost every hour. Other geysers may go months, or even years, between eruptions. Geysers are one of the true wonders of nature.

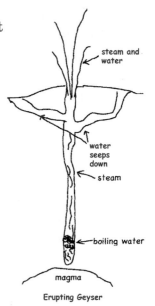

steam and water

water seeps down

steam

boiling water

magma

Erupting Geyser

TEKS 6.17C
ELPS 3E

Writing Tips

Before you write . . .

- **Read the article more than once.**
  Make sure you thoroughly understand the article.
- **Organize your thoughts.**
  Write a focus statement based on your understanding of the article and what you want to say in your response.

During your writing . . .

- **Share specific details.**
  Choose details that will help explain the topic of the article to the reader. Provide details and evidence from the text that demonstrate your understanding of the article.
- **Use comparisons or illustrations.**
  Make comparisons to help the reader understand surprising or difficult facts presented in the article. Also consider including drawings. In the sample essay, the writer uses a simple drawing to explain why geysers erupt.

After you've written a first draft . . .

- **Ask for another opinion.**
  Let several of your classmates read the essay. Do they understand it? Remember that the purpose of your essay is to respond to an article.
- **Check for organization.**
  Review each paragraph and sentence to make sure each thought leads naturally to the next thought.

EXPOSITORY

 Write an expository essay in response to an article on nature. Think of things like weather, landforms, and the oceans. Read the article and write a short response essay in which you provide evidence from the text to demonstrate your understanding. Share your response and what you learned with your classmates.

 TEKS 6.17B

Practical Writing:
Drafting Directions in an Informal Letter

One reason for writing an informal letter is to give directions. To write good directions, give the information in short, clear sentences in a logical order. In the letter below, a member of a middle school marching band gives directions to the place where the band must meet.

The writer uses appropriate conventions.

First paragraph conveys the controlling idea of the letter.

Directions include all important information.

Last paragraph brings the letter to a close.

May 25, 2011

Dear Marching Band members,

This is just a quick note to remind you that the band will be marching in the city parade on Memorial Day, Monday, May 31. Plan to be at the band room by 8:00 Monday, in uniform, to tune up. At 8:20, Mr. Roberts will walk the group to the parade meeting place. Here are the directions:

1. Leave from the front door of the school and turn left on Evans Street.
2. Walk to the railroad tracks. Look for trains and cross the tracks.
3. Continue on Evans Street until it meets Randolf Street.
4. Turn left on Randolf Street.
5. Follow Randolf around a sharp curve and over a bridge.
6. Turn right on Jenkins Street. The Lincoln statue is on the right.
7. Wait in the parking lot just beyond the statue.

The total walk is one mile and should take about half an hour. Be ready!

Sincerely,

Brad Bunsen

TEKS 6.17B
ELPS 3E, 3G, 5G

Writing Tips

Before you write . . .

- **Think about the start and finish of the route.**
  Choose a path that is direct, easy to follow, and safe.
- **Check a map.**
  Trace the route from start to finish. Include a basic map.

During your writing . . .

- **Use appropriate letter writing conventions.**
  Include the date and a salutation. Demonstrate a sense of
  closure by including a closing line and signature.
- **Provide specific street names.**
  Give the name of each street, as well as details about the
  street. ("Follow Randolf around a sharp curve.")
- **List landmarks.**
  Mention spots along the way that will help your friends
  know they are on the right course. ("Walk to the railroad
  tracks" or the "Lincoln statue is on the right.")
- **Provide times, distances, and directions.**
  Tell your friend how long the trip is. ("The total walk is
  one mile and should take about a half hour.") Explain
  which way to turn. Use left/right, north/south, or east/
  west. ("Turn right on Jenkins Street.")

After you've written a first draft . . .

- **Follow your own directions.**
  If possible, walk the route to test your directions.
- **Check the details.**
  Double-check all the turns, streets, and landmarks carefully.
  Make sure you conveyed important ideas and information.

EXPOSITORY

Try It   Write an informal letter to an out-of-town friend giving directions
from your school to an important location in your city or town. Make
sure the letter conveys important information and details. Use
appropriate conventions and include a closing. Then trade letters
with a partner. Discuss your opinions of each other's letters.

Expository Writing
Writing for the Texas Assessment

When you take state tests in Texas, you often have to write. The prompt tells you what to write about and gives some things to remember. Read the following prompt.

Prompt

Write a composition about the value of respect for others.

Use the information below to help you write your composition.

REMEMBER THAT YOU SHOULD—

- [ ] write about learning respect for others.

- [ ] make sure each sentence helps readers understand your composition.

- [ ] include specific details about your ideas to make sure readers fully understand what you have to say.

- [ ] try to use correct grammar, punctuation, capitalization, sentence structure, and spelling.

TEKS 6.14A

Prewriting Selecting a Form

The prompt doesn't tell you what form of writing to use. How can you decide which one? Think about which form best fits what you want to say.

Do you want to:
- give information?
- describe a place or person?
- explain something?
- share a personal experience?
- persuade someone to do something?
- offer a solution to a problem?

Answering these questions will help you decide on a form.

Latisha wanted to explain something. She decided the best form was an expository essay because it allowed her to tell how she learned to respect others.

Organizing Ideas and Details

Latisha remembered that her first-grade teacher taught her about showing respect to others. She decided to write about the kinds of actions that her teacher taught. To plan her draft, Latisha made a three-column chart. It helped her organize her ideas and related details.

EXPOSITORY

Sharing	Being polite	Following rules
– crayons and paper	– kickball	– listening with respect
– playground equipment		– taking turns when talking
– board games		– not cutting in line

Drafting **Writing the Essay**

Next, Latisha used her chart to write her expository essay. Read Latisha's essay.

The **beginning** states the focus or thesis. (underlined).

My first grade teacher, Mrs. Kloften, made a big impression on me. In one important way, she was a lot like my mom because she taught me about getting along and respecting other people. Everything we did in Mrs. Kloften's classroom centered around becoming respectful classmates.

The **middle** paragraphs build on the ideas in the first paragraph.

We had to share everything in her class. We shared crayons and markers and paper. On the playground, we had to share all of the equipment, and during classroom playtime, everyone got a chance to play with the best board games. At first, we may not have liked all of that sharing, but it helped us become better classmates and friends.

When we played any outdoor games, especially kickball, Mrs. Kloften expected us to follow certain rules. Her main rule was, "Everyone who wants to play gets to play." Also, everyone got a chance to be pitcher and cover first base as well as to kick. If a student was caught making fun of someone, that person had to apologize

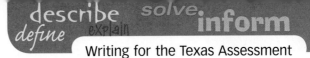

ELPS 3D, 3E, 3G, 3H

or take a time out. With these rules, Mrs. Kloften was trying to teach us about being good sports.

Mrs. Kloften also wanted us to be polite, at all times. During class work, we had to be good listeners, and we had to wait our turn to talk. When we were given something, we had to say, "Thank you." When we left the room, we had to line up by the door without taking "cuts" and wait until everyone was quiet.

My first-grade teacher taught us a lot about reading and math, too. She also made science a lot of fun, especially when we studied animals. But the most important thing Mrs. Kloften taught us was how to act in class. She wanted to make sure that we became good classroom citizens, and I respect her for that.

The **ending** paragraph reflects on the experience.

EXPOSITORY

Respond to the reading. Answer the following questions about the sample response. Discuss with a partner.

☐ **Focus and Coherence** **(1)** What is the focus of the writer's explanation? **(2)** What key words in the prompt also appear in the essay?

☐ **Organization** **(3)** What is the topic of each middle chapter?

☐ **Voice** **(4)** What details make the writer's voice vivid?

Literature Connection: You can find an example of an expository essay in the handbook excerpt "Wilderness Survival."

 **TEKS** 6.14A
ELPS 5G

Writing Tips

Before you write . . .

- **Understand the prompt and select the appropriate genre.**
  Remember that an expository prompt asks you to explain. Use the genre that is appropriate for conveying the intended meaning to your audience.
- **Plan your time wisely.**
  Spend several minutes planning before you start writing. Use a graphic organizer (cluster) to help you gather ideas.

Cluster

Detail   Detail

Person

Detail   Detail

During your writing . . .

- **Decide on a focus for your essay.**
  Keep your main idea or purpose in mind as you write.
- **Choose carefully.**
  Use clear examples and explanations.
- **End in a meaningful way.**
  Remind readers about the importance of the topic at the end of your explanation.

After you've written a first draft . . .

- **Check for completeness and correctness.**
  Write your supporting details in logical order and correct any errors in capitalization, punctuation, spelling, and grammar.

 Plan and write a response. Respond to the prompt listed on page 220. Remember to select a form and use the tips above to help you as you write.

Expository Writing in Review

Purpose: In expository writing, you *explain something* to readers.
Topics: Explain . . .

how to do or make something
the causes of something
the kinds of something
the definition of something

Prewriting

Select a topic that you know a lot about or one that you want to learn about. (See pages 170–171.)

Write a focus statement, telling the controlling idea you plan to cover. (See page 172.)

Gather the important steps or details and organize them according to the organizational strategy you have chosen. (See pages 172–174.)

Drafting

In the beginning part, introduce your topic and state your controlling idea. (See page 177.)

In the middle, give the details and examples that explain the focus. Use transitions between paragraphs to help guide the reader. (See pages 178–179.)

In the ending, summarize your writing and make a final comment about the controlling idea. (See page 180.)

Revising

Review your focus and coherence, organization, and development of ideas. Then check for **voice.** (See pages 182–190.)

Editing

Check your writing for conventions. Also have a trusted classmate edit your writing. (See pages 192–196.)

Make a final copy and proofread it for errors before sharing it. (See page 197.)

Assessing

Use the expository rubric to assess your finished writing. (See pages 198–203.)

EXPOSITORY

persuade
argue

ELPS 2C, 3E, 3H, 4G

Persuasive Writing

Writing Focus

- Persuasive Paragraph
- Persuasive Essay
- Pet-Peeve Essay

Grammar Focus

- Predicate Adjectives
- Subject-Verb Agreement

Learning Language

Work with a partner. Read the meanings and share answers to the questions.

1. You **convince** people of something by making them feel sure about it.
   Convince a classmate that you like to read.

2. An idea you believe in or work for is a **cause**.
   Name a cause that you support.

3. When you **gather support** you get many people to agree with you.
   When could you gather support for something?

convince
reason support

Persuasive Writing

Persuasive Paragraph

If you could change one thing at school or at home, what would it be? How would you change it? Do you think you could convince other people to go along with the change?

Persuasive writing is your chance to get people to think the way you do about something. Advertisements, editorials, and even some letters are common kinds of persuasive writing.

In the next few pages, you'll write a persuasive paragraph about a change you'd like to make.

Writing Guidelines

Subject:	An important change
Purpose:	To convince readers to agree with you
Form:	Persuasive paragraph
Audience:	Classmates, parents, guardians, or school officials

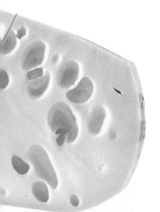

ELPS 2C, 2G, 3E,3H, 4K

Persuasive Paragraph

In a persuasive paragraph, the topic sentence establishes an opinion, the body sentences give evidence and sound reasoning to support it, and the closing sentence restates the opinion. The following paragraph was written by a student concerned about access to the school stage.

The **topic sentence** establishes an opinion.

The **body** includes evidence and sound reasoning.

The **closing sentence** restates the opinion.

Ramp It Up!

Bryant Middle School needs to add a ramp to its auditorium stage. State law says that everyone has to have equal access to important parts of the school, and the stage is important. In this year's spring play, the student who is playing the Wizard of Oz is in a wheelchair. A ramp is needed so he can get up on the stage and also move down into the audience during performances. A ramp also would open drama to more students. That's the most important reason for it. Putting in a ramp isn't just about state laws or one student. The ramp should be added because it would give more students the chance to perform.

Respond to the reading. Write answers to the following questions. Discuss your answers with a partner.

☐ **Focus and Coherence** (1) What is the topic of the paragraph?

☐ **Organization** (2) How is the paragraph organized—by time, by location, or by order of importance?

☐ **Voice** (3) What specific words or phrases make this paragraph persuasive?

TEKS 6.14A, 6.14B

Prewriting Selecting a Topic

Think about the places where you spend the most time. What important changes would you like to make in each of those places? A chart like the one below is a strategy that can help you think about important changes.

Chart

Home	School	Martin Luther King, Jr., Park
Less dish duty	Make stage accessible	Remove leash law
Get cable	Improve school food	Clean up graffiti

Think about important changes. Create a chart like the one above as an organizational strategy. Write down three places where you spend time. Under each one, list at least two changes you would like to make. Choose one change to write about in a persuasive paragraph.

Gathering Reasons

Everyone has opinions. To convince others to agree with your position, you need to provide sound reasoning with detailed evidence. The writer of the sample paragraph on page 228 used listing to gather support for her opinion and plan her organizational strategy.

List

> *Bryant Middle School needs to build a ramp to the stage.*
>
> - *State law says important spots need to be accessible.*
> - *The actor playing the Wizard of Oz has a wheelchair.*
> - *Anybody who wants to be in drama should be able to get onto our stage.*

List your reasons. At the top of your paper, write the important change you chose to write about. Under it, write as many reasons as you can think of to support your opinion. Try to come up with at least three.

TEKS 6.14D

Drafting Developing the First Draft

Write the first draft of your paragraph. Use the following tips:

- Start with a sentence that clearly states your position.
- In the body, write sentences that give your supporting reasons and evidence.
- End with a sentence that restates your opinion.

Write your first draft. When you write your first draft, include at least three good reasons with evidence to support your opinion.

Revising Improving Your Writing

After you complete the first draft of your paragraph, you are ready to revise it. Check your *focus and coherence, organization, development of ideas, voice,* and *conventions.*

Revise your paragraph. Make the necessary changes to improve your first draft, using the questions below as a guide.

1 Does the topic sentence state a clear opinion?

2 What details should be added or removed?

3 Do I sound persuasive?

4 Have I used specific nouns and strong verbs?

5 Have I written complete sentences that flow smoothly?

Editing Checking for Conventions

Once you have revised your paragraph, check it for *conventions.*

Edit your paragraph. Ask yourself the questions below.

1 Have I checked for errors in usage *(to, too, two; it's, its; there, their, they're)* and other grammar errors?

2 Have I used correct spelling, punctuation, and capitalization?

Proofread your paragraph. After making a neat final copy of your paragraph, check it one more time for errors.

Persuasive Writing

Promoting a Cause

"Save the whales!" "Alba Moreno for class president!" "Reuse and recycle!" Each of these statements identifies a cause. Like most people, you probably have worthy causes that you support, too. If you feel strongly enough about them, you will want to persuade others to support them as well.

Persuasive writing is one way to get others to think the way that you do. To do this, you must express a thoughtful opinion that shows your position and give strong reasons and evidence to support it. In this unit, you will be asked to write an essay that persuades others to support one of the causes that you believe in.

Writing Guidelines

Subject:	A cause that you believe in
Purpose:	To persuade others to agree with you
Form:	Persuasive essay
Audience:	Classmates

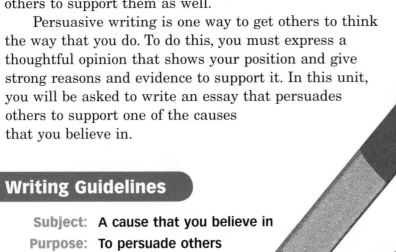

Understanding Your Goal

Your goal in this chapter is to write a persuasive essay convincing others to support a cause you believe in. The traits listed below will help you meet that goal. The scoring rubric on pages 48–49 will also help you. Refer to it often to improve your writing.

Traits of Persuasive Writing

Focus and Coherence

Choose one cause that you support. State it clearly at the beginning. Make sure that your position is supported by detailed evidence and sound reasoning. Wrap up your essay by restating your position including consideration of alternatives at the end.

Organization

Create a smooth flow of ideas from the beginning through the middle to the ending. Build each paragraph on the one before it.

Development of Ideas

Give evidence to support your opinions about the cause.

Voice

Sound confident and sincere about your cause.

Conventions

Check your writing for errors in grammar, punctuation, capitalization, and spelling.

Literature Connection. You can find an example of persuasive writing in the public service announcement, "Start the Day Right."

Persuasive Essay

The focus of this persuasive essay is avoiding exotic pets, a cause that the writer feels strongly about. The writer begins by getting the reader's attention and stating a position. Then the writer supports the opinion with reasons, and ends with a call to action that considers an alternative.

Beginning

The beginning introduces the topic and establishes the writer's position (underlined).

Middle

The middle paragraphs show sound reasoning and detailed evidence that support the opinion (underlined).

Avoiding Exotic Pets

Last year, a neighbor got a dingo. As a puppy, this Australian wild dog was very friendly. By the time it was six months old, though, the dingo was big and mean. After it attacked another dog, Animal Control had to take the dingo away. What if this neighbor buys a baby crocodile next? Exotic pets might be interesting, but they can also cause a lot of trouble. People should think carefully before buying unusual pets.

One problem is that owners often don't think about what will happen when the animal grows. For example, potbellied pigs are cute when they're little, but they can be hard to handle later on. In fact, pigs may turn over furniture or dig up the backyard looking for something to eat. Owners may become frustrated with their pet's behavior.

Another problem is that owners who grow tired of their exotic pets have trouble finding new homes for them. Often, shelters can't take these pets, so owners turn them loose. Releasing exotic animals can be very harmful to native animals and dangerous for people. For example, foreign fish that have been released into lakes and rivers are wiping out native fish like bass and trout.

TEKS 6.18A
ELPS 3E, 3G, 4J, 4K

Relevant evidence is included to strengthen the position.

Scarier yet, when a woman in Wisconsin reached into her flower garden, a large tropical snake attacked her.

The most serious problem is that exotic pets may carry dangerous diseases. For instance, monkey pox has become a problem in this country because infected animals brought it here from Africa. Even worse, some imported pets could also carry the deadly Ebola virus to the United States.

Ending
• • • • • • • • • • • • • •

The ending summarizes the main points and asks the reader to consider alternatives (underlined) and makes a call to action.

Even though some owners are well prepared to keep exotic pets, most of these animals were never meant to be pets like dogs and cats. A big dog may cause some damage once in a while, but a pet wolf can chew through doors. Is it really worth it to keep an animal that can be destructive or even dangerous? If a person insists on keeping an unusual pet, he or she should educate themselves. Perhaps people should be required to earn a certification before being allowed to keep an unusual pet. However, it would be best for the sake of these animals and the environment, that people avoid having unusual pets.

Respond to the Reading. Answer the following questions. Discuss your answers with a partner.

☐ Focus and Coherence (1) What is the writer's opinion about the topic? (2) What are the three reasons given in the body that support the opinion?

☐ Organization (3) How are these reasons organized?

☐ Voice (4) Does the writer sound confident and sincere? (5) What words or phrases tell you so?

Go Online!

Prewriting

PREWRITE · REVISE · PUBLISH · DRAFT · EDIT

Prewriting is the first step in the writing process. It involves selecting a topic, gathering specific details, and organizing your ideas.

Keys to Effective Prewriting

1. Select a cause that you care about and that fits the assignment.

2. Gather details about the cause.

3. Write a clear focus statement that establishes your position. Use it to guide you as you write.

4. Write topic sentences and paragraphs that include sound reasoning and evidence that supports your position.

5. Create a list or an outline as a planning guide.

PROD. NO.
SCENE   TAKE   ROLL
SOUND
DATE

PERSUASIVE

Prewriting Selecting a Topic

To get started, use a strategy to determine your topic. Think of a worthwhile cause to write about. For example, if your school district is thinking about dropping art classes, you might write an essay opposing this proposal.

A chart like the one below can help you find causes that you feel strongly about. Different causes are listed under four separate categories.

Chart

Animals	Community	Sports	School
Support animal shelters *Clean up after pets	*Build a skateboard park Improve the library	Add soccer teams Schedule games so parents can watch	*Keep art classes Expand school menus

Create a chart. Make a chart like the one above. Under each category (animals, community, sports, school), list causes you feel strongly about. When you finish, put a star (✳) next to two or three causes that interest you the most. Ask yourself the following questions about each one.

1 Why is this cause important to me?

2 Why would this cause interest my readers?

Choose a topic and controlling idea. After you have answered the questions above, choose your best topic and determine what your controlling idea will be.

Focus on the Texas Traits

Development of Ideas Choose a cause that you feel strongly about so that you have plenty of convincing things to say about it. You will need at least three strong sound reasons to support your opinion.

Gathering Ideas and Information

Once you select a topic, the next step is to gather your first thoughts about it. The writer of the essay on pages 233–234 did this by answering three basic questions: *Why is this cause important to me? What do I already know about it? What evidence do I need to find?* The answers will establish his position and help him find sound reasoning. Review his answers below.

First Thoughts

CAUSE: KEEPING ART CLASSES

Why is this cause important to me?

- *Art is one of my favorite subjects.*
- *Art allows me to use my imagination.*
- *It is a nice break from regular classes.*

What do I already know about it?

- *Art classes might be cut next year.*
- *The school board says that it doesn't have money for the program.*
- *When I asked the principal what I could do, she told me that parents should contact school board members.*

What evidence do I need to find?

- *I need more background information about this topic.*
- *How can schools solve money problems?*
- *Are there other reasons why we should keep art?*

Prewrite

Gather your thoughts. Answer the three questions above about your own topic. This will help you determine your position and organize your reasons and evidence.

1 Start by writing your cause on the top of a piece of paper.

2 Then list each question, leaving space after each one for your answers.

3 Write a sentence establishing your position. Put a star next to sound reasons and evidence that you will find and use in your essay.

Prewriting **Understanding Opinions and Facts**

At this point, make sure that you are clear about the difference between facts and opinions. An opinion is a feeling or belief; a fact is a detail that can be used to support an opinion. Opinions and positions must be supported with facts and reasons that are logical to the cause.

Opinion vs. Fact

Opinion: *School officials should keep art in our schools.*
(This statement expresses a feeling and cannot be checked.)

Fact: *The school administration has proposed to cut art classes.* (This statement can be checked.)

 Number a piece of paper from 1 to 6. Then decide if each statement below is a fact or an opinion. Write "O" for opinion and "F" for fact.

1. Carlos should run for class president.

2. Carlos has a 4-point average.

3. Our band room is the size of a regular classroom.

4. Park Middle School needs a new band room.

5. Josie is the tallest player on our basketball team.

6. Josie is the best player on the team.

Writing a Position Statement

Your position statement must establish your opinion by identifying (1) your cause and (2) your feeling about it. Review the examples that follow.

Position Statements

People should think carefully (feeling) *before buying exotic pets* (cause).
Art classes (cause) *should be kept in our school* (feeling).

 Write a position statement. Remember that your position statement should establish your true feelings and opinion about your cause. Write more than one version of your statement. Pick the best one.

persuade convince support
argue reason

Making a Plan

Once you have written your position statement, the next step is to list the sound, logical supporting reasons. See the list of reasons below.

Reasons List

Position Statement: *Schools in our district should keep art classes.*

First reason: *encourages creativity and trying new things*

Second reason: *fun way to learn about other subjects*

Third reason: *best place for many kids to make art*

Identify your supporting reasons. Write your position statement and then list at least three sound reasons that support your opinion.

Writing Topic Sentences

Each of your main reasons becomes a topic sentence for a supporting paragraph in your essay. Study the example that follows.

Reason: *encourages creativity and trying new things*

Topic sentence: *Art encourages people to be creative and try something new.*

Write your topic sentences. Turn each of your sound reasons into a strong topic sentence. Use the example above as a guide.

Texas Traits

Focus on the Texas Traits

Organization Think about the arrangement of your reasons. In persuasive essays, many writers either start with their most important reason or end with it.

PERSUASIVE

 **TEKS** 6.14B, 6.18A

Prewriting Organizing Your Ideas

Once you've written your topic sentences, use an appropriate organizational strategy to plan your draft. See the directions below.

Directions   **Organized List**

> **Write your position statement.**
>
> *Schools in our district should keep art classes.*

> **Write your first topic sentence.**
>
> *Art encourages people to be creative and try something new.*

> **List reasons and evidence.**
>
> *– Have freedom to imagine*
> *– Able to experiment*
> *– Make ceramics, paintings, and drawings*

> **Write your second topic sentence.**
>
> *Art is a fun way to learn about other subjects.*

> **List reasons and evidence.**
>
> *– Study Native American culture in social studies*
> *– In art, create Native American pouches*

> **Write your third topic sentence.**
>
> *School is the best place for many kids to make art.*

> **List reasons and evidence.**
>
> *– Need special supplies not found in most homes*
> *– Peers can offer support*

Make an organized list. To create your list and organize your writing, follow the directions above. Use this list as a guide when you write.

Focus on the Texas Traits

Voice In a persuasive essay, it's important to sound convincing, and you will sound convincing if you know a lot about your cause.

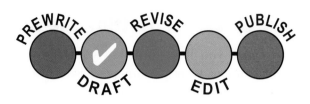

Drafting

A first draft lets you get all your ideas down on paper. You're ready to write a first draft when you have written a clear opinion statement and gathered supporting details.

Keys to Effective Writing

1. Use your organized list or outline as a planning guide.

2. Get all your ideas on paper in your first draft.

3. Write a clear position statement; use topic sentences in the middle paragraphs that support your position.

4. Add sound reasons and evidence to support your topic sentences and interest the reader.

5. Use transitions to tie everything together.

6. Write with your purpose, form, and audience in mind. Ask yourself these questions as you write:
   • What is my purpose for writing?
   • Am I keeping to the correct form?
   • Who is my audience?

 **TEKS** 6.18A
ELPS 5G

Drafting Getting the Big Picture

Once you have finished your prewriting, you are ready to begin the first draft of your persuasive essay. Remember, you are trying to convince the reader to agree with your feeling about a cause—and perhaps also to do something as a result.

The graphic below shows how the different parts of a persuasive essay fit together. (The examples are from the student essay on pages **243–246**.)

Beginning

The **beginning** grabs the reader's attention and establishes the position.

Position Statement
Schools in our district should keep art classes.

Middle

The **middle** includes sound supporting reasons and detailed and relevant evidence.

Topic Sentences
Art encourages people to be creative and try something new.

In addition, art is a fun way to learn more about other subjects.

Besides, school is the best place for many kids to make art.

Ending

The **ending** summarizes the argument, includes consideration of alternatives, and makes a call to action.

Closing Sentences
Instead of cutting subjects the district should think of ways to raise money to keep art classes.

We need to stand together against this, or it might actually happen. I don't want to live in a world without art, do you?

TEKS 6.18A
ELPS 5G

persuade convince support
argue reason
Promoting a Cause
243

Starting Your Essay

Once you have written a position statement and organized your thinking, you're ready to start writing your essay. In the beginning paragraph of a persuasive essay, you should grab the reader's attention and establish your position. Here are several good ways to begin:

Beginning

Middle

Ending

- **Give some interesting information about your topic.**
- **Ask a question.**
- **Quote someone.**
- **Share an experience.**

Beginning Paragraph

The writer of the following essay captures the reader's attention with a question and some interesting information and then shares a opinion statement (underlined).

The topic is introduced.	*Can anyone imagine a world without art? Take away colorful paintings, metal sculptures, and beautiful photographs. Erase the artwork from book covers, magazine ads, and comic books. Who would want to live in a world without art? Students in Burnley might have to. The school board is planning to cut art class. But this is wrong. Schools in Burnley should keep art classes.*
The paragraph ends with a clear position statement (underlined).	

Write an opening. Write the beginning paragraph of your persuasive essay. Make sure that you grab the reader's attention and include a statement that establishes your position.

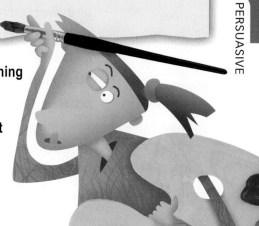

PERSUASIVE

TEKS 6.18A
ELPS 5G

Drafting Developing the Middle Part

After writing your opening paragraph, you are ready to develop the middle part of your essay. The middle paragraphs must present sound reasoning that supports the position statement. Detailed and relevant evidence is used to support each reason. As you move from paragraph to paragraph, be sure to use transitions like *besides, in addition,* and so on, to help the reader follow your argument. (See pages **620–622**.)

The following middle paragraphs are from the persuasive essay about keeping art classes in school. Each paragraph has three parts:

1 The **topic sentence** (underlined) states a reason that supports the opinion statement. Transitions are often used in topic sentences to tie the paragraphs together.

2 The **body** provides details and evidence that support the reason, including **facts** and **examples**.

3 The **closing sentence** summarizes the information in the paragraph.

Middle Paragraphs

The topic sentence states a sound reason.	<u>Art encourages people to be creative and try something new.</u> In art, students make ceramics, paintings, and drawings. Even though art teachers give directions, students have the freedom to follow their imaginations. Students experiment and make mistakes as they try to capture their dreams using clay, paint, and paper. There is no better place for creative thinking than in an art class.
The body provides facts.	
The closing sentence gives a summary.	
The next topic sentence includes a transition.	<u>In addition, art is a fun way to learn more</u> about other subjects. For example, students in

persuade convince support
argue reason
Promoting a Cause
245

TEKS 6.18A
ELPS 5G

The body includes detailed and relevant evidence.

The topic sentence includes a transition.

Detailed and relevant evidence is presented.

The closing sentence repeats the sound reasoning given in the essay.

social studies class study Native American culture by reading books and surfing the Internet. In art class, they work with leather to make pouches like Native Americans do. Students feel a personal connection with the Native American tribes they are studying. Hands-on projects are an important way for students to learn more about other subjects.

Besides, school is the best place for many kids to make art. Some kinds of art require lots of special supplies like clay, glazes, canvases, paints, and brushes. These expensive materials and tools are provided in art classes. Many students can't afford to have these things at home. It would be unfair to take away the students' chances to explore different kinds of art.

Draft

Write your middle paragraphs. Make sure that each paragraph includes one sound reason that is supported with relevant evidence.

Drafting Tips

- **Follow your prewriting** plan as you begin to write. Establish your position in your position statement.
- **Provide detailed evidence and sound reasoning** that supports your position statement and topic sentences.
- **Use a voice** that sounds confident and positive.
- **Write freely** and focus on organizing your ideas.

PERSUASIVE

 **TEKS** 6.14C, 6.18A
ELPS 5G

Drafting **Ending Your Essay**

The ending of your persuasive essay may be a good place to address a possible concern or objection to your opinion and to consider the alternatives to your cause. It's also a good place to restate your position and make a call to action. A call to action encourages the reader to do something or to think a certain way.

Examples of a call to action

- Help save our energy resources by walking or riding a bike.
- Join us at the rally to save music in our schools.
- Don't let your pet run loose.

Ending Paragraph

An objection is addressed (underlined), and the opinion is stated again.
The call to action encourages the reader to think about the problem.

Everyone knows that the district has money problems. But instead of cutting subjects, the district should think of ways to raise money to keep art classes. Art connects everything else that is learned. It's hard to imagine a school dropping reading or math, but the school board plans to drop art class. Students need to stand together against this, or it might actually happen. No one wants to live in a world without art, do they?

Write your ending. Write the last paragraph of your essay. Remember to state your position again and make a call to action as an alternative to your cause. Also try to include a strong final sentence.

Form a complete first draft. Write a complete copy of your essay. Leave room between lines for revising. Read your draft. Rethink how well questions of purpose, genre, and audience were addressed.

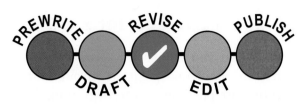

Revising

A first draft can usually be improved in a number of ways. Paragraphs may need to be shifted around, and parts of the argument may need to be clearer. You revise your writing in order to fix problems like these.

Keys to Effective Revising

1. Read through your entire draft to get a feeling of how well your essay works.

2. Make sure your position is stated clearly.

3. Check your paragraphs to make sure your topic sentences support your position and your evidence supports your topic sentences.

4. Fine-tune your voice to sound confident and convincing.

5. Check your words and sentences.

6. Use the editing and proofreading marks inside the back cover of this book.

PERSUASIVE

 **TEKS** 6.14C
ELPS 2H, 3E, 4I, 4J

Revising for Focus and Coherence

When you revise for *focus and coherence*, you make sure you have written about one position throughout your writing. You want to clearly state your position at the beginning. You continue to clarify your position throughout your essay by providing sound reasoning with detailed evidence to support it. This will help convince others to agree with you.

Is my beginning clear and focused?

Your opening paragraph should grab the reader's attention about your cause and then clearly state your position. Don't include unnecessary information. Stay focused on your position statement.

 Read the beginning paragraph below. With a partner, identify the writer's position. Then decide which sentences or larger units of text should be deleted because they don't support the position and confuse the reader. Discuss your thoughts with your partner.

> Coach Alcaraz always says, "Healthy food is like fuel for your brain and junk food makes you run on empty." He also says that gym shoes without proper support will ruin your feet. So why bring candy, cupcakes, and soda for classroom treats? This question has lots of parents and kids talking. But the answer is simple. Only healthy treats should be allowed for classroom parties and special school events. It is also important for parents and kids to talk to each other about school issues. Parents need to be involved in all parts of their kids' school life, not just homework.

 Check your persuasive essay. Review your essay. Look for sentences or larger units of text that do not directly support your position. Delete these sentences or text units from your writing. Revise your paper so that it is clear and flows smoothly from one idea to the next.

Do I stay focused on my position throughout my essay?

You stay focused by including only sound reasoning and detailed and relevant evidence to support your position.

Read the position statement. Then review each of the detail sentences. Which sentences would support the position and keep the essay focused and coherent?

Position Statement: Only healthy treats should be allowed in school.

1. Healthy treats are my favorite.
2. Research shows that healthy treats improve memory.
3. Junk food has been shown to cause health problems like obesity.
4. The cost of school lunches should remain the same for next year.
5. Eating healthy treats in school promotes a healthy lifestyle.

Check your details. Make sure your details, reasons, and evidence support your position and help you convince others to support your cause. Delete sentences that don't apply or break the flow of ideas.

Focus and Coherence
A large unit of text is deleted because it did not support the focus statement.

Learning to choose nutritious snacks in school will also help kids make better choices when they are not in school. This will improve their lifestyle and overall health. It will also train them to make good decisions about food when they are adults. ~~There are other things we can train kids to do in school that will help them when they are adults. For example, learning how to budget, cook, and fix things around the house are life skills that will benefit them when they are older.~~ *Healthy eating is a great start to a healthy life.*

PERSUASIVE

Revising **for** Organization

When you check your essay's *organization,* look for a smooth flow of ideas both within each paragraph and from one paragraph to the next. Use transitional words and phrases to help the organization of your writing.

How can I check the transitions in my sentences?

To check your sentences for transition words and phrases, read them carefully, making certain that each sentence moves logically into the next.

 Read the first paragraph. The sentences in the first paragraph have no transitions. It sounds choppy. Read the second paragraph. The transitions in the second paragraph help the reader understand how the details relate to each other. The sentences flow.

Without Transitional Words and Phrases

Kids who grow up in the city should go to a wilderness summer camp at least once. Kids will learn survival skills. They will learn how to purify water, to keep warm, and to stay calm during an emergency. Camping in the wilderness gives kids many new experiences and teaches them that not all wildlife is dangerous. Kids will come to enjoy and respect the world of nature.

With Transitional Words and Phrases

Kids who grow up in the city should go to a wilderness summer camp at least once. <u>First of all</u>, kids will learn survival skills. <u>For example</u>, they will learn how to purify water, to keep warm, and to stay calm during an emergency. Camping in the wilderness <u>also</u> gives kids many new experiences and teaches them that not all wildlife is dangerous. <u>As a result</u>, kids will come to enjoy and respect the world of nature.

 Connect your sentences. Review the sentences in your essay. Do you need to add a few transitions to show how your details relate to each other? Add any needed transitional words or phrases. See pages 620–621 for a list of transitions.

How can transitions link my paragraphs?

Transitional words and phrases can help show how the ideas in one paragraph are related to the ideas in others. Read the topic sentences below from a persuasive essay about improving a neighborhood playground. As you'll see, the transitional words and phrases (in blue) show how the paragraphs' ideas are related.

To begin with, **the playground at 6th Street and Rio Grande is a health hazard.**

In addition, **the playground is an eyesore.**

Finally, **fixing up the playground will send a positive message to neighborhood kids.**

Read the following topic sentences from a persuasive essay about tutoring. Rewrite them, adding transitional words and phrases that help show how the ideas are related. Choose from the following transitions: *First of all, Also, In addition, As a result,* and *Lastly.*

1. A tutoring program could help struggling students.
2. Tutoring would give teachers a break.
3. The program would let advanced students share what they know.

Connect your paragraphs. Review the paragraphs in your essay. Do you need to add a few transitions to show how your paragraphs flow from one idea to the next? Add any needed transitional words or phrases to improve your organization. See pages 620–621 for a list of transitions.

Organization
A transition is added between paragraphs.

Besides,
   ∧*School is the best place for many kids to*

make art. Some kinds of art require lots of special

supplies like clay, glazes, canvases, paints, and . . .

 **TEKS** 6.14E, 6.18A
ELPS 2I, 3E, 4I

Revising for Development of Ideas

When you revise for *development of ideas,* you want to make sure your position is clear and supported by sound reasoning and detailed, relevant evidence. It is also important to present possible alternative actions to support your position.

How can I recognize "fuzzy thinking" in my writing?

You have used fuzzy thinking when an idea is not sound and cannot be supported with detailed, relevant evidence. This makes it difficult to establish your position. Here are three types of fuzzy thinking.

Jumping to Conclusions
Avoid using reasoning that is not sound to reach a big conclusion.

Last year, a kid got sick after lunch, so cafeteria food isn't healthy.

Bandwagoning
Avoid using a group's opinion as if it were relevant evidence.

None of my classmates think that metal detectors make schools safer.

Take It, or Leave It
Avoid statements that don't leave room for discussion.

Either the pep band will sell 1,000 pizzas, or it will never play again.

 Read the following examples. Then identify the type of fuzzy thinking each one contains. How could it be improved?

1. Either the principal will remove the metal detectors, or this school will be a prison.

2. Our pep band didn't raise much money this year, so nobody appreciates us.

3. Everybody knows that restaurant food is healthier than cafeteria food.

 Revise fuzzy thinking. Review your essay and look for places where you have used fuzzy thinking. Revise your writing by replacing the errors with sound reasoning and detailed, relevant evidence. Ask a classmate to read and check that there is no fuzzy thinking in your essay. Listen to his or her feedback and revise as needed.

How can qualifiers make my ideas easier to support?

Ideas that suggest "all" or "nothing" are difficult to support and do not allow for consideration of alternatives. That's why *qualifiers*—terms such as *most* and *usually*—are important in persuasive writing. Read the two ideas below. Notice the qualifier in the second sentence.

Students in study hall can't work because of lunchroom noise.
Many students in study hall can't work because of lunchroom noise.

The qualifier *many* limits the idea, making it easier to support. It also opens the possibility to consider alternatives that an "all" or "nothing" position does not allow. Other helpful qualifiers include *most, often, usually, some,* and *in many cases.*

 Rewrite the following four statements. Add a different qualifier to each one.

1. Students think teachers assign too much homework.
2. Classrooms are crowded.
3. Students don't work hard.
4. Parents are too busy to help with homework.

 Revise "all-or-nothing" ideas. Look for ideas that are difficult to support. Add qualifiers to limit these ideas. Check that you have an alternative solution to your cause.

Development of Ideas
A qualifier is added which makes it possible to consider alternative actions.

Many
Students in study hall can't work because the
So I think
lunchroom noise. The study hall classroom should be moved
to a different part of the building.
Those students should be able to study in quieter room.

Texas Traits

Revising for Voice

When you revise for *voice,* check to see how your essay sounds. You should try to sound authentic and original with your own writing style. You want your individual personality to show through.

How can I make my voice sound authentic?

You can make your essay sound authentic by writing sentences that flow smoothly and engage your reader. As you revise, try combining sentences or larger units of text so that your writing will sound natural and more like you. Read the two examples below. Notice that by combining sentences the second example sounds much more authentic and natural than the first.

> **Unauthentic Writing Voice**
>
> Students should learn to swim. They should learn to swim before they graduate high school. Swimming is a life skill. Swimming is great exercise.
>
> **Authentic Writing Voice**
>
> Students should learn to swim before they graduate high school. Swimming is a life skill, and it is also great exercise!

 Read the following paragraph. Combine sentences or larger units of text to enhance your style and make the voice sound more authentic and natural. Share your work with a partner. Did you combine text in the same way? Explain your thinking.

> Lifeguarding is a great summer job for teens that swim well. Teaching swimming lessons is a great summer job for teens that swim well. Swimming is a fun activity. It can also be a chance for future employment.

 Check your voice. Review your essay to see if your style sounds authentic and original. Look for places where you can combine sentences and text units to make your writing flow and sound more natural.

How can I make my writing sound unique?

You can make your writing sound unique by letting your personality show through. Always use strong, positive words that let your reader know your viewpoint and connect with you personally.

You know your writing sounds unique if it:
- uses language that makes your reader feel your emotions.
- helps your reader connect to your topic and to you.
- makes the reader understand your personal viewpoint.
- genuinely reflects what you believe about your position.

 Use the tips above to rewrite the following sentences. Make each sentence unique to your own voice.

1. Oh no. Our school won't have a marching band next year.

2. I don't like the rule against wearing hats.

3. People should exercise to be healthy.

 Revise for voice. Review your essay for language that engages your reader and clearly expresses your unique, personal viewpoint.

Voice	
Language that expresses a unique viewpoint is added.	*connects everything else that is learned.* *Art ~~is important.~~ It's hard to imagine a school* *but,* *dropping reading or math. The school board plans to* *or,* *drop art. Students need to stand against this. It might* *actually happen.* No one wants to live in a world without art. Do they?

Revising Using a Checklist

Check your revising. On a piece of paper, write the numbers 1 to 10. If you can answer "yes" to a question, put a check mark after that number. If not, continue to work with that part of your essay.

Focus and Coherence

_____ **1.** Do I state a clear, focused topic at the beginning?

_____ **2.** Do I grab the reader's attention?

_____ **3.** Do I stay focused on my position throughout my essay?

Organization

_____ **4.** Do I have a clear beginning, middle, and ending?

_____ **5.** Do I use transitions within and between paragraphs?

Development of Ideas

_____ **6.** Do I avoid fuzzy thinking in my writing?

_____ **7.** Do I include sound reasoning and detailed, relevant evidence to support my position?

_____ **8.** Do I use qualifiers to make my ideas easier to support and allow for consideration of alternatives?

Voice

_____ **9.** Did I combine sentences to make my writing sound natural?

_____ **10.** Does my voice sound unique?

Make a clean copy. Ask a classmate to read and respond to your essay. Make any needed revisions. Create a clean copy for editing.

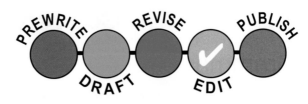

Editing

After you've finished revising your essay, it's time to edit it for your use of conventions: grammar, mechanics, sentence structure, and spelling.

Keys to Effective Editing

1. Use a dictionary, a thesaurus, and the "Proofreader's Guide" in the back of this book.

2. Check for any words or phrases that may be confusing to the reader.

3. Check your writing for correctness of grammar, mechanics (punctuation and capitalization), sentence structure, and spelling.

4. If possible, edit on a printed computer copy. Then enter your changes on the computer.

5. Use the editing and proofreading marks inside the back cover of this book.

PERSUASIVE

Editing for Conventions

Grammar

When you edit for *grammar,* you make sure you use nouns, verbs, and other parts of speech correctly.

How do I check predicate adjectives and their comparative and superlative forms?

A predicate adjective is a describing word that is linked by a verb to the noun it modifies.

- Predicate adjectives follow linking verbs.

    The envelopes are small.

The comparative form of a predicate adjective compares two people, places, things, or ideas that are the subject of the sentence. (Also see page 533.)

- One way to make the comparative form is to add the suffix *er.*

    Rosario is smarter.

- If the word has two or more syllables, add the word *more* to make it comparative.

    The flowers are more beautiful.

The superlative form of a predicate adjective compares three or more people, places, things, or ideas that are the subject of the sentence. (See page 533).

- One way to make the superlative form is to add the suffix *est.*

    My sister was the loudest.

- If the word has two or more syllables, add the word *most* to make it superlative.

    Our cheer team was the most enthusiastic.

 For each of the subject/adjective pairs below, write two sentences: one using its comparative form and one its superlative form.

    subject/difficult   **animal/wild**   **child/happy**

 Check for predicate adjectives. Edit your essay for proper form for predicate adjectives, including comparative and superlative forms.

Do I use too many general adjectives?

Your adjectives should be specific and meaningful to the reader. Remember that adjectives describe nouns so you want to avoid using common words like *nice*, *good*, and *bad* that weaken your writing.

General Adjective	Specific Adjective
big	enormous
sad	depressed
short	petite

Study the pairs of sentences below. Which sentence in each pair sends a clear, specific message? Explain your choice.

1. a. The information in the morning message is good.
   b. The information in the morning message is valuable.

2. a. That new girl is friendly.
   b. That new girl is nice.

3. a. The sound of the pencil sharpener was awful.
   b. The sound of the pencil sharpener was bad.

4. a. Tanya's little brother is interesting.
   b. Tanya's little brother is clever.

Check your adjectives. Replace any general predicate adjectives with adjectives that send clear, specific messages.

Learning Language

Words that mean almost the same thing are called synonyms. To replace a common adjective, you will need to find a synonym for it. Below is a list of common words and their synonyms. With a partner, practice using these synonyms in a conversation.

Common Word	Synonyms		
bad	awful	terrible	naughty
cold	frigid	icy	chilly
old	ancient	aged	elderly
hard	firm	tough	stiff

PERSUASIVE

 TEKS 6.19C

Sentence Structure

When you revise for *sentence structure,* you make sure you include a variety of sentence types and have subject-verb agreement.

Have I used a variety of sentence types?

You can check your writing by seeing how many simple and compound sentences you use. (See pages **555–557.**)

- A **simple sentence** is a subject and predicate forming one complete thought.

    The school board is planning to cut art class.

- A **compound sentence** is two simple sentences joined by a comma and a coordinating conjunction such as *and, but, or, so, for,* or *yet.*

    I don't want to live in a world without art, but I might have to.

 Read the following sentences. For each one, identify whether it is simple or compound.

1. It's hard to concentrate, and the smell of food is distracting.
2. Bellwood needs a different study hall.

 Check your sentence variety. Read each paragraph of your essay. If too many simple sentences appear together, rewrite some of them as compound sentences.

Do my subjects and verbs agree in my sentences?

Check both parts of your compound sentences for agreement. Subjects and verbs in sentences must agree. Singular subjects take a singular verb. Plural subjects take a plural verb. (See page **555.**)

 Rewrite each sentence below correcting the errors in subject-verb agreement.

1. The cafeteria are too loud, and the sound fill the study hall.
2. People in the cafeteria is rude.
3. Artwork make the school look more beautiful.

 Check your subject-verb agreement. Check your simple and compound sentences to make sure the subjects and verbs agree.

TEKS 6.20A(iii)

Mechanics: Capitalization

When you edit for *mechanics*, you check for correct use of capitalization and punctuation. To edit your capitalization, make sure you have correctly capitalized the first word in each sentence and all proper nouns.

How do I know when to capitalize organizations?

You need to capitalize the name of an organization, an association, or a team and its members. (See page **670**.)

Examples of Organizations

Republican Party	Democrats
Texas Longhorns	Houston Visitors Bureau
Better Business Bureau	Boy Scouts of America

Do not capitalize words that describe general groups of people or things.

baseball players politicians banks

 Number your paper from 1 to 4. In each sentence, if the name of an organization needs a capital letter, write the correction on your paper.

1. The members of congress make the laws.
2. My brother is a fan of the dallas cowboys.
3. The american red cross helps people after natural disasters.
4. My father works at the odessa chamber of commerce.

 Edit for conventions. Check your essay to make sure you have capitalized the names of organizations.

Conventions
Proper names
are capitalized.

Members of the longhorn american indian council spoke to students about the tribes they are studying. These talks and presentations are an important way for...

Editing **Using a Checklist**

Check your editing. On a piece of paper, write the numbers 1 to 10. If you can answer "yes" to a question, put a check mark after that number. If not, continue to edit for that convention.

Conventions

GRAMMAR

_____ **1.** Do I correctly use predicate adjectives?

_____ **2.** Do I use comparative and superlative forms correctly?

_____ **3.** Do I use strong adjectives in my writing?

MECHANICS (Punctuation and Capitalization)

_____ **4.** Did I correctly capitalize the names of organizations?

_____ **5.** Did I capitalize the first word in every sentence?

_____ **6.** Do I use end punctuation after all my sentences?

SENTENCE STRUCTURE

_____ **7.** Do I use a variety of simple and compound sentences?

_____ **8.** Do the subjects and verbs agree in my sentences?

SPELLING

_____ **9.** Have I spelled all my words correctly?

_____ **10.** Have I doubled-checked the words my spell-check may have missed?

Creating a Title

- Restate the call to action: **Shelter the Animals**
- Write a slogan: **Let's Band Together**
- Be creative: **Where Art Thou, Art?**

Go Online!

Publishing

PREWRITE · DRAFT · REVISE · EDIT · PUBLISH ✓

Sharing Your Essay

After you have worked so hard to write and improve your essay, make a neat final copy to share. You may also present your persuasive essay as an editorial, a speech, or a multimedia presentation.

Make a final copy. Follow your teacher's instructions or use the guidelines below to format your essay. (If you are using a computer, see page 60.) Create a clean final copy of your essay and carefully proofread it.

Focus on Presentation

- Use blue or black ink and write neatly.
- Write your name in the upper left corner of page 1.
- Skip a line and center your title; skip another line and start your writing.
- Indent every paragraph and leave a one-inch margin on all four sides.
- Write your last name and the page number in the upper right corner of every page after the first one.

Give a Speech

Present your persuasive essay to your classmates in the form of a speech.

Go Online!

Upload your persuasive essay to share with others.

Create a Multimedia Presentation

Turn your persuasive essay into a multimedia presentation. See pages 443–451 for more information.

PERSUASIVE

Evaluating a Persuasive Essay

To learn how to evaluate a persuasive essay, you'll use the scoring rubric on pages **48–49** and the essays that follow. These essays are examples of writing for each score on the rubric.

Notice that this first persuasive essay received a score of 4. Read the description for a score of 4 on pages **48–49**. Then read the essay. Use the same steps to study the other examples. Always remember to think about the overall quality of the writing.

Writing that fits a score of 4 is very strong.

Keep Libraries Open!

Yesterday evening I walked to my neighborhood branch of the public library to return some books and take out new ones. I got to the front door and started to push it open, but it wouldn't open. Then I noticed the sign on the door: "We apologize that the Douglass branch will no longer be open after 6 p.m." I was so disappointed! The library is one of my favorite places on Earth. Cutting back library hours is not fair to the people of this city. I think the government should keep the hours the same as they used to be.

First, reducing the hours hurts students. Students depend on the library when we have to look up things for school papers. My older sister is in high school and she's always in the library doing research. In addition to school work, students need books to read independently so that they can enrich their minds.

Starts with a strong position statement

The writer gives detailed reasons and evidence.

Confident, authentic voice

In addition, reducing library hours is unfair to people who don't have money to spend on new books or Internet service. Libraries are one of the best things that help improve the people's lives. Where else can you find so much valuable information and enjoyment without having to pay? Some people can buy books and computers and Internet service, but others cannot afford those things. By using the Internet at the library, a person can find jobs and services and learn skills. My uncle studied for the firefighters exam totally at the library. Now he's a firefighter. The library is a way for people to improve their lives. Isn't that worth it?

Finally, libraries are important for culture, just like museums, sports teams, parks, and theaters. Our city is growing, and we're trying to get people to move here who are well-educated and have a lot to contribute.

Consideration of alternatives

I know that some people say we need to save money by cutting library hours. It's true that the city needs money, but I don't think they'll save so much money on this way that it's worth hurting people.

Libraries are for everyone, but if the library closes at 6, many working people will not be able to go to it, and they may lose the opportunity to better themselves.

Focuses on the purpose

The city government should think about this before it decides to cut hours any more. I am going to send an e-mail to the mayor, and people who agree with me should, too.

PERSUASIVE

Writing that fits a score of 3 is strong in most ways.

Wanted: A Park at 37th Street

Have you ever seen the vacant lot at the corner of 37th Street and Marshall Drive? I have. It's a mess. There are weeds and rocks all over the lot, and there's even broken glass. Considering that some kids who don't know any better actually play in the lot, it's a danger to the community. A friend of mine once fell there and cut himself on a broken bottle and had to get twelve stitches! So what can be done about a situation like that? The answer is completely obvious. We have got to get rid of the vacant lot. How do you get rid of a vacant lot, do you just throw it away? No, you can't. What you can do is turn the vacant lot into a park, so that is what I recommend.

Some people say, Who cares about a vacant lot, we have more important things to do? My answer is that all the people who live near 37th and Marshall care about it, and we need to do something so that more kids and other people don't have to go to the emergency room.

First, a park would be good at that corner because it would bring families and other people to the corner who would enjoy it and keep it clean. If that corner was a park, the police would probably come around more often and keep it safe, and getting rid of the glass and rocks would also be a safety factor, which I mentioned already.

Strong beginning shows the writer's sincere interest.

Consideration of alternatives

Sound reasoning and evidence

There could even be a garden that the community people could work on.

Another reason for turning the vacant lot into a park is that putting a park on that street would make the whole street look nicer. As you may know, Marshall Drive at around 37th Street is not the most beautiful place in the city. Many people avoid that area. People talk about turning the area around. Well, if you want to turn the area around, put a park there! If there's one nice place on the street, maybe other nice places will appear too, like a store opening.

Finally, kids need a place to play. A vacant lot is not a good place to play, because of the environment and because of the people who hang around there. Kids want to play ball and run around without having to worry. A park provides the perfect place to do that.

In conclusion, the city needs to think about the needs of its people. People have been talking about getting rid of that vacant lot for years, but it never happens. But that doesn't mean it never will happen. All it takes is for people to make enough noise. We want our park and we want it now!

Too much repetition

Good use of varied sentence lengths, beginnings, and types

PERSUASIVE

Writing that fits a score of 2 is strong in some ways.

Voice is confident and sincere.

Flow of ideas is not smooth.

Many repeated words.

No consideration of alternatives

Red Light!

Everybody knows that red light means stop. And that's what people don't do on my street, Spaulding Street, they don't stop. Drivers just zoom past like no one lives there. Meanwile there are kids with tricycles, old people, parents pushing their kids in strollers, and just plain people crossing the street. People around here complain about it. What they've got to do is the city should put a traffic light on the corner.

For one reason, without the light there are more accidents than if there would be a light I'm sure of that. Last month a little kid on my block was almost run over when he started to cross the street and the driver wasn't looking and the driver didn't stop. If there was a light there, the kid would of stopped if the light was red and went if the light was green and so would the driver. But a lady from the nayborhood had to get a hold of the kid by pure luck to stop him.

For another reason, it's important to teach traffic safety. This traffic light would be an example of traffic safety for all to see. And for the last reason if traffic is messed up on one street it's going to be messed up on the next street too, but if it's going smoothly on one street it'll be going smoothly on the next street too, because each one effects the other.

So for many reasons we need a light on Spaulding Street. Let's not wait until somebody realy gets hurt.

Writing that fits a score of 1 is weak.

Errors in conventions

Reasoning is not sound.

Focus is not on the genre and purpose.

Flow of ideas is not smooth.

Kids shoud Stop Eating Junk Food

Kids shoud stop eating junk food. Junk food means fast food such as burgers with fries and a 32 oz drink. Nobody needs that much. This kind of food is not good for you it has to many calories and too much fat and not enogh vitamins. It makes peple fat. Which is a problem because the whole country is eating junk and getting fat so medical care is skyroketing.

Some people say I shoud mind my own bizniss instead of telling them to stop eating junk food. Well, they have a point there. Who wants somebody telling them how to live? I agree, but it's more important to get people to eat healthy, so that's what I'm going to do.

If you want to stop eating junk food, first you have to know when your eating it and second you have to find something else to eat. Lets say your ordering a cheeseburger. What could you get instead of a cheeseburger? Maybe a salad. Instead of a big soda you could get water. Or you could not go to the fast food place at all. Try making something for yourself at home, maybe a penut butter sandwich with a glass of milk. That fills you up as much as anthing. Then you could eat a banana with it.

People shoud not eat junk food. Better if you never eat it, but if not, just eat less of it.

PERSUASIVE

Evaluating and Reflecting on Your Writing

You've worked hard to complete your persuasive essay. Now take some time to score and think about your writing. One your own paper, finish each sentence starter below. To score your writing, refer to the scoring rubric on pages **48–49** and the examples you just read.

My Persuasive Essay

1. *The best score for my persuasive essay is . . .*

2. *It's the best score because . . .*

3. *The best part of my essay is . . .*

4. *The part that still needs work is . . .*

5. *The main thing I learned about writing a persuasive essay is . . .*

Persuasive Writing

Pet-Peeve Essay

"I'm peeved" is an old-fashioned expression meaning "I'm irritated." A pet peeve may be something that bothers you a little bit more than it bothers others.

Writing about a pet peeve is another form of persuasive writing. In this form, a writer complains about something annoying but doesn't really expect to change it.

We all have pet peeves: people who chew gum with their mouths open, kids who always cut in line, parents who think they can rap. A pet-peeve essay gives you a chance to vent some frustration as you complain in a humorous way about something that irritates you.

Writing Guidelines

Subject:	Something that annoys you
Purpose:	To complain
Form:	A pet-peeve essay
Audience:	Classmates

Pet-Peeve Essay

The following pet-peeve essay was written by a student annoyed by the food served in the school cafeteria.

Beginning

The beginning introduces the pet peeve and establishes the writer's position.

Middle

The middle includes sound reasoning.

No More Mystery Meat

The cafeteria served "mystery meat" for lunch again today. At least, I think it was meat. It was chunky, brown, and coated with a yellow sauce. I've seen that stuff before. Sometimes the meat is served with noodles. Sometimes it's baked, and sometimes it's fried, but what it really is remains a mystery.

Now, I don't like to complain. Still, it seems to me that after we spend a long morning of working math problems and studying science, the school could at least give us something good to eat. Imagine getting a slice of steaming hot pizza, covered with lots of cheese! Picture some fried chicken or even a hot dog with all the fixings. We get these types of lunches at times, but not enough.

No, instead, we usually get something that doesn't even look like food. What is that tough brown stuff? All I know is that it certainly doesn't look like lunch to me! But it keeps showing up on our trays,

TEKS 6.18A
ELPS 3D, 3E, 4I, 4K

persuade convince support
argue reason

273

Pet-Peeve Essay

Middle
Detailed
and
relevant
evidence

and we can either choke it down or go hungry. That's not much of a choice.

I have been keeping track, and we have mystery meat at least once a week. I interviewed the cafeteria supervisor to find out the nutritional values in the meat. It just meets the standards that are required for schools to meet in the lunches. I think that the school should be more concerned about the students' nutrition and look for an alternative that is healthier and more appetizing. No matter how they might try to disguise this mystery meat, we will always recognize it.

Ending

The last
paragraph
offers a
humorous
solution.

I have a better use for mystery meat. Next time it's served, I'll take it home to my dog, Jiggs. He likes chewing on old shoe leather like this.

Respond to the reading. On paper, answer the following questions about the sample essay. Discuss your answers with a partner.

☐ **Focus and Coherence** (1) What is the writer's position on "mystery meat"?

☐ **Development of Ideas** (2) What reasons and evidence did the writer provide to support the position? What alternatives could you offer to the school?

☐ **Voice** (3) What words and phrases show the writer's irritation?

⭐ **TEKS** 6.14A, 6.18A

Prewriting Selecting a Topic

To determine an appropriate topic for a pet-peeve essay, think of everyday annoyances—things that "bug" you. Does riding the bus drive you crazy? Are the school lunches boring?

Use a strategy to find your topic. The writer of the sample pet-peeve essay used freewriting.

Freewriting

> *What bugs me? Let's see, I hate the way my sister follows me around. She always wants to meet my friends and talk to them. But I guess my friends kind of like her, and anyway, she's not that bad. The school bus! That's something I don't like. Well, except it's fun when José and Rick and I get the back seat and bounce over the railroad tracks. School isn't so bad, either. How about lunch—ack! What is that stuff? How come the cafeteria thinks we can eat fried shoe leather? . . .*

Prewrite **Choose your topic.** Freewrite about your life. Go through your day and think about things that irritate you. Keep going until you settle on a topic that you can establish a firm position on. If you have trouble getting started, answer the question "What things bug me the most?"

Adding Humorous Details

Humor makes a pet-peeve essay fun to read. These techniques can help.

- **Make comparisons.** Comparing your pet peeve with something else can emphasize your feelings. In the sample essay, the writer compares mystery meat to an old piece of shoe leather.

- **Use exaggeration.** A writer can add humor to an essay by exaggerating. In the sample essay, the writer suggests that the mystery meat comes by the truckload.

Prewrite **Create humorous details.** Write at least one comparison and one exaggeration that you could use in your essay.

Drafting **Organizing a Pet Peeve**

When you write a persuasive essay, order of importance is an effective organizational strategy. With order of importance, you tell the most important reason first or last.

However, you can also arrange the reasons in a way that simply makes the best sense, called *logical order*. With this order, one reason is no more important than the one before or after it. This is the type of organization that is used in the pet peeve on pages **272–273**.

Using logical order is like fitting the pieces in a jigsaw puzzle. The graphic below shows how the three main reasons in the pet peeve fit together.

Logical Order

After a long morning, we need something good to eat.

But usually we get some tough mystery meat.

The school should look for a healthier alternative.

Creating Your First Draft

Though an essay about a pet peeve is a lighter kind of persuasive essay, it still has a definite form. As you write your essay, follow these guidelines.

- **Introduce your pet peeve.** Maybe you could begin with a funny story about an annoying experience you had. Be sure to establish your position so your reader will know how you feel.

- **Discuss the pet peeve.** Help the reader understand why the topic annoys you. Add humor with comparisons and exaggeration, but also use sound reasoning and give detailed, relevant evidence to support your position. Use an appropriate organizational strategy.

- **Close your essay by offering a solution.** Your solution might be reasonable, or it might be funny. Also include consideration of alternatives.

Write your first draft. Establish your position, and support it with sound reasoning and evidence. Remember to consider alternatives.

TEKS 6.14E

Revising Improving Your Writing

As you revise, ask yourself the following questions to make your writing better.

- ☐ **Focus and Coherence** Have I stated my complaint clearly? Have I included any comparisons or used any exaggerations? Do I need to cut any details that are off the subject?

- ☐ **Organization** Are the points in the paragraphs in the best order? Should I add, delete, combine, or rearrange any sentences or larger chunks of text?

- ☐ **Development of Ideas** Have I supported my thoughts with strong details? Could I add any details to make my complaint more believable?

- ☐ **Voice** Does my personality show through in my writing? What would make my writing voice stronger?

Revise your writing. Improve your first draft, using the questions above as a guide. Make changes and then create a clean copy for editing.

Editing Checking for Conventions

As you edit your essay, focus on the following questions.

- ☐ **Conventions** Have I carefully checked my work for errors in grammar, mechanics, sentence structure, and spelling? Have I also checked for errors in usage?

Edit your work. Use the questions above to decide how to edit your essay. After making your changes, create a final copy and check it one more time for errors.

Persuasive Writing
Across the Curriculum

You can use the valuable skill of writing persuasively throughout the school day. For example, your social studies teacher may assign an editorial cartoon about a social problem. Your math teacher may require convincing proof for some mathematical fact. In science, you may need to argue for or against some scientific theory. In or out of school, you may need to write persuasive letters to convince others to take a certain action.

You may also need to be persuasive on writing tests. The model and tips at the end of this chapter will help you.

What's Ahead

- **Social Studies:** Creating an Editorial Cartoon
- **Math:** Presenting a Proof
- **Science:** Supporting a Theory
- **Practical Writing:** Drafting a Persuasive Letter

Social Studies:
Creating an Editorial Cartoon

A picture is worth a thousand words, especially when the picture is an editorial cartoon. An editorial cartoon is a drawing that pokes fun at a political or social problem.

The following editorial cartoon was created for a social studies class. While the paragraph explains the social problem, the cartoon does most of the persuading. What position is the cartoon taking? What sound reasoning is used in the paragraph? What evidence is presented in the cartoon? What alternatives could be considered?

The paragraph explains the problem.

The drawing illustrates the problem.

Social Problem: Some people think that oil companies should be allowed to drill for oil in some national parks and wildlife refuges. This is a bad idea. If it really is a wildlife refuge, animals ought to be able to live there safely and naturally. The cartoon expresses this opinion.

Writing Tips

Before you write . . .

- **Choose a problem you care about.**
  Think of things that worry you about your city, the country, or the world.
- **Do your research.**
  Read articles and gather information.
- **Think of symbols.**
  Consider symbols to use in your cartoon. In the example, the oil well symbolizes the oil industry.
- **Use pictures as models.**
  Find a picture of an oil well, for example, if you need to draw an oil well.

During your writing . . .

- **Establish your position.**
  Explain clearly how you feel about the problem.
- **Explain the problem.**
  Tell why the problem concerns you. Use sound reasoning and strong evidence. Include consideration of alternatives.
- **Draw your cartoon.**
  Concentrate on one or two images.
- **Write a caption below the cartoon, if necessary.**
  If your cartoon needs explaining, create a sentence or paragraph that will get your point across.

After you've written a first draft . . .

- **Review your opening explanation.**
  Make sure that all of your ideas are clear.
- **Study your cartoon.**
  Redraw any parts that could be better.

PERSUASIVE

Create an editorial cartoon about a social problem. Include your position, sound reasons, evidence, and alternatives.

Math: Presenting a Proof

The best way to show that a given math concept is correct is to prove it. This type of writing is called a "proof."

The **beginning** names the concept.

The **middle** shows two proofs.

The **ending** restates the concept.

Long Division Is Short Subtraction

Concept: Division is a quick form of subtraction.

Proof 1: One way to solve 42 ÷ 7 would be to subtract 7 from 42 until the answer is 0.

$$42 - 7 = 35$$
$$35 - 7 = 28$$
$$28 - 7 = 21$$
$$21 - 7 = 14$$
$$14 - 7 = 7$$
$$7 - 7 = 0$$

How many 7's would need to be subtracted to reach 0? The answer is 6. Of course, 42 ÷ 7 = 6.

Proof 2: Here is a harder problem: 209 ÷ 46 = ?

$$209 - 46 = 163$$
$$163 - 46 = 117$$
$$117 - 46 = 71$$
$$71 - 46 = 25$$
$$25 - 46 = ?$$

The last subtraction would end with a negative number. That means 25 is the remainder. Then we count how many 46's were subtracted. The answer is 4, with a remainder of 25. Dividing it out brings the same answer (209 ÷ 46 = 4, remainder 25).

Conclusion: A division problem can be solved by using either division or subtraction.

TEKS 6.14D

Writing Tips

Before you write . . .

- **Choose a math concept.**
  Think of math concepts you understand well. Make a list and choose one.
- **Study the concept.**
  Review the idea until you thoroughly understand it.
- **Experiment with ways to prove it.**
  Recall how your teacher first taught the idea to the class. Think of how you could prove the concept. Check books and Internet articles for other ways.
- **Plan your proof.**
  List the steps for proving the concept.

During your writing . . .

- **Introduce the math concept.**
  State what you will prove.
- **Give the proof or proofs.**
  Present the information in a step-by-step process.
- **Summarize your proof.**
  Restate your concept.

After you've written a first draft . . .

- **Check for completeness.**
  Include all of the information the reader will need.
- **Check for correctness.**
  Make sure there are no errors in your math, spelling, punctuation, and grammar.

 Choose a math concept to prove. (Here is an example: An even number plus or minus another even number will always equal an even number.) Then follow the tips above to present your proof.

Science: Supporting a Theory

A scientific theory is an idea or group of ideas that explains an event. When you support a theory, you back your position with sound reasoning and evidence, and you should include consideration for alternatives. The following essay supports one theory about how dinosaurs became extinct.

What Happened to the Dinosaurs?

The **beginning** introduces the topic and the theory.

There are many mysteries about dinosaurs. One of the most interesting is this question: "Why did they become extinct?" Scientists have been arguing about this since the first fossils were discovered. The most popular theory says that the earth was struck by a gigantic meteor or asteroid when dinosaurs lived all over the world.

The **middle** paragraphs describe the theory.

According to the theory, the huge meteor caused a shock wave of heat and strong winds that killed many dinosaurs. A big cloud of dust darkened the skies for years. That made the world grow colder because the sun couldn't shine through all the dust. There wasn't enough light for plants to grow. Without plant life, the dinosaurs couldn't survive.

Research backs up this theory. Scientists have found a crater in the Gulf of Mexico that was caused by a huge force at about the time the dinosaurs disappeared. They also have found in many places a layer of dirt that is made up of materials found in meteors. This layer was probably formed when the huge dust cloud settled to the ground.

The **ending** summarizes the writer's support for the theory.

Right now, no one knows for sure why the dinosaurs died, but every day scientists dig up new clues. Someday they may be able to prove the meteor theory. For now, it seems like a good explanation.

Writing Tips

Before you write . . .

- **Choose a topic.**
  List scientific theories you are studying. Choose one to support.
- **Research your topic.**
  Read about the theory and make sure you understand it. Find strong, sound reasons to support the theory.
- **Take notes.**
  Jot down facts, reasons, and examples.

Table Diagram

Opinion		
Reason	Reason	Reason

During your writing . . .

- **Introduce the topic, theory, and your position.**
  Give the reader necessary background information. Establish your position.
- **Develop the middle paragraphs.**
  Explain how the theory works and support the explanation. Present sound reasons and evidence.
- **End your essay.**
  Summarize your support for the theory with final details. Provide any alternatives.

After you've written a first draft . . .

- **Check for completeness.**
  Make sure you have clearly explained the theory with reasons, facts, and examples.
- **Check for conventions.**
  Make sure there are no errors in spelling, punctuation, and grammar.

PERSUASIVE

 Select a scientific theory that you agree with—for example, the theory of global warming. Your teacher may suggest other topics. Do some research and then write a persuasive essay supporting the theory.

Practical Writing:
Drafting a Persuasive Letter

A polite, persuasive informal letter can influence people and get things done. This sample letter talks about a dangerous intersection and what should be done about it.

The letter follows the correct format. (See pages 286–287.)

The writer includes important information.

The letter conveys the problem and ideas to fix it.

The letter uses appropriate conventions.

1414 Johnson Street
Walvan, WI 53000
April 20, 2011

Phillip Smith
111 Main Street
Walvan, WI 53000

Dear Phil,

Hello. How have you been? I think we have a problem in our neighborhood and I might need your help. We need a stoplight at the intersection of 34th Avenue and Cottage Street (two blocks away from our school) so we can get to school safely.

Cars drive so fast on 34th Avenue. It's dangerous for us trying to cross the street going to and from school. I think that the city should put up a stoplight before someone gets hurt.

Would you be willing to help me get signatures for a petition asking for a stoplight? We could get some other kids and parents involved. I think it's the best solution. Let me know if you can help.

Thank you,

Ruby Keast

Writing Tips

Before you write . . .

- **Choose a topic you care about.**
  Think of problems that you would like to solve.
- **Form your opinion.**
  Write freely about the topic to understand it better.
- **Gather information as needed.**
  Collect details and evidence that support your position.
- **Establish your position.**
  Clearly state your opinion, and support it with sound reasoning and detailed, relevant evidence.

During your writing . . .

- **Keep it short.**
  Convey ideas and important information. The letter should not be longer than one page. Offer any alternatives. If you have extra information, such as the petition in the example letter, include it on separate pages.
- **Stay on the topic.**
  Make sure every sentence supports your argument.

After you've written a first draft . . .

- **Check for completeness.**
  Add any important reasons you forgot to include. Don't end the letter abruptly, but instead build a sense of closure.
- **Check for correctness.**
  Read the letter several times. If possible, have someone else read it as well. Make sure that you used appropriate conventions and your letter is free of errors. Make sure that all names are capitalized and spelled correctly.

PERSUASIVE

 Think of a problem in your community. Write a persuasive letter to a friend asking her to help you solve it. Convey your ideas and important information in your letter, and use correct conventions.

TEKS 6.17B

Parts of a Letter

1 The heading includes your address and the date. Write the heading at least one inch from the top of the page at the left-hand margin. Note: informal letters do not have to have a heading.

2 The inside address includes the name, title, and address of the person or organization you are writing to. Note: informal letters do not always include an inside address.

- If the person has a title, make sure to include it. (If the title is short, write it on the same line as the name. If the title is long, write it on the next line.)

- In a formal letter, if you are writing to an organization or a business but not to a specific person, begin the inside address with the name of the organization or business.

3 The salutation is the greeting followed by a comma.

- If you know the person's name, use it in your greeting.
   Dear Christopher,

- In a formal letter, when you don't know the name of the person, use a salutation like one of these:
   Dear Store Owner:
   Dear Madison Soccer Club:

4 The body is the main part of the letter where you convey ideas and include all important information.

5 The closing is placed after the body and will demonstrate a sense of closure. Use a line such as **Yours truly** or **Sincerely** to close a letter. Capitalize only the first word of the closing and put a comma after it.

6 The signature ends the letter. If you are using a computer to type a formal letter, leave four spaces after the closing; then type your name. Write your signature between the closing and the typed name.

Turn to page **668** for more about writing letters, as well as a set of guidelines for addressing envelopes properly.

TEKS 6.17B
ELPS 3D, 3E, 4I

Letter Format

1

2

3

4

5

6

}—— **Four to Seven Spaces**

:

}—— **Double Space**

}—— **Double Space**

}—— **Double Space**

}—— **Double Space**

,

}—— **Double Space**

}—— **Four Spaces**

PERSUASIVE

 Write a letter to your teacher that might persuade him or her to give you less homework. Remember to use appropriate conventions. Read it to a classmate to see and discuss if it sounds persuasive.

Practical Writing:
Drafting a Persuasive Letter

A persuasive letter is a great way to invite people to assist you with a project or task. This sample letter asks for help in running a fundraising event at school.

This is the correct format for an informal letter. The writer uses appropriate conventions.

951 Walla Walls Road
Dallas, TX 75201
September 30, 2011

The **beginning** conveys the idea of what the writer is asking for.

Dear Uncle Joaquin,

You know that I am a member of the band at Lone Star Middle School. We are planning a pancake breakfast fundraiser at the school on the last Saturday of the month.

The **body** of the letter tells the important information about the event.

We are hoping to raise money to purchase new band uniforms for a competition next summer. I know how much you love to cook, and I was hoping that you would be able to help us out. The breakfast will start at 9:00 a.m. Would you be able to come at 7:30 a.m. to help us set up the grills and begin cooking the pancakes? Your shift would last until 10:00 a.m. As a thank you, you are invited to stay and have a free breakfast.

The **closing** demonstrates a sense of closure by asking for a specific action.

This is a really important event at our school, and we are looking for the best crew to help us out. I know that with your kitchen skills and positive attitude, you would be perfect! Please let me know if you are able to help us or not. I look forward to hearing from you soon!

Sincerely,

Elissa

TEKS 6.17B

Writing Tips

Before you write . . .

- **Define your need.**
  Know exactly what you need help with.
- **Form your request.**
  Think about it so that you can clearly explain it.
- **Gather information as needed.**
  Collect details and facts that your reader will need to know.
- **Find someone to help.**
  Find a person or an organization that might be able to help you with your request.

During your writing . . .

- **Keep it short.**
  Stick to important details. The letter should not be longer than one page. Give your reader only the information he or she needs to know in order to make a decision.
- **Demonstrate a sense of closure.**
  Find a way to wrap up your letter and ask for the reader to respond. Be sure to give the reader specific instructions on how to reply to your request.

After you've written a first draft . . .

- **Check for completeness.**
  Add any important information you forgot to include.
- **Check for correctness.**
  Read the letter several times. If possible, have someone else read it as well. Make sure that your letter is free of errors and that all names are capitalized and spelled correctly.

PERSUASIVE

Think of something that you or your school needs help with. Write a persuasive letter to someone you know asking to help. Convey your idea and share important information. Check your conventions.

Narrative Writing
Writing for the Texas Assessment

When you take state tests in Texas, you often have to write. The prompt tells you what to write about and gives some things to remember. Read the following prompt.

Prompt

> Write a composition convincing your teachers to give more or less homework.

Use the information below to help you write your composition.

REMEMBER THAT YOU SHOULD–

☐ write to convince your teachers to give either more or less homework.

☐ clearly state your position.

☐ include sound reasoning and detailed, relevant evidence to support your position.

☐ try to use correct grammar, punctuation, capitalization, and spelling.

Prewriting Select a Form

The prompt doesn't tell you what form of writing to use. How will you figure out which one? Consider what you have learned and think about which form best fits what you want to say.

Do you want to:
- describe a person or place?
- offer a solution to a problem?
- explain an object?
- share a personal experience?
- give information?
- persuade someone to do something?

Answering these questions will help you decide on a form.

Eduardo wanted to persuade his teacher. He decided the best form was a persuasive essay because it allowed him to state his position and tell why he thinks others should feel the same way.

Identify Details

Eduardo decided on his position. To plan his draft, he used a table diagram. It helped him identify details and evidence that supported his position.

Teachers need to give less homework		
Students have many after school activities	Students need more time to spend with their families	Less homework will make students like school more and not feel like giving up.

PERSUASIVE

Drafting **Writing the Essay**

Next, Eduardo used his table diagram to write his persuasive essay. Read Eduardo's persuasive essay.

The **beginning** includes the position statement (**underlined**).

"I have too much homework" is a complaint that lots of students have. But has anyone considered that they might be right? Some homework can help kids learn, but too much homework can make learning harder. <u>Ridge Middle School students need less homework, not more.</u>

Most Ridge students have very full schedules. School goes from 8:00 in the morning to 3:00 in the afternoon. Kids who ride the bus may spend an extra hour just getting to school and back home. Then some kids stay after school for an hour or two of sports, and other kids have music lessons or club meetings. Add a couple of hours of homework, and that makes an 11-hour day!

Each **middle** paragraph gives sound reasoning and detailed, relevant evidence to support the position.

The little time kids have when they are not scheduled for class or lessons should be spent enjoying time with their families. Kids need time to play. They also need to enjoy their families and just get to be kids. Free time is short. Spending all their extra time working on homework causes them to be away from family time.

When there's too much homework, some kids feel like giving up. Teachers at Ridge might say that they only give 20 minutes of homework a day. Still, if six teachers each give just 20 minutes of homework, that's two full hours of work! Kids will have no time to relax, and they will be too tired for school the next day. All this will make them not like to learn.

Some homework is a good thing. It does help you learn concepts better and gives you a chance to practice skills. But too much homework causes problems. Kids work too many hours with no rest, they don't have time to spend with their families, and they end up not liking to learn at all. Teachers at Ridge Middle School should give less homework. Then maybe their students will learn even more.

The **ending** includes consideration of alternatives and restates the position statement.

Respond to the reading. Answer the following questions to see how the traits were used in Eduardo's responses.

☐ **Focus and Coherence** (1) What is the position in the response? (2) What key words in the prompt does Eduardo use?

☐ **Development of Ideas** (3) What details and evidence does Eduardo use in his essay?

☐ **Voice** (4) How does Eduardo share his personal views?

Literature Connection: Read another example of persuasive writing in the article "Metric Metric: It's so nice, we'll say it twice!"

PERSUASIVE

 **TEKS** 6.14A1, 6.18A

Writing Tips

Before you write . . .

- **Understand the prompt.**
  Remember that a persuasive prompt asks you to state and support a position.
- **Plan your persuasive essay.**
  Use a graphic organizer like a table diagram to help with your planning.

Table Diagram

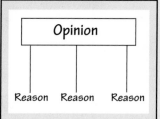

During your writing . . .

- **Establish a position.**
  Choose a position and state it clearly.
- **Build your argument.**
  Choose sound reasoning and detailed, related evidence to support your position.
- **End effectively.**
  Be sure to include consideration of alternatives. Summarize your argument and restate your opinion.

After you've written a first draft . . .

- **Check for focus and coherence.**
  Make sure you stayed focused and on topic.
- **Check for conventions.**
  Correct errors in grammar, punctuation, and spelling.

 Plan and write a response. Respond to the prompt on page 290. Remember to select a form and to use the tips above.

Persuasive Writing in Review

In persuasive writing, you work to convince people to think the way you do about something. You express a thoughtful position and give strong reasons to support it. Then you offer an alternative to the situation or ask for a call to action.

Prewriting

Select a topic that you care about, one that you can present confidently and that is appropriate for your audience. (See page 236.)

Gather ideas about your topic. (See page 237.)

Write a position statement that identifies your "cause + feeling." (See page 238.)

Organize your ideas in a list or an outline with your position statement at the top, followed by topic sentences with sound reasoning and detailed, relevant evidence. (See pages 240.)

Drafting

In the beginning, grab the reader's attention and clearly state your position. (See page 243.)

In the middle, devote a paragraph to each reason with detailed and relevant evidence. (See pages 244–245.)

In the ending, include consideration of alternatives, restate your position, and make a call to action. (See page 246.)

Revising

Review your focus and coherence, organization, and development of ideas first. Then check for **voice.** (See pages 248–255.)

Editing

Check your writing for conventions. Ask a friend to edit the writing, too. (See pages 258–261.)

Make a final copy and proofread it for errors before sharing it with your audience. (See page 263.)

Assessing

Use the persuasive rubric as a guide to assess your finished writing. (See pages 264–269.)

PERSUASIVE

experience
answer

ELPS 2C, 3E, 3H, 4G

Responding to Texts

Writing Focus

- Response Paragraph
- Book Review
- Response to a Magazine Article

Grammar Focus

- Passive and Active Verbs
- Compound Sentences

Learning Language

With a partner, read the prompts and share your answers.

1. A modifier is a word that describes.
   Which word modifies the noun *ship* in this sentence? Explain your answer. *The ship is tall.*

2. Someone who is knowledgeable knows a lot of information.
   Name someone who is knowledgeable about sports.

evaluate
REACT
preview

Responding to Texts

Response Paragraph

You're sitting in a movie theater, the lights dim, and the "Coming Attractions" begin. Each preview highlights a new movie. In a very short time, you know whether or not you want to see it.

A response to literature in the form of a paragraph is much like a movie preview. The writing must get right to the point and say something meaningful about the story. This type of response usually highlights an important event.

On the next page, you will read a sample paragraph that responds to a book. Then you will write a response paragraph of your own.

Writing Guidelines

Subject: An important event in a book or short story

Purpose: To respond to a story

Form: A paragraph

Audience: Classmates

Response Paragraph

When you write a paragraph about something you've read, it should focus on one event. The **topic sentence** identifies the story, the author, and the event. The details in the **body** of the paragraph describe the event, and the **closing sentence** tells why the event is important.

In the following response, Shandra writes about the book *Bridge to Terabithia*. She shares an event she thinks is very important.

Topic Sentence
• • • • • • • • • • • • • •

Body

Closing Sentence
• • • • • • • • • • • • • •

A Friendship Fort

The most important event in Katherine Paterson's *Bridge to Terabithia* is when Jess and Leslie build their fort. Jess is a shy boy who wants to be an artist, and Leslie is the new girl in the neighborhood. They don't fit in with other kids, but they get along with each other. Together, Jess and Leslie create Terabithia, a secret meeting place in the woods. To get there, they must cross a creek by swinging on an old rope. Jess and Leslie build a wooden fort in Terabithia and spend a lot of time there. Their little wooden fort takes them to a thousand places. The day Jess and Leslie create Terabithia is the day they begin to build their friendship.

Respond to the reading. On your own paper, answer the following questions. Discuss your answers with a partner.

☐ **Development of Ideas** (1) What part of the story does the writer think is most important? (2) Why is it important?

☐ **Organization** (3) Is this paragraph organized by time, by order of importance, or by some other logical order?

☐ **Voice** (4) Does the writer sound knowledgeable about the story? (5) What words or phrases tell you so?

TEKS 6.14A
ELPS 5G

Prewriting Selecting a Topic

Your first step in writing a response to literature is using strategies to determine your topic. Sofia began by listing novels and stories she had read and could respond to. (See pages **646** and **648** for punctuation of titles.)

List

Books	Short Stories
Holes	"The Gift of the Magi"
The Cay	"The Bell"
Bridge to Terabithia	"The Legend of Sleepy Hollow"

Prewrite

Choose a book or short story. Use the list strategy to determine an appropriate topic. On your own paper, list some of your favorite books or short stories. Circle the one that interests you the most.

Focusing on an Important Event

Think about things that happen in the story you've chosen. Focus on events that affect the whole story. You will develop your paragraph's controlling idea based on one event. A cluster can help you find events.

Cluster

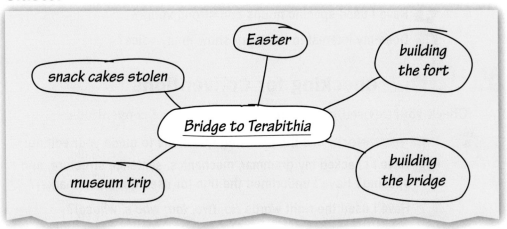

Easter

snack cakes stolen

building the fort

Bridge to Terabithia

museum trip

building the bridge

Prewrite

Create a cluster. In the center of your cluster, write the title of the book or short story. Around it, write a number of important events. Then choose one event around which you can develop a controlling idea.

RESPONSE

 **TEKS** 6.14D
ELPS 3E, 5G

Drafting **Creating Your First Draft**

Remember that a paragraph has three main parts: a topic sentence, the body, and a closing sentence. (See the sample on page **298**.)

- **Topic sentence:** Write a sentence that names the book, short story, or expository text, its author, and the main event you will focus on.
- **Body:** Write sentences that describe and explain the event.
- **Closing sentence:** End with a sentence that tells why the event is important.

Write the first draft of your paragraph. Use the information above as a guide.

Revising **Improving Your Paragraph**

After you've written your first draft, you need to revise your paragraph for *focus and coherence, organization, development of ideas*, and *voice*.

Review your paragraph. Use the following questions as a guide when you revise.

1 Have I written about an important event?

2 Do I need to rearrange my sentences to be in the best order?

3 Do my sentences flow smoothly?

4 Have I used specific nouns and strong verbs?

5 Does my interest in the story show in my voice?

Editing **Checking for Conventions**

Check your revised paragraph for correct use of conventions.

Edit your work. Use the following questions to guide your editing:

1 Have I checked my grammar, mechanics, sentence structure, and spelling? Have I underlined the title (or used quotation marks)?

2 Have I used the right words *(to, two, too; who's, whose)*?

Proofread your paragraph. After making a neat copy of your final paragraph, check it one more time for errors. Read your paragraph aloud to a partner.

Responding to Texts

Writing a Book Review

Have you ever been carried away by a book? You start to read but soon lose track of where you are and what time it is. For a while, nothing exists outside of the story, and you and the book soar together on a flight of fancy.

Writing a response to a book helps you relive those flights of fancy. In this assignment, you will write about an insight you have discovered in a book or story. As you recap the important events, you'll soar once more.

Writing Guidelines

Subject: A book or a story
Purpose: To share an insight
Form: An essay
Audience: Classmates

Understanding Your Goal

How do you know what to include in your response? For starters, your response must clearly and concisely retell the story and develop an insight. The traits listed below will help you meet your goal. The scoring rubric on pages 48–49 will also help you. Refer to it often to improve your writing.

Traits of a Book Review

Focus and Coherence

Build on ideas and insights to create a focused, coherent piece of writing.

Organization

Organize your response using an appropriate organizational strategy.

Development of Ideas

Tell what your insight is and support it with carefully selected details.

Voice

Be sure your voice reflects your personality and fits the assignment and the audience.

Conventions

Be sure your grammar is correct. Use complete sentences. Check for correct punctuation, capitalization, and spelling.

Literature Connection: You can find a response similar to a book review by reading the film review "Twain's Tale Transplanted to Today."

Writing a Book Review

The following essay was written by a student who tells how the events in the story *Brothers* lead to his understanding and insight.

Beginning

The beginning introduces the book and shows the writer's understanding in the focus statement (underlined).

Middle

The middle paragraphs summarize events that lead to the writer's understanding.

Brothers

Brothers by Justin Lang is a story about a young boy who realizes that family members need each other when things get tough. The story is about a boy, Luis. <u>The story shows that Luis deeply wants to be mature and respected.</u>

Luis's father is away on a military tour, and Luis helps his mother around the house a lot. She calls him her "little man," and hugs his shoulders. "My little man," she laughs, "you help me more than your father ever did."

Luis and his older brother Miguel have very little in common. Miguel spends time away from home, working and going to school. When he's home, he calls Luis "little man," which makes Luis feel like a child. When their father was home, he and Miguel would whisper together and make each other laugh. Miguel was allowed to stay up late, but Luis and the little ones were sent to bed.

One weekend, Miguel stays home from work because he is sick. Luis takes care of him. When Miguel begins to feel better, he tells Luis, "You know, Dad would be proud of you. You help Mom so much. I wrote to Dad, and I told him that you make it possible for me to go to school and work long hours. I know you're taking care of things at home, so I never have to worry." Luis's eyes open wide. Suddenly, he sees that the "little man" is important to the family.

 **TEKS** 6.17C
ELPS 3E, 3G, 4J

Middle
This paragraph shares details that continue to develop the writer's understanding.

Miguel starts to resent getting up when it's still dark out to finish his homework. Luis notices and begins to realize what a burden his older brother has been shouldering. He tries to think of a way to help.

A few days later, Luis persuades the corner storekeeper to let him help for two hours every day after school. At home, this news is shared by Luis. He waits until Miguel gets home so he can tell his mother and Miguel at the same time. He wants to make a big announcement. I can tell from this that he is excited about his news, and that shows how much he wanted to help his family. When he hears the news, Miguel grabs Luis, gives him a rough hug and says, "I'm very impressed, man." Luis is very proud

Ending

The ending paragraph sums up the writer's understanding of this story.

One of the best parts of the story, in my opinion, is when Miguel responds to Luis' news about his job. Out of habit, he begins by calling him "little man." Then he finishes by switching to "man." Luis has matured by the story's end. He has proved his maturity by recognizing a problem and solving it. In the process, Luis learns that respect comes to those who pitch in to help when they are needed.

Respond to the reading. Answer the following questions about the sample response. Discuss your answers with a partner.

☐ **Focus and Coherence** **(1) Which sentences explain the writer's focus?**

☐ **Organization** **(2) How is the last paragraph like the first paragraph?**

☐ **Development of Ideas** **(3) What events from the story support the writer's insight?**

evaluate
react
PREVIEW
answer
experience
305

Writing a Book Review

Go Online!

Prewriting

PREWRITE ✓ DRAFT REVISE EDIT PUBLISH

Prewriting is the first step in the writing process. It involves selecting a book or story to write about, listing important events in the plot, writing a focus statement, and planning your paragraphs.

Keys to Effective Prewriting

1. Select a book, story, or piece of expository writing you have recently read and would like to write about.

2. Use a cluster to help you remember key details or events that support your central focus.

3. Write an opening and clear focus statement to guide your writing.

4. Review the events or ideas and pick those you can explain in detail to support your controlling idea.

5. Provide evidence from the text to demonstrate your understanding and support your controlling idea.

PROD. NO.
SCENE
TAKE
ROLL
SOUND

RESPONSE

 **TEKS** 6.14A, 6.17C
ELPS 5G

Prewriting Selecting a Topic

Use a strategy to choose an appropriate topic. Start by making a list of novels, short stories, or expository writing you have read and know well.

Chart your choices. After you list titles, make a chart. In the first column, fill in three or four titles of stories you've read recently. In the second column, write a sentence that sums up the story.

Chart

Title	Story Summary
* <u>Prairie Days</u>	A woman recalls life on the prairie and its influence on her development.
"An Unforgettable Life"	A short story about a man's dream of success.
<u>Dog Days of Summer</u>	A book about a boy growing up in a small town.

I choose <u>Prairie Days</u> because I like the way the author uses historical details to help the story seem realistic.

Determine your topic. Review your chart and put a star next to the title you will write about. Beneath the chart, explain the reason for your choice. Provide evidence from the text to show your understanding.

Focus on the Texas Traits

Development of Ideas Each story or article contains ideas that help readers draw conclusions and form ideas from the text. Pay attention to the organization of the story or text and make note of the key events or ideas that give you insight into understanding the text. These examples serve as your evidence.

TEKS 6.14B, 6.17C

Gathering Details

Once you select a story or book to review, the next step is to identify the important events in the plot. A time line like the one below allows you to list the events in the order in which they happened. In planning your review, focus on the events and evidence from the text that you will use to demonstrate your understanding. Use the time line to help you choose the appropriate organizational strategy to use for your draft.

Time Line

Summary: A woman recalls life on the prairie and its influence on her development.

Edna's family built their home from scratch.

Edna's father taught his children how to be self-sufficient.

Edna's mother taught her the virtue of simple living.

Edna's experience with neighbors reinforces her belief that people can accomplish a lot if they work together.

Edna learns to appreciate nature and not fear it.

Insight: Edna's childhood was hard, but she is grateful for what she learned: how to work hard, love life, and rely on herself.

Prewrite

Make a time line. List the key events in the order in which they happened. (Try to list five or six events.) Study the events to help you discover how they lead up to your insight about the book you've read.

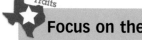
Texas
Traits

Focus on the Texas Traits

Voice There's a good chance your writing will have a strong, confident voice if you know and understand the book you are reviewing. Be sure to carefully review all the details of the story.

RESPONSE

 **TEKS** 6.14A, 6.14B, 6.17C

ELPS 5G

Prewriting Writing a Focus Statement

In any story, the events will change the main character in some way. For example, the events in *Prairie Days* teach Edna to rely on herself and be strong.

In the time line you created (page **307**), you listed the important events in the story. Use the events and your insight or understanding to develop the controlling idea for your review. Build on the controlling idea to create a focused, organized, and coherent piece of writing. Here is a formula that will help you write a focus statement to guide your writing.

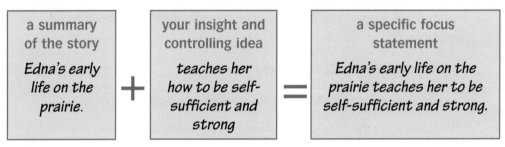

a summary of the story		your insight and controlling idea		a specific focus statement
Edna's early life on the prairie.	**+**	*teaches her how to be self-sufficient and strong*	**=**	*Edna's early life on the prairie teaches her to be self-sufficient and strong.*

 Form a focus. Decide on the controlling idea that will be the focus of your review. Write a focus statement using the formula above.

Planning the Middle Part of Your Review

The next step is to plan the middle part of your review. The first middle paragraph should cover events in your time line that happened early in the story. The second paragraph should cover the later events. Paragraphs should flow smoothly and be coherent. Use evidence from the text to show your insight and demonstrate your understanding of the events.

 Plan your middle paragraphs. Use your time line as an organizational strategy. Use the prompts below to plan your paragraphs.

1 Put one check next to the events that happen early in the story. (These events will be in your first middle paragraph.)

2 Put two checks next to the events that happen later on. (These events will be in your other middle paragraphs.)

3 Write topic sentences for each paragraph that flow logically. Bullet point notes on the evidence from the text you will use to show your insight. (See pages 600–601 for more information.)

Drafting

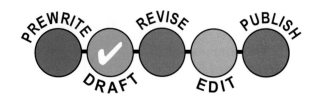

PREWRITE · DRAFT · REVISE · EDIT · PUBLISH

When you write your first draft, you turn your prewriting ideas into an essay. Your time line, focus statement, paragraph plan, and topic sentences will help you write your essay.

Keys to Effective Writing

1. Let your focus statement and topic sentences guide you.

2. Add specific details and evidence from the text to support your topic sentences and provide to interest the reader.

3. Use transitions to tie everything together.

4. Write with your purpose, form, and audience in mind.
   Ask yourself:
   - Have I conveyed my focus and my understanding clearly?
   - Have I used evidence from the text to show my insight?
   - Is my voice appropriate for my audience?

RESPONSE

TEKS 6.17C
ELPS 5G

Drafting Getting the Big Picture

The chart below shows how the parts of a book review fit together. (The examples are from the essay about Prairie Days on pages **311–314**.) You're ready to write your review once you . . .

- understand the story,
- state your topic in a clear, two-part focus statement, and
- plan your paragraphs.

Beginning

The **beginning** paragraph introduces the story and states the writer's insight in a focus statement.

Focus Statement
Edna's early life on the prairie teaches her to be self-sufficient and strong.

Middle

The **middle** paragraphs cover events in the story. They provide evidence from the story that lead to the reviewer's insight.

Two Topic Sentences
During her childhood, Edna works hard and learns to respect simple living.

Edna and her neighbors live through a harsh winter together.

Ending

The **ending** explains the writer's insight into the story.

Closing Sentences
Edna comes to realize that her childhood taught her strength, an appreciation of simple things, and the importance of working with others for the common good.

TEKS 6.14B, 6.17C
ELPS 5G

Starting Your Review

The beginning paragraph should introduce the story and state your controlling idea in a focus statement.

Beginning

Middle

Ending

Beginning Paragraph

Read the beginning paragraph below. Notice how this paragraph begins with a general introduction, provides evidence from the text, and ends with a specific focus statement with the controlling idea and the writer's insight.

The first part introduces the story.	*Prairie Days by Carla Ferber is about the growing-up years of Edna Chester who, with her family, moves to the wilderness to seek a better life for themselves. Edna and her family have to do everything themselves, from building their home to working the dry earth to grow crops. They even make their own*
The focus statement includes the writer's insight (underlined).	*clothes. They face illness, hunger, and a harsh winter, and still they always come out on top. This is because of their hard work and belief in themselves.* <u>*Edna's early life on the prairie teaches her to be self-sufficient and strong.*</u>

Retelling in the Present Tense

A book review can be written in the past or present tense. The verbs in the sample paragraph above are all in the present tense (*is, make, face, teaches*). Because the events in a story happen again and again each time the story is read, it makes sense to discuss them in the present tense. In the essay you are about to write, you also should use the present tense.

Draft

Write your beginning. Write the first paragraph of your review. Be sure to include information that introduces the story and state your insight and controlling idea in a focus statement. Present the controlling idea that you will build on to create a focused, organized, coherent review.

RESPONSE

 **TEKS** 6.14B, 6.17C, 6.19A(viii)
ELPS 5G

Drafting **Developing the Middle Part**

The middle paragraphs build on ideas to create a focused, organized, coherent piece of writing. These paragraphs provide evidence of events from the story that support your insights and understanding.

First Middle Paragraph

The first middle paragraph tells about the important events and explains evidence in the first part of the story.

The topic sentence introduces the paragraph.	<u>When the Chester family first arrives in the middle of the prairie,</u> everyone stays busy. Mama and the girls clean, make clothes, cook, and try to raise crops and care for the animals they acquire. Dad and the boys build the house, all the furniture, and venture out to meet neighbors and become part of the community. <u>Later,</u> a neighbor's barn catches fire, and Mr. Chester says "We need to rely on ourselves. But we also need to ask for help if we need it and be ready to help our neighbors." <u>Then,</u> the Chesters and the rest of the community provide food and clothes for the family.
Transitions (<u>underlined</u>) **connect the events.**	

Transitions

The transitions below show time. These words help make the ideas in your writing and speaking easier to follow. (See pages **620–621**.)

about	before	later	soon	tomorrow
after	during	meanwhile	then	until
as soon as	finally	next	third	when
at	first	second	today	yesterday

TEKS 6.14B, 6.17C, 6.19A(viii)
ELPS 2I, 3D, 3E, 5G

Second Middle Paragraph

The second middle paragraph tells about events and explains evidence that happen later in the story. Write additional paragraphs as needed.

The transition word (underlined) helps introduce the paragraph. Evidence from the text demonstrates the writer's understanding.	*<u>Later,</u> Edna and her family experience more problems. Edna and her family have no control over the weather! When storms come or when they are faced with weeks of drought, crops die and the family goes hungry. In times of plenty, Mama and the girls pickle and can food to store for lean times. Edna thinks to herself often "Do not to despair. Times change. Life goes on." Edna and her family learn to appreciate simple things and each other, especially during challenging times. They learn to turn to neighbors for support and friendship, and offer the same in return.*

Draft

Write the middle of your review. Using the following tips, write the middle paragraphs of your essay. (Look again at the sample paragraphs.)

Drafting Tips

- **Talk about the story** with a classmate before you begin to write this part. Ask for and listen to feedback.
- **Review your time line** to make sure you've included all the significant events. Use transitions make events flow.
- **Include important details and evidence** from the text that will help the reader understand your insight. Build on ideas. Keep your writing focused, organized, and coherent.
- **Write as freely as you can,** without being too concerned about neatness.

Drafting Ending Your Book Review

Your focus statement introduced your insight and basic understanding of the story, and your closing paragraph should restate it. Ask yourself the following questions:

- Beginning
- Middle
- Ending

- Have I built on ideas to keep my writing focused, organized, and coherent?
- Have I provided enough evidence from the text to demonstrate my understanding of the story?
- Have I used transitions to help the reader follow the organization of my review?
- How should I state my insight in the conclusion?

tip Your insight is the message you want to leave with your readers. It often centers around *growing up* or *learning a lesson*.

Ending Paragraph

Read the ending paragraph below. The writer states that Edna learns an important lesson about life and what is important.

> The ending restates the writer's insight.

> As an adult, Edna thinks back to her growing-up years and what those years on the prairie taught her. She realizes that her family taught her a valuable lesson: how to be strong in good times and in bad. Edna knows her early years prepared her to appreciate the simple things in life that make living most worthwhile: being productive, raising a family, and being an active member of a community. She knows that she is strong and self-sufficient because of her childhood.

Write your ending. In your last paragraph, be sure to explain how the evidence in the story helped you develop your insight.

Form a complete first draft. Make a complete copy of your review. Read it. Rethink how you handled purpose, audience, and form.

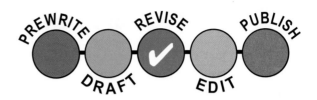

Revising

A first draft is never perfect. One of the paragraphs might be missing an important idea. Another might appear in the wrong place. Revising your essay can fix problems like these.

Keys to Effective Revising

1. Read through your entire draft to get a feeling of how well your essay works.

2. Make sure your focus statement clearly states your insight into the story.

3. Check your paragraphs to make sure the details of events provide evidence for your insights.

4. Look for sentences or text that you can delete, combine, or rearrange to help with focus and organization.

5. Use the editing and proofreading marks inside the back cover of this book.

Revising **for** Focus and Coherence

When you revise for *focus and coherence,* you make sure you are focused on one controlling idea. All events and details in your essay should provide evidence of that idea. Your writing should present a complete whole.

Does my focus statement work?

Your focus statement works if it clearly introduces the story and includes your insight. Be sure you have used the formula below to write your focus statement.

Effective Focus Statement

> Edna's early life on the prairie *(summary of the story)*
> teaches her to be self-sufficeient and strong *(a specific insight).*

 Read each pair of focus statements below. For each pair, decide which statement works better. Be prepared to explain why.

1. a. **As Jody cares for his pony, he works really hard.**
    b. As Jody cares for his pony, he learns about love and loss.

2. a. **Buck's trials and challenges increase his courage and leadership qualities.**
    b. Buck tries hard, unlike his owners.

3. a. **Meg's journey to save her father makes her more confident.**
    b. Meg's journey to save her father is long.

4. a. **The team's efforts to make the finals were valuable.**
    b. The team's efforts to make the finals helped them realize that everyone has unique talents.

 Review your focus statement. Make sure that your focus statement introduces the story and clearly presents your controlling idea, which is your insight into the story. Share your focus statement with a teacher or a classmate to see if it works.

evaluate PREVIEW experience
react answer
317

 **TEKS** 6.14C
ELPS 3E, 4I, 4K

Writing a Book Review

Have I cut unnecessary details?

When summarizing a story, you should include only the key details so that your writing is clear. All other information should be cut. You should delete sentences or larger units of text that are:

- repeating the same information.
- unnecessary details or evidence.
- unimportant personal thoughts and feelings.

 Rewrite the paragraph below on your own paper. Using the list above as a guide, cut any sentences or words that are unnecessary. Afterward, share and evaluate your work with a classmate.

1   "Dog's Eye View" is a pretty good story about a dog named
2   Moose. Lots of people give their pets funny names. My friend named
3   her dog Sandwich. That's funny. One day, Moose slips out of his
4   owner's apartment and goes exploring. The story follows Moose all
5   around New York City. I love New York City. Moose meets lots of
6   interesting New Yorkers.

 Review your essay. Make sure your review contains the main points and no unnecessary details. Delete details for clarity as needed.

Focus and Coherence
An unnecessary detail and personal comment are deleted.

~~Prairie Days, by Carla Ferber is a lot like her other book,~~ ~~To The Wilderness, which I also liked.~~ Edna Chester, the main character in Praire Days by Carla Ferber, learns at an early age that life is full of challenges.

TEKS 6.14C

Revising for Organization

When you revise for *organization,* make sure your writing is easy for your readers to follow. Your sentences and paragraphs should be logically linked together. Each paragraph should build on the one before it. If not, then you need to rearrange sentences or larger units of text. You may also have to add sentences to provide a link from one paragraph to another.

Is my beginning organized properly?

Your beginning paragraph for this essay should start with general information about your book and end with a specific insight or focus. Review the beginning paragraph below from the sample essay on page **303.**

General ideas

Specific insight or focus

Brothers by Justin Lang is a story about a young boy who realizes that family members need each other when things get tough. The story is about a boy, Luis, and his family. Luis deeply wants to be mature and to be respected by his older brother, Miguel.

Rearrange the sentences in the following paragraph to fix their organization and how they flow. Put them in order from general information to a specific focus.

The story begins on a hot, dusty August day when Mimi wanders on he trail in the woods near her home. Just as Mimi is about to cross the stream, her life changes, and she must make a big decision. The novel *The Trail Outside* by Eva Lopez is the story of 10-year-old girl named Mimi. In her experience on the trail that day, Mimi realizes something very important about herself.

Check your beginning. Carefully review your beginning paragraph to make sure that it is organized from general to specific. Rearrange sentences or larger units of text as needed to have them in a logical order.

TEKS 6.19A(viii)

What is the best way to connect my ideas?

One of the best ways to connect the sentences and paragraphs in your essay is to use transitions. Usually, you will use transition words that show time: *first, next, then, finally.* (See pages **602–603.**)

 Read the paragraph below. On your own paper, write a revised version that adds a few more transition words or phrases. One transition word *(underlined)* has been added to get you started.

1   In the story "How to Win a Date," Carlos decides to make
2   a girl like him enough to go to the movies with him. He starts
3   out by helping her in a variety of ways. <u>First</u>, he offers to help
4   Louisa with her math homework. He offers to babysit her little
5   brother with her to help pass the time. He helps her parents
6   clean out their garage and run a sale. Louisa agrees to go to the
7   movies with him. But, Carlos is so tired that he falls asleep and
8   misses their date.

 Review your first draft. Check to make sure that you have included enough transition words and phrases in your essay. Check again to make sure they are in the correct order. Rearrange sentences and text as necessary.

Organization
Transitions are added to make the ideas easier to follow.

> *First,*
> Delores creates a background of a stormy night. *Then,* In the
>
> foreground, she paints a house with shutters blown
>
> *Last,*
> open by the wind. Delores adds a panicked face in the
>
> window. (Delores was making scenery for the play.)

 **TEKS** 6.14C, 6.17C
ELPS 3E, 4I, 4K

Revising for Development of Ideas

When you revise your writing for development of ideas, you make sure you include the details and evidence that not only support your insight but also bring the story to life. When you write about events from the story, use the details to add interest and to show you understand.

Have I developed my ideas in depth?

In order to develop an idea in depth, every sentence you write must relate or add to your controlling idea. Think of every possible way to explore your ideas with words and sentences that paint a picture. Revise your writing by keeping only ideas and details that enhance your controlling idea, making it more interesting.

Try IT Read the following paragraph. With a partner, discuss the following questions. Which sentences or words paint a picture? Which details enhance the controlling idea and make it more interesting?

"Moon Cakes" is the story of Yen's experience in her new country, the United States. When she first comes to this country from Vietnam, Yen feels isolated and out of place. She wants to return home because she doesn't understand the language or customs. She feels like she doesn't fit in with the other students in school. Then one day the teacher asks everyone to bring in foods from home. Yen brings moon cakes. Sharing food from one's culture is a good ice-breaker. Yen and her classmates learn from each other as they share foods from their home cultures.

Review details. In your essay, revise for details that enhance the controlling idea and make it more interesting. Remember to use words that show your insight and understanding of the text.

TEKS 6.14C
ELPS 3E, 4I, 4K

Do my ideas support my understanding of the story?

The goal of your book review is to advance your understanding of the story by providing evidence from the text. Any details that do not support your insight and understanding of the story do not belong.

 Read the following paragraph. Which ideas are not related to the understanding of the story or do not provide insight? Discuss with a partner.

> Caring for animals taught Ameer about love and loss. He had been very self-involved as a young boy. He did his own thing. Ameer helped his father birth colts. He cleaned the stalls and talked to the mares every morning. When one was ill, he and his father nursed it back to health. It was unusual for animals to get sick. The worst day of his life was the day Ameer had to bring some horses to market. Selling them felt like parting with a relative or dear friend.

 Remove extra ideas. Read through your essay and cut any ideas that do not support your understanding of the story. Remove extra words, phrases, and sentences, or large units of text.

Development of Ideas
The sentence that does not aid the development is removed.

Paul wanted to play basketball more than anything. He practiced every day. He tried out for the team. But he was never quite good enough. ~~Running came naturally to him.~~ His father said, "Think of something you do well. Use that skill to get ahead." Paul had long legs and could jump distances. He decided to try out for track and field. Sure enough! He made the team.

RESPONSE

Revising for Voice

When you revise for *voice,* you check your essay's language for understanding and interest. Is your voice confident and knowledgeable? The information that follows will help you revise your review for voice.

How do I know if my voice is strong and knowledgeable?

A *knowledgeable* voice is confident in its choice and presentation of events that support the writer's insight. The voice in the first paragraph below does not present relevant events. It results in a general feeling and not a specific insight.

General Feeling

> I really loved reading *Private Nobody.* At first, I was bored when the main character was joining the army. After all, who cares about the 1960s? Then I got a little interested because of all the fights. Those fights sure seemed real to me.

The voice in the next paragraph is knowledgeable because it focuses on facts that help the writer share a specific insight.

Specific Insight

> *Private Nobody* by Greg Washington is about a young man named Larry who joins the United States Army in the late 1960s. He is sent to Vietnam and gets into lots of fights. However, the fights are with his fellow soldiers, not the enemy. The fights show that the young man was filled with anger even before he arrived in Vietnam.

Check for a knowledgeable voice. Review your essay, looking for places where you focus on your opinions or feelings instead of on events and a specific insight. Revise to make your voice more knowledgeable.

How do I know if my writing is formal enough?

When you speak to friends, you say things like "Hey, what's up?" or you use casual language. However, the language in a book review should be more formal. Formality of language contributes to a writer's voice. When you write, be sure to use the correct voice for your audience. To sound formal, avoid street talk or slang.

 Read the following informal paragraph. On your own paper, list at least three words, phrases, or clauses that make the writing too informal. One phrase is underlined for you.

1
2   One night, Larry gets into a <u>giant smackdown</u>. He's on
3   guard duty when this one dude comes out of nowhere! Larry
4   tries to take off running, but he gets bashed. Larry wakes
5   up in an army hospital with this big humongous bandage on
6   his head and no memory at all. He can't even remember his
7   own name. He's like totally wacko. Letters from his mom and
8   girlfriend help him regain his memory, and eventually Larry gets
        a Purple Heart medal.

 Check your level of language. As you revise your book review, delete words and phrases that sound too informal. Revise to write for your audience.

Voice
A formal voice
matches the
audience.

After her journey, Billie ~~gets a clue. I think~~ understands that nature speaks to everyone.

~~this part is the coolest.~~ She sees that the

animals really have been talking to her all along . . .

TEKS 6.14E

Revising Using a Checklist

Check your revising. On a piece of paper, write the numbers 1 to 10. If you can answer "yes" to a question, put a check mark after that number. If not, continue to work with that part of your essay.

Focus and Coherence

_____ **1.** Have I included my insight in a clear focus statement?

_____ **2.** Have I cut unnecessary details from events that provide evidence for my insight?

_____ **3.** Have I developed a controlling idea in a focused, organized, and coherent way?

Organization

_____ **4.** Do I use transitions to connect my thoughts?

_____ **5.** Do I present events in the best possible order?

_____ **6.** Do I have a beginning, middle, and ending?

Development of Ideas

_____ **7.** Do I include only the events that provide evidence for my insight and understanding?

_____ **8.** Have I reordered parts that are out of place?

Voice

_____ **9.** Do I show interest in and understanding of my topic?

_____ **10.** Is my voice knowledgeable and formal to suit the audience?

Make a clean copy. Ask a classmate to read and respond to your book review. Make any needed revisions. Create a clean copy for editing.

Editing

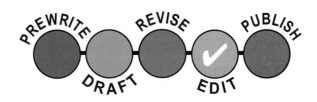

PREWRITE · REVISE · PUBLISH · DRAFT · EDIT ✓

After you've finished revising your essay, it's time to edit it for your use of conventions: grammar, mechanics, sentence structure, and spelling.

Keys to Effective Editing

1. Use a dictionary, a thesaurus, and the "Proofreader's Guide" in the back of this book.

2. Check for any words or phrases that may be confusing to the reader.

3. Check your writing for correctness of grammar, mechanics, sentence structure, and spelling.

4. If you are using a computer, edit on a printed computer copy. Then enter your changes on the computer.

5. Use the editing and proofreading marks inside the back cover of this book.

RESPONSE

TEKS 6.19A(i), 6.19B
ELPS 2I, 3E, 3G, 4K

Editing for Conventions

Grammar

When you edit for grammar, you make sure you use nouns, verbs, and other parts of speech correctly.

How can I make my verbs more active?

A verb in the active voice expresses action if its subject is doing the action. A verb in the passive voice expresses an action done to its subject. Below, the word *attack* is used as both a passive and an active verb. In a passive sentence, the verb phrase always includes the form of *be*.

Passive Verb

The panther is attacked by the alligator. (The panther receives the action.)

Active Verb

The alligator attacks the panther. (The alligator is doing the action.)

 Read the following sentences, which have active and passive verbs. For each sentence, ask yourself who or what is doing the action. Discuss each sentence with a partner. Work together to rewrite the sentences, changing the passive verb to an active verb or the active verb to a passive verb.

1. Billie Wind saves the panther cub.
2. The men in the swamp are avoided by her.
3. Her friendship with Petang, the otter, is enjoyed by Billie.

 Edit for active voice. Read through your essay for active and passive voice. Remember that active voice is stronger and more direct, while passive voice may use more words. Generally, you want to use active voice in your writing. Edit your verbs as needed to sound more active.

Have I used too many modifiers?

Once Mark Twain wrote: "When you catch an adjective, kill it." He knew that too many adjectives and adverbs can make writing sound fake or unnatural. A sentence such as "Jasper quite loudly shouts for greatly needed help" would sound clearer as "Jasper shouts for help."

Read the following paragraph. With a partner, find five adjectives or adverbs that should be removed. Explain your answers.

1   Jasper has never been in such a dark pit. He pulls out his
2   wonderful glow-stick, which glows really bright in the big dark
3   cave. On the floor of the cave, Jasper sees a shiny, gleaming piece
4   of gold. It is a beautifully lovely treasure coin. Jasper grabs the
5   coin and quickly and rapidly puts it in pocket. That's when he
6   hears a scary and frightening sound—the low scary growl of a
7   creature he doesn't know.

Remove extra modifiers. Read through your essay and cut out any unneeded adjectives and adverbs that you find. Tell a partner the adjectives you cut. Listen as they tell you the modifiers they cut.

Conventions
Extra modifiers are removed and a passive sentence is made active.

Later, the wind ~~gets so very much quieter and quieter.~~ *quiets down.*

Billie and the boy start to go outside, ~~but the fact that~~ *they notice that*

the panther is not budging from the cave ~~is noticed by~~

~~them.~~ Billie and the boy decide . . .

Learning Language

Adjectives are words that describe nouns or other adjectives.

big house   big, old house   tall tree

Adverbs are words that describe verbs and other adverbs.

run quickly   run very quickly   sing loudly   glows brightly

Using adjectives and adverbs, describe your vacation to a partner.

RESPONSE

Mechanics: Punctuation

When you edit for *mechanics,* you check for correct use of capitalization and punctuation. To edit your punctuation, look for correct use of periods, commas, question marks, and other punctuation marks.

How do you use a comma in a compound sentence?

A compound sentence is made up of two independent clauses. Each has a subject and a verb and can stand alone as a sentence. When they appear as a single sentence, they are joined by a comma and a coordinating conjunction such as *and, or, but, nor, for, so, yet.*

> You can buy this bike, or you can rent this bike.
> A single flower is beautiful, but many flowers create a bouquet.
> It was a beautiful day, so we went outside to play.

 On your own paper, join the two independent clauses of each pair to make a single sentence. Use a comma and a coordinating conjunction to join the two parts of the sentence.

1. We can go bowling.
   We can go to the movies.

2. My dog Bo chases squirrels.
   My dog Peep just sleeps.

3. Faisal wanted to join us.
   Chanry did not want to come.

4. I've finished my homework.
   I can watch TV.

5. Marianna is good at math.
   Kim is good in science.

6. We wanted to throw him a party.
   Felipe doesn't like surprises.

 Check compound sentences. Make sure that you have some compound sentences in your writing to add variety. Check to make sure you have used the correct conjunction and punctuation. Edit your sentences as needed.

TEKS 6.20C

Mechanics: Italics and Underlining

When do I use quotations, underline, or italics?

When you refer to a title of a book, you use italics if you are working on a computer. If you are writing by hand about a book, you underline the title. Short stories and poems should be enclosed by quotation marks.

Gone with the Wind **is a classic novel by Margaret Mitchell.**

Herman Melville wrote the book, <u>Moby Dick</u>.

My favorite poem is "The Road Not Taken" **by Robert Frost.**

 Read the following sentences. On a separate piece of paper, rewrite the titles correctly using underlines, italics (if you type them), or quotation marks.

1. Tuck Everlasting by Natalie Babbitt is one of my favorite books.
2. Eleven by Sandra Cisneros is a short story about a girl who does not like her name.
3. Too Many Tamales by Gary Soto is a funny, inspiring book.
4. My favorite book is Scorpions by Walter Dean Myers.
5. Shel Silverstein writes funny poems kids can relate to, such as Messy Room.
6. The Wolf and the Crane is a short story by Aesop that has a moral, or lesson.
7. When I was young, Amelia Bedelia was my favorite book.
8. Beverly Cleary writes books for kids, such as Henry and Mudge.

 Check titles. In your book review, check your writing carefully for correct use of underlining, italics, or quotations of titles. Edit any titles as needed.

 **TEKS** 6.14D

Editing Using a Checklist

Check your editing. On a piece of paper, write the numbers 1 to 11. If you can answer "yes" to a question, put a check mark after that number. If not, continue to edit for that convention.

Conventions

GRAMMAR

_____ **1.** Do I keep all my verbs in the same tense?

_____ **2.** Do I use the active and passive verb tenses correctly?

MECHANICS (Punctuation and Capitalization)

_____ **3.** Did I punctuate titles correctly?

_____ **4.** Did I underline or use italics for a book title?

_____ **5.** Did I use quotes for the title of an essay or piece of expository writing?

_____ **6.** Did I use commas in all my compound sentences?

_____ **7.** Did I start all sentences with capital letters?

SENTENCE STRUCTURE

_____ **8.** Did I use a comma and coordinating conjunction (*and, or, but, so, for*) in each compound sentence?

_____ **9.** Did I use different sentence structures for variety?

SPELLING

_____ **10.** Have I spelled all my words correctly?

_____ **11.** Have I double-checked the words my spell-check may have missed?

Creating a Title

- Use the title of the book: *Prairie Days*
- Describe the main idea: **Edna Learns to be Strong**
- Be creative: **Little Lessons on the Prairie**

Go Online!

Publishing

Sharing Your Essay

After you have worked so hard to write and improve your essay, you'll want to make a neat-looking copy to share. You may also decide to present your essay in some other form: an illustration, a reading, or an online posting. (See the suggestions in the boxes below.)

Publish | **Make a final copy.** Follow your teacher's instructions or use the guidelines below to format your paper. (If you are writing with a computer, see page 60.) Write a final copy of your essay and proofread it for errors.

Focus on Presentation

- Use blue or black ink and write neatly.
- Write your name in the upper left corner of page 1.
- Skip a line and center your title; skip another line and start your writing.
- Indent every paragraph and leave a 1-inch margin on all four sides.
- Write your last name and the page number in the upper right corner of every page after the first one.

Illustrate Your Summary

Draw a picture that shows an important event in the story. Post your essay and illustration in your classroom.

Go Online

Upload your book review for others to read.

Give a Recitation

Read aloud a part of the story in which an important event occurs. Then tell the class how the event helped you find an insight.

RESPONSE

Evaluating a Book Review

To learn how to evaluate a book review, you'll use the scoring rubric on pages **48–49** and the book reviews that follow. These book reviews are examples of writing for each score on the rubric.

Notice that this first book review received a score of 4. Read the description for a score of 4 on pages **48–49**. Then read the book review. Use the same steps to study the other examples. Always remember to think about the overall quality of the writing.

Writing that fits a score of 4 is very strong.

Strong two-part focus statement

Follows organizational pattern

Knowledge-able, formal voice

Shutterbugs

At the beginning of Scott Morton's novel <u>Shutterbugs</u>, sixth grader Carlene Glendower hates school and most of the rest of her life too. Then, one day, her English teacher Mr. Oliva passes out a disposable camera to each student in the class. He tells them to photograph what they see during their lives outside of school. "When you put it in a camera frame, even a blade of grass, is interesting," Mr. Oliva tells them. All the students are doubtful, including Carlene. But by taking photographs of her life, Carlene comes to belief in herself and in the beauty of human beings.

The story begins with Carlene seeming very negative and then, as the semester goes by, feeling more and more positive. When she first comes home with the camera, her parents don't respond and her brother makes fun of her. At that point, Carlene takes her first photographs—she takes photos of her family. Just by seeing the photos, Carlene starts to feel like she understands her life better.

Carlene soon starts shooting pictures all over her neighborhood. She takes pictures of the stores, the street corners where people hang out, the fire station, and more. In English class, the students exchange photos, writing about their own pictures and each other's. The students think that Carlene's pictures are the best in the class. It is the first time she has ever thought of herself as the best at anything.

Later, Carlene asks a homeless woman if she can take her picture. Louise, the woman, has had a hard life. Friendship with Louise changes Carlene. Carlene sees that a person who she thought was unpleasant and dirty was actually kind, wise, and even a hero. Carlene realizes that if Louise had hidden qualities like that, then everyone must—including herself. And, at the end of the semester party, the pictures of Louise are the highlight.

Shutterbugs shows that there can be goodness or greatness in everybody, and that when we realize this, we appreciate the world around us much more. Carlene is a character that many young people could identify with. Maybe not everyone is a photographer; someone might be a scientist or a soccer player or just a good friend. But this book says that everyone is special, and human beings are all beautiful in some way.

Detailed evidence from the text

Writer remembers purpose, form, and audience.

RESPONSE

Writing that fits a score of 3 is strong in most ways.

Good focus statement

Evidence from the text

Whose Woods are These

<u>Whose Wood are These</u> is a great science fiction novel by M. Jeanne Prudeaux. It is about a shy young boy named Kelvin who lives in the future and who is flying to a colony planet when the spaceship crashes, killing everyone on board except himself. His parents, his sister and the whole crew and all the other passengers are all dead. Kelvin has to survive all by himself. Can he make it? Against all odds, Kelvin figures out how to do things like build shelter, make fire, and catch fish, and he grows up into being a strong leader.

The planet the ship crashed on isn't even the colony planet they were headed to, it's a different planet on the way there. At first, Kelvin misses his family. Then, he realizes that in order to survive he must snap out of it, and that his family would want him to survive. At that point Kelvin is the only character, so we learn about him by the thoughts that the author, M. Jeanne Prudeaux, tell us, such as, "This was his first test, and he had passed."

Kelvin passes many more tests as time goes on. He learns to make his own shelter, catch fish, make a spear, trap little animals that are like rabbits, and cook them. Also he explored the island and even drew a rough map on a big green leaf with a dry twig. Kelvin was feeling

Inconsistent verb tense

Rambling sentences

Forgetting purpose: not enough insights and too much summary.

confidant. Then a huge, unexpected surprise came. Kelvin discovered aliens on the planet! They were living in the tops of the trees and they were watching Kelvin the whole time. They wanted to see if he would survive. Now that he did, they welcome him into their group, and here Kelvin faces a struggle that's even harder: fitting in with creatures who are not even his speces (they look almost human, but smaller, so Kelvin is the size of an adult).

It turns out that the aliens are not very good with technology, and they have been watching Kelvin to see how he made things out of raw materials. They figure that if he can do all that by himself, he would be able to lead them in inventing new tools. Sure enough, Kelvin is able to do it. However, he has an enemy, one of the members of the tribe, Fl'in'kaff, who is jealous of him. They have a fight, and Kelvin wins but he lets Fl'in'kaff go free instead of enslaving him, and so Kelvin teaches the tribe a better way of behaving.

It's amazing how much Kelvin changes over one year in the book, but it's all believable because you think that if you were in his shoes you might do the same things. This book shows that when people are in a dangerous sitation they can become heroes. Maybe you won't become the leader of an alien planet but you can do anything here on Earth if you try!

RESPONSE

Writing that fits a score of 2 is strong in some ways.

Strong focus statement

Middle is not organized.

Ending is too short.

Brodie

Brodie is the name of the dog that Habib finds in this book. The book's name is also <u>Brodie</u>. Brodie is injured when Habib finds him. Taking care of Brodie helps Habib understand that everyone needs someone and that everyone can help someone else.

The way he finds the dog is, Habib has been running away from a buly. The buly was making fun of Habib and saying he was going to beat him up. Habib doesn't like to fight. He hid behind a big rock in the park. Suddenly he heard wimpering behind him. It was Brodie. Habib caries him home and bandages his paw. Habib and Brodie become good friends and meanwhile he had to put up a poster saying he found a lost dog. No one answerred the poster, and secritly Habib was glad because he didn't want to lose Brodie. He understands now that him and Brodie are taking care of each other. It teaches Habib a lot of things. He isn't afraid of the buly anymore because he has a big dog to protect him—with a fixed paw, ha ha! Most of all Habib feels good because he has helped Brodie. Habib used to be lonely but now he isn't anymore. Because if you help someone else you're not lonely anymore.

I liked this book a lot. I made me feel like I could help someone too.

Writing that fits a score of 1 is weak.

No focus statement or organization.

Little use of transitions.

Many errors in conventions.

All plot summary, no insight or sense of purpose.

"The Mystery of the Stolen Statue"

This book is a mystery story. It's about these two kids, boy and girl named Hao and Aurora, who solve crimes. I didn't think they were such grate crimes but it was a good book.

First someone dicscovers the statue in the middle of town is missing. No sine of it anywere. Police don't have a clue. Who would want to steel the statue. It wasn't worth anything besides how could they carry it. They look for a wile and don't find anything. Hao & Aurora see something unusaul. They find a code message. It fell out of the trash can when the garbage truck came and picked up the trash in the park next to where the statue was. They have been studying about codes and they re-read the books they have been reading about it. The message was instructions on how to steel the statue and where to put it.

Hao and Aurora go there but the criminals ty them up. They get away by rubbing the rope against a place on the statue where it chipped off so its sharp. They show a chip from the statue to Prof Wilkins who sees its the rigt kind of rock they realy did find it. Police go to the cave and arest the robers. They robed it becase there was trsaure in it.

So the trasure gos to the city and the kids solved the case. I liked this book because it was exiting.

Evaluating and Reflecting on Your Writing

You've put a lot of time and effort into your book review. Now take some time to score and think about your writing. On your own paper, finish each sentence starter below. To score your writing, refer to the scoring rubric on pages **48–49** and the examples you just read.

My Book Review

1. The best score for my book review is . . .

2. It's the best score because . . .

3. The best part of my book review is . . .

4. The part that still needs work is . . .

5. The main thing I learned about writing a book review is . . .

Responding to Texts

Response to a Magazine Article

If humans have eleven bones in their necks, how many neck bones do you think giraffes have? The answer is eleven! Are you surprised?

Do you enjoy finding out interesting facts? Perhaps you like to read about outer space or sports. Expository writing is writing that explains facts or ideas. You find this kind of writing in articles and magazines. A response to expository writing is different from a response to a story. This type of response highlights important facts or information contained in the article.

On the next page, you will read a sample paragraph that responds to an article. Then you will write a response paragraph of your own.

Writing Guidelines

Subject:	**Information in a magazine article**
Purpose:	**To respond to an article**
Form:	**Response paragraph**
Audience:	**Classmates**

 **TEKS** 6.17C

Response to a Magazine Article

When you respond to an article, you provide evidence from the text to demonstrate your understanding of the material. In this student sample, the writer has just read an article about butterflies that fly thousands of miles each fall. The notes will help you understand this type of writing.

The Magic of Butterflies

The **beginning** tells what the article is about in an interesting way.

Like me, you may see orange and black butterflies during the summer. But when summer is over, they're gone! According to scientists in the article "Where do the Butterflies Go?," the monarch butterflies migrate, or fly, to a warmer region to spend the winter. Many monarchs travel all the way to central Mexico! The article goes on to say that these migrating monarchs will also fly back to the same place.

The **middle** gives facts that support the understanding of the subject.

Scientists think the butterflies "travel by instinct", since none has ever made the trip before. Monarchs are especially interesting because it is only "the fourth generation in a year" that makes the migration. So the monarchs that go to Mexico are the great, great grandchildren of the previous generation that made the same trip last year.

TEKS 6.17C
ELPS 3E, 3G, 4I, 4J, 4K

I was amazed to find out that the fourth generation has the longest life span of all the others. The first three generations complete their life cycles within three months. The butterfly from the first generation dies after laying eggs for the second generation. This continues until the fourth generation. It's only the last generation that lives up to eight months. This allows the butterflies to make the migration and start the process all over again.

So how do the monarchs know where to go? Are they "programmed"? I guess it is another one of nature's great mysteries.

The **ending** refers back to the controlling idea.

Respond to the reading. Answer the following questions about these traits in the repsonse. Discuss your answers with a partner.

☐ **Focus and Coherence** (1) What is the controlling idea of the response?

☐ **Organization** (2) Does the writer use time order, order of importance, or order of location?

☐ **Voice** (3) Is the writer knowledgeable about the topic? (4) What words or phrases show the writer's personality?

RESPONSE

 **TEKS** 6.14A, 6.17C

Prewriting **Selecting an Article**

Determine your topic by selecting an article from a newspaper or magazine you would like to write about. Think about the reasons you find the article interesting. Think of the facts you learned. What ideas did you think about as you read the article? Choose an article that leaves you with a lot to say.

If you have trouble choosing an article, you may want to visit the library. Search the magazines and find an interesting article. A helpful strategy is to make a list of articles you have read, and choose the best one.

List

> "The Big Cattle Drive"   ✱ "Where do the Butterflies Go?"
>
> "The Politics of Bees"

List articles that you have read. Make a list of articles that you've enjoyed and would like to write about. Put a star (✱) next to the one that you liked the most.

Selecting Evidence

Think about the article you have chosen. Consider the facts from the article that demonstrate your understanding of the subject matter.

Select evidence. On your own paper, make a chart like the one below. Name the article, its main idea, and list evidence from the article.

Evidence Chart

> Name of article: "Where do the Butterflies Go?"
>
> Main idea: Monarch butterflies seem "programmed" to fly south to Mexico without every having been there before.
>
> Evidence: Author states, "A new generation (different from the previous one) flies south each year."

evaluate *PREVIEW* experience
react answer
343

TEKS 6.14B, 6.17C
ELPS 3D, 3E, 3H, 5G

Response to a Magazine Article

Drafting **Creating Your First Draft**

You will develop a draft that builds on ideas to create a focused, organized, and coherent piece of writing. Consider the following points as you begin to write.

- **Focus on the main or controlling idea of the article.**
  What is this article about?

- **Find evidence in the text that supports the main idea.**
  What details support the main idea of the article?

- **Respond to the text.**
  What facts and details will you select to show your understanding and insight of the article?

 Read the following part of an article. Write a short response to this article. Afterward, share your results with a classmate.

1	In Ancient Egypt, people melted and shaped silver into tiny
2	bars. The bars were stamped with their weight and used as
3	money. In Ancient Greece, coins were pieces of metal that had
4	pictures or designs on them. The use of coins spread to many
5	lands. They came in many shapes, but most were round. They
6	were decorated with pictures of leaders or symbols. Metal money
7	was popular because it was easy to carry and it didn't wear out.
8	But in ancient China, there wasn't enough metal for making
9	coins. To solve the problem, the Chinese invented paper money!

 Write your response. After selecting an article and gathering evidence, write a response to the article discussing your insights. Use the points at the top of this page to guide your writing. (Also review the sample response on pages 340 and 341.)

 **TEKS** 6.14E, 6.20C
ELPS 3D, 3E, 4!

Revising **Improving Your Writing**

After you finish the first draft of your response, you need to revise for the following traits.

- ☐ **Focus and Coherence** Have I presented a clear focus statement?
- ☐ **Organization** Have I arranged the information in an appropriate order?
- ☐ **Development of Ideas** Do I include evidence that supports my understanding of what I've read?
- ☐ **Voice** Do I sound interested and knowledgeable about what I read in the article?

 Review your writing. Ask yourself the questions above as you revise your response. Have a teacher and a classmate read it too. Revise according to the feedback you receive from them.

Editing **Checking for Conventions**

When you edit your draft, focus your attention on the conventions of writing.

- ☐ **Conventions** Do I use proper mechanics of italics and underlining for book titles and quotation marks for short stories or articles? Have I checked grammar, punctuation, capitalization, sentence structure, and spelling?

 Edit your work. Ask yourself the questions above to help you edit your response. Also check the "Proofreader's Guide" for additional editing help.

Publishing **Sharing Your Writing**

Once you've finished your response to a magazine article, it's time to share it with your classmates.

 Write your final copy. Create a final copy of your response. Proofread this copy carefully before sharing it with others.

Responding to Texts
Across the Curriculum

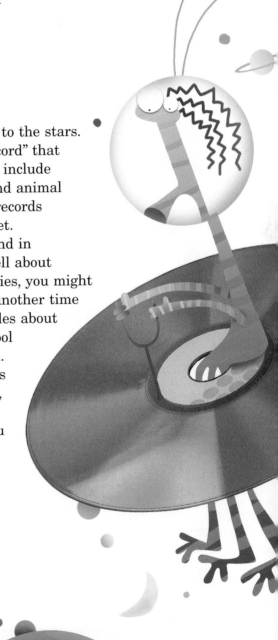

In 1977, Earth sent two ambassadors to the stars. *Voyager 1* and *2* each carried a "golden record" that contained sounds from Earth. The records include greetings in 55 languages, whale songs, and animal calls. Any space travelers who find these records could learn about life in 1977 on our planet.

Literature and expository writing found in magazines is also a golden record. They tell about events long ago or far away. In social studies, you might read a biography about a person's life in another time and place. In science, you could read articles about distant worlds. Even a poster in your school hallway can open up new horizons for you.

After working with the different forms of response writing in the following pages, you will be able to practice responding to a timed test prompt and analyze what you have learned.

What's Ahead

- **Social Studies:** Reviewing a Biography
- **Science:** Summarizing an Article
- **Practical Writing:** Writing a Blog Entry

Social Studies:
Reviewing a Biography

Social studies explores the way people have lived in different places and at different times. A good biography can teach you about both.

In his social studies class, Josh read a biography about brave men and women fighting for freedom in South Africa.

The beginning names the book and author.

The middle presents evidence from the book to support his opinion.

The ending tells about the importance of the book and the person's life.

Freedom Fighters

Hear Our Voices, by Ali Tungi, tells about the brave men and women who fought to end South Africa's cruel system of "apartheid." As the name suggests, apartheid kept blacks separate from whites. This racial discrimination made it hard for black Africans to get good educations, jobs, or housing.

Hear Our Voices focuses on the life and work of one man who fought tirelessly with others to win equal rights. The book starts with a description of Kali's life as a child in a segregated community and chronicles the injustices he and his family faced daily. It shows how the early events of Kali's life led to his belief in justice and his fight to win freedom for himself and others like him.

Kali was rounded up by police and arrested many time for protests he helped organize. He spent months at a time in jail, but never gave up his fight. Finally in 1994, apartheid came to an end and Kali and others voted in their first free election. They voted for Nelson Mandela who became South Africa's first black president.

This biography was very inspiring to read. It shows how important it is for people never to stop fighting injustice. It shows how average people can have a voice in changing the world.

TEKS 6.17C

Writing Tips

When you write a response to a biography, consider these tips.

Before you write . . .

- **Imagine being the person in this biography.**
  Think about what it must have been like to live in another time and place.
- **Think about why this person's life is important.**
  Ask yourself how the person's actions changed society, both in the past and in the present.

Cluster

Detail   Detail

Person

Detail   Detail

During your writing . . .

- **Provide evidence that demonstrates your understanding.**
  Choose events from the person's life that contribute to understanding what he or she stands for.
- **Share interesting details.**
  Select details that show what the person was really like.

After you've written a first draft . . .

- **Revise for ideas, organization, and voice.**
  Make sure the details are well organized and that your voice is formal enough.
- **Double-check important facts.**
  Make sure that the names and dates are correct.
- **Edit and proofread.**
  Check your review for punctuation, capitalization, spelling, and grammar. Then make a final copy of your work and proofread it for errors.

 Try It Search the classroom, the library, or the Internet for a biography that interests you. Then read the biography and write a review of it using the tips above as a guide.

TEKS 6.17C

Science: Summarizing an Article

A summary paragraph captures the main idea of a longer piece of writing. The student's response to the article provides evidence from the text to demonstrate his understanding of the information in the article.

Is There Life on Europa?

Scientists are planning to send a probe to one of Jupiter's moons to look for signs of life. The first inkling that the moon Europa might have life came in 1997 when the *Galileo* space probe flew past and photographed its frozen surface. The photographs revealed a possible sea under the ice and showed volcanic activity. Scientists theorize that where there is liquid water and a source of heat, life could exist.

Ironically, the very space probe that discovered the possibility of life on Europa became a threat to further missions. By 2003, the *Galileo* space probe was losing power. If it had accidentally crashed on Europa, it could have spread micro-organisms from Earth on the world. Then, if later probes found life, scientists wouldn't know whether the life originated on Earth. Instead of possibly "contaminating" Europa with terrestrial life forms, NASA scientists decided to steer *Galileo* into Jupiter, where it burned up.

If life does exist on Europa, it may be bacterial, such as life forms found in geothermal pools in Yellowstone. On the other hand, scientists have discovered six-foot-long tube worms living beside volcanic vents at the bottom of Earth's oceans. Perhaps larger life forms such as those could exist on Europa.

A NASA probe will be sent to Europa 2015. Until then, scientists will have to wait to find out whether Jupiter's satellite contains extraterrestrial life.

The writer states the controlling idea of the article.

The writer gives evidence from the article.

The writer revisits the controlling idea.

Extraterrestrial Life?

In 1997, the <u>Galileo</u> space probe discovered that one of Jupiter's moons could have life on it. The moon was Europa, and photos taken from <u>Galileo</u> showed that under the moon's frozen surface there may be a sea and volcanoes. Scientists believe that life might exist where there is liquid water and heat. If life does exist, it could be as small as bacteria or as large as a tubeworm. NASA wants to send another probe to find out if Europa has life. Unfortunately, they'll have to wait until 2015. Until then, we just have to wonder: Does extraterrestrial life exist?

Writing Tips

Before you write . . .

- **Read and reread.**
  Read the article to get a sense of its controlling idea. Then reread the article, focusing on details.
- **Mark up the article and make notes.**
  Ask yourself, "What is the controlling idea of this article?" Write it down in a single sentence. Then underline important details that support the controlling idea.
- **Plan your paragraph.**
  Write a topic sentence that sums up the main idea of the article. Consider which facts you will use in the middle. Finally, decide on an interesting closing sentence.

During your writing . . .

- **Be brief.**
  Write a summary that is a third the size of the original—or even smaller. Focus on the controlling idea of the article and provide evidence that demonstrates your understanding of it. This will help your readers understand it.
- **Paraphrase the information.**
  Put details from the article into your own words. Avoid copying phrases and sentences from the original source.

After you've written a first draft . . .

- **Revise your paragraph.**
  Ask yourself whether you have summed up the controlling idea and provided the most important details as evidence. Revise parts that are incomplete or unclear.
- **Check your paragraph for correctness.**
  Make sure there are no mistakes in grammar, punctuation, capitalization, sentence structure and spelling.

Try IT Look for a science-related article in a newspaper or magazine, or use the article that your teacher hands out to you. Follow the tips above as you write a paragraph that summarizes the article.

RESPONSE

Practical Writing: Writing a Blog Entry

Blogs allow you to write about your life and share experiences online. In this blog entry, the writer tells about an interesting web article. She uses evidence taken straight from the article to explain her point of view.

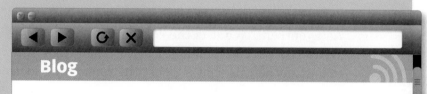

Blog

The writer introduces the topic of the entry.

To Sail Among Stars . . .
Posted on October 6, 2011, by Jani

What goes up like a rocket and comes down like a plane? The Space Shuttle! I just read an amazing article about how astronauts live aboard the Space Shuttle. Did you know that the word astronaut means "star sailor"? I think that's a perfect name to describe someone who sails into space and visits faraway stars.

The writer shares interesting details and evidence.

I've always wondered about a life aboard the space shuttle. Did you know that astronauts wear ordinary clothes and eat ordinary food, like sandwiches. Some foods come sealed in pouches, like nuts or cookies. Other food comes in dehydrated forms. The astronauts have to mix in water to make them edible.

Astronauts have to keep the inside of the Shuttle very clean so no one catches germs. They change their socks and underwear every two days. They take "sponge showers." It's important that astronauts exercise so their muscles stay strong in low-gravity conditions.

When they're not working, astronauts read books, write, or play games. When it's time for sleep, they either "free float" or strap themselves in to special berths.

The writer personalizes the details of the article by imagining being up in space, too.

If I lived on the Shuttle, I know how I'd spend my time. I'd look out the window and "star gaze." Then I'd tell my friends what I see. The question is: Would my cell phone work from outer space?

TEKS 6.17C
ELPS 3D, 3E, 3H, 3G

Writing Tips

Use the following tips to guide you to write a blog entry.

Before you write . . .

- **Choose a place to post.**
  If you don't have your own blog, find a class or school blog. Make sure your teacher and parents say it's okay to post.
- **Select a topic.**
  Think of an interesting event or article you've read.

During your writing . . .

- **Convey your ideas.**
  Tell how you feel about what the article says.
- **Include important information.**
  Select details and information you find interesting. Your readers will probably find them interesting too.
- **Use a friendly voice.**
  Show your interest in your topic and your readers. Blogs are informal writing.
- **Add a catchy title.**
  Create a title that will grab your readers' attention.
- **Demonstrate a sense of closure.**
  Don't end abruptly. Lead up to your closing and give a final thought. It can be humorous or serious.

After you've written your first draft . . .

- **Edit for correctness.**
  Read your whole entry and correct all errors in conventions.

 Find or create a blog you are interested in. Write a response using the tips as a guide. Share your ideas and blog with your class.

RESPONSE

imagine

entertain

Creative Writing

Writing Focus

- Stories
- Poems

Learning Language

Work with a partner. Read the meanings and share answers to the questions.

1. People who work together cooperate with each other.
   What do you do at home to cooperate with family members?

2. A flashback is a part of a story that tells about an event that happened before the story's beginning.
   If you wrote a flashback of your day, what would it include?

3. Something believable seems true. Something unbelievable does not.
   Name one believable thing and one unbelievable thing about you.

show

create

discover

Creative Writing

Writing Stories

People have always told stories. Early on, they gathered around campfires and spoke of heroes and heroines, kings and queens, beasts and battles. Over time, people began writing their stories down, acting them out, and producing them for the screen. Stories entertain us, and they teach us about life.

Almost all stories include the same elements: a clearly defined focus, plot and point of view; a specific believable setting created through the use of sensory details; and dialogue that develops the story. The many stories you have heard, read, or written, contain these elements and they should be part of your own thinking. As a result, writing a story will come naturally to you.

In this chapter, you will read a sample story about the future and then develop a story of your own to share.

Writing Guidelines

Subject:	**Future event**
Purpose:	**To entertain**
Form:	**Short story**
Audience:	**Classmates**

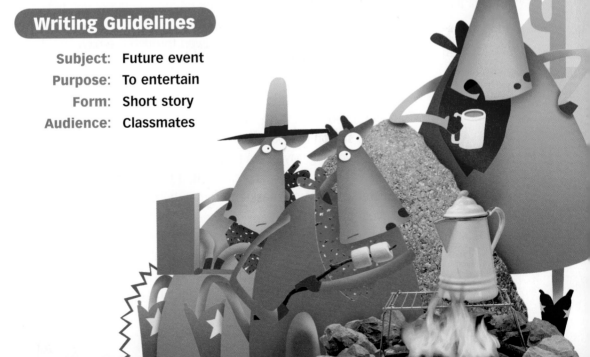

 **TEKS** 6.15A(i)

Short Story

In many stories, events change the main character in some way. The character may learn something new, gain a friend, achieve a goal, or lose a prized possession. The way a character faces a problem or challenge is what makes a story interesting, and defines the focus and plot.

Imagine an important event or challenge that you might face in the future. In the story below, Sarah imagined her journey up the slopes of Mount Everest and the problems she faced. The side notes identify the different parts of the story.

Journey to the Top of the World

Beginning

The beginning introduces the main characters, the setting, and clearly defines the focus of the story.

I opened my eyes and stared up at the orange roof of my tent. The world was silent. What a wonderful sound! All night, winds had whistled and snow had pounded the tent walls. At last, the storm was over. Today I could head up from Camp 5 to the summit of Mount Everest, achieving my long-awaited dream.

After dressing in my gear and eating an energy bar, I came out of my tent. The sun shone brightly, and wind had carried away much of the snow. Even through the oxygen mask I wore, I could feel the cold, biting air.

"Ready for the climb?" asked Kami, our guide. She stood with the other team members near their tents.

I replied, "I've been ready since fifth grade."

We slid on our backpacks, grabbed our ice axes, and started climbing. My boots bit into the snow, and I paused with each step. Even going slow, I had to fight for breath. I adjusted my oxygen mask and remembered the first time I'd worn one of these.

Rising Action

The rising action adds a conflict, increases the suspense, and moves along the defined plot.

Just after turning 11, I had my first serious asthma attack. My parents took me to the hospital, and the doctor gave me oxygen and bitter medicine. That night, I saw a National Geographic special about climbing Mount Everest.

TEKS 6.15A(i)
ELPS 3E, 3G

CREATIVE

A flashback with background details can help keep the plot clear and defined.

The people in the show were short of breath and wore oxygen masks just like me. I decided that someday I would climb Mount Everest. Today that dream would come true.

I looked up the trail. The peak looked so high and black, it made me dizzy. My legs felt like lead. Worst of all, my throat started to tighten up. I stopped walking and dropped to my knees. I couldn't breathe.

"Are you okay?" asked Kami, checking my oxygen mask. "Do you need to go back?"

I shook my head and closed my eyes. Just as I had learned to do in fifth grade, I calmed my heart and relaxed my throat. It took a minute, but I slowly got my throat to open again. "I'll be fine," I gasped.

High Point

At the high point in this story, the main character succeeds.

I stood up and began to walk. My feet soon fell into a regular pace, and my breathing did, too. One step at a time, I would make it to the top.

Just after 1:00 p.m., I stood at the top of the world. The sun couldn't fight off the bitter cold, but my heart burned with joy. The mountains all around me seemed small next to Everest.

Ending

The ending tells how the main character has changed.

Suddenly I knew I could do anything I set my mind to doing. I silently thanked my fifth-grade self for that long-ago decision. That's really when this amazing journey up the mountain began.

Respond to the reading. Review the story and answer the following questions. Discuss your answers with a partner.

☐ **Development of Ideas** **(1) How does Sarah make the idea clear that climbing Mount Everest is very important to her? (2) What details make her climb believable?**

☐ **Organization** **(3) Explain why the first paragraph logically leads to the second paragraph.**

☐ **Voice** **(4) How does the writer use voice and words to show the main character's mood change?**

Prewriting **Selecting a Topic**

It's fun to think about the things you might do in the future. Sarah planned her first draft by using the freewriting strategy to dream about her future. She kept writing until she determined an appropriate topic for her story. Sarah then developed a focus and started to define her plot.

Freewriting

I'm supposed to think about a future event. Well, if I became a vet, maybe I could work with animals. Or maybe I could be a forest ranger and help save spotted owls. I hope I'm not allergic to spotted owls. My allergies have been awful since that asthma attack last year. That's when I decided I wanted to climb Mount Everest. That might make a cool story. I can focus my story on what it would be like to climb up and how hard it would be. It would be amazing to reach the top. How would that feel? What would happen? This is what I will write about...

Prewrite

Freewrite to select a topic. Use freewriting or another strategy to explore events in your future. Write until you discover an appropriate topic and controlling idea. As you write, think about giving your story a clearly defined focus and plot.

Texas Traits

Focus on the Texas Traits

Organization

The plot should be organized so that each action leads logically to the next. Each action should be "built" on the one before it. Each part of the plot should be clearly defined.

PLOT LINE	High Point
Rising Action	
Beginning	Ending

- The **beginning** introduces the characters and setting.
- The **rising action** adds a conflict—a problem for the characters.
- The **high point** is the most exciting part.
- The **ending** tells how the main character has changed.

TEKS 6.15A(i), 6.15A(iii)
ELPS 21, 3E, 3H

CREATIVE

Creating a Point of View

Sarah thought about what it would be like to climb Mount Everest. She had her plot, but who should tell the story? Another character? A narrator? A narrator would speak in third person using pronouns like *he, she,* and *they.* In the first-person, Sarah would use pronouns like *I, me,* and *we.* She decided that telling her story in first person would have more impact. (For more information about point of view, see pages **362–364**).

> *I opened my eyes and stared up at the roof of my tent. Today I could head up from Camp 5 to the summit of Mount Everest.*

Create a point of view. Practice writing and rewriting sample sentences from your story in first person or third person. Determine from what point of view your story will be told. Be consistent in the point of view from sentence to sentence.

Using Dialogue

The words that characters speak to each other are dialogue. Dialogue helps to develop a story. Sarah wrote the following dialogue between herself and another character.

> *I was at the base of the mountain and it was time to start our climb.*
> *"Are you ready for breakfast before we start?" asked Jim.*
> *"I'm starved," I said.*
> *"We'll have to eat fast," said Jim. "We want to get an early start."*

Use dialogue. Think about the characters in your story. What will they say? How does this help move the story along? Write several lines of dialogue between characters to develop your story. Practice speaking your dialogue with a partner to see if it sounds natural and realistic.

 TEKS 6.14B, 6.15A(i), 6.15A(ii)

Prewriting Creating a Plot

Before drafting, Sarah wanted the focus (climbing Mt. Everest) and plot (what happens) to be clear. Charting the events helped Sarah do this.

Plot Chart

Beginning	Rising Action	High Point	Ending
The story starts at the camp. I wake up and greet the team.	We start to climb. I remember why I want to do this: the bad asthma attack in fifth grade.	Suddenly I can't breathe! The guide checks my oxygen. I calm myself and keep going.	Victory! I know I can do anything I set my mind to doing.

 Create a plot chart. Make a plot chart like the one above. Organize the events in your plot from the beginning to the end. Check that your events move your plot along and build upon your focus.

Using Sensory Details to Create Setting

We all experience a place or setting through our five senses. The same is true in a story. Sarah decided to organize the sensory details of her setting before she wrote her first draft. She created the chart below to gather sensory details for her story. She thought of things that related to the setting of Mount Everest and categorized them by each sense.

Sensory Chart

See	Hear	Smell	Taste	Touch/Feel
orange tent, bright sun, tall mountain, rugged rock	whistling wind, snow hitting the tent	fresh air, oxygen mask	bitter medicine, energy bar	cold air, tight throat, spiky shoes, tired legs

 Organizing sensory details. Create a sensory chart like the one above for your story. Write down the things you would see, hear, smell, taste, and feel in the story's setting. Be specific with the images you choose.

TEKS 6.15A(ii)

CREATIVE

Create a Believable Setting

A story with a specific, well-described setting allows the reader to enter the world the characters live in. To make your setting believable and specific, use strong sensory details. Sarah wrote the following paragraph using sensory details to picture her setting.

> I woke up to the shrill whistling of the wind outside my tent. I threw on more clothes and pulled back the tent flap. Icy, arctic air hit my face like a sharp slap. I stepped out and gazed up at the tall mountain in the bright sun. The rich smell of coffee brewing wafted through the cold air. I pulled an energy bar from my pocket and bit in. It was sweet and tasty.

Prewrite

Create a believable setting. Write a paragraph like the one above. Build a picture of a setting of your choice by using sensory details. It may even help to draw a picture of your setting and think about the images that come to mind. Include at least one example of things you would see, hear, smell, taste, and feel.

Texas Traits

Focus on the Texas Traits

Development of Ideas

Paint a picture for the reader when you create your setting. Use the setting to help develop your story, making it as important to your plot as another character. Ask these questions when developing ideas around your setting.

- **Do I have sensory details that create an image for the reader?**
- **Can this story only happen in this setting?**
- **How does this setting impact the plot and the characters?**

 **TEKS** 6.14C, 6.15A(i), 6.15A(ii), 6.15A(iii)

Drafting Developing Your First Draft

You now have everything you need to begin writing your story. As you write, keep the following tips in mind.

1 Use sensory details to create your setting.

Instead of . . . **It was cold.**
    Write . . . My skin shivered from the icy cold.

2 Use dialogue to move the story along.

Instead of . . . **I said I would be fine, but it was hard to talk.**
    Write . . . "I'll be fine," I gasped.

3 Clearly define each action in the plot by showing what happens, not just telling about it.

Instead of . . . **I couldn't go on because of an asthma attack.**
    Write . . . I stopped walking and dropped to my knees. I couldn't breathe.

 Write your first draft. Use your plot chart and sensory chart as you write your first draft. Remember to describe your setting using sensory details. Use dialogue to move the story forward and show what happens in the plot rather than tell it. Enjoy writing your story!

Revising Improving Your Writing

Once you finish your first draft, set it aside. Later, check for all the traits. Make any revisions that will make your story better.

☐ **Development of Ideas** Do I develop ideas clearly in my story so the reader can understand?

☐ **Organization** Is the development of the plot clear from paragraph to paragraph? Do I add larger units of text to clarify the plot where they are needed?

 Revise your story. Use the questions above as a guide when you revise your draft. Remember to add text to clarify ideas in your writing.

CREATIVE

⭐ **TEKS** 6.14D, 6.14E
ELPS 3E, 4C

Editing Checking for Conventions

Once you have completed your revisions, it is time to edit your story for *conventions*.

☐ **Conventions** Have I corrected any errors in grammar, mechanics, sentence structure, and spelling? Have I included end punctuation for each sentence? Do I use quotation marks correctly when writing dialogue? Do I use specific nouns and verbs in the correct tense?

Edit your story. Use the questions above to guide your editing. Create a title using the tips below. Then write a final copy and proofread it.

Creating a Title

The title of your story should catch the reader's interest. Here are three strategies for writing story titles.

- ■ Use words from the story: **Journey to the Top of the World**
- ■ Use colorful words: **A Breathless Victory**
- ■ Be creative: **Conquering Asthma in the Himalayas**

Publishing Sharing Your Story

Here are three suggestions for sharing your story with others.

- ● **Hold a storytelling session.** Practice reading your story out loud. Then read it to others. Ask them to read their stories, too.

- ● **Act out your story.** Choose some friends to act out the story with you. Then present your skit to your class or family.

- ● **Post your story online.** Search for a Web page that accepts student writing and post your story there. Make sure to get permission from a parent or guardian before doing this.

Present your story. Choose one of the ideas above or make up your own. Then read your story aloud to a partner and listen when he or she reads.

TEKS 6.15A(i), 6.15A(ii), 6.15A(iii)

Fiction Elements

Imaginative stories should include a clear focus, plot, point of view, setting, and believable dialogue. Here are descriptions of each element.

Focus	The focus is the main idea of a story. Everything in the story should be focused on this idea.
Plot	The plot is the action that makes up the story. The plot should be clear as it moves forward from event to event. The events should logically lead from one to another. If a main character goes on a journey, the plot might be made up of obstacles the hero faces and how she overcomes each one.
Point of View	The point of view is the angle from which the story is told. If a character in the story is telling it, it is in first person. In third person, someone from outside the story is telling it.
	First person: **I was nervous when I arrived at the softball try-outs.**
	Third person: **She was nervous when she arrived at softball try-outs.**
Setting	The setting is the place and the time period in which a story takes place. Sensory details make the setting come alive for readers.
	The hospital room smelled of cleaning fluid and medicine.
Dialogue	Dialogue is the words spoken between two or more characters. Dialogue should help define who a character is and move the action of the story forward.
	"Where are you going?" John's father asked.
	"I don't know," John replied. "Just out."

 Look at an older piece of your own writing and search for the fiction elements in it. If any elements are missing, revise your writing.

TEKS 6.14A, 6.15A(i), 6.15A(iii)

CREATIVE

Glossary of Elements

The following list includes many terms used to describe the elements or parts of literature. This information will help you discuss and write about the novels, poetry, essays, and other literary works you read.

Action: Everything that happens in a story

Antagonist: The person or force that works against the hero of the story (See *protagonist.*)

Character: A person or an animal in a story

Characterization: The way in which a writer develops a character, making him or her seem believable

Here are three methods:

● Sharing the character's thoughts, actions, and dialogue

● Describing his or her appearance

● Revealing what others in the story think or say about this character

Conflict: A problem or clash between two forces in a story

There are five basic conflicts:

● **Person Against Person** A problem between characters

● **Person Against Himself or Herself** A problem within a character's own mind

● **Person Against Society** A problem between a character and society, the law, or some tradition

● **Person Against Nature** A problem with some element of nature, such as a blizzard or a hurricane

● **Person Against Destiny** A problem or struggle that appears to be beyond a character's control

Dialogue: The words spoken between two or more characters

Focus: The controlling idea of a story

Foil: The character who acts as a villain or challenges the main character

Mood: The feeling or emotion a piece of literature or writing creates in a reader

Moral: The lesson a story teaches

Narrator: The person or character who actually tells the story

Plot: The action that makes up the story, following a plan called the plot line

Plot Line: The planned action or series of events in a story (The basic parts of the plot line are the beginning, the rising action, the high point, and the ending.)

PLOT LINE — High Point — Rising Action — Beginning — Ending

● The **beginning** introduces the characters and the setting.

● The **rising action** adds a conflict—a problem for the characters.

● The **high point** is the moment when the conflict is strongest.

● The **ending** tells how the main characters have changed.

TEKS 6.15A(i), 6.15A(ii)
ELPS 3E, 3G

Point of View: The angle from which a story is told (The angle depends upon the narrator, or person telling the story.)

- **First-Person Point of View**

  This means that one of the characters is telling the story: "We're just friends—that's all—but that means everything to us."

- **Third-Person Point of View**

  In third person, someone from outside the story is telling it: "They're just friends—that's all—but that means everything to them." There are three third-person points of view: *omniscient, limited omniscient,* and *camera view.* (See the illustrations on the right.)

Protagonist: The main character or hero in a story (See *antagonist.*)

Setting: The place and the time period in which a story takes place

Theme: The message about life or human nature that is "hidden" in the story that the writer tells

Tone: The writer's attitude toward his or her subject (can be described by words like *angry* and *humorous*)

Total Effect: The overall influence or impact that a story has on a reader

Third-Person Points of View

Omniscient point of view allows the narrator to tell the thoughts and feelings of all the characters.

Limited omniscient point of view allows the narrator to tell the thoughts and feelings of only one character at a time.

Camera view (objective view) allows the story's narrator to record the action from his or her own point of view without telling any of the characters' thoughts or feelings.

Look closely at the different points of view. Choose a short story you know well and rewrite from a different point of view. Be creative in telling the story from whole different perspective. Read and discuss with a partner.

Creative Writing

Writing Poems

Poets love words. They love the way words sound and the way they look on the page. They love the way words create pictures and unlock ideas. Today many poets write free-verse poems, which don't follow a regular pattern. With free-verse, writers can play with the sounds and arrangement of their words, as in the poem to the right.

In the following chapter, you will write a free-verse poem about an animal that you would like to be. You'll also find other types of poetry that you could try. The last pages of the chapter tell about special techniques you can use when writing poetry.

I stretch,
I stretch,
my ostrich
neck.
Crack!
Crack!
The kinks
are back!

Writing Guidelines

Subject:	An animal you would like to be
Purpose:	To entertain
Form:	Free-verse poem
Audience:	Classmates

TEKS 6.15B(iii)

Free-Verse Poem

Many free-verse poems contain sensory details. Sights, sounds, smells, and other sensations let the reader "experience" the topic of the poem. Graphic elements such as capital letters or varied line lengths can add interest and emphasis to a poem. Caleb Carter wrote the following poem about the life of a firehouse dog.

White Flame

People call me White Flame.
I ride on a wailing fire truck
    as it roars down crowded streets.
I leap off to sniff the smoky air
    and face the blazing flames.
I splash through the hose's spray
    and sit by the little gray girl
    and lick the salty tears
    from her sooty cheeks.

Respond to the reading. On your own paper, reflect on the ideas, organization, and voice of the free-verse poem.

☐ **Development of Ideas** **(1) List five details that refer to the senses.**

☐ **Organization** **(2) What words and letter sounds are repeated in this poem?**

☐ **Voice** **(3) Who is the speaker in the poem? (4) How does the writer's use of graphic elements affect your reading of the poem?**

Prewriting Selecting a Topic

Poets are inspired by all sorts of things. You will be writing a poem about an animal you would like to be. Caleb used a clustering strategy to determine an appropriate animal for the topic of his poem.

Cluster

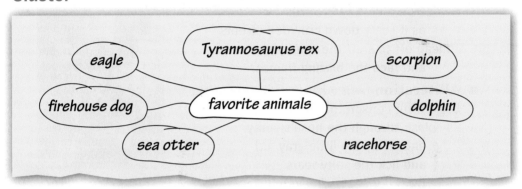

Create a cluster. Plan the first draft of your poem by organizing your idea for a topic using a cluster as Caleb has. Write "favorite animals" and cluster names of animals you would like to be. Choose your favorite.

Gathering Details

Sensory details are key to creating vivid images in the mind of the reader of a poem. They are a good way to organize the draft of your poem. Caleb created the following sensory chart to help him plan.

Sensory Chart

See	Hear	Smell	Taste	Touch
black/white	barking	dog breath	biscuit	hot fire
gray	siren wailing	people smells	salty tears	cold water
fire truck	splash	ash		spray
flames	crying	smoke		

Gather sensory details. Develop a draft of your poem by first creating a sensory chart like the one above. Organize your chart to include details about the animal and about the setting of your poem.

 TEKS 6.15B(i)
ELPS 3E, 3H, 5G

Prewriting **Using Poetry Techniques**

Poets play with the sounds of words. Two simple techniques will help you create poetic sounds as you write your free-verse poem.

- **Onomatopoeia** *(ŏn´ə-măt´ə-pē´ə)* is using words that sound like the noises they name.

    I ride on a wailing fire truck
       as it roars down crowded streets.
    I leap off to sniff the smoky air
       and face the blazing flames.

- **Alliteration** *(ə-lĭt´ə-rā´shən)* is repeating beginning consonant sounds.

    I splash through the hose's spray
       and sit by the little gray girl
       and lick the salty tears
       from her sooty cheeks.

 Use poetry techniques. Look back at your sensory chart. Circle any words that sound like the noise they name (onomatopoeia). Then underline words that start with the same consonant (alliteration). Add a few more of each kind of word. Share your findings with a partner.

Drafting **Developing Your First Draft**

Now that you have gathered sensory details and learned two poetry techniques, you are ready to write the first draft of a poem. Try these tips.

- **Imagine being the animal.** What things do you sense? What thoughts do you think? How do you feel about your world?
- **Tell your story.** What important things do you do? What will be happening in your poem? (Your animal should be doing something.)
- **Play with words.** Use poetic techniques to add interest. Think about fun ways you can use words, letters, and line lengths.

 Write your first draft. Create the first draft of your poem. Write as if you were the animal, telling about something that happens in your life. Use poetic techniques, like onomatopoeia or alliteration, to add interest to your poem. Read your poem to a classmate. Discuss the techniques.

TEKS 6.14D, 6.14E
ELPS 3E, 3G, 4K

CREATIVE

Revising Improving Your Poem

Exchange your first draft with a partner and think about these traits of writing as you make suggestions for revision.

- [ ] **Development of Ideas** Are the ideas in the poem developed clearly? Does each line add meaning to the one before it?

- [ ] **Organization** Does one thought lead to another?

- [ ] **Voice** Does my writing voice express how the animal thinks and feels? Do I use poetic techniques to show my individual voice?

Revise your writing. Make changes to improve your poem using the new feedback you have received from your partner. Continue working with your poem until you like the way it looks and sounds.

Editing Fine-Tuning Your Poem

Focus on the conventions of writing as you edit your poem.

- [ ] **Conventions** Is my grammar correct throughout? Have I used the mechanics of punctuation and capitalization correctly and effectively? Is my work free of spelling errors?

Edit your work. Edit your poem for grammar, mechanics, and spelling. Make a final copy of your poem and proofread it again for these errors.

Publishing Sharing Your Poem

Think of the best way to publish or share your poem with the appropriate audience.

- **Perform it.** Read the poem to your classmates or to your family.
- **Post it.** Display your poem where people can read it—on a bulletin board, on a Web site, or on your refrigerator.
- **Send it out.** Submit your work to a local or student newspaper.

Present your work. Choose one of the presentation suggestions above or come up with one of your own. Share your poem with the class.

 **TEKS** 6.15B(iii)

Writing Haiku

Another form of poetry is *haiku*. This type of Japanese poetry presents a picture of nature, so an animal makes a perfect topic. A haiku poem has certain graphic element requirements. It is three lines long. The first line has five syllables, the second has seven, and the third has five. Guess what animal is described in each of the following haiku poems.

Mud smears on pink skin—
soft grunts rumble from its snout—
it loves to wallow.

Guards all dressed in black,
patrolling from the treetops,
nod and caw commands.

Huge gray beasts lift their
ears and eyes and nostrils from
muddy waterways.

Spreading hood and fangs,
it slithers from the basket
to the charmer's tune.

Writing Tips

- **Select a topic.** Think of an interesting animal.
- **Gather details.** List things about the animal that you would see, hear, smell, or feel.
- **Follow the graphic elements pattern.** Make sure you use five syllables each in the first and last lines and seven in the middle line.

Create your haiku. Choose an animal and write your haiku poem. Make sure each line has the right number of syllables. Make sure to meet the graphic elements requirements.

TEKS 6.15B(i), 6.15B(ii), 6.15B(iii)

CREATIVE

Writing Other Forms of Poetry

Poems take many forms. Here are three other forms that work well for describing animals.

Limerick

A *limerick* is a humorous poem of five lines. Notice the graphic element of varying line lengths that is used: The first, second, and last lines rhyme with each other, as do the third and fourth. The first, second, and last lines have three accented syllables. The third and fourth have two.

> **A mon**key **named** Joe **plans to** save
> **His** money **to pur**chase a shave.
> **But** razors **can't** hack
> **All the** hair **on his** back,
> **And** barbers **in** town **aren't that** brave.

Name Poem

A *name poem* uses the letters in a name to begin each line, another graphic element. The repeated sound of /f/ shows alliteration.

> Feline
> Loudly
> Utters her
> Fierce but
> Funny-sounding
> Yowl

Phrase Poem

A *phrase poem* states an idea with a list of phrases. This phrase poem contains figurative language. Note the use of a simile in line three.

> Into the lake
> with a swoosh
> like falling rain
> over flapping wings
> across bright feathers

Draft

Write a poem. Choose one of the forms of poetry on this page to write. Use poetic techniques, figurative language, and graphic elements.

TEKS 6.15B(i), 6.15B(ii)

Using Special Poetry Techniques

On the next two pages, you will find a number of special poetic techniques and figurative language that poets use to develop poems.

Figurative Language

Poets use the following techniques to create strong images in their poems. These techniques are called *figures of speech*.

■ A **simile** *(sĭm´ə-lē)* compares two different things using the word *like* or *as*.

The branch curved like a claw.

■ A **metaphor** *(mĕt´ə-fôr)* compares two different things without using the word *like* or *as*.

Her eyes were flashlights in the dark.

■ **Personification** *(pər-sŏn´ə-fĭ-kā´shən)* gives human traits to something that is not human.

The leaves gossiped among themselves.

■ **Hyperbole** *(hī-pûr´bə-lē)* is an exaggeration.

My heart hit the floor.

Poetic Techniques

Poets use the following special techniques to add pleasing and interesting sounds to their poems. (Also see page 368.)

■ **Alliteration** *(ə-lĭt´ə-rā´shən)* is the repetition of beginning consonant sounds.

The kids rode a carousel of cartoon characters.

■ **Assonance** *(ăs´ə-nəns)* is the repetition of vowel sounds in words.

A green apple gleams at me from the tree.

 Try IT Write a simile or metaphor about a topic that interests you. Use the figurative language you just wrote to write a free-verse poem. Share your poem with a classmate.

TEKS 6.15B(i), 6.15B(ii)
ELPS 3E, 4I

- **End rhyme** *(ĕnd\\rīm)* is the use of rhyming words at the ends of two or more lines.

    My country, 'tis of thee,
    sweet land of liberty . . .

- **Internal rhyme** *(ĭn-tûr′nəl\\rīm)* is the use of rhyming words within a line of poetry.

    The smoke **could** choke **a chimney.**

- **Onomatopoeia** *(ŏn′ə-măt′ə-pē′ə)* is the use of words that sound like the noise they name.

    The crackling **bag** crumpled **in his fist.**

- **Repetition** *(rĕp′ĭ-tĭsh′ən)* is the use of the same word, idea, or phrase for rhythm or organization.

    We ran **above.**
    We ran **below.**
    We ran **where no one else would go.**

- **Rhythm** *(rĭth′əm)* is the way a poem flows from one idea to the next. In free-verse poetry, the rhythm follows the poet's natural voice. In traditional poetry, a regular rhythm is created. Notice how the poet William Blake accented certain syllables to create a regular rhythm.

    Tiger, Tiger, burning bright
    In **the** forests **of the** night, . . .

Write a poem. In your poem, write about an amazing animal. Include at least one example of figurative language, such as a simile, and use at least one special poetic technique. Share your poem with the class.

Draft

organize

NOTE

ELPS 2G, 3E, 4C, 4G

TEXAS
WRITE
SOURCE
Online
www.hmheducation.com/tx/writesource

Research Writing

Writing Focus

- **Research Report**
- **Oral Presentation**
- **Multimedia Presentation**

Grammar Focus

- **Subordinating Conjunctions**
- **Subject-Verb Agreement**
- **Parentheses, Brackets, and Ellipses**

Learning Language

Work with a partner. Read the meanings and share your answers to the prompts.

1. A source is a book, person, Web site, newspaper, or other thing that gives information.
   Name a source where you could find out about zebras.
2. Something that is consistent is the same all the time.
   Name something consistent in your daily routine.
3. Relevant ideas relate directly to the topic being discussed.
   In math class, what ideas are relevant to discuss?

summarize

RESEARCH

cite

Research Writing

Building Skills

Research is a form of exploration. It can take you to remote corners of the world or down to the depths of the ocean. By using the right tools and digging into your subject, you can discover amazing things.

Of course, the tools of your research probably won't include a mini-sub. Instead, you'll use tools such as a computer catalog, periodical guides, reference materials, and Internet searches. But once you know how to use these tools of research, you will be ready to explore your world.

What's Ahead

- **The Research Process**
- **Gathering Sources**
- **Researching on the Internet**
- **Using the Library**
- **Using Reference Materials**
- **Evaluating Sources**

 **TEKS** 6.22A, 6.22B, 6.23A–E
ELPS 2H, 3E, 3G

The Research Process

Follow these steps in the research process to create a focused, organized, informative report.

1 Create a Research Plan.

- Think of things that interest you. Brainstorm ideas and topics.
- Consult with others to ask for feedback on your topics. Use this information to decide what will be interesting to your audience.
- Think of a major research question to develop your controlling idea. Formulate open-ended questions to guide your research.
- Finally make a research plan for gathering useful information for your topic, such as how, when, and where you will find sources.

 Which is the better research question for the topic *Ancient Egypt?* Discuss your answer with a partner.

1. What are the reasons this ancient civilization thrived?
2. What was Ancient Egypt like?

2 Gather Sources.

- Collect information from a variety of sources. Use both print (books, periodicals, etc.) and electronic sources (Web sites). You can also interview an expert on your topic. Experts are reliable sources.
- Know the difference between primary and secondary sources.
- Using your sources, take careful, thorough notes on your topic. Look at charts, diagrams, and time lines for important data. Use a computer programming tool to help you map or outline the information from visual aids to your written notes.
- Make sure to identify the source of your information in your notes. Carefully record information to create a bibliography.
- Remember to paraphrase or quote your sources to avoid plagiarism.

 Suppose you are writing a report on Colonial America. Which experts would you consider reliable and valid? Explain.

1. A professor of American History from a local college.
2. A director at a "living museum" that employs people to recreate colonial times accurately.
3. A cashier at a store selling American memorabilia.

3 Synthesize Information.

- Bring all your research together to develop your controlling idea. Think about your major research question and review your notes. Ask yourself more specific, detailed questions about your topic to refine your major research question.
- Evaluate all of your sources. Which sources are related to your topic? Which sources can you trust? Which sources give true information? Use the most relevant, reliable, and valid sources.

 For each pair below, choose the best source that could be used.

1. Your friend's opinion about your topic
   An expert's opinion about your topic

2. An online source written by average people
   An official encyclopedia written by a trusted publisher

4 Organize and Present Your Ideas.

- Now you can synthesize your research into an organized written or oral presentation. Start by using the notes from your sources.
- Summarize and present your findings in a consistent format and style. Make sure your report sounds the same all the way through.
- Develop topic sentences for your paragraphs or presentation from the questions that helped to refine your major research question.
- Use evidence to support your topic sentences, ideas, and conclusions. In an oral presentation, you can use evidence to help you answer questions from the audience.
- Use quotations that stand out from your sources or experts to support your ideas. These will grab the audience's interest.
- In an oral presentation, present your findings so your audience can follow along. Use visual aids to help your audience understand.
- Always cite the sources of your research in the correct format to show that your information is reliable.

 If you were researching what happens on the space shuttle, which quote would be appropriate and relevant? Discuss with a partner.

a. "The space shuttle is costing taxpayers too much money."
   -- quote from member of Congress

b. "We took breaks from work to exercise and play games."
   -- quote from astronaut who had lived on the space shuttle

 TEKS 6.23A, 6.23B

Gathering Sources

When you gather your sources, follow your research plan to collect data from a varied range of print and electronic sources, or from authors and experts themselves. As you gather sources, you should know the difference between primary and secondary sources.

Primary sources of information are original sources. They give you firsthand information. You're working with a primary source when you visit a place to learn about your topic, ask experts questions about your subject, or conduct a survey or experiment.

Secondary sources contain information that has been gathered by someone else. Most nonfiction books, newspapers, magazines, and Web sites are secondary sources of information. You're working with secondary sources when you read a magazine article about your subject, check out a reference book or visit a Web site.

Primary Sources

1
Visiting a
health-food store

2
Interviewing
a vegetarian

3
Cooking a
vegetarian meal

Secondary Sources

1
Article about
vegetarians

2
Encyclopedia entry
on vegetarian diets

3
TV documentary
about vegetarians

 Decide whether each of the following is a primary or a secondary source of information.

A Web-site review of a vegetarian cookbook

A taste test of vegetarian foods

What other resources can you imagine for this topic? Think of one more primary or secondary source about vegetarianism.

Types of Primary Sources

Primary sources of information provide you with firsthand details. Review the following list of primary sources.

Diaries, Journals, and Letters

Reading the diaries, journals, and letters of other people (especially historical figures) is an interesting way to gather information. You can find this sort of information in libraries and museums. If you used an article about them, the article would be a secondary source.

Presentations

Visiting historical sites or museums can provide you with firsthand information. You can also listen to guest speakers or see demonstrations.

Interviews

In an interview, you can talk with someone who is an expert on your subject. You can conduct the interview in person, over the phone, by e-mail, or through the mail. If you saw an interview in a documentary on television, that would be considered a secondary source.

Surveys and Questionnaires

You can also use a survey or questionnaire to gather firsthand information. Begin by making a list of the questions you would like answered. Then give copies of your questions to people who can answer them. Collect the completed surveys or questionnaires and study the results. An article in your school paper about a survey would be a secondary source.

Observation and Participation

Observing people, places, and things is one method of gathering information. Taking part in an event also supplies firsthand details. For example, to research ethnic foods, be sure to taste some yourself.

 Gather information by observing students in your cafeteria. During lunch, make note of what is served and what students select and eat. Also make note of what they avoid. If possible, use this method of research when you do a research report. Would this be a primary or secondary source? Explain.

TEKS 6.23A
ELPS 3E

Researching on the Internet

The Internet allows people all around the world to publish information, making it a great place to do research. Following your research plan, you should collect data from multiple sources found on the Internet.

> Since information on the Internet comes from a variety of people and places, you need to evaluate each source carefully to be sure it is valid and reliable.

Points to Remember

- **Use the Web carefully.** Look for sites that have *.edu,* or *.gov* in the address. These are educational or government Web sites and offer reliable information. Use *.org* addresses with caution. Depending on the organization, these sites may be unreliable. If you are unsure sure about a site, check with your teacher.

- **Use a search site.** Search engines are like computer catalogs for the Internet. You can enter keywords to find Web pages about your subject. Use only trusted search engines or Web sites.

- **Look for links.** Often, a Web page includes links to other pages dealing with your topic. Take advantage of these links.

- **Be patient.** The Web is huge and searches can get complicated. New pages are added all the time, and old ones may change addresses or even disappear completely.

- **Know your school's Internet policy.** To avoid trouble, be sure to follow your school's Internet policy. Also follow whatever guidelines your parents may have set up for you.

 Search the Internet for information about space exploration. Collect data from a range of sources by checking at least three different Web sites. Write down three facts from three different sources, then share what you found with a partner.

TEKS 6.23A
ELPS 3E

NOTE *RESEARCH*
organize summarize *cite*

381

Building Skills

RESEARCH

Using the Library

Libraries provide a variety of resources for people seeking information, including books, periodicals, CD's, and much more.

1 **Books** are usually divided into three sections.

- The **fiction** section includes stories and novels. These books are arranged in alphabetical order by the authors' last names.

- The **nonfiction** section contains books that are based on fact. They are arranged according to the Dewey decimal system.

- The **reference** section has encyclopedias, atlases, dictionaries, directories, and almanacs.

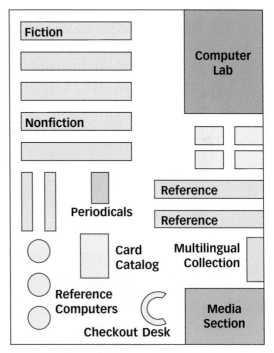

2 The periodicals section includes magazines and newspapers.

3 The computer lab has computers, often connected to the Internet. You usually sign up to use a computer.

4 The media section includes music CD's, cassettes, DVD's, videotapes, and CD-ROM's. Computer software (encyclopedias, games, and so on) may be found in this section as well.

Try It Visit your school library and look around. Notice where each of the above areas is located. Then draw a map of the library and label each area. Discuss your findings with a partner.

TEKS 6.23A
ELPS 3E, 3G, 4C

Searching a Computer Catalog

Searching a computer catalog for sources is an important step in the research process. The first time you use a particular computer catalog, check the instructions for using it or ask a librarian for help. With a computer catalog, you can find information on the same book in three ways:

1 If you know the book's **title**, enter the title.

2 If you know the book's **author**, enter the author's name. (When the library has more than one book by the same author, there will be more than one entry.)

3 Finally, if you know only the **subject** you want to learn about, enter either the subject or a keyword. (A *keyword* is a word or phrase that is related to the subject.)

If your subject is . . .	**your keywords might be . . .**
ethnic cooking in the United States,	Mexican meals, southwestern cooking, or Native American recipes.

Computer Catalog Screen

Author:	Hunt, Deborah
Title:	Cooking of the American Southwest
Published:	Sunlight Publishing, 2010
Subjects:	Southwestern Cooking Spanish, Mexican, Anglo, and Native American recipes

STATUS:	CALL NUMBER:
Available	641.6987D

LOCATION:
General collection

Try IT Make a plan to research cooking. When in your plan would you use a computer catalog? How? Practice with a partner.

Finding Books

Once you've searched for books, you then have to find them. Each catalog entry for a book includes a **call number**. Use the call number to help you to find the book you are looking for. Most libraries use the Dewey decimal system to arrange books. Here, the nonfiction books are in 10 categories.

000-099	**General Works**	500-599	**Sciences**
100-199	**Philosophy**	600-699	**Technology**
200-299	**Religion**	700-799	**Arts and Recreation**
300-399	**Social Sciences**	800-899	**Literature**
400-499	**Languages**	900-999	**History and Geography**

Using Call Numbers

A call number often has a decimal in it, followed by the first letters of an author's name. (See the illustration below.) Look first for the number when searching for a book, and then for the alphabetized letters.

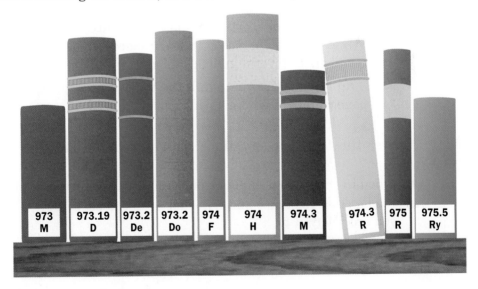

| 973 M | 973.19 D | 973.2 De | 973.2 Do | 974 F | 974 H | 974.3 M | 974.3 R | 975 R | 975.5 Ry |

Find the title of your favorite book in the computer or card catalog of your library. Write down the call number and see if you can find the book on the shelves.

Understanding the Parts of a Book

Understanding the parts of a nonfiction book can help you to use that book efficiently when researching a topic.

- The **title page** is usually the first page. It tells the title of the book, the author's name, and the publisher's name and city.
- The **copyright page** comes next. It tells the year the book was published. This can be important. Some information in an old book may no longer be correct.
- An **acknowledgement** or **preface** may follow. It may tell what the book is about, why it was written, and how to use it.
- The **table of contents** shows how the book is organized. It gives the names and page numbers of the sections and chapters.
- A **cross-reference** sends the reader to another page for more information. *Example:* (See page **372**.)
- An **appendix** has extra information, such as maps, tables, lists, and so on.
- A **glossary** explains special words used in the book. It's like a mini-dictionary.
- A **bibliography** lists books, articles, and other sources that the author used while writing the book. To learn more about the topic, read the materials listed in the bibliography.
- The **index** is an alphabetical list of all the topics in the book. It gives the page numbers where each topic is covered.

 Answer the following questions. Discuss your findings with a partner.

1. When in your research plan would you use a nonfiction book?
2. Find a cross-reference and tell what is on the page you are referred to.
3. On what page does the index begin?

TEKS 6.23A
ELPS 3E

Using Reference Materials

Using reference materials should be part of your research plan. The reference section in a library contains reference materials such as atlases, encyclopedias, and dictionaries. The sources often lead to other sources.

Using Encyclopedias

An **encyclopedia** is a set of books or a CD with articles on almost every topic you can imagine. The tips below can guide your use of encyclopedias.

- If the article is long, skim any subheadings to find specific information.
- Encyclopedia articles are written with the most basic information first, followed by more detailed information.
- At the end of an article, you may find a list of related topics. Look them up to learn more about your topic.
- The index lists all the places in the encyclopedia where you will find more information about your topic. (See the sample below.) The index is usually in the back of the last volume of a printed set.

Encyclopedia Index

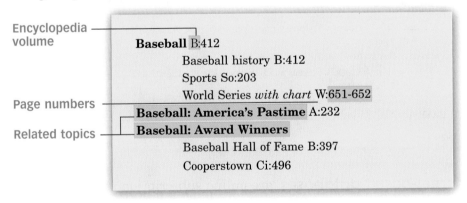

Encyclopedia volume
Page numbers
Related topics

Baseball B:412
    Baseball history B:412
    Sports So:203
    World Series *with chart* W:651-652
Baseball: America's Pastime A:232
Baseball: Award Winners
    Baseball Hall of Fame B:397
    Cooperstown Ci:496

Check the index entries above; then list the volume and page where you might find the following information. Discuss with a partner.

1. A list of teams that have played in the World Series
2. A description of the first baseball game
3. The names of players in the Baseball Hall of Fame

Finding Magazine Articles

Periodical guides are found in the reference section of the library and list magazine articles about many different topics.

- **Locate the right edition** of the periodical guide in your library. The latest edition will have the newest information, but you may need information from an older edition.

- **Look up your subject.** Subjects are listed alphabetically. If your subject is not listed, try another word related to it.

- **Write down the information** about the article. Include the name of the magazine, the issue date, the name of the article, and its page numbers.

- **Find the magazine.** Ask the librarian for help if necessary.

Sample Format

BAKE SALES	Subject Entry
Bake sale. G. Watson. *Working* v32 no10 p12 O 2009.	
Fundraising for fun and profit. *School Administrator* v23 no3 p52-55 Fe 2010.	Name, Volume, and Number of Magazine
BAKER, KENNETH	
Kite-flying Tricks. *Back Yard Magazine* p60-65 My/Ag 2011.	Author Entry
BAKERY	
Appetites grow for pastry. A. Greeley. *Chef Central Journal* v6 no18 pC1 D 31 2009.	Name of Author
Bread basics. *Restaurant News* v32 no2 Je 5 2008.	
Tabletop treats for tots. K. Stevens and R. Samuel. *Parent's Pal* v17 no2 p12-17 Je 26 2011.	Title of Article
Valentine's day cakes and cookies. *Eating Well* no341 p84 Fe 2010.	Page Number/Date
BAKESHOP *See* Bakery	
	Cross-Reference

Internet-based databases are online subscription services that allow you to search for and read periodicals on the Internet.

 Use the sample periodical guide to answer each question.

1. When and how would using a periodical guide fit into your research plan?

2. If your research topic is how to bake sweets, which articles could you possibly use in your research?

TEKS 6.23E
ELPS 2G, 3E, 3G

Differentiating Between Paraphrasing and Plagiarism

When you do research, you will find many interesting facts that support your research topic or question. Do not write the exact words that you find in your research without properly citing the source. This is called plagiarism. You can avoid plagiarism by paraphrasing your source. When you paraphrase, you put the ideas from a source into your own words. You also give credit to the original source in the appropriate format.

What is plagiarism?

Read the original text and the student version that follows to see an example of plagiarism.

Original Text

Greek myths, which are still popular today, are stories about gods and heroes. In one, Daedalus makes wings for himself and his son Icarus so they can escape from a maze in which they've been imprisoned. The wings Daedalus makes are attached with wax. When Icarus flies too close to the Sun, the wax melts, causing him to fall into the Aegean Sea and drown.

Student Text

Greek myths are stories about gods and heroes. They are still popular today. In one, Daedalus makes wings for himself and son so they can fly out of a maze in which they've been imprisoned. Daedalus attaches the wings with wax. Icarus flies too close to the Sun and the wax melts. This causes Icarus to drop into the sea and drown.

What makes this passage plagiarism? The writer has only changed around a few words and phrases and has not cited, or given credit to the source, for any of the ideas. (See page **405**.)

 Write an acceptable paraphrase for the original text. Share with a partner and check each other's work. Give your thoughts and opinions on whether he or she has paraphrased correctly, and listen as your partner shares opinions on your work.

Citing Sources

When you cite a source in your research you are showing where the information that you are using came from. It is not only important to give credit to the source, but checking the source for author, title, publisher, and year will help you determine if it is valid and reliable.

Always cite sources when:

- using another person's idea, opinion, or theory
- quoting a person's spoken or written words
- paraphrasing a person's spoken or written words
- using facts, statistics, graphs—any piece of information— from a reference source.

Always cite your sources in an appropriate format, such as a bibliography at the end of your research, or within your research. See the examples.

1. A sentence with paraphrased information has the author's last name and book's page number in parentheses after the sentence.

2. A sentence with paraphrased (or quoted) information and author's name has only the page number in parentheses.

3. Cite the source after a quotation without the author's name using parentheses, author's name, and page number.

Examples of citations within a report:

1. Greek myths are stories about gods and heroes (Joseph 384).

2. As Natalie Joseph says in her book Favorite Greek Myths, the myths are as popular today as they were in ancient Greece (28).

3. "Myths are an early form of storytelling that still captivate us today," says the prominent author in her latest book (Joseph 3).

Try IT Create a citation for a book you have read. Choose a sentence from the book, and cite it three ways as shown above. Then write the bibliographic information for the book.

TEKS 6.23D

Identifying Notes and Bibliographic Information

When you take notes, you identify the title, author, and page number for the source of each piece of information. You can quote the source directly or paraphrase the source for your notes.

A bibliography appears at the end of your paper or presentation. It lists all the sources you used for your research in alphabetical order. You should follow the standard format for a bibliography. The following entry is an example of a bibliographic entry for a book. Notice the punctuation.

> Joseph, Natalie. Favorite Greek Myths. Chicago: Mulberry Park Press, 2011. Print.

Always note these things for your bibliography:

- the author and date (copyright or date of article) of the source.
- the publisher (publishing house, magazine, or Web site).
- the medium (print, Web, etc.) of the source.

 If you cannot find all of the information you need, write down all that you can. You still need to identify your source as completely as possible.

 Write a bibliographic entry for the source used in the note shown below. Use the standard format shown in the example in blue.

"Athena and Poseidon both loved a city in Greece. They decided to hold a contest. Whoever could give the best gift could claim the city as his or her own. Poseidon struck the side of a cliff with his trident, and water sprung from the ground. The people were amazed and excited, until they realized the water was salty and they could not use it. Athena's gift was an olive tree that gave the people food, oil, and wood. The people decided Athena had won, and she named the city Athens."

From the book: Myths: Tales of the Gods, by Paul Stern, page 42, San Francisco, CA, Peace Press, August 2010.

RESEARCH

TEKS 6.23B, 6.23E, 6.24B

ELPS 3E, 3G, 4C

Evaluating Sources

You don't want to give false information in your report so you must decide if your sources are trustworthy. Ask yourself the following questions to help judge the reliability, relevance, and overall value of your sources.

Is the source a primary or a secondary source?

Firsthand facts are often more trustworthy than secondhand facts. However, secondary sources, such as references, can also be trustworthy.

Is the source an expert or written by an expert?

An expert is an authority on a certain subject. You may need to ask a teacher, parent, or librarian for help evaluating how reliable a source is.

Is the information valid?

Sources that are well respected are more likely to be accurate. For example, a journal written by experts is more valid than a tabloid.

Is the information complete?

If a source of information provides some facts about a subject, but you still have questions, find another source. This source is not as relevant as one that answers many of your questions.

Is the information reliable?

Be sure you have the most up-to-date information on a subject. Check for copyright dates of books and articles and for posting dates of online information to evaluate the reliability of your sources.

Is the source biased?

A source is biased when it presents information that is one-sided. A biased source is not accurate. Some organizations, for example, have something to gain by using only some of the facts. Avoid such sources.

Try IT For your next research paper, look at the sources you gather. With a partner, answer the questions above. Explain your thoughts.

Research Writing

Research Report

Today, it is easier than ever to find answers to your questions. You might be wondering about new ways to treat some disease. Perhaps you're interested in learning about a strange-looking fish. You can find answers quickly by surfing the Internet. Of course, you can also find answers by talking to people or reading books, magazines, and newspapers. This question-and-answer work is called research.

In this unit, you will write a report about a natural event or formation that affects people. As you develop your report, you will *describe* the formation or event, *explain* some things about it, and *summarize* information from other sources. Then you will organize your ideas and facts into an interesting, informative report.

Writing Guidelines

Subject: **A natural event or formation that affects people**

Purpose: **To research and share information about nature's effect on people**

Form: **Research report**

Audience: **Classmates**

 TEKS 6.14A, 6.25B

Research Report

The following research report is about the natural occurring weather event, the hurricane. Notice how important information is presented. The side notes point out key features in the report.

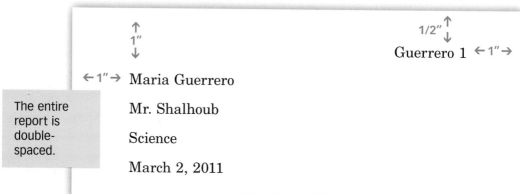

↑ 1" ↓

1/2" ↑↓

Guerrero 1 ←1"→

←1"→ Maria Guerrero

The entire report is double-spaced.

Mr. Shalhoub

Science

March 2, 2011

Hurricane Havoc

Beginning

The opening gives important background information.

Does the thought of a hurricane scare you? It should. Hurricanes cause a lot of damage every year, especially along the south eastern coast of the United States. <u>To understand these storms, scientists are studying how hurricanes form, move, and cause destruction.</u>

The writer develops a controlling idea and states it in a thesis sentence (underlined).

Every hurricane forms because of heat, moisture, and wind. When cool air lies above a warm ocean, moisture begins to rise, causing a thunderstorm. If the thunderstorm gets strong enough, it is called a tropical storm. "If the winds reach at least 74 miles per hour, it [the storm]

↑ 1" ↓

TEKS 6.25A, 6.25B, 6.25D

Guerrero 2

becomes a hurricane" (Acker 4).

Middle
The writer compiles and synthesizes information from multiple sources.

Hurricanes move in circular motion. The strongest winds of a hurricane are closest to the center or "eye" (Sklar). My uncle, Arnie Rasmussen, remembers when Hurricane Hugo hit Charleston, South Carolina, in 1989. "When that eye came after all the pounding wind and rain, the quiet was eerie. A high wall of clouds swirled around us. We knew that when the eye passed, the pounding would begin again."

The writer uses an appropriate form of documentation to acknowledge sources.

The author's name and page number appear in parentheses, unless the author is mentioned in the text.

Hurricanes can destroy buildings, ruin crops, and cause serious injury and even death to people and animals. The sudden flood and high winds do most of the damage. Scientists use a 5-point scale to measure the strength of a hurricane. Category 1 is the weakest, with winds from 74 to 95 miles per hour and waves more than 18 feet above normal (Moser 12). Uncle Arnie said, "If it [Hugo] was a category 4 storm, I never want to see a category 5!"

The writer summarizes findings and uses evidence to support the controlling idea.

TEKS 6.20B(iii), 6.25A, 6.25B

Guerrero 3

HURRICANE CATEGORIES

Categories	Wind Speed	Description
1	74 – 95 mph	Weak
2	96 – 110 mph	Moderate
3	111 – 130 mph	Strong
4	131 – 155 mph	Very Strong
5	greater than 155 mph	Devastating

However, only about five hurricanes form near the United States each year. Just two of those hurricanes reach land, and only one of those is a category 3 or stronger (Moser 13). In 1900, the worst hurricane in United States history hit Galveston, Texas. "A storm surge two stories high broke over the city . . . causing 20-foot floods and more than 8,000 deaths" (Sklar).

Hurricanes are very dangerous storms. They can cause destruction, injury (harm to people), and death over a large area. It's important to learn how these storms form and move, and that's why scientists spend so much studying hurricanes. Hurricanes cannot be stopped, so people must learn how to protect themselves and their belongings when one strikes.

TEKS 6.25A, 6.25B, 6.25D
ELPS 3G, 3E

Guerrero 4

Works Cited

Aker, Mike C. Hurricanes. Boston: Urban Press, 2011. Print.

Moser, Jonathan. "Fly in the Eye of the Storm." Science Discovery 18 May 2010: 12–14. Print.

Rassmusen, Arnold. Personal interview. 13, March 2011

Sklar, Rachel. "Forces of Hurricanes." hurrcat. com. 6 June 2010. Pacific Environmental Laboratory in Seattle, Washington. 12 March 2010 <http://hurrcat.com/rof.html>.

The sources used in the report are listed alphabetically.

RESEARCH

Respond to the reading. After reading the sample research report, answer the following questions about important traits of writing. Discuss your opinions and ideas with a partner.

☐ Organization **(1) How are the middle paragraphs arranged? List the main idea for each of these paragraphs.**

☐ Development of Ideas **(2) What did you learn from reading the report? List at least one idea and two supporting details.**

☐ Voice **(3) List words and phrases that show the writer's interest in the topic.**

With a partner, find a topic that interests you. Gather three sources and synthesize your findings into one controlling idea. Discuss how you could put your controlling idea into a topic sentence.

Prewriting

Selecting a Topic

Selecting a topic is an important part of your research plan. Brainstorm ideas for topics—either a natural event or a natural formation. One way to do this is to create a cluster for the word "nature" as seen below.

Cluster

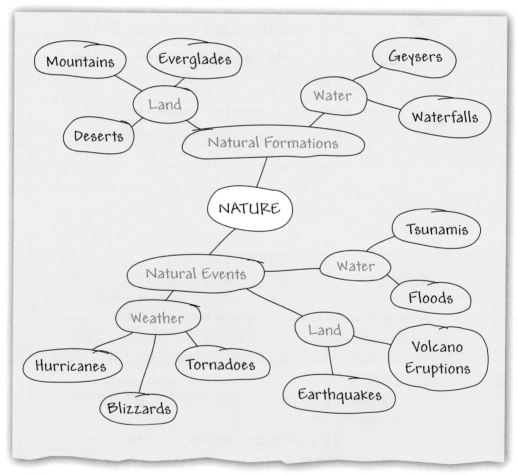

Create your cluster. Using the example above, create your own cluster. Brainstorm as many ideas as you can. Look at an atlas, a science book, or a geography book if you need help. Choose a topic that interests you—one that you would like to learn more about.

TEKS 6.22A, 6.24A
ELPS 2I, 3G

Consulting with Others

Part of your research plan should include asking others for feedback. This will help you decide your topic or encourage decisions you have already made. Consult with your classmates as you brainstorm ideas and questions for your topic. Your peers can help you decide on which ideas work best.

Start by listing questions that you want to answer. Ask a peer to help you. If you cannot think of at least three questions, you should choose a broader topic. If you have more than five questions, you should narrow your topic. Look at the lists of narrow, broad and focused topics below.

Lists

RESEARCH

Too Narrow

SLEET
– What is sleet?
– How does it affect people?

Well–Focused

HURRICANES
– What are they?
– What causes them?
– How strong are their winds?
– How often do they occur?

Too Broad

WEATHER
– What causes wind?
– Where is it windiest?
– What are clouds?
– How many types of clouds are there?
– What causes rain?
– What places get the most rain?
– What places get the least rain?
– What causes snow?
– What places get the most snow?
– How is sleet different from rain or snow?
– How is hail different from sleet?
– How is an ice storm different from hail or sleet?
– What causes frost?

Prewrite

Consult with others. Work with classmates to brainstorm ideas as you continue to choose and narrow your topic. Ask thoughtful questions about a topic that interests you in order to help you figure out what your major research question will be.

 **TEKS** 6.22A, 6.24A
ELPS 2I, 3D, 3E, 4K

Prewriting Formulating the Questions

You should always ask questions throughout your research process. This will help you adjust your research and refine or focus the major research question you are trying to answer. Open-ended questions that answer *Who, What, Where, When, Why,* and *How* help create ideas and thoughts about your topic. Below are example questions about hurricanes that help refine what this writer wants to research. By answering these questions, the writer focuses her research mostly on the data that scientists provide.

- Who is affected by hurricanes?
- What are hurricanes?
- Where do they start?
- When do they happen?
- What causes them?
- How strong are their winds?

 With a partner, look at the list of questions below. These questions are too broad for one report. Choose which questions should go with which report. Explain your choices to your partner.

"Hurricanes" "Tracking Hurricanes" "How to Survive a Hurricane"

---

1. What are hurricanes?
2. How strong are their winds?
3. How do scientists identify the start of a hurricane?
4. What tools do scientists use to study hurricanes?
5. How do hurricanes form?
6. What do hurricanes look like?
7. Why do scientists clock the speed of hurricanes?
8. Where do hurricanes usually hit?
9. How can people prepare for hurricanes?
10. What should people do if a hurricane is predicted?

 Choose a topic. Formulate new open-ended questions or revise old questions about your topic to better address your major research question. With a partner, make sure they are not too broad or too narrow.

TEKS 6.22B, 6.25A
ELPS 3E, 4J

Generating a Research Plan

After you have asked questions and decided upon a topic, you can look for sources. You must plan how to gather your research. Think about where and how you will find the best information. Keep these things in mind as you make your plan:

- List possible sources and where to find them, such as your school or local library, or the Internet.
- Think of the places you could visit, such as museums.
- Who could you interview as an expert?

Prewrite

Generate your research plan. Use the tips above to create your own research plan. List the kinds of sources you want to find and where to find them. As you gather research, track where you find your best sources.

Compiling Information from Multiple Sources

After you gather sources, you will have to take notes and compile the information. Look for common ideas and answers to your research questions. Remember to copy the information you will need for a bibliography. Write the source and page number for all notes you take, like the examples below.

"Hurricanes," p. 379: "These giant tropical storms can pack wind speeds of more than 160 miles per hour (257 kilometers)."

"Hurricanes are also known as tropical cyclones and are capable of churning up the sea so waves are 50 feet high (15 meters)."

See how one student used information for his research. Is this an example of plagiarism or paraphrasing? Discuss your answer.

> *Hurricanes are giant tropical storms. Wind speeds can be greater than 160 miles an hour! ("Hurricanes," p. 379) "The heavy rain and strong winds of hurricanes stir up ocean waters like an eggbeater."*

Prewrite

Compile Information. As you gather sources and take notes, look for the information that answers the questions you asked about your topic. Which ideas are common in your findings? As you note the information, avoid plagiarizing. Quoting your sources in your notes will help you decide what to paraphrase later.

 **TEKS** 6.23A, 6.24B
ELPS 3E, 3G

Prewriting
Gathering Information: Online Sources

Your research plan should include collecting information from both print and electronic sources, like articles on the Internet. Use a trusted search engine while conducting research on the Internet. Cite only trustworthy and accurate Web sites. To do this, look for the person, organization, or company who provides the Web site.

Searching the Internet for Reliable Sources

Sofia is doing a report on Ancient Egypt. She types "Ancient Egypt" into her search engine. Then she lists the Web sites that appear and writes a short description of each. Look at her list below. Sofia starred the sources she thought were reliable and relevant. How do you think she decided?

Ancient Egypt search results

www.egyptpedia.com
   A free encyclopedia written by a person who loves ancient
   Egyptian culture.
* www.ancientegyptmuseum.org
   a museum in Britain specializing in ancient Egyptian artifacts
www.letsgobackintime.com/ancientegypt
   a fun look at times past
* www.samsonuniversity.edu/archaeology/egypt
   an accredited university with a famous Ancient Civilization
   department

Gather information from online sources. As part of your research plan, use a trusted search engine to look for Web sites, online articles, and other sources that will give reliable and relevant information on your topic.

Gathering Information: Reference and Periodicals

Libraries have much more than books. You can find encyclopedias, almanacs, and many periodicals, such as newspapers, journals, and magazines. Ask your librarian to help you find these reliable and valuable sources.

Starting With an Encyclopedia

When planning your research, encyclopedias are a good place to start. Encyclopedias have information in alphabetical order on many different topics. Encyclopedias can be found in both print and electronic formats. There are also whole encyclopedias on special topics, such as music or science.

Using Journals

A journal is a special periodical focusing on one subject. There are journals about space, archaeology, history, nature, medicine, and many more topics. Journals have articles, reports, or studies written by experts on that subject. For example, you may find a journal published about weather. This journal could include studies by scientists on how hurricanes begin. Check to see if there is a periodical written just for your topic.

Searching Newspapers and Magazines

Newspapers and magazines can be great resources for finding interesting facts and stories about your topic. In your research report, you want to provide facts, but you also want to make it interesting. You can find a story in a magazine or newspaper. Old newspapers that are stored electronically at your library can help you search far into the past.

Prewrite

Gather information using reference materials and periodicals.
As part of your research plan, visit the school or local library. Use encyclopedias, journals, and periodicals to help you find relevant and reliable information about your topic.

TEKS 6.23B, 6.24B

Evaluating Sources

Before you use any information in your report, ask yourself: Is this information related to my topic? Is the source trustworthy? Here are some things to consider when you evaluate the relevance and reliability of sources.

Is the source a primary or a secondary source?

You must be able to distinguish between a primary source, such as an expert or someone who kept a diary during a time in history, and a secondary source, such as an encyclopedia that gives facts about your topic.

Is the source reliable?

Are you quoting an expert or an authority on a topic, such as a scientist? Does the person have the credentials to be trusted, or is the person merely an interested person? Is the information you are getting related or relevant to your topic?

Is the information accurate and trustworthy?

A nonfiction reference book about hurricanes would have reliable, objective information. Still, how trustworthy is the opinion of a person who watched a hurricane? The person could be trusted to give the feeling, which will add interest, but not scientific data.

Is the information current?

Be sure you have up-to-date information on a subject. Check the copyright dates of books and articles. In some cases, online information from reliable Web sites might have the most up-to-date information.

Evaluate your sources. Make sure that the sources you have collected for your research are reliable, accurate, and trustworthy. Use the questions and explanations above to check that your sources work the best for your topic. See also page 390.

TEKS 6.23C, 6.23D, 6.24B

Prewriting **Using a Gathering Grid**

One way to organize the data you collected from print and electronic sources is to use a gathering grid. Maria created this grid on a computer for her research report. It helps identify the sources of notes by name and type. She can quickly reference which notes are where.

Gathering Grid

Hurricanes	Hurricane Center (Internet)	National Weather (magazine)	Hurricanes (book)	World Wide Encyclopedia (encyclopedia)
What are they?				Largest type of storm
How strong are their winds?	Up to 250 mph!		From 74 mph to more than 155 mph!	

Create a gathering grid. Use a computer to help you organize your research questions and notes and to identify your sources in the grid. Replace any sources that are not relevant or reliable.

Using a Graphic Organizer

Use technology to help with other graphic organizers. As Maria interviewed her uncle, she organized her notes in a timeline. This helped her make the connection between ideas and identify the evidence she would use in her report.

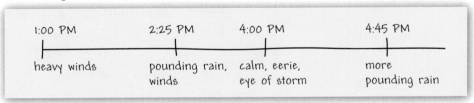

1:00 PM	2:25 PM	4:00 PM	4:45 PM
heavy winds	pounding rain, winds	calm, eerie, eye of storm	more pounding rain

Create a graphic organizer. Use a computer to help you organize your research notes. Make connections between ideas and to decide on which evidence to include in your report.

 **TEKS** 6.23C, 6.23D, 6.25B, 6.25D

Prewriting **Creating Note Cards**

Use note cards to expand the notes from your grid. Number each card and write a question at the top. Underneath the question, write a quotation, paraphrase information, or summarize your findings from charts and graphs. The answers are support and evidence for the conclusions that you make about your topic. At the bottom, identify the source of each note. Be sure you have recorded all bibliographic information for each source. Here are three sample note cards for the report about hurricanes.

Card number
Question
Answer (paraphrase)
Source

1. What causes hurricanes?

Cool air draws heat and moisture from ocean water, causing winds and thunderstorms. If this continues, it may make a tropical storm. A tropical storm may become a hurricane.

Science Discovery Magazine
pages 12–14

2. How big was hurricane Hugo?

"It was a category 4. If Hugo was a category 4 storm, I never want to see a category 5!" — Answer (quotation)
interview with
Uncle Arnie

3. When is hurricane season?

Answer (list)
– Starts in June
– Peaks in September
– Ends in November
www.hurrcat.com/

Create note cards. Use note cards to expand your findings into written notes as stated above and to identify each source.

Prewrite

TEKS 6.23E, 6.25D
ELPS 3E

Avoiding Plagiarism

As you do your research, you will find many interesting ideas, facts, and comments that will help you make your point. It is important to cite every source you use so you don't plagiarize. Also, you **must not copy** these words and ideas and pretend they are yours. This is called *plagiarism,* and it is stealing. You can avoid plagiarism in one of two ways.

- **Quoting exact words:** If the exact words of a source capture an idea perfectly, you may include them in quotation marks and give credit to the source.

- **Paraphrasing:** You may also put the ideas from a source into your own words. This is called *paraphrasing.* However, you must still give credit to the original source in the appropriate format.

---

4. How do hurricanes cause destruction?

Quoting Exact Words

"A category 5 hurricane can produce a 20-foot storm surge, torrential rains, and even tornadoes."

Zephyrs Web site

Paraphrasing

4. How do hurricanes cause destruction?

In addition to high winds, big hurricanes cause destruction through storm surges, downpours, and tornadoes.

Zephyrs Web site

Prewrite

Quote exact words or paraphrase. Discuss with a partner your work, the differences between plagiarism and paraphrasing, and why it is important to cite your sources. Pick out notes you have taken from your research. Decide whether you should paraphrase or quote the material. Share your findings with a classmate and ask for feedback.

 TEKS 6.23D

Prewriting Identifying Your Sources

Whenever you find a valid and reliable source of information for your report, record the following bibliographic information about it in the standard format below. Then use it for your works-cited page.

- **Encyclopedia entry:** Author's name (if listed). Entry title. Encyclopedia title. Edition (if given). Publication date. Medium.
- **Book:** Author's name. Title. Publisher. City. Copyright date. Medium.
- **Magazine:** Author's name. Article title. Title. Date published. Page numbers. Medium of publication.
- **Internet:** Author's name (if listed). Page title. Site title. Date posted or copyright (if listed). Date found. Electronic address.
- **Interview:** Person's name. Type of interview (personal, telephone, mail, or e-mail). Date.

My Source Notes

Encyclopedia
"Hurricane." World View Encyclopedia. 2011. Print.

Book
Mike C. Aker. Hurricanes. Urban Press. Boston. 2011. Print.

Magazine
Jonothan Moser. "Fly in the Eye of the Storm." Science Discovery Magazine. May 18, 2010. Pages 12–14. Print.

Internet
Rachel Sklar. "Forces of Hurricanes." hurrcat.com Pacific Marine Environmental Lab. Seattle, WA March 12, 2010. <www.hurricat.com/0312/storm>.

Interview
Arnold Rasmussen. Personal interview. March 13, 2011.

Prewrite

Identify sources. List the bibliographic information from each of your sources. Be sure to use the correct standard formatting. Update your list whenever you find new sources.

TEKS 6.24A
ELPS 3E

Refining Your Research Question

After you have completed researching your topic, revisit your questions. Did you answer all the questions? Do your answers lead to more questions? Is any information being repeated? By looking at all the questions and answers, your controlling idea and major research question should become more clear.

Read the questions below.

HURRICANES
- *What are hurricanes?*
- *What causes them?*
- *How strong are their winds?*
- *How often do they occur?*
- *Why are they named after people?*

 Which question or questions would you eliminate to keep the focus on hurricanes as natural disasters? Which questions seem like details to a bigger question? Which question could you use as the major research question? Discuss with your partner.

Reviewing Your Materials

When you finish your research, you may have more information than you really need. Some facts may be interesting, but they may not be relevant to your controlling idea or focus of the report. Write the controlling idea of your report or a one-sentence summary. Then review your notes to see which notes are relevant and which are not.

 Refine your questions. Look at your list of questions. Look at the research you have gathered and decide if you have more questions. Refine your major research question if necessary.

 **TEKS** 6.14A, 6.25B

Prewriting **Writing Your Thesis Statement**

When you finish your research and are ready to plan a draft, you must develop your thesis. The thesis, or focus, should remain the same throughout your report. It is based on your controlling idea, the part of your topic that you emphasize. This formula will help you write a thesis statement.

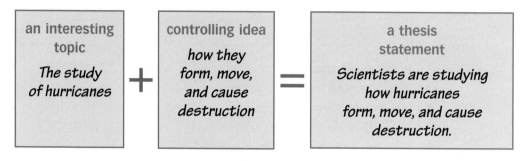

an interesting topic	controlling idea	a thesis statement
The study of hurricanes	+ how they form, move, and cause destruction	= Scientists are studying how hurricanes form, move, and cause destruction.

Sample Thesis Statements

Deserts seem like lifeless stretches of sand (an interesting topic), *but they are actually home to many plants and animals* (controlling idea).

The Florida Everglades (an interesting topic) *is truly one of North America's most unique environments* (controlling idea).

Prewrite

Form your thesis statement. After reviewing your research notes and list of research questions, decide on two main points you could make about your topic. Develop a separate thesis statement for each of these controlling ideas, using the formula above. Finally, put a star (✱) next to the statement that says most clearly what you want to share. From this, you can also develop your topic sentence for your beginning paragraph.

TEKS 6.17A(iii), 6.25A, 6.25B

Outlining Your Ideas

One way to plan your report is to make an outline. An outline helps you compile and organize information from many sources. It is a list of specific facts organized in a particular structure. Key ideas and supporting evidence can be listed as words or phrases or in complete sentences.

Sentence Outline

Below is the first part of a sentence outline for a report on hurricanes. Notice that the outline begins with the thesis statement and then organizes ideas below it. Compare the outline with the opening paragraph and first middle paragraph of the report.

Thesis Statement	*THESIS STATEMENT: Scientists are studying how hurricanes form, move, and cause destruction.*
I. Topic Sentence (for first middle paragraph)	*I. Every hurricane forms because of heat, moisture, and wind.*
	A. These combine to make a thunderstorm.
A. B. C. **Specific examples, or evidence for key ideas are listed in logical order.**	*B. If winds do not blow the storm apart, it grows into a tropical storm.*
	C. When winds reach 74 miles per hour, the storm becomes a hurricane.
	II. Hurricanes move in a circular motion.
	A. . . .
Continue . . .	*B. . . .*

Your outline begins with your thesis statement. It lists the topic sentences of paragraphs that will support your controlling idea. Examples, or evidence, that support each key idea is listed as well. Remember, in an outline, if you have a I, you must have at least a II. If you have an A, you must have at least a B.

Prewrite

Create your outline. Review your research notes and create a thesis statement and outline for your report. Be sure that each topic sentence (I, II, III, . . .) supports your thesis statement and that each detail (A, B, C, . . .) supports the topic sentence above it. Use your outline as a guide when you write the first draft of your report.

TEKS 6.14A, 6.25A, 6.25C
ELPS 5G

Drafting

Starting Your Research Report

The opening paragraph of your report should grab your reader's interest, introduce your topic, and share your thesis (focus) statement. Below are two possible ways that you could write the beginning of a report on hurricanes.

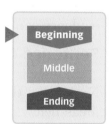

Beginning Paragraphs

This paragraph uses important information from sources to develop the thesis (focus) statement.

> Nature's most powerful storms are hurricanes. These huge, spinning storms build up over the ocean and sometimes move onto land. Hurricanes can cause a lot of damage before they weaken and turn into common thunderstorms. <u>To understand these storms, scientists are studying how hurricanes form, move, and cause destruction.</u>

This paragraph stays in a consistent format by ending with the thesis statement.

> Should everyone be scared by the thought of a hurricane? Hurricanes cause a lot of damage every year, especially along the southeastern coast of the United States. <u>To understand these storms, scientists are studying how hurricanes affect people and their environment.</u>

Write your opening paragraph. Compile important information from many sources and use it to develop your opening paragraph. Be sure to get your reader's interest, introduce your topic in a topic sentence, and make a clear thesis statement.

TEKS 6.20B(iii), 6.25C, 6.25D

Citing Sources in Your Report

As you write your report, remember to give credit to sources that you paraphrase or quote directly. Your findings should be presented appropriately throughout your report.

When You Have All the Information

■ The most common type of credit (citation) lists the author's last name and the page number in parentheses.

> If the winds reach 74 miles per hour, the storm becomes a hurricane (Aker 4).

■ If you already name the author in your report, just include the page number in parentheses.

> Jonothan Moser explains that cool air draws heat and moisture from warm bodies of water to form a storm (13).

When Some Information Is Missing

■ Some sources do not list an author. In those cases, use the title and page number.

> The winds of a hurricane are most violent around the eye ("Hurricane" 7).

■ Some sources do not use page numbers. In those cases, list just the author.

> Hurricanes in the Indian Ocean are called cyclones (Tyson).

■ If a source does not list the author or page number, use the title.

> In Southeast Asia, they are called typhoons ("Big Storm").

 Use the information above to document a source correctly. Rewrite the following sentence giving credit to Jennifer Garcia's article "Hurricanes: Life's Great Storms" from *National Weather Magazine,* page 6.

Hurricanes in the Pacific Ocean are called typhoons and generally are limited to the coast of Southeast Asia.

TEKS 6.23E, 6.25B, 6.25D

Drafting   Developing the Middle Part

Once you have grabbed the reader's attention in the introduction, begin writing the middle paragraphs.

Include a topic sentence for each paragraph that supports your controlling idea. In each paragraph, summarize your research by including facts, details, and quotations that support your topic sentences. In this way, you provide evidence to support your conclusions.

Be sure your ideas are coherent and your sentences flow from one to the next so the reader can follow along. Use your sentence outline as a guide to keep your writing organized as Maria did in her draft.

Middle Paragraphs

Each topic sentence (underlined) summarizes a finding.

The rest of the paragraph supports its single idea.

The writer paraphrases information and cites the source.

A quote from a primary source adds interest and is documented appropriately.

Every hurricane forms because of heat, moisture, and wind. When cool air lies above a warm ocean, moisture begins to rise, causing a thunderstorm. If the thunderstorm gets strong enough, it is called a tropical storm. If the winds reach at least 74 miles per hour, the storm becomes a hurricane (Aker 4).

Hurricanes move in a circular motion. The strongest winds of a hurricane are the closest to the center or the eye (Sklar). The weather is calm and clear in the eye. My uncle, Arnie Rasmussen, remembers when Hurricane Hugo hit Charleston, South Carolina, in 1989. "When that eye came after all the pounding wind and rain, the quiet was eerie. A high wall of clouds swirled around us. But we knew that when the eye passed, the pounding would begin again."

Hurricanes can destroy buildings, ruin crops, and cause serious injury and even death to people

TEKS 6.20B(iii), 6.23E, 6.25B, 6.25C, 6.25D
ELPS 5G

Evidence from sources is paraphrased and used to support conclusions.

A quotation is used to support an idea.

Brackets help to clarify the quotation.

A chart helps summarize findings.

Sources are acknowledged and documented in parentheses.

RESEARCH

and animals. The sudden flood and high winds do most of the damage. Scientists use a 5-point scale to measure the strength of a hurricane. Category 1 is the weakest, with winds from 74 to 95 miles per hour and waves about 4 to 5 feet above normal tides. The category 5 hurricane is the strongest, with winds of at least 155 miles per hour and waves more than 18 feet above normal (Moser 12). Uncle Arnie said, "If it [Hugo] was a category 4 storm, I never want to see a category 5!"

Hurricane Categories

Categories	Wind Speed	Description
1	74–95 mph	Weak
2	96–110 mph	Moderate
3	111–130 mph	Strong
4	131–155 mph	Very Strong
5	greater than 155 mph	Devastating

However, only about five hurricanes form near the United States each year. Just two of those hurricanes reach land, and only one of those is a category 3 or stronger (Moser 13). In 1900, the worst hurricane in United States history hit Galveston, Texas. "A storm surge almost two stories high broke over the city . . . causing 20-foot floods and more than 8,000 deaths" (Sklar).

Draft

Write your middle paragraphs. Develop a topic sentence, and then use quotations and evidence to support it. When you summarize your findings, remember to paraphrase to avoid plagiarism and to acknowledge your sources in the proper format. Present your findings in the same way from beginning to end to keep your writing coherent.

TEKS 6.17A(i), 6.25B
ELPS 5G

Drafting **Ending Your Research Report**

Your ending paragraph should bring your report to a thoughtful close in order to be effective. Make sure all your findings have been summarized. Include the following ideas in your closing paragraph.

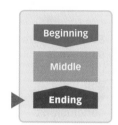

- **Remind the reader about the thesis of the report.**
- **Tell one last interesting piece of evidence about the topic to support your conclusion.**
- **Make a final observation about the topic.**

Ending Paragraph

An effective concluding paragraph includes restating the thesis (underlined) and a final observation.	Hurricanes are very dangerous storms. They can cause destruction, injury (harm to people), and death over a very large area. <u>It's important to learn how these storms form and move, and that's why scientists spend so much time studying hurricanes.</u> Hurricanes cannot be stopped, so people must learn how to protect themselves and their belongings when one strikes.

Write your final paragraph.
On your paper, write your final paragraph, summarizing your findings and using evidence to support your conclusions.

Look over your draft. Read your first draft, looking over your notes and outline to see if you included all the necessary details and evidence. Make notes about possible changes. You are now ready to begin revising.

Creating Your Works-Cited Page

The first step to creating a works-cited page is to format your sources according to standard format. The two following pages show formats for common types of sources.

Books

Author or editor (last name first). Title (underlined or italics if typed). City where published: Publisher, copyright date. Medium of publication *[Print]*.

Magazines

Author (last name first). Article title (quotation marks). Title of the magazine (underlined or italics if typed). Date (day, month, year): Page numbers of the article. Medium of publication *[Print]*.

Internet

Author (if available). Page title (if available, quotation). Site title (underlined or italics if typed). Name of sponsor (if available). Date published (if available). Medium of publication *[Web]*. Date found. <Electronic address>.

Books

Aker, Mike, C. Hurricanes. Boston: Urban
    Press, 2011. Print.

Magazines

Garcia, Jennifer. "Hurricanes: Life's Great
    Storms." National Weather Magazine.
    17 Nov. 2010: 4–6. Print.

Internet

Nugyen, Tamk,. "The Force of the Storm."
    Hurricane Research Association.
    Hurricane Research Association.
    May 21, 2010. Web. <http://www.
    hurricaneresearchassociation.
    com/0312/storm/>.

Encyclopedia

Author (if available). Article title (in quotation marks). Title of the encyclopedia (underlined or italics if typed). Edition (if available). Date published. Medium of publication *[Print]*.

Interview

Person interviewed (last name first). Type of interview (personal, phone, mail, e-mail). Date.

Encyclopedia

"Hurricane." <u>World View Encyclopedia</u>. 2011. Print.

Interview

Rasmussen, Arnold. Personal interview. 13 Mar. 2011.

Format your sources. Check your notes, report and your list of sources. Acknowledge your sources with the appropriate documentation on your works cited page. Create the works cited page using the guidelines below.

1 Identify your sources by making a list using the guidelines above and on the previous page. Write them on paper or note cards.

2 Alphabetize your sources.

3 Write bibliographic information in the correct format on your page.

Works Cited

Miles, Michael C. <u>Hurricane Force</u>. Philadelphia:
Countryside Press, 2009.

Rasmussen, Arnold. Personal interview. 13 Mar. 2011.

Skelton, Renee. "Flying into the Eye of a Hurricane."
<u>Phenomenal Weather Kids</u>. National Weather.
12 Mar. 2004 <http://www.nationalweatherkids.com/
nwkids/0308/hurricane/>.

Go Online!

PREWRITE REVISE PUBLISH
DRAFT EDIT

Revising

A solid research report can rarely be written in one draft. Some ideas in the first draft may not be fully developed, or it may need to be organized in a different order. The voice may be boring in spots, and the focus may be weak. Revision can turn your first draft into a clear and informative report. To revise your draft effectively, use these keys as a guide.

Keys to Effective Revision

1. Read your entire draft to yourself.

2. Ask yourself these questions:
   - Have I achieved the purpose of my report and shared what I wanted to?
   - Have I used the correct format for the research report genre?
   - Who is my audience? Have I addressed them using the correct voice?

3. Mark anything you see that needs to be changed.

4. Revise for focus and coherence, organization, development of ideas, and voice.

5. Use the editing and proofreading marks inside the back cover of this book.

 **TEKS** 6.14B, 6.14C
ELPS 3E, 4I, 4K

Revising for Focus and Coherence

When you revise for *focus* and *coherence,* you check that the evidence and details you provide support the controlling idea throughout your writing.

- The beginning states the controlling idea in a thesis statement.
- The middle provides evidence for the controlling idea.
- The ending refers back to the thesis and offers a meaningful reflection about it.

Have I stayed focused on my controlling idea?

You know your writing is focused when all your facts relate to the controlling idea. The facts should also be points of interest that hook the reader. Check each sentence and ask "Is it interesting? Is it relevant?" If it is interesting but not relevant to understanding the controlling idea, delete it.

 Read the paragraphs below. With a partner, identify the facts or details that do not belong. Discuss your findings.

> The Emergency Services Training Institute in College Station, Texas, is a unique school. It trains firefighters and emergency workers. Students rarely sit at desks! The training is realistic and hands-on.
>
> A special feature of the school is "Disaster City." It is a collection of fake buildings, such as a mall, office buildings, homes, and apartment buildings. The school uses these structures to train emergency workers, such as firefighters, police, and search-and-rescue workers. The buildings are designed to collapse the way buildings would during a real earthquake, hurricane, or tornado. The practice drills are intense. Firefighter trainees have had to work with 200-pound hoses to put out fires. Some have fallen through burning floors or off roofs. Students role-play and learn to deal with many injured people at once. They learn to search for people buried in a fallen building.

 Check your focus. Read through your first draft. Be sure all ideas are connected to your thesis statement and controlling idea. Delete sentences or larger units of text that do not belong.

TEKS 6.14C, 6.14E, 6.17A(i)

ELPS 3E, 4I

Does my beginning clearly introduce my thesis?

Read the beginning paragraph of your report. Look to see if you have clearly stated your thesis. Will it be clear to your reader? If you think it needs work, revisit your list of questions that helped you create your major research question.

Your opening paragraph also needs to hook your reader and make them want to read more about your topic. Does your opening grab the reader's attention?

Have a partner read your beginning and answer these questions:

1. **Is my thesis statement clearly stated?**

2. **Does it grab my reader's attention?**

3. **Is my major research question clear?**

Review your beginning paragraph. Have you done your best to interest your readers in the topic and make your thesis clear? If not, revise your introduction. Ask a partner to review it and give you feedback. Revise according to the feedback you receive.

Have I addressed my thesis in my ending paragraph?

A strong ending stays focused and refers back to your thesis to bring your report to a close. It should also leave your reader with something to think about. You can do this by leaving them with an interesting thought, or one last piece of supporting evidence. Remember to do one or more of the following:

- Refer back to your thesis and summarize your topic.
- Share one last thought or piece of evidence.
- Make a final observation about your topic.

Check your ending. Does your ending give the reader something to think about? Does it refer back to the thesis statement and provide a final observation about the topic? If not, revise your ending. Ask a classmate for his or her response to it.

TEKS 6.14C, 6.25B

Revising **for** Organization

When you revise for *organization*, check that your writing is logical and easy to follow from beginning to end. Have you introduced your ideas and evidence in a logical order? If not, rearrange sentences or larger units of text to help keep your report organized.

Have I followed my outline?

If you follow the outline you developed in your research plan, your report should be organized. Each paragraph should support your thesis statement with a particular idea. This idea is a topic sentence of a paragraph. All sentences that follow provide details and evidence that support the topic sentence. Review your outline for this pattern.

Try IT Copy this outline onto your own paper. Then write the following details where they belong in the outline. Rewrite the outline in a paragraph, adding or rearranging information as needed. How did this outline help organize the paragraph?

> I. The Romans were master builders.
>
>   A. They created elaborate temples, stadiums, and public buildings.
>
>   _____
>
>   B. They invented the dome and expanded the use of the arch.
>
>   _____

    1. Some of these stadiums still stand today.

    2. Some parts of the public buildings are on display in museums.

Review your organization. Look at your outline and compare it to what you have written. Do your ideas flow logically from one idea to the next? Check your report to see whether your sentences follow the ideas in your outline. Rearrange sentences or information that is out of place.

Are my paragraphs and sentences linked?

An organized report will have paragraphs, sentences, and ideas that link together. Each idea leads to the next in a logical way. The paragraphs and sentences move the reader forward, deepening his or her understanding of the controlling idea.

Read the following report. Most of the sentences lead logically to the next. A detail sentence was moved in order to support the topic. With that revision, all the sentences are linked in a way that makes sense.

Organization
The ideas are logically linked from sentence to sentence.

The humpback whale is one of the largest whales. No wonder it makes such BIG sounds. The humpback is the only whale that "sings." Only the male whales sing. The songs can go for hours. Scientists have been trying to understand its songs for years. They have discovered interesting facts about Humpbacks in the process.

The "singers" change their song as the breeding season moves along. Humpbacks don't have vocal cords. Scientists think that muscles in the whale's breathing system allow it to produce sounds. In a given area, all the whales sing the same song. The song heard at the end of the season is different from the song heard at the beginning. Scientists think the songs are meant to attract females or keep other male singers away.

Review for organization. Review the way your paper is written from beginning to end. Check that each paragraph flows into the next. Rearrange sentences, paragraphs, or larger units of text to make your ideas flow in a logical way.

Revise

 **TEKS** 6.25B
ELPS 3E, 4K

Revising **for** Development of Ideas

When you revise for *development of ideas,* you make sure that you've included enough details to describe your ideas. Are your ideas developed enough so readers can understand and appreciate them? In a research report, make sure your ideas and conclusions are supported with evidence from your sources.

How can I include details to develop my ideas?

Think of how you developed your topic. Check to see if you've answered the 5 W's *(Who, What, When, Where, Why).* Revisit your research report. Think about these questions:

- Are there details that answer all the 5 W questions?
- Could I add more interesting and relevant details or evidence?
- Do my ideas and evidence support the conclusion?

Try It Read the writing below. How and where does it answer the 5 W questions? Discuss your findings with a partner. The first two have been done for you.

> Country music **[what]** grew up and changed much the same way our country did. The settlers **[who]** who came to America brought music from their homelands with them. Scottish, Irish, and English people had their own kind of tunes. As people began to mingle, so did their music. Different sounds started up in different areas. In Appalachia, people played guitars, banjos and fiddles in their own way.
>
> Music and people mixed even more after records and radio were invented. They had a big impact on music. One could hear what people were playing and listening to all over the country.
>
> Country music mixes with these many styles. You can have country bluegrass, or country western, or country rock. Country music keeps changing as new singers and musicians add their own touches. It will keep changing as our country grows.

 Review your details. Check that you have included important details and evidence to answer the 5 W's. Look for places where you can add sentences that provide strong evidence to support your ideas.

TEKS 6.25D
ELPS 3E, 4K

What is the best way to present my ideas?

As a writer, you want your audience to connect to your ideas. You want them to "buy into" your conclusions. In order to connect to the audience in a meaningful way, you should support your thinking. This shows you know your topic. Quotations from sources can add depth to your ideas and get readers to think "Wow, I didn't know that! This writer knows his stuff!"

 Read this paragraph. Tell a partner the details and/or quotations that you think add interest and depth.

> When we think of money, we usually think in terms of how much we have, or want, or need. But did you ever stop to wonder how money got started in the first place? "Long ago, people didn't even need money! They made or grew the things they needed," says Abby Longman in her book The History of Money (34). They traded with other people, too. Later, coins were invented. After a while, people came up with common measures of value. Different cultures used different things for money. They used shells, leaves, feathers —even dried fish! In ancient Rome, soldiers were paid in "salt." That's how our word "salary" came to be.

How can I support my ideas in an interesting way?

Using quotations is a credible way to present and support an idea. Most often when you are using sources, you will paraphrase the information that the sources provide. Sometimes, however, a piece of information will be so important that you want to say it exactly as it is shown in the source text. When that happens, use quotations to present the information that supports your ideas and thesis.

 Check your ideas. Be sure your report includes enough interesting facts and details to surprise your readers and keep them reading. Use quotations along with paraphrasing to support your ideas in an interesting way.

ELPS 3E, 3H, 4K

Revising for Voice

When you revise for *voice*, you make sure your writing sounds authentic, like you. Also, you want your reader to know that you are telling them important information. You want your writing to sound natural and engaging, but for a research report, you need to sound formal and knowledgeable too. You have to strike a balance.

How can my voice sound natural and credible?

When writing a research report, you need to make sure that your readers can trust the information you are giving them, so you want to sound formal, knowledgeable, and credible. However, it is also important to connect with your reader so that they want to continue reading. Read the examples below.

> **Natural and Credible**
>
> Did you know that there is no paper in paper money? Bills are printed on material that is made from cotton and linen. This material lasts longer than paper.
>
> **Too Formal**
>
> Our United States government created a dollar coin in 1979. It was a silver coin. It had the face of Susan B. Anthony on it. She was a leader in women's rights in the late 1800s. The government thought that people would like to have dollar coins. However, the coins were easily confused with quarters, so few were ever circulated.

 Compare the two examples above. With a partner, discuss the following questions. How are these examples different? Which one makes you want to keep reading? Why?

 Check your voice. Read through your report. Revise sentences that sound too formal or not formal enough. Think about how you can revise your writing to connect with your audience.

How can I let the real me come through?

Your personality is what makes you unique. Sometimes, it can get lost in a research report. It is very important to give information, state your thesis, and support your controlling idea with evidence. But you need to remember that your reader wants to be engaged.

 Read the paragraphs below. With a partner, rewrite them so they sound more natural.

> In the United States, all bills are green. Other countries have colorful money. It comes in all shapes and sizes. The United States has a law about who can be pictured on coins and paper bills. No living person can be shown. The law was passed to keep a person, like a king, from minting money.

> Most countries make their own money. Each country has its own special paper and ink. The processes for making coins and paper money is kept secret. This prevents people from making counterfeit copies.

 Read your report carefully. Make sure your voice matches your personality.

Voice
Sentences are revised to make the voice more natural.

What will money be like in the future? Experts say that ~~perhaps~~ *maybe* we will not need money at all. ~~It is possible~~ *Maybe* ~~that~~ debit and credit cards will replace money completely. Perhaps we will begin using our computers to send and receive digital money. Who can tell what the future holds in store for us ~~when it comes to money~~?

TEKS 6.14E
ELPS 2G

Revising Using a Checklist

Revise

Check your revising. On a piece of paper, write the numbers 1 to 10. If you can answer "yes" to a question, put a check mark after that number. If not, continue to work with that part of your report.

Focus and Coherence

_____ **1.** Is my controlling idea and major research topic the focus throughout my report?

_____ **2.** Have I clearly introduced my thesis at the beginning and addressed it again in my conclusion?

Organization

_____ **3.** Is the outline I created organized logically?

_____ **4.** Does my report follow my outline?

_____ **5.** Do my ideas, sentences, and paragraphs flow in a logical order?

Development of Ideas

_____ **6.** Have I included enough details to develop my ideas?

_____ **7.** Have I supported my thesis with evidence?

_____ **8.** Do I use quotations to create interest and add credibility?

Voice

_____ **9.** Does my voice sound credible?

_____ **10.** Does the real me come through while still giving important information to my readers?

Revise

Make a clean copy. Ask a classmate to read and respond to your report. Revise based on his or her feedback. Then create a clean copy for editing.

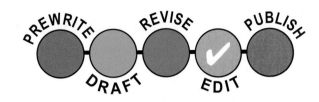

TEKS 6.25C

PREWRITE • • REVISE • ✓ PUBLISH
DRAFT EDIT

Editing

After you've finished revising, it's time to edit your work for grammar, mechanics, sentence structure, and spelling. To edit your draft effectively, use the keys as a guide.

Keys to Effective Editing

1. Use a dictionary, a thesaurus, your computer's spell checker, and the "Proofreader's Guide."

2. Read your report out loud and listen for words or phrases that may be incorrect.

3. Look for errors in grammar, punctuation, capitalization, and spelling.

4. Check your report for consistent formatting.

5. Edit on a printed computer copy. Then enter your changes on the computer.

6. Use the editing and proofreading marks inside the back cover of this book.

RESEARCH

 **TEKS** 6.19A(vii)
ELPS 3D

Editing for Conventions

Grammar

When you edit for *conventions*, you make sure you have used correct grammar, punctuation, capitalization, sentence structure, and spelling.

Do I use subordinating conjunctions?

A *subordinating conjunction* connects two ideas by making one idea depend on the other. The subordinating conjunction always comes before the dependent clause. It connects that dependent idea to the main idea. It can come at the beginning or in the middle of the sentence.

Examples

1. While **you were out, the paper was delivered.**
2. Although **Cesar was a good player, he did not win the game.**
3. **We cannot leave** until **the babysitter comes.**
4. **We were happy** when **the show started.**

Subordinating Conjunctions				
after	although	as	because	before
during	even though	if	in order that	now that
since	so that	than	though	unless
until	when	whether	whenever	while

GRAMMAR
Try It

Use a subordinating conjunction to link sentence pairs into one new sentence. Remember, the subordinating conjunction connects a dependent idea to the main idea. With a partner, share your new sentences and discuss which idea is dependent on the other.

1. Sam practiced his music. He could try out for the band.
2. There weren't enough crayons. The children had to share.
3. Sarah played the piano. Ari sang.
4. She has a pretty voice. She didn't want to sing in the chorus.

Edit

Check for subordinating conjunctions. Using subordinating conjunctions can allow you to combine sentences and add variety to your writing. Check your report for sentences that can be combined. See that you have used subordinating conjunctions properly. Practice using the conjunction as you speak or in an oral presentation.

TEKS 6.19C
ELPS 2I, 3D, 3E

Do the subjects and verbs in my sentences agree?

A verb should always agree with its subject in number.

Singular subjects take singular verbs.

> **Example:** **My** dog barks **when it** wants **to go outside.**

Plural subjects take plural verbs.

> **Example:** **Our** dogs bark **when they** want **to go outside.**

Compound subjects joined by *and* **usually take plural verbs.**

> **Example:** **Both** giraffes and zebras live **on African plains.**

Two or more singular subjects joined by the word *or* **or the word** *nor* **have a singular verb.**

> **Example:** **Either** Ms. Ross or Mr. Perez teach **English in 6th Grade.**

 Choose the verb that belongs in each sentence. With a partner, take turns reading the sentences aloud.

1. Ali and David always (arrives, arrive) on time.
2. Neither Jake nor Carmen (want, wants) to stay after school.
3. Both kangaroos and wallabies (live, lives) in Australia.
4. Walruses have tusks that (weigh, weighs) up to nine pounds.

 Edit for subject-verb agreement. Reread your report. Make sure your subjects and verbs agree in number.

Learning Language

For many verbs, the letter *s* shows the difference between the singular form of a verb from the plural form.

> live / lives   run / runs   play / plays

Some verbs change spelling entirely to show singular and plural.

> is / are   was / were   has / have

With a partner, practice speaking sentences with different subject and verb agreement. Use the verbs above or find your own verbs to use. Listen to your partner's sentences. Discuss the subject-verb agreement.

RESEARCH

 TEKS 6.20B(iii)
ELPS 2I, 3E, 4K

Mechanics: Punctuation

Have I used parentheses correctly?

When you use parentheses, you are enclosing information that isn't necessary to the meaning of the sentence. It is additional information.

> The strongest winds of the hurricane are the closest to the center (also called the eye).

Parentheses are also used in research reports to enclose source citations.

> If the winds reach 74 miles per hour, the storm becomes a hurricane (Aker 4).

 Put parentheses around the words that contain the additional information. Try writing your own sentence that uses parentheses. With a partner, listen to each other's sentences to see if you can hear where the parentheses should be.

1. Rio Grande known in Mexico as Rio Bravo separates Mexico from Texas.
2. A quart 32 ounces can be shared by four people.
3. The Rio Grande is the 4th largest river in the Unites States Smythe 589.

How can I use brackets to clarify information?

Use brackets when you need to add something to a quotation. Brackets offer explanations that the source did not have. They clarify, or make certain information more clear.

> "If it [Hugo] was a category 4 storm, I never want to see a category 5!"

 Look in magazines or newspapers for brackets in the text. Share your findings with a partner and discuss how the brackets are used.

 Edit for parentheses, brackets. Reread your report. In sentences that need more detail, add them in parentheses if possible. Make sure your citations are enclosed. Look for quotations that are unclear. Add brackets and the necessary information to any quotations that need to be clarified.

TEKS 6.20B(iii)
ELPS 3E, 3H

How can I shorten quotations without changing the meaning?

As you research, you will want to use the best quotes from your sources. Sometimes, the quotation that you want to use will be too long, or it will have information that is not relevant to the idea you want to share. That is when you can use an ellipsis. An ellipsis is a series of three marks that show the reader where words have been omitted or left out of a quotation.

In this example, the student wanted to share the idea that hurricanes are large, scary, and amazingly destructive. The source included extra information that the student did not need. See how this student used an ellipsis to omit or leave out the information that was not relevant.

From the source:

A storm surge almost two stories high broke over the city. Meanwhile, people miles away had no idea what was happening. They went about their daily lives while the hurricane hit, causing 20-foot floods and more than 8,000 deaths.

From the report:

"A storm surge almost two stories high broke over the city . . . causing 20-foot floods and more than 8,000 deaths" (Sklar).

Read the following quotation about the Great Depression. On your own paper, rewrite the quotation to show only the most relevant information. Use an ellipsis to omit information you do not need. Explain your choice with a partner.

"Living through the Great Depression was hard for my family. We cheered ourselves with stories and games, but were hungry much of the time. Many families we knew went hungry and there was nothing we could do to help them. It was very sad."

Edit for ellipses. Go back to your report. Were there any quotations that were too long or had extra information in them? Are there words you should omit to refine your quotations? Edit any quotations that have too much information using an ellipsis.

Editing   **Using a Checklist**

Edit

Check your editing. On a piece of paper, write the numbers 1 to 11. If you can answer "yes" to a question, put a check mark after that number. If not, continue to edit for that convention.

Conventions

GRAMMAR

_____ **1.** Do I use correct forms of verbs *(had gone,* not *had went)*?

_____ **2.** Do my subjects and verbs agree in number?
(Hurricanes *are* dangerous, not Hurricanes *is* dangerous.)

_____ **3.** Have I used the correct subordinating conjunctions in my sentences?

MECHANICS (PUNCTUATION and CAPITALIZATION)

_____ **4.** Have I correctly punctuated my works-cited page?

_____ **5.** Have I correctly placed citations in my report in parentheses?

_____ **6.** Do I capitalize proper nouns and titles?

SENTENCE STRUCTURE

_____ **7.** Have I used ellipses to shorten quotations that are too long?

_____ **8.** Do I have a variety of sentence lengths?

SPELLING

_____ **9.** Do I spell my words correctly?

_____ **10.** Have I double-checked the spelling of names in my report?

_____ **11.** Have I double-checked the spelling of authors' names on my works-cited page?

Creating a Title

■ Describe the main idea: **Destructive Hurricanes**

■ Be creative: **Hurricane Havoc**

Go Online!

Publishing

PREWRITE · DRAFT · REVISE · EDIT · PUBLISH ✓

Sharing Your Report

After you have worked so hard to write and improve your report, you'll want to make a neat-looking final copy to share. You may also decide to prepare your report as an electronic presentation, an online essay, or an illustrated report.

Publish

Make a final copy. Follow your teacher's instructions or use the following guidelines to format your report. Create a clean final copy and carefully proofread it.

RESEARCH

Focus on **Presentation**

- Use blue or black ink and double-space the entire paper.
- Write your name, your teacher's name, the class, and the date in the upper left corner of page 1.
- Skip a line and center your title; skip another line and start your writing.
- Indent every paragraph and leave a one-inch margin on all four sides.
- Write your last name and the page number in the upper right corner of every page of your report.

Develop Visual Aids

Draw a diagram or prepare a model to illustrate an important part of your topic. (For example, if you wrote about geysers, you might draw a diagram showing how a geyser works.)

Make a Multimedia Presentation

Prepare a multimedia presentation of your report. (See "Multimedia Presentations" on pages 443–451 for more information.)

Go Online
Upload your research for others to read.

TEKS 6.22A–B, 6.23A–E, 6.24A–B, 6.25A, 6.25C–D

Research Report Checklist

Use the following checklist for your written or oral research report. If you can answer "yes" to a question, check the number. If not, apply these items to your next published piece.

Creating a Topic and Research Plan

_____ **1.** Did I brainstorm and consult with others to decide on a topic?

_____ **2.** Did the open-ended questions I formulated help me to decide on and address my major research question? Did I refine my major research question?

_____ **3.** Did I generate a good research plan to gather relevant and reliable information about my topic?

Gathering Sources

_____ **4.** Did I follow my research plan to search for a variety of print, electronic, and expert sources?

_____ **5.** Did I use both primary and secondary sources? Are my sources valid, relevant, and reliable?

Collecting Data

_____ **6.** Did I take careful notes, identify the source in my notes, and record bibliographic information in a standard format?

_____ **7.** Did I use data from charts and graphs in my written notes?

_____ **8.** Did I use technology to help me organize my notes?

Synthesizing and Presenting Information

_____ **9.** Did I compile important information from multiple sources into an organized, focused report?

_____ **10.** Did I include quotations to support my ideas and use an appropriate form of documentation to show the source?

_____ **11.** Did I carefully check to make sure I have not plagiarized an author's work?

_____ **12.** Is my report presented in a consistent format?

_____ **13.** Did I reread my draft to check for **focus and coherence, organization, development of ideas,** and **voice**? Did I edit my presentation for **conventions**?

Making Oral Presentations

You have probably already given lots of oral presentations—from your first show-and-tell in kindergarten to book reports, group projects, and demonstration speeches. Speaking in front of other people is an important lifelong skill, and the more you practice speaking now, the more your skill and confidence will grow.

In this chapter, you will learn how to present a research report you have already written. You will also find some tips on effective speaking and how to apply them to your own presentation. Finally, you'll get some helpful hints on how to relax during your presentation.

What's Ahead

- **Preparing Your Presentation**
- **Organizing a Research Report Presentation**
- **Delivering Your Speech**

 **TEKS** 6.25A. 6.25D
ELPS 5B, 5G

Preparing Your Presentation

When you prepare an oral presentation from something you have already written, you have gathered that information, developed your topic and the details you want to use. Here are some tips to help you organize and present your ideas.

- Start with an exciting opening to grab the audience's attention.
- Ask a question, tell a surprising fact, or make a strong statement.
- Repeat a famous quotation.

Rewriting in Action

Look at the two introductions below. The first is from the written report on hurricanes. The second is the same introduction that has been rewritten for an oral report. What is the same? What has been added? Which would be more interesting to hear if you were in the audience?

Does the thought of a hurricane scare you? It should. Hurricanes cause a lot of damage every year. Especially along the southeastern coast of the Unites States. To understand these storms, scientists are studying how hurricanes, form, move, and cause destruction.

Does the thought of a hurricane scare you? It should. A little more than 100 years ago, the deadliest storm in the history of the United States roared out of the Gulf of Mexico and crashed into the island of Galveston, Texas. The hurricane that hit on September 8, 1900 was a Category 4 storm. More than 10,000 people died. The island was destroyed by 15-foot waves and 130-mile-an-hour winds. In addition to lives, the devastation cost about $700 million in today's dollars.

What exactly are hurricanes? What causes them? That's what we're here today to find out.

 Rethink and rewrite your material. Review the written report you will present. Rewrite parts that won't sound interesting to an audience using the tips above.

TEKS 6.25B
ELPS 5B, 5G

Using Visual Aids

Once you have finished writing (or rewriting) your essay or report, you are ready to prepare your presentation. Use visual aids like the ones listed below to summarize your findings and show evidence to support your ideas. They will help make your presentation clear and interesting.

Posters	show words, pictures, or both.
Photographs	help your audience "see" who or what you are talking about.
Charts	compare ideas or explain main points.
Transparencies	highlight key words, ideas, or graphics.
Maps	show specific places being discussed.
Objects	allow your audience to see the real thing.

Here are some tips for preparing your visual aids.

1 **Choose them carefully.** Use visual aids that help explain or clarify a main point.

2 **Make them big.** Be sure your visual aids can be seen from the back of the room.

3 **Keep them clear.** Choose words and graphics that are to the point and easy to read at a glance.

4 **Use a good design.** Make visual aids colorful and attractive.

List visual aids. List a number of possible visual aids you could use for a presentation of a hurricane report. Then select two that you think will work best.

> *List of visual aids*
> *＊photographs of hurricanes or hurricane damage*
> *＊maps of areas where hurricanes have occurred*
> *＊graphs or charts to show statistics clearly*
> *＊actual objects that survived a hurricane*

 TEKS 6.25C
ELPS 3E

Organizing a Research Report Presentation

If you are asked to give a presentation in any of your classes, there are a few things you should know. When you give a presentation, you want to give your audience information, but you need to make it interesting, too. Follow these suggestions:

1 Use visual aids, props, and other materials to help your audience *see* what you are telling them.

2 Use a more formal voice during your presentation, but try to infuse your personality. You want to sound knowledgeable and natural.

3 Present your findings in an organized, step-by-step way.

Using Note Cards

One way to organize your ideas is to use note cards. Because you will have a lot of important information to share, you need to put it in an easy-to-handle form.

For example, the writer of the hurricane report decided to present her research report. She rewrote the main ideas on note cards. Then, as she gave her presentation, she was able to see the next point by simply glancing at the next card.

Note-Card Guidelines

- Write out your introduction word for word.
- Number your cards and use a separate card for each idea.
- Write the idea at the top of the card. Underneath, add specific details and evidence supporting that idea you want to present.
- At the appropriate points, show your visual aids.
- Write out your ending word for word.

 Create your note cards. Look over the example note cards on the next page. Create note cards in a consistent format with the topics, findings, and evidence that you will present. Add notes to yourself about visual aids.

1

Introduction (grab my audience)
        Does the thought of a hurricane scare you? It should. A little more than 100 years ago, the deadliest storm in the history of the United States roared out of the Gulf of Mexico and crashed into the island of Galveston, Texas. The hurricane that hit on September 8, 1900 was a Category 4 storm. More than 10,000 people died. The island was destroyed by 15-foot (5 meter) waves and 130-mile-an-hour (210-kilome-

2

Hurricanes (controlling idea/thesis statement)
        Hurricanes are nature's most powerful storms. They build up over the ocean and sometimes move onto land. They can cause devastating damage.
– Visual: Show photographs of destruction caused by a hurricane.

3

Evidence (discuss scientific data)
        Scientists use a 5-point scale to measure the strength of a hurricane. The category 5 hurricane is the strongest.
– Visual: Show and explain the chart of hurricane categories.

4

Ending (support my conclusion)
        Hurricanes can cause destruction, injury and death. My Uncle Arnie lived through Hurricane Hugo in 1989. He remembers his fear and the pounding of the wind and rain. He says "If Hugo was a category 4 storm, I never want to see a category 5!" I don't blame him!

 **ELPS** 3D, 3G, 3H

Delivering Your Presentation

Every time you speak, you use both your voice and your body to communicate your message. The way you speak and move helps you connect with your listeners. This is especially important during an oral presentation. The following suggestions should be helpful.

Using Body Language

1 **Stand up straight.** Relax, but don't slouch. When you relax, it helps your audience to relax, too. They will enjoy your presentation more.

2 **Take a deep breath.** Breathe deeply to relax. Give yourself a moment to think about what you will say next.

3 **Look up.** Make eye contact with your audience. If looking at your audience is hard for you, look slightly over their heads.

4 **Look interested.** Use facial expressions to show the audience that you care about your topic.

5 **Use your hands.** Use simple hand gestures, such as pointing to a visual aid, to add emphasis and interest.

Using Your Voice

Along with your body, your voice helps you communicate clearly. The most important features of your speaking voice are *volume, tone,* and *speed.*

Volume	Practice speaking loudly enough so that everyone in the room will be able to hear you.
Tone	Stress certain words if you want to add feeling or emphasize an idea.
Speed	Practice your presentation. Remember that too slow is boring, but too fast can be confusing. Vary your speed of delivery depending on what you want to emphasize.

 Practice and present. Practice your presentation using the tips and suggestions above and the checklist on the next page. Have a family member or friend listen to you practice and offer suggestions.

RESEARCH

Overcoming Stage Fright

Most people feel nervous in front of a group. You may feel that way, too. Here are some ways to help you relax and reduce your "stage fright."

1 Practice and be prepared.

Know your presentation. That means you should practice every chance you get. Practice by delivering it in front of a mirror, family, or friends. Also consider videotaping your presentation to evaluate your delivery.

2 Warm up.

Before you begin your presentation, stretch your arms, neck, and shoulders. Breathe deeply.

3 Focus.

Often, nervousness or stage fright comes from losing your focus. When you are making your presentation, concentrate on what you are doing and on what comes next.

Using a Checklist

Whenever you practice your presentation, use the checklist below. If possible, record yourself or have someone else watch your presentation and offer suggestions.

_____ **1.** My posture is relaxed, but I don't slouch.

_____ **2.** I look up from my notes, have eye contact with my audience, and move naturally.

_____ **3.** I speak clearly and loudly enough to be heard and understood by everyone.

_____ **4.** I look and sound like I'm interested in my topic.

_____ **5.** I control and vary my speed (not too fast, not too slow).

_____ **6.** I avoid unnecessary sounds and words: *um, er, like.*

_____ **7.** My visual aids are clear and large enough for all to see.

_____ **8.** I use my hands to hold my notes and to point out my visual aids.

 ELPS 3D, 3E, 3G, 3H

Presentation Tips

Before your presentation . . .

- **Gather all the materials you will need.**
  Practice your presentation as much as you can.
- **Time your presentation.**
  If it is too short, add information, details, and evidence.
- **Be prepared.**
  Put all your main ideas and important details on
  note cards.

During your presentation . . .

- **Hold up your visual aids as you refer to them.**
  Be sure that everyone can see them.
- **Speak up.** Be sure everyone can hear you.
- **Talk slowly.** You want your audience to understand you.
  Repeat important information if necessary.
- **Keep talking throughout the presentation.**
  Stay focused on your topic,
  and keep your report moving.
- **Remind your audience of
  your thesis statement.** In your
  conclusion, make a final
  observation, linking the idea
  back to your thesis statement.

After your presentation . . .

- **Answer any questions.**
  Ask if anyone has a question
  about the topic.
- **Then collect your materials**
  and walk to your seat.

Practice and present. Have a final practice with a friend or someone
at home. Ask for feedback and make changes. Then, after your classroom
demonstration, listen to suggestions from your teacher and classmates.

Developing

Multimedia Presentations

If you've just written your best report or essay ever, you may want to share it with a larger audience. By creating a multimedia presentation or a Web page using a computer, you'll be able to reach a larger audience, as well as add special effects to your report.

There are several kinds of software that you can use to produce multimedia presentations and Web pages. Just add a little imagination, and you'll be connecting with your audience in a new, dynamic way.

What's Ahead

- **Electronic Slideshow**
- **Web Page**

 **TEKS** 6.14A, 6.17D, 6.25A,

Creating an Electronic Slideshow

With the help of a computer, you can create an electronic slideshow that includes computer-generated slides with text, graphics and sound effects. These "extras" can make the important points of your presentation clearer and more interesting.

Prewriting Selecting a Topic and Details

For this presentation, you may want to use something you've already written that interests both you and your audience. Choose your topic, conduct the necessary research, and list your ideas. Then find or create one or more of the graphics or sound effects to match your ideas:

- **Pictures** such as photos or "click art"
- **Animations** that show a process or tell a story
- **Videos** of something you've filmed yourself
- **Sounds** and **music** to use as background or to make a point

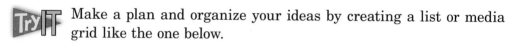 Make a plan and organize your ideas by creating a list or media grid like the one below.

Media Grid

Words on Slides	Visuals	Animations or Music	Sounds
1. Hurricanes cause a lot of damage each year.	photos	background music	
2. Scientists study the storms to understand them better.	charts	hurricane animation	storm sound effects

 Gather details. Select ideas from your list or media grid for different graphics and sounds to include with each slide. Create them yourself or find them on the Internet. Save these images and sounds on your computer in a special folder created for this assignment.

Drafting **Preparing the Electronic Slideshow**

Make a *storyboard*. A storyboard is a "map" of the slides you plan to use in your presentation. (See the sample storyboard on the next page.) Use your list or media grid as a guide. Follow these tips:

- Include one box for each main idea in the storyboard.
- Use your computer software to design the slides.
- If you include words, choose a typestyle that is easy to read.
- Use the graphics and sounds you found earlier.
- Use bulleted lists and graphs to organize your information.
- Have each slide lead to the next in a coherent, organized way.

Create a storyboard. Refer to your list or media grid to help you map out your storyboard. Using the tips above, include ideas that your audience will see and hear. This will give you an idea of how the slides should look.

Revising **Improving Your Presentation**

Match the spoken parts of your presentation to the slides. To work well, everything in your presentation must be tied together so that it flows smoothly. Practice your presentation with family and friends. Ask for any suggestions they may have for making your presentation even better.

Rehearse your report. As you rehearse, fix the parts that don't flow smoothly. Make whatever changes using your peers best suggestions.

Editing **Checking for Conventions**

Check the text on each slide for grammar, punctuation, capitalization, and spelling. Ask your teacher and/or a classmate to check your slides, too.

Make corrections. Make edits based on the feedback you receive. Go through the presentation once more to make sure it works well.

You can save your presentation on a disk or CD to share with others. Make sure you copy all the necessary files.

TEKS 6.17D

Interactive Report Storyboard

Here is the storyboard for the electronic slideshow based on the student research report about hurricanes. The author reads each slide and adds details from the report as the slides are presented.

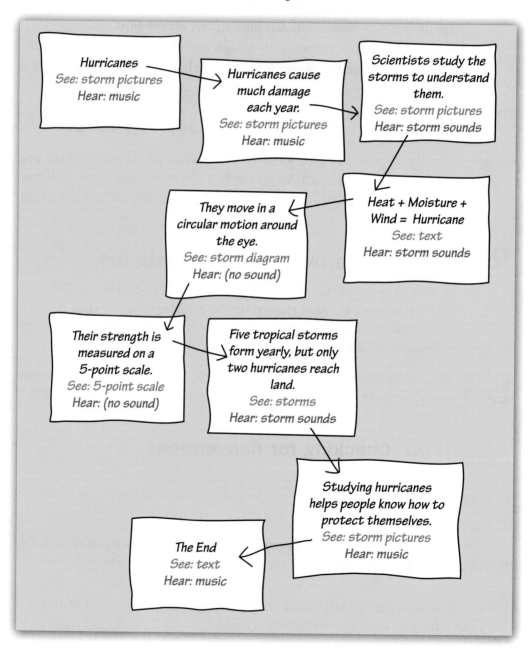

Hurricanes
See: storm pictures
Hear: music

Hurricanes cause
much damage
each year.
See: storm pictures
Hear: music

Scientists study the
storms to understand
them.
See: storm pictures
Hear: storm sounds

They move in a
circular motion around
the eye.
See: storm diagram
Hear: (no sound)

Heat + Moisture +
Wind = Hurricane
See: text
Hear: storm sounds

Their strength is
measured on a
5-point scale.
See: 5-point scale
Hear: (no sound)

Five tropical storms
form yearly, but only
two hurricanes reach
land.
See: storms
Hear: storm sounds

Studying hurricanes
helps people know how to
protect themselves.
See: storm pictures
Hear: music

The End
See: text
Hear: music

TEKS 6.17D

RESEARCH

Slideshow Checklist

Use the following checklist to make sure your slideshow presentation is the best it can be. When you can answer all of the questions with a "yes," you're ready to present!

Focus and Coherence

_____ **1.** Did I introduce my topic clearly in the beginning?

_____ **2.** Did I include the important relevant main points?

_____ **3.** Did I end with a summary or wrap-up thought to support the ideas I presented at the beginning?

Organization

_____ **4.** Did I organize my storyboard in a logical way so that my slideshow would be ordered in a logical way?

_____ **5.** Does my presentation flow smoothly from slide to slide?

Development of Ideas

_____ **6.** Did I choose a report for my slideshow that could be developed in-depth?

_____ **7.** Do my graphics help communicate my ideas clearly?

Voice

_____ **8.** Did I use an interesting, somewhat formal voice?

_____ **9.** Does my voice fit my audience and topic?

Conventions

_____ **10.** Is my presentation free of errors in grammar, mechanics, sentence structure, and spelling?

Multimedia Choices

_____ **11.** Are all of my graphics and visuals relevant to my topic?

_____ **12.** Did I choose the best pictures and sounds for my ideas?

 **TEKS** 6.17D, 6.25A, 6.25B, 6.25D

Creating a Video

Suppose you wrote a report that contains information you would like to share. You can create a video to present it to an audience larger than your own class. Using video allows you to add music, sound, animation, and graphics to help bring your report to life. With permission from your parents or teachers, you might even want to post your video on a Web site.

Prewriting Selecting a Topic and Details

When you plan your video, follow similar guidelines as when you create an oral presentation or a written report. First, select the topic you will cover. You can use a report you have already written. Compile information from multiple sources, develop a thesis statement to focus your report, and then summarize your findings using evidence to support your conclusions.

- **Plan your information.** Choose the material from your report that you want to use. List it, and check to make sure it is interesting and informative.

- **Plan your presentation.** Look at your list. Arrange it in a logical order so that your video will flow smoothly.

- **Plan your graphics.** Think about what you could include in your video to add interest. What keeps you interested when you are watching an informative video? Use photos, animation, sound effects, music, or interviews to vary what your audience sees.

 Make a plan for your video by making a Planning Chart like the one below that shows what you will talk about, or narrate, and what will be shown at the same time.

Video Planning Chart

Information	Visual
What are hurricanes? How are they formed? Share a personal story.	movie of a hurricane in action animation of a hurricane forming interview with Uncle Arnie

 Gather details. Select ideas, findings, and evidence from your list to include. Document your sources in your credits at the end of your video.

TEKS 6.17D, 6.25B–D
ELPS 3H, 5B, 5G

Drafting **Preparing your Video**

Create a *storyboard* similar to the one for a slideshow. Just like a real filmmaker, a storyboard will help you plan the scenes you want to show in your video. (See the page **450**.) Use your planning list as a guide. Include one box in the storyboard for each main idea.

On each panel in the storyboard, include what the audience will hear and what they will see at the same time. To help make it interesting, you can narrate while the video is being shown. This means that your audience will hear your voice while they see something else. Be sure to present your video in a consistent format so that it is easy to follow.

Create a storyboard. Refer to your planning list to help you map out your storyboard including evidence to support your ideas. Include exactly what your audience will see and hear. Plan your video carefully before you start filming so that everything is in place when you begin the process.

Revising **Improving Your Video**

Once you have recorded your video, you will need to make sure that it is organized in a logical way. Your narration should match the visual you are showing. Listen to the evidence you have presented to support your ideas. Have you informed and entertained your audience? Show your video to family and friends and listen to any feedback they may have for making your video even better.

Review your video. As you watch your video, you may notice parts that you can improve with details or better visuals. Make whatever changes are necessary.

Editing **Checking for Conventions**

If you have included credits, visuals, or graphics using words, check the text for grammar, punctuation, capitalization, and spelling errors. As you are crediting your sources, it is very important to spell names and document them correctly.

Make corrections. After you've edited for the things above and made corrections, watch the video one more time to make sure it works well.

Video Storyboard

Here is the storyboard for a video based on a report about hurricanes. The author planned what the audience would hear and see. If the author is narrating, he notes that by writing the narration in black.

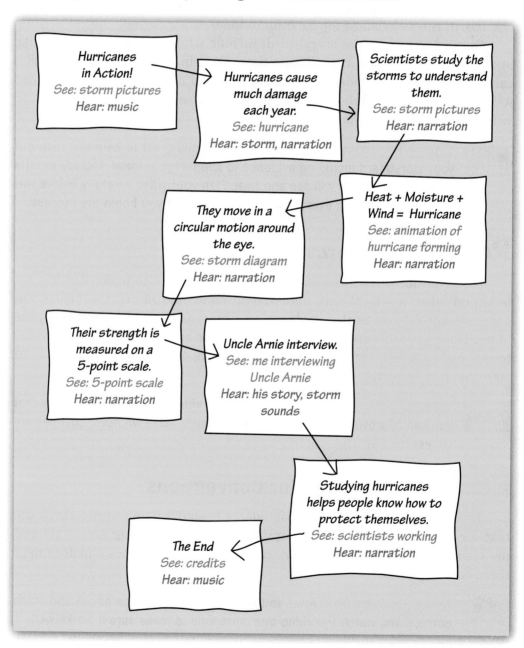

Hurricanes
in Action!
See: storm pictures
Hear: music

Hurricanes cause
much damage
each year.
See: hurricane
Hear: storm, narration

Scientists study the
storms to understand
them.
See: storm pictures
Hear: narration

They move in a
circular motion around
the eye.
See: storm diagram
Hear: narration

Heat + Moisture +
Wind = Hurricane
See: animation of
hurricane forming
Hear: narration

Their strength is
measured on a
5-point scale.
See: 5-point scale
Hear: narration

Uncle Arnie interview.
See: me interviewing
Uncle Arnie
Hear: his story, storm
sounds

Studying hurricanes
helps people know how to
protect themselves.
See: scientists working
Hear: narration

The End
See: credits
Hear: music

Video Checklist

Use the following checklist to make sure your video is the best it can be. When you can answer all of the questions with a "yes," you're ready to share your video!

Focus and Coherence

_____ **1.** Did I introduce my topic clearly in the beginning?

_____ **2.** Did I include the important relevant main points?

_____ **3.** Did I end with a summary or wrap-up thought to support the ideas I showed at the beginning?

Organization

_____ **4.** Did I organize my storyboard in a logical and consistent way so that my audience can follow my video?

_____ **5.** Does my video flow smoothly from scene to scene?

Development of Ideas

_____ **6.** Did I develop my topic, summarize findings, and show evidence visually and in a meaningful way?

_____ **7.** Do I have quotes to support my ideas?

Voice

_____ **8.** Did my narration sound knowledgeable and natural?

_____ **9.** Does my voice fit my audience and topic?

Conventions

_____ **10.** Is my video text free of errors in grammar and spelling?

Video Choices

_____ **11.** Does my narration always match my visuals?

_____ **12.** Did I choose the best visuals and sounds for my ideas?

LISTEN
respect

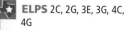
ELPS 2C, 2G, 3E, 3G, 4C, 4G

TEXAS
WRITE
SOURCE
Online
www.hmheducation.com/tx/writesource

The Tools of Language

Learning Language

Work with a partner. Read the meanings and share answers to the questions.

1. The purpose is the reason for doing something.
   What is the purpose of turning off lights when you leave a room?

2. To revise is to change something and make it better.
   Tell one thing you would like to revise about the last essay you wrote for class.

3. Feedback is comments and opinions about something.
   Suppose you could give feedback to the director of the last movie you saw. Tell a partner what you would say.

clarify speak observe

Listening and Speaking

No matter where you are in school—in the classroom, in the gym, on the stage—you need to listen carefully. This means paying attention to everything that is being said. Why is this important? For one thing, you don't want to miss anything. Teachers introduce new ideas, coaches explain new strategies, and directors give stage directions. Listening is one of the most important classroom skills you can master.

Speaking, which goes hand in hand with listening, is another key classroom skill. When you have mastered these two skills, you will be able to work better with others. You will also be more confident in your ability to learn and to succeed.

What's Ahead

- **Listening in Class**
- **Participating in a Group**
- **Speaking in Class**

ELPS 2C, 2D, 2I, 5G

Listening in Class

Listening involves more than just hearing. It means *paying attention, staying focused,* and *thinking about the speaker's ideas.* The following tips will help you become a better listener—in and out of school.

1 **Figure out your purpose for listening.** Is it to learn new information, understand an assignment, review for a test?

2 **Show that you are listening.** Let the speaker know that you are listening by looking at him or her and staying focused. Looking around the room tells the speaker that you don't care very much about what's being said.

3 **Listen carefully.** Hearing is not the same as listening. Hearing involves only your ears; listening involves your ears *and* your mind. To listen, you need to think about what you hear. If you don't understand what you've heard, ask the teacher to explain.

4 **Listen and watch for signals.** Many speakers, especially teachers, will use signals to tell you what is important. Here are some common phrases to listen for.

And don't forget . . .	**This all means that . . .**
The two main reasons for . . .	**The bottom line is . . .**

Sometimes speakers use their voice as a signal. Their voice gets higher or lower, louder or softer to help make a point. Speakers also use body language and facial expressions as signals.

Keep a signal log. Make a chart like the one below for one of your classes. List the specific activities and what signals each teacher uses.

SIGNAL LOG

Class	Date	Activity	Signals
Spanish	Sept. 10	Reviewing for a test	The most important . . . Lo más importante . . .

A Closer Look at Listening

Good listening is one of the keys to successful learning. As you become a better listener, you will also become a better student. As you practice listening skills, you learn to . . .

- give your full attention to the speaker;
- notice the speaker's body language and tone of voice;
- consider how the speaker's message applies to you;
- take notes and form questions.

 Test your speaking and listening skills by doing the activity below with a classmate.

1. Draw a simple picture using three or four different geometric shapes. (See the ***Original*** illustration below.)
2. Then have a classmate re-create your picture following your spoken directions. Do **not** let your classmate see the drawing!
3. After you have finished, compare the pictures. (See the ***Copy*** below.) How close are they? Why do you think they are not exactly alike?
4. Now switch and have your partner draw a picture and give you the directions. What did this activity teach you about speaking and listening?

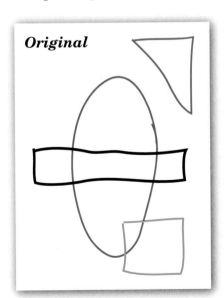

Original

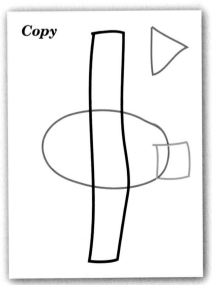

Copy

LANGUAGE

ELPS 3E, 5G

Participating in a Group

Nearly everything you say and do in a group is a response or reaction to what someone else has said or done. That's why it's important to follow basic rules of respect for yourself and for others.

Respect yourself by . . .

- believing that your own ideas are important.
- sharing your ideas clearly and politely.
- taking responsibility for what you say.

Respect others by . . .

- listening carefully to what others have to say.
- waiting for an opening before speaking, or interrupting politely by raising your hand and saying, "May I add something?"
- complimenting speakers when you can.
- encouraging everyone to participate.

> Remember, everyone has a right to his or her opinion or idea.

 Sam is participating in a classroom group. Read about him below and then write a few sentences telling what you think Sam should do in each situation. Refer to the rules of respect above.

Situation 1

Sam has an idea to add, but he's not sure if he should share it immediately. What should Sam do?

Situation 2

Sam has been selected group leader. As the group brainstorms for project ideas, Sam notices that one of the students isn't saying anything. What should Sam do?

ELPS 2D, 3E, 3G

Group Skills

You now know why listening and speaking politely are so important to group work. Here are three skills you can use to make working in a group a truly positive experience. All members of a group need to use these skills: *observing, cooperating,* and *clarifying.*

Observe the speaker's . . .
- body language (facial expressions, eye contact, posture).
- tone of voice (for excitement, nervousness, shyness).

Cooperate by . . .
- staying positive and waiting your turn.
- avoiding put-downs.
- disagreeing in a polite way.

Clarify, or make something clearer, by . . .
- asking if there are any questions you can answer.
- restating a speaker's idea if necessary to be sure you understand everything.

LANGUAGE

 Read the statements and questions below about group skills. Then discuss your answers with a classmate.

1. Ivan speaks very softly while looking down at his notes. What message is Ivan sending with his tone of voice and body language? How could he improve his message?

2. Juan keeps saying that everything the group is doing is stupid. What does Juan need to learn about working in a group?

3. Lacey listens to her group, but she doesn't understand what she is supposed to do. How can Lacey make sure that she understands everything?

Speaking in Class

To speak effectively in class or in small groups, follow the helpful guidelines listed below.

Pay attention. Listen carefully and limit your comments to the topic being discussed.

Think before you speak. Be sure your comments and ideas add to the discussion.

Be respectful. Respond politely to all speakers.

Make eye contact. Respect whomever you are talking to by looking at them. You can also listen more effectively when you watch a speaker's expressions and gestures.

Wait your turn. Show that you care about the opinions and ideas of others by listening until they are finished. Then they will be more willing to listen to you.

> Speak up so that everyone in class can hear your ideas.

Get to the point. Make your point quickly so that others have a chance to respond and join in the discussion.

 Follow the rules. On your own paper, write down one of the six speaking rules above that you think is especially important.

1 List all the reasons why you think this is a good rule to follow.

2 Give examples of what might happen if this rule is not followed.

3 Share your responses in small groups.

Learning Language

When it comes to writing, there are many new words and ideas to learn. The *writing process,* the *traits of writing, prewriting, drafting,* and *revising* are just a few of them.

If you play basketball, you know that there is a vocabulary, or certain group of words, related to this sport. Without words such as *lay up, jump shot, dribble,* and *rebound,* you would have a hard time playing the game.

The vocabulary related to writing works in the same way. Without knowing the meaning of *prewriting, drafting,* and *revising,* you would have a hard time writing a strong story or report. This chapter will help you learn all about the language of writing so you can do your best work!

What's Ahead

- Language of the Writing Process
- Language of the Writing Traits
- Language of the Writing Forms

⭐ ELPS 2C, 2D, 2G, 2H, 3D, 3H

Language Strategies

You hear new words in conversation every day. Here are some strategies to help you understand, remember, and use the new language you hear.

Listen for Language Patterns

In a language pattern, a word or phrase is repeated. Paying attention to this repetition helps you understand the meaning.

You hear: **I have been** waiting since lunch.
You hear: **I have been** wanting this forever.
You can say: **I have been** studying for an hour.

 Turn to a partner. Say two more sentences that include the phrase *I have been*.

Ask For Help

When you don't know a word you hear, ask others for help. Wait for the explanation and then thank the person for his or her help.

You can say: I just heard a new word—antique. What is an antique?

 Listen to a partner tell you about a favorite place. Ask your partner to define new words that you hear.

Use Academic Language

Your teachers may use unfamiliar words in class. Repeating the words will help you remember them.

You hear: Choose a topic that interests you.
You repeat: topic

 Listen in class and repeat words you think you may not remember. Then try using them in different sentences.

ELPS 2C, 2D, 2G, 2I, 3D, 3H, 5G

Talk Around a Problem Word

When you don't know a word, describe the word or talk around it. Then ask someone to tell you the word you don't know.

You say: This building has a moving staircase. Is that what it's called?
Your classmate says: That's called an escalator.

 Find an object that you don't know the name of. Describe it to a friend. Then ask your friend to tell you the word.

Teach a Friend

Teaching a friend, family member, or classmate about a new word can help you remember it.

You hear: Honey bees communicate by doing dances at the hive.
You can say: We communicate by talking and using our hands.

 Explain something to a classmate using a new word you have learned. Help him or her understand the new word.

Take Notes or Draw a Picture

Writing new words in a notebook gives you a way to study them later. In your notebook, jot down details or make drawings that help you understand the meaning of the word.

You hear: Snakes and lizards are examples of reptiles.
What you do: You write *reptiles* and draw a small picture of a snake and a lizard.

You hear: For good nutrition, choose foods from the four food groups.
What you do: You prepare to list the four food groups under the heading "good nutrition."

 Start and keep a vocabulary journal. The next time you hear a word you want to remember, write or draw about it in your journal.

LANGUAGE

Language of the Writing Process

Read each of the terms. Then read about what they mean.

Prewrite

The first step in the writing process is to prewrite, or plan your writing. During prewriting, you think about possible topics as well as your audience, purpose, and genre. After choosing a topic, you collect details and develop a controlling idea for your piece of writing.

When you are learning about writing, sometimes the purpose, audience, and genre are given to you. You learn many ways to generate ideas, such as brainstorming. You also learn to plan ways to arrange your ideas.

Draft

When you write a first draft, you turn your ideas and details into sentences. You build on your prewriting ideas, keeping in mind your controlling idea. You group your sentences into paragraphs as you go and, at the same, you make sure your ideas are well developed and well connected.

Revise

Next, you read over your draft and revise, or make changes. When you revise, you make sure that all the parts of your writing support your controlling idea. You check that your ideas and details are clear, complete, and organized. You also evaluate your word choices for purpose and audience.

Edit

When you edit, you correct mistakes in grammar, mechanics, and spelling, and you ensure that your sentences make sense.

Publish

In this step, you get feedback from your audience, such as your classmates or your teacher, and make any last changes. Then you publish your work by making a neat final copy.

Vocabulary: Writing Process

audience	**draft**	**edit**
mechanics	**prewrite**	**publish**
revise		

1. **Say the word.** Listen as your teacher says and points to each written word. Then repeat each word. Some words have consonant clusters, such as *dr*, *pr*, and *sh*. Which vocabulary words have consonant clusters? Practice pronouncing each word.

2. **Discover the meaning.** Working with a partner, make a three-column chart. List the vocabulary words in the first column, the meanings in the second column, and an example sentence in the third. Start with the words you already know. Discuss what you think the other words mean.

3. **Learn more.** Listen as your teacher explains the meaning of each word. Work with your partner to change what you wrote in the second column, if needed.

4. **Show your understanding.** Use your notebook to answer the questions below.
   - What do you do first—publish or edit?
   - Should you fix a spelling mistake when you edit or when you revise?
   - What is something you might do when you prewrite?

5. **Write it, show it.** In your journal, make notes and drawings to help you remember what the new words mean. For example, you might draw a pencil for the word *draft* to help you understand this step.

LANGUAGE

ELPS 2I, 4C

The Writing Process in Action

You have learned the language of the writing process. Now it's time to see the process in action! First, your teacher will show you how to do each step of the writing process. Then, you will write together, using the questions below. As you write together, your teacher will ask you to do things. These questions are called *requests*. Be sure to respond to each request.

Prewrite

1. Choose a topic. For example, select a place that you like to go to with friends.
2. Summarize what is interesting about this place.
3. What writing genre, or form, will you use to write?
4. Who is your audience for this piece of writing?

Draft

5. How can you group your ideas, or put them into categories?
6. How can you organize your ideas into paragraphs that support your controlling idea?

The Writing Process in Action

These pages from the first unit in your book show the writing process in action.

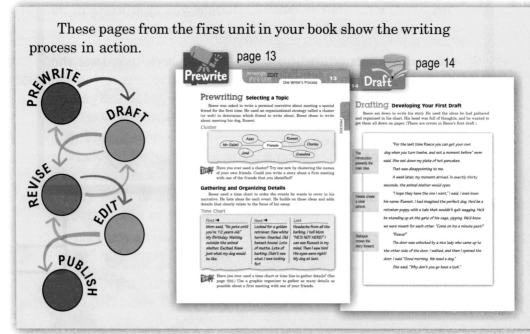

ELPS 2I, 3D, 3E, 3G, 3H, 4C

Revise

1. Do all of your sentences support your controlling idea?
2. Are there any sentences you should add or take out?
3. Does each sentence and paragraph build on the one before it?
4. Did you choose the right words for your audience?

Edit

5. Did you follow all the rules of grammar and mechanics?
6. Are the sentences put together correctly?
7. Are all the words spelled correctly?

Publish

8. Have you used the feedback you received to improve your writing?
9. Is your writing neat and easy to read?

Turn and Talk

Talk to a classmate about which step is the most important. Listen to his or her opinions.

The most important step is_____.

LANGUAGE

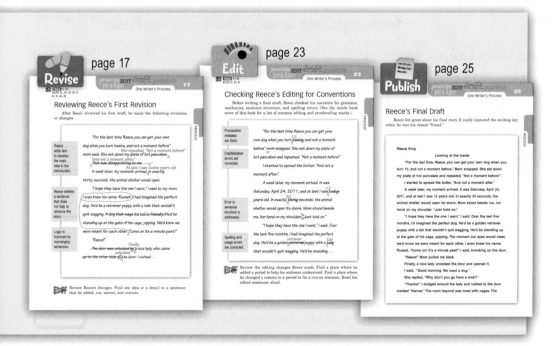

Language of the Writing Traits

Read each of these terms. Then read about what they mean.

Focus and Coherence

If your writing has focus, all your sentences connect to the main idea of your piece of writing. Coherence means that the sentences all work together for one purpose. When your writing has focus and coherence, your audience will understand your ideas.

Organization

Your writing should be organized, or arranged, in a way that makes it easy to follow from beginning to end. Each sentence should lead logically to the next. In the same way, each paragraph should be linked to the ones before and after it.

Development of Ideas

It is important to develop your ideas in depth, or completely. That means supporting the main idea in each paragraph with important and interesting details. Each sentence should add meaning to the sentence that comes before it.

Voice

Your writing voice should show the way you think and feel. It should also reflect your personality. Your voice is part of what keeps the reader interested in your ideas or information.

Conventions

Conventions refer to the rules for using grammar, mechanics, sentence structure, and spelling. Writing that is free of errors in conventions is easier to read and understand.

⭐ **ELPS** 2C, 2D, 2G, 2H, 3D, 3E, 3G, 5B

Vocabulary: Writing Traits

coherence	conventions	depth
focus	organization	voice

1 **Say the word.** Listen as your teacher reads the words aloud. For example, notice two words that have the long *o* sound. Repeat each word.

2 **Discover the meaning.** Write the words you already know in your vocabulary journal. Then, use this book to find more information about the other words. Add the new information to your journal. Write each word in a sentence. Compare your notes with a partner.

3 **Learn more.** Listen as your teacher explains the meaning of each word. Work with your partner to restate the meanings.

4 **Show your understanding.** With a partner, read the questions below and discuss your answers.
- Why is focus important when taking a photograph? Why is focus important when writing? Give an example.
- How does your speaking voice show how you feel? How could your writing voice show how you feel? Give an example.

5 **Write it, show it.** In your journal, add any last notes or drawings to help you remember what the words mean. Use a chart or other graphic organizer to add sentences that use each vocabulary word.

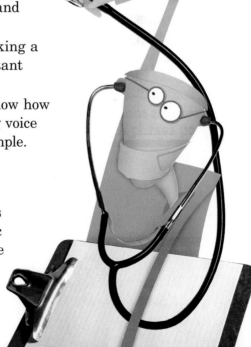

ELPS 3G, 3H, 4C

Language of Descriptive Writing

Descriptive writing is writing that describes a person, place, thing, event, or how to do something. Usually, descriptive essays have the same basic organization. A beginning paragraph tells the topic and grabs the reader's interest. Three or four body, or middle, paragraphs describe the topic. An ending paragraph concludes the description of the topic.

Descriptive Essay Organization

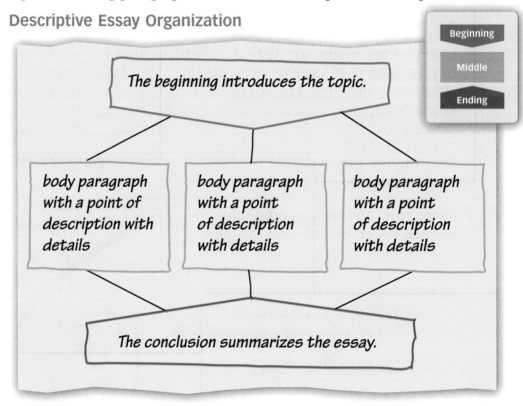

Beginning

Middle

Ending

The beginning introduces the topic.

body paragraph with a point of description with details

body paragraph with a point of description with details

body paragraph with a point of description with details

The conclusion summarizes the essay.

Turn and Talk

Talk with a partner about how the middle part of the graphic organizer helps a writer plan a descriptive essay.

The middle part of the graphic organizer _____.

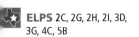

ELPS 2C, 2G, 2H, 2I, 3D, 3G, 4C, 5B

Vocabulary: Descriptive Writing

description	location	sensory details
surroundings	sights	encounter

1 **Say the word or phrase.** Listen as your teacher says and points to each word on the chalkboard. Then repeat each word.

2 **Discover the meaning.** Most of these vocabulary words appear in the margin notes next to the writing model on pages **76–77**. Work with a partner to find the words. Write notes about what you think the words mean.

3 **Learn more.** Listen as your teacher explains the meaning of each word. Work with a partner to find examples of these words in the writing model on pages **76–77**.

4 **Show your understanding.** Use your notebook to answer the questions below.
- What sights and sounds might you use in a description of a gym class?
- List three sensory words that could describe a pet cat.
- Describe your surroundings right now.

5 **Speak it, show it.** With a partner, take turns saying sentences that use one of the vocabulary words.

LANGUAGE

 ELPS 2G, 2I, 5B

Reading the Descriptive Model

What Do You Know?

Next you will read *The Watcher in the Water*, a model descriptive essay about observing a frog, on pages **76–77**. What do you know about frogs? Maybe you have seen or heard a frog in nature. What kind of sound do frogs make? What do they look like?

Build Background

A frog is a small animal that usually lives near water. It has smooth skin, large eyes, and long rear legs that allow it to leap long distances. Frogs spend the early part of their life in water but live on land when they are grown. A bullfrog is a large type of frog.

Listening

Listen as your teacher or a classmate reads *The Watcher in the Water* aloud. As you listen, make notes about the sensory details the writer uses. Note details about how the bullfrog looks, sounds, and moves, and about the scene, or surroundings. Be ready to answer the questions below.

1. How does the frog blend in with its surroundings?
2. What words and phrases describe the noise made by the bullfrog?
3. How does the writer feel during her encounter with the bullfrog?

Key Descriptive Words

olive green	slimy	echoed
ripples	acrobat	drumming

Look at the words in the box. These are some of the descriptive words the writer uses. You will see these words when you read the writing model. With a partner, decide which sense each word appeals to: sight, sound, touch, smell, or taste. Then use the words to talk about places, things, or events you have observed. Use the key words to write sentences based on your discussion.

Read Along

Now it's your turn to read. Read along as your teacher or classmate reads aloud pages **76–77**. As you read, think about the sensory details.

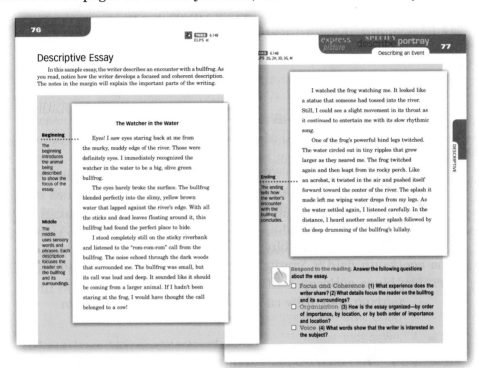

76 TEKS 6.14B ELPS 4I

Descriptive Essay

In this sample essay, the writer describes an encounter with a bullfrog. As you read, notice how the writer develops a focused and coherent description. The notes in the margin will explain the important parts of the writing.

The Watcher in the Water

Beginning
The beginning introduces the animal being described to show the focus of the essay.

Eyes! I saw eyes staring back at me from the murky, muddy edge of the river. Those were definitely eyes. I immediately recognized the watcher in the water to be a big, olive green bullfrog.

The eyes barely broke the surface. The bullfrog blended perfectly into the slimy, yellow brown water that lapped against the river's edge. With all the sticks and dead leaves floating around it, this bullfrog had found the perfect place to hide.

Middle
The middle uses sensory words and phrases. Each description focuses the reader on the bullfrog and its surroundings.

I stood completely still on the sticky riverbank and listened to the "rom-rom-rom" call from the bullfrog. The noise echoed through the dark woods that surrounded me. The bullfrog was small, but its call was loud and deep. It sounded like it should be coming from a larger animal. If I hadn't been staring at the frog, I would have thought the call belonged to a cow!

express picture *SPECIFY* describe portray **77**

Describing an Event

TEKS 6.14B ELPS 2G, 2H, 3D, 3G, 4I

I watched the frog watching me. It looked like a statue that someone had tossed into the river. Still, I could see a slight movement in its throat as it continued to entertain me with its slow rhythmic song.

One of the frog's powerful hind legs twitched. The water circled out in tiny ripples that grew larger as they neared me. The frog twitched again and then leapt from its rocky perch. Like an acrobat, it twisted in the air and pushed itself forward toward the center of the river. The splash it made left me wiping water drops from my legs. As the water settled again, I listened carefully. In the distance, I heard another smaller splash followed by the deep drumming of the bullfrog's lullaby.

Ending
The ending tells how the writer's encounter with the bullfrog concludes.

Respond to the reading. Answer the following questions about the essay.

☐ Focus and Coherence **(1)** What experience does the writer share? **(2)** What details focus the reader on the bullfrog and its surroundings?

☐ Organization **(3)** How is the essay organized—by order of importance, by location, or by both order of importance and location?

☐ Voice **(4)** What words show that the writer is interested in the subject?

DESCRIPTIVE

LANGUAGE

After Reading

Copy the following chart on a piece of paper and fill it in with words and phrases the writer uses that appeal to the senses. With a partner, use your chart to discuss your favorite parts of the descriptive essay.

Sight	Sound	Touch

Oral Language: Descriptive Writing

The person or people who will listen to you or read your writing are called the audience. When you speak or write, it is important to choose the best words to reach your audience. When you write a description, your tone, or way of writing, will be different for each audience.

 Read about the situation below. Then choose two audiences from the bottom of the page. With a partner, discuss how the words you choose might be different for each audience.

Situation

It's a winter day with plenty of snow on the ground, and you have decided to go sledding with several friends. You will describe this event to someone in a way that shows how much you enjoyed it. The description will include sights, sounds, textures, tastes, or smells that were part of the experience.

Audiences

- Your class
- A friend who has never seen snow
- A newspaper editor

ELPS 2G, 2I, 3G, 3H, 5G

Effective Talk

When you answer a question, you might use a few words, a sentence, or a few sentences. When you describe something, you should include details that help bring to life the event, place, person, or thing you are describing. When you use a lot of specific details, your description becomes richer and clearer.

Read the question and the answers below. In the first box, there are only two words. In the second box, there is a short sentence. The third answer has more detail and does a better job answering the question.

What is your favorite activity to do with friends?

play basketball

We play basketball at the indoor court.

We like to play basketball at the indoor court. The lines are faded, and the hoop has no net. We don't notice, though, because we are too busy running, passing, and shooting. Our shoes squeak on the wooden floor as we dart around the court.

Try IT Choose a question to talk about with a partner. Write down two or three ideas for answering the question. Next, add details that will help your partner understand your ideas. Finally, use your notes to discuss your answers to the questions.

1. At what restaurant or whose home do you like most to eat meals?
2. What musical event have you attended recently?

⭐ ELPS 3G, 3H

Language of Narrative Writing

A narrative essay is writing that tells about a true experience in a person's life. Narrative essays all have the same basic organization: a beginning paragraph, middle paragraphs, and an ending paragraph. The beginning introduces the story and often gives some background. The middle paragraphs tell about the experience in time, or chronological order. The ending paragraph concludes the story.

Narrative Essay Organization

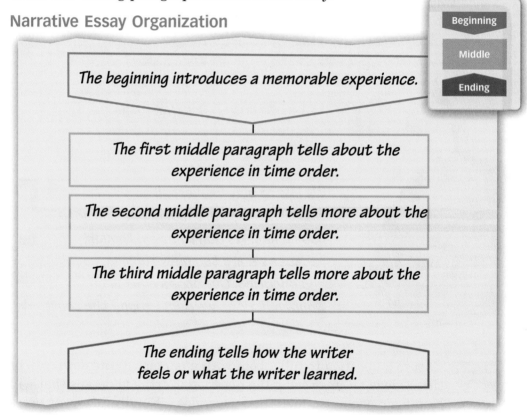

The beginning introduces a memorable experience.

The first middle paragraph tells about the experience in time order.

The second middle paragraph tells more about the experience in time order.

The third middle paragraph tells more about the experience in time order.

The ending tells how the writer feels or what the writer learned.

Beginning

Middle

Ending

Turn and Talk

Talk with a partner about how the parts of the graphic organizer fit together.

The graphic organizer _____.

⭐ **ELPS** 2C, 2G, 2H, 2I, 3D, 4C

Vocabulary: Narrative Writing

action	**chronological order**	**dialogue**
experience	**narrative**	**personality**
sensory details		

1. **Say the word or phrase.** Listen as your teacher says and points to each written word. Then repeat each word.

2. **Discover the meaning.** Some of these vocabulary words appear next to the writing model on pages **99–100**. Work with a partner to find these words. Write notes about what you think the words mean. Discuss what the other words might mean.

3. **Learn more.** Listen as your teacher explains the meaning of each word or phrase. Work with your partner to find examples of these words in the writing model on pages **99–100**.

4. **Show your understanding.** With a partner, take turns asking and answering the questions below. After listening to your partner, summarize his or her answer.
   - How does action help keep readers interested in a narrative?
   - Why is giving some background information at the beginning a good idea?
   - Tell about doing a chore in chronological order.

5. **Write it, show it.** In your journal, draw pictures to help you remember what each word means. You may wish to add other synonyms, or words that mean the same thing. For example, next to the word *dialogue*, you could draw a person's head with a speech bubble, as in a comic strip, and write the word *speech*.

LANGUAGE

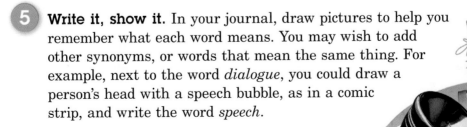

★ ELPS 2C, 2G, 2H, 2I, 3E, 4C, 5G

Reading the Narrative Model

What Do You Know?

Next, you will read *Turtle Rescue*, a model narrative essay about one student's experience with turtles. What do you know about turtles? What do they look like and where do they live? Have you ever seen a turtle in the wild or at the zoo? What impression did it make on you? Talk with a partner about your impressions.

Build Background

Turtles know how to swim, and some turtles called sea turtles live in the ocean. Female sea turtles, however, crawl onto land when it is time to lay their eggs. They do this once a year. When the eggs hatch later, the baby turtles walk back to the sea on their own. On some beaches in the United States, you can see this happen.

Listening

Listen as your teacher or a classmate reads aloud *Turtle Rescue*. As you listen, make brief notes. At the beginning, listen for the *who, where, when, what,* and *why* of the story. As you listen to the middle, make notes about the events in order. As you listen to the end, note the narrator's feeling about the experience. Then answer the questions below.

1. What is the first example of dialogue in the narrative?

2. What main event occurs first? What occurs several months later?

3. How did the narrator feel about the turtle rescue?

Key Words: Chronological Order

after	every	first
next	soon	when

Look at the words in the box. You will see these words and phrases when you read the writing model. With a partner, use some of the words to narrate an experience at school.

Read Along

Now it's your turn to read. Read along as your teacher or classmate reads aloud pages **99–100**. Think about the organization of the essay.

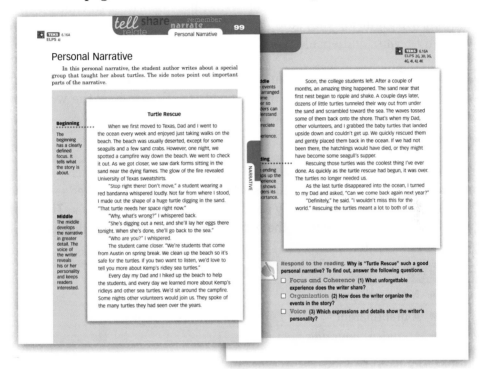

After Reading

Copy the following time line on a piece of paper. Fill it in with key events in the narrative in the correct order. Use your time line to retell the story *Turtle Rescue* to a partner.

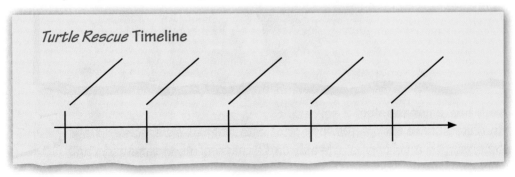

Turtle Rescue Timeline

ELPS 3G, 3H

Oral Language: Narrative Writing

The way in which you write a narrative description depends, in part, on your audience. When you speak or write, it's important to choose words that are right for your audience. You also adjust the tone, or way of writing, to fit your audience.

 Read about the situation below. Then choose two audiences from the bottom of the page. With a partner, discuss how the words you choose might be different for each audience.

Situation

You and three friends are spending time at the beach. After tossing a ball for a while, you decide to take a walk along the edge of the water. You will tell a story about what happens on your walk. The story will present events in the order they happened and use dialogue and sensory details.

Audiences

- A second grader
- A grandparent
- A student your age

ELPS 2G, 2I, 3E, 3G, 3H, 4C, 5B

Effective Talk

You can answer a question in different ways—in a few words, a sentence, or a few sentences. If you are asked to tell a story about something, including details will help your listener enjoy and understand the story.

Read the question and answers below. The first box shows only a three-word answer. In the second box, the answer is a short sentence. In the third box, the answer includes more details. It does a better job of answering the question.

What happened during your walk on the beach?

saw some kites

We saw four people flying kites.

First, we saw four people flying kites. Each one was a different color—red, blue, yellow, and green. Then we walked farther and spotted an upside-down lifeboat on the sand. A gull perched on top of it squawked as we passed. On the way back, we ran and splashed in the salty water.

Try IT Think of another question you would like to talk about with a partner. The question should be about an experience you would like to share. Before you answer the question, make notes about the events you want to relate in the right order. Also note sensory details that will help make the story vivid and interesting. Then use your notes to tell your story to your partner.

Language of Expository Writing

Expository writing is writing that explains information to the writer's audience. This type of writing might explain a subject, or it might explain a process step by step. Most often, expository essays have the same basic organization: an introduction to the topic or process, supporting details or steps in the process, and a conclusion.

Expository Essay Organization

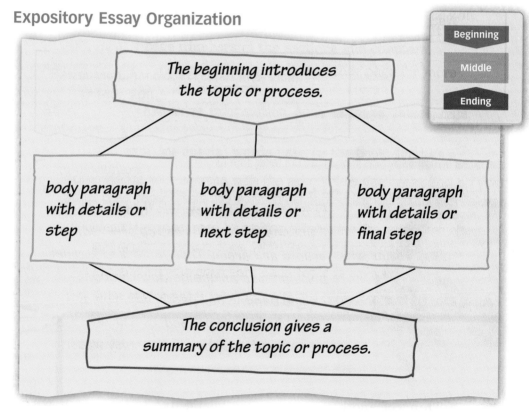

Beginning

Middle

Ending

The beginning introduces the topic or process.

body paragraph with details or step

body paragraph with details or next step

body paragraph with details or final step

The conclusion gives a summary of the topic or process.

Turn and Talk

Explain to a partner the purpose of the conclusion.

The purpose of the conclusion is _____.

ELPS 2C, 2G, 2H, 2I, 3G, 5B

Vocabulary: Expository Writing

conclusion	expository	focus statement
introduction	step-by-step explanation	
middle paragraphs	supporting detail	transitions

1 **Say the word.** Listen as your teacher says and points to each written word. Then repeat each word.

2 **Discover the meaning.** Most of these vocabulary words appear in the margin notes next to the writing model on pages 167–168. Work with a partner to find the words. Write notes about what you think each word or phrase means.

3 **Learn more.** Listen as your teacher explains the meaning of each word. Work with a partner to find examples of these words in the writing model on pages 167–168.

4 **Show your understanding.** In your notebook, answer the questions below. Your teacher will give you directions. When following directions, listen for such action words as *write* and signal words such as *next*. They tell you what to do and when.
   - Which is an example of a step-by-step explanation: a report on tigers or game instructions? Give another example.
   - Which is an example of a transition: *very* or *afterward*? Give another example.

5 **Write it, show it.** In your journal, copy each vocabulary word or phrase. You can add pictures or drawings to help you remember a word's meaning. For example, for *transition*, you might draw an arrow because a transition, like an arrow, directs someone's attention. You can also write synonyms, such as the word *ending* for *conclusion*.

LANGUAGE

 ELPS 2G, 2I, 3E, 4C, 5B

Reading the Expository Model

What Do You Know?

Next you will read *How to Give a Dog a Bath*, a model expository essay on pages 167–168. It gives step-by-step instructions for doing a task. Have you ever given a dog a bath? If not, can you imagine what the steps might be? Do you think this task is, or would be, easy or difficult?

Build Background

Many people have dogs as pets. Part of being a dog owner is making sure your pet gets the care it needs. That includes washing the dog. Many dogs spend time outdoors, where they can get muddy paws or roll in something that smells unpleasant. They might even meet up with a skunk! Even dogs that live mainly indoors need baths from time to time.

Listening

Listen as your teacher or a classmate reads aloud *How to Give a Dog a Bath*. As you listen, take notes. At the beginning, listen for the focus statement, or the main idea that the writer is emphasizing. Then listen for each step in the process. Be prepared to answer the questions below.

  1. What is the writer's focus, or main idea about giving a dog a bath?

  2. What are the main steps in washing a dog?

  3. Did you hear transition words mainly in the introduction, middle, or conclusion?

Key Words and Phrases: Transitions

to begin	**next**	**to continue**
then	**after that**	**to finish**

Look at the words in the chart. You will see some of the words when you read the writing model. With a partner, use the words to talk about how to make a simple breakfast. Then use these words to write sentences based on your discussion.

ELPS 4G, 4I, 5B

Read Along

Now it's your turn to read. Follow as your teacher or classmate reads pages **167–168** aloud. As you read, think about the steps in the process.

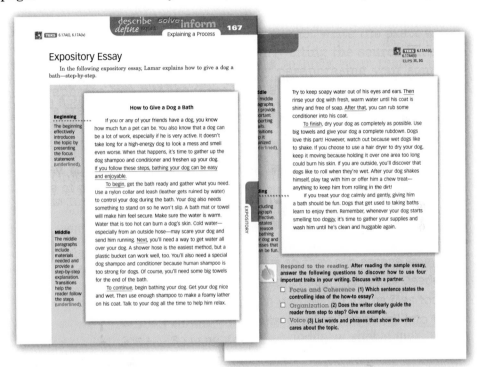

describe solve inform
define explain
Explaining a Process 167

TEKS 6.17A(i), 6.17A(iv)

Expository Essay

In the following expository essay, Lamar explains how to give a dog a bath—step-by-step.

How to Give a Dog a Bath

Beginning
The beginning effectively introduces the topic by presenting the focus statement (underlined).

If you or any of your friends have a dog, you know how much fun a pet can be. You also know that a dog can be a lot of work, especially if he is very active. It doesn't take long for a high-energy dog to look a mess and smell even worse. When that happens, it's time to gather up the dog shampoo and conditioner and freshen up your dog. If you follow these steps, bathing your dog can be easy and enjoyable.

To begin, get the bath ready and gather what you need. Use a nylon collar and leash (leather gets ruined by water) to control your dog during the bath. Your dog also needs something to stand on so he won't slip. A bath mat or towel will make him feel secure. Make sure the water is warm. Water that is too hot can burn a dog's skin. Cold water—especially from an outside hose—may scare your dog and send him running. Next, you'll need a way to get water all over your dog. A shower hose is the easiest method, but a plastic bucket can work well, too. You'll also need a special dog shampoo and conditioner because human shampoo is too strong for dogs. Of course, you'll need some big towels for the end of the bath.

To continue, begin bathing your dog. Get your dog nice and wet. Then use enough shampoo to make a foamy lather on his coat. Talk to your dog all the time to help him relax.

Middle
The middle paragraphs include materials needed and provide a step-by-step explanation. Transitions help the reader follow the steps (underlined).

TEKS 6.17A1(i), 6.17A(iii)
ELPS 3E, 3G

Try to keep soapy water out of his eyes and ears. Then rinse your dog with fresh, warm water until his coat is shiny and free of soap. After that, you can rub some conditioner into his coat.

To finish, dry your dog as completely as possible. Use big towels and give your dog a complete rubdown. Dogs love this part! However, watch out because wet dogs like to shake. If you choose to use a hair dryer to dry your dog, keep it moving because holding it over one area too long could burn his skin. If you are outside, you'll discover that dogs like to roll when they're wet. After your dog shakes himself, play tag with him or offer him a chew treat—anything to keep him from rolling in the dirt!

If you treat your dog calmly and gently, giving him a bath should be fun. Dogs that get used to taking baths learn to enjoy them. Remember, whenever your dog starts smelling too doggy, it's time to gather your supplies and wash him until he's clean and huggable again.

Respond to the reading. After reading the sample essay, answer the following questions to discover how to use four important traits in your writing. Discuss with a partner.

☐ **Focus and Coherence** (1) Which sentence states the controlling idea of the how-to essay?

☐ **Organization** (2) Does the writer clearly guide the reader from step to step? Give an example.

☐ **Voice** (3) List words and phrases that show the writer cares about the topic.

EXPOSITORY

LANGUAGE

After Reading

Copy the following chart on a piece of paper. With a partner, work to fill in the chart with the main idea and details for each step in *How to Give a Dog a Bath*.

To begin	To continue	To finish

Oral Language: Expository Writing

The person or people who listen to you or read your writing are called the audience. When you speak or write, the words you choose should fit your specific audience. In writing, the tone, or the way you write, will be different for each audience.

 Read about the situation below. Then choose two audiences from the bottom of the page. With a partner, discuss how the words you choose might be different for each audience.

Situation

You are teaching another person how to do something new. You are very familiar with the steps in the process, but the other person is not. For example, you might be teaching how to fix a bike, how to skateboard safely, or how to make something. You explain the process from start to finish.

Audiences

- A friend
- A first grader
- Your elderly neighbor

Effective Talk

When you answer a question, you might use one word, a few words, a sentence, or a few sentences. When writing a how-to explanation, you should include enough details so that the reader has a clear picture of what to do.

Read the question and the answers below. The answer in the first box is only a phrase. The answer in the second box is a short sentence. The third answer contains more detail, so it more clearly and completely answers the question.

How do you use the index of a book?

> *turn to the back of the book*

▽

> *You should turn to the back of the book and find the index.*

▽

> *First, turn to the the back of the book. and find the index. Then, search the alphabetical list to find the topic. At the end of the line, look for the page number. Turn to that page in the book, and skim the page to find the topic.*

Try IT Choose a question about how to do something, and share your answer with a partner. First, make notes about the steps. Next, add details that will make the steps clear. Then, use your notes to explain the process. Ask your partner for feedback.

Here are some ideas to get you started.

1. How do you make your favorite kind of sandwich?
2. What are the steps for riding a city bus?

ELPS 3G, 3H

Language of Persuasive Writing

A persuasive essay is writing that attempts to convince others to agree with the writer about a topic. Most persuasive essays have the same basic organization: a beginning paragraph introduces the topic and establishes the writer's position, the middle paragraphs discuss the topic and support the writer's position, and the ending presents an alternative solution and calls the reader to action.

Persuasive Essay Organization

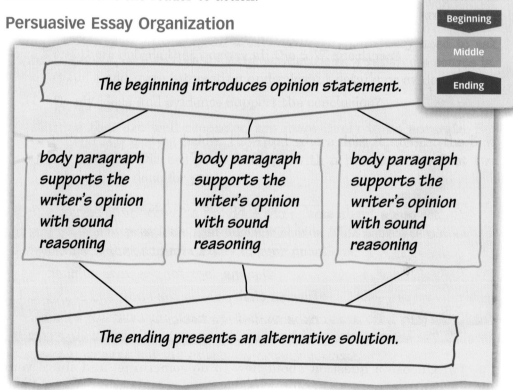

Beginning

Middle

Ending

The beginning introduces opinion statement.

body paragraph supports the writer's opinion with sound reasoning

body paragraph supports the writer's opinion with sound reasoning

body paragraph supports the writer's opinion with sound reasoning

The ending presents an alternative solution.

Turn and Talk

Talk with a partner about how the graphic organizer helps writers support an opinion in a persuasive text.

The graphic organizer _____.

ELPS 2C, 2G, 2H, 3A, 3D, 3G, 4C, 5B

Vocabulary: Persuasive Writing

alternative	call to action	evidence
objection	opinion	persuasive
propose	quotation	solution

1 **Say the word or phrase.** Listen as your teacher reads each word aloud and points to the written word. Listen for the words with the long *o* sound, as in the word *boat*. Then repeat each word, practicing the correct pronunciation of words with long *o*.

2 **Discover the meaning.** Work with a partner to find some of the vocabulary words in the boxes next to the writing model on pages **233–234**. Write notes to show what you think the words mean.

3 **Learn more.** Listen as your teacher explains the meaning of each word or phrase. Work with your partner to check and correct your earlier notes. Write the meanings for the words you didn't know. Find examples of these words in the model on pages **233–234**.

4 **Show your understanding.** Use your notebook to answer the questions below.
- What words might you find in a call to action at the end of a persuasive essay?
- What's the difference between an opinion and evidence?

5 **Explain it.** Take turns explaining to a partner what each word means.

LANGUAGE

 ELPS 2G, 2I, 4C, 5B

Reading the Persuasive Model

What Do You Know?

Next you will read *Avoiding Exotic Pets*, a model persuasive essay about problems caused when people adopt unusual pets. Can you name some kinds of exotic, or unusual pets? What kinds of problems can they cause? Have you ever seen an exotic pet? Describe what you saw.

Build Background

Dogs, cats, and other common pets are domesticated animals. This means they have grown used to living with people. Exotic pets are wild animals and are not used to living in people's homes. Some exotic pets are wolves, monkeys, skunks, raccoons, and poisonous snakes.

Listening

Listen as your teacher or a classmate reads *Avoiding Exotic Pets* aloud. As you listen, make a note about how the writer uses an example to introduce the topic. Then listen for the different problems that the writer describes. Finally, listen for what the writer believes should be done about exotic pets. Work with a partner to answer the questions.

1. What exotic pets does the writer describe?
2. What are three problems with exotic pets, according to the writer?
3. What is the writer's proposed solution?

Key Persuasive Words

even though	**for example**	**for instance**
however	**in fact**	**often**
perhaps	**should**	

Look at the words in the box. You will see these words when you read the writing model. With a partner, use the words to talk about problems that can occur with exotic pets. Think about possible alternatives. Use the words above to write a short essay explaining your ideas.

ELPS 4C, 4G, 4I, 5G

Read Along

Now it's your turn to read. Read along as your teacher or a classmate reads pages 233–234 aloud. As you read, think about the writer's opinion.

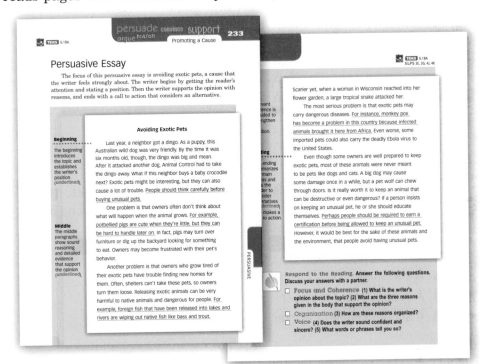

persuade convince **support**
argue reason
Promoting a Cause
233

TEKS 6.18A

Persuasive Essay

The focus of this persuasive essay is avoiding exotic pets, a cause that the writer feels strongly about. The writer begins by getting the reader's attention and stating a position. Then the writer supports the opinion with reasons, and ends with a call to action that considers an alternative.

Avoiding Exotic Pets

Beginning
The beginning introduces the topic and establishes the writer's position (underlined).

Last year, a neighbor got a dingo. As a puppy, this Australian wild dog was very friendly. By the time it was six months old, though, the dingo was big and mean. After it attacked another dog, Animal Control had to take the dingo away. What if this neighbor buys a baby crocodile next? Exotic pets might be interesting, but they can also cause a lot of trouble. People should think carefully before buying unusual pets.

One problem is that owners often don't think about what will happen when the animal grows. For example, potbellied pigs are cute when they're little, but they can be hard to handle later on. In fact, pigs may turn over furniture or dig up the backyard looking for something to eat. Owners may become frustrated with their pet's behavior.

Middle
The middle paragraphs show sound reasoning and detailed evidence that support the opinion (underlined).

Another problem is that owners who grow tired of their exotic pets have trouble finding new homes for them. Often, shelters can't take these pets, so owners turn them loose. Releasing exotic animals can be very harmful to native animals and dangerous for people. For example, foreign fish that have been released into lakes and rivers are wiping out native fish like bass and trout.

PERSUASIVE

TEKS 6.18A
ELPS 3E, 3G, 4I, 4K

Scarier yet, when a woman in Wisconsin reached into her flower garden, a large tropical snake attacked her.

The most serious problem is that exotic pets may carry dangerous diseases. For instance, monkey pox has become a problem in this country because infected animals brought it here from Africa. Even worse, some imported pets could also carry the deadly Ebola virus to the United States.

Even though some owners are well prepared to keep exotic pets, most of these animals were never meant to be pets like dogs and cats. A big dog may cause some damage once in a while, but a pet wolf can chew through doors. Is it really worth it to keep an animal that can be destructive or even dangerous? If a person insists on keeping an unusual pet, he or she should educate themselves. Perhaps people should be required to earn a certification before being allowed to keep an unusual pet. However, it would be best for the sake of these animals and the environment, that people avoid having unusual pets.

Respond to the Reading. Answer the following questions. Discuss your answers with a partner.

☐ **Focus and Coherence** (1) What is the writer's opinion about the topic? (2) What are the three reasons given in the body that support the opinion?

☐ **Organization** (3) How are these reasons organized?

☐ **Voice** (4) Does the writer sound confident and sincere? (5) What words or phrases tell you so?

LANGUAGE

After Reading

Copy the following chart on a sheet of paper and fill it in with the writer's opinion, reasoning, and the alternative solution. Compare and discuss your chart with a partner.

Opinion:	
Reason 1	
Reason 2	
Reason 3	
Alternative	

⭐ ELPS 3G, 3H, 4C

Oral Language: Persuasive Writing

The person or people who will listen to you or read your writing are called the *audience*. It is important to think about the right words to use so your audience will understand your topic and your position on it. The tone, or the way you write, will be different for each audience.

 Read about the situation below. Then choose two audiences from the bottom of the page. With a partner, discuss how the words you choose might be different for each audience.

Situation

Several students at your school have begun a campaign. Their goal is to have the school cafeteria serve more fruits, vegetables, whole grains, and low-fat foods. You will try to persuade someone to support or to not support the campaign.

Audiences

- A classmate
- A school board member
- A school cafeteria worker

ELPS 2G, 2I, 3E, 3G, 3H, 5G

Effective Talk

When you answer a question, you might use one word, a few words, a sentence, or a few sentences to explain your ideas. Persuasive essays include details that help readers understand. When you use more details to tell about something, the reader will have a better understanding.

Read the question and the answers below. In the first box, there is only one word. In the second box, there is a short sentence that answers the question. The third answer contains more details and does a better job of answering the question.

How can students be sure to eat more healthful foods?

fruit

Serve fruit in the cafeteria.

One way is to offer a choice of fruits and vegetables in the cafeteria. It is also possible to limit or take away soft drink machines and replace them with juice machines.

Try IT Choose a question to talk about with a partner. Write two or three ideas for answering the questions. Next, add details that will help your partner understand your ideas. Finally, use your notes as you and your partner discuss your answers to the questions.

Here are some ideas to get you started.

1. How can we persuade people at our school to stop littering?
2. How can we persuade students to volunteer?

LANGUAGE

⭐ **ELPS** 3D, 3E, 3G, 3H

Language of Response Writing

A response to text is writing that tells about something you have read. In this type of writing, you analyze characters and themes and share insight about the story. The response essay has a beginning paragraph that states the focus, middle paragraphs that explain important events and describe the characters, and an ending paragraph that summarizes your insight.

Response Writing Organization

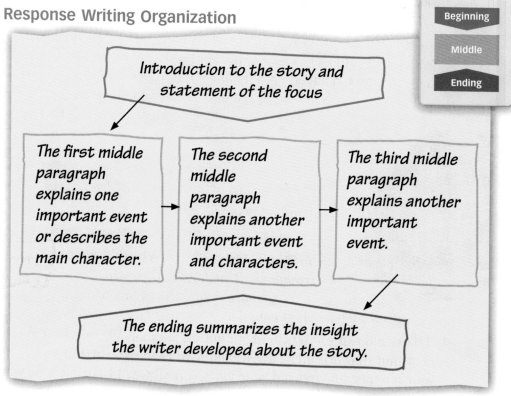

Beginning

Middle

Ending

Introduction to the story and statement of the focus

The first middle paragraph explains one important event or describes the main character.

The second middle paragraph explains another important event and characters.

The third middle paragraph explains another important event.

The ending summarizes the insight the writer developed about the story.

Turn and Talk

Talk with a partner about how the graphic organizer helps writers explain their response to different texts.

The graphic organizer helps to respond by _____.

ELPS 2C, 2G, 2H, 2I, 3G, 4C, 5B

Vocabulary: Response Writing

characters	details	events
experience	focus	insight
interpretation	summary	theme

1 **Say the word.** Listen as your teacher reads each word aloud. Then repeat each word.

2 **Discover the meaning.** Work with a partner to find some of the vocabulary words in the boxes next to the writing model on pages **303–304**. Write notes to show what you think the words mean.

3 **Learn more.** Listen as your teacher explains the meaning of each word or phrase. Work with your partner to check and correct your earlier notes. Write the meanings for the words you didn't know. Find examples of these words in the model on pages **303–304**.

4 **Show your understanding.** Work with a partner to answer the questions below. Have your partner answer the first question. Then use your own words to summarize his or her answer. Finally, switch roles to answer the second question.

- Why do details make a response to literature stronger?
- What is the difference between a summary and an interpretation?

5 **Explain it.** Draw pictures in your notebook to help you remember what each word means.

LANGUAGE

Reading the Response Model

What Do You Know?

Next you will read *Brothers*, a response to literature about a story that features two brothers. The book describes the brothers' relationship and their roles in the family. What is your role in your family? How has it changed as you have gotten older?

Build Background

It's not always easy being a younger brother or sister. It can be hard to get other members of the family to take you seriously. The feeling of wanting to take on more responsibility is one many people can understand. If you're one of these people, this story would appeal to you, like it did to the writer of the model.

Listening

Listen as your teacher or a classmate reads *Brothers* aloud. As you listen, make a note about how the writer uses details about the characters and events of the story in the middle paragraphs to support his insight. Then listen for how the writer summarizes and reinforces the insight at the end. Work with a partner to answer the questions.

1. Who are the important characters in the story?
2. What events does the writer use to explain his insight?
3. Summarize the writer's understanding of the story.

Key Response Words

about	opinion	process
realize	suddenly	tell

Look at the words in the box. You will see some of these words when you read the writing model. Others are words you can use when talking about the writing model. With a partner, use some of the words to talk about a book or story that you have read and enjoyed.

ELPS 4C, 4G, 4I

Read Along

Now it's your turn to read. Read along as your teacher or a classmate reads pages 303–304 aloud. As you read, think about the writer's insight.

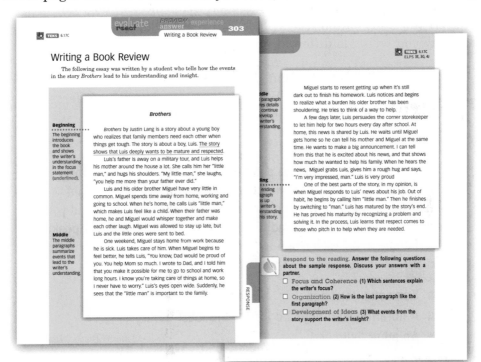

TEKS 6.17C

evaluate *PREVIEW* experience
react answer
Writing a Book Review **303**

Writing a Book Review

The following essay was written by a student who tells how the events in the story *Brothers* lead to his understanding and insight.

Brothers

Beginning
The beginning introduces the book and shows the writer's understanding in the focus statement (underlined).

Brothers by Justin Lang is a story about a young boy who realizes that family members need each other when things get tough. The story is about a boy, Luis. The story shows that Luis deeply wants to be mature and respected.

Luis's father is away on a military tour, and Luis helps his mother around the house a lot. She calls him her "little man," and hugs his shoulders. "My little man," she laughs, "you help me more than your father ever did."

Luis and his older brother Miguel have very little in common. Miguel spends time away from home, working and going to school. When he's home, he calls Luis "little man," which makes Luis feel like a child. When their father was home, he and Miguel would whisper together and make each other laugh. Miguel was allowed to stay up late, but Luis and the little ones were sent to bed.

Middle
The middle paragraphs summarize events that lead to the writer's understanding.

One weekend, Miguel stays home from work because he is sick. Luis takes care of him. When Miguel begins to feel better, he tells Luis, "You know, Dad would be proud of you. You help Mom so much. I wrote to Dad, and I told him that you make it possible for me to go to school and work long hours. I know you're taking care of things at home, so I never have to worry." Luis's eyes open wide. Suddenly, he sees that the "little man" is important to the family.

RESPONSE

TEKS 6.17C
ELPS 3E, 3G, 4I

Miguel starts to resent getting up when it's still dark out to finish his homework. Luis notices and begins to realize what a burden his older brother has been shouldering. He tries to think of a way to help.

A few days later, Luis persuades the corner storekeeper to let him help for two hours every day after school. At home, this news is shared by Luis. He waits until Miguel gets home so he can tell his mother and Miguel at the same time. He wants to make a big announcement. I can tell from this that he is excited about his news, and that shows how much he wanted to help his family. When he hears the news, Miguel grabs Luis, gives him a rough hug and says, "I'm very impressed, man." Luis is very proud

One of the best parts of the story, in my opinion, is when Miguel responds to Luis' news about his job. Out of habit, he begins by calling him "little man." Then he finishes by switching to "man." Luis has matured by the story's end. He has proved his maturity by recognizing a problem and solving it. In the process, Luis learns that respect comes to those who pitch in to help when they are needed.

Respond to the reading. Answer the following questions about the sample response. Discuss your answers with a partner.

☐ Focus and Coherence **(1)** Which sentences explain the writer's focus?

☐ Organization **(2)** How is the last paragraph like the first paragraph?

☐ Development of Ideas **(3)** What events from the story support the writer's insight?

LANGUAGE

After Reading

Copy the following chart on a piece of paper and fill in the events used to show the writer's insight. With a partner, use your chart to discuss what each event shows.

Insight: _____.
Event	
Event	
Event	

ELPS 3H, 3G, 4C, 4I, 4K

Oral Language: Response Writing

The people who will read your writing are called the *audience*. It is important to use the right words so readers will understand your insight as well as the information that helped you reach your insight. The tone, or the way you write, is different for each audience.

 Read about the situation below. Then choose two audiences from the bottom of the page. With a partner, discuss the different words you chose for each audience and why you chose them.

Situation

You have been asked to present a response to a book, story, movie, or play of your own choosing. You will share your insight about it and talk about whether or not you liked it. You will read your response on a community radio station program called Kids Speaking Out. People of all ages listen to this radio show.

Audiences

- Someone your age
- A librarian who buys books for the local library
- An adult listener

ELPS 2G, 2H, 2I, 3E, 3G, 3H, 5G

Effective Talk

When you answer a question, you might use one word, a few words, a sentence, or a few sentences to explain your ideas. Explanations include details that help readers understand. When you use more details to tell about something, the reader will have a better understanding.

Read the question and the answers below. In the first box, there is only one word. In the second box, there is a short sentence that answers the question. The third answer contains more details and does a better job of answering the question.

What did you think about the last book you read?

good

The last book I read was very good.

The last book I read was very good. It was called The Owl. In it, a boy grows up and learns to be strong. At the beginning of the story, the boy acts very young and silly. After a tragedy occurs, he has to grow up fast.

LANGUAGE

Try IT Choose a statement to talk about with a partner. Write two or three ideas for responding to the statement. Next, add details that will help your partner understand your ideas. Finally, use your notes as you and your partner discuss your responses to the statements.

Here are some ideas to get you started.

1. Tell how you feel about a book you have read recently.
2. Tell about your favorite book and how it makes you feel.

ELPS 3D, 3E, 3G

Language of Creative Writing

The purpose of creative writing is to express thoughts, feelings and emotions, not simply convey information. In many cases, creative writing tells a story. Stories have characters, a setting, a point of view, plot events, dialogue, and a theme. Often, the main character has a conflict, or problem, and has to make a difficult decision. The story builds on this and gets more exciting. The decision usually happens at the high point of the story somewhere in the middle paragraphs. The ending tells how the character changes or what has been learned.

Creative Writing Plot Line

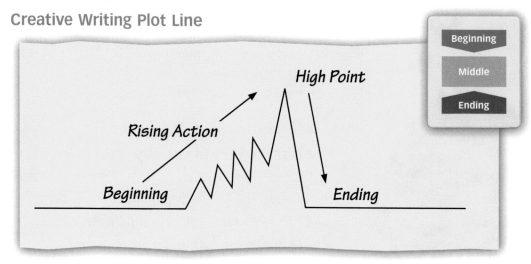

Turn and Talk

Talk with a partner about why it is important for a story to follow a plot line.

It is important because _____.

ELPS 2C, 2G, 2H, 2I, 3D, 3E, 3G, 4C, 5B

Vocabulary: Creative Writing

| conflict | dialogue | point of view |
| high point | rising action | setting |

1 **Say the word or phrase.** Listen as your teacher reads each word aloud and points to the written word. Then repeat each word.

2 **Discover the meaning.** Work with a partner to find some of the vocabulary words in the boxes next to the writing model on pages 354-355. Write notes to show what you think the words mean.

3 **Learn more.** Listen as your teacher explains the meaning of each word or phrase. Work with your partner to check and correct your earlier notes. Write the meanings for the words you didn't know. Look for examples of these words in the writing sample on pages 354–355.

4 **Show your understanding.** Work with a partner to answer the questions below. Have your partner answer the first question. Then, use your own words to summarize his or her answer. Finally, switch roles to answer the second question.
- Which comes first, the high point or the rising action?
- Why does a story need dialogue?

5 **Explain it.** Work with a partner. Take turns explaining the meanings of the words on the list.

LANGUAGE

★ ELPS 2G, 2I, 3G, 3H, 4C, 5G

Reading the Creative Model

What Do You Know?

Next you will read *Journey to the Top of the World*, a story about a character who overcomes obstacles to achieve her dream of climbing the world's highest mountain. Have you seen television shows about mountain climbers? What kinds of challenges do they face?

Build Background

Mountain climbing is a very dangerous sport. At high altitudes, breathing becomes more difficult. Climbers usually carry oxygen tanks to help them breathe. Asthma is a disease that can make breathing difficult.

Listening

Listen as your teacher or a classmate reads *Journey to the Top of the World* aloud. As you listen, make notes about how the writer introduces characters, describes events, and presents dialogue. Also listen for the high point of the plot. Then take turns with a partner answering the questions below.

1. What details does the writer include that make the story seem more real?
2. What additional problem does the narrator face, besides the challenge of climbing the mountain?
3. What is the high point of the story?

Key Creative Writing Words

decided	just	paused
remembered	replied	some day

Look at the words above. You will see them when you read the model or use them when talking about the model. With a partner, use the words to describe something you dream of doing. How would you write about it?

Write a few sentences to describe your dream.

Read Along

Now it's your turn to read. Read along as your teacher or a classmate reads pages 354–355 aloud. As you read, think about the rising action.

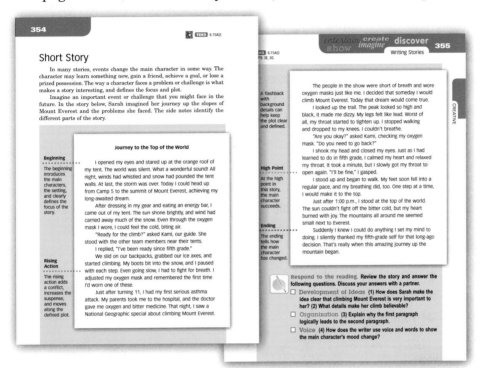

354

TEKS 6.15A(i)

Short Story

In many stories, events change the main character in some way. The character may learn something new, gain a friend, achieve a goal, or lose a prized possession. The way a character faces a problem or challenge is what makes a story interesting, and defines the focus and plot.

Imagine an important event or challenge that you might face in the future. In the story below, Sarah imagined her journey up the slopes of Mount Everest and the problems she faced. The side notes identify the different parts of the story.

Beginning

The beginning introduces the main characters, the setting, and clearly defines the focus of the story.

Rising Action

The rising action adds a conflict, increases the suspense, and moves along the defined plot.

Journey to the Top of the World

I opened my eyes and stared up at the orange roof of my tent. The world was silent. What a wonderful sound! All night, winds had whistled and snow had pounded the tent walls. At last, the storm was over. Today I could head up from Camp 5 to the summit of Mount Everest, achieving my long-awaited dream.

After dressing in my gear and eating an energy bar, I came out of my tent. The sun shone brightly, and wind had carried away much of the snow. Even through the oxygen mask I wore, I could feel the cold, biting air.

"Ready for the climb?" asked Kami, our guide. She stood with the other team members near their tents.

I replied, "I've been ready since fifth grade."

We slid on our backpacks, grabbed our ice axes, and started climbing. My boots bit into the snow, and I paused with each step. Even going slow, I had to fight for breath. I adjusted my oxygen mask and remembered the first time I'd worn one of these.

Just after turning 11, I had my first serious asthma attack. My parents took me to the hospital, and the doctor gave me oxygen and bitter medicine. That night, I saw a National Geographic special about climbing Mount Everest.

355

entertain create discover
show imagine
Writing Stories

TEKS 6.15A(i)
ELPS 3E, 3G

A flashback with background details can help keep the plot clear and defined.

High Point

At the high point in this story, the main character succeeds.

Ending

The ending tells how the main character has changed.

CREATIVE

The people in the show were short of breath and wore oxygen masks just like me. I decided that someday I would climb Mount Everest. Today that dream would come true.

I looked up the trail. The peak looked so high and black, it made me dizzy. My legs felt like lead. Worst of all, my throat started to tighten up. I stopped walking and dropped to my knees. I couldn't breathe.

"Are you okay?" asked Kami, checking my oxygen mask. "Do you need to go back?"

I shook my head and closed my eyes. Just as I had learned to do in fifth grade, I calmed my heart and relaxed my throat. It took a minute, but I slowly got my throat to open again. "I'll be fine," I gasped.

I stood up and began to walk. My feet soon fell into a regular pace, and my breathing did, too. One step at a time, I would make it to the top.

Just after 1:00 p.m., I stood at the top of the world. The sun couldn't fight off the bitter cold, but my heart burned with joy. The mountains all around me seemed small next to Everest.

Suddenly I knew I could do anything I set my mind to doing. I silently thanked my fifth-grade self for that long-ago decision. That's really when this amazing journey up the mountain began.

Respond to the reading. Review the story and answer the following questions. Discuss your answers with a partner.

☐ Development of Ideas **(1)** How does Sarah make the idea clear that climbing Mount Everest is very important to her? **(2)** What details make her climb believable?

☐ Organization **(3)** Explain why the first paragraph logically leads to the second paragraph.

☐ Voice **(4)** How does the writer use voice and words to show the main character's mood change?

LANGUAGE

After Reading

Work with a partner, taking turns rereading the model aloud, alternating paragraphs. Then draw the plot line on your own paper, and work together to name what happens at each point.

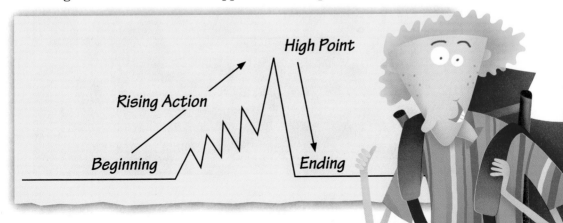

Oral Language: Creative Writing

The people who will listen to you or read your writing are called the *audience*. It is important to think about the right words to use so your audience will understand your plot, setting, dialogue, and other parts of your story. The tone, or the way you write, is different for each audience.

 Read about the situation below. Then choose two audiences from the bottom of the page. With a partner, discuss how the words you choose might be different for each audience.

Situation

You and some friends have received mysterious letters asking you to meet at a clubhouse. You have found the clubhouse, but there is no one inside. On the table is a strange object. You will write a story that begins with this event.

Audiences

- Your best friend
- A kindergartner
- Your teacher

ELPS 2G, 2H, 2I, 3E, 3G, 3H, 5G

Effective Talk

When you answer a question, you might use one word, a few words, a sentence, or a few sentences to explain your ideas. Stories include details that help readers understand. When you use more details to tell about something, the reader will have a better understanding.

Read the question and the answers below. In the first box, there is only one word. In the second box, there is a short sentence that answers the question. The third answer contains more details and does a better job of answering the question.

What was the strange object on the table in the clubhouse?

key

It was an old-fashioned key.

On the table lay a dusty old key, like you might find for an old-fashioned castle door. It seemed to glow strangely in the dark clubhouse.

Try IT Choose a question to talk about with a partner. Write two or three ideas for answering the questions. Next, add details that will help your partner understand your ideas. Finally, use your notes as you and your partner discuss your answers to the questions.

Here are some ideas to get you started.

1. What did the mysterious key on the table in the clubhouse unlock?
2. Who sent the letters to meet at the clubhouse?

ELPS 3E, 3G, 3H, 4C

Language of Research Writing

When you research, you investigate a topic. A research report shares the result of that investigation. The beginning of most research writing explains what you learned from your research. This explanation is called the thesis statement. Middle paragraphs provide details about the topic. The ending sums up the writing and often leaves the reader with another interesting fact. Sources are listed on a separate sheet of paper.

Research Report Organization

Beginning
Middle
Ending

I. Beginning
   A. gets the reader excited about the subject
   B. introduces the thesis statement, or controlling idea

II. Middle
   A. explains the subject
   B. provides details and evidence

III. Ending
   A. summarizes the paper
   B. often includes another interesting fact

IV. Separate sheet for sources

Turn and Talk

Talk with a partner about the main purposes of the beginning of a research report.

The beginning of a research report _____.

Vocabulary: Research Writing

alphabetically	**background**	**documentation**
double-spaced	**evidence**	**pronunciation**
thesis	**topic sentence**	

1 **Say the word.** Listen as your teacher reads each word aloud. Then repeat each word. Listen for the consonant digraphs *th* and *ph,* as in the words *third* and *phobia.* Consonant digraphs are two consonants that join together to make one sound. Practice pronouncing these words.

2 **Discover the meaning.** Work with a partner to find the vocabulary words in the boxes next to the writing model on pages **392–395**. Write notes to show what you think the words mean.

3 **Learn more.** Listen as your teacher explains the meaning of each word or phrase. Work with your partner to check and correct your earlier notes. Write the meanings for the words you didn't know. Find examples of these words in the model on pages **392–395**.

4 **Show your understanding.** Take turns with your partner answering the questions and summarizing answers. Then switch roles to answer the second question.
- Why do you need to provide background information for your readers?
- Why should you include pronunciation guides in your report?

5 **Explain it.** Listen to your partner pronounce each word. Offer advice if you hear mistakes. Then pronounce the words as your partner listens.

ELPS 2G, 2I, 4C, 5B

Reading the Research Model

What Do You Know?

Next you will read *Exploring the Ring of Fire*, a research report about an interesting place. Have you ever experienced an earthquake or seen one on television? Can you describe what happens when a volcano erupts? Have you seen a report about a tsunami or volcano erupting on the news?

Build Background

Volcano eruptions, earthquakes, and tidal waves are caused by natural forces inside the earth. One part of the earth that is especially affected by these natural forces is the Ring of Fire. The Ring of Fire is the area that circles the Pacific Ocean.

Listening

Listen as your teacher or a classmate reads *Exploring the Ring of Fire* aloud. As you listen, make notes on a separate piece of paper about earthquakes, volcanoes, tidal waves, and the natural forces that cause them. Be prepared to answer the questions below.

1. What is the writer's thesis, or controlling idea?

2. What evidence is there in the essay that the writer did research?

3. What kinds of details does the writer include to support the thesis?

Key Research Writing Words

another	average	because
caused	experts	investigate
scientists		

Look at the words in the box. You will see these words when you read the writing sample. Others you can use to talk about this topic. With a partner, use some of the words to talk about the scientists who study natural disasters. Use one of the words in a sentence about them.

Read Along

Now it's your turn to read. Read along as your teacher or a classmate reads pages 392–395 aloud. Listen for the writer's facts and evidence.

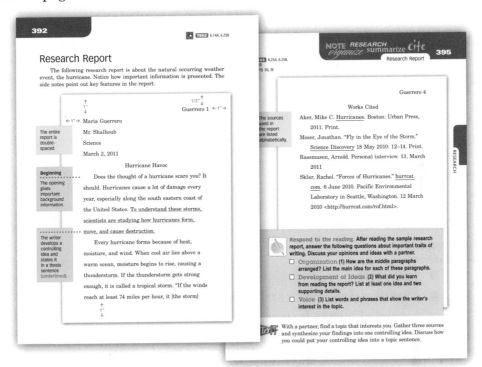

392

TEKS 6.14A, 6.25B

Research Report

The following research report is about the natural occurring weather event, the hurricane. Notice how important information is presented. The side notes point out key features in the report.

Guerrero 1

Maria Guerrero
Mr. Shalhoub
Science
March 2, 2011

The entire report is double-spaced.

Hurricane Havoc

Beginning
The opening gives important background information.

Does the thought of a hurricane scare you? It should. Hurricanes cause a lot of damage every year, especially along the south eastern coast of the United States. To understand these storms, scientists are studying how hurricanes form, move, and cause destruction.

The writer develops a controlling idea and states it in a thesis sentence (underlined).

Every hurricane forms because of heat, moisture, and wind. When cool air lies above a warm ocean, moisture begins to rise, causing a thunderstorm. If the thunderstorm gets strong enough, it is called a tropical storm. "If the winds reach at least 74 miles per hour, it [the storm]

NOTE RESEARCH *organize* summarize cite **395**
Research Report

Guerrero 4

Works Cited

The sources used in the report are listed alphabetically.

Aker, Mike C. Hurricanes. Boston: Urban Press, 2011. Print.

Moser, Jonathan. "Fly in the Eye of the Storm." Science Discovery 18 May 2010: 12–14. Print.

Rassmusen, Arnold. Personal interview. 13, March 2011

Sklar, Rachel. "Forces of Hurricanes." hurrcat. com. 6 June 2010. Pacific Environmental Laboratory in Seattle, Washington. 12 March 2010 <http://hurrcat.com/rof.html>.

Respond to the reading. After reading the sample research report, answer the following questions about important traits of writing. Discuss your opinions and ideas with a partner.

☐ Organization **(1)** How are the middle paragraphs arranged? List the main idea for each of these paragraphs.

☐ Development of Ideas **(2)** What did you learn from reading the report? List at least one idea and two supporting details.

☐ Voice **(3)** List words and phrases that show the writer's interest in the topic.

With a partner, find a topic that interests you. Gather three sources and synthesize your findings into one controlling idea. Discuss how you could put your controlling idea into a topic sentence.

LANGUAGE

After Reading

Copy the following outline structure on your own paper. Fill it in with the information you find in the model. You can add or delete levels as you think necessary. Compare and discuss your outline with a partner.

Model Outline

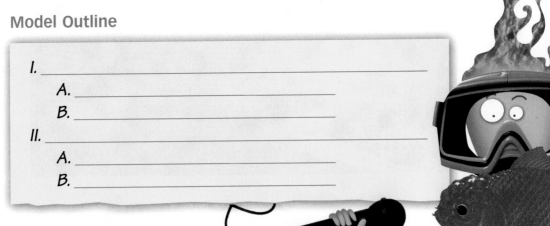

I. _____

   A. _____

   B. _____

II. _____

   A. _____

   B. _____

ELPS 3G, 3H, 4C

Oral Language: Research Writing

The person or people who will listen to you or read your writing are called the *audience*. It is important to think about the right words to use so your audience will understand your thesis and your supporting details. The tone, or the way you write, will be different for each audience.

 Read about the situation below. Then choose two audiences from the bottom of the page. With a partner, discuss how the words you choose to use in a report might be different for each audience.

Situation

You are a member of a small group. Your assignment is to create a research report. Your report must be written. However, you will also use your report to make a classroom multimedia presentation with illustrations, models, displays, video, audio, and other elements.

Audiences

- Your peers
- A fourth grade class learning about your topic
- A panel of judges for a writing contest

ELPS 2G, 2H, 2I, 3E, 3G, 3H, 5G

Effective Talk

When you answer a question, you might use one word, a few words, a sentence, or a few sentences to explain your ideas. Stories include details that help readers understand. When you use more details to tell about something, the reader will have a better understanding.

Read the question and the answers below. In the first box, there is only one word. In the second box, there is a short sentence that answers the question. The third answer contains more details and does a better job of answering the question.

How will your group divide up responsibilities for the presentation?

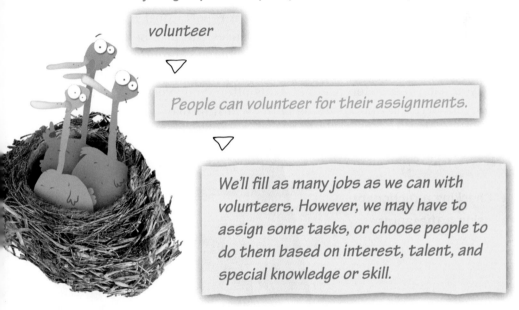

volunteer

People can volunteer for their assignments.

We'll fill as many jobs as we can with volunteers. However, we may have to assign some tasks, or choose people to do them based on interest, talent, and special knowledge or skill.

LANGUAGE

Try IT Choose a question to talk about with a partner. Write two or three ideas for answering the questions. Next add details that will help your partner understand your ideas. Finally, use your notes as you and your partner discuss your answers to the questions.

Here are some ideas to get you started.

1. How does the weather and climate affect the lives of people in our community?

2. What should people do in case of a natural disaster?

Using Reference Materials

Do you want to find a fact quickly? Reference materials can help. They provide useful and reliable facts and information. For your schoolwork, you will often need to use references. For example, you might use an encyclopedia to do research for a report. Most libraries have a range of reference books. Many references can also be found online. You can access these from a library or home computer.

A dictionary and thesaurus can help you spell and understand words. If you use these reference materials often, your vocabulary will grow, and your writing and speaking skills will improve.

What's Ahead

- Checking a Dictionary
- Using a Thesaurus

Checking a Dictionary

A dictionary is the most reliable source for learning the meanings of words. It offers the following aids and information:

- **Guide words** are located at the top of every page. They show the first and last entry words on a page, so you can tell whether the word you're looking up is listed on that page.

- **Entry words** are the words that are defined on the dictionary page. They are listed in alphabetical order for easy searching.

- **Parts of speech** labels tell you the different ways a word can be used. For example, the word *Carboniferous* can be used as a noun or as an adjective.

- **Syllable divisions** show where you can divide a word into syllables.

- **Spelling and capitalization** (if appropriate) are given for every entry word. If an entry is capitalized, capitalize it in your writing, too

- **Spelling of verb forms** is shown. Watch for irregular forms.

- **Illustrations** are often provided to make a definition clearer.

- **Accent marks** show which syllable or syllables should be stressed when you say a word.

- **Pronunciations** are special spellings of a word to help you say the word correctly.

- **Pronunciation keys** give symbols to help you say or pronounce the entry words correctly.

- **Etymology** gives the history of a word [in brackets]. Knowing a little about a word's history can make it easier to remember.

(*Remember:* Each word may have several definitions. It's important to read all of the meanings and select the one that is best for you.)

 Open a dictionary to any page and find the following information.
1. Write down the guide words on that page.
2. Find a multisyllabic word and write it out by syllables. Jot down the word's part of speech. (There may be more than one.)
3. Find an entry that includes spelling of verb forms and write them down.

LANGUAGE

ELPS 4C, 4I

Dictionary Page

Guide words ———— **carbon dioxide | carburetor**   150

Entry word ————

carbon dioxide *n.* A colorless or odorless gas that does not burn, composed of carbon and oxygen in the proportion CO_2 and present in the atmosphere or formed when any fuel containing carbon is burned. It is exhaled from an animal's lungs during respiration and is used by plants in photosynthesis. Carbon dioxide is used in refrigeration, in fire extinguishers, and in carbonated drinks.

Part of speech ————

carbonic acid *n.* A weak acid having the formula H_2CO_3. It exists only in solution and decomposes readily into carbon dioxide and water.

Syllable division ————

car·bon·if·er·ous (kär′bə-**nĭf**′ər-əs) *adj.* Producing or containing carbon or coal.

Spelling and capitalization ————

Carboniferous *n.* The geologic time comprising the Mississippian (or Lower Carboniferous) and Pennsylvanian (or Upper Carboniferous) Periods of the Paleozoic Era, from about 360 to 286 million years ago. During the Carboniferous, widespread swamps formed in which plant remains accumulated and later hardened into coal. See table at **geologic time.—Carboniferous** *adj.*

Spelling of verb forms ————

car·bon·ize (kär′bə-nīz′) *tr. v.* **car·bon·ized, car·bon·iz·ing, car·bon·iz·es 1.** To change an organic compound into carbon by heating. **2.** To treat, coat, or combine with carbon.—**car′bon·i·za′tion** (kär′be-nī-zā′shən) *n.*

Illustration ————

air
air filter
choke valve
gas
gas and air mixture
float
venturi
throttle valve
float chamber

carburetor
cross section of a carburetor

carbon monoxide *n.* A colorless odorless gas that is extremely poisonous and has the formula CO. Carbon monoxide is formed when carbon or a compound that contains carbon burns incompletely. It is present in the exhaust gases of automobile engines.

carbon paper *n.* A paper coated on one side with a dark coloring matter, placed between two sheets of blank paper so that the bottom sheet will receive a copy of what is typed or written on the top sheet.

Accent marks ————

carbon tet·ra·chlor·ide (tĕt′rə-**klôr**′īd′) *n.* A colorless poisonous liquid that is composed of carbon and chlorine, has the formula CCl_4, and does not burn although it vaporizes easily. It is used in fire extinguishers and as a dry-cleaning fluid.

Car·bo·run·dum (kär′bə-**rŭn**′dəm) A trademark for an abrasive made of silicon carbide, used to cut, grind, and polish.

Pronunciation ————

Pronunciation key ————

ă	pat	ôr	core
ā	pay	oi	boy
âr	care	ou	out
ä	father	ŏŏ	took
ĕ	pet	ŏŏr	lure
ē	be	ōō	boot
ĭ	pit	ŭ	cut
ī	bite	ûr	urge
îr	pier	th	thin
ŏ	pot	th	this
ō	toe	zh	vision
ô	paw	ə	about

car·bun·cle (kär′bŭng kəl) *n.* **1.** A painful inflammation in the tissue under the skin that is somewhat like a boil but releases pus from several openings. **2.** A deep-red garnet.

car·bu·re·tor (kär′bə-rā′tər *or* kär′byə-rā′tər) *n.* A device in a gasoline engine that vaporizes the gasoline with air to form an explosive mixture. [First written down in 1866 in English, from *carburet*, carbide, from Latin *carbō*, carbon.]

Etymology ————

Using a Thesaurus

A thesaurus is a book of words and their synonyms, or words with similar meanings. It is organized from A to Z. In each entry, synonyms that share a similar meaning are grouped. If a word can be used in different ways, there are different entries for each meaning. For example, you might find results like these for the word *view* as a verb and as a noun.

> **view** (*n.*)   appearance, aspect, look, outlook, panorama, scene, show, spectacle, way.
>
> **view** (*v.*)   behold, discover, glare, inspect, look for, observe, peep, peer, perceive, scan, see, survey, watch.

When Should I Use a Thesaurus?

As a writer, you should always try to vary your word usage. A thesaurus can help. You can use a thesaurus when you:

- find yourself using the same words over and over.
- want to find just the right word to express your meaning.
- need a different word that fits your purpose or audience.
- are looking for a new word to replace a word you already know.

What Should I Know When I Use a Thesaurus?

Using a thesaurus is like using a dictionary. Words are listed in alphabetical order. Follow these tips when you use a thesaurus:

- When looking at synonyms grouped by meaning, pick the meaning you need. As in the example shown above, the word *view* can be used as either a noun or a verb. Be sure to choose the correct form.
- Scan the list of relevant synonyms to choose the one you want.
- Use a dictionary to check meanings of unfamiliar synonyms.
- If you do not find an entry for a word, look up a word that is similar to your word.

 Use a thesaurus to find a new word to replace each blue word in the sentences below. Rewrite the sentences and share them with a partner.

1. My new jacket got wet in the rain.
2. I think a clown contest would be interesting.
3. The elephant at the zoo is very large.

LANGUAGE

compare

vary

ELPS 2C, 3E, 3G, 4C, 4G

Basic Grammar and Writing

Writing Focus

Learning Language

Work with a partner. Read the meanings and share answers to the questions.

1. Dependent means to need something else for support.
   How is a child dependent on a parent?

2. A fragment is a broken off or detached piece of something.
   What would a fragment of a map look like?

3. To ramble is to move or talk in a wandering way.
   How would it sound to ramble when answering the question "How are you?"

4. Building blocks are the basic, or essential, parts of something big.
   What are the building blocks of a good education?

MODIFY CONNECT

choose

Working with Words

Writing is like cooking. You have eight basic ingredients, called the parts of speech. Take a cupful of specific nouns and add a tablespoon of colorful adjectives. Then blend in a pint of action verbs, seasoned with adverbs. Finally, mix in the pronouns, interjections, prepositions, and conjunctions, and you'll be cooking with words!

Specific *nouns* will help you write clearly, and *pronouns* will help you write smoothly. Action *verbs* will add drama to whatever you are writing, and *conjunctions* will help by connecting the words in your writing.

Besides some basic information about each part of speech, this section answers the question,

"How can I use words effectively in my own writing?"

What's Ahead

- **Using Nouns**
- **Using Pronouns**
- **Choosing Verbs**
- **Describing with Adjectives**
- **Describing with Adverbs**
- **Connecting with Prepositions**
- **Connecting with Conjunctions**

Using Nouns

A noun is a word that names a person, a place, a thing, or an idea in your writing. (See page **738**.)

Person	actor, Denzel Washington, students, President Adams
Place	state, Arizona, kitchen, San Diego, middle school
Thing	bird, Baltimore oriole, books, clock
Idea	holiday, Veterans Day, courage, thought

 On your own paper, rewrite the sentences below by filling in each blank with the type of noun shown.

1. _____*(a place)*_____ has spectacular fall colors.

2. The park contains hundreds of _____*(things)*_____ .

3. _____*(a person)*_____ can spot wildlife throughout the park.

4. The destruction of wilderness areas may lead to the _____*(an idea)*_____ of certain animals.

Concrete, Abstract, and Collective Nouns

Concrete nouns name things that can be seen or touched.

Abstract nouns name things that you can think about but cannot see or touch.

Concrete	clown	valentine	school	heart
Abstract	happiness	February	education	love

Write four concrete nouns and four related abstract nouns. For example, a *heart* (concrete) is a symbol of *love* (abstract).

Collective nouns name a collection of persons, animals, or things.

Persons	class	family	jury	audience	committee
Animals	herd	flock	pack	school	pod

 List two more collective nouns for both persons and animals. (See page **738** for help.) Share your words with a partner.

Proper and Common Nouns

Proper nouns name a specific person, place, thing, or idea. They are always capitalized. A **common noun** is any noun that's not a proper one.

	Person	Place	Thing	Idea
Common	ranger	park	pet	holiday
Proper	Tom	Yosemite	Fido	Labor Day

Common **The club visited the national park last weekend.**

Proper **The Dyer Biking Club visited Yosemite National Park last Saturday.**

 Make a chart like the one above. Add your own common and proper nouns (four of each). Be sure to capitalize the proper nouns.

General and Specific Nouns

Specific nouns give a clearer picture than general nouns.

General	actress	stadium	pants	emotion
Specific	Julia Roberts	Wrigley Field	blue jeans	happiness

General **People like challenges.**

Specific **Climbers like steep rock walls.**

 Write the sentences replacing general nouns with specific nouns.

1. The student biked to a recreational area.
2. The storm blew things around the place.

Noncount Nouns

A **noncount noun** is a noun that cannot be counted with a number and always takes a singular form (you can't add an *s* to the end).

Countable	pencil/s	pen/s	chair/s	smile/s
Noncountable	weather	ink	furniture	jelly

Countable **I only have two chairs at my table.**

Noncountable **I will have to buy more furniture for the dinner party.**

 List four more noncount nouns. Write sentences using each noun. Read and discuss your sentences to a partner.

BASIC GRAMMAR

What can I do with nouns in my writing?

Identify People, Places, Things, and Ideas

You use nouns to identify the people, places, things, and ideas you are talking about in your writing. You can add variety to your writing by using these different types of nouns as subjects.

Yosemite National Park **is amazing.** *(a place)*

Ansel Adams **took many photographs in Yosemite.** *(a person)*

His pictures **captured** images **in black and white.** *(things)*

In the park, breathtaking beauty **surrounds you.** *(an idea)*

Find the subject in each of the following sentences. Is it a person, a place, a thing, or an idea?

■ In 1890, John Muir helped establish Yosemite National Park.
  John Muir, person

1. Muir wrote many magazine stories about the park's beauty.

2. The Sierra Club lists Muir as one of its founders.

3. His love of nature turned into a photography career.

Rename the Subject

A predicate noun follows a "be" verb *(am, is, are, was, were, will be)* and renames the subject of the sentence. Predicate nouns are useful for making simple, natural comparisons.

My favorite vacation **is a** visit **to the mountains.**
(The predicate noun "visit" renames the subject "vacation.")

Write a sentence for each of the subjects and predicate nouns below using a "be" verb.

Subject	Predicate Noun
■ mountain hike	experience

A mountain hike is an invigorating experience.

1. walking and climbing	activities
2. fresh air	medicine
3. eagles and deer	companions

Complete the Action of the Verb

Readers may ask questions like *who?* and *what?* after many action verbs. You can use concise nouns to answer these questions and complete the action of the verb.

Campers must plan. (*What* must they plan?)

Yosemite offers an overnight permit. (*Who* gets a permit?)

See how the nouns below—*trips* and *visitors*—answer the questions *what?* or *who?* and complete the action of the verb.

Campers must plan overnight trips. (This answers *what?*)

Yosemite offers overnight visitors a permit. (This answers *who?*)

Nouns that answer the question *what?* after a verb are called **direct objects**. Nouns that answer the question *who?* after a verb that has a direct object are called **indirect objects**. (See **730.4–730.5**.)

Number your paper from 1 to 4. Write a noun that answers each *what* and *who* question in the sentences below.

1. Long-distance hikers need good ___*(what?)*___ for their feet.

2. The wilderness offers ___*(who?)*___ sightings of rare birds.

3. Hikers can find ___*(what?)*___ growing along the trail.

4. Maps give ___*(who?)*___ specific trail information.

Add Specific Information

Prepositional phrases add information to your sentences. Using a specific noun as the **object of a preposition** makes your writing clearer. (See **774.1**.) Notice how all of the nouns highlighted below add details to the passage.

A first-aid kit offers hikers medical supplies for minor problems like blisters. A new product, called "second skin," provides moist treatment for blisters and other wounds. Salt packets are also an important first-aid supply. They can prevent dehydration.

Object of Preposition

Direct Object

Indirect Object

Predicate Noun

Subject

Using Pronouns

A pronoun is a word used in place of a noun. The noun replaced, or referred to, by the pronoun is called the pronoun's **antecedent**. The arrows below point to each pronoun's antecedent. (Also see page **742**.)

> Edgar Allan Poe rented a home in Philadelphia, and it is now a national historical site.

> Amanda read a Poe story before she visited the site.

The personal pronouns listed below are used as subjects and objects. (For a complete list of personal pronouns, see page **746**.)

Personal pronouns						
I	you	he	she	it	we	they
me		him	her		us	them

Person and Number of a Pronoun

Pronouns show "person" and "number" in writing. The following chart shows which pronouns are used for the three different persons (*first, second, third*) and the two different numbers (*singular* or *plural*). (See page **748**.)

		Singular	Plural
First Person	(The person speaking)	I call.	We call.
Second Person	(The person spoken to)	You call.	You call.
Third Person	(The person or thing spoken about)	He calls. It calls.	They call.

 GRAMMAR Try IT Number your paper from 1 to 4. Write sentences that use the pronouns described below as subjects.

- first-person singular pronoun
  I want to visit the White House.

1. third-person singular pronoun
2. third-person plural pronoun
3. second-person singular pronoun
4. first-person plural pronoun

TEKS 6.19A(vi)
ELPS 3E

Indefinite Pronouns

An indefinite pronoun refers to people or things that are not named or known. The chart below lists which indefinite pronouns are singular, which are plural, and which can be singular or plural.

Indefinite Pronouns				Plural	Singular or Plural
Singular					
another	either	nobody	someone	both	all
anybody	everybody	no one	something	few	any
anyone	everyone	nothing		many	most
anything	everything	one		several	none
each	neither	somebody			

> When you use indefinite pronouns as subjects, the verbs and other pronouns used in the sentence must agree with the subject in number.

Singular
Everybody needs to take his or her notebook on the field trip.

Plural
Several of the boys took notes on their trip to Lincoln's birthplace.

Singular or Plural
Most of the information is printed on handouts. (singular)
Most of the students are working on their research papers. (plural)

GRAMMAR
Try IT

Number your paper from 1 to 5. Choose the correct pronoun to complete each of the following sentences. Read them to a partner.

1. Many of the boys will write about *(his, their)* favorite heroes.
2. Everyone posts *(his or her, their)* report on the school Web page.
3. All of the students will send *(his or her, their)* reports to the paper.
4. Someone named Leah sent *(their, her)* comments to the editor.
5. Both of my friends read *(his or her, their)* reports aloud.

> If using *his or her* is clumsy, try changing the singular pronoun to a plural pronoun. For example, the first sample sentence above could be rewritten like this: **All** *of the students need to take* **their** *notebooks on the field trip.*

BASIC GRAMMAR

How can I produce better writing with pronouns?

Avoid Repeating Nouns

You can use pronouns in your writing to avoid repeating the same nouns over and over again. (See pages **742–750**.) Read the sample paragraph below. How many times did the writer use "Mary Pickersgill"?

Without Pronouns

Mary Pickersgill, a famous flag maker, is the subject of today's lesson. Mary Pickersgill made the flag that inspired "The Star-Spangled Banner." During the War of 1812, Mary Pickersgill made the flag that flew over Fort McHenry. The flag, which Mary Pickersgill's family helped Mary Pickersgill make, measured 30 feet by 42 feet.

Now read the revised sample below. The writer has replaced some of the nouns with pronouns. Which pronouns refer to Mary Pickersgill?

With Pronouns

Mary Pickersgill, a famous flag maker, is the subject of today's lesson. She made the flag that inspired "The Star-Spangled Banner." During the War of 1812, she made the flag that flew over Fort McHenry. The flag, which her family helped her make, measured 30 feet by 42 feet.

Read the following paragraph. On your own paper, rewrite the paragraph changing some of the underlined nouns to pronouns so that the paragraph reads more smoothly.

(1) Mary Pickersgill learned flag making from **(2)** Mary Pickersgill's mother, Rebecca Flower. **(3)** Mary Pickersgill and Mary Pickersgill's mother worked together to create the huge flag that flew over Fort McHenry during the Battle of Baltimore. This was **(4)** Mary Pickersgill's most famous flag. Francis Scott Key wrote a poem about the flag. **(5)** Francis Scott Key's poem became "The Star-Spangled Banner," the national anthem of the United States.

Improve Sentence Flow

Pronouns can be used to help the reader move easily from one sentence to the next. In the following paragraph, notice how the pronouns (in blue) improve the flow of the sentences. The arrows point to the antecedents (the words the pronouns replace).

Our class went on a field trip. We toured the two-story brick

Star-Spangled Banner Flag House in Baltimore, Maryland. It was

the home of Mary Pickersgill. In 1807, she moved there with her

mother and daughter. Later, they helped Mary sew the 30- by

42-foot flag that inspired "The Star-Spangled Banner". It was Mary's

most famous flag. She earned her living making flags to be flown

from the masts of ships. Our class wants to visit this site again.

 Number your paper from 1 to 5. Add pronouns from the list below to help improve the sentence flow. (You may use some pronouns more than once.) Then write the antecedent for each pronoun.

| it | you | we | them | they | us |

■ **pronoun:** *They*   **antecedent:** *landmarks*

The students in my class studied national historic landmarks.
___*They*___ represent the history of the United States in a very
important way. **(1)** _____ discovered that landmarks are
special building sites and structures including Mount Vernon, Pearl
Harbor, and Alcatraz. Becoming a national historic landmark is a
long process. **(2)** _____ starts with filling out lots of forms
and ends when the secretary of the interior gives approval. There
are thousands of historic places in America. Only about 2500 of
(3) _____ are national historic landmarks. The Flag House in
Baltimore, Maryland is one of **(4)** _____.
(5) _____ became a national historic landmark in 1969.

How can I use pronouns properly?

Avoid Agreement Problems

You can make your writing clearer by using pronouns properly. You must use pronouns that agree with their antecedents. (An antecedent is the noun or pronoun that a pronoun replaces or refers to. See pages **520** and **742**.) Pronouns must agree with their antecedents in number, person, and gender.

The Henry Ford Museum and Greenfield Village are known for their historic importance.

Henry Ford is best known for his automobiles.

Agreement in Number

The **number** of a pronoun is either singular or plural. The pronoun must match the antecedent in number.

■ A singular pronoun refers to a singular antecedent.

Henry Ford invented his own self-propelled vehicle—the quadricycle.

■ A plural pronoun refers to a plural antecedent.

The Ford children grew up on their family's farm in Dearborn, Michigan.

 Number your paper from 1 to 3 and write the correct pronoun for each sentence. Then write the antecedent each pronoun refers to.

■ Henry Ford changed the world when *(he, they)* built assembly-line automobiles.
  he, Henry Ford

1. So that people could learn more about *(his or her, their)* nation's history, Henry Ford also built a museum.

2. The chair Abraham Lincoln sat in at the time of *(their, his)* assassination is at the Henry Ford Museum.

3. The bus on which Rosa Parks refused to give up *(their, her)* seat is also on exhibit.

Agreement in Gender

The **gender** of a pronoun *(her, his, its)* must be the same as the gender of its antecedent. Singular pronouns can be feminine (female), masculine (male), or neuter (neither male nor female).

The Henry Ford Museum got its name in honor of Henry Ford.

Manuel went to Greenfield Village with his family.

 Number your paper from 1 to 5. Correct each underlined pronoun so that it agrees with its antecedent in gender.

1   Manuel enjoyed her visit to Greenfield Village. He liked

2 his old buildings and the people in historical costumes. Manuel

3 visited Henry Ford's childhood home and she saw a model of

4 the factory where Mr. Ford made its first automobile. At the

5 end of the tour she even took a ride in a Model-T car.

Shift in Person

When you use pronouns, you must choose either first-, second-, or third-person pronouns. Using more than one "person" to express an idea may cause an error called a pronoun shift.

Pronoun shift: **If Jerry and I want to see whales you must be patient.**

Correct: **If Jerry and I want to see whales we must be patient.**

 In the sentences below, change each underlined pronoun so that it doesn't cause a shift in person. Use all first-person pronouns. (See the chart on page **750**.)

1. My friend Jerry and I live near the ocean where you sometimes see whales.

2. When we know whales are migrating, you set up a telescope.

3. We wait and wait, watching through your telescope.

4. When we come home, Dad asks if they have seen any whales.

BASIC GRAMMAR

Choosing Verbs

Writers must constantly make choices, and one of their most important choices is which verb to use to express their thoughts clearly.

Action Verbs

An **action verb** tells what the subject is doing. Action verbs help bring writing to life. (Also see page **752**.)

During World War II, many women worked in wartime industries.

They built tanks and tested airplanes to help win the war.

Linking Verbs

A **linking verb** connects (links) a subject to a noun or an adjective in the predicate. (Also see page **752**.)

Common Linking Verbs	
Forms of "be"	be, is, are, was, were, am, been, being
Other linking verbs	appear, become, feel, grow, look, remain, seem, smell, sound, taste

Rosie the Riveter was an imaginary character.
(The linking verb "was" connects the subject "Rosie the Riveter" to the noun "character." "Character" is a *predicate noun*.)

She became popular during World War II.
(The linking verb "became" connects the subject "she" to the adjective "popular." "Popular" is a *predicate adjective*.)

 For each sentence below, write the linking verb and the predicate noun or predicate adjective. (One sentence has three predicate nouns.) Share your answers with a partner.

■ "Rosie Riveters" were women who got jobs during World War II.
Linking verb: were   *predicate noun:* women

1. These women were skilled in a number of ways.

2. They became riveters, welders, and shipbuilders.

3. A park in Richmond, California, is a memorial to these women.

4. Richmond was home to four shipyards where the "Rosies" worked.

 **TEKS** 6.19A(i)
ELPS 3E

Irregular Verbs

Verbs in the English language can be either *regular* or *irregular*.

Regular Verbs

Most verbs in the English language are regular. A writer adds *ed* to regular verbs to show a past action. A writer can also use *has, have,* or *had* with the past participle to form other verb tenses. (See the chart below.)

Present	Past	Past Participle
I watch.	**Yesterday I** watched.	**I** had watched.
He watches.	**Yesterday he** watched.	**He** had watched.

Irregular Verbs

Irregular verbs do not follow the *ed* rule. Instead of adding *ed* to show a past action, the word might change. (See the two examples below.)

Present	Past	Past Participle
I speak.	**Yesterday I** spoke.	**I** have spoken.
She runs.	**Yesterday she** ran.	**She** has run.

Writers use the correct forms of irregular verbs by using them over and over. Since the 10 most common verbs in English are irregular, you should understand them first. The chart below gives the principal parts of these 10 irregular verbs. (See the list of irregular verbs on page 756.)

 GRAMMAR Choose three of these verbs and write a short sentence for each principal part (*present, past,* and *past participle*). Exchange sentences with a partner, and read each other's aloud.

Present	Past	Past Participle
is	was	(has) been
come	came	(has) come
do	did	(has) done
get	got	(has) gotten
go	went	(has) gone
have	had	(has) had
make	made	(has) made
say	said	(has) said
see	saw	(has) seen
take	took	(has) taken

BASIC GRAMMAR

TEKS 6.19A(i), 6.19B
ELPS 3E, 3G

How can I use more effective verbs?

Show Powerful Action

You can use strong action verbs to help show the reader exactly what is happening (or has happened).

> **Ordinary Action Verbs**
>
> Louis Armstrong played a new kind of music—jazz.
> He performed with many bands.
>
> **Powerful Action Verbs**
>
> Notes poured out of Louis Armstrong's horn.
> When jazz became popular, Armstrong exploded into fame.

Try to avoid using linking verbs *(is, are, was, were)* too much. Often, a stronger action verb can be made from another word in the same sentence.

> Joe "King" Oliver was Armstrong's trumpet teacher. (linking verb)

> Joe "King" Oliver taught Armstrong to play the trumpet.
> (The action verb "taught" is made from the word "teacher.")

Create Active Voice

A verb is in the active voice if the subject is doing the action. To sound direct, use active voice more than passive voice. (See page **760**.)

> The trumpet was played by Louis Armstrong like no one else. (passive)

> Louis Armstrong played the trumpet like no one else. (active)

GRAMMAR Try IT Rewrite the sentences below, changing the passive voice verbs to active verbs. Read and discuss your sentences with a partner.

- ■ Hit songs were recorded by Louis Armstrong for five decades.
  Louis Armstrong recorded hit songs for five decades.

1. Many music awards were also won by him.
2. The nickname "Satchmo" was given to Louis Armstrong by a group of musicians.
3. His home, a national historic landmark in Queens, New York, can be visited by people.

Show When Something Happens

You can use different verb tenses to "tell time" in sentences. The three simple tenses are *present, past,* and *future.* (Also see page **754**.)

The Three Simple Tenses of Verbs	Singular	Plural
Present	I dance. You dance. He or she dances.	We dance. You dance. They dance.
Past	I danced. You danced. He or she danced.	We danced. You danced. They danced.
Future	I will dance. You will dance. He or she will dance.	We will dance. You will dance. They will dance.

 Identify the tense of the underlined verbs in the sentences below.

■ Students <u>enjoy</u> reading books that Laura Ingalls Wilder <u>wrote</u>.

present, past

1. Laura <u>wrote</u> about many "little houses."

2. You <u>will enjoy</u> learning about one of the houses that <u>remains</u>.

3. It is the house where Laura <u>lived</u> in Burr Oak, Iowa.

4. Maybe someday it <u>will become</u> a national historic landmark.

 Find and correct the six incorrect verb tenses used in the following paragraph. (The first verb is correct.)

1   Laura Ingalls' adventures <u>began</u> in Pepin, Wisconsin, in the

2   1870s. Laura and her family are pioneers, and they move often

3   when Laura is a child. Many years later, Laura writes books

4   about her childhood adventures. Today, they were published

5   in America and in many foreign countries. In the future, new

6   "Little House" fans continue to read the stories.

 Choose verbs carefully to tell exactly when the actions in your writing happen.

BASIC GRAMMAR

What else can I do with verbs?

Show Special Types of Action

You need perfect tense verbs to express certain types of actions. (See page 758 in the "Proofreader's Guide.") There are three perfect tenses.

sing, sang, sung	Singular	Plural
Present perfect tense states an action that *began in the past but continues or is completed in the present.*		
Present perfect (use *has* or *have* + past participle)	I have sung. You have sung. He or she has sung.	We have sung. You have sung. They have sung.
Past perfect tense states an action that *began in the past and was completed in the past.*		
Past perfect (use *had* + past participle)	I had sung. You had sung. He or she had sung.	We had sung. You had sung. They had sung.
Future perfect tense states an action that *will begin in the future and will be completed by a specific time in the future.*		
Future perfect (use *will have* + past participle)	I will have sung. You will have sung. He or she will have sung.	We will have sung. You will have sung. They will have sung.

Identify the tense of each underlined verb in the following paragraph. The first one has been done for you.

■ *present perfect*

Probably, you <u>have learned</u> of the midnight ride of Paul Revere. Once you read this paragraph, you **(1)** <u>will have learned</u> about Revere's house. His wooden home in Boston's North End **(2)** <u>has stood</u> since about 1680. Paul Revere and his family moved into the house in 1770. They **(3)** <u>had lived</u> there only 10 years when Revere decided to sell the house. By 1902, his great-grandson **(4)** <u>had seen</u> what bad condition the house was in and bought it. Today it is a national historic landmark. Over the years, many people **(5)** <u>have visited</u> Revere's house at 19 North Square, Boston, Massachusetts.

ELPS 3E, 5G

Share the Right Feeling

The verbs that you use should have the right connotation. (*Connotation* means "the feelings suggested by a word.") For example, you could say that a loud noise *alarmed* someone. But that word may not express the right feeling. Perhaps the word *terrified* or *excited* would better share your meaning.

Below are five words similar to *laugh*, but each of these words has a slightly different meaning.

Laugh	Definitions
giggle	to laugh with repeated, brief, soft sounds
snicker	to laugh slyly
chuckle	to laugh quietly to oneself
cackle	to laugh sharply and loudly
guffaw	to burst out in laughter

Complete a chart like the one above for the word *run, cry,* or *talk.* Use a thesaurus to help you create your list of five similar words. Then define each word with the help of a dictionary.

To get a specific feeling across, writers try to use verbs with the right connotation. In the paragraph below, the underlined verbs create a *rushed* feeling.

Paul Revere <u>devoured</u> his food and <u>gulped</u> from his cup. He then <u>threw</u> his napkin on the table before <u>charging</u> out the door. A sound in the yard caught his attention, and he <u>dashed</u> to the lighthouse. He <u>tore</u> up the stairs and <u>grabbed</u> a lantern.

Rewrite the paragraph above. Replace the underlined verbs in the paragraph with verbs that create a different feeling—*slow,* rather than *rushed.* Be sure that all your verbs match the new feeling you want to create. Share your new paragraph with a partner.

BASIC GRAMMAR

Describing with Adjectives

Adjectives are words that describe or modify nouns or pronouns. Sensory adjectives help the reader see, hear, feel, smell, and taste what writers are describing. (Also see pages **766–769**.)

Without Adjectives

> The world is full of landmarks. From the ring of Big Ben in England to the roar of Niagara Falls, landmarks are everywhere.

With Adjectives

> The world is full of mysterious and beautiful landmarks. From the deep-sounding ring of Big Ben in England to the thunderous roar of Niagara Falls, landmarks are everywhere.

Adjectives can answer three questions: *What kind? How many (much)? Which one?* Remember that proper adjectives can be made from proper nouns (England, *English;* Italy, *Italian*) and are capitalized.

What Kind?	Chinese **food**	pea **soup**	red **shoes**
How Many (Much)?	two **kittens**	a little **sugar**	some **bugs**
Which One?	this **book**	these **students**	those **cars**

GRAMMAR Try IT For each blank in the sentences below, write an adjective of the type called for in parentheses.

1. When you visit the historical site of the great Chicago fire, you can almost smell the *(what kind?)* blaze of 1871.

2. You'll hear *(how many?)* explosions as work continues on the Crazy Horse Memorial in South Dakota.

3. *(what kind?)* wildflowers cover *(how many?)* areas of the park.

4. The circle of stone called the Medicine Wheel, at Lovell, Wyoming, is a/an *(what kind?)* symbol of native civilization.

5. The Eiffel Tower in Paris is *(what kind?)* landmark known around the world.

6. *(which one?)* structure is made of iron.

TEKS 6.19A(iii)
ELPS 3E

vary compare
modify CONNECT
choose
Working with Words
533

Comparative and Superlative Adjectives

You can use comparative adjectives to compare two things. For most one-syllable adjectives, add *er* to make the **comparative form**. To compare three or more things, add *est* to make the **superlative form**. (See page **768**.)

Positive	Comparative	Superlative
large	larger	largest

Comparative: **The Sears Tower is taller than the John Hancock Building.**
Superlative: **The Sears Tower is the tallest building in the United States.**

Add *er* and *est* to some two-syllable words and use *more* or *most* (or *less* or *least*) with others. Always use *more* or *most* with three-syllable adjectives.

Positive	Comparative	Superlative
joyful	more joyful	most joyful

Comparative: **The Chrysler Building is a more complex structure than other skyscrapers.**
Superlative: **The most complex structure in my town is a long bridge.**

Write the comparative and superlative forms of the adjective in each of the following sentences. Read aloud with a partner.

1. While Washington, D.C., is an exciting city, New York is a _____ city. Javier thinks Rio de Janeiro is the _____ city in the world.

2. There was a long line to get into the Lincoln Memorial. There was a _____ line than that to get into the Capitol, but the _____ line was at the White House.

3. The Constitution is an important document. Some people think the Declaration of Independence is a _____ document than the Constitution, but I think the Constitution is our country's _____ document.

4. A beautiful park called Lafayette Square overlooks the White House. A _____ park than this one is located nearby in Great Falls, Virginia, and the _____ park I've ever visited is Great Smoky Mountains National Park.

5. The Postal Museum is a small part of the Smithsonian Institution. The American Indian Museum is a bit _____, and the Sackler Gallery is the _____.

BASIC GRAMMAR

How can I strengthen my writing with adjectives?

Create Stronger Descriptions

Strong adjectives help readers use their senses. For example, "Black Thunder is a cool waterslide" creates a basic picture of the slide, but "Black Thunder is a hair-raising, monster waterslide" creates a sharper picture.

> **Avoid ho-hum adjectives.** Some adjectives really don't provide a clear picture for the reader. Replacing vague words like *nice, good,* and *big* with vivid adjectives will make your writing more effective.

 Replace each underlined adjective in the sentences below with a stronger adjective. (A thesaurus can help you.)

1. Listen to the roar of Niagara Falls, a <u>big</u> waterfall.
2. The Liberty Bell is a <u>good</u> symbol of this country.
3. The <u>strong</u> Colorado River carved the Grand Canyon's <u>tall</u> cliffs.
4. San Francisco's cable cars are <u>different</u> landmarks.

Form "Extra-Strength" Modifiers

Compound adjectives are made of two or more words. Some are spelled as one word; others are hyphenated. (Use a dictionary to check spelling.)

Many natural but little-visited landmarks enjoy worldwide recognition.

 For each of the following sentences, write a compound adjective to fill in the blank. Make your compound adjectives by combining words from the following list.

earth	first	taking	wind	breath	rate	blown	shaking

■ There are _____ hiking trails in Glacier Park, Montana.
first-rate

1. Chicago could be called a _____ city.
2. You get a _____ view from the Statue of Liberty.
3. Mauna Loa in Hawaii has _____ volcanic eruptions.

Use Sensory Details

Writers often use adjectives to create sensory details. This kind of detail forms pictures in the reader's mind. As you read the paragraph below, think about the pictures formed by the sensory details. Then consider how the underlined adjectives help to create the sensory details.

A thumping "rom-rom-rom" echoes across the muddy Mississippi River. I hurry on. My toes make squishing sounds in the sticky riverbank mud. The smell of rotting leaves and decaying fish doesn't bother me. I see an olive green lump at the edge of the river—a bullfrog! It sits still except for its vibrating yellow throat.

 Draw a chart like the one below and list all the sensory details that are underlined in the paragraph above.

sight	sound	smell	texture (feeling)
olive green lump			

Try to get into the habit of using sensory details whenever you write. Practice focusing on one sense at a time. See if you can learn to be more aware of what is going on around you.

 List one or two ideas of sensory details in response to each of the following statements. (An example is provided for each.) Share your ideas with a partner, then decide which one you like best.

1. Identify the smells you like.
   Just-baked bread

2. Identify things you like to touch or feel.
   A gentle wind

3. Identify favorite tastes.
   A sour apple

4. Identify sights that you look forward to seeing.
   The fall colors

5. Identify the sounds that you like to hear.
   The 3:00 dismissal bell

Describing with Adverbs

Adverbs describe or modify verbs, adjectives, or other adverbs. You can use adverbs to answer *how? when? (or how often?) where?* or *how much?* (See pages **770–771**.)

How?	slowly	**Kiet counts slowly to 20.**
When?	yesterday	**Tyisha went on a field trip yesterday.**
Where?	outside	**My classmates are waiting outside.**
How Much?	barely	**Falling debris barely missed the workers.**

GRAMMAR Try IT For each of the following sentences, write the adverbs you find. (The number of adverbs is shown in parentheses.) Tell what word each adverb describes and what question it answers.

■ Quietly, our class explored the Indian burial grounds. *(1)*
   quietly (explored, how)

1. I often go to Mexico City with my father. *(1)*

2. It may be hot outside, but Mammoth Cave is very cool. *(2)*

3. I never knew that Boston had landmarks everywhere. *(2)*

4. My uncle frequently travels to the East Coast. *(1)*

5. Recently we went to San Antonio, Texas, to see the Alamo. *(1)*

6. A famous battle was fought there. *(1)*

7. Our guide turned left and walked quickly away. *(3)*

8. Today I learned that Research Cave has been badly damaged. *(2)*

9. I instantly recognized the White House when I saw it for the first time. *(1)*

Comparative and Superlative Adverbs

You can use adverbs to compare two things. The **comparative form** of an adverb compares two people, places, things, or ideas. The **superlative form** of an adverb compares three or more people, places, things, or ideas.

 For most one-syllable adverbs, add *er* to make the comparative form and *est* to make the superlative form.

Positive	Comparative	Superlative
soon	sooner	soonest

Comparative: I arrived later than Sheila did.

Superlative: Kayla arrived latest of all.

While you add *er* and *est* to some two-syllable adverbs, you need to use *more* or *most* (or *less* or *least*) with others. Always use *more* or *most* with three-syllable adverbs.

Positive	Comparative	Superlative
quickly	more quickly	most quickly

Comparative: Ed has visited the Sears Tower more frequently than I have.

Superlative: Of all of us, Ed visits the Sears Tower most frequently.

 When you use the comparative form, make sure that you state a complete comparison: *I arrived later than Sheila did,* not *I arrived later than Sheila.*

 Write a sentence for each adverb below.

■ later (comparative)
  I arrived at Marengo Cave later than the rest of my friends.

1. harder (comparative)
2. slowly (superlative)
3. more effectively (comparative)
4. fastest (superlative)

BASIC GRAMMAR

How can I use adverbs effectively?

Describe Actions

You can make your writing more descriptive by using adverbs. You can add *ly* to some adjectives to create adverbs.

> **bad** badly   **amazing** amazingly   **tight** tightly
>
> **The cat was lazy. / The cat stretched out** lazily **on the windowsill.**

When you add *ly* to form an adverb, you need to remember these three spelling rules.

- Add *ly* to some words: **neat** neatly
- Drop the *e* and add *ly* to others: **terrible** terribly
- Change the *y* to *i* and add *ly* to still others: **sleepy** sleepily

Rewrite the following sentences by changing the underlined adjectives to adverbs. (Change other words as needed.)

- The <u>swift</u> river ran under the bridge in the park.
  The river ran swiftly under the bridge in the park.

1. I was <u>happy</u> to walk over the bridge.
2. The woman heard a <u>sudden</u> cry.
3. Her <u>gentle</u> voice calmed the child.

Add Emphasis

You can stress the importance of something with adverbs. Generally, use adverbs of degree—those that answer *how much?*—for this job.

> **San Antonio's Riverwalk is** absolutely **beautiful.**
>
> I really **want to explore it.**

Rewrite the following sentences. Add emphasis by using adverbs to modify the underlined words.

- I <u>agree</u> with you.
  I completely agree with you!

1. I <u>suggest</u> that you visit the Riverwalk in the evening.
2. It is <u>scenic</u>.
3. We had an <u>exciting</u> time there last year.

Modify Adjectives

With adverbs, you can describe how often something is a certain way. Adverbs that tell how often include *sometimes, often, usually, occasionally, always,* and so on.

The Badlands are always **spectacular.**

A visit there is rarely **disappointing.**

Rewrite the following sentences, using a *how often* adverb to modify each underlined adjective.

■ The Badlands' Fossil Exhibit Trail is <u>fascinating</u>.

The Badlands' Fossil Exhibit Trail is always fascinating.

1. The yucca plants are <u>interesting</u> to see.

2. Bison are <u>visible</u> on Sage Creek Rim Road.

3. Turkey vultures are <u>overhead</u>.

4. It is <u>rainy</u> in the Badlands.

5. People are <u>amazed</u> at the Badlands formations.

Be Precise

With adverbs, you can tell the reader exactly when *(then, yesterday, now)* or where *(there, nearby, inside)* something happens.

We are going to the Milwaukee Zoo tomorrow.

The buses will pick us up here **at 9:00.**

Add an adverb that tells *when* or *where* to each one of the following sentences.

■ We need to turn in our permission slips.

We need to turn in our permission slips today.

1. I handed mine in.

2. Sheniqua wants to visit the primate house.

3. Carl spotted a bonobo, an African chimpanzee.

4. I will sit on this bench.

TEKS 6.19A(v)
ELPS 3E, 5G

Connecting with Prepositions

A preposition is a word (or words) that shows how one word or idea is related to another. A preposition is the first word of a prepositional phrase like *over the hill* and *near the river*. (See page **774** for a complete list of prepositions.)

The Gila Cliff Dwellings National Monument is located in New Mexico. (The preposition "in" shows the relationship between the verb "is located" and the object of the preposition "New Mexico." The prepositional phrase acts as an adverb telling "where.")

The monument in the Gila Wilderness **has 50,000 visitors annually.** (The preposition "in" shows the relationship between the noun "monument" and the object of the preposition "Gila Wilderness." The prepositional phrase acts as an adjective telling "which one.")

Avoid confusing prepositions and adverbs. If a word that can also be used as a preposition appears alone in a sentence, it is being used as an adverb.

Two students lagged behind the group.
(*Behind the group* is a prepositional phrase.)

Two students lagged behind, **so we waited.**
(*Behind* is an adverb that modifies the verb, *lagged.*)

What can I do with prepositions?

Show Location

Prepositional phrases are often used to show location, or where something is or happens. Some prepositions used in theses phrases are *at, near, by, outside, near, in, on, above,* and *below.*

You can see many geysers at Yellowstone National Park.

Dad parked the car near the visitor's center.

Write a prepositional phrase to describe the location of each subject below. Use your phrases in sentences and share with a partner.

1. flowers   **3.** school

2. river   **4.** window

TEKS 6.19A(v)
ELPS 3E, 3G, 3H

Show Time

Prepositional phrases can also be used to convey time, or *when* something happens. Example prepositions in these phrases include *after, before, at, in, on, during, around,* and *since.*

> **The geyser erupted** at 9:58 a.m.
>
> On the next day, **we were the first people to arrive.**

 With a partner, read each sentence aloud. Identify the prepositional phrases that answer the question *when?*

> **1.** Yellowstone National Park was established in 1872.
>
> **2.** The geyser erupts on a regular schedule.

Show Direction

Prepositional phrases can also convey direction when used with verbs that show movement. Example prepositions in these phrases include *across, between, into, around, through,* and *toward.*

> **As we walked** toward the geyser, **it erupted.**
>
> **The water sprayed high** into the air.

 With a partner, take turns adding a prepositional phrase that shows direction in each sentence.

> **1.** They wandered _____.   **3.** Chandra ran _____.
>
> **2.** The snake slithered _____.   **4.** The hikers marched _____.

Add Details

Prepositional phrases that describe a noun or pronoun can add details. When acting as an adjective, a prepositional phrase may answer the questions *which one? what kind?* or *how many?*

> **The geyser** near Firehole River **is impressive.**
>
> **The campsites** with electrical hookups **are more expensive.**

 Describe a topic (your room, a book, etc.) to a partner using sentences with prepositional phrases that add details. Have your partner identify the prepositional phrases.

BASIC GRAMMAR

TEKS 6.19A(vii)
ELPS 3E, 4C

Connecting with Conjunctions

Conjunctions connect words, groups of words, and sentences. There are three kinds of conjunctions: *coordinating, subordinating,* and *correlative.* The following sentences show some of the ways to use conjunctions. (See page 776 for a list of common conjunctions.)

Coordinating Conjunctions Connect Words

Artists come to Crazy Horse near Mt. Rushmore in the Black Hills to sketch or paint the memorial.

Skilled crews shape the mountain with explosives and torches.

Connect Compound Subjects and Predicates

Today, a museum and a cultural center are part of the memorial.

Visitors view exhibits and meet Native American craftspeople there.

Connect Sentences

Work on Crazy Horse Memorial began in 1948, yet it is not finished.

The sculptor of Crazy Horse, Korczak Ziolkowski, died in 1982, so his family continues his work.

Subordinating Conjunctions Connect Dependent Clauses to Independent Clauses

For several years, Ziolkowski worked alone while he sculpted the memorial.

Before he started Crazy Horse, he worked as a sculptor on nearby Mt. Rushmore.

Correlative Conjunctions Connect Noun Phrases and Verb Phrases

Both foggy days and moonlit nights make Crazy Horse look mysterious.

People not only watch the work on Crazy Horse from a distance but also ride buses to the base of the huge project.

GRAMMAR Try IT Write three sentences using the three different types of conjunctions: *coordinating, subordinating,* and *correlative.* Underline the conjunctions you use. Read your sentences to a classmate.

What can I do with conjunctions?
Connect a Series of Ideas

You can use conjunctions to connect a series of three or more words or phrases in a row. Place commas between the words or phrases and place a conjunction before the final item.

> **People hike up the mountain, stand on the statue, and enjoy the view.**
> (The conjunction connects three verb phrases.)

> **Wild iris, pine trees, and cone flowers greet the hikers.**
> (The conjunction connects three noun phrases.)

 Copy the following sentences and place commas where they are needed. Underline the conjunctions.

1. I gaze out over the rocks trees and hills of the Black Hills.
2. I tilt my head back stare up at the face and feel very small.
3. Crazy Horse cared for the children the elderly and the sick.

Expand Sentences (with Coordinating Conjunctions)

You can use **coordinating conjunctions** *(and, but, or, nor, for, so, yet)* to make compound subjects and predicates and to write compound sentences.

> **Ziolkowski and his sons carved stone for almost 36 years, but they didn't finish the sculpture.**
> (In this sentence, "and" creates a compound subject, and the conjunction "but" creates a compound sentence.)

 For each blank, write a coordinating conjunction. Tell whether it connects a compound subject, a compound predicate, or a compound sentence.

Native Americans have lived in the Black Hills for 12,000 years,
(1) _____ several tribes consider the area to be sacred land.
Its noble history **(2)** _____ spiritual power are valued greatly. It
was fitting to honor Crazy Horse with a carving in the Black Hills,
(3) _____ the chosen sculptor was, surprisingly, not a Native
American. Korczak Ziolkowski, a sculptor of Polish descent, worked
on the mountain until his death **(4)** _____ did not finish the
sculpture. His family continues to work on the monument.

BASIC GRAMMAR

 **TEKS** 6.19A(vii)
ELPS 3E, 4C

Expand Sentences (with Subordinating Conjunctions)

You can use a **subordinating conjunction** to connect a dependent clause to another sentence. A dependent clause (one that *cannot* stand alone as a sentence) must be connected to an independent clause (one that *can* stand alone as a sentence). In the expanded sentences below, the dependent clause is underlined, and the subordinating conjunction is in blue.

> Gutzon Borglum worked on Mt. Rushmore from 1927 <u>until he died in 1941.</u>
>
> <u>When he started his work on the mountain,</u> he planned to include an area to keep historical documents.

 Choose a subordinating conjunction *(before, although, because, while, when)* to complete each sentence in the paragraph below. Then read your final paragraph to a classmate.

> Borglum chose Mt. Rushmore **(1)** _____ he knew the granite would last for thousands of years. **(2)** _____ any carving was done, workers used dynamite to blast out large chunks of the mountainside. **(3)** _____ the sculptors got to work, they used jackhammers, drills, and chisels on the hard rock. Weather and financial problems halted the work several times **(4)** _____ the sculpture was in progress. **(5)** _____ it took 14 years to finish, sculptors actually worked on the monument for only 6 of those years.

Show a Relationship

You can use **correlative conjunctions** to show a relationship between two words, phrases, or clauses. Correlative conjunctions are always used in pairs: *both/and, not only/but also, neither/nor, either/or, whether/or.*

> Either Gutzon Borglum or his son, Lincoln, supervised the people working on Mount Rushmore.
>
> They weren't sure whether they would find skilled workers in South Dakota or they would have to train workers.

 For each of the blanks in the sentences below, write the correlative conjunctions that make the most sense.

1. _____ bad weather _____ a lack of money could stop the work.

2. _____ the hard work _____ the tough conditions scared the workers away.

Building Effective Sentences

Imagine eating the same thing every day, at every meal. Eventually, you would dislike even the cheesiest pizza or the most scrumptious cake. People just naturally like variety.

The same is true with writing. A story with one long sentence after another, or one short sentence after another, would soon become boring. Sometimes a short sentence expresses feeling in a way that a long sentence cannot, and a long sentence does a better job of explaining a complicated idea. One key to clear writing is using a variety of sentences.

What's Ahead

You will learn about . . .

- writing complete sentences.
- fixing sentence problems.
- adding variety to your sentences.
- combining sentences.
- using different types of sentences.
- expanding and modeling sentences.

Writing Complete Sentences

A sentence is a group of words that forms a complete thought. Writers use complete sentences in order to communicate clearly. Here is a group of words that does not form a complete thought:

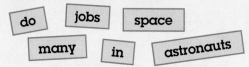

The jumble of words above makes no sense. When these same words are rearranged into a sentence, however, they do make sense. They communicate a clear, complete thought:

 On your own paper, unscramble the word groups below to create complete sentences. Some sentences can be arranged in more than one way. Remember to capitalize and punctuate each sentence correctly.

■ developed NASA the in 1970s the shuttle space
  NASA developed the space shuttle in the 1970s.

1. a like shuttle a launches rocket
2. airplane an like lands it
3. used rockets be only can once most
4. be again shuttle can again a used and
5. 1981 first launched shuttle in was the
6. satellites orbit shuttles the to carried first
7. carry and now people shuttles cargo
8. is crew flown a flight by shuttle a
9. do to job member each crew has a special

Write **Write three or four sentences about space exploration. On another sheet,**
NOW **mix up the words and leave out punctuation and capitalization. Ask a**
classmate to rearrange the words so they form complete sentences.

Basic Parts of a Sentence

Every sentence has two basic parts: a complete subject—which tells who or what is doing something—and a complete predicate—which tells what the subject is doing. (See pages **728** and **730**.)

Complete Subject	Complete Predicate
Who or what did something?	*What did the subject do?*
Scientists	explored the idea of flight.
George Cayley, an engineer,	studied flight for many years.

Divide a piece of paper into two columns. For each of the sentences below, write the complete subject in the left column and write the complete predicate in the right column.

> In the following sentences, the words that come before the verb are the *complete subject*. The verb and all the words that follow it are the *complete predicate*.

■ Sir George Cayley discovered the principles of flight.
  Sir George Cayley | discovered the principles of flight.

1. Cayley learned from birds soaring long distances.
2. A flying toy top was one of his first inventions.
3. It had a three-bladed propeller.
4. A model of the first glider flew successfully in 1804.
5. A small boy became the first person in history to fly.
6. He made a short flight in Cayley's glider.
7. Cayley prepared the way for other inventors.

 Write three or four sentences about what you think it was like to fly in Cayley's glider. Draw a line between the complete subject and the complete predicate in each of your sentences.

BASIC WRITING

Simple Subjects and Predicates

A simple subject is the subject of a sentence without the words that modify it. A simple predicate is the verb without the words that modify it or complete the thought. In the sentences below, the simple subjects are orange and the simple predicates are blue. (See also pages **728** and **730**.)

Complete Subject	Complete Predicate
Governments **in many countries**	developed **airplanes.**
Airplanes	changed **how people traveled.**

 Divide a piece of paper into two columns. For each of the sentences below, write the complete subject in the left column and write the complete predicate in the right column. Then underline the simple subjects and predicates.

■ Leonardo da Vinci drew designs of aircraft in the 1400s.

   Leonardo da Vinci | *drew designs of aircraft in the 1400s.*

1. He gathered data about birds.

2. His first aircraft moved like a bird's wings.

3. Paul Cornu of France built a man-carrying helicopter in 1907.

4. Charles Lindbergh flew the first solo flight across the Atlantic.

5. Jumbo jets carry almost 500 passengers today.

6. These planes weigh nearly 460 tons!

7. The supersonic *Concorde* began passenger service in 1976.

8. It flew faster than the speed of sound.

9. Some airports need longer runways now.

 Write three sentences about airplanes or airports. Ask a classmate to find and underline the simple subject and simple predicate in each sentence.

Compound Subjects and Predicates

Some sentences have compound subjects or compound predicates, and some have both.

- A compound subject includes two or more subjects that share the same predicate (or predicates).
- A compound predicate includes two or more predicates that share the same subject (or subjects).

Compound Subject	Compound Predicate
Hospitals and trauma centers	**build and maintain heliports.**

Number your paper from 1 to 7. For each sentence below, write any compound subject and any compound predicate.

- Leonardo da Vinci, Louis Bréguet, and Paul Cornu designed and illustrated early helicopters.

  Leonardo da Vinci, Louis Bréguet, and Paul Cornu designed and illustrated

1. A huge whirling blade lifts a helicopter and keeps it in the air.

2. Helicopters carry seriously ill people to hospitals and save people from floods.

3. Radio reporters and television newspeople spot and describe traffic delays from helicopters.

4. The coast guard, police departments, and fire departments sometimes use helicopters in emergencies.

5. People explore wilderness areas and search for missing persons from helicopters.

6. Directors and photographers use helicopters for bird's-eye views of movie scenes.

7. A helicopter pilot can even find and track a whale.

Write
NOW Write one sentence with a compound subject and another one with a compound predicate. Then write a sentence with both a compound subject and a compound predicate.

How can I make sure my sentences are complete?

Check Your Subjects and Predicates

Sentence fragments are incomplete sentences. They may be missing a subject, a predicate, or both. You can learn how to fix sentence fragments by reading the examples below.

Fragment	Sentence
Is a place where airplanes take off and land. *(The subject is missing.)*	**An airport is a place where airplanes take off and land.**
In 2003, Atlanta's Hartsfield Airport, the world's busiest airport. *(The predicate is missing.)*	**In 2003, Atlanta's Hartsfield Airport was the world's busiest airport.**
At a small airport near Detroit. *(The subject and predicate are missing.)*	**My uncle keeps his plane at a small airport near Detroit.**

 Number your paper from 1 to 7. For each sentence, write "S" next to the number. For each fragment, write "F." Also tell which part or parts are missing: "subject," "predicate," or "both."

■ Are like small cities.

  F – subject

1. Each year, more than 100 million people travel through large airports.
2. Most of the visitors to airports passengers.
3. At areas for ticketing, check-in, and baggage handling.
4. Some concourses hold restaurants and shops.
5. Can eat, shop, and relax.
6. Passengers are only one type of airport customer.
7. Airfreight companies as well.

 Rewrite the fragments above. Add the missing parts so that each fragment is now a complete sentence.

Edit Your Writing Carefully

Sentence fragments may be difficult to spot in your writing. At first glance, a fragment may look like a sentence. It starts with a capital letter, and it ends with a punctuation mark. Reading a sentence out loud can help you figure out if something is missing.

In the examples below, the writer found and underlined a number of fragments. Then she turned the fragments into complete sentences, some by combining the fragments with nearby sentences.

Fragment	Sentence
An airport is a busy place. On the ground and in the air. An airport doesn't have just planes and jets. Cars, buses, and trains, too.	An airport is a busy place both on the ground and in the air. An airport doesn't have just planes and jets. It has cars, buses, and trains, too.
You might see fire trucks and police cars. Or motorized carts that carry luggage.	You might see fire trucks, police cars, or motorized carts that carry luggage.

 Read the following paragraph and check for fragments. Then on your own paper, tell how many fragments you found. Rewrite the paragraph, correcting each of the fragments.

1   At an airport. You don't see just airplanes. Busy airports
2   also rely on ground vehicles. Like cars and buses. People drive
3   their cars to and from airports. Buses take passengers to local
4   hotels and car-rental offices. Also limousines and taxis. Trains
5   and subways, too. Ground transportation helps passengers get
6   to the airport on time. To catch their flights. It also helps them
7   get back home again.

 Write a short paragraph about an airport, a train or bus station, or a busy street in your town. Have a classmate check your writing for fragments.

Fixing Sentence Problems

Check for Run-On Sentences

Sometimes you may accidentally write a **run-on sentence**. A run-on sentence is two or more sentences that run together. Sometimes it is called a *comma splice* because it is connected with a comma instead of a period. Other run-ons may have no punctuation at all.

One way to fix run-on sentences is to divide them into two or more complete sentences. Another way is to add a comma and a conjunction.

Run-On Sentence	Corrected Sentences
This year, I learned what flight attendants do I think I might like to be one someday.	This year, I learned what flight attendants do. I think I might like to be one someday.
	This year, I learned what flight attendants do, and I think I might like to be one someday.

 On your own paper, correct the run-on sentences below by dividing them into two or more shorter sentences.

■ Flight attendants welcome passengers aboard they also help passengers find their seats.

Flight attendants welcome passengers aboard. They also help passengers find their seats.

1. First they check to see that seat belts are fastened then they check to make sure carry-on items are stored safely.
2. Flight attendants are trained for emergencies they know what to do if something unexpected happens.
3. They keep the passengers comfortable they serve food and beverages and supply blankets and pillows.
4. Flight attendants sometimes go to "career days" students can learn a lot by asking flight attendants questions.

 Choose two of the above run-on sentences and correct them by using a comma and the conjunction "and."

Eliminate Rambling Sentences

A **rambling sentence** happens when you join too many sentences with the word *and*, as in the example below. Notice that there are two ways shown to correct a rambling sentence.

 Of course, some *and*'s are necessary in sentences. See the blue **and** used in the following rambling sentence.

Rambling Sentence	Corrected Sentences
Air traffic controllers work in the control towers at airports and they have very important jobs and they must know where all the planes are, both in the air **and** on the ground.	**Air traffic controllers work in the control towers at airports, and they have very important jobs**. **They must know where all the planes are, both in the air and on the ground.** (Add a comma before the first *and*. Drop the second *and* to make two sentences.)
	Air traffic controllers work in the control towers at airports. **They have very important jobs and must know where all the planes are, both in the air and on the ground.** (Drop the first *and* to make two sentences. Drop *they* in the second sentence to make a compound predicate.)

 Correct the following rambling sentences on your own paper. (Watch for three *and*'s that are necessary.)

1. Controllers keep track of planes flying around the airport and they direct planes in and out of the airport and they even guide the planes on the ground.

2. Controllers warn pilots about weather changes and they also report on ground conditions and they tell pilots when and where to land.

3. Miles from the airport, the pilot contacts the tower and a controller in the tower watches the plane on radar and makes sure that the plane lands safely and once the plane lands, a ground controller directs it to its gate.

 Choose one of the rambling sentences above and correct it by rewriting it in a different way than you did at first.

BASIC WRITING

 **TEKS** 6.19C
ELPS 3E

What can I do to write clear sentences?
Make Subjects and Verbs Agree

Writers must be careful to make the subjects and verbs in each of their sentences agree. That means a singular subject needs a singular verb, and a plural subject needs a plural verb.

Singular or Plural Subjects

A verb must agree with its subject in number.

■ If a subject is singular (refers to one person, place, thing, or idea), the verb must be singular, too.

> Luis enjoys **airport field trips.**

■ If a subject is plural (refers to more than one person, place, thing, or idea), the verb must be plural.

> **My** classmates enjoy **airport field trips.**

(Don't forget that most nouns ending in *s* or *es* are plural, and most verbs ending in *s* are singular.)

 Number your paper from 1 to 6. For each of these simple sentences, write the correct verb (or verbs). Make sure each verb agrees with its subject.

■ Each May, the sixth graders goes on a field trip to Atlanta's Hartsfield International Airport.

go

1. A plane arrive there every 40 seconds, 24 hours a day!
2. Almost 150 million passengers passes through the airport yearly.
3. People rides a "people mover" train to get around the airport.
4. The terminal buildings covers about 130 acres.
5. Shops, restaurants, and benches lines the long concourses.
6. People working at the airport helps keep passengers safe.

 Write one sentence using the subject "pilots" and another using the subject "airplane." Make sure your subjects and verbs agree. Read your sentences aloud, and listen as a classmate reads his or hers.

agree model EXPAND
order *combine*

555

Building Effective Sentences

TEKS 6.19C
ELPS 3E

Compound Subjects Connected by "And"

A compound subject connected by the word *and* needs a plural verb.

Miss Gonzales **and** Mr. Peet **take** us on the field trip.

Compound Subjects Connected by "Or"

A compound subject connected by the word *or* needs a verb that agrees in number with the subject nearest to it.

The teachers **or the** principal **organizes the field trip.**

(*Principal*, the subject nearer the verb, is singular, so the singular verb *organizes* is used.)

GRAMMAR
Try IT

Number your paper from 1 to 8. Write the correct verb choice for each of these sentences.

■ Airports and air travel *(is, are)* quite safe.
are

1. Airport rules and airline employees *(help, helps)* passengers stay safe.

2. Each passenger or airline employee *(carry, carries)* personal identification everywhere in the airport.

3. Metal detectors and X-ray scanners *(check, checks)* passengers and luggage.

4. An electronic game or a cell phone *(is, are)* not harmed by X-ray equipment.

5. Passengers or a lost kid *(sets, set)* off security detectors sometimes.

6. Even small scissors and nail files *(cause, causes)* alarms to go off.

7. Security guards or an airport police officer *(question, questions)* passengers who carry metal objects.

8. Checkpoints and security guards *(keep, keeps)* passengers and visitors safe.

Write
NOW

Rewrite sentence 5 above using a plural verb. Rewrite sentence 6 using a singular verb. Say the new verbs aloud. Listen as a classmate says the verbs in his or her sentences.

BASIC WRITING

 **TEKS** 6.19C
ELPS 3E

How can I write simple sentences with correct subject-verb agreement?

In simple sentences, you can sometimes hear when a subject and verb agree in number.

> **The** birds fly **from tree to tree.**
>
> **A** bird flies **high into the sky.**

Making sure the subject and verb agree can be harder when a phrase or appositive come between the subject and verb.

Phrase Between the Subject and Verb

A prepositional phrase after the subject does not affect the number of the verb. The verb should always agree with the subject.

> One **of my favorite Greek myths** is **the story of Icarus and Daedalus.**
>
> (The subject is *one*, so the verb *is* singular.)

Appositive Between the Subject and Verb

An appositive is a noun that follows another noun to identify or explain it. An appositive after the subject does not affect the number of the verb.

> Daedalus, **a man of many inventions,** builds **a pair of wings.**
>
> (The subject is *Daedalus*, so the verb *builds* is singular.)

Number your paper from 1 to 5. With a partner, read each sentence silently. Discuss which verb is correct. Read the sentence aloud with the correct verb. Then write the sentence on your paper.

1. The wings of a bird *(is, are)* his inspiration, so Daedalus makes them by gluing feathers to a frame.

2. Icarus, the dearest of sons, *(is, are)* called upon to test the wings.

3. Daedalus, like other inventors, *(has, have)* both knowledge and ambition.

4. Many myths of ancient Greece *(explore, explores)* the theme of a fate that cannot be escaped.

5. None of us *(know, knows)* if the myth is about a real person.

TEKS 6.19C
ELPS 3E

How can I write compound sentences with correct subject-verb agreement?

A compound sentence has two clauses, each with its own subject and verb. Each clause expresses a complete thought.

> **Ducks migrate** south each year, and **they stay** south for the winter.

The clauses are joined by a coordinating conjunction such as *and, or, but, for, so,* or *yet,* and a comma is used before the conjunction. In each clause, the subject and verb should agree in number.

Singular Subjects in Both Clauses

> **The** frog **suddenly** leaps **into the air, and** it glides **a long distance.**

Plural Subjects in Both Clauses

> **Many** dolphins **in the ocean** leap **into the air, but** they **also** splash **loudly over the surface of the water.**

Singular and Plural Subjects in Different Clauses

> **I** enjoy **unusual animals, so the** guides are taking **me out to see some flying fish.**

Number your paper from 1 to 5. With a partner, read each compound sentence. Identify the subject in each clause. Discuss which verb is correct. Read the sentence aloud with the correct verb. Then write the sentence on your paper.

1. The wildlife tour *(is/are)* amazing, but the boat *(is/are)* crowded with people.

2. A flying fish *(swishes/swish)* its tail very fast, and it *(gains/gain)* enough speed from this to burst into the air.

3. The birds *(sits/sit)* in the trees, and nearby a turtle *(crawls/crawl)* slowly to the shore.

4. I *(am/are)* hungry at the end of the tour, and the guides *(treats/treat)* all of us to sandwiches and juice.

5. All of the tourists *(am/are)* happy with the tour, and the guides *(am/are)* exhausted from the day.

BASIC WRITING

What should I do to avoid nonstandard sentences?

Avoid Double Negatives

A **double negative** happens when two negative words are used together (*don't never, can't hardly*) in the same sentence. Using double negatives is incorrect in both spoken and written language. Your writing will seem careless—or even inaccurate—if you use double negatives.

Negative Words				
nothing	nowhere	neither	never	not
barely	hardly	nobody	none	no
Be Careful: Contractions that end in *n't* are also negative words.				
don't	can't	won't	shouldn't	
wouldn't	couldn't	didn't	hadn't	

 Read aloud the paragraph below to find sentences with the double negatives. On your own paper, rewrite those sentences correctly. (There is usually more than one way to correct a double negative.)

Example: The family couldn't hardly wait to fly.
Corrected: The family could hardly wait to fly.
Corrected: The family couldn't wait to fly.

1   Almost since the beginning of time, people have wanted
2   to fly like the birds. None of the early inventions were no good.
3   They didn't fly at all. At first, the Wright brothers didn't have no
4   success either. Finally, they found a way to keep their plane in
5   flight. That changed things forever. Other inventors improved
6   on the Wright brothers' idea. Eventually, airplanes were
7   everywhere. Today, there aren't hardly any places that you
8   can't never reach by flying.

 Write a short paragraph about a time when you were frustrated. Use some negative expressions but avoid using any double negatives.

TEKS 6.14C
ELPS 3E

Enhancing Your Sentence Style

There are a number of ways to add variety to your sentences and enhance your writing style. Here are four of the most common ways.

1 **Combine short sentences.**

2 **Use different types of sentences.**

3 **Expand sentences by adding words and phrases.**

4 **Model sentences of other writers.**

What happens when too many sentences in a paragraph are the same length or follow the same pattern? Read the following paragraph to find out.

Little Variety

> I visited the Smithsonian's National Air and Space Museum. I saw part of the *Apollo 11* spacecraft. Three astronauts flew in this craft. Astronauts Armstrong, Aldrin, and Collins went to the moon in 1969. They worked, ate, and slept in the command module. They were there for eight days. The command module was very small.

Using a variety of sentences would keep this paragraph from sounding choppy and better transition between ideas. Read the following version.

Good Variety

> When I visited the Smithsonian's National Air and Space Museum, I saw part of the *Apollo 11* spacecraft. In 1969, astronauts Armstrong, Aldrin, and Collins flew this craft to the moon. The command module was very small, but the astronauts worked, ate, and slept there for eight days.

BASIC WRITING

GRAMMAR

Read the paragraph below. Then, on your own paper, change the paragraph by creating more sentence variety. Take turns with a partner reading and listening to your paragraphs.

1 I visited Kitty Hawk last summer. Kitty Hawk is in North
2 Carolina. That is where the Wright brothers first flew their
3 airplane. They flew it in 1903. I liked the museum. I loved walking
4 on the sand and climbing up Kill Devil Hill. I saw the memorial
5 tower up there.

 **TEKS** 6.14C
ELPS 3E, 3G

How can I make my sentences flow more smoothly?

Writers often combine sentences to help their writing flow more smoothly. Too many short sentences will sound choppy and will not transition well from one idea to the next. Combining some of the sentences will add variety, help your writing flow, and enhance your overall writing style.

Combine with Key Words or Phrases

One way to combine sentences is to use key words or phrases.

Moving a Key Word From One Sentence to Another	
Short Sentences	*Combined Sentences*
Katherine Stinson was a flier. She was a stunt flier.	**Katherine Stinson was a stunt flier.**

Moving a Key Phrase From One Sentence to Another	
Bessie Coleman, the first African American aviator, earned an international pilot's license. She earned it in 1922.	**In 1922, Bessie Coleman, the first African American aviator, earned an international pilot's license.**

 Combine each pair of sentences below by moving a key word or phrase from one sentence to another.

■ Bessie Coleman wanted to open a school for young African Americans. She wanted to open a flight school.
Bessie Coleman wanted to open a flight school for young African Americans.

1. In 1910, Blanche Stuart Scott flew solo in the United States. She became the first woman to do that.

2. Amelia Earhart was the first person to fly alone from Honolulu, Hawaii, to California. She made the flight in 1935.

3. Anne Morrow Lindbergh was a copilot for her husband, Charles Lindbergh. She was also a radio operator for him.

 Review an essay you wrote, such as your personal narrative. Revise sentences to help your ideas flow more smoothly and to add variety. Make sure your sentences can be combined using a key word or phrase. Read your revisions to a partner. Discuss how your writing has been improved.

TEKS 6.14C
ELPS 3E, 3G

Combine with a Series of Words

Sentences and larger units of text can also be combined using a series of words or phrases. Put similar ideas in the same sentence and don't repeat words. Combining ideas like this makes your writing easier to understand.

Combining with a Series of Words or Phrases	
Short Sentences	*Combined Sentences and Text Units*
Hot-air balloons can be made of nylon. They can be made of acrylic. They can be made of polyester.	**Hot-air balloons can be made of** nylon, acrylic, **or** polyester.
The hot-air balloon is an aircraft that has an envelope to hold hot air. It has a basket to carry people. It has a heating system to warm the air in the balloon.	**The hot-air balloon is an aircraft that has** an envelope **to hold hot air,** a basket **to carry people, and** a heating system **to warm the air in the balloon.**

Be sure to use commas between the words or phrases in your series. (See page **630**.) The items in any series must be alike (or parallel). For example, if the first item is a phrase, all the items must be phrases. The same is true for series containing words or clauses.

 Combine the following groups of sentences with a series of words or phrases. (You may need to change some words to make the sentences work.)

1. The mathematician Archimedes explored the idea of flying in balloons. The English scientist Roger Bacon did, too. So did the German philosopher Albertus Magnus.

2. In 1783, Joseph and Etienne Montgolfier powered the first hot-air balloon by burning straw in a fire pit attached to the bottom of the balloon. They burned wood in the fire pit, too. They also burned other materials in the fire pit.

Write **NOW** Review the same essay you used for *Write Now* on page 560. Look for sentences to revise that repeat words or ideas. Make sure that your sentences can be combined using a series of words or phrases. Read your revisions to a partner. Discuss whether your writing is easier to understand.

BASIC WRITING

Combine with Subjects and Predicates

Another way to combine sentences is to move a subject or predicate from one sentence to another. When you do this, you create a compound subject or a compound predicate. (See page **549**.)

Combining with Compound Subjects and Predicates	
Short Sentences	*Combined with a Compound Subject*
Orville Wright was a pilot. Wilbur Wright was a pilot, too.	Orville and Wilbur **Wright were pilots.**
Short Sentences	*Combined with a Compound Predicate*
The brothers owned a bicycle shop. They explored the idea of flying.	**The brothers** owned **a bicycle shop and** explored **the idea of flying.**

 Combine each set of sentences below by using a compound subject or a compound predicate (change the verb when necessary).

- Orville Wright was an inventor. So was Wilbur Wright.
  Orville and Wilbur Wright were inventors.

1. The brothers built the first airplane. They flew the first airplane.

2. The first flights covered short distances. The first flights lasted less than a minute.

3. Orville made changes to the design. Wilbur made changes to the design.

4. In 1908, the brothers demonstrated the plane. They set several records.

5. Americans were interested in the plane. Europeans were interested, too.

6. The United States government ordered Wright airplanes. Countries in Europe ordered them, too.

7. The Wright brothers formed a company. They built their planes.

8. The brothers earned awards. They received honors.

 Write two related sentences for your classmates to combine. Make sure they can be combined using a compound subject or a compound predicate.

What can I do to add variety to my writing?

Writers use different types of sentences to add variety to their writing and make it sound interesting. The three common types of sentences are **simple, compound,** and **complex**. By learning to write these three types of sentences effectively, you can create sentence variety in your writing.

Write Simple Sentences

A **simple sentence** is one independent clause. (An independent clause is a group of words that can stand alone as a sentence.) A complete simple sentence may contain a single or compound subject and a single or compound predicate, and the subjects and verb should agree.

> **Simple Sentence = One Independent Clause**
>
> **Simple Subject with a Simple Predicate**
> The early <u>days</u> of aviation <u>had</u> many heroes.
>
> **Simple Subject with a Compound Predicate**
> <u>Pilots</u> <u>faced</u> and <u>overcame</u> dangerous situations.
>
> **Compound Subject with a Simple Predicate**
> <u>Amelia Earhart</u> and <u>Charles Lindbergh</u> <u>flew</u> on heroic flights.

 Find the five simple sentences in the paragraph below and copy them. Underline the subjects once and the predicates twice.

1. Charles Lindbergh was a famous American pilot. Lindbergh flew
2. his airplane nonstop from New York City to Paris. The plane was
3. called the *Spirit of St. Louis.* Lindbergh made the flight because he
4. wanted to win a $25,000 prize. He flew across the Atlantic Ocean
5. and landed in Paris, France. Americans and Europeans cheered for
6. Lindbergh. He had made the first successful transatlantic flight, so
7. people called him a hero.

 NOW Revise a paragraph from one of your essays using the guidelines below. Think about how the different sentence styles add variety.

1 Write one with a simple subject and simple predicate.

2 Write one with a simple subject and compound predicate.

3 Write one with a compound subject and simple predicate.

 TEKS 6.14C, 6.19C
ELPS 3E, 3G

Create Compound Sentences

A **compound sentence** is made up of two or more simple sentences joined together. Often, they are joined with a coordinating conjunction and a comma. (Coordinating conjunctions are words like *and, but,* and *so.*) A complete compound sentence includes a subject and a predicate with correct subject-verb agreement.

> **Compound Sentence = Two Independent Clauses**
>
> **Yuri Gagarin was a Russian cosmonaut, and he became the first person to orbit Earth.** (A comma and the conjunction *and* join the two independent clauses.)
>
> **Russia was the first country to enter the "space race," but the United States quickly followed.** (A comma and the conjunction *but* join the two independent clauses.)

 On your own paper, combine the pairs of simple sentences below to create compound sentences. Use commas and the coordinating conjunctions *and, but,* or *so.*

■ The United States launched its first manned spacecraft in 1961. Alan Shepard became the first American astronaut in space.

The United States launched its first manned spacecraft in 1961, and Alan Shepard became the first American astronaut in space.

1. The first phase of space travel in this country used *Mercury* spacecraft. The second phase used bigger *Gemini* spacecraft.

2. The *Apollo* spacecraft were the third phase. They were created to explore the moon.

3. In 1969, Neil Armstrong stepped onto the moon. He said, "That's one small step for man, one giant leap for mankind."

 Write **NOW** Review a writing assignment you are currently working on. Add variety to your writing by revising it for compound sentences. Read your revisions to a partner. Discuss how these sentences add variety and enhance your writing style.

Develop Complex Sentences

A **complex sentence** has both an independent clause and at least one dependent clause. Because a dependent clause cannot stand alone as a sentence, it must be connected to an independent clause.

Complex sentences may contain a subordinating conjunction, such as *after, although, because, before, until, when,* and *while.* (See page **776** for more subordinating conjunctions.) Complex sentences may also contain a relative pronoun such as *that, which,* and *who.* (See page **746** for more.)

Complex Sentence =

An Independent Clause	+	A Dependent Clause
Airplanes have instruments		**that pilots use in bad weather.**

A Dependent Clause	+	An Independent Clause
When pilots fly in a storm,		**they have to trust their gauges.**

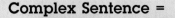 Number your paper from 1 to 6. Then write the dependent clause found in each sentence below.

■ Since pilots can't always see where they are flying, they use flight instruments to get valuable information.

Since pilots can't always see where they are flying

1. If pilots study their instruments, they will know the plane's altitude, speed, and fuel supply.

2. A compass, which shows the airplane's direction, helps the pilot stay on course.

3. Another gauge measures cabin pressure because planes fly so high.

4. Before they land, pilots get directions from radio air controllers on the ground.

5. Unless planes have altimeters, pilots won't know how high they are above sea level.

6. Some people like to fly planes while others prefer being passengers.

 Write NOW Write two complex sentences about an airplane or an airplane flight you've taken or heard about. (Be sure to use commas correctly.)

BASIC WRITING

Use Questions and Commands

Writers use a variety of sentences to make statements, ask questions, give commands, or show strong emotion. See the chart below.

Kinds of Sentences			
Declarative ▪	Makes a statement about a person, a place, a thing, or an idea	Amelia Earhart flew across the Atlantic Ocean alone.	**This is the most common kind of sentence.**
Interrogative **?**	Asks a question	Can you tell me more about Amelia Earhart?	**A question gets the reader's attention.**
Imperative ▪	Gives a command	Read about Earhart on the FAA Web site.	**Commands often appear in dialogue or directions.**
Exclamatory **!**	Shows strong emotion or feeling	Amelia's plane disappeared!	**Use these sentences for occasional emphasis.**

 On a piece of paper, write the numbers 1 to 7. Identify each of the sentences shown below by writing "D" for declarative, "INT" for interrogative, "IMP" for imperative, or "EX" for exclamatory.

1. In 1932, Amelia Earhart flew across the Atlantic Ocean in 14 hours and 56 minutes.
2. Amelia Earhart had incredible courage!
3. In 1937, she began a flight around the world with her navigator, Frederick Noonan.
4. Imagine how she must have felt as that plane left the ground.
5. What happened to her and her navigator?
6. When her plane never arrived at Howland Island, southwest of Hawaii, a search found nothing.
7. Can you believe people are still looking for her plane?

 Write four sentences—one of each kind—about someone you feel showed courage.

TEKS 6.19A(v)
ELPS 3E

What can I do to add details to my sentences?

Expand with Prepositional Phrases

Writers use prepositional phrases to add details and information to their sentences. The chart below shows how this is done. Prepositional phrases act like adjectives or adverbs and can be used to convey location, time, direction, or details. *Remember:* A prepositional phrase includes a preposition, the object of a preposition, and any words that modify the object. (See page **774** for a list of prepositions.)

Prepositional Phrase	Used in a Sentence
Early biplanes had two pairs of wings.	The phrase acts as an **adjective** to describe the noun "pairs."
Pilots took passengers on short flights.	The phrase acts as an **adverb** to modify the verb "took."

- Prepositional phrases that are used as adjectives answer the adjective questions: *How many? Which one? What color? What size?*

- Prepositional phrases used as adverbs answer the adverb questions: *When? How? How often? How long? Where? How much?*

Number a piece of paper from 1 to 5. Write the prepositional phrase or phrases that you find in each of these sentences.

- During the 1920s, the most popular planes were biplanes.

  During the 1920s

1. These planes were made of wood and fabric.
2. Supports and wire between the wings gave the biplane strength.
3. Sometimes the front edge of the wooden propeller was covered with metal.
4. There were few airports, so pilots often landed in farm pastures.
5. Pilots called barnstormers flew in air shows across the country.

Write **NOW** Add one or two prepositional phrases to the sentences below. Read your sentences, and listen as a classmate reads his or her sentences.

1 Biplanes were popular planes.

2 Pilots wore goggles.

3 The planes had wooden propellers.

BASIC WRITING

Expand with Appositive Phrases

Writers sometimes make their sentences more interesting by adding appositive phrases. An **appositive phrase** renames the noun or pronoun before it and is set off from the rest of the sentence with commas.

> ### Appositive Phrases
>
> **The Tuskegee Airmen,** a group of fighter pilots, **helped win the war.**
> (The appositive "a group of fighter pilots" renames the noun "Tuskegee Airmen.")
>
> **General Daniel "Chappie" James,** a Tuskegee pilot, **became a hero.**
> (The appositive "a Tuskegee pilot" renames the noun "General Daniel 'Chappie' James.")

On your own paper, make a chart like the one below. Read the paragraph that follows the chart and list the appositive phrases you find. Also list the noun or pronoun each appositive renames. (The first one has been done for you.)

Appositive Phrase	Noun or Pronoun It Renames
a group of fighter pilots	Tuskegee Airmen

1   The Tuskegee Airmen, a group of fighter pilots, played an
2 important role in World War II. Beginning in 1941, they served
3 with the United States Army Air Force in Tuskegee, Alabama.
4 These men, all highly trained pilots, made up the first African
5 American flying unit in the U.S. military. The first group to train
6 at Tuskegee, the 99th Pursuit Squadron, was led by Lt. Col.
7 Benjamin O. Davis. The 99th was the only escort group not to
8 lose a bomber to enemy planes. The brave Tuskegee pilots, 992
9 men in all, flew 1,578 missions and won more than 850 medals.

Write NOW Write two or three sentences about what you think life would be like as a pilot. Use an appositive in each sentence.

How can I make my sentences more interesting?

Model Sentences

You can learn a great deal about writing by imitating, or modeling, the sentences of other writers. Studying these sentences can teach you how to punctuate and how to put parts together. When you come across sentences that you like, practice writing some of your own that use the same pattern.

Professional Model	Student Models
The mountains have been my lifelong companions, and I still make my home at their feet.	The gym has been my favorite hangout, but I sometimes ride my unicycle at the playground.
Marisa marveled at the open-air market with stalls of vegetables and cheese, people laughing and chatting, and music blaring. —*International Traveler*	My little sister clapped for the parade of clowns in huge shoes and curly wigs, horses snorting and prancing, and bands marching.

Guidelines for Modeling

- Find a sentence or a short passage that you like and write it down.
- Follow the pattern of the sentence or passage as you write about your own subject. (You do not have to follow the model exactly.)
- Build each sentence one part at a time and check your work when you are finished. (Take your time.)
- Find other sentences to model and keep practicing. Share your sentences with a classmate.

Write NOW On your own paper, model the following sentences. Remember, you do not have to follow the model sentence exactly.

1 The hill was steep and slick, but I knew there was no turning back.

2 Having completed the work, Joshua carefully packed his toolbox and went home.

Develop a Sentence Style

Modeling sentences can help you make your writing more exciting, lively, and appealing. The following writing techniques will also help you improve your style. (Also see page **43**.)

Varying Sentence Beginnings

Do too many of your sentences begin with a subject and a verb? Try beginning with a dependent clause or with a phrase, as in the sentences below. This adds variety to the subject-verb pattern.

When I awoke, **there were snowflakes on my eyes**.
—True Grit by Charles Portis

Hobbling on one foot, **Wanda opened the closet door and turned on the light**.
—Summer of the Swans by Betsy Byars

From the stable, **the pair of oxen bellowed and rolled their eyes in terror**.
—The Book of Three by Lloyd Alexander

Moving Adjectives

Usually, you write adjectives before the nouns they modify. Notice how these writers emphasized the adjectives by placing them after the nouns.

The children, shouting and screaming, **came charging back into their homeroom**.
—The Friends by Rosa Guy

Her brown face, upraised, **was stained with tears**.
—The Red Badge of Courage by Stephen Crane

Repeating a Word

You can repeat a word to emphasize a particular idea or feeling.

. . . that government of the people, **by** the people, **for** the people **shall not perish from the earth**.
—"Gettysburg Address" by Abraham Lincoln

Life is an exciting **business and most** exciting **when it is lived for others**.
*—*Interview with Helen Keller

 On your own paper, model one sentence from each of the three categories listed above.

Constructing Strong Paragraphs

If you can write a paragraph well, you can write anything. Writer Donald Hall calls a paragraph a "maxi-sentence" or a "mini-essay." Think of it as an important building block for all of your writing. If you can create strong, well-organized paragraphs, you can also create effective essays, book reviews, and reports.

A paragraph is made up of a group of sentences focused on one topic. Each sentence should add something to the overall picture. A paragraph can explain a process, share an opinion, describe something, or tell a story.

What's Ahead

You will learn about . . .
- the parts of a paragraph.
- types of paragraphs.
- writing effective paragraphs.
- adding details to paragraphs.
- gathering details.
- organizing your details.
- refining your details.
- turning paragraphs into essays.
- using a checklist.

The Parts of a Paragraph

Most paragraphs have three main parts: a topic sentence, a body, and a closing sentence. A paragraph usually begins with a *topic sentence* that tells what the paragraph is about. The sentences in the *body* share details about the topic, and the *closing sentence* brings the paragraph to a close.

Topic Sentence

Body

Closing Sentence

Striking It Rich

During the California gold rush, Levi Strauss invented blue jeans. In 1850, when so many gold diggers arrived in California, Strauss took bolts of canvas to San Francisco. He planned to make tents to sell to the miners. When that didn't work out, Strauss used the canvas to make pants that miners could wear for their rough work. Miners bought these pants as fast as Strauss could make them. These pants became the very first Levi jeans, and they changed the clothing world forever. Later, Strauss made the pants out of blue denim instead of canvas and added copper rivets. Since that time, blue jeans have become popular throughout the United States and around the world.

Respond to the reading. What common item of clothing is discussed in this paragraph? Based on the history of Levi jeans, what is the double meaning of the title?

⭐ **TEKS** 6.14A

A Closer Look at the Parts

The Topic Sentence

The topic sentence tells the reader the controlling idea of a paragraph, or what a paragraph is going to be about. A good topic sentence (1) *names the topic* and (2) *states the controlling idea or a feeling* about it. Here is a simple formula for writing a topic sentence.

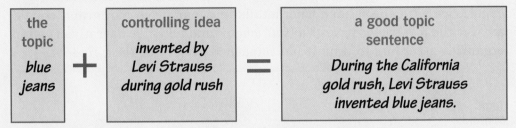

the topic		controlling idea		a good topic sentence
blue jeans	**+**	*invented by Levi Strauss during gold rush*	**=**	*During the California gold rush, Levi Strauss invented blue jeans.*

The topic sentence is usually the first sentence in a paragraph, although sometimes it comes later. It guides the direction of the sentences in the rest of the paragraph.

During the California gold rush, Levi Strauss invented blue jeans.

The Body

The sentences in the body of the paragraph include the details needed to understand the topic.

- **Use specific details to make your paragraph interesting.**
  The specific details below are shown in red.
  Later, Strauss made the pants out of blue denim instead of canvas and added copper rivets.

- **Organize your sentences in the best possible order.**
  Three common ways to organize sentences are chronological (time) order, order of location, and order of importance. (See page 599.)

The Closing Sentence

The closing sentence comes after all the details in the body. It will often restate the topic, give the reader something to think about, or provide a transition to the following paragraph.

Since that time, blue jeans have become popular throughout the United States and around the world.

BASIC WRITING

Types of Paragraphs

There are four types of paragraphs: *narrative, descriptive, expository,* and *persuasive.* Each type requires a different way of thinking and planning.

Compose Narrative Paragraphs

In a **narrative paragraph**, you share a personal story or an important experience with the reader. The details in a narrative paragraph should answer the 5 W's *(who? what? when? where?* and *why?).* A narrative is often organized according to time (what happened *first, next, then, finally).*

Topic Sentence
· · · · · · · · · · · · · ·

Body

Closing Sentence
· · · · · · · · · · · · ·

A Play Day

It was Saturday morning, and I was ready for my first Service Day. Our school requires each student to volunteer for community service once a semester. My friends and I decided to work at Smith House, a place for families who need somewhere to stay. We walked inside the house, and before we could take off our coats, 10 little kids ambushed us and begged, "Please play with us!" We read books, played board games, and even went outside to shoot hoops. When we left at noon, our new playmates hugged us and gave us loads of high fives. My friends and I agreed that a day of playing with young kids was the perfect service project for us.

Respond to the reading. Find the key word repeated in the topic sentence and the closing sentence. Does this paragraph answer the 5 W's?

Write your own paragraph. Write a paragraph that tells about an experience you've had recently. Be sure to include the 5 W's and whatever details are needed.

Create Descriptive Paragraphs

When you write a **descriptive paragraph**, you give a detailed picture of a person, a place, an object, or an event. Descriptive paragraphs include many sensory details *(sight, sound, smell, taste, touch)*. The following sample describes the sights, sounds, smells, and feelings of a local soup kitchen.

Topic Sentence

Body

Closing Sentence

Soup's On

One Friday night, my family decided to help at a local soup kitchen. By the time we arrived, the kitchen was filled with noisy people doing all sorts of things. Across the room beside the sink, some of them were washing vegetables, while others were peeling and chopping. Several people gathered around the stove that was in the middle of the kitchen. They added chopped vegetables to the steaming soup pots. Soon the smell of hot vegetable soup filled the room. On the counter between the kitchen and the dining area, another group worked like an assembly line putting together huge stacks of ham and cheese sandwiches. I set the paper plates, salt-and-pepper shakers, and butter plates on the tables. Finally, a stream of hungry people arrived. They seemed to really enjoy the meal and thanked us for everything.

BASIC WRITING

Respond to the reading. Which of the five senses are covered in the paragraph? Which two or three details are especially descriptive?

Draft

Write your own paragraph. Write a paragraph that describes a place with lots of sights, sounds, and so on.

TEKS 6.19A(viii)
ELPS 3E

Write Expository Paragraphs

In an **expository paragraph**, you share information. You can explain a subject, give directions, or show how to do something. Transition words like *first, next, then,* and *finally* are often used in expository writing.

Topic Sentence
· · · · · · · · · · · · · ·

Body

Closing Sentence
· · · · · · · · · · · · · ·

> ### How to Start a Pet Pantry
>
> A pet pantry is a place for citizens with low incomes to get free food and supplies for their pets. To create a pet pantry follow these steps. First, meet with the people at a local humane society. See if they will suggest a location for the pantry and a way to distribute food and supplies. Then talk with grocery-store managers and local veterinarians. Ask if they will allow donation containers in their stores and clinics. Next, contact local newspapers and television stations to get the word out. Also make posters and flyers to make sure that people know about the pet pantry. Finally, ask adults to help with the collection of pet food and supplies and to take them to the pantry. A well-run pet pantry can help keep people and their pets together.

Respond to the reading. List the transitions used between sentences in the paragraph above. How many transitions did the writer use? (See pages 620–621 for a list of transitions.)

Write an expository paragraph. Write a paragraph that explains how to do something—like play a game, make a snack, or plant a garden. Be sure to use transitions to connect your ideas. Read your paragraph to the class, and listen as your classmates read their paragraphs.

Develop Persuasive Paragraphs

In a **persuasive paragraph**, you give your position (or strong feeling) about a topic. To be persuasive, you must include plenty of reasons, facts, and details to support your opinion. Persuasive writing is usually organized by order of importance or by logical order (as in the paragraph below).

Topic Sentence

Body

Closing Sentence

Get Involved in a Trash Bash

Participating in a trash bash or neighborhood cleanup is a great way to improve a community. First of all, it will help the city's trash collectors get rid of some of the garbage in places where it is hard to pick up. This will save the city time and money. In addition, cleaning up piles of trash will make a neighborhood a more pleasant place to live and play. Most importantly, participating in a cleanup will make a neighborhood safer. Piles of garbage can contain things like broken glass and dangerous chemicals. Germs produced by piles of garbage can make people sick. There are many good reasons to clean up the environment, and a trash bash is one way to do it.

BASIC WRITING

Respond to the reading. What is the writer's position in the paragraph? What reasons does she give to support her opinion? When is the most important reason given?

Prewrite
Give your opinion. Write a position about an environmental topic. Then list three strong reasons to support your opinion.

 **TEKS** 6.14A, 6.14B, 6.14C, 6.14D

Writing Effective Paragraphs

Whenever you write paragraphs, use the following general guidelines.

Prewriting
Selecting a Topic and Developing a Controlling Idea

- Use one or more strategies to select a topic.
- Collect facts, examples, and details about your topic.
- Write a topic sentence that presents the controlling idea.
- Choose an appropriate organizational strategy.

Drafting Creating the First Draft

- Start your paragraph with a focused topic sentence.
- Write sentences in the body that support your topic.
- Present the details you collected in an organized way.
- Connect sentences with transitions to create a coherent whole.
- End with a sentence that rounds out the paragraph and transitions or leads to the next.

Revising Improving Your Writing

- Add simple or compound sentences to say more about your topic.
- Add, delete, or move sentences to help your ideas flow smoothly.
- Delete repeated or unnecessary details to clarify your writing.
- Combine sentences to add variety and enhance your style.

Editing Checking for Conventions

- Check the revised version of your writing for grammar, mechanics, sentence structure, and spelling.
- Then write a neat final copy and proofread it.

 When you write a paragraph, remember that readers want . . .
- original ideas. *(They want something new and interesting.)*
- personality. *(They want to hear the writer's voice.)*

How can I find interesting details?

No paragraph is complete without good supporting details. Here are some types of details you can use in expository and persuasive paragraphs: facts, explanations, definitions, reasons, examples, and comparisons. You might get these details from personal knowledge and memories or from other sources of information.

Use Personal Details

For narrative and descriptive writing, personal details can add interest. Personal details can include sensory, memory, and reflective details.

- **Sensory details** are things that you see, hear, smell, taste, and touch. (These details are important in descriptive paragraphs.)

  Soon the smell of hot vegetable soup filled the room.

- **Memory details** are things you remember from experience. (These details are important in narrative paragraphs.)

  When we left at noon, our new playmates hugged us and gave us loads of high fives.

- **Reflective details** are things you think about or hope for. (These details are often used in narrative and descriptive paragraphs.)

  I felt good about helping at the soup kitchen, and I hope my family decides to do it again soon.

Use Other Sources of Details

To collect details from other sources, use the following tips.

1. **Talk with someone you know.** Parents, neighbors, friends, or teachers may know a lot about your topic.

2. **Write for information.** If you think a museum, a business, or a government office has information you need, send for it.

3. **Read about your topic.** Gather details from books, magazines, and newspapers.

4. **Use the Internet.** The quickest source of information is the Internet. Remember to check Web sites carefully for reliability.

BASIC WRITING

How do I know what kinds of details to gather?

Here are tips that will help you collect the right kinds of details when you write paragraphs about people, places, objects, and events—and also when you write definitions.

Writing About a Person

When writing about or describing a person, make sure you collect plenty of information. The following guidelines will help.

Observe ■ If possible, carefully watch the person. Maybe the person laughs in a special way or wears a certain type of clothing.

Interview ■ Talk with your subject. Write down words and phrases that the person uses.

Research ■ Use whatever sources are necessary—books, articles, the Internet—to find out more about this person.

Compare ■ Could your subject be compared to some other person?

Writing About a Place

When describing or writing about a place, use details that help the reader understand why the place is important to you.

Observe ■ Study the place you plan to write about. Use photos, postcards, or videos if you can't observe the place in person.

Remember ■ Think of a story (or an anecdote) about this place.

Describe ■ Include the sights, sounds, and smells of the place.

Compare ■ Compare your place to other places.

Writing About an Object

When writing about an object, tell your reader what kind of object it is, what it looks like, how it is used, and why this object is important to you.

Observe ■ Think about these questions: How is the object used? Who uses it? How does it work? What does it look like?

Research ■ Learn about the object. Try to find out when it was first made and used. Ask other people about it.

Define ■ What class or category does this object fit into? (See "Writing a Definition" on page 581.)

Writing About an Event

When writing about or describing an event, focus on the important actions or on one interesting part. Also include sensory details and answer the 5 W's. The following guidelines will help.

Observe ■ Study the event carefully. What sights, sounds, tastes, and smells come to mind? Listen to what people around you are saying.

Remember ■ When you write about something that happened to you, recall as many details connected with the event as you can.

List ■ Answer the *who? what? when? where?* and *why?* questions for facts about the event.

Writing a Definition

When you write a definition, you need to think about three things.

- First put the **term** you are defining *(coyote)* into a **class** or category of similar things *(wild member of the dog family)*.

- Then list special **characteristics** that make this individual different from others in that class *(like a wolf, only smaller)*.

> **Term**—*A coyote*
>
> **Class**—*is a wild member of the dog family*
>
> **Characteristic**—*that is like a wolf, only smaller.*

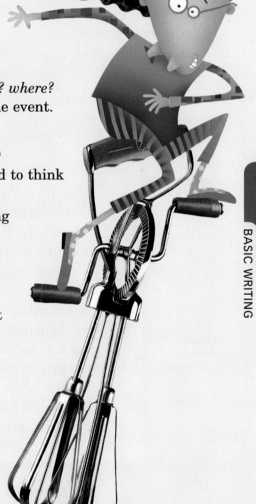

What can I do to organize my details effectively?

After you've gathered your details, you need to organize them by using an appropriate organizational strategy. You can organize a paragraph by *time, location, importance,* or *comparison.* Graphic organizers can help you keep your details in order.

Use Chronological Order

Chronological means "according to time." Transition words and phrases that tell days, months, and years are often used in chronological paragraphs. So are words like *first, second, then,* and *finally.* A time line can help you organize your details.

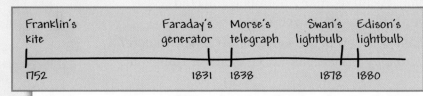

Franklin's Kite		Faraday's generator	Morse's telegraph	Swan's lightbulb	Edison's lightbulb
1752		1831	1838	1878	1880

Topic Sentence

Body

Closing Sentence

From Kites to Lights

In 1752, Benjamin Franklin flew a kite in a thunderstorm and proved that lightning is a form of electricity. But there was no easy way to capture electricity. Almost 80 years after Franklin's discovery, the British inventor Michael Faraday created the first electric generator. It was simply a magnet moving inside a coil of copper wire. Seven years later, Samuel Morse put the new type of power to good use. He demonstrated his telegraph, which used electricity to send messages. Still, it took another 40 years before Sir Joseph Swan (in England) and Thomas Edison (in America) created the most famous electrical invention, the lightbulb.

 Respond to the reading. How are dates given in the time line? How are they given in the paragraph?

TEKS 6.14B

Use Order of Location

Often, you can arrange descriptive details by using an organizational strategy such as order of location. For example, a description may move from left to right, from top to bottom, or from one direction (north) to another (south). Words or phrases like *next to, before, above, below, east, west, north,* and *south* are used to show location. A drawing or map can help you organize your details.

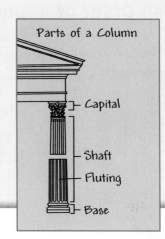

Parts of a Column

- Capital
- Shaft
- Fluting
- Base

Topic Sentence · · · · · · · · · · · · ·

Body

Closing Sentence · · · · · · · · · · · · · ·

Parts of a Corinthian Column

A Corinthian column has three main parts: a base, a shaft, and a capital. The base is a large disk of stone that looks like rings stacked up. It has to be very strong to hold the weight of everything above it. The shaft stands on top of the base. This long cylinder is built from shorter sections of stone. Grooves called "flutes" run up and down its sides. On top of the column is the capital. It's shaped like an upside-down bell. Stone carvings of leaves surround the capital. All these parts come together to form a column that is both strong and beautiful.

BASIC WRITING

Respond to the reading. On the drawing, why is the column shown in two sections? In the paragraph, with what part of the column does the description begin? Where does it end?

Use Order of Importance

Persuasive and expository paragraphs are often organized by order of importance—from *most* to *least* important, or from *least* to *most* important.

Most important
1. _____
2. _____
3. _____
Least important

or

Least important
3. _____
2. _____
1. _____
Most important

Topic Sentence
• • • • • • • • • • • •

The Aztecs

    Aztec civilization clearly was the most advanced culture in the Americas at one time. The Aztecs were the first people to make hot cocoa and other chocolate treats. They also wrote books and made colorful paintings.

Body

Aztec miners found gold, silver, and turquoise that artists used for jewelry and carvings. Engineers built a city named Tenochtitlan that had palaces, temples, and the world's largest pyramid. Astronomers watched the movements

Closing Sentence
• • • • • • • • • • • •

of the sun, the moon, and the stars to create calendars. If you still aren't sure that the Aztecs were the most advanced people of their time, here is one last fact: They could even predict the coming of comets!

Respond to the reading. How are the details organized in this paragraph? On your own paper, list them in reverse order (most to least, least to most). Which order works better?

TEKS 6.14B

Use Comparison-Contrast Order

When you write a comparison-contrast paragraph, you want to show how two subjects are both alike and different. A Venn diagram can be used to show differences (**A** and **B**) and similarities (**C**).

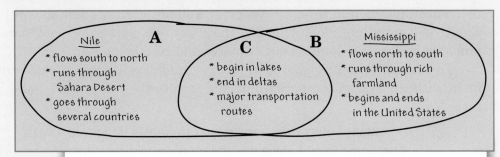

A Nile
* flows south to north
* runs through Sahara Desert
* goes through several countries

C
* begin in lakes
* end in deltas
* major transportation routes

B Mississippi
* flows north to south
* runs through rich farmland
* begins and ends in the United States

Topic Sentence
· · · · · · · · · · · ·

Body

Closing Sentence
· · · · · · · · · · · ·

Two Mighty Rivers

The Nile and the Mississippi Rivers are alike in many ways, but they are also very different. Each of these long rivers begins in a lake and ends in a delta, but they flow in different directions. The Mississippi flows from north to south in the United States, while the Nile flows from south to north through several countries. These rivers run through very different types of land. The Mississippi travels through rich farmland, while the Nile flows through the Sahara Desert. Both rivers are major transportation routes for business and wildlife. These two great rivers are truly wonders of nature.

BASIC WRITING

Respond to the reading. Find two body sentences that include contrasting details about the two rivers. What two words are used to show the contrast?

Draft

Write a paragraph. Choose two rivers, lakes, or oceans to compare. Use a Venn diagram to list the details. Then write your paragraph.

 **TEKS** 6.14B

How can I be sure all my details work well?

Create Unity in Your Writing

In a focused and organized paragraph, each detail tells something about the controlling idea in a logical order. If a detail does not tell something about the controlling idea, it breaks the *unity* of a paragraph and should probably be cut. If a detail is out of place, it should be moved.

The detail (sentence) shown in blue in the following passage does not fit in with the rest of the paragraph. It disrupts the unity and should be cut.

> **Many young boys served in both armies during the Civil War. Some fought alongside the men and did everything soldiers normally do.** One thing these soldiers didn't do was shave regularly. **Most boys, however, were either drummers or flag bearers.**

 In the paragraph below, find three details (sentences) that do not support the controlling idea. Then read the paragraph aloud without those sentences. Did the unity of the paragraph improve?

1   Did you know that many famous writers played roles in
2 the Civil War? Probably other creative people also took part in
3 the war. Harriet Beecher Stowe wrote a novel called *Uncle Tom's*
4 *Cabin* that showed how slavery was wrong. My grandma has a
5 copy of that book. Louisa May Alcott, who wrote *Little Women*,
6 was a wartime nurse in an army hospital. Her novel was made
7 into a movie. Walt Whitman was a wartime nurse, too. After the
8 war, he wrote a poem about President Lincoln's death called
9 "O Captain! My Captain!" The poet Julia Ward Howe edited a
10 magazine that was against slavery. Each of these writers did
11 what they could to help with the war.

 Look at your paragraph. Study the comparison-contrast paragraph you wrote on page 585. Do all your details support your topic? Would the unity of your paragraph be improved if you cut a detail or two?

TEKS 6.14B

Develop Coherence from Start to Finish

An effective paragraph reads smoothly and clearly. When all the details in a paragraph are tied together well, the paragraph has *coherence* and is easy for the reader to follow. One way to make your writing smooth and coherent is to use transitions.

Number your paper 1 to 7. Use the transitions listed below to help tie the essay together. (Use each transition only once.) When you finish, read the paragraph. Does it read smoothly? If not, switch some transitions.

first	in addition	besides	although
then	also	second	

A well-trained dog has many career opportunities. _____ ,
                                                    (1)
there are jobs herding cattle and sheep. _____ , there are
                                          (2)
jobs in law enforcement. _____ tracking down criminals,
                          (3)
dogs can keep the suspects under control once they're caught.

_____ there are opportunities for dogs in the social services.
(4)
Of course, dogs can be trained to guide people who are blind.

They can _____ pick up objects for people in wheelchairs or
          (5)
cheer up people in nursing homes. _____ , dogs are natural
                                   (6)
athletes and entertainers. The entertainment industry is always

looking for a few good dogs. _____ dogs have so many career
                              (7)
opportunities, most dog owners are happy that their dogs are

content to be pets.

Read your paragraph. Read your comparison-contrast paragraph from page 585. Underline any parts that don't flow smoothly. Then use transitions to make the writing smoother. (See pages 620–621.)

BASIC WRITING

How can I turn my paragraphs into essays?

Use an Essay Plan

Creating a focused and well-organized essay takes planning. Of course, each paragraph needs to be well written and well constructed. Here are some additional tips to follow.

1 Select an organizational strategy.

Organize your essay in a way that fits your topic—time order, order of importance, order of location, and so on.

2 State the topic and focus in the first paragraph.

Use an interesting fact, example, or story to catch the reader's interest. Then tell what your essay is about in a focus statement, which includes the topic and a main idea or feeling about it.

3 Develop your ideas in the middle paragraphs.

Use each paragraph in the body of your essay to explain and support the main ideas that relate to your controlling idea. Each paragraph should build on the one before it.

4 End with a concluding paragraph.

The final paragraph is usually a review of the main points in the essay. Your ending may emphasize the importance of the topic, or it may leave the reader with something to think about.

5 Use transitional words and phrases.

Use transitions as needed to link individual sentences as well as paragraphs. In the examples below, the transitions are shown in red. For a complete list of transitions, see pages **620–621**.

> In addition to **jeans, athletic shoes and sports jerseys are worn in nearly every nation in the world.**
>
> For many reasons, **clothing trends have begun in the United States.**

How do I know if I have a strong paragraph?

Use a Paragraph Checklist

You'll know you have a strong paragraph if it gives the reader complete information and presents it in an engaging and understandable way.

Focus and Coherence

_____ **1.** Does my topic sentence make the focus clear?

_____ **2.** Do all the details fit together to form a whole?

Organization

_____ **3.** Have I arranged the details in the best order?

_____ **4.** Do transitions help guide the reader through the paragraph?

Development of Ideas

_____ **5.** Do the details help the reader understand my ideas?

_____ **6.** Do I provide enough details?

_____ **7.** Have I removed any sentences that do not relate to my focus?

Voice

_____ **8.** Do I show interest in and knowledge of my topic?

_____ **9.** Is my voice the same throughout the paragraph?

Conventions

_____ **10.** Is my sentence structure correct?

_____ **11.** Have I avoided errors in grammar, mechanics, and spelling?

BASIC WRITING

improve
support

ELPS 3E, 3G, 3H, 4C

A Writer's Resource

Learning Language

Work with a partner. Read the meanings and share your answers to the prompts and questions.

1. Something that is full of variety and interest is colorful.
   Name a colorful character in a movie you have seen.

2. People who know everything about a subject are experts.
   If you are a scuba diving expert, what do you know?

3. Body language is how your face and gestures send a message.
   What body language shows you are tired?

organize
REFERENCE
select

A Writer's Resource

If you're like most students, you often have questions when you are in the middle of a writing assignment. If a question pops up when you're in class, you can ask your teacher or a classmate. If, however, a question pops up when you're not in class, you need another source to ask or check. This "Writer's Resource" chapter can be a great source of information for answering many of your questions, like "How can I find the best topics to write about?" or "How can I make my voice more colorful?" or "What can I do to make my final copy look better?"

What's Ahead

You will learn how to . . .

- find topics and get started.
- collect and organize details.
- write terrific topic sentences.
- improve your writing style.
- use new forms and techniques.
- increase your vocabulary.
- improve your final copy.

 **TEKS** 6.14A

How can I find the best topics to write about?

Try a Topic-Selecting Strategy

A distinguished writer once said, "There are few experiences quite so satisfactory as getting a good writing idea. You're pleased with it, and feel good about it." Many writing assignments are related to a general subject area you are studying. Let's say, for example, you are asked to write a report about a current health issue as part of a science unit. Your job would be to select a certain part of that subject—a specific topic—to write about.

> **General Subject Area:** Current health and medicine
> **Specific Writing Topic:** Exercising to improve strength

The following strategies will help you select effective, appropriate topics that are specific to your subject area that you can feel good about.

Notebook Writing Write on a regular basis in a notebook, recording your thoughts and experiences. Review your entries from time to time and underline ideas that you would like to write more about later.

Clustering Begin a cluster (also called a web) with a key word. Select a general term or idea that is related to your writing assignment. Then cluster related words around the key word, as in the model below.

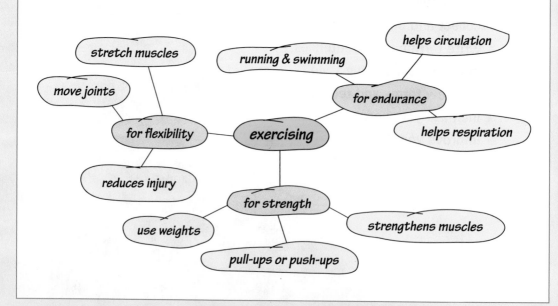

TEKS 6.14A

Listing Freely list ideas as they come to mind when you think about your assignment. Keep your list going as long as you can. Then look for words in your list that you feel would make good writing topics.

Freewriting Write nonstop for 5 to 10 minutes to discover possible writing ideas. Begin writing with a particular idea in mind (one related to your writing assignment). Underline ideas that might work as topics for your assignment.

Sentence Completion Complete an open-ended sentence in as many ways as you can. Try to word your sentence so that it leads you to a topic you can use for a particular writing assignment.

I wonder how . . .	I hope our school . . .	Television is . . .
Too many people . . .	I just learned . . .	Cars can be . . .
The good thing about . . .	One place I enjoy . . .	Grades are . . .

Review the "Basics of Life" List

The words listed below name many of the categories or groups of things that people need in order to live a full life. The list provides an endless variety of possibilities for topics. Consider the first category, *clothing*. You could write about . . .

- the wardrobe of a friend or a family member,
- your all-time favorite piece of clothing, or
- clothing as a statement (the "we are what we wear" idea).

clothing	machines	rules/laws
housing	intelligence	tools/utensils
food	history/records	heat/fuel
communication	agriculture	natural resources
exercise	land/property	personality/identity
education	work/occupation	recreation/hobby
family	community	trade/money
friends	science	literature/books
purpose/goals	plants/vegetation	health/medicine
love	freedom/rights	art/music
senses	energy	faith/religion

RESOURCE

 **TEKS** 6.14A

What can I do to get started?

Use a List of Writing Topics

The writing prompts listed below and the sample topics listed on the next page provide plenty of starting points for writing assignments.

Writing Prompts

Every day is full of experiences that make you think. You do things that you feel good about. You hear things that make you mad. You wonder how different things work. You're reminded of a past experience. These common, everyday thoughts can make excellent prompts for writing, which can then be used to determine a genre and topic for your writing.

Describe (Descriptive)
A bull moose, a fawn, a camel
A parrot, a guinea pig, a ferret
Newborn lambs, calves, chickens
Stalking cats, galloping horses
Pioneer days, wagon-train life
Life in ancient Egypt, Greece, or Rome
Solar or lunar eclipses, rainbows
Meteor showers, hailstorms, sun dogs

Tell Your Story (Narrative)
Meeting an unusual person
Learning something amazing, surprising
Visiting a special place
Overcoming a challenge
A sudden or a big change
Learning a lesson
Another person's triumph or
    determination

How-To (Expository)
Skateboard, snowboard, surf
Do a headstand, a flip, or a swan dive
Saddle a horse, show a dog, lift weights
Recognize constellations
Do origami, build a radio
Be patient, kind, brave, or helpful
Make or bake a favorite food
Get from one place to another

Parts of the Whole (Expository)
Types of workouts
Kinds of clouds, weather
Different games
Personality types
Variety of musical styles
Clothing styles

Promote (Persuasive)
Individual sports in school
An environment-friendly idea
Ways to help your community
Supporting a worthwhile cause
Ideas for avoiding boredom
Putting an end to something unfair
More field trips for students

Respond to Literary or Expository Texts
A book that changed your thinking
A poem that helped explain something
An interesting magazine article
The biography of someone you admire

Research (Report)
Aquifers, oil wells, salt mines
Hot springs, mud slides, droughts
Importance of natural forest fires
Deserts, tide pools, glaciers

Sample Topics

The writing topic you choose will depend on the genre you have selected or on one that has been chosen for you. To determine if a topic below is appropriate, try different strategies to record ideas and details you might include in your writing, such as freewriting about it for a few minutes or creating a concept web.

Descriptive

People: teacher, relative, classmate, coach, neighbor, bus driver, hero, someone you spend time with, someone you admire, brothers and sisters, someone with a special talent, someone from history

Places: hangout, garage, room, rooftop, historical place, zoo, park, hallway, barn, bayou, lake, cupboard, yard, empty lot, alley, valley, campsite, river, city street

Things: billboard, poster, video game, cell phone, bus, frostbite, boat, gift, drawing, rainbow, doll, junk drawer, flood, mascot, movie

Animals: dolphin, elephant, snake, armadillo, eagle, deer, toad, spoonbill, squirrel, pigeon, pet, coyote, catfish, octopus, beaver, turtle

Narrative

just last week, a big mistake, a reunion, a surprise, getting hurt, learning to _____, getting wet, getting caught, cleaning up, being a friend, a scary time, solving a problem, an important lesson, making a decision

Expository

How to . . . make a taco, improve your memory, care for a pet, entertain a child, impress your teacher, earn extra money, get in shape, overcome fear, get organized, plan a party

The causes of . . . sunburn, acne, hiccups, tornadoes, dropouts, rust, computer viruses, arguments, success, failure

Kinds of . . . crowds, friends, commercials, dreams, neighbors, pain, clouds, joy, stereos, heroes, chores, homework, frustration

Definition of . . . a good time, a grandmother, one type of music, advice, courage, strength, fun, freedom, pride

Persuasive

dieting, homework, testing, air bags, teen centers, something that needs improving, something that deserves support, something that's unfair, something that everyone should see, need for more or less of something, healthful habits, dangerous situations, education issues, protecting the environment, preserving historical places, preventing accidents

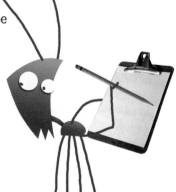

TEKS 6.14B

How can I collect details for my writing?

Try Graphic Organizers

Graphic organizers can help you gather and organize your details for writing. Clustering is one method. (See page **592**.) These two pages list other useful organizers.

Cause-Effect Organizer

Use to collect and organize details for cause-effect essays.

Subject: _____

Causes	Effects
•	•
•	•
•	•
•	•
•	•

Problem-Solution Web

Use to map out problem-solution essays.

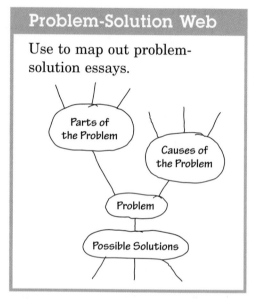

Time Line

Use to collect details for personal narratives and how-to essays.

Subject: _____

(Chronological Order)

① —
② —
③ —
④ —

Before-After Organizer

Use to collect details for a before-after essay.

Subject: _____

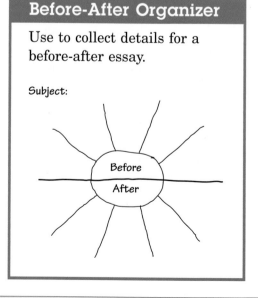

Venn Diagram

Use to collect details to compare and contrast two subjects.

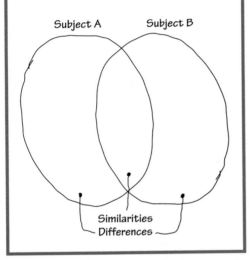

Subject A   Subject B

Similarities
Differences

5 W's Chart

Use to collect the *Who? What? When? Where?* and *Why?* details for personal narratives and news stories.

Subject: _____

Who?	What?	When?	Where?	Why?

Sensory Chart

Use to collect details for descriptive essays and observation reports.

Subject: _____

Sights	Sounds	Smells	Tastes	Feelings

Process (Cycle)

Use to collect details for science-related writing, such as how a process or cycle works.

Subject: _____

(Chronological Order)

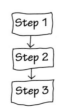

Step 1
↓
Step 2
↓
Step 3

RESOURCE

TEKS 6.14B

What can I do to organize my details better?

Make Lists and Outlines

List Your Details

You can use a variety of organizational strategies to organize details as you prepare to write an essay or a report. For most writing, you can make a simple list.

Manatees
— eat 80 to 120 lbs. of water plants a day
— grow to 10 feet in length and live for 60 years
— are fun to watch in tropical areas
— can get caught in locks and dams
— are endangered—about 3,000 in U.S.
People hurt manatees
— drive boats that hit, injure, and kill manatees
— destroy manatee habitat
People help manatees
— enforce slow boat speeds in manatee areas
— install safety devices on locks and dams
— pass laws to protect manatee habitat

Outline Your Information

After gathering facts and details, select two or three main points that best support your focus. Write an outline to organize your information.

I. Manatees worth saving
  A. Keep rivers clear of plants
  B. Fun for people to watch these gentle giants
  C. Save an endangered animal
II. People harming manatees
  A. Injuring and killing in boating collisions
  B. Trapping in locks and dams
  C. Destroying habitat
III. People rescuing manatees
  A. Enforcing boat speed laws
  B. Installing lock and dam safety devices
  C. Protecting habitat

Use Organizational Strategies

■ **Chronological (Time) Order** or **Step-by-Step** You can arrange your details in the order in which they happen (*first, then, next,* and so on). Use these patterns for narratives, history reports, directions, how-to essays, and explaining a process. (See pages **38** and **582**.)

> You can make a delicious omelet even if you've never cooked before. First, break the eggs into a bowl and add the milk. Second, mix everything with the beater until it is foamy. Next, heat . . .

■ **Order of Location** You can arrange details in the order in which they are located (*above, below, beside,* and so on). Use order of location for descriptions, explanations, and directions. (See pages **38** and **583**.)

> From my mom's office window, I can see the west and south sides of the city. The town hall with its square clock tower is directly in front of me. To my left I see the top of the oldest church in town. . . .

■ **Order of Importance** You can arrange details in your writing from the most important to the least—or from the least important to the most. Persuasive and expository essays are often organized this way. (See pages **38** and **584**.)

> Participating in a neighborhood cleanup is a great way to improve your community. First of all, you will help the city get rid of some of the garbage. In addition, if you help clean up piles of trash, you will make your neighborhood cleaner. Most importantly, if you . . .

■ **Comparison-Contrast** You can write about two or more subjects by showing how they are alike and how they are different. Compare subjects by talking about each separately or by talking about both, point by point, as in the following example. (See page **585**.)

> The Nile and the Mississippi Rivers are alike in many ways, but they are also very different. Each of these long rivers begins with a lake and ends in a delta, but they flow in different directions. The Mississippi flows from north to south, while the Nile flows from . . .

■ **Logical Order** Use this pattern to organize information in a way that makes sense. Begin with a main idea followed by details, or lead up to a main point. (See page **38**.)

> Hurricanes are very dangerous storms. They can cause destruction, injury, and death over a very large area. It's important to learn how these storms form and move. That's why scientists spend so much time studying hurricanes. . . .

 TEKS 6.14A

How can I write terrific topic sentences?

Try Eight Special Strategies

Writing a good topic sentence and developing a strong controlling idea is a key to writing a great paragraph. A good topic sentence names the topic and states a specific feeling about it. Use the following strategies the next time you need to write a terrific topic sentence. (Also see page 573.)

Use a Number

Topic sentences can use number words to tell what the paragraph will be about.

Number Words		
two	couple	a pair
few	three	a number
several	four	many
a variety	five	a list

Each cell has three main parts.

Ms. Chen should change the menu for several reasons.

Create a List

A topic sentence can list the things the paragraph will talk about.

Egyptians built step pyramids, bent pyramids, and straight pyramids.

To stay healthy and alert, get eight hours of sleep, eat a good breakfast, and walk a mile every day.

Start with "To" and a Verb

A topic sentence that starts with "to" and a verb helps the reader know why the information in the paragraph is important.

To learn a one-and-a-half flip, divers first need to learn a single flip.

To understand rock and roll, people should first learn about the blues.

Use Word Pairs

Conjunctions that come in pairs can help organize a topic sentence.

Word Pairs
if . . . then
either . . . or
not only . . . but also
both . . . and
whether . . . or
as . . . so

Connelly Middle School needs not only a new track but also new bleachers.

Some scientists debate whether T. rex was a hunter or a scavenger.

Join Two Ideas

A topic sentence can state two equal ideas. You can do this by writing a compound sentence. (See page **564**.)

> A tree fort is easy to build, and even beginning carpenters can lend a hand.
>
> The principal wants to ban hats in school, but some students don't think that's a good idea.

Use a "Why-What" Word

A "why-what" word is a subordinating conjunction that shows how ideas are connected.

> So that everyone can hear the candidates' ideas, the student council should hold a debate.
>
> Because you want a smooth texture, use a mixer or blender.

Why-What Words	
So that	Once
Before	Since
Until	Whenever
Because	While
If	As long as
As	After
In order that	When

Use a "Yes, But" Word

A "yes, but" word is a subordinating conjunction that tells how two ideas are different.

> Instead of just complaining about it, students should help clean up roadside litter.
>
> Even though the writers' group is small, the members have written lots of material.

"Yes, But" Words
However
Instead of
Although
Even though
Even if
Unless
Whether
Whereas

Quote an Expert

Sometimes the best way to start a paragraph is to quote someone who knows about your topic.

> Michael Jordan once said, "You have to expect things of yourself before you can do them."
>
> Amelia Earhart put it best: "It is far easier to start something than to finish it."

RESOURCE

What other forms can I use for my writing?

Try These Forms of Writing

Finding the right *form* (genre) for your writing is just as important as finding the right topic. When selecting a form, be sure to ask yourself who you're writing for (your audience) and why you're writing (your purpose).

Anecdote	A brief story that makes a point
Autobiography	A writer's story of his or her own life
Biography	A writer's story of some other person's life
Book review	A brief essay giving a response or an opinion about a book (See pages **301–314.**)
Character sketch	Writing that describes a specific character in a story
Composition	A longer piece of writing, such as a story or an essay
Descriptive writing	Writing that uses details to help the reader clearly imagine a certain person, place, thing, or idea (See pages **71–91.**)
Editorial	Newspaper letters or articles giving an opinion
Essay	A piece of writing in which ideas are presented, explained, argued, or described in an interesting way
Expository writing	Writing that explains by presenting the steps, the causes, or the kinds of something (See pages **161–225.**)
Fable	A short story that often uses talking animals as the main characters and teaches a lesson or moral
Fantasy	A story set in an imaginary world in which the characters usually have supernatural powers or abilities
Freewriting	Writing whatever comes to mind about any topic
Historical fiction	A made-up story based on something real in history in which fact is mixed with fiction
Myth	A traditional story intended to explain a mystery of nature, religion, or culture
Narrative	Writing that tells about an event, an experience, or a story (See pages **93–159.**)

Novel	A book-length story with several characters and a well-developed plot
Personal narrative	Writing that shares an event or experience in the writer's personal life (See pages **97–112**.)
Persuasive writing	Writing that is meant to persuade the reader to agree with the writer about someone or something (See pages **227–295**.)
Play	A form that uses dialogue to tell a story and is meant to be performed in front of an audience
Poem	Writing that uses rhythm, rhyme, and imagery (See pages **365–373**.)
Proposal	Writing that includes specific information about an idea or a project that is being considered for approval
Research report	An essay that shares information on a topic that has been researched well and organized carefully
Response to literary or expository text	Writing that is a summary or a reaction to something the writer has read (novel, short story, poem, article, and so on)
Science fiction	Writing based on real or imaginary science and often set in the future
Short story	A short piece of literature with only a few characters and one problem or conflict (See pages **353–364**.)
Summary	Writing that presents only the most important ideas from a longer piece of writing
Tall tale	A humorous, exaggerated story (often based on the life of a real person) about a character who does impossible things
Tragedy	Literature in which the hero is destroyed because of some serious flaw or defect in his or her character

RESOURCE

TEKS 6.15A(iii), 6.20B(ii)

How can I make my voice more colorful?

You can make your writing voice more colorful and develop your story by using strong dialogue and by "showing" instead of "telling."

Use Dialogue

Each person you write about has a unique way of saying things, and well-written dialogue lets the reader *hear* the speaker's personality and thoughts. For example, notice how the following message can be spoken in several different ways.

> *Message:* Your new car is impressive.
>
> *Speaker 1:* "Whoa Dad! Cool new wheels!"
>
> *Speaker 2:* "Nice coupe, Bill. I've always been a sedan man myself."
>
> *Speaker 3:* "Such a fancy car, Son! Hope you didnt spend too much."

Each of these speakers delivers the same message in a unique way. The dialogue tells as much about the speaker as it does about the topic.

One way to improve your dialogue is to think about the speaker and his or her personality. Look at the three personality webs below and try to decide which one is *Speaker 1, Speaker 2,* or *Speaker 3* from above. How does the dialogue show their personalities?

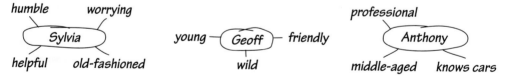

humble   worrying
Sylvia
helpful   old-fashioned

young — **Geoff** — friendly
wild

professional
Anthony
middle-aged   knows cars

Tips for Punctuating Dialogue

- Indent every time a different person speaks.
- Put the exact words of a speaker in quotation marks.
- Set off the quoted words from the rest of the sentence by using a comma.
- At the end of quoted words, put a period or comma inside the quotation marks.

(For more information and examples on how to punctuate dialogue, see pages **636**, **644**, and **646** in the "Proofreader's Guide.")

Show, Don't Tell

The old saying "Seeing is believing" is especially true in writing. You can "show" a reader your story by using sensory details to create a specific, believable setting and using dialogue. Notice the difference between the two paragraphs below.

Telling: I rode on the roller coaster. It was frightening but fun.

Showing: As the roller coaster topped the first big hill, I could see my mom down below. She looked so small. Then the coaster began to surge down the hill. My hands went up, my heart jumped into my throat, and I let out a sound that was half laugh and half scream. Then I yelled, "This is amazing!"

The first paragraph *tells* the reader that the roller coaster ride was "frightening but fun." The second paragraph *shows* just how "frightening but fun" it really was.

Key Strategies for Showing

Next time you realize your writing is telling rather than showing, try one of these strategies.

- **Add sensory details.** Include sights, sounds, smells, tastes, and touch sensations. That way, the reader can "experience" the event.

  Telling: Swimming was refreshing.

  Showing: All morning the sun beat down on us as we painted the garage, but we escaped all afternoon in the cool, refreshing water of Watkins Pond.

- **Explain body language.** Write about facial expressions and the way people stand, gesture, and move.

  Telling: Sharissa was upset with me.

  Showing: Sharissa glared at me, tapped her foot, pursed her lips, and snorted.

- **Use dialogue.** Let people in your writing speak for themselves.

  Telling: Sharon Whitecloud wanted to go to the Art Institute.

  Showing: Sharon Whitecloud piped up, "You're not going to the Art Institute without me!"

What can I do to enhance my writing style?

Learn Some Writing Techniques

Writers put special effects in their stories, essays, and poems in different ways. Look over the following writing techniques and then experiment with some of them in your own writing.

Analogy : A comparison of similar objects to help clarify one of the objects

Personal journals are like photograph albums. They both share personal details and tell a story.

Anecdote : A brief story used to illustrate or make a point

Abe Lincoln walked two miles to return several pennies he had overcharged a customer. (This anecdote shows Lincoln's honesty.)

Exaggeration : An overstatement or a stretching of the truth used to make a point or paint a clearer picture (See *overstatement*.)

After getting home from summer camp, I slept for a month.

Foreshadowing : Hints or clues that a writer uses to suggest what will happen next in a story

Halfway home, Sarah wondered whether she had locked her locker.

Irony : A technique that uses a word or phrase to mean the opposite of its normal meaning

Marshall just loves cleaning his room.

Local color : The use of details that are common in a certain place or local area (A story taking place on a seacoast would contain details about the water and the life and people near it.)

Everybody wore flannel shirts to the Friday fish fry.

Metaphor : A figure of speech that compares two things without using the word *like* or *as* (See page **372**.)

In our community, high school football is king.

Overstatement : An exaggeration or a stretching of the truth (See *exaggeration*.)

When he saw my grades, my dad hit the roof.

Parallelism	Repeating similar words, phrases, or sentences to give writing rhythm (See page 570.) **We will swim in the ocean, lie on the beach, and sleep under the stars.**
Personification	A figure of speech in which a nonhuman thing (an idea, object, or animal) is given human characteristics (See page 372.) **Rosie's old car coughs and wheezes on cold days.**
Pun	A phrase that uses words in a way that gives them a humorous effect **The lumberjack logged on to the site to order new boots.**
Sarcasm	The use of praise to make fun of or "put down" someone or something (The expression is not sincere and is actually intended to mean the opposite thing.) **Micah's a real gourmet; he loves peanut butter and jelly sandwiches.** (A *gourmet* is a "lover of fine foods.")
Sensory details	Specific details that help the reader see, feel, smell, taste, and/or hear what is being described (See page 535.) **As Lamont took his driver's test, his heart thumped, his hands went cold, and his face began to sweat.**
Simile	A figure of speech that compares two things using the word *like* or *as* (See page 372.) **Faye's little brother darts around like a water bug.** **Yesterday the lake was as smooth as glass.**
Slang	Informal words or phrases used by particular groups of people when they talk to each other **chill out hang loose totally awesome**
Symbol	An object that is used to stand for an idea **The American flag is a symbol of the United States. The stars stand for the 50 states, and the stripes stand for the 13 original U.S. colonies.**
Understatement	Very calm language (the opposite of exaggeration) used to bring special attention to an object or an idea **These hot red peppers may make your mouth tingle a bit.**

RESOURCE

How can I expand my writing vocabulary?

Study Writing Terms

This glossary includes terms used to describe the parts of the writing process. It also includes terms that explain special ways of stating an idea.

Antonym : A word that means the opposite of another word: *happy* and *sad; large* and *small* (See page 611.)

Audience : The people who read or hear what has been written

Body : The main or middle part in a piece of writing that comes between the *beginning* and the *ending* and includes the main points

Brainstorming : Collecting ideas by thinking freely about all the possibilities

Closing : The ending or final part in a piece of writing (In a paragraph, the closing is the last sentence. In an essay or a report, the closing is the final paragraph.)

Coherence : Tying ideas together in your writing (See page 587.)

Connotation : The "feeling" a word suggests (See page 531.)

Denotation : The dictionary meaning of a word

Dialogue : Written conversation between two or more people

Figurative language : Special comparisons, often called figures of speech, that make your writing more creative (See page 372.)

Focus statement : The statement focuses the controlling idea and tells what specific part of a topic is written about in an essay (See *thesis statement* and page 35.)

Form : A type of writing or the way a piece of writing is put together (See pages 602–603.)

Grammar : The structure of language; the rules and guidelines that you follow in order to speak and write acceptably

Jargon : The special language of a certain group, occupation, or field
  Computer jargon: byte   digital   upload

Journal : A notebook for writing down thoughts, experiences, ideas, and information

Limiting the subject	Taking a general subject and narrowing it down to a specific topic
	General subject → Specific topic
	sports → golf → golf skills → putting
Modifiers	Words, phrases, or clauses that describe another word
	Our black **cat** slowly **stretched and** then **leaped** onto the wicker chair. (Without the blue modifiers, all we know is that a "cat stretched and leaped.")
Point of view	The angle from which a story is told (See page 364.)
Purpose	The specific reason that a person has for writing
	to describe to narrate to persuade to explain
Style	How an author writes (choice of words and sentences)
Supporting details	Facts or ideas used to tell a story, explain a topic, describe something, or prove a point
Synonym	A word that means the same thing as another word (*dog* and *canine*) (See page 611.)
Theme	The main point, message, or lesson in a piece of writing
Thesis statement	A statement that gives the main idea of an essay (See *focus statement*.)
Tone	A writer's attitude toward his or her subject
	serious humorous sarcastic
Topic	The specific subject of a piece of writing
Topic sentence	The sentence that contains the main idea of a paragraph (See page 573.)
	Blue jeans are a popular piece of American clothing.
Transition	A word or phrase that connects or ties two ideas together smoothly (See pages 620–621.)
	also however lastly later next
Usage	The way in which people use language (*Standard usage* generally follows the rules of good grammar. Most of the writing you do in school will require standard usage.)
Voice	A writer's unique, personal tone or feeling that comes across in a piece of writing

RESOURCE

How can I mark changes in my writing?

Use the symbols below to show where and how your writing needs to be changed. Your teachers may also use these symbols to point out errors in your writing.

Symbols	Meaning	Example	Corrected Example
≡	Capitalize a letter.	Beverly Cleary wrote the novel *Dear Mr. henshaw.*	Beverly Cleary wrote the novel *Dear Mr. Henshaw.*
/	Make a capital letter lowercase.	The main Character is Leigh Botts.	The main character is Leigh Botts.
⊙	Insert (add) a period.	Leigh writes to Mr. Henshaw He writes back.	Leigh writes to Mr. Henshaw. He writes back.
◯ or *sp.*	Correct spelling.	Leigh has trubble in school.	Leigh has trouble in school.
ℓ	Delete (take out) or replace.	Leigh he wants to be an author.	Leigh wants to be an author.
∧	Insert here.	Mr. Henshaw writes *to* Leigh.	Mr. Henshaw writes to Leigh.
∧ ∧ ∧	Insert a comma, a colon, or a semicolon.	Leigh lives in Pacific Grove California.	Leigh lives in Pacific Grove, California.
∨ ∨ ∨	Insert an apostrophe or quotation marks.	Bandit is the name of Leighs dog.	Bandit is the name of Leigh's dog.
? ! ∧ ∧	Insert a question mark or an exclamation point.	Who is the lunchroom thief	Who is the lunchroom thief?
∼	Switch words or letters.	Leigh invents a alarm burglar for his lunch box.	Leigh invents a burglar alarm for his lunch box.
¶	Start a new paragraph.	Leigh receives a postcard from Mr. Henshaw.¶One day his dad . . .	Leigh receives a postcard from Mr. Henshaw. One day his dad . . .

What can I do to increase my vocabulary skills?

Use Context

When you come across a word you don't know, you can often figure out its meaning from the other words in the sentence. The other words form a familiar context, or setting, for the unfamiliar word. Looking closely at these surrounding words will give you clues to the meaning of the word.

When you come to a word you don't know . . .

◼ **Look for a synonym**—a word or words that have the same meaning as the unknown word.

> Sara had an ominous feeling when she woke up, but the feeling was less threatening when she saw she was in her own room.
> (An *ominous* feeling is a threatening one.)

◼ **Look for an antonym**—a word that has the opposite meaning from the unknown word.

> Ben had always been agile, but he looked stiff after the game.
> (*stiff* is the opposite of *agile*.)

◼ **Look for a comparison or contrast.**

> Riding a mountain bike in a remote area is my idea of fun. I wonder why people ride motorcycles on busy six-lane highways.
> (A *remote* area is out of the way, in contrast to a busy area.)

◼ **Look for a definition or description.**

> Manatees, large aquatic mammals (sometimes called sea cows), can be found in the warm coastal waters of Florida.
> (An *aquatic* mammal is one that lives in the water.)

◼ **Look for words that appear in a series.**

> The campers spotted sparrows, chickadees, and indigo buntings on Saturday morning.
> (An *indigo bunting,* like a *sparrow* or *chickadee,* is a bird.)

◼ **Look for a cause-and-effect relationship.**

> The amount of traffic at 6th and Main doubled last year, so crossing lights were placed at that corner to avert an accident.
> (*Avert* means "to prevent.")

RESOURCE

How can I build my vocabulary across the curriculum?

On the next several pages, you will find many of the most common prefixes, suffixes, and roots in the English language. Learning these word parts can help you increase your spelling and writing vocabulary.

Learn About Prefixes

A **prefix** is a word part that is added before a word to change the meaning of the word. For example, when the prefix *un* is added to the word *fair (unfair),* it changes the word's meaning from "fair" to "not fair."

ambi *[both]*
ambidextrous (skilled with both hands)

anti *[against]*
antifreeze (a liquid that works against freezing)
antiwar (against wars and fighting)

astro *[star]*
astronaut (person who travels among the stars)
astronomy (study of the stars)

auto *[self]*
autobiography (writing that is about yourself)

bi *[two]*
bilingual (using or speaking two languages)
biped (having two feet)

circum *[in a circle, around]*
circumference (the line or distance around a circle)
circumnavigate (to sail around)

co *[together, with]*
cooperate (to work together)
coordinate (to put things together)

ex *[out]*
exhale (to breathe out)
exit (the act of going out)

fore *[before, in front of]*
foremost (in the first place, before everyone or everything else)
foretell (to tell or show beforehand)

hemi *[half]*
hemisphere (half of a sphere or globe)

hyper *[over]*
hyperactive (overactive)

im *[not, opposite of]*
impatient (not patient)
impossible (not possible)

in *[not, opposite of]*
inactive (not active)
incomplete (not complete)

inter *[between, among]*
international (between or among nations)
interplanetary (between the planets)

macro *[large]*
macrocosm (the entire universe)

mal *[bad, poor]*
malnutrition (poor nutrition)

micro *[small]*
microscope (an instrument used to see very small things)

organize
select support
REFERENCE
improve
613
A Writer's Resource
TEKS 6.21

mono *[one]*
monolingual (using or speaking only one language)

non *[not, opposite of]*
nonfat (without the normal fat content)
nonfiction (based on facts; not made-up)

over *[too much, extra]*
overeat (to eat too much)
overtime (extra time; time beyond regular hours)

poly *[many]*
polygon (a figure or shape with three or more sides)
polysyllable (a word with more than three syllables)

post *[after]*
postscript (a note added at the end of a letter, after the signature)
postwar (after a war)

pre *[before]*
pregame (activities that occur before a game)
preheat (to heat before using)

re *[again, back]*
repay (to pay back)
rewrite (to write again or revise)

semi *[half, partly]*
semicircle (half a circle)
semiconscious (half conscious; not fully conscious)

sub *[under, below]*
submarine (a boat that can operate underwater)
submerge (to put underwater)

trans *[across, over; change]*
transcontinental (across a continent)
transform (to change from one form to another)

tri *[three]*
triangle (a figure that has three sides and three angles)
tricycle (a three-wheeled vehicle)

un *[not]*
uncomfortable (not comfortable)
unhappy (not happy; sad)

under *[below, beneath]*
underage (below or less than the usual or required age)
undersea (beneath the surface of the sea)

uni *[one]*
unicycle (a one-wheeled vehicle)
unisex (a single style that is worn by both males and females)

Numerical Prefixes

deci *[tenth part]*
decimal system (a number system based on units of 10)

centi *[hundredth part]*
centimeter (a unit of length equal to 1/100 meter)

milli *[thousandth part]*
millimeter (a unit of length equal to 1/1000 meter)

micro *[millionth part]*
micrometer (one-millionth of a meter)

deca or **dec** *[ten]*
decade (a period of 10 years)
decathlon (a contest with 10 events)

hecto or **hect** *[one hundred]*
hectare (a metric unit of land equal to 100 ares)

kilo *[one thousand]*
kilogram (a unit of mass equal to 1,000 grams)

mega *[one million]*
megabit (one million bits)

RESOURCE

Study Suffixes

A **suffix** is a word part that is added after a word. Sometimes a suffix will tell you what part of speech a word is. For example, many adverbs end in the suffix *ly*. Use this pattern to also help you spell words correctly.

able *[able, can do]*
agreeable (able or willing to agree)
doable (can be done)

al *[of, like]*
magical (like magic)
optical (of the eye)

ed *[past tense]*
called (past tense of call)
learned (past tense of learn)

ess *[female]*
lioness (a female lion)

ful *[full of]*
helpful (giving help; full of help)

ic *[like, having to do with]*
symbolic (having to do with symbols)

ily *[in some manner]*
happily (in a happy manner)

ish *[somewhat like or near]*
childish (somewhat like a child)

ism *[characteristic of]*
heroism (characteristic of a hero)

less *[without]*
careless (without care)

ly *[in some manner]*
calmly (in a calm manner)

ology *[study, science]*
biology (the study of living things)

s *[more than one; plural noun]*
books (more than one book)

ward *[in the direction of]*
westward (in the direction of west)

y *[containing, full of]*
salty (containing salt)

Comparative Suffixes

er *[comparing two things]*
faster, later, neater, stronger

est *[comparing more than two]*
fastest, latest, neatest, strongest

Noun-Forming Suffixes

er *[one who]*
painter (one who paints)

ing *[the result of]*
painting (the result of a painter's work)

ion *[act of, state of]*
perfection (the state of being perfect)

ist *[one who]*
violinist (one who plays the violin)

ment *[act of, result of]*
amendment (the result of amending, or changing)
improvement (the result of improving)

ness *[state of]*
goodness (the state of being good)

or *[one who]*
actor (one who acts)

Understand Roots

A **root** is a word or word base from which other words are made by adding a prefix or a suffix. Knowing the common roots can help you figure out the meaning and spelling of difficult words.

aster *[star]*
aster (star flower)
asterisk (starlike symbol [*])

aud *[hear, listen]*
audible (can be heard)
auditorium (a place to listen to speeches and performances)

bibl *[book]*
Bible (sacred book of Christianity)
bibliography (list of books)

bio *[life]*
biography (book about a person's life)
biology (the study of life)

chrome *[color]*
monochrome (having one color)
polychrome (having many colors)

chron *[time]*
chronological (in time order)
synchronize (to make happen at the same time)

cide *[the killing of; killer]*
homicide (the killing of one person by another person)
pesticide (pest [bug] killer)

cise *[cut]*
incision (a thin, clean cut)
incisors (the teeth that cut or tear food)
precise (cut exactly right)

cord, cor *[heart]*
cordial (heartfelt)
coronary (relating to the heart)

corp *[body]*
corporation (a legal body; business)
corpse (a dead human body)

cycl, cyclo *[wheel, circular]*
bicycle (a vehicle with two wheels)
cyclone (a very strong circular wind)

dem *[people]*
democracy (ruled by the people)
epidemic (affecting many people at the same time)

dent, dont *[tooth]*
dentures (false teeth)
orthodontist (dentist who straightens teeth)

derm *[skin]*
dermatology (the study of skin)
epidermis (outer layer of skin)

fac, fact *[do, make]*
factory (a place where people make things)
manufacture (to make by hand or machine)

fin *[end]*
final (the last of something)
infinite (having no end)

flex *[bend]*
flexible (able to bend)
reflex (bending or springing back)

flu *[flowing]*
fluent (flowing smoothly or easily)
fluid (waterlike, flowing substance)

forc, fort *[strong]*
force (strength or power)
fortify (to make strong)

fract, frag *[break]*
fracture (to break)
fragment (a piece broken from the whole)

Learn More Roots

gen *[birth, produce]*
congenital (existing at birth)
genetics (the study of inborn traits)

geo *[of the earth]*
geography (the study of places on the earth)
geology (the study of the earth's physical features)

graph *[write]*
autograph (writing one's name)
graphology (the study of handwriting)

homo *[same]*
homogeneous (of the same birth or kind)
homogenize (to blend into a uniform mixture)

hydr *[water]*
dehydrate (to take the water out of)
hydrophobia (the fear of water)

ject *[throw]*
eject (to throw out)
project (to throw forward)

log, logo *[word, thought, speech]*
dialogue (speech between two people)
logic (thinking or reasoning)

luc, lum *[light]*
illuminate (to light up)
translucent (letting light come through)

magn *[great]*
magnificent (great)
magnify (to make bigger or greater)

man *[hand]*
manicure (to fix the hands)
manual (done by hand)

mania *[insanity]*
kleptomania (abnormal desire to steal)
maniac (an insane person)

mar *[sea, pool]*
marine (of or found in the sea)
mariner (sailor)

mega *[large]*
megalith (large stone)
megaphone (large horn used to make voices louder)

meter *[measure]*
meter (unit of measure)
voltmeter (device to measure volts)

mit, miss *[send]*
emit (to send out; give off)
transmission (sending over)

multi *[many, much]*
multicultural (of or including many cultures)
multiped (an animal with many feet)

numer *[number]*
innumerable (too many to count)
numerous (large in number)

omni *[all, completely]*
omnipresent (present everywhere at the same time)
omnivorous (eating all kinds of food)

onym *[name]*
anonymous (without a name)
pseudonym (false name)

ped *[foot]*
pedal (lever worked by the foot)
pedestrian (one who travels by foot)

phil *[love]*
Philadelphia (city of brotherly love)
philosophy (the love of wisdom)

organize
select support
REFERENCE
improve
617
A Writer's Resource

phobia *[fear]*
acrophobia (a fear of high places)
agoraphobia (a fear of public, open places)

phon *[sound]*
phonics (related to sounds)
symphony (sounds made together)

photo *[light]*
photo-essay (a story told mainly with photographs)
photograph (picture made using light rays)

pop *[people]*
population (number of people in an area)
populous (full of people)

port *[carry]*
export (to carry out)
portable (able to be carried)

psych *[mind, soul]*
psychiatry (treatment of the mind)
psychology (science of mind and behavior)

sci *[know]*
conscious (being aware)
omniscient (knowing everything)

scope *[instrument for viewing]*
kaleidoscope (instrument for viewing patterns and shapes)
periscope (instrument used to see above the water)

scrib, script *[write]*
manuscript (something written by hand)
scribble (to write quickly)

spec *[look]*
inspect (to look at carefully)
specimen (an example to look at)

spir *[breath]*
expire (to breathe out; die)
inspire (to breathe into; give life to)

tele *[over a long distance; far]*
telephone (machine used to speak to people over a distance)
telescope (machine used to see things that are very far away)

tempo *[time]*
contemporary (from the current time period)
temporary (lasting for a short time)

tend, tens *[stretch, strain]*
extend (to stretch and make longer)
tension (stretching something tight)

terra *[earth]*
terrain (the earth or ground)
terrestrial (relating to the earth)

therm *[heat]*
thermal (related to heat)
thermostat (a device for controlling heat)

tom *[cut]*
anatomy (the science of cutting apart plants and animals for study)
atom (a particle that cannot be cut or divided)

tract *[draw, pull]*
traction (the act of pulling)
tractor (a machine for pulling)

typ *[print]*
prototype (the first printing or model)
typo (a printing error)

vac *[empty]*
vacant (empty)
vacuum (an empty space)

vid, vis *[see]*
supervise (to oversee or watch over)
videotape (record on tape for viewing)

vor *[eat]*
carnivorous (flesh-eating)
herbivorous (plant-eating)

zoo *[animal or animals]*
zoo (a place where animals are kept)
zoology (the study of animal life)

RESOURCE

What can I do to write more effective sentences?

Study Sentence Patterns

Sentences in the English language follow the basic patterns below. Use a variety of patterns to add interest to your writing. (Also see page 619.)

1 Subject + Action Verb

S AV
Gus giggles. (Some action verbs, like *giggles*, are intransitive. This means that they *do not need* a direct object to express a complete thought. See 762.3.)

2 Subject + Action Verb + Direct Object

S AV DO
Jesse tells ghost stories at camp. (Some action verbs, like *tells*, are transitive. This means that they *need* a direct object to express a complete thought. See 762.2.)

3 Subject + Action Verb + Indirect Object + Direct Object

S AV IO DO
Mom gave me this book.

4 Subject + Action Verb + Direct Object + Object Complement

S AV DO OC
We named Jamaal the best storyteller.

5 Subject + Linking Verb + Predicate Noun

S LV PN
Christina is a beautiful singer.

6 Subject + Linking Verb + Predicate Adjective

S LV PA
My teacher was terrific.

In the patterns above, the subject comes before the verb. In the patterns below, the subject (called a *delayed subject)* comes after the verb.

LV S PN
7 **Is Larisa a poet?** (A question)

LV S
8 **There was a meeting.** (A sentence beginning with *there* or *here*)

Practice Sentence Diagramming

Diagramming sentences can help you understand how the parts of a sentence fit together. Here are the most common diagrams. (See page 618.)

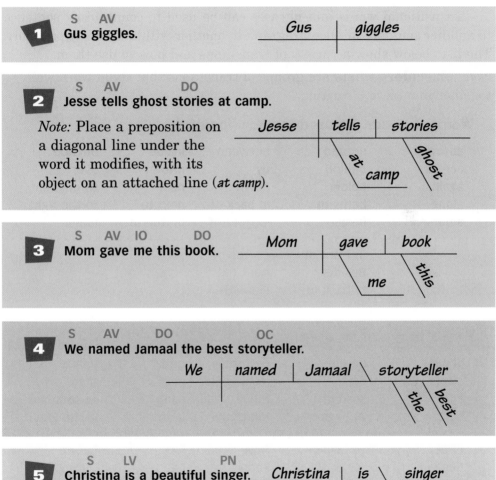

1   S   AV
Gus giggles.

        Gus | giggles

2   S   AV   DO
Jesse tells ghost stories at camp.

Note: Place a preposition on a diagonal line under the word it modifies, with its object on an attached line (*at camp*).

      Jesse | tells | stories
           at camp   ghost

3   S   AV   IO   DO
Mom gave me this book.

      Mom | gave | book
           me   this

4   S   AV   DO   OC
We named Jamaal the best storyteller.

      We | named | Jamaal \ storyteller
           the   best

5   S   LV   PN
Christina is a beautiful singer.

Note: Place an adjective or adverb on a diagonal line under the word it modifies.

      Christina | is \ singer
           a   beautiful

6   S   LV   PA
My teacher was terrific.

      teacher | was \ terrific
           My

RESOURCE

 **TEKS** 6.17A(iv), 6.19A(viii)

How can I connect my sentences and paragraphs?

Use Transitions

Transitional words and phrases can be used to connect one sentence to another sentence or one paragraph to another within an essay or report. The lists below show a variety of transitions and how to use them.

Note: The **colored lists** are groups of transitions that could work well together in a piece of writing.

Words that can be used to show location

above	around	between	inside	outside
across	behind	by	into	over
against	below	down	near	throughout
along	beneath	in back of	next to	to the right
among	beside	in front of	on top of	under

Above	In front of	On top of
Below	Beside	Next to
To the left	In back of	Beneath
To the right		

Words that can be used to show time

about	during	yesterday	until	finally
after	first	meanwhile	next	then
at	second	today	soon	as soon as
before	to begin	tomorrow	later	in the end

First	To begin	Now	First	Before
Second	To continue	Soon	Then	During
Third	To conclude	Later	Next	After
Finally			In the end	

Words that can be used to compare two things

likewise	as	in the same way	one way
like	also	similarly	both

In the same way	One way
Also	Another way
Similarly	Both

Words that can be used to contrast things (show differences)

| but | still | although | on the other hand |
| however | yet | otherwise | even though |

On the other hand	Although
Even though	Yet
Still	Nevertheless

Words that can be used to emphasize a point

| again | truly | especially | for this reason |
| to repeat | in fact | to emphasize | |

| For this reason | Truly | In fact |
| Especially | To emphasize | To repeat |

Words that can be used to conclude or summarize

| finally | as a result | to sum up | in conclusion |
| lastly | therefore | all in all | because |

Because	As a result	To sum it up	Therefore
In conclusion	All in all	Because	Finally
		Therefore	

Words that can be used to add information

again	another	for instance	for example
also	and	moreover	additionally
as well	besides	along with	other
next	finally	in addition	

For example	For instance	Next	Another
Additionally	Besides	Moreover	Along with
Finally	Next	Also	As well

Words that can be used to clarify

| in other words | for instance | that is |

| For instance | For example |
| In other words | Equally important |

What can I do to make my final copy look better?

Add Graphics to Your Writing

You can add information to reports in a multimedia presentation by adding text and graphics. Use the internet or computer programs to help you create interesting graphics showing your research.

Diagrams are drawings that show the parts of something. A diagram may include simple text to show only the parts you need to learn.

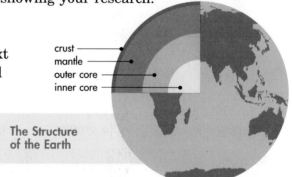

crust
mantle
outer core
inner core

The Structure of the Earth

Picture diagrams show how something is put together.

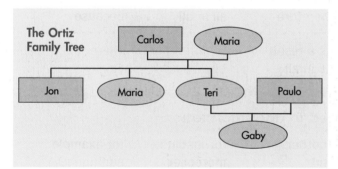

The Ortiz Family Tree

Carlos — Maria

Jon · Maria · Teri · Paulo

Gaby

Line diagrams also show how something is put together, but they show something you can't really see. Instead of objects, line diagrams show ideas and relationships.

Tables have two parts: rows and columns. Rows go across and show one kind of information or data. Columns go up and down and show a different kind of data.

To read a table, find where a row and a column meet. In the table to the right, if the wind speed is 15 and the air temperature is 20, the windchill factor is 6.

Windchill Chart												
	Temperature (°F)											
Calm	40	35	30	25	20	15	10	5	0	-5	-10	-15
5	36	31	25	19	13	7	1	-5	-11	-16	-22	-28
10	34	27	21	15	9	3	-4	-10	-16	-22	-28	-35
15	32	25	19	13	6	0	-7	-13	-19	-26	-32	-39
20	30	24	17	11	4	-2	-9	-15	-22	-29	-35	-42
25	29	23	16	9	3	-4	-11	-17	-24	-31	-37	-44
30	28	22	15	8	1	-5	-12	-19	-26	-33	-39	-46

Wind Speed (mph)

Graphs are pictures of information. **Bar graphs** show how things compare to one another. The bars may be vertical or horizontal. (*Vertical* means "up and down." *Horizontal* means "from side to side.") Sometimes the

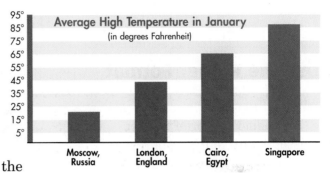

bars on graphs are called *columns*. The part that shows numbers is called the *scale*. Look for the text at the bottom for helpful information.

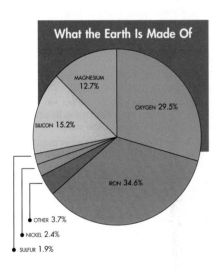

Pie graphs show how all the parts of something add up to make the whole. A pie graph often shows percentages. (A percentage is the part of a whole stated in hundredths: 35% = 35/100.) It's called a pie graph because it is usually in the shape of a pie or circle.

Line graphs show how something changes as time goes by. A line graph always begins with an L-shaped grid. One line of the grid shows passing time; the other line shows numbers.

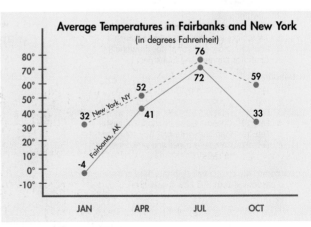

How should I set up my practical writing?

Use the Proper Format

Memos

A memo is a brief written message that you can share with a teacher, a coach, or a principal. Memos create a flow of information—asking and answering questions, giving instructions, describing work to be done, or reminding people about meetings.

Date: March 16, 2010

To: Mr. Ortega

From: Rebecca Ehly

Subject: Mid-Project Report on Training Rats

The goal of my science fair project is to train my rat Carmel to play basketball. I want to teach him to do four things:

1. Go to the rubber ball (about 1" in diameter).

2. Push the ball with his nose across the basketball court that I made in his cage.

3. Pick up the ball with his forepaws.

4. Put the ball through the hoop (about 2" above the floor of the cage).

Carmel has learned two steps: (1) go to the ball and (2) push it. I taught him how to do these things by luring him with pieces of cheddar cheese (extra sharp).

Unfortunately, I haven't been able to get Carmel to do ʳ̶ers 3 and 4. He won't lift the ball. I'm not sure what ᵗ̶ next. Do you have any suggestions?

Castle Construction for History Project

Description: For my history project on medieval life, I plan to build a scale model (2′ x 2′ x 2′) of an English castle and write an essay on the construction of castles for protection.

Materials:

1. Books on medieval life and on castles
2. 3′ x 3′ plywood board (for base)
3. Clay (for walls)
4. Toilet paper rolls (for frame of towers)
5. Toothpicks and glue (for ladders, gates)
6. Popsicle sticks and string (for drawbridge)
7. Cloth (for banners and tapestries)

Deadlines:

1. Jan. 25   Research medieval castles
2. Feb. 1   Choose a castle to build
3. Feb. 3   Design my model on paper as a blueprint
4. Feb. 10   Construct a scale model of castle
5. Feb. 16   Plan and write first draft of paper
6. Feb. 22   Complete paper and present project to class

Outcome: My project will help the class understand how a castle was built and how it was used.

Proposals

A proposal is a detailed plan for doing a project, solving a problem, or meeting a need.

Follow Guidelines

Letters

A letter is a written message sent through the mail. Letters can be formal, like a business letter, or informal, like a friendly letter. Formal letters follow a set format, including important contact information, a salutation or greeting, a body, and a closing signature. (See pages **284–289** for more information.)

> 1414 Johnson Street
> Walvan, WI 53000
> April 20, 2009
>
> Mayor Phillip Smith
> Walvan City Hall
> 111 Main Street
> Walvan, WI 53000
>
> Dear Mayor Smith:
>
> I am a student at Parker Lane Middle School. At a city council meeting last October, I asked the council to put up a stoplight at the intersection of 34th Avenue and Cottage Street. Six months later, cars are still going by too fast on 34th Avenue.
>
> I am not the only one who thinks this corner is dangerous. I passed around a petition asking for the stoplight, and more than 400 students, teachers, parents, and neighbors signed it. I have enclosed my petition. Mayor Smith, please vote for putting a traffic light at 34th Avenue and Cottage Street.
>
> Sincerely,
>
> *Ruby Keast*
> Ruby Keast

Envelope Addresses

Place the return address in the upper left corner, the destination address in the center, and the correct postage in the upper right corner.

> RUBY KEAST
> 1414 JOHNSON ST
> WALVAN WI 53000
>
>
>
> MAYOR PHILLIP SMITH
> WALVAN CITY HALL
> 111 MAIN ST
> WALVAN WI 53000

U.S. Postal Service Guidelines

1. Capitalize everything and leave out ALL punctuation.
2. Use the list of common abbreviations found on **676.1**. Use numerals rather than words for numbered streets and avenues (9TH AVE NE, 3RD ST SW).
3. If you know the ZIP + 4 code, use it.

RESOURCE

ELPS 2C, 3E, 4C, 4G

Proofreader's Guide

Learning Language

With a partner, read the prompts and share your answers.

1. Confusion is what you feel when you don't know what is happening.
   When could you experience confusion?

2. Initials are the first letters of a person's full name.
   What are your initials?

3. When you dot your *i*'s and cross your *t*'s, you are careful and precise about doing something.
   Explain a time when you would dot your *i*'s and cross your *t*'s.

improve edit

Editing for Mechanics

Periods

Use a **period** to end a sentence. Also use a period after initials, after abbreviations, and as a decimal point.

MECHANICS

627.1
At the End of Sentences

Use a period to end a sentence that makes a statement or a request. Also use a period for a mild command, one that does not need an exclamation point. (See page 566.)

> **The Southern Ocean surrounds Antarctica.** (statement)
>
> **Please point out the world's largest ocean on a map.** (request)
>
> **Do not use a laser pointer.** (mild command)

NOTE It is not necessary to place a period after a statement that has parentheses around it if it is part of another sentence.

> **The Southern Ocean is the fourth-largest ocean (it is larger than the Atlantic).**

627.2
After Initials

Place a period after an initial.

> **J. K. Rowling** (author)
>
> **Colin L. Powell** (politician)

627.3
After Abbreviations

Place a period after each part of an abbreviation. Do not use periods with acronyms or initialisms. (See page 678.)

> Abbreviations: **Mr. Mrs. Ms. Dr. B.C.E. C.E.**
>
> Acronyms: **AIDS NASA**
>
> Initialisms: **NBC FBI**

NOTE When an abbreviation is the last word in a sentence, use only one period at the end of the sentence.

> **My grandfather's full name is William Ryan James Koenig, Jr.**

627.4
As Decimal Points

Use a period to separate dollars and cents and as a decimal point.

> **The price of a loaf of bread was $1.54 in 1992.**
>
> **That price was only 35 cents, or 77.3 percent less, in 1972.**

ELPS 4C

Question Marks

A **question mark** is used after an interrogative sentence and also to show doubt about the correctness of a fact or figure. (See page **566**.)

628.1
At the End of Direct Questions

Use a question mark at the end of a direct question (an interrogative sentence).

Is a vegan a person who eats only vegetables?

628.2
At the End of Indirect Questions

No question mark is used after an indirect question. (An indirect question tells about a question you or someone else asked.)

Because I do not eat meat, I'm often asked if I am a vegetarian.

I asked the doctor if going meatless is harmful to my health.

628.3
To Show Doubt

Place a question mark within parentheses to show that you are unsure that a fact or figure is correct.

By the year 2020 (?) the number of vegetarians in the United States may approach 15 percent of the population.

Exclamation Points

An **exclamation point** may be placed after a word, a phrase, or a sentence to show emotion. (The exclamation point should not be overused.)

628.4
To Express Strong Feelings

Use an exclamation point to show excitement or strong feeling.

Yeah! Wow! Oh my!

Surprise! You've won the million-dollar sweepstakes!

Caution: Never use more than one exclamation point in writing assignments.

Incorrect: **Don't ever do that to me again!!!**

Correct: **Don't ever do that to me again!**

ELPS 3G

 **Practice**

End Punctuation

 On your own paper, write whether each of the following sentences needs a period, a question mark, or an exclamation point at the end.

Example: Wow, listen to that alarm ringing

exclamation point

1. Uh-oh, it's a fire drill

2. How many fire drills do you have at your school

3. Drills are held to make sure everyone knows how to get out of the building in an emergency

4. What can you do to make sure you will safely get out of a burning building

5. Should you take all of your books and belongings with you

6. You should simply get up and quickly walk out without taking anything with you

7. To prevent confusion and panic, everyone needs to exit calmly

8. Absolutely no pushing is allowed

9. Make sure those with a disability are assisted to the exit

10. Close the door on your way out to prevent a fire from spreading

11. Would you know another way out if the first exit was blocked

12. Meet at a chosen place to make sure everyone got out

13. Firefighter Jim asked us if we should go back into a burning building for any reason

14. The answer was a loud no

Next Step: Write about a fire drill you had. End at least one sentence with a period, one with a question mark, and one with an exclamation point. Read them aloud with feeling.

MECHANICS

ELPS 4C

Commas . . .

Use a **comma** to indicate a pause or a change in thought. This helps to keep words and ideas from running together, so writing is easier to read. For a writer, no other form of punctuation is more important to understand than the comma.

630.1
Between Items in a Series

Use commas between words, phrases, or clauses in a series. (A series contains at least three items.) (See page 561.)

Chinese, English, and Hindi are the three most widely used languages in the world. (words)

Being comfortable with technology, working well with others, and knowing another language are important skills for today's workers. (phrases)

My dad works in a factory, my mom works in an office, and I work in school. (clauses)

630.2
To Keep Numbers Clear

Use commas to separate the digits in a number in order to distinguish hundreds, thousands, millions, and so on.

More than 104,000 people live in Kingston, the capital of Jamaica.

The population of the entire country of Liechtenstein is only 29,000.

NOTE Commas are not used in years.

The world population was 6.1 billion by 2003.

630.3
In Dates and Addresses

Use commas to distinguish items in an address and items in a date.

On August 28, 1963, Martin Luther King, Jr., gave his famous "I Have a Dream" speech.

The address of the King Center is 449 Auburn Avenue NE, Atlanta, Georgia 30312.

NOTE No comma is placed between the state and ZIP code. Also, when only the month and year are given, no comma is needed.

In January 2029 we will celebrate the 100th anniversary of Reverend King's birth.

Practice

Commas 1

- ■ Between Items in a Series
- ■ To Keep Numbers Clear
- ■ In Dates and Addresses

For each sentence below, write the series, date, address, or number that should include a comma. Add the comma.

Example: A democracy, as Abraham Lincoln said, is a government of the people by the people and for the people.

of the people, by the people, and for the people

1. The first democracy was created in ancient Greece over 2000 years ago.

2. When colonial Americans declared independence from England on July 4 1776, they created a democracy.

3. Benjamin Franklin Thomas Jefferson and George Washington were men who worked to create an independent country.

4. Jefferson wrote the Declaration of Independence Franklin edited it and they both signed it.

5. The reasons for declaring independence included complaints about the king of England a wish to give power to the people and the desire for individual freedoms.

6. The people wanted the right to "life liberty and the pursuit of happiness."

7. The Declaration was signed on August 2 1776 in Philadelphia, which had a population at the time of about 25000.

8. The original document is kept in the National Archives Building 700 Pennsylvania Avenue Washington DC 20408.

Next Step: Write a sentence telling what you think your world would be like if the Declaration of Independence had not been adopted. Include commas between items in a series.

Commas . . .

632.1
To Set Off Nonrestrictive Phrases and Clauses

Use commas to set off nonrestrictive phrases and clauses—those not necessary to the basic meaning of the sentence.

People get drinking water from surface water or groundwater, which makes up only 1 percent of the earth's water supply.
(The clause *which makes up only 1 percent of the earth's water supply* is additional information; it is nonrestrictive—not required. If the clause was left out, the meaning of the sentence would remain clear.)

Restrictive phrases or clauses—those that are needed in the sentence—restrict or limit the meaning of the sentence; they are not set off with commas.

Groundwater that is free from harmful pollutants is rare.
(The clause *that is free from harmful pollutants* is restrictive; it is needed to complete the meaning of the basic sentence and is not set off with commas.)

632.2
To Set Off Titles or Initials

Use commas to set off a title, a name, or initials that follow a person's last name. (Use only one period if an initial comes at the end of a sentence.)

Melanie Prokat, M.D., is our family's doctor. However, she is listed in the phone book only as Prokat, M.

NOTE Although commas are not necessary to set off "Jr." and "Sr." after a name, they may be used as long as a comma is used both before and after the abbreviation.

632.3
To Set Off Interruptions

Use commas to set off a word, phrase, or clause that interrupts the main thought of a sentence. These interruptions usually can be identified through the following tests:

1. You can leave them out of a sentence without changing its meaning.

2. You can place them other places in the sentence without changing its meaning.

Our school, as we all know, is becoming overcrowded again. (clause)

The gym, not the cafeteria, was expanded a while ago. (phrase)

My history class, for example, has 42 students in it. (phrase)

There are, indeed, about 1,000 people in my school. (word)

The building, however, has room for only 850 students. (word)

ELPS 3E

Practice

Commas 2

- ■ To Set Off Nonrestrictive Phrases and Clauses
- ■ To Set Off Titles or Initials
- ■ To Set Off Interruptions

 Rewrite each of the following sentences, placing commas where they are needed.

Example: Dr. Martin Luther King Jr. was originally named Michael.

Dr. Martin Luther King, Jr., was originally named Michael.

1. His parents Alberta and Martin Luther King Sr. renamed their son Martin when he was about six years old.

2. Benjamin Mays Ph.D. convinced Martin to begin a religious career when he finished college in 1948.

3. Reverend King became a very important leader as you may already know in the civil rights movement.

4. He believed that all people no matter what race or gender should be able to live and work together.

5. His nonviolent efforts toward peace which won him the Nobel Peace Prize in 1964 made him unpopular with some people.

6. His home for instance was bombed, and he was arrested several times.

7. King's assassination in 1968 however did not end his work.

8. His birthday in fact is a national holiday that is celebrated on the third Monday of January.

9. George Washington and Abraham Lincoln whose birthdays are also celebrated as national holidays are two other Americans who are honored in this way.

Next Step: Write a short paragraph describing what your school does for Martin Luther King, Jr., Day. Use sentences with commas that set off nonrestrictive phrases/clauses, titles/ initials, and interruptions. Share your paragraph aloud.

ELPS 4C

Commas . . .

634.1
To Set Off Appositives

Commas set off an appositive from the rest of the sentence. An appositive is a word or phrase that identifies or renames a noun or pronoun. (See page 568.)

The capital of Cyprus, Nicosia, has a population of almost 643,000. (*Nicosia* renames *capital of Cyprus,* so the word is set off with commas.)

Cyprus, an island in the Mediterranean Sea, is about half the size of Connecticut. (*An island in the Mediterranean Sea* identifies *Cyprus,* so the phrase is set off with commas.)

Do not use commas with appositives that are necessary to the basic meaning of the sentence.

The Mediterranean island Cyprus is about half the size of Connecticut. (*Cyprus* is not set off because it is needed to make the sentence clear.)

634.2
To Separate Equal Adjectives

Use commas to separate two or more adjectives that equally modify the same noun.

Comfortable, efficient cars are becoming more important to drivers. (*Comfortable* and *efficient* are separated by a comma because they modify *cars* equally.)

Some automobiles run on clean, renewable sources of energy. (*Clean* and *renewable* are separated by a comma because they modify *sources* equally.)

Conventional gasoline engines emit a lot of pollution. (*Conventional* and *gasoline* do not modify *engines* equally; therefore, no comma separates the two.)

Use these tests to help you decide if adjectives modify equally:

1. Switch the order of the adjectives; if the sentence is clear, the adjectives modify equally.

Yes: Efficient, comfortable cars are becoming more important to drivers.

No: Gasoline conventional engines emit a lot of pollution.

2. Put the word *and* between the adjectives; if the sentence is clear, use a comma when *and* is taken out.

Yes: Comfortable and efficient cars are becoming more important to drivers.

No: Conventional and gasoline engines emit a lot of pollution.

MECHANICS

Practice

Commas 3

■ **To Set Off Appositives**

For each sentence below, write the appositive phrase and the noun it renames. Set off the appositive with commas.

Example: "Mexamerica" the region between Houston and Los Angeles is the location of choice for many people.

"Mexamerica," the region between Houston and Los Angeles,

1. San Diego California's second-largest city boasts some of the best weather in the country.

2. Austin the capital of Texas has a strong Tejano music scene.

3. San Antonio another Texas city hosts the annual Fiesta San Antonio to remember its war heroes.

4. Las Cruces, New Mexico, was ranked by *Forbes* a financial newsmagazine as the best small city to live and work in.

■ **To Separate Equal Adjectives**

For each numbered sentence below, write the adjectives that need commas between them. Add the commas.

Example: Los Angeles is located along the rugged sandy coast of southern California.

rugged, sandy

(1) Considered the "capital" of Mexamerica by some, Los Angeles is an exciting spread-out city. **(2)** It is full of lively unique neighborhoods. **(3)** Although many people live an enjoyable rewarding life in Los Angeles, the city also has its problems. **(4)** Everyone seems to know about the slow-moving congested traffic and the very high cost of living. **(5)** Despite the city's troubles, many people still like living in golden sunny Los Angeles.

 **TEKS** 6.20B(ii)
ELPS 4C

Commas . . .

636.1
To Set Off Dialogue

Use commas to set off the exact words of a speaker from the rest of the sentence. (Also see page 604.)

> The firefighter said, "When we cannot successfully put out a fire, we try to keep it from spreading."

> "When we cannot successfully put out a fire, we try to keep it from spreading," the firefighter said.

NOTE Do not use a comma or quotation marks for indirect quotations. The words *if* and *that* often signal dialogue that is being reported rather than quoted.

> The firefighter said that when they cannot successfully put out a fire, they try to keep it from spreading. (These are not the speaker's exact words.)

636.2
In Direct Address

Use commas to separate a noun of direct address from the rest of the sentence. (A noun of direct address is a noun that names a person spoken to in the sentence.)

> Hanae, did you know that an interior decorator can change wallpaper and fabrics on a computer screen?

> Sure, Jack, and an architect can use a computer to see how light will fall in different parts of a building.

636.3
To Set Off Interjections

Use commas to separate an interjection or a weak exclamation from the rest of the sentence.

> No kidding, you mean that one teacher has to manage a class of 42 pupils? (weak exclamation)

> Uh-huh, and that teacher has other classes that size. (interjection)

636.4
To Set Off Explanatory Phrases

Use commas to separate an explanatory phrase from the rest of the sentence.

> English, the language computers speak worldwide, is also the most widely used language in science and medicine.

> More than 750 million people, about an eighth of the world's population, speak English as a foreign language.

Practice

Commas 4

- ■ To Set Off Dialogue
- ■ In Direct Address
- ■ To Set Off Interjections
- ■ To Set Off Explanatory Phrases

Rewrite each of the following sentences, placing commas where they are needed.

Example: Whales are warm-blooded mammals breathing air through their blowholes and are found in all oceans.

Whales are warm-blooded mammals, breathing air through their blowholes, and are found in all oceans.

1. While most whales swim in groups, others like fin whales swim alone or in pairs.

2. Ms. Smith asked "Laticia did you know the longest dive by a sperm whale lasted more than an hour?"

3. Laticia replied "Uh-uh but I know sperm whales can dive to depths of more than a mile."

4. Jeremy said "Well that's hard to believe. Ms. Smith how do they do that?"

5. "Fish swim by moving their tails from side to side, but whales swim by pumping their tails up and down" she said.

6. Some of the sea creatures we know as dolphins are actually whales such as the killer whale and the pilot whale.

7. Humpback whales named for the hump behind the dorsal fin are an endangered species.

8. Laticia said "Other whales including the right and blue whales are also endangered."

Next Step: Write a brief, imagined conversation between whales. Use commas correctly to set off dialogue and nouns of direct address.

MECHANICS

TEKS 6.20B(i)
ELPS 4C

Commas

638.1

To Separate Introductory Clauses and Phrases

Use a comma to separate an adverb clause or a long phrase from the independent clause that follows it.

If every automobile in the country were a light shade of red, we'd live in a pink-car nation. (adverb clause)

According to some experts, solar-powered cars will soon be common. (long modifying phrase)

638.2

In Compound Sentences

Use a comma between two independent clauses that are joined by a coordinating conjunction (such as *and, but, or, nor, for, so,* and *yet*), forming a compound sentence. An independent clause expresses a complete thought and can stand alone as a sentence. (Also see page **564**.)

Many students enjoy working on computers, so teachers are finding new ways to use them in the classroom.

Computers can be valuable in education, but many schools cannot afford enough of them.

Avoid Comma Splices: A comma splice results when two independent clauses are "spliced" together with only a comma—and no conjunction. (See page **552**.)

SCHOOL DAZE

Ann, we've completed two-thirds of the quarter, and you haven't turned in one assignment. What do you have to say for yourself?

Ah . . . is there anything I can do for extra credit?

Practice

Commas 5

■ **To Separate Introductory Clauses and Phrases**
■ **In Compound Sentences**

For each sentence below, write the word or words that should be followed by a comma. Add the comma.

Example: I sat down to eat lunch and I began to slurp my soup.

lunch,

1. Aunt Marianna wanted me to improve my table manners so she enrolled me in a class.

2. After the teacher, Ms. Wyatt, introduced herself she said, "The main thing to remember is to be polite."

3. If you are a guest at someone else's house don't sit down at the table or begin eating before the host does.

4. Along with Ms. Wyatt we sat at a beautifully set table.

5. Ramón wanted to sip some of his water but he didn't know which glass was his.

6. Your glass is always placed to the right of your plate and your bread plate goes on the left.

7. Before doing anything else put your napkin on your lap.

8. When you want to butter your bread put some butter on your bread plate first.

9. Since there was more than one fork at each place setting Ms. Wyatt said that we should use the utensils from the outside in.

10. Then she said, "While you're eating take your time yet try to keep pace with the other guests."

Next Step: Write two sentences telling how your table manners could be improved. Include an introductory phrase or clause in one sentence; the other should be a compound sentence. Use commas correctly.

TEKS 6.19A(iv)
ELPS 4C

Semicolons

Use a **semicolon** to suggest a stronger pause than a comma indicates. A semicolon may also serve in place of a period.

640.1
To Join Two Independent Clauses

In a compound sentence, use a semicolon to join two independent clauses that are not connected with a coordinating conjunction. (See page **776**.)

> **The United States has more computers than any other country; its residents own more than 164 million of them.**

640.2
With Conjunctive Adverbs

A semicolon is also used to join two independent clauses when the clauses are connected by a conjunctive adverb (such as *as a result, for example, however, therefore,* and *instead*). (See page **772**.)

> **Japan is next on that list; however, the Japanese have only 50 million computers.**

> **You might think that the billion people of China own a lot of computers; instead, the smaller country of Germany has twice as many computers as China.**

640.3
To Separate Groups That Contain Commas

Use a semicolon between groups of words in a series when one or more of the groups already contain commas.

> **Many of our community's residents separate their garbage into bins for newspapers, cardboard, and junk mail; glass, metal, and plastic; and nonrecyclable trash.**

SCHOOL DAZE

It's true that I have only a few minutes to finish this; **however,** I am not worried.

Well, that makes one of us.

TEKS 6.19A(iv)

MECHANICS

Practice

Semicolons

For each of the following sentences, write the word or words that should be followed by a semicolon. Add the semicolon. If a conjunctive adverb is used, write it next to the semicolon.

Example: Go to the library first then do your homework.
first;

1. Mom said I could go to Jean's house however, I have to do the dishes before I go.

2. Cam must be an artist this drawing is fantastic!

3. Sanjay is sick therefore, he can't go to Manny's party.

4. I have already read this book it's about a two-headed monster.

The following directions will help you create a sentence that uses semicolons. The semicolons will separate groups of words that already contain commas.

1. Think of three toys that involve imagination and write down their names.

2. Next write a list of three games.

3. Finally, write three toys a child would use outside.

4. Now copy and complete the following sentence. Fill in the blanks with your own toy lists. Make sure to include both the commas and the semicolons to separate your lists.

My little sister Keisha's favorite toys are her _____, _____, and _____; her _____ game, _____ game, and _____ game; and her _____, _____, and _____.

Next Step: Write three sentences about your favorite foods. Think of plenty of choices. Use semicolons between groups of words in a series, as in the example above. Use a conjunctive adverb in at least one sentence.

Colons

A **colon** may be used to introduce a list or an important point. Colons are also used in business letters and between the numbers in time.

642.1
To Introduce Lists

Use a colon to introduce a list. The colon usually comes after words describing the subject of the list (as in the first example below) or after summary words, such as *the following* or *these things*. Do not use a colon after a verb or preposition.

> Certain items are still difficult to recycle: foam cups, car tires, and toxic chemicals.

> To conserve water, you should do the following three things: fix drippy faucets, install a low-flow showerhead, and turn the water off while brushing your teeth.

> Incorrect: To conserve water, you should: install a low-flow showerhead, turn the water off while brushing your teeth, and fix drippy faucets.

642.2
To Introduce Sentences

A colon may be used to introduce a sentence, a question, or a quotation.

> This is why air pollution is bad: We are sacrificing our health and the health of all other life on the planet.

> Answer this question for me: Why aren't more people concerned about global warming?

> Joaquin shared this with us: "Iceland is the world's leader in the use of renewable energy."

642.3
After Salutations

A colon may be used after the salutation of a business letter.

> Dear Ms. Manners: Dear Dr. Warmle: Dear Professor Potter:
> Dear Captain Elliot: Dear Senator:

642.4
For Emphasis

Use a colon to emphasize a word or phrase.

> The newest alternative energy is also the most common element on earth: hydrogen.

> Here's one thing to help save energy: a programmable thermostat.

642.5
Between Numbers in Time

Use a colon between the parts of a number that indicate time.

> My thermostat automatically turns the heat down at 11:00 p.m.

MECHANICS

Practice

Colons

The following letter needs colons placed correctly. Write the words or numbers that need colons. Then add them.

Example: These are a few reasons to go to the dentist to have your teeth cleaned, to relieve a toothache, and to get a cavity filled.

dentist:

1 Dear Dr. Meyer

2   It was 330 p.m. last Thursday, almost time to have my cavity

3 filled. I was a bit nervous. As I was gnawing on my fingernails, I

4 thought of a question What are these things made of, anyway?

5   I remember hearing that fingernails are made of the same stuff

6 as these other things horses' hooves, birds' feathers, and bulls' horns.

7 They're also made of the same substance as another thing hair.

8   One great thing about nails and hair is that it doesn't hurt to

9 cut into them. By 400, as the drill was making the hole in my tooth

10 even bigger, I had this thought It would be fantastic to have teeth

11 like nails and hair, too! Just think, Dr. Meyer—without using any

12 anesthetic, you could do any of these procedures fill a cavity, fix a

13 broken tooth, or file a chipped tooth.

14   Well, Dr. Meyer, it doesn't hurt to dream! Thanks for helping

15 me take care of something very important to me my teeth.

16 Sincerely,

17 James Ormon

Next Step: Write a sentence containing a colon; after the colon, list all the different ways a colon can be used.

 **TEKS** 6.20B(ii)
ELPS 4C

Quotation Marks . . .

Quotation marks are used in a number of ways:
- to set off the exact words of a speaker,
- to punctuate material quoted from another source,
- to punctuate words used in a special way, and
- to punctuate certain titles.

644.1

To Set Off a Speaker's Exact Words

Place quotation marks before and after a speaker's words in dialogue. Only the exact words of the speaker are placed within quotation marks.

> Marla said, "I've decided to become a firefighter."

> "A firefighter," said Juan, "can help people in many ways."

644.2

For Quotations Within Quotations

Use single quotation marks to punctuate a quotation within a quotation.

> Sung Kim asked, "Did Marla just say, 'I've decided to become a firefighter'?"

When titles occur within a quotation, use single quotation marks to punctuate those that require quotation marks.

> Juan said, "Springsteen's song 'The Rising' really inspired her."

644.3

To Set Off Quoted Material

When quoting material from another source, place quotation marks before and after the source's exact words.

> In her book *Living the Life You Deserve,* Tess Spyeder explains, "Choose a job you'll enjoy doing day after day over one that will fatten your bank account."

644.4

To Set Off Long Quoted Material

If more than one paragraph is quoted from a single source, quotation marks are placed before each paragraph and at the end of the last paragraph.

Quotations that are more than four lines are usually set off from the rest of the paper by indenting each line 10 spaces from the left. Quotations that are set off in this way require no quotation marks either before or after the quoted material.

TEKS 6.20B(ii)
ELPS 3E

Practice

Quotation Marks 1

■ To Set Off a Speaker's Exact Words
■ For Quotations Within Quotations

Rewrite the following conversation, using quotation marks correctly.

Example: Ms. Green said, Don't forget that your book reports are due next week.

Ms. Green said, "Don't forget that your book reports are due next week."

1 Reneé asked, What book will you use for your book report?

2 Fadi said, I've always liked the first Harry Potter book, so I'll
3 probably use that.

4 I just read a new book called *Hoot,* Reneé said. That's what I'm
5 going to report on.

6 I haven't heard of that book. What's it about? asked Fadi.

7 It's about three kids who help save some endangered miniature
8 owls. See, this big company wants to build a pancake house where
9 the owls' nest is, she said.

10 When you say, build a pancake house, do you mean they want
11 to build a house out of pancakes? Fadi asked.

12 Very funny, said Reneé. I think you know what I mean. It's a
13 restaurant that sells pancakes.

14 And so the kids stop this restaurant from being built? Fadi
15 asked.

16 I'm not going to tell you, Reneé said. You'll have to read the
17 book yourself if you want to find out!

Next Step: Imagine a conversation you have with a friend about
a book you've read recently. Write a few lines of this
dialogue. Make sure you use quotation marks correctly.
Then practice the dialogue with a partner.

MECHANICS

Quotation Marks

646.1
Placement of Punctuation

Always place periods and commas inside quotation marks.

"I don't know," said Lac.

Lac said, "I don't know."

Place an exclamation point or a question mark inside the quotation marks when it punctuates the quotation.

Ms. Wiley asked, "Can you actually tour the Smithsonian on the Internet?"

Place it outside when it punctuates the main sentence.

Did I hear you say, "Now we can tour the Smithsonian on the Internet"?

Place semicolons or colons outside quotation marks.

First I will read the article "Sonny's Blues"; then I will read "The Star Café" in my favorite music magazine.

646.2
For Special Words

Quotation marks also may be used (1) to set apart a word that is being discussed, (2) to indicate that a word is slang, or (3) to point out that a word or phrase is being used in a special way.

1. **Renny uses the word "like" entirely too much.**
2. **Man, your car is really "phat."**
3. **Aunt Lulu, an editor at a weekly magazine, says she has "issues."**

646.3
To Punctuate Titles

Use quotation marks to punctuate titles of songs, poems, short stories, lectures, episodes of radio or television programs, chapters of books, and articles found in magazines, newspapers, or encyclopedias. (Also see **648.3**.)

"21 Questions" (song)

"The Reed Flute's Song" (poem)

"Old Man at the Bridge" (short story)

"Birthday Boys" (a television episode)

"The Foolish and the Weak" (a chapter in a book)

"Science Careers Today" (lecture)

"Teen Rescues Stranded Dolphin" (newspaper article)

NOTE When you punctuate a title, capitalize the first word, last word, and every word in between—except for articles (*a, an, the*), short prepositions (*at, to, with,* and so on), and coordinating conjunctions (*and, but, or*). (See **668.2**.)

TEKS 6.20B(ii)

MECHANICS

Practice

Quotation Marks 2

■ **Placement of Punctuation**

Rewrite the following sentences, placing commas and end punctuation where needed.

Example: "We're learning some new songs in chorus" said Ryan.

"We're learning some new songs in chorus," said Ryan.

1. "I hear that's a fun class" said Elisa.

2. "Who is the new teacher" she asked.

3. Ryan said, "Mr. Pescados"

4. "Did you say 'Mr. Pescados' If you did, that's funny" Elisa said.

5. She continued, "*Pescados* means 'fish' in Spanish"

■ **To Punctuate Titles**

For each of the following sentences, write the title that needs quotation marks. (Be careful to place commas or periods correctly.)

Example: The article Remember When talks about pleasant childhood memories.

"Remember When"

1. When I was little, I've Been Workin' on the Railroad was my favorite song.

2. I also remember learning the poem One, Two, Buckle My Shoe.

3. Mom read short bedtime stories from *Grimms' Fairy Tales,* and I never got tired of listening to Rapunzel.

4. I must have watched Day of the Dumpster, the pilot episode of *Mighty Morphin' Power Rangers,* a dozen times!

5. The recent *Time for Kids* magazine article Having a Blast in the Past made me think of all these memories.

TEKS 6.20C
ELPS 4C

Italics and Underlining

Italics is slightly slanted type. In this sentence, the word *happiness* is typed in italics. In handwritten material, each word or letter that should be in italics is **underlined**.

648.1

In Printed Material

Print words in italics when you are using a computer.

In *Tuck Everlasting,* the author explores what it would be like to live forever.

648.2

In Handwritten Material

Underline words that should be italicized when you are writing by hand.

In <u>Tuck Everlasting</u>, the author explores what it would be like to live forever.

648.3

In Titles

Italicize (or underline) the titles of books, plays, book-length poems, magazines, newspapers, radio and television programs, movies, videos, cassettes, CD's, and the names of aircraft and ships.

Walk Two Moons (book)	*Teen People* (magazine)
Fairies and Dragons (movie)	*Everwood* (TV program)
The Young and the Hopeless (CD)	*U.S.S. Arizona* (ship)
Columbia (space shuttle)	*Daily Herald* (newspaper)

Exception: Do not italicize or put quotation marks around your own title at the top of your written work.

A Day Without Water (personal writing: do not italicize)

648.4

For Scientific and Foreign Words

Italicize (or underline) scientific and foreign words that are not commonly used in everyday English.

Spinacia oleracea is the scientific term for spinach.

Many store owners who can help Spanish-speaking customers display an *Hablamos Español* sign in their windows.

648.5

For Special Uses

Italicize (or underline) a number, letter, or word that is being discussed or used in a special way. (Sometimes quotation marks are used for this same reason.)

Matt's hat has a bright red *A* on it.

TEKS 6.20C

Practice

Italics and Underlining

Write the word or words that should be italicized in each sentence. Underline the words.

Example: I just finished reading an article in Teen People.

Teen People

1. In the article, it says that one of the singers in Coldplay has 007 on his license plate.

2. Yes, he's a James Bond fan—his favorite movie is Thunderball.

3. You might say some of the characters in this movie, featuring some amazing underwater action, are benthic (they're bottom-dwellers).

4. James Bond, introduced in Ian Fleming's novel Casino Royale, first appeared on film in the television series Climax! in 1954.

5. Bond works for the British Secret Service; an actual British navy ship, the Devonshire, was used in the Bond movie Tomorrow Never Dies.

6. Two of Bond's associates have the letters M and Q for their names.

7. His boss used the word prism in telegrams as a sign of approval.

8. Did Bond's enemies ever say non, merci (no, thanks) to him?

9. A French media company publishes James Bond Magazine, and 007 Magazine is available to members of the James Bond International Fan Club.

10. Almost all the Bond movies have a soundtrack available on CD, and my favorite is The World Is Not Enough.

Next Step: Write some sentences that include the names of your favorite CD, movie, and book or magazine. Use italics (underlining) correctly.

MECHANICS

Apostrophes . . .

Use **apostrophes** to form contractions, to form certain plurals, or to show possession.

650.1
In Contractions

Use an apostrophe to form a contraction, showing that one or more letters have been left out of a word.

Common Contractions

can't (cannot)	**couldn't** (could not)	**didn't** (did not)
doesn't (does not)	**don't** (do not)	**hasn't** (has not)
haven't (have not)	**isn't** (is not)	**I'll** (I will)
I'd (I would)	**I'm** (I am)	**I've** (I have)
they'll (they will)	**they'd** (they would)	**they've** (they have)
they're (they are)	**won't** (will not)	**wouldn't** (would not)
you'll (you will)	**you'd** (you would)	**you've** (you have)
you're (you are)		

650.2
In Place of Omitted Letters or Numbers

Use an apostrophe to show that one or more digits have been left out of a number, or that one or more letters have been left out of a word to show a special pronunciation.

> **class of '99** (*19* is left out)

> **g'bye** (the letters *ood* are left out of *good-bye*)

NOTE Letters and numbers should not be omitted in most writing assignments; however, they may be omitted in dialogue to make it sound like real people are talking.

650.3
To Form Some Plurals

Use an apostrophe and *s* to form the plural of a letter, a sign, a number, or a word being discussed as a word.

> **A's   8's   +'s   *to*'s**

> **Don't use too many *and*'s in your writing.**

650.4
To Form Singular Possessives

To form the possessive of a singular noun, add an apostrophe and *s*.

> **the game's directions   Dr. Mill's theory**
> **Ross's bike   Roz's hair**

NOTE When a singular noun with more than one syllable ends with an *s* or *z* sound, the possessive may be formed by adding just an apostrophe.

> **Texas' oil** (or) **Texas's oil   Carlos' mother** (or) **Carlos's mother**

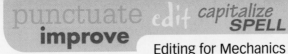

Practice

MECHANICS

Apostrophes 1

■ In Contractions
■ In Place of Omitted Letters or Numbers

In the following sentences, apostrophes are missing from numbers or words. Write the words or numbers with their apostrophes.

Example: Comets arent solid rock, but when Grandpa was in school (the class of 65), people thought they were.

aren't   '65

1. Jermaine enjoys reading his science book, published in 98.

2. The book says that space travelers wouldnt be able to take enough food and fuel for a trip to the stars.

3. Theyd run out of supplies long before they reached Pluto.

4. Back in 79, astronomers saw Pluto cross Neptune's orbit.

5. For the next 20 years, Pluto wasnt the most distant planet in our solar system—Neptune was.

■ To Form Some Plurals
■ To Form Singular Possessives

In the following sentences, apostrophes are missing from some words. Write the words with their apostrophes.

Example: A rocket must travel 25,000 miles per hour or about 7 miles per second, to escape Earths gravity.

Earth's

1. How many 0s are needed to show the distance already covered by the space probe *Voyager 2?*

2. *Voyagers* cameras took pictures around Jupiter and Neptune.

3. In 2005, the Hubbles powerful telescope helped astronomers photograph the Carina Nebula maelstrom.

4. Today, the worlds most powerful telescopes allow us to see galaxies that are 13 billion light-years away.

TEKS 6.19A(vi)
ELPS 4C

Apostrophes

652.1
To Form Plural Possessives

The possessive form of plural nouns ending in *s* is usually made by adding just an apostrophe.

> students' homework   teachers' lounge

For plural nouns not ending in *s,* an apostrophe and *s* must be added.

> children's book   people's opinions

Remember: The word immediately before the apostrophe is the owner.

> student's project (*student* is the owner)
> students' project (*students* are the owners)

652.2
To Show Shared Possession

When possession is shared by more than one noun, add an apostrophe and *s* to the last noun in the series.

> Uncle Reggie, Aunt Rosie, and my mom's garden
> (All three own the garden.)

> Uncle Reggie's, Aunt Rosie's, and my mom's gardens
> (Each person owns a garden.)

652.3
To Form Possessives with Compound Nouns

The possessive of a compound noun is formed by placing the possessive ending after the last word.

> her sister-in-law's hip-hop music (singular)
> her sisters-in-law's tastes in music (plural)
> the secretary of state's husband (singular)
> the secretaries of state's husbands (plural)

652.4
To Form Possessives with Indefinite Pronouns

The possessive of an indefinite pronoun is formed by adding an apostrophe and *s.*

> no one's   anyone's   somebody's

NOTE In pronouns that use *else,* add an apostrophe and *s* to the second word.

> somebody else's   anyone else's

652.5
To Express Time or Amount

Use an apostrophe with an adjective that is part of an expression indicating time (month, day, hour) or amount.

> In today's Spanish class, we talked about going to Spain.
> My father lost more than an hour's work when that thunderstorm knocked out our power.
> I bought a couple dollars' worth of grapes at the roadside stand.

 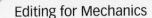
 **TEKS** 6.19A(vi)

Practice

Apostrophes 2

- To Form Plural Possessives
- To Show Shared Possession
- To Form Possessives with Compound Nouns
- To Form Possessives with Indefinite Pronouns
- To Express Time or Amount

 In each of the following sentences, one or more words are missing an apostrophe. Write the words with the apostrophes placed correctly.

Example: James Madison and Alexander Hamiltons report called for revising the Articles of Confederation.
Hamilton's

1. More than four years work was needed to create the new Constitution of the United States.

2. Our forefathers first ideas for a United States government were written in 1781 as the Articles of Confederation.

3. George Washington had accepted the commander in chiefs role in the Continental Army.

4. By 1787, however, he was not sure that the Articles truly represented everyones best interests.

5. Twelve of the original thirteen states delegates met to discuss the country's future, and Washington was named president of this Constitutional Convention.

6. It was an opportunity for everybodys ideas to be heard.

7. The delegates new document, called the Constitution of the United States, was the product of the convention.

8. George Washingtons, Benjamin Franklins, and Alexander Hamiltons signatures all appeared on that document.

9. The summers efforts had been successful.

10. In 1788, two final states votes for the Constitution meant that nine states had ratified it, and it became law.

Hyphens . . .

Use a **hyphen** to divide words at the end of a line and to form compound words. Also use a hyphen between the numbers in a fraction and to join numbers that indicate the life span of an individual, the scores of a game, and so on.

654.1
To Divide Words

Use a hyphen to divide a word when you run out of room at the end of a line. A word may be divided only between syllables. Here are some additional guidelines:

- Never divide a one-syllable word: *raised, through.*
- Avoid dividing a word of five letters or less: *paper, study.*
- Never divide a one-letter syllable from the rest of the word: *omit-ted,* **not** *o-mitted.*
- Never divide abbreviations or contractions: *NASA, wouldn't.*
- Never divide the last word in more than two lines in a row or the last word in a paragraph.
- When a vowel is a syllable by itself, divide the word after the vowel: *epi-sode,* **not** *ep-isode.*

NOTE Refer to a dictionary if you're not sure how to divide a word.

654.2
In Compound Words

A hyphen is used in some compound words, including numbers from twenty-one to ninety-nine.

about-face	warm-up	time-out
down-to-earth	ice-skating	high-rise
thirty-three	seventy-five	

654.3
To Create New Words

A hyphen is often used to form new words beginning with the prefixes *self, ex, all,* and *great.* A hyphen is also used with suffixes such as *elect* and *free.*

self-cleaning	ex-friend	all-natural	germ-free
self-esteem	ex-president	great-aunt	mayor-elect

654.4
Between Numbers in a Fraction

Use a hyphen between the numbers in a fraction. Do not, however, use a hyphen between the numerator and denominator when one or both are already hyphenated.

four-tenths	five-sixteenths	seven thirty-seconds (7/32)

Practice

Hyphens 1

- ■ To Divide Words
- ■ In Compound Words

If the underlined words are presented correctly, write "correct." If not, write the correct form. Check a dictionary if you are not sure.

Example: Twenty-one gym students went outside just as a <u>po-werful</u> storm soaked the playing field.
correct, power-ful or *pow-erful*

1. <u>Fifty five</u> minutes of exercise is required each week, and that doesn't include a <u>warm-up</u>.

2. A <u>top-notch</u> physical-education teacher instructs students <u>a-bout</u> the value of regular exercise.

3. We'd rather play a game than do calisthenics, but that <u>would-n't</u> make us sweat enough, I guess.

4. Still, playing <u>volleyball</u> is more fun than doing <u>pushups</u>.

- ■ To Create New Words
- ■ Between Numbers in a Fraction

For each of the following sentences, write the correct form of the underlined words.

Example: The coach was surprised that <u>three fourths</u> of his students were very fast runners.
three-fourths

1. Jamal saw that <u>two thirds</u> of his class ran faster than he could.

2. Since the coach was an <u>exrunner</u>, he knew that Jamal might be a better sprinter.

3. Jamal ran the 50-yard dash and beat <u>ninetenths</u> of the class.

4. Now Jamal is <u>self motivated</u> to improve his running skills.

5. He told his <u>greatgrandmother</u> about his new goal.

ELPS 4C

Hyphens

656.1
To Form Adjectives

Use a hyphen to join two or more words that work together to form a single-thought adjective before a noun. Generally, hyphenate any compound adjective that might be misread if it is not hyphenated—use common sense. (See page 534.)

smiley-face sticker   dress-up clothes   fresh-breeze scent

Use the tests below to determine if a hyphen is needed.

1. When a compound adjective is made of a noun plus an adjective, it should be hyphenated.

microwave-safe cookware   book-smart student

2. When the compound adjective is made of a noun plus a participle (*ing* or *ed* form of a verb), it should be hyphenated.

bone-chilling story   vitamin-enriched cereal

3. Hyphenate a compound adjective that is a phrase (includes conjunctions or prepositions).

heat-and-serve meals   refrigerator-to-oven dishes

Do *not* hyphenate compound adjectives in these instances:

1. When words forming the adjective come after the noun, do not hyphenate.

This cookware is microwave safe.
The cereal was vitamin enriched.

2. If the first of the two words ends in *ly,* do not hyphenate.

newly designed computer   rarely seen species

3. Do not use a hyphen when a number or letter is the final part of a one-thought adjective.

grade A milk   level 6 textbook

656.2
To Join Letters to Words

Use a hyphen to join a capital letter to a noun or participle.

U-turn   Y-axis   T-bar   A-frame
PG-rated movie   X-ray

656.3
To Avoid Confusion

Use a hyphen with prefixes or suffixes to avoid confusion or awkward spelling.

Re-collect (not recollect) **the reports we handed back last week.**

It has a shell-like (not shelllike) **texture.**

Practice

Hyphens 2

- ■ **To Form Adjectives**
- ■ **To Join Letters to Words**

 For each of the following sentences, write the word or words that should be joined by a hyphen.

Example: Truc found his T shirt rolled up in a ball under his bed.

T-shirt

1. The tie dyed shirt was all wrinkled, but he didn't have time to iron it.

2. Truc put the shirt on and looked for his acid washed jeans.

3. He raced from his fifth floor apartment to the sidewalk in front of the building.

4. It was early October, and he could smell a burning leaves odor in the air.

5. He ran back up to the apartment and grabbed his V neck sweater.

6. He decided to take his fleece lined jacket, too, just in case it got colder.

7. Truc was meeting Matt, and they were going to see a G rated, animated movie at the new theater in town.

8. Matt said it looked like a color blind designer had painted the lobby of the theater.

9. Truc and Matt sat in the top row seats of the balcony and settled in to watch the movie.

Next Step: Write two sentences about the movie Truc and Matt saw. Include a hyphenated adjective in each sentence.

Dashes

The **dash** can be used to show a sudden break in a sentence, to emphasize a word or clause, and to show that someone's speech is being interrupted. There is no space before or after a dash.

658.1
To Indicate a Sudden Break

A dash can be used to show a sudden break in a sentence.

> The three of us came down with colds, lost our voices, and missed the football game—all because we had practiced in the rain.

658.2
For Emphasis

A dash may be used to emphasize or explain a word, a series of words, a phrase, or a clause.

> Vitamins and minerals—important dietary supplements—can improve your diet.

> The benefits of vitamin A—better vision and a stronger immune system—are well known.

658.3
To Indicate Interrupted Speech

Use a dash to show that someone's speech is being interrupted by another person.

NOTE In typed material, if you don't know the keyboard shortcut for a dash, you can type two hyphens without a space before or after.

> Well—yes, I understand—no, I remember—oh—okay, thank you.

Parentheses and Brackets

Parentheses and **brackets** are used around words that are included in a sentence to add information or to help make an idea clearer.

658.4
To Add Information

Use parentheses when adding information or clarifying an idea.

> Cures for diseases (from arthritis to cancer) may be found in plants in the rain forest.

Use brackets to add information to help make quoted material clear.

> "Only about 10 percent of the [plant] species in the world have been studied."

Practice

Dashes

The following sentences use dashes in different ways. Using each as a model, write your own sentence.

Example: Yes, Dara, I know that green is your favorite color—it's mine, too!

Why, Evan, I thought that green was a natural color—it's organic, man!

1. Yellow—the color of happiness—is often used for decorations at celebrations.

2. A person who feels blue—as in sad—would probably not wear bright red.

3. Hey, Maurice, how did—no, I didn't know—okay, no shorts.

4. She wants to paint her room—why, I'll never understand—purple and red.

5. Maybe she thinks purple and red will make her feel "royal"—like a queen.

Parentheses and Brackets

Rewrite the following groups of sentences. Combine them using parentheses or brackets.

Example: Ancient people believed in healing with colors. Egyptians, Chinese, and Greeks are examples of people who believed in this type of healing.

Ancient people (Egyptians, Chinese, and Greeks) believed in healing with colors.

1. Warm colors remind people of excitement and activity, while cool colors are calming. Red, yellow, and orange are warm colors. Blue, green, and violet are cool colors.

2. "Our reactions to color are based on our experiences," Dr. Soto said. "That includes both cultural and emotional experiences."

**TEKS** 6.20B(iii)
ELPS 4C

Ellipses

Use an **ellipsis** (three periods) to show a pause in dialogue or to show that words or sentences have been left out. Leave one space before, after, and between each period.

660.1
To Show Pauses

Use an ellipsis to show a pause in dialogue.

> "My report," said Reggie, "is on . . . ah . . . cars of the future. One place that I . . . uh . . . checked on the Internet said that cars would someday run on sunshine.

660.2
To Show Omitted Words

Use an ellipsis to show that one or more words have been left out of a quotation. Read this statement about hibernation.

> Some animals, such as the chipmunk and the woodchuck, hibernate in winter. During this time, the animal's heart beats very slowly—only a few times per minute. Its body cools down so much that it nearly freezes, and this is called going into torpor.

Here's how you would type part of the above quotation, leaving some of the words out. If the words left out are at the end of a sentence, use a period followed by three dots.

> Some animals . . . hibernate in winter. During this time, the animal's heart beats very slowly . . . and this is called going into torpor.

SCHOOL DAZE

Max, where is your project? Today is the last day to turn it in!

Well . . . ah . . . can I fax it to you before midnight?

 6.20B(iii)

MECHANICS

Practice

Ellipses

■ **To Show Pauses**

 Rewrite the following brief conversation, inserting ellipses where appropriate to show a pause in dialogue.

Example: "Please open your books to um page 23."

"Please open your books to . . . um . . . page 23."

"Mr. O'Dell, why is it like so *important* to learn about civil rights?"

"Hmm well, we need to know how unfair life was how hard it was for people who were denied their civil rights, so we can make sure that it doesn't happen again."

"I see. That uh makes sense."

■ **To Show Omitted Words**

 Rewrite the following paragraph, leaving out extra words or information in three places. Use ellipses to show where you have left out words.

Some civil rights, such as freedom of speech, freedom of the press, the right to vote, and the right to equality, can be taken for granted. It is important for these rights to be spelled out in our laws so that our nation can avoid discrimination. The United States Constitution, with a number of amendments, makes sure that people's rights are protected. Under the Civil Rights Act of 1964, discrimination based on race, color, or religion against any person in a public place is illegal.

Next Step: Write two sentences about why freedom of speech is important. Trade papers with a classmate and rewrite each other's sentences, omitting words in two places.

 **TEKS** 6.20A(ii)
ELPS 4C

Capitalization . . .

662.1

Proper Nouns and Adjectives

Capitalize all proper nouns and all proper adjectives. A proper noun is the name of a particular person, place, thing, or idea. A proper adjective is an adjective formed from a proper noun.

Common Noun:	country, president, continent
Proper Noun:	Canada, Andrew Jackson, Asia
Proper Adjective:	Canadian, Jacksonian, Asian

662.2

Names and Initials of People

Capitalize the names of people and also the initials or abbreviations that stand for those names.

Samuel L. Jackson   **Aung San Suu Kyi**

Mary Sanchez-Gomez   **P. J. Lipton**

662.3

Titles Used with Names

Capitalize titles used with names of persons; also capitalize abbreviations standing for those titles.

President Mohammed Hosni Mubarak   **Dr. Linda Trout**

Governor Michael Easley   **Rev. Jim Zavaski**

Senator John McCain

662.4

Words Used as Names

Capitalize words such as *mother, father, aunt,* and *uncle* when these words are used as names.

Uncle Marius **started to sit on the couch.** (*Uncle* is a name; the speaker calls this person "Uncle Marius.")

Then Uncle **stopped in midair.** (*Uncle* is used as a name.)

"So, Mom, **what are you doing here?" I asked.** (*Mom* is used as a name.)

Words such as *aunt, uncle, mom, dad, grandma,* and *grandpa* are usually not capitalized if they come after a possessive pronoun (*my, his, our*).

My aunt **had just called him.** (The word *aunt* describes this person but is not used as a name.)

Then my dad **and** mom **walked into the room.** (The words *dad* and *mom* are not used as names in this sentence.)

 **TEKS** 6.20A(ii)

MECHANICS

Practice

Capitalization 1

- Proper Nouns and Adjectives
- Names and Initials of People
- Titles Used with Names
- Words Used as Names

 Number your paper from 1 to 10. In one column, capitalize the words in each sentence that should be capitalized. In the other column, change the words that are incorrectly capitalized.

Example: Edgar Rice burroughs wrote science Fiction Books.

Burroughs   fiction, books

1. Jules verne began writing science fiction in 1851.

2. Science fiction is a mix of Reality and the imagination.

3. h. g. wells became a famous science-fiction writer in 1898 when he published *War of the Worlds*.

4. In 1938, orson welles broadcast *War of the Worlds* on the Radio.

5. Because mr. Welles used a real american town in New jersey as the setting for the broadcast, it caused people to panic.

6. Douglas Adams, Author of *The Hitchhiker's Guide to the Galaxy*, wrote science fiction in a humorous way.

7. *Jurassic Park,* by michael crichton, was published in 1990 and released as a Movie in 1993.

8. In the science-fiction Movie *The Empire Strikes Back,* the villain Darth vader told commander Luke Skywalker, "I am your Father."

9. *The Matrix* introduced the villain agent smith to the world.

10. In *i, robot,* will smith plays the part of a detective who believes robots will take over the world.

Next Step: Think about a science-fiction book you have read. List three proper nouns, three proper adjectives, and the name and initials of the author.

Capitalization . . .

664.1
School Subjects

Capitalize the name of a specific educational course, but not the name of a general subject. (Exception—the names of all languages are proper nouns and are always capitalized: *French, English, Hindi, German, Latin*.)

> **Roberto is studying** accounting **at the technical college.**
> (Because *accounting* is a general subject, it is not capitalized.)

> **He likes the professor who teaches** Accounting Principles.
> (The specific course name is capitalized.)

664.2
Official Names

Capitalize the names of businesses and the official names of their products. (These are called trade names.) Do not, however, capitalize a general word like "toothpaste" when it follows the trade name.

Old Navy	**Best Buy**	**Microsoft**	**Kodak**
Sony Playstation	**Tombstone pizza**	**Mudd jeans**	

664.3
**Races,
Languages,
Nationalities,
Religions**

Capitalize the names of languages, races, nationalities, and religions, as well as the proper adjectives formed from them.

Arab	**Spanish**	**Judaism**	**Catholicism**
African art	**Irish linen**	**Swedish meatballs**	

664.4
**Days, Months,
Holidays**

Capitalize the names of days of the week, months of the year, and special holidays.

Thursday	**Friday**	**Saturday**
July	**August**	**September**
Arbor Day	**Independence Day**	

Do not capitalize the names of seasons.

> **winter, spring, summer, fall (autumn)**

664.5
**Historical
Events**

Capitalize the names of historical events, documents, and periods of time.

World War II	**the Bill of Rights**	**the Magna Carta**
the Middle Ages	**the Paleozoic Era**	

punctuate *edit* capitalize
SPELL
improve

Editing for Mechanics

665

MECHANICS

Practice

Capitalization 2

■ School Subjects
■ Days, Months, Holidays
■ Historical Events

For each numbered sentence below, write the word or words that should be capitalized.

Example: What is armistice day?

Armistice Day

(1) Last friday Mr. Allis, who teaches biology II, told us that veterans day was celebrated on the fourth monday of october between 1968 and 1978. **(2)** In world history, we learned that veterans day was originally called armistice day. **(3)** The holiday was a remembrance of the day in 1918 when world war I ended. **(4)** That day, in the eleventh hour of the eleventh day of the eleventh month (november), a truce was signed to end the fighting. **(5)** Now we remember veterans of all wars, including world war II, the vietnam war, and the gulf war, on november 11 every year.

■ Official Names
■ Races, Languages, Nationalities, Religions

Write the word or words that should be capitalized in each sentence.

1. Textiles are an important part of Pakistan's economy; proline footbags are made there, as are nizam tents.

2. A pakistani company supplies jeans to american companies such as wal-mart and the gap.

3. Pakistan was established in 1947 by indian muslims.

4. Only 3 percent of pakistanis are christian or hindu.

5. Only 8 percent of the population speaks urdu, the official language, but 48 percent speak punjabi.

ELPS 4C

Capitalization . . .

Capitalize the following geographic names.

Planets and heavenly bodies . . . . Venus, Jupiter, Milky Way

Lowercase the word "earth" except when used as the proper name of our planet, especially when mentioned with other planet names.

What on earth are you doing here?

Sam has traveled across the face of the earth several times.

Jupiter's diameter is 11 times larger than Earth's.

The four inner planets are Mercury, Venus, Earth, and Mars.

Continents . . . . **Europe, Asia, South America, Australia, Africa**

Countries . . . **Morocco, Haiti, Greece, Chile, United Arab Emirates**

States . . . . **New Mexico, Alabama, West Virginia, Delaware, Iowa**

Provinces . . . . **Alberta, British Columbia, Quebec, Ontario**

Counties . . . . **Sioux County, Kandiyohi County, Bell County**

Cities . . . . **Montreal, Baton Rouge, Albuquerque, Portland**

Bodies of water . . . . **Delaware Bay, Chickamunga Lake, Indian Ocean, Gulf of Mexico, Skunk Creek**

Landforms . . . . **Appalachian Mountains, Bitterroot Range**

Public areas . . . . . . **Tiananmen Square, Sequoia National Forest, Mount Rushmore, Open Space Park, Vietnam Memorial**

Roads and highways . . . . **New Jersey Turnpike, Interstate 80, Central Avenue, Chisholm Trail, Mutt's Road**

Buildings . . **Pentagon, Paske High School, Empire State Building**

Monuments . . . . **Eiffel Tower, Statue of Liberty**

Capitalize words that indicate particular sections of the country. Also capitalize proper adjectives formed from names of specific sections of a country.

Having grown up on the hectic East Coast, I find life in the South to be refreshing.

Here in Georgia, Southern hospitality is a way of life.

Words that simply indicate a direction are not capitalized; nor are adjectives that are formed from words that simply indicate direction.

The town where I live, located east of Memphis, is typical of others found in western Tennessee.

MECHANICS

Practice

Capitalization 3

■ Geographic Names
■ Particular Sections of the Country

Write the word or words that should be capitalized in each sentence.

Example: The united states, canada, and mexico have many national parks.

United States, Canada, Mexico

1. One of the most famous parks is yellowstone national park, located in wyoming, idaho, and montana.

2. Just south of yellowstone, on rockefeller parkway, is grand teton national park.

3. The park's string lake is reserved for nonmotorized boats.

4. There are many national parks in the west, but the midwest has some interesting parks, too.

5. Sleeping bear dunes national lakeshore is located on the eastern shore of lake michigan.

6. The appalachian national scenic trail runs from katahdin, maine, to springer mountain in the northern part of georgia.

7. You might see polar bears at wapusk national park in manitoba, canada.

8. Some islands in a national park located on the saint lawrence river in ontario, canada, can be reached only by boat.

9. El chico was the first national park in mexico.

10. Copper canyon in chihuahua, mexico, is deeper than the grand canyon.

Next Step: Use complete sentences to answer the following questions. Be sure to use proper capitalization.

● In what section of the country is your state found?
● What large city is closest to your home?

Capitalization . . .

668.1
First Words

Capitalize the first word of every sentence and the first word in a direct quotation.

> In many families, pets are treated like people, according to an article in the *Kansas City Star*. (sentence)

> Marty Becker, coauthor of *Chicken Soup for the Pet Lover's Soul,* reports, "Seven out of ten people let their pets sleep on the bed." (direct quotation)

> "I get my 15 minutes of fame," he says, "every time I come home." (Notice that *every* is not capitalized because it does not begin a new sentence.)

> "It's like being treated like a rock star," says Becker. "Now I have to tell you that feels pretty good."

Do not capitalize the first word in an indirect quotation.

> Becker says that in the last 10 years, pets have moved out of kennels and basements and into living rooms and bedrooms. (indirect quotation)

668.2
Titles

Capitalize the first word of a title, the last word, and every word in between except articles *(a, an, the),* short prepositions, and coordinating conjunctions. Follow this rule for titles of books, newspapers, magazines, poems, plays, songs, articles, movies, works of art, pictures, stories, and essays. (See **646.3**.)

> *Locked in Time* (book)

> *Boston Globe* (newspaper)

> *Dog Fancy* (magazine)

> "Roses Are Red" (poem)

> *The Phantom of the Opera* (play)

> *Daddy Day Care* (movie)

> "Intuition" (song)

> **Mona Lisa** (work of art)

Practice

Capitalization 4

■ First Words
■ Titles

Number your paper from 1 to 3. As you read the following paragraphs, write the words that should be capitalized in each.

Example: *The Natural History book of dinosaurs says the Tyrannosaurus rex died out 65 million years ago.*
Book   Dinosaurs

1. Because dinosaurs lived long before people, no one really knows how they behaved. for example, scientists have long thought that *Tyrannosaurus rex* was a fierce, meat-eating predator. In the movie *jurassic park,* the *T. rex* chases other dinosaurs and people.

2. Recently, however, Dr. Jack Horner determined that *T. rex* was actually a scavenger. In an article in *national geographic* magazine, Dr. Horner compared the teeth of *T. rex* with those of other hunters. He also studied the dinosaur's leg bones and compared them with those of modern predators. he thinks that *T. rex* could not move fast enough to be a predator. in addition, he points to its tiny arms, which could not hold a struggling animal.

3. Another expert, Dr. Angela Milner, says that more information is needed to be sure that *T. rex* was only a scavenger. here is what we do know: a *T. rex* could grow to be over 40 feet long, stand 15 feet tall, and weigh about 6 tons. would *the mysterious Tyrannosaurus rex* make a good title for a book on this subject?

Next Step: Write a short paragraph about a book, movie, or poem you like. Exchange papers with a classmate. Are first words and titles capitalized correctly?

 **TEKS** 6.20A(i), 6.20A(iii)
ELPS 4C

Capitalization

670.1
Abbreviations

Capitalize abbreviations of titles and organizations.

Dr. (Doctor)   **M.D.** (Doctor of Medicine)

Mr. (Mister)   **UPS** (United Parcel Service)

SADD (Students Against Destructive Decisions)

670.2
Organizations

Capitalize the name of an organization, an association, or a team.

New York State Historical Society   **the Red Cross**

General Motors Corporation   **the Miami Dolphins**

Republicans   **the Democratic Party**

670.3
Letters

Capitalize the letters used to indicate form or shape.

T-shirt   U-turn   A-frame   T-ball

Capitalize	Do Not Capitalize
American	un-American
January, February	winter, spring
Missouri and Ohio Rivers	the rivers Missouri and Ohio
The South is humid in summer.	Turn south at the stop sign.
Duluth Middle School	a Duluth middle school
Governor Bob Taft	Bob Taft, our governor
President Luiz Lula Da Silva	Luiz Lula Da Silva, Brazil's president
Nissan Altima	a Nissan automobile
The planet Earth is egg shaped.	The earth on Grandpa's farm is rich.
I'm taking World Cultures.	I'm taking social studies.

MECHANICS

Practice

Capitalization 5

- **Abbreviations**
- **Organizations**
- **Letters**

Write the words or abbreviations that should be capitalized in each sentence below.

Example: Dad took me to see dr. Zani Patell.
    Dr.

1. The two major political parties in this country are the democrats and the republicans.

2. One of the most successful professional football teams in the country is the Dallas cowboys.

3. When a tornado hits a community, the red Cross sends help.

4. Our new social studies teacher is ms. Kenal.

5. An organization of mothers who try to prevent people from driving after drinking alcohol is called madd.

6. The b-pillar on a car is located right behind the front door.

7. America's space program is run by nasa.

8. The city building code says steel i-beams must be used in new skyscrapers.

9. Some of the biggest companies in the world include GE, ibm, AT&T, and gm.

10. The washing machine repairman replaced an o-ring.

Next Step: Write a paragraph about a teacher you have now. Use an abbreviated title (such as *Ms., Dr.,* and so on) for this person in your paragraph. Check your capitalization.

Plurals . . .

672.1
Most Nouns

The **plurals** of most nouns are formed by adding *s* to the singular.

cheerleader — **cheerleaders**   wheel — **wheels**

bubble — **bubbles**

672.2
Nouns Ending in *ch, sh, s, x,* and *z*

The plural form of nouns ending in *ch, sh, s, x,* and *z* is made by adding *es* to the singular.

lunch — **lunches**   dish — **dishes**   mess — **messes**

buzz — **buzzes**   fox — **foxes**

672.3
Nouns Ending in *o*

The plurals of nouns ending in *o* with a vowel just before the *o* are formed by adding *s*.

radio — **radios**   studio — **studios**   rodeo — **rodeos**

The plurals of most nouns ending in *o* with a consonant just before the *o* are formed by adding *es*.

echo — **echoes**   hero — **heroes**   tomato — **tomatoes**

Exceptions: Musical terms and words of Spanish origin always form plurals by adding *s*.

alto — **altos**   banjo — **banjos**   taco — **tacos**

solo — **solos**   piano — **pianos**   burro — **burros**

672.4
Nouns Ending in *ful*

The plurals of nouns that end with *ful* are formed by adding an *s* at the end of the word.

three platefuls   **six tankfuls**   **four cupfuls**   **five pailfuls**

672.5
Nouns Ending in *f* or *fe*

The plurals of nouns that end in *f* or *fe* are formed in one of two ways: If the final *f* sound is still heard in the plural form of the word, simply add *s*; if the final sound is a *v* sound, change the *f* to *ve* and add *s*.

roof — roofs   **chief — chiefs**   **belief — beliefs**
(plural ends with *f* sound)

wife — wives   **loaf — loaves**   **leaf — leaves**
(plural ends with *v* sound)

Grammar Practice

Plurals 1

- ■ Nouns Ending in *ch, sh, s, x,* and *z*
- ■ Nouns Ending in *o*
- ■ Nouns Ending in *ful*
- ■ Nouns Ending in *f* or *fe*

 For each of the following sentences, write the plural form of the word or words in parentheses.

Example: Tawon and Richard grabbed *(handful)* of popcorn.
handfuls

1. Every fall, as the *(leaf)* change colors, football season begins.

2. People can see the games on their *(television)* or at *(stadium)*, or they can listen to the games on their *(radio)*.

3. At high school and college football games, marching *(band)* play during halftime.

4. At one game, a trumpet player in the band played two *(solo)*.

5. That made him so thirsty that he drank two *(glassful)* of water.

6. A few football *(stadium)*, called domes, have *(roof)*.

7. Some professional football *(player)* are like *(hero)* to their fans.

8. Even when these guys end up with *(helmetful)* of mud and grass, *(echo)* of adoration from their fans can be heard on the field.

9. For many of the *(player)*, their professional *(life)* are rather short—many end up playing for only a few *(year)*.

10. I wonder what some of these men think when they look back on their short *(career)*.

Next Step: Write two sentences about an outdoor activity. Use plurals in your sentences. Then double-check to make sure all the plural words are correct.

ELPS 4C

Plurals

Nouns Ending in _y_

The plurals of common nouns that end in _y_ with a consonant letter just before the _y_ are formed by changing the _y_ to _i_ and adding _es._

    fly — **flies**   baby — **babies**   cavity — **cavities**

The plurals of common nouns that end in _y_ with a vowel before the _y_ are formed by adding only _s._

    key — **keys**   holiday — **holidays**   attorney — **attorneys**

The plurals of proper nouns ending in _y_ are formed by adding _s._

    There are three Circuit Citys in our metro area.

Compound Nouns

The plurals of some compound nouns are formed by adding _s_ or _es_ to the main word in the compound.

    brothers-in-law   maids of honor   secretaries of state

Plurals That Do Not Change

The plurals of some words are the same in singular and plural form.

    deer   sheep   trout   aircraft

Irregular Spelling

Some words (including many foreign words) form a plural by taking on an irregular spelling; others are now acceptable with the commonly used _s_ or _es_ ending.

    child — **children**   woman — **women**   man — **men**

    goose — **geese**   mouse — **mice**   ox — **oxen**

    tooth — **teeth**   octopus — **octopuses** or **octopi**

    index — **indexes** or **indices**

Adding an _'s_

The plurals of letters, figures, symbols, and words discussed as words are formed by adding an apostrophe and an _s._

    Dr. Walters has two Ph.D.'s.

    My dad's license plate has three 2's between two B's.

    You've got too many _but_'s and _so_'s in that sentence.

For information on forming plural possessives, see 652.1.

MECHANICS

Grammar Practice

Plurals 2

- ■ Nouns Ending in *y*
- ■ Compound Nouns
- ■ Plurals That Do Not Change
- ■ Irregular Spelling
- ■ Adding an *'s*

For each of the following sentences, write the plural form of the word or words in parentheses. You may need to use a dictionary.

Example: There are about a dozen *(fish)* in Ashlee's tank.

fish

1. Have you heard the story of Santa and his eight tiny *(reindeer)*?

2. I got one A, three *(B)*, and two *(C)* on my report card.

3. The *(monkey)* escaped from the lab and ran down the *(hallway)*.

4. I have many *(ability)*, but writing *(essay)* is one skill that I definitely need to work on.

5. Nishan broke one of his *(foot)* and chipped two *(tooth)*.

6. A few *(Kennedy)* have held political office.

7. We're not supposed to use any *(&)* or *(#)* in our final papers.

8. Fresh foods do not have *(bar code)* printed on them.

9. Aunt Patti's job is to take customer satisfaction *(survey)* for different *(company)*.

10. It's not uncommon to see *(moose)* in northern Maine.

Learning Language With a partner, think of things that you can identify as singular (zebra) and then as plural (zebras). Have the words relate to the same topic, such as animals you would see in the wild. Practice using these words in a dialogue about your topic. Use as many plural and singular nouns as you can think of from the rules 674.1–674.5.

TEKS 6.20A(i)
ELPS 4C

Abbreviations . . .

676.1
Abbreviations

An **abbreviation** is the shortened form of a word or phrase. The following abbreviations are always acceptable in any kind of writing:

Mr.   **Mrs.**   **Ms.**   **Dr.**   **a.m., p.m.** (A.M., P.M.)

B.C.E. (before the Common Era)   **C.E.** (Common Era)

B.A.   **M.A.**   **Ph.D.**   **M.D.**   **Sr.**   **Jr.**

Caution: Do not abbreviate the names of states, countries, months, days, or units of measure in formal writing. Also, do not use signs or symbols (%, &) in place of words.

Common Abbreviations

AC alternating current	**kg** kilogram	**pd.** paid
a.m. ante meridiem	**km** kilometer	**pg.** (or p.) page
ASAP as soon as possible	**kW** kilowatt	**p.m.** post meridiem
COD cash on delivery	**l** liter	**ppd.** postpaid, prepaid
DA district attorney	**lb.** pound	**qt.** quart
DC direct current	**m** meter	**R.S.V.P.** please reply
etc. and so forth	**M.D.** doctor of medicine	**tbs., tbsp.** tablespoon
F Fahrenheit	**mfg.** manufacturing	**tsp.** teaspoon
FM frequency modulation	**mpg** miles per gallon	**vol.** volume
GNP gross national product	**mph** miles per hour	**vs.** versus
i.e. that is (Latin *id est*)	**oz.** ounce	**yd.** yard

Address Abbreviations

	Standard	Postal		Standard	Postal		Standard	Postal
Avenue	Ave.	AVE	Lake	L.	LK	Route	RT.	RTE
Boulevard	Blvd.	BLVD	Lane	Ln.	LN	South	S.	S
Court	Ct.	CT	North	N.	N	Square	Sq.	SQ
Drive	Dr.	DR	Park	Pk.	PK	Station	Sta.	STA
East	E.	E	Parkway	Pky.	PKY	Street	St.	ST
Expressway	Expy.	EXPY	Place	Pl.	PL	Terrace	Ter.	TER
Heights	Hts.	HTS	Plaza	Plaza	PLZ	Turnpike	Tpke.	TPKE
Highway	Hwy.	HWY	Road	Rd.	RD	West	W.	W

TEKS 6.20A(i)

Grammar Practice

Abbreviations 1

For each of the following sentences, write the correct abbreviation for the underlined word or words.

Example: Last week I talked to <u>Doctor</u> Wesley Brown.
Dr.

1. He earned his <u>doctor of medicine</u> degree from Franklin University.

2. The electric appliances in most homes and apartments use <u>alternating current</u> electricity.

3. Flashlights and other battery-operated items use <u>direct current</u> electricity.

4. This fan will use about one <u>kilowatt</u> of electricity every day.

5. Next week the city will elect a new <u>district attorney</u>.

6. <u>Mister</u> Hawthorn expects his science students to do their best.

7. He asked me to bring in my extra-credit project <u>as soon as possible</u>.

8. Our assignment was to convert 15 degrees <u>Fahrenheit</u> to its metric equivalent.

9. The <u>gross national product</u> of the United States in 2000 was $10.5 trillion.

10. My mom's hybrid car is supposed to get 60 <u>miles per gallon</u>.

11. The top speed for an electric car is 100 <u>miles per hour</u>.

12. Some fast-food places offer 32-<u>ounce</u> soft drinks.

13. The recipe includes a cup of flour, a <u>tablespoon</u> of cinnamon, and a <u>teaspoon</u> of salt.

Next Step: Write the words for these postal abbreviations: AVE, CT, EXPY, and RD. Now write the postal abbreviations for your own state. Write directions from your home to a location near you. Use the abbreviations appropriately.

MECHANICS

 **TEKS** 6.20A(ii)
ELPS 4C

Abbreviations

678.1
Acronyms

An **acronym** is an abbreviation that can be pronounced as a word. It does not require periods.

WHO — World Health Organization   **ROM** — read-only memory

FAQ — frequently asked question

678.2
Initialisms

An **initialism** is similar to an acronym except that it cannot be pronounced as a word; the initials are pronounced individually.

PBS — Public Broadcasting Service

BLM — Bureau of Land Management

WNBA — Women's National Basketball Association

Common Acronyms and Initialisms

ACLU	American Civil Liberties Union	**ORV**	off-road vehicle
CETA	Comprehensive Employment and Training Act	**OSHA**	Occupational Safety and Health Administration
CIA	Central Intelligence Agency	**PAC**	political action committee
FAA	Federal Aviation Administration	**PIN**	personal identification number
FBI	Federal Bureau of Investigation	**PSA**	public service announcement
FCC	Federal Communications Commission	**ROTC**	Reserve Officers' Training Corps
FDA	Food and Drug Administration	**SADD**	Students Against Destructive Decisions
FDIC	Federal Deposit Insurance Corporation	**SSA**	Social Security Administration
FHA	Federal Housing Administration	**SUV**	sport-utility vehicle
FTC	Federal Trade Commission	**SWAT**	special weapons and tactics
HTML	Hypertext Markup Language	**TDD**	telecommunications device for the deaf
IRS	Internal Revenue Service	**TMJ**	temporomandibular joint
MADD	Mothers Against Drunk Driving	**TVA**	Tennessee Valley Authority
NAFTA	North American Free Trade Agreement	**VA**	Veterans Administration
NASA	National Aeronautics and Space Administration	**VISTA**	Volunteers in Service to America
NATO	North Atlantic Treaty Organization	**WAC**	Women's Army Corps
OEO	Office of Economic Opportunity	**WAVES**	Women Accepted for Volunteer Emergency Service
OEP	Office of Emergency Preparedness		

TEKS 6.20A(ii)
ELPS 3E

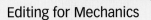

Grammar Practice

Abbreviations 2

- ■ Acronyms
- ■ Initialisms

Number your paper from 1 to 15. For each name or phrase on the left, write the letter of the abbreviation on the right that matches it.

1. all-terrain vehicle

2. telecommunications device for the deaf

3. magnetic resonance imaging

4. special weapons and tactics

5. Federal Bureau of Investigation

6. computer-aided design

7. World Health Organization

8. parental guidance

9. North Atlantic Treaty Organization

10. light amplification by stimulated emission of radiation

11. Organization of Petroleum Exporting Countries

12. personal identification number

13. master of business administration

14. attention deficit disorder

15. certified public accountant

A. ADD

B. ATV

C. CAD

D. CPA

E. FBI

F. LASER

G. MBA

H. MRI

I. NATO

J. OPEC

K. PG

L. PIN

M. SWAT

N. TDD

O. WHO

Next Step: Make up an organization name that can be abbreviated as an acronym. Share your new abbreviation—and what it stands for—with the class.

MECHANICS

Numbers . . .

680.1
Numbers Under 10

Numbers from one to nine are usually written as words; all numbers 10 and over are usually written as numerals.

two   seven   nine   10   25   106

680.2
Numerals Only

Use numerals to express any of the following forms:

money $2.39

decimals 26.2

percentages . . . . .8 percent

chapters . . . . .chapter 7

pages . . . . pages 287–289

time (with "a.m." or "p.m.") . . . . .4:30 p.m.

telephone numbers 1-800-555-1212

dates . . . . .44 B.C.E.; July 6, 1942

identification numbers . . . . .Highway 36

addresses . . . . 2125 Cairn Road

ZIP codes 60004

statistics . . . . .a vote of 23 to 4

When abbreviations and symbols are used (for instance, in science or math), always use numerals with them.

12° C   7%   33 kg   9 cm   55 mph

680.3
Very Large Numbers

You may use a combination of numerals and words for very large numbers.

Of the 17 million residents of the three Midwestern states, only 1.3 million are blondes.

You may spell out a large number that can be written as two words. If more than two words are needed, use the numeral.

More than nine thousand people attended the concert.

About 3,500 people missed the opening act.

Grammar Practice

Numbers 1

- ■ Numbers Under 10
- ■ Numerals Only
- ■ Very Large Numbers

Each sentence below has a choice of how a number should be written. Write the answers that make the sentences correct.

Example: There are *(eight, 8)* planets in our solar system.

    nine

1. The sun is one of more than *(100 billion, 100,000,000,000)* stars in our galaxy.

2. The sun's diameter is *(one million three hundred ninety thousand, 1.39 million)* kilometers.

3. The sun contains more than *(99 percent, ninety-nine percent)* of the total mass of the solar system.

4. Is Earth about *(4 billion, 4,000,000,000)* years old?

5. While Mars has *(two, 2)* moons, Earth has only *(one, 1)*.

6. On July *(twentieth, 20)*, 1969, the first humans landed on the moon.

7. Just six hours after *Apollo 11* landed at *(4:17, four-seventeen)* p.m. eastern daylight time, the astronauts stepped onto the moon's surface.

8. That summer, you could buy a model of *Apollo 11* for only $*(2.50, two-fifty)*.

9. The last astronauts to land on the moon were those in *Apollo 17* in December *(nineteen seventy-two, 1972)*.

Next Step: Use complete sentences to ask and answer the following questions with another student. Use numbers correctly.

- ● On what day and in what year were you born?
- ● What time is it right now?

MECHANICS

Numbers

682.1
Comparing Numbers

If you are comparing two or more numbers in a sentence, write all of them the same way: as numerals or as words.

Students from 9 to 14 years old are invited.

Students from nine to fourteen years old are invited.

682.2
Numbers in Compound Modifiers

A compound modifier may include a numeral.

The floorboards come in 10-foot lengths.

When a number comes before a compound modifier that includes a numeral, use words instead of numerals.

We need five 10-foot lengths to finish the floor.

Ms. Brown must grade twenty 12-page reports.

682.3
Sentence Beginnings

Use words, not numerals, to begin a sentence.

Nine students had turned in their homework. Fourteen students said they were unable to finish the assignment.

682.4
Time and Money

When time or money is expressed with a symbol, use numerals. When either is expressed with words, spell out the number.

6:00 a.m. (or) **six o'clock**

$25 (or) **twenty-five dollars**

SCHOOL DAZE

Jerry, haven't you finished your paper yet?

No, it's not due until **three o'clock**, and Mrs. Wright told me to add a few new twists and wrinkles.

Grammar Practice

Numbers 2

■ Comparing Numbers

Rewrite the underlined parts of the following sentences so that they are correct.

Example: Depending on which staircase I use, I have to climb eight or 11 stairs on my way to our apartment.

8 or 11 (or) *eight or eleven*

1. The renters of the top-floor apartment sometimes have five to 15 guests at once.

2. The children in that apartment are from nine to 18 years old.

3. Apartments may have from two to 10 windows.

4. They usually have nine to 20 electrical outlets.

5. Our building has seven furnished and 11 unfurnished units.

■ Sentence Beginnings
■ Time and Money

Rewrite the following sentences so that the numbers are correct.

Example: 9 apartments will be rented for 825 dollars per month.

Nine apartments will be rented for $825 per month.

1. The manager has agreed to show the apartment at eight p.m. tonight.

2. 60 people have already called about the new apartment complex.

3. Some people are interested in the smaller units renting for $6 hundred a month.

4. Three apartments were rented by 9 o'clock this morning.

5. 20 units remain available for rent.

TEKS 6.21

Improving Spelling

684.1
i* before *e

Write *i* before *e* except after *c*, or when sounded like *a* as in *neighbor* and *weigh*.

Some Exceptions to the Rule: *counterfeit, either, financier, foreign, height, heir, leisure, neither, science, seize, sheik, species, their, weird.*

684.2
Silent *e*

If a word ends with a silent *e*, drop the *e* before adding a suffix that begins with a vowel. There are exceptions, for example, *knowledgeable* and *changeable.*

state—stating—statement   use—using—useful
like—liking—likeness

NOTE You do not drop the *e* when the suffix begins with a consonant. Exceptions include *truly, argument,* and *ninth.*

684.3
Words Ending in *y*

When *y* is the last letter in a word and the *y* comes just after a consonant, change the *y* to *i* before adding any suffix except those beginning with *i*.

fry—fries—frying   happy—happiness
hurry—hurried—hurrying   beauty—beautiful
lady—ladies

When forming the plural of a word that ends with a *y* that comes just after a vowel, add *s*.

toy—toys   play—plays   monkey—monkeys

684.4
Consonant Endings

When a one-syllable word ends in a consonant (*bat*) preceded by one vowel (*ba̱t*), double the final consonant before adding a suffix that begins with a vowel (*ba̱tting*).

sum—summary   god—goddess

When a multisyllable word ends in a consonant preceded by one vowel (*control*), the accent is on the last syllable (*contról*), and the suffix begins with a vowel (*ing*)—the same rule holds true: double the final consonant (*contro̱lling*).

prefer—preferred   begin—beginning

Practice

Spelling 1

- *i* before *e*
- Silent *e*

If the underlined word is spelled correctly, write "correct." If it is spelled incorrectly, spell the word the right way.

Example: Jorge's family enjoys <u>dineing</u> out now and then.
> *dining*

1. Jorge can't hide his <u>excitment</u> at seeing flan on the menu.
2. He likes <u>useing</u> lots of chocolate sauce on his dessert.
3. Jorge says he could eat <u>nineteen</u> scoops of chocolate.
4. We don't <u>beleive</u> that's possible.
5. But Jorge's best <u>friend</u> saw him eat that much once.
6. We're surprised he doesn't gain a lot of <u>wieght</u>!

- Words Ending in *y*
- Consonant Endings

If the underlined word is spelled correctly, write "correct." If it is spelled incorrectly, spell the word the right way.

Example: Buses are an important means of transportation in many <u>cityes</u>.
> *cities*

1. Although buses must stop often, they always seem to be <u>hurrying</u> along city streets.
2. During the evening, some routes are <u>omited</u> from the schedule.
3. On most <u>holidaies</u>, buses run on a reduced schedule.
4. One passenger was <u>carriing</u> four bags of <u>groceries</u> on a bus.
5. When he asked if he was on the right bus, the driver <u>refered</u> him to another bus route.

Practice

Spelling 2

- ■ *i* before *e*
- ■ Silent *e*

Find the misspelled word or words in each sentence and write the words the right way.

Example: The largeest state in the union is Alaska.

largest

1. Hawaii recieves the most rainfall of all the states, so umbrellas are quite usful for its residents.

2. Niether Connecticut nor Delaware is the smallest state.

3. In Wyoming, Yellowstone Park is part of an anceint volcano.

4. Ohio and New York are loseing many older people who prefer liveing in warmer states like Florida or Arizona.

- ■ Words Ending in *y*
- ■ Consonant Endings

If the underlined word is spelled correctly, write "correct." If it is spelled incorrectly, spell the word the right way.

Example: The mountains and <u>valleies</u> in the Smoky Mountains of Tennessee attract tourists.

valleys

1. A volcanic explosion, which <u>occured</u> a long time ago, formed Crater Lake in Oregon.

2. Squirrels <u>burying</u> nuts are a common sight in the Midwestern states of Iowa and Missouri.

3. In North Dakota, you can see jackrabbits <u>hoping</u> across the fields.

4. The new governor of California is <u>planing</u> next year's budget.

5. The warm sun on the plains of Montana <u>dryed</u> our rain-soaked tent.

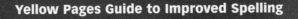

TEKS 6.21

Yellow Pages Guide to Improved Spelling

Be patient. Becoming a good speller takes time.

Check your spelling by using a dictionary or list of commonly misspelled words (like the list that follows). When using a computer, you can use the spell-check option in addition to word lists or a dictionary.

Learn the correct pronunciation of each word you are trying to spell. Knowing the correct pronunciation of a word will help you remember how it's spelled.

Look up the meaning of each word as you are checking the dictionary for pronunciation. (Knowing how to spell a word is of little use if you don't know what it means.)

Practice spelling the word before you close the dictionary. Look away from the page and try to see the word in your mind's eye. Write the word on a piece of paper. Check the spelling in the dictionary and repeat the process until you are able to spell the word correctly.

Keep a list of the words that you misspell.

Write often. As noted educator Frank Smith said, "There is little point in learning to spell if you have little intention of writing."

A

	account	after	almost
	accurate	afternoon	already
	accustom (ed)	afterward	although
abbreviate	ache	again	altogether
aboard	achieve (ment)	against	aluminum
about	acre	agreeable	always
above	across	agree (ment)	amateur
absence	actual	ah	ambulance
absent	adapt	aid	amendment
absolute (ly)	addition (al)	airy	among
abundance	address	aisle	amount
accelerate	adequate	alarm	analyze
accident	adjust (ment)	alcohol	ancient
accidental (ly)	admire	alike	angel
accompany	adventure	alive	anger
accomplice	advertise (ment)	alley	angle
accomplish	advertising	allowance	angry
according	afraid	all right	animal

anniversary
announce
annoyance
annual
anonymous
another
answer
Antarctic
anticipate
anxiety
anxious
anybody
anyhow
anyone
anything
anyway
anywhere
apartment
apiece
apologize
apparent (ly)
appeal
appearance
appetite
appliance
application
appointment
appreciate
approach
appropriate
approval
approximate
architect
Arctic
aren't
argument
arithmetic
around
arouse
arrange (ment)
arrival
article
artificial

asleep
assassin
assign (ment)
assistance
associate
association
assume
athlete
athletic
attach
attack (ed)
attempt
attendance
attention
attitude
attorney
attractive
audience
August
author
authority
automobile
autumn
available
avenue
average
awful (ly)
awkward

B

baggage
baking
balance
balloon
ballot
banana
bandage
bankrupt
barber
bargain
barrel

basement
basis
basket
battery
beautiful
beauty
because
become
becoming
before
began
beggar
beginning
behave
behavior
being
belief
believe
belong
beneath
benefit (ed)
between
bicycle
biscuit
blackboard
blanket
blizzard
bother
bottle
bottom
bough
bought
bounce
boundary
breakfast
breast
breath (n.)
breathe (v.)
breeze
bridge
brief
bright
brilliant

brother
brought
bruise
bubble
bucket
buckle
budget
building
bulletin
buoyant
bureau
burglar
bury
business
busy
button

C

cabbage
cafeteria
calendar
campaign
canal
cancel (ed)
candidate
candle
canister
cannon
cannot
canoe
can't
canyon
capacity
captain
carburetor
cardboard
career
careful
careless
carpenter
carriage

carrot
cashier
casserole
casualty
catalog
catastrophe
catcher
caterpillar
catsup
ceiling
celebration
cemetery
census
century
certain (ly)
certificate
challenge
champion
changeable
character (istic)
chief
children
chimney
chocolate
choice
chorus
circumstance
citizen
civilization
classmates
classroom
climate
climb
closet
clothing
coach
cocoa
cocoon
coffee
collar
college
colonel
color

colossal
column
comedy
coming
commercial
commission
commit
commitment
committed
committee
communicate
community
company
comparison
competition
competitive (ly)
complain
complete (ly)
complexion
compromise
conceive
concerning
concert
concession
concrete
condemn
condition
conductor
conference
confidence
congratulate
connect
conscience
conscious
conservative
constitution
continue
continuous
control
controversy
convenience
convince
coolly

cooperate
corporation
correspond
cough
couldn't
counter
counterfeit
country
county
courage
courageous
court
courteous
courtesy
cousin
coverage
cozy
cracker
cranky
crawl
creditor
cried
criticize
cruel
crumb
crumble
cupboard
curiosity
curious
current
custom
customer
cylinder

D

daily
dairy
damage
danger (ous)
daughter
dealt

deceive
decided
decision
declaration
decorate
defense
definite (ly)
definition
delicious
dependent
depot
describe
description
desert
deserve
design
desirable
despair
dessert
deteriorate
determine
develop (ment)
device (n.)
devise (v.)
diamond
diaphragm
diary
dictionary
difference
different
difficulty
dining
diploma
director
disagreeable
disappear
disappoint
disapprove
disastrous
discipline
discover
discuss
discussion

SPELLING

disease
dissatisfied
distinguish
distribute
divide
divine
divisible
division
doctor
doesn't
dollar
dormitory
doubt
dough
dual
duplicate

eager (ly)
economy
edge
edition
efficiency
eight
eighth
either
elaborate
electricity
elephant
eligible
ellipse
embarrass
emergency
emphasize
employee
employment
enclose
encourage
engineer
enormous
enough

entertain
enthusiastic
entirely
entrance
envelop (v.)
envelope (n.)
environment
equipment
equipped
equivalent
escape
especially
essential
establish
every
evidence
exaggerate
exceed
excellent
except
exceptional (ly)
excite
exercise
exhaust (ed)
exhibition
existence
expect
expensive
experience
explain
explanation
expression
extension
extinct
extraordinary
extreme (ly)

facilities
familiar
family

famous
fascinate
fashion
fatigue (d)
faucet
favorite
feature
February
federal
fertile
field
fierce
fiery
fifty
finally
financial (ly)
foliage
forcible
foreign
forfeit
formal (ly)
former (ly)
forth
fortunate
forty
forward
fountain
fourth
fragile
freight
friend (ly)
frighten
fulfill
fundamental
further
furthermore

gadget
gauge
generally

generous
genius
gentle
genuine
geography
ghetto
ghost
gnaw
government
governor
graduation
grammar
grateful
grease
grief
grocery
grudge
gruesome
guarantee
guard
guardian
guess
guidance
guide
guilty
gymnasium

H

hammer
handkerchief
handle (d)
handsome
haphazard
happen
happiness
harass
hastily
having
hazardous
headache
height

hemorrhage
hesitate
history
hoarse
holiday
honor
hoping
hopping
horrible
hospital
humorous
hurriedly
hydraulic
hygiene
hymn

icicle
identical
illegible
illiterate
illustrate
imaginary
imaginative
imagine
imitation
immediate (ly)
immense
immigrant
immortal
impatient
importance
impossible
improvement
inconvenience
incredible
indefinitely
independence
independent
individual
industrial

inferior
infinite
inflammable
influential
initial
initiation
innocence
innocent
installation
instance
instead
insurance
intelligence
intention
interested
interesting
interfere
interpret
interrupt
interview
investigate
invitation
irrigate
island
issue

jealous (y)
jewelry
journal
journey
judgment
juicy

kitchen
knew
knife
knives

knock
knowledge
knuckles

L

label
laboratory
ladies
language
laugh
laundry
lawyer
league
lecture
legal
legible
legislature
leisure
length
liable
library
license
lieutenant
lightning
likable
likely
liquid
listen
literature
living
loaves
loneliness
loose
lose
loser
losing
lovable
lovely

M

machinery
magazine
magnificent
maintain
majority
making
manual
manufacture
marriage
material
mathematics
maximum
mayor
meant
measure
medicine
medium
message
mileage
miniature
minimum
minute
mirror
miscellaneous
mischievous
miserable
missile
misspell
moisture
molecule
monotonous
monument
mortgage
mountain
muscle
musician
mysterious

SPELLING

N

naive
natural (ly)
necessary
negotiate
neighbor (hood)
neither
nickel
niece
nineteen
nineteenth
ninety
ninth
noisy
noticeable
nuclear
nuisance

O

obedience
obey
obstacle
occasion
occasional (ly)
occur
occurred
offense
official
often
omission
omitted
operate
opinion
opponent
opportunity
opposite
ordinarily
original
outrageous

P

package
paid
pamphlet
paradise
paragraph
parallel
paralyze
parentheses
partial
participant
participate
particular (ly)
pasture
patience
peculiar
people
perhaps
permanent
perpendicular
persistent
personal (ly)
personnel
perspiration
persuade
phase
physician
piece
pitcher
planned
plateau
playwright
pleasant
pleasure
pneumonia
politician
possess
possible
practical (ly)
prairie
precede
precious

precise (ly)
precision
preferable
preferred
prejudice
preparation
presence
previous
primitive
principal
principle
prisoner
privilege
probably
procedure
proceed
professor
prominent
pronounce
pronunciation
protein
psychology
pumpkin
pure

Q

quarter
questionnaire
quiet
quite
quotient

R

raise
realize
really
receipt
receive
received

recipe
recognize
recommend
reign
relieve
religious
remember
repetition
representative
reservoir
resistance
respectfully
responsibility
restaurant
review
rhyme
rhythm
ridiculous
route

S

safety
salad
salary
sandwich
satisfactory
Saturday
scene
scenery
schedule
science
scissors
scream
screen
season
secretary
seize
sensible
sentence
separate
several

TEKS 6.21

sheriff
shining
similar
since
sincere (ly)
skiing
sleigh
soldier
souvenir
spaghetti
specific
sphere
sprinkle
squeeze
squirrel
statue
stature
statute
stomach
stopped
straight
strength
stretched
studying
subtle
succeed
success
sufficient
summarize
supplement
suppose
surely
surprise
syllable
sympathy
symptom

 T

tariff
technique
temperature
temporary
terrible
territory
thankful
theater
their
there
therefore
thief
thorough (ly)
though
throughout
tired
tobacco
together
tomorrow
tongue
touch
tournament
toward
tragedy
treasurer
tried
tries
trouble
truly
Tuesday
typical

U

unconscious
unfortunate (ly)
unique
university
unnecessary
until
usable
useful
using
usual (ly)
utensil

 V

vacation
vacuum
valuable
variety
various
vegetable
vehicle
very
vicinity
view
villain
violence
visible
visitor
voice
volume
voluntary
volunteer

 W

wander
wasn't
weather
Wednesday
weigh
weird
welcome
welfare
whale
where
whether
which
whole
wholly
whose
width
women
worthwhile
wouldn't
wreckage
writing
written

 Y

yellow
yesterday
yield

SPELLING

TEKS 6.21
ELPS 4C, 5B

Using the Right Word

694.1
a, an

A is used before words that begin with a consonant sound; *an* is used before words that begin with any vowel sound except long "u."

a heap, a cat, an idol, an elephant, an honor, a historian, an umbrella, a unicorn

694.2
accept, except

The verb *accept* means "to receive"; the preposition *except* means "other than."

Melissa graciously accepted defeat. (verb)

All the boys except Zach were here. (preposition)

694.3
affect, effect

Affect is almost always a verb; it means "to influence." *Effect* can be a verb, but it is most often used as a noun that means "the result."

How does population growth affect us?

What are the effects of population growth?

694.4
allowed, aloud

The verb *allowed* means "permitted" or "let happen"; *aloud* is an adverb that means "in a normal voice."

We aren't allowed to read aloud in the library.

694.5
allusion, illusion

An *allusion* is a brief reference to or hint of something (person, place, thing, or idea). An *illusion* is a false impression or idea.

The Great Dontini, a magician, made an allusion to Houdini as he created the illusion of sawing his assistant in half.

694.6
a lot

A lot is not one word, but two; it is a general descriptive phrase meaning "plenty." (It should be avoided in formal writing.)

694.7
all right

All right is not one word, but two; it is a phrase meaning "satisfactory" or "okay." (Please note, the following *are* spelled correctly: *always, altogether, already, almost.*)

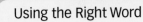

TEKS 6.21
ELPS 5B

Grammar Practice

Using the Right Word 1

■ a, an; accept, except; affect, effect; allowed, aloud

For each of the following sentences, write a word from the list above to fill in the blank.

Example: Louis Braille had _____ accident that left him blind when he was three years old.

an

1. At the school he attended, everyone _____ Louis Braille could see.

2. Not being able to read can _____ anyone's life dramatically.

3. Louis Braille was _____ to become a teacher in 1926, when he was only 15 years old.

4. He created _____ alphabet of raised dots to make teaching easier.

5. It was _____ marvelous invention.

6. These dots _____ a blind person to read and write.

7. The Braille alphabet had quite an _____ on the blind population.

8. Most sight-impaired students _____ the challenge of learning the Braille system.

9. Today, people can also hear many books read _____ on cassettes or CD's.

10. This has had an _____ on my mom (who is not blind) because now she can "read" while driving her car!

Next Step: Write a brief paragraph about learning a new skill. Use the words *a lot* and *all right* correctly.

RIGHT WORD

TEKS 6.21
ELPS 4C, 5B

696.1
already,
all ready

Already is an adverb that tells when. *All ready* is a phrase meaning "completely ready."

We have already eaten breakfast; now we are all ready for school.

696.2
altogether,
all together

Altogether is always an adverb meaning "completely."
All together is used to describe people or things that are gathered in one place at one time.

Ms. Monces held her baton in the air and said, "Okay, class, all together now: sing!"

Unfortunately, there was altogether too much street noise for us to hear her.

696.3
among, between

Among is used when speaking of more than two persons or things. *Between* is used when speaking of only two.

The three friends talked among themselves as they tried to choose between trumpet or trombone lessons.

696.4
amount, number

Amount is used to describe things that you cannot count. *Number* is used when you can actually count the persons or things.

The amount of interest in playing the tuba is shown by the number of kids learning to play the instrument.

696.5
annual,
biannual,
semiannual,
biennial,
perennial

An *annual* event happens once every year. A *biannual* (or *semiannual*) event happens twice a year. A *biennial* event happens once every two years. A *perennial* event happens year after year.

The annual PTA rummage sale is so successful that it will now be a semiannual event.

The neighbor has some wonderful perennial flowers.

696.6
ant, aunt

An *ant* is an insect. An *aunt* is a female relative (the sister of a person's mother or father).

My aunt is an entomologist, a scientist who studies ants and other insects.

696.7
ascent, assent

Ascent is the act of rising or climbing; *assent* is agreement.

After the group's ascent of five flights of stairs to the meeting room, plans for elevator repairs met with quick assent.

TEKS 6.21
ELPS 5B

Grammar Practice

Using the Right Word 2

■ already, all ready; altogether, all together; among, between; amount, number; ant, aunt

For each of the following sentences, write the correct choice from each set of words in parentheses.

Example: We *(already, all ready)* have plans for the holiday.

> *already*

1. Every Memorial Day my family meets at my *(ant's, aunt's)* house for a family picnic.

2. Many members of the family *(all ready, already)* live in the same town she lives in.

3. When the out-of-town people arrive, there are 53 of us *(all together, altogether)*.

4. Last year, as we were *(all ready, already)* to start eating our food, a large *(amount, number)* of *(ants, aunts)* invaded the picnic area.

5. The family was *(all together, altogether)* disappointed in that year's picnic.

6. As the adults talked *(among, between)* themselves, I heard them say we should get together more often.

7. All my cousins expressed a strong *(amount, number)* of interest when they heard this idea.

8. Maybe we can squeeze in another family gathering sometime *(among, between)* Independence Day and Labor Day.

Next Step: Write three sentences that show your understanding of these words: *amount, among,* and *between.*

RIGHT WORD

698.1
bare, bear

The adjective *bare* means "naked." A *bear* is a large, heavy animal with shaggy hair.

> **Despite his bare feet, the man chased the polar bear across the snow.**

The verb *bear* means "to put up with" or "to carry."

> **Dwayne could not bear another of his older brother's lectures.**

698.2
base, bass

Base is the foundation or the lower part of something. *Bass* (pronounced like "base") is a deep sound or tone.

> **The stereo speakers are on a base so solid that even the loudest bass tones don't rattle it.**

Bass (rhymes with "mass") is a fish.

> **Jim hooked a record-setting bass, but it got away . . . so he says.**

698.3
beat, beet

The verb *beat* means "to strike, to defeat," and the noun *beat* is a musical term for rhythm or tempo. A *beet* is a carrot-like vegetable (often red).

> **The beat of the drum in the marching band encouraged the fans to cheer on the team. After they beat West High's team four games to one, many team members were as red as a beet.**

698.4
berth, birth

Berth is a space or compartment. *Birth* is the process of being born.

> **We pulled aside the curtain in our train berth to view the birth of a new day outside our window.**

698.5
beside, besides

Beside means "by the side of." *Besides* means "in addition to."

> **Besides a flashlight, Kedar likes to keep his pet boa beside his bed at night.**

698.6
billed, build

Billed means either "to be given a bill" or "to have a beak." The verb *build* means "to construct."

> **We asked the carpenter to build us a birdhouse. She billed us for time and materials.**

698.7
blew, blue

Blew is the past tense of "blow." *Blue* is a color and is also used to mean "feeling low in spirits."

> **As the wind blew out the candles in the dark blue room, I felt more blue than ever.**

TEKS 6.21
ELPS 5B

Grammar Practice

Using the Right Word 3

■ bare, bear; base, bass; beat, beet; billed, build; blew, blue

 For each pair of words in parentheses below, write the line number and the correct choice.

Example: 1   The city decided to *(billed, build)* a skateboard
2   park near the baseball diamond.

1 build

1   In 1958, ocean surfers became frustrated by small waves

2 and bad weather. They couldn't *(bare, bear)* being off their boards

3 for long, so they took to the streets with skateboards. Soon

4 skateboarding became a craze on the West Coast.

5   The first contest to see who could *(beat, beet)* all the other

6 competitors was held in Hermosa, California, in 1963. Some guided

7 their skateboards with their *(bare, bear)* feet, but most wore gym

8 shoes. However, it would be almost 10 years before boarders could

9 *(billed, build)* up the sport's popularity nationwide. By this time,

10 better wheels and trucks (the metal parts that hold the wheels to

11 the board) made jumps and other tricks possible. Skateboarders

12 now seemed to sail right into the *(blew, blue)* sky as their boards

13 climbed up specially built, steep walls.

14   A strong *(base, bass)* of support among the real competitors

15 kept the sport going. In 2003, skateboarding *(blew, blue)* past

16 artificial wall climbing and paintball to become the fastest growing

17 extreme sport in the country.

Next Step: Write three sentences that show your understanding of these words: *bare, billed,* and *bass.*

RIGHT WORD

700.1
board, bored

A *board* is a piece of wood. *Board* also means "a group or council that helps run an organization."

The school board approved the purchase of 50 pine boards for the woodworking classes.

Bored means "to become weary or tired of something." It can also mean "made a hole by drilling."

Dulé bored a hole in the ice and dropped in a fishing line.
Waiting and waiting for a bite bored him.

700.2
borrow, lend

Borrow means "to *receive* for temporary use." *Lend* means "to *give* for temporary use."

I asked Mom, "May I borrow $15 for a CD?"

She said, "I can lend you $15 until next Friday."

700.3
brake, break

A *brake* is a device used to stop a vehicle. The verb *break* means "to split, crack, or destroy"; as a noun, *break* means "gap or interruption."

After the brake on my bike failed, I took a break to fix it so I wouldn't break a bone.

700.4
bring, take

Use *bring* when the action is moving toward the speaker; use *take* when the action is moving away from the speaker.

Grandpa asked me to take the garbage out and bring him today's paper.

700.5
by, buy, bye

By is a preposition meaning "near" or "not later than." *Buy* is a verb meaning "to purchase."

By tomorrow I hope to buy tickets for the final match of the tournament.

Bye is the position of being automatically advanced to the next tournament round without playing.

Our soccer team received a bye because of our winning record.

700.6
can, may

Can means "able to," while *may* means "permitted to."

"Can I go to the library?"

(This actually means "Are my mind and body strong enough to get me there?")

"May I go?"

(This means "Do I have your permission to go?")

punctuate *edit* *capitalize*
SPELL
improve
701

 TEKS 6.21

Using the Right Word

Grammar Practice

Using the Right Word 4

■ board, bored; brake, break; bring, take; by, buy; can, may

 For each numbered sentence below, write the word "correct" if the underlined word is used correctly. If it is incorrect, write the right word.

Example: A tornado can drive a <u>bored</u> into a tree.

board

(1) A tornado is a powerful, twisting windstorm that <u>can</u> destroy just about anything in its path. **(2)** A tornado will easily <u>brake</u> a wooden house into many pieces. **(3)** A tornado <u>takes</u> destruction wherever it touches down.

(4) <u>Buy</u> the time a storm has passed, relief workers are on their way to the scene. **(5)** Usually, only residents or relief workers <u>may</u> enter an area damaged by a tornado.

 For each of the following sentences, write the correct choice from each set of words in parentheses.

Example: An elevator has a special *(break, brake)* to prevent accidents.

brake

1. Would you please *(bring, take)* that garbage out to the dumpster?

2. Dad, *(can, may)* I use your set of wrenches?

3. Leander plans to *(by, buy)* a new CD next week.

4. Someone bumped the table, causing the glass to *(brake, break)*.

5. Pablo has to walk *(by, buy)* an abandoned building every day.

6. Mrs. Serbins said we *(can, may)* stay inside for recess today.

7. Johar is always complaining that he is *(board, bored)* and has nothing to do.

8. Felipe said, "Please *(bring, take)* me a glass of water."

RIGHT WORD

702.1
canvas, canvass

Canvas is a heavy cloth; *canvass* means "ask people for votes or opinions."

Our old canvas tent leaks.

Someone with a clipboard is canvassing the neighborhood.

702.2
capital, capitol

Capital can be either a noun, referring to a city or to money, or an adjective, meaning "major or important." *Capitol* is used only when talking about a building.

The capitol building is in the capital city for a capital (major) reason: The city government contributed the capital (money) for the building project.

702.3
cell, sell

Cell means "a small room" or "a small unit of life basic to all plants and animals." *Sell* is a verb meaning "to give up for a price."

Today we looked at a human skin cell under a microscope.

Let's sell those old bicycles at the rummage sale.

702.4
cent, sent, scent

Cent (1/100 of a dollar) is a coin; *sent* is the past tense of the verb "send"; *scent* is an odor or a smell.

After our car hit a skunk, we sent our friends a postcard that said, "One cent doesn't go far, but skunk scent seems to last forever."

702.5
chord, cord

Chord may mean "an emotion or a feeling," but it is more often used to mean "the sound of three or more musical tones played at the same time." A *cord* is a string or rope.

The band struck a chord at the exact moment the mayor pulled the cord on the drape covering the new statue.

702.6
chose, choose

Chose (chōz) is the past tense of the verb *choose* (cho͞oz).

This afternoon Mom chose tacos and hot sauce; this evening she will choose an antacid.

702.7
coarse, course

Coarse means "rough or crude." *Course* means "a path" or "a class or series of studies."

In our cooking course, we learned to use coarse salt and freshly ground pepper in salads.

TEKS 6.21
ELPS 5B

Grammar Practice

Using the Right Word 5

■ capital, capitol; cell, sell; sent, scent; chose, choose;
coarse, course

For each of the following sentences, write the correct choice from each set of words in parentheses.

Example: Carlos's Coffee Shops *(sell, cell)* the world's best breakfast burritos.

sell

1. If I had lots of *(capital, capitol)* to spend, I'd buy a big-screen TV.

2. Is your state's *(capital, capitol)* building located on the highest ground in your *(capital, capitol)* city?

3. Johnson City's old jailhouse, which had only three *(cells, sells),* is now a small restaurant.

4. Rigid walls surround the *(cells, sells)* of most plants, bacteria, fungi, and algae.

5. Reggie's older sister is taking a creative writing *(course, coarse)* at the community center.

6. We often smell the *(sent, scent)* from the Bread Factory drifting up to our second-floor apartment.

7. I even *(sent, scent)* my cousin Cade an e-mail to tell him how good it smells!

8. On Monday, Rhea *(chose, choose)* to color her hair pink, but tomorrow she may *(chose, choose)* to make it bright green.

9. Did Leroy and Tamra use fine or *(course, coarse)* sandpaper to make the sand dunes for their geography project?

Next Step: Write four sentences that show your understanding of the following words: *choose, scent, capitol,* and *sell.*

RIGHT WORD

TEKS 6.21
ELPS 4C, 5B

704.1 complement, compliment

Complement means "to complete or go with." *Compliment* is an expression of admiration or praise.

Aunt Athena said, "Your cheese sauce really complements this cauliflower!"

"Thank you for the compliment," I replied.

704.2 continual, continuous

Continual refers to something that happens again and again; *continuous* refers to something that doesn't stop happening.

Sunlight hits Peoria, Iowa, on a continual basis; but sunlight hits the earth continuously.

704.3 counsel, council

When used as a noun, *counsel* means "advice"; when used as a verb, *counsel* means "to advise." *Council* refers to a group that advises.

The student council asked for counsel from its trusted adviser.

704.4 creak, creek

A *creak* is a squeaking sound; a *creek* is a stream.

I heard a creak from the old dock under my feet as I fished in the creek.

704.5 cymbal, symbol

A *cymbal* is a metal instrument shaped like a plate. A *symbol* is something (usually visible) that stands for or represents another thing or idea (usually invisible).

The damaged cymbal lying on the stage was a symbol of the band's final concert.

704.6 dear, deer

Dear means "loved or valued"; *deer* are animals.

My dear, old great-grandmother leaves corn and salt licks in her yard to attract deer.

704.7 desert, dessert

A *desert* is a barren wilderness. *Dessert* is a food served at the end of a meal.

In the desert, cold water is more inviting than even the richest dessert.

The verb *desert* means "to abandon"; the noun *desert* (pronounced like the verb) means "deserving reward or punishment."

A spy who deserts his country will receive his just deserts if he is caught.

TEKS 6.21
ELPS 5B

Grammar Practice

Using the Right Word 6

■ counsel, council; **creak, creek;** cymbal, symbol;
dear, deer; desert, dessert

**For each of the following sentences, write the correct choice from each
set of words in parentheses.**

Example: My dad's shed door *(creaks, creeks)* every time it opens.
creaks

1. I heard a fish splash in the *(creek, creak)*.

2. Sometimes we see *(deer, dear)* drinking water from a nearby
   pond.

3. Last year when we were in the *(dessert, desert)*, we saw
   vultures flying overhead.

4. The bald eagle is our country's *(cymbal, symbol)* of freedom.

5. Our family dinners at Grandma's are always followed by
   (dessert, desert).

6. After such a big meal, Grandpa's old wooden chair begins to
   (creek, creak).

7. The leader of the band *(councils, counsels)* students to store
   their instruments properly.

8. After the school concert, Janelle put her *(cymbal, symbol)* away.

9. Her *(deer, dear)* grandfather was so proud of her performance.

10. The student *(counsel, council)* decided that another concert
    should be scheduled.

11. If the floodwaters continue to rise, we will be forced to
    (dessert, desert) our house.

Next Step: Write three sentences that show your understanding of
these words: *symbol, dessert,* and *counsel.*

RIGHT WORD

6.21
ELPS 4C, 5B

706.1
die, dye

Die (dying) means "to stop living." *Dye* (dyeing) is used to change the color of something.

The young girl hoped that her sick goldfish wouldn't die.

My sister dyes her hair with coloring that washes out.

706.2
faint, feign, feint

Faint means "feeble, without strength" or "to fall unconscious." *Feign* is a verb that means "to pretend or make up." *Feint* is a noun that means "a move or an activity that is pretended in order to divert attention."

The actors feigned a sword duel. One man staggered and fell in a feint. The audience gave faint applause.

706.3
farther, further

Farther is used when you are writing about a physical distance. *Further* means "additional."

Alaska reaches farther north than Iceland. For further information, check your local library.

706.4
fewer, less

Fewer refers to the number of separate units; *less* refers to bulk quantity.

I may have less money than you have, but I have fewer worries.

706.5
fir, fur

Fir refers to a type of evergreen tree; *fur* is animal hair.

The Douglas fir tree is named after a Scottish botanist.

An arctic fox has white fur in the winter.

706.6
flair, flare

Flair means "a natural talent" or "style"; *flare* means "to light up quickly" or "burst out" (or an object that does so).

Jenrette has a flair for remaining calm when other people's tempers flare.

706.7
for, four

The preposition *for* means "because of" or "directed to"; *four* is the number 4.

Mary had grilled steaks and chicken for the party, but the dog had stolen one of the four steaks.

TEKS 6.21
ELPS 5B

Grammar Practice

Using the Right Word 7

■ die, dye; farther, further; fewer, less; fir, fur; for, four

 For each of the following sentences, write the correct choice from each set of words in parentheses.

Example: Yesterday I spent *(fewer, less)* money at the mall than I did last time I was there.

less

1. An elephant separates itself from the rest of the herd when it is about to *(dye, die)*.

2. Leona walks six blocks *(further, farther)* to school than Tomei does.

3. I spend *(less, fewer)* time studying than my brother does, so I have *(less, fewer)* A's on my report card than he does.

4. Sometimes, when cattle and horses rub against *(fur, fir)* trees, bits of their *(fur, fir)* get stuck in the rough bark.

5. Do you want to *(dye, die)* your shoes orange or chartreuse for "Crazy Shoe Day"?

6. Sloan wants to trade her lunch *(four, for)* yours.

7. Sloan's lunch is a day-old sandwich, soggy potato chips, and *(four, for)* rock-hard chocolate chip cookies.

8. Ramón is helping his dad plant some Douglas *(furs, firs)* in their yard.

9. Does Seattle, Washington, or Portland, Oregon, have *(less, fewer)* sunny days?

10. If you need *(further, farther)* help with the assignment, call me after dinner.

Next Step: Show your understanding of the words *dye, further,* and *fewer* by using each of them correctly in a sentence.

RIGHT WORD

708.1 good, well

Good is an adjective; *well* is nearly always an adverb.

The strange flying machines flew well. (The adverb *well* modifies *flew*.)

They looked good as they flew overhead. (The adjective *good* modifies *they*.)

When used in writing about health, *well* is an adjective.

The pilots did not feel well, however, after the long, hard race.

708.2 hare, hair

A *hare* is an animal similar to a rabbit; *hair* refers to the growth covering the head and body of mammals and human beings.

When a hare darted out in front of our car, the hair on my head stood up.

708.3 heal, heel

Heal means "to mend or restore to health." *Heel* is the back part of a human foot.

I got a blister on my heel from wearing my new shoes. It won't heal unless I wear my old ones.

708.4 hear, here

You *hear* sounds with your ears. *Here* is the opposite of *there* and means "nearby."

708.5 heard, herd

Heard is the past tense of the verb "to hear"; *herd* is a group of animals.

The herd of grazing sheep raised their heads when they heard the collie barking in the distance.

708.6 heir, air

An *heir* is a person who inherits something; *air* is what we breathe.

Will the next generation be heir to terminally polluted air?

708.7 hole, whole

A *hole* is a cavity or hollow place. *Whole* means "entire or complete."

The hole in the ozone layer is a serious problem requiring the attention of the whole world.

708.8 immigrate, emigrate

Immigrate means "to come into a new country or area." *Emigrate* means "to go out of one country to live in another."

Martin Ulferts immigrated to this country in 1882. He was only three years old when he emigrated from Germany.

TEKS 6.21
ELPS 5B

Grammar Practice

Using the Right Word 8

■ good, well; hare, hair; hear, here; heard, herd; heir, air; hole, whole

For each of the following sentences, write the correct choice from each set of words in parentheses.

Example: Mammals are animals covered with *(hare, hair)*.

hair

1. A wood duck looks for a *(hole, whole)* in a tree to build a nest.

2. Although you can't see turtles' ears, they can *(hear, here)* very *(good, well)*.

3. The peregrine falcon can dive through the *(heir, air)* at 200 miles per hour.

4. I'd say that's a pretty *(good, well)* speed!

5. Caribou always travel in a large *(heard, herd)*.

6. The sounds a whale makes underwater can be *(heard, herd)* for miles.

7. A *(hare, hair)* has long ears and very long hind legs.

8. The sailfish can swim from *(hear, here)* to there faster than any other fish.

9. While humans grow *(hare, hair)* in just a few places, most mammals are covered with it.

10. As an *(heir, air)* of his uncle, Rashid was given the scarlet macaw.

11. Listen! The *(hole, whole)* forest is filled with singing birds.

12. They sound *(good, well)*, don't they?

Next Step: Write three sentences about animals. Show your understanding of these words: *herd, whole,* and *hair.*

RIGHT WORD

⭐ **TEKS** 6.21
ELPS 4C, 5B

710.1
imply, infer

Imply means "to suggest indirectly"; *infer* means "to draw a conclusion from facts."

"Since you have to work, may I infer that you won't come to my party?" Guy asked.

"No, I only meant to imply that I would be late," Rochelle responded.

710.2
it's, its

It's is the contraction of "it is." *Its* is the possessive form of "it."

It's a fact that a minnow's teeth are in its throat.

710.3
knew, new

Knew is the past tense of the verb "know." *New* means "recent or modern."

If I knew how to fix it, I would not need a new one!

710.4
know, no

Know means "to recognize or understand." *No* means "the opposite of yes."

Phil, do you know Cheri?

No, I've never met her.

710.5
later, latter

Later means "after a period of time." *Latter* refers to the second of two things mentioned.

The band arrived later and set up the speakers and the lights. The latter made the stage look like a carnival ride.

710.6
lay, lie

Lay means "to place." (*Lay* is a transitive verb; that means it needs a word to complete the meaning.) *Lie* means "to recline." (*Lie* is an intransitive verb.)

Lay your sleeping bag on the floor before you lie down on it. (*Lay* needs the word *bag* to complete its meaning.)

710.7
lead, led

Lead (lēd) is a present tense verb meaning "to guide." The past tense of the verb is *led* (lĕd). The noun *lead* (lĕd) is the metal.

Guides planned to lead the settlers to safe quarters. Instead, they led them into a winter storm.

Peeling paint in old houses may contain lead.

710.8
learn, teach

Learn means "to get information"; *teach* means "to give information."

I want to learn how to sew. Will you teach me?

TEKS 6.21
ELPS 5B

Grammar Practice

Using the Right Word 9

■ it's, its; knew, new; know, no; lay, lie; lead, led; learn, teach

 For each numbered sentence below, write the correct choice from each set of words in parentheses.

Example: Ancient stone carvings show that the Egyptians *(new, knew)* about swimming 5,000 years ago.

knew

(1) Doctors *(no, know)* that swimming is good exercise. **(2)** All children should *(learn, teach)* how to swim, but parents need to make sure they *(lie, lay)* down the ground rules about water safety.

Some kids take swimming lessons. **(3)** After a short talk, the swimming instructor will *(led, lead)* students to the pool and *(learn, teach)* them basic strokes. The most common stroke is called the front crawl. **(4)** *(Its, It's)* how most people swim. **(5)** Some people like to *(lie, lay)* on their backs when they swim—this is called the backstroke. **(6)** Some Olympic swimmers have *(lead, led)* the race doing the butterfly stroke. **(7)** A *(new, knew)* swimmer might think that this stroke is too difficult to do, but *(no, know)* stroke is impossible to learn.

(8) Many people have tried to swim the English Channel; *(it's, its)* water is very cold. **(9)** Although the swimmers *(new, knew)* what a difficult task it would be, I'm sure they looked forward to going home to *(lie, lay)* down in a nice, warm bed!

Next Step: Lay and lie are challenging words to use correctly. Write two or more sentences that show you know the meanings of those words.

RIGHT WORD

TEKS 6.21
ELPS 4C, 5B

712.1
leave, let

Leave means "fail to take along." *Let* means "allow."

Rozi wanted to leave her boots at home, but Jorge wouldn't let her.

712.2
like, as

Like is a preposition meaning "similar to"; *as* is a conjunction meaning "to the same degree" or "while." *Like* usually introduces a phrase; *as* usually introduces a clause.

The glider floated like a bird. The glider floated as the pilot had hoped it would.

As we circled the airfield, we saw maintenance carts moving like ants below us.

712.3
loose, lose,
loss

Loose (lüs) means "free or untied"; *lose* (lo͞oz) means "to misplace or fail to win"; *loss* (lôs) means "something lost."

These jeans are too loose in the waist since my recent weight loss. I still want to lose a few more pounds.

712.4
made, maid

Made is the past tense of "make," which means to "create," "prepare," or "put in order." A *maid* is a female servant; *maid* is also used to describe an unmarried girl or young woman.

The hotel maid asked if our beds needed to be made.

Grandma made a chocolate cake for dessert.

A maid strolled in the garden before the concert.

712.5
mail, male

Mail refers to letters or packages handled by the postal service. *Male* refers to the masculine sex.

My little brother likes getting junk mail.

The male sea horse, not the female, takes care of the fertilized eggs.

712.6
main, mane

Main refers to the most important part. *Mane* is the long hair growing from the top or sides of the neck of certain animals, such as the horse, lion, and so on.

The main thing we noticed about the magician's tamed lion was its luxurious mane.

712.7
meat, meet

Meat is food or flesh; *meet* means "to come upon or encounter."

I'd like you to meet the butcher who sells the leanest meat in town.

TEKS 6.21
ELPS 5B

Grammar Practice

Using the Right Word 10

■ leave, let; like, as; loose, lose, loss; main, mane; meat, meet

 For each of the following sentences, write the correct choice from each set of words in parentheses.

Example: Emme and James swim *(as, like)* fish.
like

1. They glide across the surface *(as, like)* water bugs *(as, like)* we sit and watch.

2. Your tomcat's *(mane, main)* makes him look like a miniature lion.

3. Don't *(leave, let)* the dog eat cake anymore.

4. The straps on Brad's backpack are very *(loose, lose)*.

5. If he's not careful, he may *(loose, lose)* it.

6. The *(lose, loss)* of his valuable art supplies would be a disaster!

7. Mom wouldn't *(leave, let)* me go to Jule's party until 6:30.

8. At this weekend's *(main, mane)* event, Vegan Fest, no one will be eating any *(meat, meet)*.

9. At the stable, a woman was braiding her horse's *(main, mane)*.

10. *(As, Like)* a ballerina, Marta pranced across her room, twirling and hopping.

11. I don't want to *(lose, loss)* my ring while I'm swimming, so I'll *(leave, let)* it at home.

12. "I'm happy to finally *(meat, meet)* you," said Rocco's pen pal.

13. "You look *(as, like)* your picture," he said.

Next Step: Write two sentences that show your understanding of the words *leave* and *let*.

RIGHT WORD

TEKS 6.21
ELPS 4C, 5B

714.1
medal, metal, meddle, mettle

A *medal* is an award. *Metal* is an element like iron or gold. *Meddle* means "to interfere." *Mettle,* a noun, refers to quality of character.

Grandpa's friend received a medal for showing his mettle in battle. Grandma, who loves to meddle in others' business, asked if the award was a precious metal.

714.2
miner, minor

A *miner* digs in the ground for valuable ore. A *minor* is a person who is not legally an adult. *Minor* means "of no great importance" when used as an adjective.

The use of minors as miners is no minor problem.

714.3
moral, morale

Moral relates to what is right or wrong or to the lesson to be drawn from a story. *Morale* refers to a person's attitude or mental condition.

The moral of this story is "Everybody loves a winner."

After the unexpected win at football, morale was high throughout the town.

714.4
morning, mourning

Morning refers to the first part of the day (before noon); *mourning* means "showing sorrow."

Abby was mourning her test grades all morning.

714.5
oar, or, ore

An *oar* is a paddle used in rowing or steering a boat. *Or* is a conjunction indicating choice. *Ore* refers to a mineral made up of several different kinds of material, as in iron ore.

Either use one oar to push us away from the dock, or start the boat's motor.

Silver-copper ore is smelted and refined to extract each metal.

714.6
pain, pane

Pain is the feeling of being hurt. A *pane* is a section or part of something.

Dad looked like he was in pain when he found out we broke a pane of glass in the neighbor's front door.

714.7
pair, pare, pear

A *pair* is a couple (two); *pare* is a verb meaning "to peel"; *pear* is the fruit.

A pair of doves nested in the pear tree.

Please pare the apples for the pie.

TEKS 6.21
ELPS 5B

Grammar Practice

Using the Right Word 11

■ medal, metal; miner, minor; oar, ore, or; pain, pane;
pair, pare, pear

For each of the following sentences, write the correct choice from each set of words in parentheses.

Example: *(Miners, Minors)* work underground to find *(oar, ore)* used in manufacturing.

Miners, ore

1. Should I use my *(oar, or)* on the left side of the boat *(ore, or)* on the right side?

2. We are required to wear a *(pare, pair)* of blue socks with our uniforms.

3. A first-place winner in the Olympic Games receives a *(metal, medal)* made of a precious *(metal, medal)*—gold.

4. Do you know that some states still call people between the ages of 18 and 21 *(minors, miners)*?

5. When Abe stumbled and fell, he felt a sharp *(pane, pain)* as his arm went through a *(pane, pain)* of glass in the patio door.

6. Juan received our school's *(metal, medal)* of excellence during the graduation ceremony.

7. If you are going to put that *(pare, pear)* in the fruit salad, you have to *(pare, pear)* it first.

8. Huge barges carry iron *(oar, ore)* to steel mills along the Mississippi River.

9. Most fine jewelry is made of *(metal, medal)*.

10. A *(pare, pair)* of red-handled scissors and a *(pare, pear)*-shaped pincushion are on Grandma Delora's sewing table.

Next Step: Write a short paragraph in which you correctly use four of the italicized words above.

RIGHT WORD

TEKS 6.21
ELPS 4C, 5B

716.1
past, passed

Passed is always a verb; it is the past tense of *pass. Past* can be used as a noun, as an adjective, or as a preposition.

A motorcycle passed my dad's 'Vette. (verb)

The old man won't forget the past. (noun)

I'm sorry, but I'd rather not talk about my past life. (adjective)

Old Blue walked right past the cat and never saw it. (preposition)

716.2
peace, piece

Peace means "harmony, or freedom from war." A *piece* is a part or fragment of something.

In order to keep peace among the triplets, each one had to have an identical piece of cake.

716.3
peak, peek, pique

A *peak* is a "high point" or a "pointed end." *Peek* means "brief look." *Pique,* as a verb, means "to excite by challenging"; as a noun, it means "a feeling of resentment."

Just a peek at Pike's Peak in the Rocky Mountains can pique a mountain climber's curiosity.

In a pique, she marched away from her giggling sisters.

716.4
personal, personnel

Personal means "private." *Personnel* are people working at a job.

Some thoughts are too personal to share.

The personnel manager will be hiring more workers.

716.5
plain, plane

A *plain* is an area of land that is flat or level; it also means "clearly seen or clearly understood" and "ordinary."

It's plain to see why the early settlers had trouble crossing the Great Plains.

Plane means "a flat, level surface" (as in geometry); it is also a tool used to smooth the surface of wood.

When I saw that the door wasn't a perfect plane, I used a plane to make it smooth.

716.6
pore, pour, poor

A *pore* is an opening in the skin. *Pour* means "to cause a flow or stream." *Poor* means "needy."

People perspire through the pores in their skin. Pour yourself a glass of water. Your poor body needs it!

TEKS 6.21
ELPS 5B

Grammar Practice

Using the Right Word 12

■ past, passed; peace, piece; peak, peek; personal, personnel; plain, plane

For each of the following sentences, write the correct choice from each set of words in parentheses.

Example: Imaginative wrapping on a gift box can make it more *(personal, personnel)*.

personal

1. Uleasha's mom said to her friends, "I like the *(personal, personnel)* gifts Uleasha gives me."

2. She can make even a simple *(peace, piece)* of *(plain, plane)* paper into a work of art.

3. As Janet *(past, passed)* the group of women, she stopped to listen.

4. Janet took a *(peak, peek)* at one of Uleasha's origami cranes.

5. She could see how it would give Uleasha's mom a feeling of *(peace, piece)*.

6. In the *(past, passed)*, origami was practiced only in the Far East.

7. Still a Japanese tradition, origami is now created everywhere— from the Great *(Plains, Planes)* to Greenland.

8. At the scene of the accident, the driver said he hadn't had a ticket in the *(past, passed)* 10 years.

9. Then the driver admitted he had been looking at a nearby mountain *(peak, peek)*.

10. "We'll need more *(personal, personnel)* to get this mess cleaned up," said the officer.

Next Step: Write three sentences in which you use the word *past* in these different ways: as an adjective, as a noun, and as a preposition.

RIGHT WORD

TEKS 6.21
ELPS 4C, 5B

718.1
principal,
principle

As an adjective, *principal* means "primary." As a noun, it can mean "a school administrator" or "a sum of money." *Principle* means "idea or doctrine."

My mom's principal goal is to save money so she can pay off the principal balance on her loan from the bank.

Hey, Charlie, I hear the principal gave you a detention.

The principle of freedom is based on the principle of self-discipline.

718.2
quiet, quit, quite

Quiet is the opposite of "noisy." *Quit* means "to stop." *Quite* means "completely or entirely."

I quit mowing even though I wasn't quite finished.

The neighborhood was quiet again.

718.3
raise, rays

Raise is a verb meaning "to lift or elevate." *Rays* are thin lines or beams.

When I raise this shade, bright rays of sunlight stream into the room.

718.4
real, very, really

Do not use the adjective *real* in place of the adverbs *very* or *really*.

The plants scattered throughout the restaurant are not real.

Hiccups are very embarrassing.

Her nose is really small.

718.5
red, read

Red is a color; *read*, pronounced the same way, is the past tense of the verb meaning "to understand the meaning of written words and symbols."

"I've read five books in two days," said the little boy.

The librarian gave him a red ribbon.

718.6
right, write, rite

Right means "correct or proper"; *right* is the opposite of "left"; it also refers to anything that a person has a legal claim to, as in "copyright." *Write* means "to record in print." *Rite* is a ritual or ceremonial act.

We have to write an essay about how our rights are protected by the Constitution.

Turn right at the next corner.

A rite of passage is a ceremony that celebrates becoming an adult.

TEKS 6.21
ELPS 5B

Grammar Practice

Using the Right Word 13

■ quiet, quit, quite; raise, rays; real, very, really;
red, read; right, write, rite

For each of the following sentences, write the correct choice from each set of words in parentheses.

Example: It's *(quiet, quite)* nice to read a good book on a
(really, real) rainy afternoon.
quite, really

1. Max's sister has beautiful *(read, red)* hair.

2. Have you ever seen the colors and patterns formed when
(raise, rays) of sunlight pass through a prism?

3. Mom pleaded, "*(Quit, Quiet)* playing that CD so loudly and be
(quite, quiet) for a while."

4. "That would make me *(quiet, quite)* happy!" she added.

5. The reporter will *(right, write)* an article about women's fight
for equal *(rights, writes)*.

6. A huge crane will *(raise, raze)* the new water tank to the top of
the new tower.

7. I *(read, red)* an article about miniature horses.

8. It's *(real, really)* hard to believe that they are horses since they
are not *(very, real)* tall.

9. I saw one in a parade once, and it definitely was a *(real, really)*
horse.

10. I think it would be an interesting hobby to *(raise, rays)* these
animals.

Next Step: Write a few sentences about a hobby that you find
interesting. Use at least four of the italicized words
above in your sentences. Then exchange papers with
a classmate and read about each other's hobby.

RIGHT WORD

TEKS 6.21
ELPS 4C, 5B

720.1
scene, seen

Scene refers to the setting or location where something happens; it also means "sight or spectacle." *Seen* is a form of the verb "see."

> The scene of the crime was roped off. We hadn't seen anyone go in or out of the building.

720.2
seam, seem

A *seam* is a line formed by connecting two pieces of material. *Seem* means "appear to exist."

> Every Thanksgiving, it seems, I stuff myself so much that my shirt seams threaten to burst.

720.3
sew, so, sow

Sew is a verb meaning "to stitch"; *so* is a conjunction meaning "in order that." The verb *sow* means "to plant."

> In Colonial times, the wife would sew the family clothes, and the husband would sow the family garden so the children could eat.

720.4
sight, cite, site

Sight means "the act of seeing" or "something that is seen." *Cite* means "to quote or refer to." A *site* is a location or position (including a Web site on the Internet).

> The Alamo at night was a sight worth the trip. I was also able to cite my visit to this historical site in my history paper.

720.5
sit, set

Sit means "to put the body in a seated position." *Set* means "to place." (*Set* is a transitive verb; that means it needs a direct object to complete its meaning.)

> How can you just sit there and watch as I set up all these chairs?

720.6
sole, soul

Sole means "single, only one"; *sole* also refers to the bottom surface of a foot or shoe. *Soul* refers to the spiritual part of a person.

> Maggie got a job for the sole purpose of saving for a car.

> The soles of these shoes are very thick.

> "Who told you dogs don't have souls?" asked the kind veterinarian.

720.7
some, sum

Some means "an unknown number or part." *Sum* means "the whole amount."

> The sum in the cash register was stolen by some thieves.

TEKS 6.21
ELPS 5B

Grammar Practice

Using the Right Word 14

■ scene, seen; sight, cite, site; sit, set; sole, soul; some, sum

For each numbered sentence below, write the correct choice from each set of words in parentheses.

Example: A student needs to *(sight, cite)* sources used for a research report.

cite

(1) Mali wants to find *(some, sum)* information about the history of bicycles. **(2)** Several Web *(sites, cites)* about it can be found on the Internet. According to one Web page, Baron von Drais invented the first bike, a wooden one without pedals, in 1817. **(3)** He would *(sit, set)* on the bike and use his feet on the ground to make the bike move. **(4)** Men riding these bikes were quite a *(sight, site)* to see!

(5) For a long time, women were only *(scene, seen)* riding tricycles. **(6)** *(Some, sum)* people did not consider it right for a woman to ride a bicycle. **(7)** If a woman rode a bike, she'd cause a *(scene, seen)*! **(8)** Now some people use bikes as their *(soul, sole)* form of transportation.

For each of the following sentences, write the correct choice from each set of words in parentheses.

Example: It *(seams, seems)* that I always have to take the garbage out.

seems

1. Maybe you'd prefer to *(sit, set)* the table for dinner every evening.
2. Allow me to *(site, cite)* my mother: "Life is not fair."
3. James said he had already *(scene, seen)* that movie.
4. Just the *(sight, site)* of a skunk makes its enemies run.
5. Grandma gave me a large *(some, sum)* of money as a gift.

RIGHT WORD

722.1
sore, soar

Sore means "painful"; to *soar* means "to rise or fly high into the air."

> Craning to watch the eagle soar overhead, we soon had sore necks.

722.2
stationary, stationery

Stationary means "not movable"; *stationery* is the paper and envelopes used to write letters.

> Grandpa designed and printed his own stationery.

> All of the built-in furniture is stationary, of course.

722.3
steal, steel

Steal means "to take something without permission"; *steel* is a metal.

> Early ironmakers had to steal recipes for producing steel.

722.4
than, then

Than is used in a comparison; *then* tells when.

> Since tomorrow's weather is supposed to be nicer than today's, we'll go to the zoo then.

722.5
their, there, they're

Their is a possessive pronoun, one that shows ownership. (See **750.2**.) *There* is an adverb that tells where. *They're* is the contraction for "they are."

> They're upset because their dog got into the garbage over there.

722.6
threw, through

Threw is the past tense of "throw." *Through* means "passing from one side to the other" or "by means of."

> Through sheer talent and long practice, Nolan Ryan threw baseballs through the strike zone at more than 100 miles per hour.

722.7
to, too, two

To is the preposition that can mean "in the direction of." (*To* also is used to form an infinitive. See **764.4**.) *Too* is an adverb meaning "very or excessive." *Too* is often used to mean "also." *Two* is the number 2.

> Only two of Columbus's first three ships returned to Spain from the New World.

> Columbus was too restless to stay in Spain for long.

TEKS 6.21
ELPS 5B

Grammar Practice

Using the Right Word 15

■ sore, soar; steal, steel; their, there, they're; threw, through; to, too, two

For each of the following sentences, write the correct choice from each set of words in parentheses.

Example: Hearing such beautiful music makes my spirits *(sore, soar)*.

soar

1. The rummage sale earned us enough money *(to, too)* buy a new computer for the school.

2. There's a little *(sore, soar)* on my dog's paw.

3. Little League coaches spend hours teaching baseball players how to *(steal, steel)* a base.

4. One of my teammates *(threw, through)* the ball too hard.

5. *(Their, They're)* parents are helping them out.

6. Watching a kite *(sore, soar)* in the afternoon sky, Rubi felt peaceful.

7. Blueprints often call for *(steel, steal)* I-beams to support large buildings.

8. Linc's legs grew *(sore, soar)* as he struggled *(to, two)* finish the marathon.

9. Ms. Ramsay pointed to room 102 and whispered, "Shhh! *(Their, They're)* taking a test in *(they're, there)*."

10. *(They're, Their)* jackets, books, and papers were scattered here, *(their, there)*, and everywhere.

11. Robin Hood would *(steel, steal)* from the rich and give to the poor.

Next Step: See if you can, in one sentence, use the words *their*, *there*, and *they're* correctly.

RIGHT WORD

TEKS 6.21
ELPS 4C, 5B

724.1
vain, vane, vein

Vain means "worthless." It may also mean "thinking too highly of one's self; stuck-up." *Vane* is a flat piece of material set up to show which way the wind blows. *Vein* refers to a blood vessel or a mineral deposit.

> The weather vane indicates the direction of wind.
>
> A blood vein determines the direction of flowing blood.
>
> The vain mind moves thinks only about itself.

724.2
vary, very

Vary is a verb that means "to change." *Very* can be an adjective meaning "in the fullest sense" or "complete"; it can also be an adverb meaning "extremely."

> Garon's version of the event would vary from day to day. His very interesting story was the very opposite of the truth.

724.3
waist, waste

Waist is the part of the body just above the hips. The verb *waste* means "to wear away" or "to use carelessly"; the noun *waste* refers to material that is unused or useless.

> Don't waste your money on fast-food. What a waste to dump food because you're concerned about the size of your waist!

724.4
wait, weight

Wait means "to stay somewhere expecting something." *Weight* is the measure of heaviness.

> When I have to wait for the bus, the weight of my backpack seems to keep increasing.

724.5
ware, wear, where

Ware means "a product to be sold." *Wear* means "to have on or to carry on one's body"; *where* asks the question "in what place or in what situation?"

> Where can you buy the best cookware to take on a campout— and the best rain gear to wear if it rains?

724.6
way, weigh

Way means "path or route" or "a series of actions." *Weigh* means "to measure weight."

> What is the correct way to weigh liquid medicines?

724.7
weather, whether

Weather refers to the condition of the atmosphere. *Whether* refers to a possibility.

> The weather will determine whether I go fishing.

724.8
week, weak

A *week* is a period of seven days; *weak* means "not strong."

> Last week when I had the flu, I felt light-headed and weak.

TEKS 6.21
ELPS 5B

Grammar Practice

Using the Right Word 16

■ very, vary; waist, waste; wait, weight; ware, wear, where; weather, whether; week, weak

 For each of the following sentences, write the correct choice from each set of words in parentheses.

Example: I am not sure what costume I will *(wear, where)* to Alberto's Halloween party.

wear

1. I thought about being a knight, but then I'd have the *(wait, weight)* of all that armor.

2. Perhaps if I just wrap a grass skirt around my *(waist, waste)*, I'll look like a hula dancer.

3. I do have a wig that I can *(wear, where)*.

4. I got it last year, but I didn't use it—what a *(waist, waste)*!

5. I will *(wait, weight)* until this weekend to decide *(weather, whether)* I will be a hula dancer.

6. I hope making my costume won't take me a *(week, weak)*.

7. I'll need at least a few days to work on it, but I can't *(waist, waste)* any time because the party is soon.

8. Mom said she will drive me to the party if the *(weather, whether)* is rainy.

9. I must look at a map to see *(wear, where)* Alberto's house is.

10. He said it's close to the public library; in fact, it's *(vary, very)* close to my house.

11. It sounds like so much fun—I can't *(wait, weight)*!

Next Step: Write three sentences that show your understanding of the words *where*, *waste*, and *weight*.

RIGHT WORD

726.1
which, witch

Which is a pronoun used to ask "what one or ones?" out of a group. A *witch* is a woman believed to have supernatural powers.

> **Which of the women in Salem in the 1600s were accused of being witches?**

726.2
who, which, that

When introducing a clause, *who* is used to refer to people; *which* refers to animals and nonliving beings but never to people (it introduces a nonrestrictive, or unnecessary, clause); *that* usually refers to animals or things but can refer to people (it introduces a restrictive, or necessary, clause).

> **The idea that pizza is junk food is crazy.**
>
> **Pizza, which is quite nutritious, can be included in a healthful diet.**
>
> **My mom, who is a dietician, said so.**

726.3
who, whom

Who is used as the subject in a sentence; *whom* is used as the object of a preposition or as a direct object.

> **Who asked you to play tennis?**
>
> **You beat whom at tennis? You played tennis with whom?**

NOTE To test for who/whom, arrange the parts of the clause in a subject–verb–direct-object order. *Who* works as the subject, *whom* as the object. (See page **618**.)

726.4
who's, whose

Who's is the contraction for "who is." *Whose* is a possessive pronoun, one that shows ownership.

> **Who's the most popular writer today?**
>
> **Whose bike is this?**

726.5
wood, would

Wood is the material that comes from trees; *would* is a form of the verb "will."

> **Sequoia trees live practically forever, but would you believe that the wood from these giants is practically useless?**

726.6
your, you're

Your is a possessive pronoun, one that shows ownership. *You're* is the contraction for "you are."

> **You're the most important person in your parents' lives.**

★ **TEKS** 6.21
ELPS 3E, 5B

Grammar Practice

Using the Right Word 17

■ which, witch; who, which, that; who, whom; who's, whose; wood, would; your, you're

For each of the following sentences, write the correct choice from each set of words in parentheses.

Example: Ms. Sebastian asked, *"(Which, Witch)* one of you has a dentist appointment coming up?"
Which

1. "It is important to keep *(your, you're)* teeth clean and healthy," she said.

2. *"(Who's, Whose)* dentist is the friendliest?" she asked.

3. Quentin said the he just read that George Washington had false teeth made of *(wood, would).*

4. I hope that my new dentist, *(whose, who's)* office is down the street, is nice.

5. The dentist *(who, which, that)* used to clean my teeth moved away.

6. One Halloween, my dentist dressed as a *(which, witch).*

7. I liked the way she *(wood, would)* she clean my teeth.

8. "You look like *(your, you're)* nervous about going to a new dentist," my Mom said.

9. My Mom convinced me everything *(wood, would)* be fine.

10. My new dentist said, *"(Your, You're)* teeth are very healthy!"

Next Step: Write two sentences using the words *which* and *that* correctly. Share your sentences with a partner. *Hint:* If the clause you're introducing is not required to understand the meaning of the sentence, use *which* and set the clause off with commas. Otherwise, use *that*—without commas—to introduce the clause.

RIGHT WORD

Understanding Sentences

Sentences

A **sentence** is a group of words that expresses a complete thought. A sentence must have both a subject and a predicate. A sentence begins with a capital letter; it ends with a period, a question mark, or an exclamation point.

> I like my teacher this year.
>
> Will we go on a field trip?
>
> We get to go to the water park!

Parts of a Sentence . . .

728.1
Subjects

A subject is the part of a sentence that does something or is talked about.

> The kids **on my block play basketball at the local park.**
>
> We **meet after school almost every day.**

728.2
Simple Subjects

The simple subject is the subject without the words that describe or modify it. (Also see page **548**.)

> My friend **Chester plays basketball on the school team.**

728.3
Complete Subjects

The complete subject is the simple subject and all the words that modify it. (Also see page **547**.)

> My friend Chester **plays basketball on the school team.**

728.4
Compound Subjects

A compound subject has two or more simple subjects. (See page **549**.)

> Chester, Malik, **and** Meshelle **play on our pickup team.**
>
> Lou **and** I **are the best shooters.**

Grammar Practice

Parts of a Sentence 1

■ Simple Subjects
■ Complete Subjects

For each sentence below, write the complete subject. Circle the simple subject.

Example: A group of people in one neighborhood wanted to make a difference in society.

A (group) of people in one neighborhood

1. A special week for doing good things was announced.
2. The positive actions of some kids were reported in the paper.
3. One boy in the neighborhood carried groceries for someone in a wheelchair.
4. Two strong, young men cleaned the hallway in their apartment building.
5. A teenage girl cleaned the kitchen in her home for her mother.
6. Kindness can be something easy to do.
7. Many people doing good things will change the world.

■ Compound Subjects

Write the compound subject in each of the following sentences.

Example: My cousin and his friends went to the movies.
cousin, friends

1. The big black box and the gray snake belong to me.
2. Did Bill or Sophia buy balloons for the party?
3. Students, teachers, and school staff enjoy good school assemblies.
4. Simone, Alister, Ramona, Shaleen, and Leia donated canned goods for the hunger drive.
5. Hoping to catch the bus, Raul and Malcolm raced across the lawn.

ELPS 4C

Parts of a Sentence . . .

730.1
Predicates

The predicate, which contains the verb, is the part of the sentence that shows action or says something about the subject.

Hunting has reduced the tiger population in India.

730.2
Simple Predicates

The simple predicate is the predicate (verb) without the words that describe or modify it. (See page 548.)

In the past, poachers **killed** too many African elephants. **Poaching** is **illegal**.

730.3
Complete Predicates

The complete predicate is the simple predicate with all the words that modify or describe it. (See page 547.)

In the past, **poachers** killed too many African elephants. **Poaching** is illegal.

730.4
Direct Objects

The complete predicate often includes a direct object. The direct object is the noun or pronoun that receives the action of the simple predicate—directly. The direct object answers the question *what* or *whom*. (See page 618.)

Many smaller animals need friends **who will speak up for them.**

The direct object may be compound.

We all need animals, plants, wetlands, deserts, **and** forests.

730.5
Indirect Objects

If a sentence has a direct object, it may also have an indirect object. An indirect object is the noun or pronoun that receives the action of the simple predicate—indirectly. An indirect object names the person *to whom* or *for whom* something is done. (See page 618.)

I showed the class **my multimedia report on endangered species.** (*Class* is the indirect object because it says *to whom* the report was shown.)

Remember, in order for a sentence to have an indirect object, it must first have a direct object.

730.6
Compound Predicates

A compound predicate is composed of two or more simple predicates. (See page 549.)

In 1990 the countries of the world met **and** banned **the sale of ivory.**

Grammar Practice

Parts of a Sentence 2

■ Simple Predicates
■ Compound Predicates

 For each numbered sentence below, write the simple or compound predicate.

Example: Henry "Hank" Aaron hit 755 home runs during his career.

hit

(1) Henry Aaron was born in Mobile, Alabama, on February 5, 1934, and became a great baseball player. **(2)** For a long time, segregation kept him from the major leagues. **(3)** Finally, he joined the Milwaukee Braves baseball team. **(4)** Hank was one of the most dependable and valuable players on the team. **(5)** He played 3,298 games and batted in 2,297 runs.

■ Complete Predicates
■ Direct and Indirect Objects

 For each numbered sentence below, write the complete predicate. Underline the direct object once. If there's an indirect object, underline it twice.

Example: Hank Aaron's career spanned 23 years.

spanned 23 years

(1) Hank won the Most Valuable Player award for 1957. **(2)** He gave baseball a very memorable moment in 1974. **(3)** "Hammerin' Hank" hit his 715th home run in the fourth inning. **(4)** That hit broke Babe Ruth's record. **(5)** Hank Aaron showed the world his determination during his successful career.

Parts of a Sentence . . .

732.1
Understood Subjects and Predicates

Either the subject or the predicate (or both) may not be stated in a sentence, but both must be clearly understood.

[You] **Get involved!** (*You* is the understood subject.)

Who needs your help? Animals [do]. (*Do* is the understood predicate.)

What do many animals face? [They face] **Extinction.** (*They* is the understood subject, and *face* is the understood predicate.)

732.2
Delayed Subjects

In sentences that begin with *there* followed by a form of the "be" verb, the subject usually follows the verb. (See page **618**.)

There are laws that protect endangered species. (The subject is *laws; are* is the verb.)

The subject is also delayed in questions.

How can we preserve the natural habitat? (*We* is the subject.)

SCHOOL DAZE

John, I've got all the projects. Now which one is yours?

I'm not sure. See if there's one with a missing piece.

732.3
Modifiers

A modifier is a word (adjective, adverb) or a group of words (phrase, clause) that changes or adds to the meaning of another word. (See pages **532–539**.)

Many North American zoos and aquariums voluntarily participate in breeding programs that help prevent extinction.

The modifiers in this sentence include the following: *many, North American* (adjectives), *voluntarily* (adverb), *in breeding programs* (phrase), *that help prevent extinction* (clause).

Grammar Practice

Parts of a Sentence 3

■ Understood Subjects and Predicates
■ Delayed Subjects

For each of the sentences below, write down the part or parts named in parentheses.

Example: Study for the math test. *(understood subject)*
        You

1. When will we have the test? *(delayed subject)*

2. Tomorrow. *(understood subject and predicate)*

3. Get some help with your homework. *(understood subject)*

4. What is the lesson on page 244? *(delayed subject)*

5. Long division. *(understood predicate)*

6. Be sure to read it carefully. *(understood subject)*

■ Modifiers

Rewrite the following simple sentences, adding modifiers to expand them.

Example: Lalita talks.
        Lalita talks endlessly on her cordless phone.

1. Dominic runs.

2. She read a book.

3. Brigitte plays basketball.

4. Theo listened.

5. Habib writes.

6. I will walk.

7. Prem asked a question.

8. Shaquana paints.

ELPS 4C

Parts of a Sentence . . .

734.1
Clauses

A clause is a group of related words that has both a subject and a verb. (Also see pages **563–565**.)

> **a whole chain of plants and animals is affected**
> (*Chain* is the subject, and *is affected* is the verb.)

> **when one species dies out completely**
> (*Species* is the subject; *dies out* is the verb.)

734.2
Independent Clauses

An independent clause presents a complete thought and can stand alone as a sentence.

> **This ancient oak tree may be cut down.**

> **This act could affect more than 200 different species of animals!**

> **Why would anyone want that to happen?**

734.3
Dependent Clauses

A dependent clause does not present a complete thought and cannot stand as a sentence. A dependent clause *depends* on being connected to an independent clause to make sense. Dependent clauses begin with either a subordinating conjunction *(after, although, because, before, if)* or a relative pronoun *(who, whose, which, that)*. (See pages **746** and **776** for complete lists.)

> If this ancient oak tree is cut down, **it could affect more than 200 different species of animals!**

> **The tree,** which experts think could be 400 years old, **provides a home to many different kinds of birds and insects.**

SCHOOL DAZE

Boy, are you in for a real blockbuster next hour!

Yeah . . . Mr. Runge is showing a movie called *A Day in the Life of a Dependent Clause.*

Grammar Practice

Parts of a Sentence 4

■ Clauses

Write the dependent clause in each numbered sentence below. If the sentence does not contain a dependent clause, write "none."

Example: Spiral notebooks, which are held together with strong wire, can be dangerous in the wrong hands.

which are held together with strong wire

(1) One day in eighth grade, I learned to be more careful around my spiral notebooks. **(2)** During science class, an end of the wire that was sticking out managed to corkscrew its way into my thumb. **(3)** Because I couldn't get it out, Mr. Gibson, my teacher, saw what had happened. **(4)** He clipped the wire from the notebook and tried unsuccessfully to pull the other part out of my thumb. **(5)** Then Mr. Zold, who was the gym teacher, had a go at it. **(6)** Since he couldn't get it out either, I went to the office. **(7)** As the secretary looked at my thumb, she decided right then to call my mother. **(8)** When my mother picked me up, she rushed me to the emergency room at St. Luke's Hospital. **(9)** I didn't have much pain through all of this, but the wire, which was still sticking out of my thumb, sure made me feel foolish. **(10)** After the doctor examined my injury, she froze my thumb and twisted the wire out with some kind of medical pliers. **(11)** From that day on, I always covered the spiral part of my notebooks with tape.

Next Step: Read the dependent clauses that you wrote. Circle the clauses that begin with a subordinating conjunction and underline those beginning with a relative pronoun.

SENTENCES

Parts of a Sentence

736.1
Phrases

A phrase is a group of related words that lacks either a subject or a predicate (or both). (See pages **567–568**.)

> **guards the house** (The predicate lacks a subject.)
>
> **the ancient oak tree** (The subject lacks a predicate.)
>
> **with crooked old limbs** (The phrase lacks both a subject and a predicate.)
>
> **The ancient oak tree with crooked old limbs guards the house.** (Together, the three phrases form a complete thought.)

736.2
Types of Phrases

Phrases usually take their names from the main words that introduce them (prepositional phrase, verb phrase, and so on). They are also named for the function they serve in a sentence (adverb phrase, adjective phrase).

> **The ancient oak tree** (noun phrase)
>
> **with crooked old limbs** (prepositional phrase)
>
> **has stood its guard,** (verb phrase)
>
> **very stubbornly,** (adverb phrase)
>
> **protecting the little house.** (verbal phrase)

For more information on verbal phrases, see page **764**.

SCHOOL DAZE

Give me an example of a **verbal phrase** used as a subject.

Hanging upside down refreshes my brain.

Grammar Practice

Parts of a Sentence 5

■ Phrases

 Write whether each of the following phrases is missing a subject, a predicate, or both. Then use the phrase in a sentence.

Example: won a prize

missing a subject

My brother won a prize at the school science fair.

1. in Kansas

2. her parents

3. ran her first race

4. was the librarian

5. at a summer festival

6. other kids in the class

7. is not feeling well

8. writes letters to his grandchildren

9. Zack's blond hair

10. between the fence and the oak tree

11. lived in Chicago

Next Step: Go back to the phrases above and identify each as a noun phrase, a verb phrase, or a prepositional phrase.

Using the Parts of Speech

Nouns . . .

A **noun** is a word that names a person, a place, a thing, or an idea.

Person: **John Ulferts** (uncle)   Thing: **"Yankee Doodle"** (song)

Place: **Mississippi** (state)   Idea: **Labor Day** (holiday)

Kinds of Nouns

738.1

Common Nouns

A common noun is any noun that does not name a specific person, place, thing, or idea. These nouns are not capitalized.

woman   museum   book   weekend

738.2

Proper Nouns

A proper noun is the name of a specific person, place, thing, or idea. Proper nouns are capitalized.

Hillary Clinton   Central Park   *Maniac McGee*   Sunday

738.3

Concrete and Abstract Nouns

A concrete noun names a thing that is physical (can be touched or seen). An abstract noun names something you can think about but cannot see or touch.

Concrete: **space station, pencil, Statue of Liberty**

Abstract: **Judaism, poverty, satisfaction, illness**

738.4

Noncount Nouns

A noncount noun names something that cannot be counted.

unease   happiness   evidence   thunder

738.5

Collective Nouns

A collective noun names a group or collection of persons, animals, places, or things.

Persons: **tribe, congregation, family, class, team**

Animals: **flock, herd, gaggle, clutch, litter**

Things: **batch, cluster, bunch**

738.6

Compound Nouns

A compound noun is made up of two or more words.

football (written as one word)

high school (written as two words)

brother-in-law (written as a hyphenated word)

Grammar Practice

Nouns 1

■ Common, Proper and Noncount Nouns

For each line of the following paragraph, write the nouns and label them either "C" for common, or "P" for proper. Add an "N" for noncount.

Example: In Iraq, date-palm trees are a source of wealth.
Iraq – P, trees – C, source – C, wealth – CN

1 The trees are passed down from one generation to the next. In

2 Europe, families often pass down jewelry or art. In America, families

3 may save fine furniture or dishes for future generations. Wherever

4 families live, most people are interested in giving their children

5 keepsakes from their past.

■ Concrete and Abstract Nouns

For each line of the following paragraph, write the underlined nouns and label them either "C" for concrete or "A" for abstract. Add an "N" for nouns that are noncount.

Example: Grandpa said he doesn't know his true age.
Grandpa – C, age – AN

1 <u>Research</u> shows that the life span of people is increasing in

2 most countries of the <u>world</u>. Georgia, a country that used to be part

3 of the Soviet Union, has many <u>people</u> who are more than 110 <u>years</u>

4 old. When one old <u>man</u> was asked for the <u>secret</u> to his long <u>life</u>, he

5 replied, "I sleep with my <u>hat</u> on."

Next Step: Write two sentences about your family. Use a common
noun in one sentence and a noncount noun in the other.
Read your sentences to a classmate.

Nouns

Number of Nouns

The number of a noun is either singular or plural.

740.1

Singular Nouns

A singular noun names one person, place, thing, or idea.

    boy   group   audience   stage   concert   hope

740.2

Plural Nouns

A plural noun names more than one person, place, thing, or idea.

    boys   groups   audiences   stages   concerts   hopes

Gender of Nouns

740.3

Noun Gender

Nouns are grouped according to gender: *feminine, masculine, neutral,* and *indefinite.*

    Feminine (female): **mother, sister, women, cow, hen**

    Masculine (male): **father, brother, men, bull, rooster**

    Neutral (neither male nor female): **tree, cobweb, closet**

    Indefinite (male or female): **president, duckling, doctor**

Uses of Nouns

740.4

Subject Nouns

A noun that is the subject of a sentence does something or is talked about in the sentence.

    The roots of rap can be traced back to West Africa and Jamaica.

740.5

Predicate Nouns

A predicate noun follows a form of the *be* verb (*am, is, are, was, were, being, been*) and renames the subject.

    In the 1970s, rap was a street art.

740.6

Possessive Nouns

A possessive noun shows possession or ownership.

    Early rap had a drummer's beat but no music.

    The rapper's words are set to music.

740.7

Object Nouns

A noun is an object noun when it is used as the direct object, the indirect object, or the object of the preposition.

    Some rappers tell people their story about life in the city. (indirect object: *people*; direct object: *story*)

    Rap is now a common music choice in this country. (object of the preposition: *country*)

punctuate *edit* capitalize
improve **SPELL** **741**
Using the Parts of Speech

Grammar Practice

Nouns 2

■ **Number and Gender of Nouns**

For each of the following sentences, write the correct singular or plural noun from the choices in parentheses. Then write whether it is masculine, feminine, neutral, or indefinite.

Example: Hanukkah is a happy Jewish *(holiday, holidays).*
holiday (neutral)

1. It usually falls during the *(month, months)* of December.

2. The holiday includes eight *(day, days)* of celebration.

3. All the *(member, members)* of the family take part.

4. My *(aunt, aunts)* makes a huge dinner.

5. My *(brother, brothers)* like to light the candles on the menorah.

■ **Subject, Predicate, Possessive, and Object Nouns**

Identify each underlined noun in the sentences below as a subject noun, a predicate noun, a possessive noun, or an object noun.

Example: One of <u>Hanukkah's</u> symbols is a <u>dreidel.</u>
possessive noun, predicate noun

1. The <u>dreidel</u> is a square-shaped top with letters on each side.

2. The <u>letters</u> on the dreidel stand for the <u>words</u> "A Great Miracle Happened There."

3. In ancient <u>times</u>, the <u>study</u> of the Jewish holy books was forbidden in some countries.

4. <u>Soldiers</u> checking Jewish <u>homes</u> would find people playing with the dreidel.

5. The <u>dreidel's</u> <u>meaning</u> is that freedom is a miracle.

Pronouns . . .

A **pronoun** is a word used in place of a noun. Some examples are *I, you, he, she, it, we, they, his, hers, her, its, me, myself, us, yours,* and so on.

Without pronouns: **Kevin said Kevin would be going to Kevin's grandmother's house this weekend.**

With pronouns: **Kevin said he would be going to his grandmother's house this weekend.**

742.1
Antecedents

An antecedent is the noun that the pronoun refers to or replaces. All pronouns (except interrogative and indefinite pronouns) have antecedents. (See page **520**.)

Jamal and Rick tried out for the team, and they both made it.

(*They* refers to *Jamal* and *Rick*; *it* refers to *team*.)

NOTE Pronouns must agree with their antecedents in number, person, and gender.

Types of Pronouns

There are several types of pronouns. The most common type is the personal pronoun. (See the chart on page **746**.)

742.2
Personal Pronouns

A personal pronoun takes the place of a specific person (or thing) in a sentence. Some common personal pronouns are *I, you, he, she, it, we,* and *they.*

Suriana would not like to live in Buffalo, New York, because she does not like snow.

742.3
Relative Pronouns

A relative pronoun is both a pronoun and a connecting word. It connects a dependent clause to an independent clause in a complex sentence. Relative pronouns include *who, whose, which,* and *that.*

Buffalo, which often gets more than eight feet of snow in a year, is on the northeast shore of Lake Erie.

The United States city that gets the most snow is Valdez, Alaska.

742.4
Interrogative Pronouns

An interrogative pronoun helps ask a question.

Who wants to go to Alaska?

Which of the cities would you visit?

Whom would you like to travel with?

What did you say?

Grammar Practice

Pronouns 1

■ Antecedents and Personal, Relative, and Interrogative Pronouns

The type of pronoun that's missing is indicated at the end of each sentence. First write the antecedent of the missing pronoun and then write a pronoun that agrees with it. (See the chart on page 746.)

NOTE An interrogative pronoun doesn't have an antecedent, so write "none" in place of the antecedent.

Example: Kathryn says _____ favorite holiday is Labor Day. *(personal)*

Kathryn – her

1. Holidays have been celebrated for a long time, and _____ were originally known as "holy days." *(personal)*

2. Because many people traveled during the holy days, tradesmen along the way were there to meet _____. *(personal)*

3. Fairs and bazaars, _____ became part of many holiday celebrations, encouraged spending. *(relative)*

4. Now that spending is a big part of these holidays, many products are associated with _____. *(personal)*

5. _____ can guess what my favorite holiday is? *(interrogative)*

6. It is a holiday _____ is celebrated each January. *(relative)*

7. Sunee, if _____ guessed New Year's Day, _____ are correct. *(personal, personal)*

8. Aunt Fabiola wishes New Year's Day were celebrated in March; _____ thinks that's when the earth is new again. *(personal)*

9. _____ of the holidays is your favorite? *(interrogative)*

Next Step: Write two sentences about a holiday. Use pronouns in both sentences. Exchange papers with a classmate and circle the antecedents in each other's sentences.

PARTS OF SPEECH

Pronouns . . .
Types of Pronouns

744.1
Demonstrative Pronouns

A demonstrative pronoun points out or identifies a noun without naming the noun. When used together in a sentence, *this* and *that* distinguish one item from another, and *these* and *those* distinguish one group from another. (See page **746**.)

This **is a great idea;** that **was a nightmare.**

These **are my favorite foods, and** those **are definitely not.**

NOTE When these words are used before a noun, they are *not* pronouns; rather, they are demonstrative adjectives.

Coming to this **picnic was fun—and** those **ants think so, too.**

744.2
Intensive Pronouns

An intensive pronoun emphasizes, or *intensifies*, the noun or pronoun it refers to. Common intensive pronouns include *itself, myself, himself, herself,* and *yourself.*

Though the chameleon's quick-change act protects it from predators, the lizard itself **can catch insects 10 inches away with its long, sticky tongue.**

When a chameleon changes its skin color—seemingly matching the background—the background colors themselves **do not affect the chameleon's color changes.**

NOTE These sentences would be complete without the intensive pronoun. The pronoun simply emphasizes a particular noun.

744.3
Reflexive Pronouns

A reflexive pronoun refers back to the subject of a sentence, and it is always an object (never a subject) in a sentence. Reflexive pronouns are the same as the intensive pronouns—*itself, myself, himself, herself, yourself,* and so on.

A chameleon protects itself **from danger by changing colors.** (direct object)

A chameleon can give itself **tasty meals of unsuspecting insects.** (indirect object)

I wish I could claim some of its amazing powers for myself. (object of the preposition)

NOTE Unlike sentences with intensive pronouns, these sentences would *not* be complete without the reflexive pronouns.

Grammar Practice

Pronouns 2

■ **Demonstrative Pronouns**

Write whether the underlined word is a demonstrative adjective or a demonstrative pronoun. *Extra challenge:* Rewrite any sentence that contains a demonstrative adjective so that the word is used as a pronoun instead.

Example: <u>This</u> pie is good!

demonstrative adjective This is good pie!

1. Is <u>that</u> ring valuable?

2. <u>Those</u> cars are the finest available.

3. <u>That</u> was useful two years ago, but not now.

4. <u>These</u> apples are expensive.

■ **Intensive Pronouns**
■ **Reflexive Pronouns**

For each sentence below, write whether the underlined pronoun is intensive or reflexive.

Example: Although Elijah McCoy <u>himself</u> was not a slave, he was the son of former slaves.

intensive

1. In 1858, Elijah McCoy traveled from Canada to Scotland to better <u>himself</u> with a college education.

2. McCoy earned a degree in engineering and then moved to Michigan, where he went into business for <u>himself</u>.

3. Elijah believed that he <u>himself</u> could invent products that would save companies both time and money.

4. He invented a tool that allowed a machine to oil <u>itself</u>.

5. Over time, the oiling tool <u>itself</u> became so popular that people would ask whether it was the "real McCoy."

Pronouns . . .
Types of Pronouns

746.1
**Indefinite
Pronouns**

An indefinite pronoun is a pronoun that does not have a specific antecedent (the noun or pronoun it replaces). (See page **521**.)

Everything about the chameleon is fascinating.

Someone donated a chameleon to our class.

Anyone who brings in a live insect can feed our chameleon.

Types of Pronouns

Personal Pronouns
I, me, mine, my, we, us, our, ours, you, your, yours, they, them, their, theirs, he, him, his, she, her, hers, it, its

Relative Pronouns
who, whose, whom, which, what, that, whoever, whomever, whichever, whatever

Interrogative Pronouns
who, whose, whom, which, what

Demonstrative Pronouns
this, that, these, those

Intensive and Reflexive Pronouns
myself, himself, herself, itself, yourself, yourselves, themselves, ourselves

Indefinite Pronouns

all	both	everything	nobody	several
another	each	few	none	some
any	each one	many	no one	somebody
anybody	either	most	nothing	someone
anyone	everybody	much	one	something
anything	everyone	neither	other	such

punctuate edit capitalize
SPELL   747
improve
Using the Parts of Speech

TEKS 6.19A(vi)

Grammar Practice

Pronouns 3

■ **Indefinite Pronouns**

Write the indefinite pronoun in each of the following sentences. Share your ideas with a partner.

Example: Rodeo events offer entertainment for everybody.

everybody

1. Most are designed to showcase a person's skill and strength.

2. Calf roping is enjoyed by many.

3. Nothing harmful is done to the animals.

4. Each must be lassoed, thrown down, and tied.

5. None are hurt, and riders earn points for speed.

6. No one can deny that bull riding is an exciting event.

Pronoun Review

For each numbered sentence below, identify the underlined pronoun as "personal," "relative," or "indefinite."

Example: In a rodeo, even the clowns have <u>their</u> own event.

personal

(1) Rodeo events can be dangerous, and sometimes <u>someone</u> gets hurt. **(2)** Bull riding, <u>which</u> is the most dangerous event, is very exciting. **(3)** The rider must stay on a bucking bull for eight seconds, holding on to a rope <u>that</u> is tied around the bull's middle.

Women riders enjoy the rodeo as well. **(4)** They have <u>their</u> own events, including barrel racing. **(5)** The contestants ride around a series of three barrels as fast as possible without knocking <u>any</u> over.

Those are just a couple of the many events featured at a rodeo. **(6)** Anyone may take part, but he or <u>she</u> had better know how to ride!

Pronouns . . .

Number of a Pronoun

Pronouns can be either singular or plural in number.

Singular: **I, you, he, she, it**   Plural: **we, you, they**

NOTE The pronouns *you, your,* and *yours* may be singular or plural.

Person of a Pronoun

The person of a pronoun tells whether the pronoun is speaking, being spoken to, or being spoken about. (See page **520**.)

A first-person pronoun is used in place of the name of the speaker or speakers.

I **am speaking.**   We **are speaking.**

A second-person pronoun is used to name the person or thing spoken to.

Eliza, will you **please take out the garbage?**

You **better stop grumbling!**

A third-person pronoun is used to name the person or thing spoken about.

Bill should listen if he **wants to learn the words to this song.**

Charisse said that she **already knows** them.

They **will perform the song in the talent show.**

Uses of Pronouns

A pronoun can be used as a subject, as an object, or to show possession. (See the chart on page **750**.)

A subject pronoun is used as the subject of a sentence *(I, you, he, she, it, we, they)*.

I **like to surf the Net.**

A subject pronoun is also used after a form of the *be* verb *(am, is, are, was, were, being, been)* if it repeats the subject. (See "Predicate Nouns," **740.5**.)

"This is she**," Mom replied into the telephone.**

"Yes, it was I**," admitted the child who had eaten the cookies.**

punctuate *edit* capitalize
SPELL
improve
749
Using the Parts of Speech

Grammar Practice

Pronouns 4

- Number of a Pronoun
- Person of a Pronoun

For each of the following sentences, write the pronouns and identify them as first, second, or third person. (See the chart on page 750.)

Example: We studied the Civil War in my history class.

We (first person), my (first person)

1. Abraham Lincoln was elected president of the United States in 1860; he was the sixteenth president.

2. In January of 1861, South Carolina decided it would leave the United States of America.

3. In class, we learned that 11 states decided to leave the United States, and they created the Confederate States of America.

4. In February of 1861, the Confederate States elected Jefferson Davis as their new president.

5. He became the first—and last—president of the Confederacy.

6. Our teacher said, "I will test you on the Civil War next week."

7. I said, "José, I am sure you can pass the test easily."

8. "Your study habits are better than mine."

9. The night before the test, we reviewed the study sheets together.

10. Dad gave us three agates and a fossil that he had found.

11. José told me, "You could try rereading each chapter carefully, Joanne."

12. He was right; it helped me get a passing grade.

Next Step: Look at your answers for the exercise above. Underline the pronouns that are singular and circle those that are plural.

Pronouns
Uses of Pronouns

An object pronoun *(me, you, him, her, it, us, them)* can be used as the object of a verb or preposition.

> I'll call her as soon as I can. (direct object)
>
> Hand me the phone book, please. (indirect object)
>
> She thinks these flowers are from you. (object of the preposition)

A possessive pronoun shows possession or ownership. These possessive pronouns function as adjectives before nouns: *my, our, his, her, their, its,* and *your.*

> School workers are painting our classroom this summer. Its walls will look much better.

These possessive pronouns can be used after verbs: *mine, ours, hers, his, theirs,* and *yours.*

> I'm pretty sure this backpack is mine and that one is his.

NOTE An apostrophe is not needed with a possessive pronoun to show possession.

Uses of Personal Pronouns

	Singular Pronouns			Plural Pronouns		
	Subject Pronouns	Possessive Pronouns	Object Pronouns	Subject Pronouns	Possessive Pronouns	Object Pronouns
First Person	I	my, mine	me	we	our, ours	us
Second Person	you	your, yours	you	you	your, yours	you
Third Person	he	his	him	they	their, theirs	them
	she	her, hers	her			
	it	its	it			

punctuate *edit* capitalize
improve SPELL **751**
Using the Parts of Speech

Grammar Practice

Pronouns 5

■ **Subject, Object, and Possessive Pronouns**

 For each numbered sentence in the paragraphs below, identify the underlined pronoun as a subject, an object, or a possessive pronoun.

Example: Roberto Clemente liked many sports, but <u>his</u> favorite sport was baseball.

possessive pronoun

(1) Roberto Clemente was born in Puerto Rico in 1934; <u>he</u> was the youngest of four children. **(2)** As a young boy, Roberto discovered sports were easy for <u>him</u>. **(3)** He played baseball for several teams, but <u>his</u> big break came when he signed with the Brooklyn Dodgers. **(4)** At first, <u>they</u> sent Roberto to play on a minor-league team. **(5)** In 1954, the Pittsburgh Pirates drafted him, and he spent 17 years with <u>them</u>. **(6)** Roberto was named the most valuable player in a World Series, and <u>it</u> was a great honor for him.

(7) For many years, Clemente helped <u>those</u> in need. **(8)** When a devastating earthquake hit Nicaragua in 1972, Clemente helped arrange relief for Nicaragua and <u>its</u> people. **(9)** Determined to see that food and other supplies got to the people, <u>he</u> chartered a plane and accompanied four others on the flight. **(10)** Before the flight, Roberto's wife said <u>she</u> was worried about his safety. **(11)** On December 31, 1972, the plane flew into storm winds that caused <u>it</u> to crash, leaving no survivors. **(12)** Today, many people remember Roberto Clemente not only for <u>his</u> baseball skills but also for his desire to help others.

Next Step: Go back to the "Colons" exercise on page **643**. Identify the pronouns in the last paragraph of the letter as subject, object, or possessive pronouns.

Verbs . . .

A **verb** is a word that shows action or links a subject to another word in a sentence.

> **Tornadoes** cause **tremendous damage.** (action verb)
>
> **The weather** is **often calm before a storm.** (linking verb)

Types of Verbs

752.1
Action Verbs

An action verb tells what the subject is doing. (See page **526**.)

> **Natural disasters** hit **the globe nearly every day.**

752.2
Linking Verbs

A linking verb connects—or links—a subject to a noun or an adjective in the predicate. The most common linking verbs are forms of the verb *be (is, are, was, were, being, been, am).* Verbs such as *smell, look, taste, feel, remain, turn, appear, become, sound, seem, grow,* and *stay* can also be linking verbs. (See page **526**.)

> **The San Andreas Fault** is **an earthquake zone in California.** (The linking verb *is* connects the subject to the predicate noun *zone.*)
>
> **Earthquakes there** are **fairly common.** (The linking verb *are* connects the subject to the predicate adjective *common.*)

752.3
Helping Verbs

A helping verb (also called an auxiliary verb) helps the main verb express tense and voice. The most common helping verbs are *shall, will, should, would, could, must, might, can, may, have, had, has, do, did,* and the forms of the verb *be—is, are, was, were, am, being, been.*

> **It** has been **estimated that 500,000 earthquakes occur around the world every year.** (These helping verbs indicate that the tense is present perfect and the voice is passive.)
>
> **Fortunately, only about 100 of those** will **cause damage.** (*Will* helps express the future tense of the verb.)

Grammar Practice

Verbs 1 ■ Action Verbs, Linking Verbs, and Helping Verbs

Number your paper from 1 to 10. Then identify the underlined verbs as action, linking, or helping verbs.

Example: The Baldwin Locomotive Works <u>built</u> 75,000 locomotives.

action

1   Matthias Baldwin <u>founded</u> the Baldwin Locomotive Works in

2 1831. His company <u>built</u> train locomotives to fit the needs of his

3 customers. Baldwin technicians <u>designed</u> powerful steam engines,

4 and buyers <u>were</u> pleased. The company <u>grew</u> bigger.

5   Steam engines eventually <u>were challenged</u> by diesel engines.

6 One steam locomotive <u>was</u> more powerful than one diesel

7 locomotive, but the train engineers <u>used</u> several diesel engines

8 hooked together to pull more freight. The Age of Steam <u>was coming</u>

9 to an end. After more than 120 years, Baldwin Works <u>closed</u> its

10 doors in 1954.

Write the linking verb in each of the following sentences. Then write the word it links the subject to and tell whether it is a noun or an adjective.

Example: Railroads were the fastest transportation in the 1800s.

were, transportation (noun)

1. The South Carolina Railroad was the first company to have a passenger train.

2. In 1852, the Pacific Railroad of Missouri became the first railroad in the West.

3. To some people, trains seemed scary.

4. Today, automobiles are the most common form of passenger travel.

5. However, many people remain fans of train travel.

Verbs . . .

Tenses of Verbs

A verb has three principal parts: *present, past,* and *past participle.* (The part used with the helping verbs *has, have,* or *had* is called the past participle.)

All six of the tenses are formed from these principal parts. The past and past participle of regular verbs are formed by adding *ed* to the present tense. The past and past participle of irregular verbs are formed with different spellings. (See the chart on page **756**.)

754.1

Present Tense Verbs

The present tense of a verb expresses action (or a state of being) that is happening now or that happens continually or regularly. (See page **529**.)

> **The universe** is **gigantic. It** takes **my breath away.**

754.2

Past Tense Verbs

The past tense of a verb expresses action (or a state of being) that was completed in the past. (See page **529**.)

> **To most people many years ago, the universe** was **the earth, the sun, and some stars. The universe** reached **only as far as the eye could see.**

754.3

Future Tense Verbs

The future tense of a verb expresses action that *will* take place. (See page **529**.)

> **Maybe I** will visit **another galaxy in my lifetime.**
>
> **Somebody** will find **a way to do it.**

SCHOOL DAZE

I **know** the answer!

Okay, but I **said** you **will have** to sing the answer . . . go ahead!

punctuate *edit* capitalize
SPELL
improve
755

ELPS 3E, 3H, 5G

Using the Parts of Speech

Grammar Practice

Verbs 2

■ Present Tense Verbs
■ Past Tense Verbs
■ Future Tense Verbs

 For each of the following sentences, write the verb or verbs and identify them as "present tense," "past tense," or "future tense."

Example: The "Great War" started in Europe more than 90 years ago.

started (past tense)

1. Now we call that war World War I.

2. The conflict began in the summer of 1914.

3. The Central Powers (Germany and Austria-Hungary) fought against the Allies.

4. England and France, two countries on the Allied side, sent more than 2 million soldiers to the battlefields.

5. England and France are still allies (friends) to this day.

6. Both countries also maintain a friendly relationship with the United States.

7. These three nations probably will remain allies for years to come.

8. Leaders of these countries meet together often.

9. These nations depend on one another economically.

10. They will support one another during times of crisis.

11. It is good to have political friends!

Learning Language With a partner, describe something you did last weekend. Write each verb down from your description. Using the same verbs, describe the event as if it is happening right now, or how it would happen in the future. Remember to use the correct verb tenses. Refer to page 754 to help you.

 **TEKS** 6.19A(i)

Common Irregular Verbs and Their Principal Parts

The principal parts of the common irregular verbs are listed below. The part used with the helping verbs *has, have,* or *had* is called the **past participle**. (Also see page **527**.)

Present Tense:	I write.	She hides.
Past Tense:	Earlier I wrote.	Earlier she hid.
Past Participle:	I have written.	She has hidden.

Present Tense	Past Tense	Past Participle	Present Tense	Past Tense	Past Participle
am, is, are	was, were	been	lead	led	led
begin	began	begun	lie (recline)	lay	lain
bid (offer)	bid	bid	lie (deceive)	lied	lied
bid (order)	bade	bidden	make	made	made
bite	bit	bitten	ride	rode	ridden
blow	blew	blown	ring	rang	rung
break	broke	broken	rise	rose	risen
bring	brought	brought	run	ran	run
burst	burst	burst	see	saw	seen
buy	bought	bought	set	set	set
catch	caught	caught	shake	shook	shaken
come	came	come	shine (polish)	shined	shined
dive	dived, dove	dived	shine (light)	shone	shone
do	did	done	shrink	shrank	shrunk
draw	drew	drawn	sing	sang, sung	sung
drink	drank	drunk	sink	sank, sunk	sunk
drive	drove	driven	sit	sat	sat
eat	ate	eaten	sleep	slept	slept
fall	fell	fallen	speak	spoke	spoken
fight	fought	fought	spring	sprang, sprung	sprung
flee	fled	fled	steal	stole	stolen
fly	flew	flown	strive	strove	striven
forsake	forsook	forsaken	swear	swore	sworn
freeze	froze	frozen	swim	swam	swum
get	got	gotten, got	swing	swung	swung
give	gave	given	take	took	taken
go	went	gone	tear	tore	torn
grow	grew	grown	throw	threw	thrown
hang (execute)	hanged	hanged	wake	woke, waked	woken, waked
hang (dangle)	hung	hung	wear	wore	worn
hide	hid	hidden, hid	weave	wove	woven
know	knew	known	wring	wrung	wrung
lay (place)	laid	laid	write	wrote	written

punctuate *edit* capitalize SPELL
improve

757

Using the Parts of Speech

TEKS 6.19A(i)
ELPS 3E

Grammar Practice

Verbs 3

- ◼ **Present Tense Verbs**
- ◼ **Past Tense Verbs**
- ◼ **Past Participle Verbs**

For each sentence below, write the correct form of the irregular verb or verbs in parentheses.

Example: I have always _____ a roller-coaster fan. *(am)*
　　　　　 been

1. Mom _____ us to the amusement park last Saturday. *(take)*

2. Alberto and Jim _____ along. *(come)*

3. They had _____ at my house the night before, and we nearly _____ with excitement. *(sleep, burst)*

4. On Saturday morning, Mom _____ us up at 7:00, and we _____ a light breakfast. *(wake, eat)*

5. As soon as we arrived at the park, we _____ in line for the super roller coaster. *(get)*

6. If we had _____ that we would wait more than an hour, we wouldn't have _____ in line. *(know, get)*

7. After we _____ the roller coaster, we _____ from the water fountain. *(ride, drink)*

8. Dad had _____ me money to purchase a souvenir. *(give)*

9. Just as I _____ my money on the counter, a gust of wind _____ it away. *(lay, blow)*

10. I _____ after it, and, luckily, I _____ it. *(run, catch)*

11. You have never _____ someone so relieved! *(see)*

12. I _____ a cap with the park's name on the front. *(buy)*

Next Step: Write three sentences using the present tense, past tense, and past participle of the word *begin*. Read your sentences to a partner.

PARTS OF SPEECH

Verbs . . .

Tenses of Verbs

758.1

Present Perfect Tense Verbs

The present perfect tense verb expresses action that began in the past but continues or is completed in the present. The present perfect tense is formed by adding *has* or *have* to the past participle. (Also see page **530**.)

I have wondered **for some time how the stars got their names.**

A visible star has emitted **light for thousands of years.**

758.2

Past Perfect Tense Verbs

The past perfect tense verb expresses action that began in the past and was completed in the past. This tense is formed by adding *had* to the past participle. (Also see page **530**.)

I had hoped **to see a shooting star on our camping trip.**

758.3

Future Perfect Tense Verbs

A future perfect tense verb expresses action that will begin in the future and will be completed by a specific time in the future. The future perfect tense is formed by adding *will have* to the past participle. (Also see page **530**.)

By the middle of this century, we probably will have discovered many more stars, planets, and galaxies.

758.4

Present Continuous Tense Verbs

A present continuous tense verb expresses action that is not completed at the time of stating it. The present continuous tense is formed by adding *am, is,* or *are* to the *ing* form of the main verb.

Scientists are learning **a great deal from their study of the sky.**

758.5

Past Continuous Tense Verbs

A past continuous tense verb expresses action that was happening at a certain time in the past. This tense is formed by adding *was* or *were* to the *ing* form of the main verb.

Astronomers were beginning **their quest for knowledge hundreds of years ago.**

758.6

Future Continuous Tense Verbs

A future continuous tense verb expresses action that will take place at a certain time in the future. This tense is formed by adding *will be* to the *ing* form of the main verb.

Someday astronauts will be going **to Mars.**

This tense can also be formed by adding a phrase noting the future *(are going to)* plus *be* to the *ing* form of the main verb.

They are going to be performing **many experiments.**

punctuate *edit* *capitalize*
SPELL
improve
759

Using the Parts of Speech

ELPS 3E, 5B, 5G

Grammar Practice

Verbs 4

- ■ Present Perfect Tense Verbs
- ■ Past Perfect Tense Verbs
- ■ Future Perfect Tense Verbs

For each of the sentences below, write the verb and identify the tense as "present perfect," "past perfect," or "future perfect."

Example: Students in the ecology club had thought quite a bit about the environment.

had thought (past perfect)

1. Progress has caused some negative effects on our world.

2. As early as the 1970s, research scientists in Antarctica had noticed the growth of a hole in our atmosphere's ozone layer.

3. Some argue that the hole had grown due to pollution.

4. This discovery has worried researchers.

5. Scientists have suggested ways to protect the ozone layer.

6. Some countries have banned the use of chlorofluorocarbons.

7. Environmental groups hope all pollution will have stopped by 2020.

8. The ecology club students had wanted to help in some way.

9. They have worked to spread the word about saving the ozone.

10. They will have made 100 posters by the end of the week.

11. The club members have promised to put the posters up this weekend.

Next Step: Write a paragraph about what your community is doing to reduce pollution. Use a perfect tense verb in each sentence. Share your paragraph with the class.

PARTS OF SPEECH

TEKS 6.19A(i), 6.19B

Verbs . . .
Forms of Verbs

760.1
Active or
Passive Voice

The voice of a verb tells you whether the subject is doing the action or is receiving the action. Use a verb in the active voice (in any tense) if the subject is doing the action in a sentence. (See page **528**.)

> **I** dream **of going to galaxies light-years from Earth.**
>
> **I** will travel **in an ultrafast spaceship.**

A verb is in the passive voice if the subject is not doing the action. The action is done *by* someone or something else. The passive voice is always indicated with a helping verb plus a past participle or a past tense verb.

> **My daydreams often** are shattered **by reality.** (The subject *daydreams* is not doing the action.)
>
> **Of course, reality** can be seen **differently by different people.** (The subject *reality* is not doing the action.)

Tense	Active Voice		Passive Voice	
	Singular	**Plural**	**Singular**	**Plural**
Present Tense	I find	we find	I am found	we are found
	you find	you find	you are found	you are found
	he/she/it finds	they find	he/she/it is found	they are found
Past Tense	I found	we found	I was found	we were found
	you found	you found	you were found	you were found
	he found	they found	he/she/it was found	they were found
Future Tense	I will find	we will find	I will be found	we will be found
	you will find	you will find	you will be found	you will be found
	he will find	they will find	he/she/it will be found	they will be found
Present Perfect	I have found	we have found	I have been found	we have been found
	you have found	you have found	you have been found	you have been found
	he has found	they have found	he/she/it has been found	they have been found
Past Perfect	I had found	we had found	I had been found	we had been found
	you had found	you had found	you had been found	you had been found
	he had found	they had found	he/she/it had been found	they had been found
Future Perfect	I will have found	we will have found	I will have been found	we will have been found
	you will have found	you will have found	you will have been found	you will have been found
	he will have found	they will have found	he/she/it will have been found	they will have been found

⭐ **TEKS** 6.19A(i), 6.19B
ELPS 3E

Grammar Practice

Verbs 5

■ Active or Passive Voice

For each sentence below, write the verb and tell whether it is active (doing the action) or passive (receiving the action).

Example: William Shakespeare has been called the greatest writer of the English language.

has been called (passive)

1. People feel his influence in many ways.

2. Many words and phrases were invented by Shakespeare.

3. He created the words "moonbeam," "elbow," and "buzzer."

4. Most people know Shakespeare best for his plays.

5. He wrote 37 plays in his lifetime.

6. Additional plays might have been written by Shakespeare and another writer.

7. Shakespeare also created beautiful poems, including many sonnets.

Rewrite each of the following sentences using the active voice. Add or delete words as necessary. Read your new sentences to a partner.

Example: Shakespeare's plays have been enjoyed by millions of people.

Millions of people have enjoyed Shakespeare's plays.

1. His plays have been explained in different ways by different audiences.

2. The play *The Taming of the Shrew* was made by Gil Junger into the movie *10 Things I Hate About You.*

3. The part of the "shrew" was played by Julia Stiles.

4. Whatever you think about the play, it will be enjoyed by you.

5. Shakespeare's plays are loved by people who have read them.

PARTS OF SPEECH

PARTS OF SPEECH

Verbs . . .
Forms of Verbs

762.1
Singular and Plural Verbs

A singular subject needs a singular verb. A plural subject needs a plural verb. For action verbs, only the third-person singular verb form is different: *I wonder, we wonder, you wonder, she wonders, they wonder.* Some linking verbs, however, have several different forms.

First Person	**Singular:**	I am **(or** was**) a good student.**
	Plural:	We are **(or** were**) good students.**
Second Person	**Singular:**	You are **(or** were**) a cheerleader.**
	Plural:	You are **(or** were**) cheerleaders.**
Third Person	**Singular:**	He is **(or** was**) on the wrestling team.**
	Plural:	They are **(or** were**) also on the team.**

762.2
Transitive Verbs

A transitive verb is a verb that transfers its action to a direct object. The object makes the meaning of the verb complete. A transitive verb is always an action verb (never a linking verb). (See page **618**.)

> **An earthquake** shook **San Francisco in 1906.** (*Shook* transfers its action to the direct object *San Francisco*. Without *San Francisco*, the meaning of the verb *shook* is incomplete.)

> **The city's people** spent **many years rebuilding.** (Without the direct object *years*, the verb's meaning is incomplete.)

A transitive verb transfers the action directly to a direct object and indirectly to an indirect object.

> **Fires** destroyed **the city.** (direct object: *city*)

> **Our teacher** gave **us the details.** (indirect object: *us*; direct object: *details*)

See **730.4** and **730.5** for more on direct and indirect objects.

762.3
Intransitive Verbs

An intransitive verb does not need an object to complete its meaning. (See page **618**.)

> **Abigail** was shopping. (The verb's meaning is complete.)

> **Her stomach** felt **queasy.** (*Queasy* is a predicate adjective describing *stomach*; there is no direct object.)

> **She** lay **down on the bench.** (Again, there is no direct object. *Down* is an adverb modifying *lay*.)

Grammar Practice

Verbs 6

■ **Singular and Plural Verbs**

For each sentence below, write the correct choice from the verb forms in parentheses and identify it as "singular" or "plural."

Example: She *(was, were)* the perfect actress for the role.
was—singular

1. I *(am, are)* going to try out for the next play.

2. We *(am, are)* fine actors.

3. We *(was, were)* in the last play.

4. She *(love, loves)* to be the star.

5. They *(are, is)* in the chorus.

6. You must *(shine, shines)* the spotlights on Kim.

■ **Transitive Verbs**
■ **Intransitive Verbs**

For each of the following sentences, write whether the underlined verb is transitive or intransitive.

Example: Nigel <u>threw</u> a forward pass to Manuel.
transitive

1. Manuel <u>turned</u> sideways to catch it.

2. Suddenly, Roger ran up to Manuel and <u>grabbed</u> the football.

3. Roger <u>carried</u> it all the way down the field for a touchdown.

4. He <u>spiked</u> the ball onto the artificial turf.

5. Then he <u>danced</u> around the end zone.

6. Unfortunately, the referee had <u>blown</u> his whistle.

7. Roger <u>looked</u> surprised that he hadn't scored the touchdown.

8. The team gloomily <u>walked</u> back up the field.

Verbs

Forms of Verbs

Some verbs can be either transitive or intransitive.

Transitive: She reads my note.   Albert ate an apple.

Intransitive: She reads aloud.   Albert ate already.

Verbals

A **verbal** is a word that is made from a verb but acts as another part of speech. Gerunds, participles, and infinitives are verbals.

A gerund is a verb form that ends in *ing* and is used as a *noun*. A gerund often begins a gerund phrase.

Worrying **is useless.** (The gerund is the subject noun.)

You should stop worrying about so many things. (The gerund phrase is the direct object.)

A participle is a verb form ending in *ing* or *ed*. A participle is used as an *adjective* and often begins a participial phrase.

The idea of the earth shaking **and** splitting **both fascinates and frightens me.** (The participles modify *earth*.)

Rattling in the cabinets, **the dishes were about to crash to the floor.** (The participial phrase modifies *dishes*.)

Why doesn't this tired **earth just stand still?** (The participle modifies *earth*.)

An infinitive is a verb form introduced by *to*. It may be used as a *noun,* an *adjective,* or an *adverb.* It often begins an infinitive phrase.

My need to whisper **is due to this secret.** (The infinitive is an adjective modifying *need.*)

I am afraid to swim. (The infinitive is an adverb modifying the predicate adjective *afraid.*)

To overcome this fear **is my goal.** (The infinitive phrase is used as a noun and is the subject of this sentence.)

punctuate edit capitalize SPELL **765**
improve
Using the Parts of Speech

Grammar Practice

Verbs 7

■ Gerunds, Participles, and Infinitives

In each numbered sentence below, identify the underlined verb form as a gerund, a participle, or an infinitive.

Example: A Michigan man, J. Sterling Morton, worked to improve agricultural practices in Nebraska.
infinitive

(1) Arbor Day began in 1872 when Morton decided <u>to settle</u> in Nebraska. **(2)** He came up with a plan to get more trees <u>growing</u> in his adopted state. **(3)** <u>Working</u> as a newspaper editor, he wrote articles that encouraged people <u>to plant</u> more trees. **(4)** He said the trees would be good for <u>blocking</u> the winds, preventing soil erosion, and making the prairie lands more beautiful. **(5)** Morton proposed that people observe a special day <u>dedicated</u> to tree planting, and in 1885, Arbor Day was named a legal holiday in Nebraska. **(6)** In the beginning, April 22 (Morton's birthday) was the <u>selected</u> date. **(7)** Today, the date for Arbor Day varies by state, depending on the best time for <u>planting</u> trees locally. **(8)** <u>Improving</u> the look of a community is a great result of Arbor Day. **(9)** The success of the holiday in the United States has caused the idea <u>to spread</u> to other countries, as well.

For each of the following sentences, write the infinitive phrase and label how it is used: noun, adjective, or adverb.

Example: To improve the natural environment is the ecology club's cause.
To improve the natural environment (noun)

1. Our efforts to plant trees will result in a more scenic landscape.
2. A local business offered to supply seedlings.
3. We are eager to make a difference in our community.
4. Would you be willing to help us?

PARTS OF SPEECH

Adjectives . . .

An **adjective** is a word used to describe a noun or a pronoun. Adjectives tell *what kind, how many (how much),* or *which one.* They usually come before the word they describe. (See pages **532–535**.)

ancient **dinosaurs**   800 **species**   that **triceratops**

Adjectives are the same whether the word they describe is singular or plural.

small **brain**—or—small **brains**   large **tooth**—or—large **teeth**

766.1
Articles

The articles *a, an,* and *the* are adjectives.

A **brontosaurus was** an **animal about 70 feet long.**

The **huge dinosaur lived on land and ate plants.**

766.2
Proper Adjectives

A proper adjective is formed from a proper noun, and it is always capitalized. (See **662.1**.)

A Chicago **museum is home to the skeleton of one of these beasts.** (*Chicago* functions as a proper adjective describing the noun *museum.*)

766.3
Common Adjectives

A common adjective is any adjective that is not proper. It is not capitalized (unless it is the first word in a sentence).

Ancient **mammoths were** huge, woolly **creatures.**

They lived in the ice **fields of Siberia.**

Special Kinds of Adjectives

766.4
Demonstrative Adjectives

A demonstrative adjective points out a particular noun. *This* and *these* point out something nearby; *that* and *those* point out something at a distance.

This **mammoth is huge, but** that **mammoth is even bigger.**

NOTE When a noun does not follow *this, these, that,* or *those,* these words are pronouns, not adjectives. (See **744.1**.)

766.5
Compound Adjectives

A compound adjective is made up of two or more words. (Sometimes it is hyphenated.)

Dinosaurs were egg-laying **animals.**

The North American **Allosaurus had sharp teeth and powerful jaws.**

punctuate *edit* *capitalize*
SPELL
improve
Using the Parts of Speech

767

Grammar Practice

Adjectives 1

- Articles
- Proper Adjectives
- Common Adjectives

Label the underlined adjectives in the following sentences by writing "article," "proper," or "common."

Example: In 1957, Althea Gibson was <u>the</u> first <u>African American</u> <u>tennis</u> player to win at Wimbledon.

article, proper, common

1. As a <u>young</u> woman, Althea set out to be <u>the</u> best woman tennis player of all time.

2. This goal motivated her to win <u>a</u> girls' <u>singles</u> championship in New York in 1942 when she was 15 years old.

3. Ms. Gibson was the <u>first</u> African American to enter the <u>American Lawn Tennis Association</u> championships in 1950.

4. After college, she entered a <u>French</u> competition in 1956, and that tournament became her first <u>major</u> victory.

5. Althea also won <u>the</u> singles competition of the U.S. Open <u>two</u> years in a row.

6. Trophies from these championships lined a <u>broad</u> glass shelf.

7. After retiring from tennis, she toured America with the <u>Harlem Globetrotters</u> basketball team.

8. Later, Althea tried <u>professional</u> golf, and she became <u>an</u> athletic advisor for the state of New Jersey.

9. Ms. Gibson enjoyed those duties for <u>several</u> years.

10. Althea Gibson died on September 28, 2003, in a <u>New Jersey</u> hospital.

Next Step: Read the sentences above again, this time looking for demonstrative adjectives (not underlined). Write them down as you find them. (There are four.)

⭐ TEKS 6.19A(iii)

Adjectives
Special Kinds of Adjectives

768.1
Indefinite Adjectives

An indefinite adjective gives approximate, or indefinite, information (*any, few, many, most,* and so on). It does not tell exactly how many or how much.

> **Some mammoths were heavier than today's elephants.**

768.2
Predicate Adjectives

A predicate adjective follows a linking verb and describes the subject.

> **Mammoths were once abundant, but now they are extinct.**

Forms of Adjectives

768.3
Positive Adjectives

The positive form describes a noun or pronoun without comparing it to anyone or anything else.

> **The Eurostar is a fast train that runs between London, Paris, and Brussels.**
>
> **It is an impressive train.**

768.4
Comparative Adjectives

The comparative form of an adjective (*er*) compares two persons, places, things, or ideas. (See page **533**.)

> **The Eurostar is faster than the Orient Express.**

Some adjectives that have more than one syllable show comparisons by their *er* suffix, but many of them use the modifiers *more* or *less*.

> **It is a speedier commuter train than the Tobu Railway trains in Japan.**
>
> **This train is more impressive than my commuter train.**

768.5
Superlative Adjectives

The superlative form (*est* or *most* or *least*) compares three or more persons, places, things, or ideas. (See page **533**.)

> **In fact, the Eurostar is the fastest train in Europe.**
>
> **It is the most impressive commuter train in the world.**

768.6
Irregular Forms

Some adjectives use completely different words to express comparison.

good, better, best	**bad, worse, worst**
many, more, most	**little, less, least**

Grammar Practice

Adjectives 2

- Indefinite Adjectives
- Predicate Adjectives

For each of the following sentences, identify and label the indefinite adjectives and the predicate adjectives.

Example: Many homes were destroyed during the great Chicago fire of 1871.
many (indefinite)

1. Before the fire, most buildings were wooden.

2. Few buildings escaped the fire.

3. Wooden sidewalks were flammable and added fuel to the fire.

4. Almost 100,000 city residents became homeless due to the fire.

5. Some residents rebuilt their homes after the fire.

- Positive, Comparative, and Superlative Adjectives

Write the correct form of the underlined adjectives in the following sentences. Take turns reading the sentences aloud with a partner.

Example: The Panama Canal was one of the underlined expensive projects ever to be built.
most expensive

1. The bad problem affecting the construction workers was disease caused by mosquito bites.

2. The engineers had to make the canal 100 feet wide than they originally planned in order to let large ships through.

3. The *Jahre Viking*, currently the large ship in the world, is too wide to pass through the canal.

4. The first toll (in 1914) of 90 cents per ton was cheap than today's rate, which is almost three dollars per ton.

5. The quick travel time through the canal is eight hours.

Adverbs . . .

An **adverb** is a word used to modify a verb, an adjective, or another adverb. It tells *how, when, where, how often,* or *how much.* Adverbs can come before or after the words they modify. (See pages **536–539**.)

Dad snores loudly. (*Loudly* modifies the verb *snores.*)

His snores are really **explosive.** (*Really* modifies the adjective *explosive.*)

Dad snores very **loudly.** (*Very* modifies the adverb *loudly.*)

Types of Adverbs

There are four basic types of adverbs: *time, place, manner,* and *degree.*

770.1

Adverbs of Time

Adverbs of time tell *when, how often,* and *how long.*

tomorrow   often   never   always

Jen rarely **has time to go swimming.**

770.2

Adverbs of Place

Adverbs of place tell *where, to where,* or *from where.*

there   backward   outside

We'll set up our tent here.

770.3

Adverbs of Manner

Adverbs of manner often end in *ly* and tell *how* something is done.

unkindly   gently   well

Ahmed boldly **entered the dark cave.**

Some words used as adverbs can be written with or without the *ly* ending. When in doubt, use the *ly* form.

slow, slowly   deep, deeply

NOTE Not all words ending in *ly* are adverbs. *Lovely,* for example, is an adjective.

770.4

Adverbs of Degree

Adverbs of degree tell *how much* or *how little.*

scarcely   entirely   generally   very   really

Jess is usually **the leader in these situations.**

punctuate edit capitalize SPELL **771**
improve
Using the Parts of Speech

ELPS 3G, 5B

Grammar Practice

Adverbs 1

- Adverbs of Time
- Adverbs of Place
- Adverbs of Manner
- Adverbs of Degree

The number of adverbs in each sentence below is indicated in parentheses at the end of the sentence. Write the adverbs and identify them as adverbs of "time," "place," "manner," or "degree."

Example: We are going to see a Chicago Cubs game tomorrow. *(1)*
tomorrow (time)

1. The Chicago Cubs always play home games at Wrigley Field, generally during the day. *(2)*

2. Cubs fans really like to watch games there. *(2)*

3. People even stand outside of the stadium, waiting patiently for home runs that completely clear the fence. *(4)*

4. The last time the Cubs were world champions was 1908; now the Cubs rarely make it to the play-offs. *(2)*

5. Their fans often say, "Wait till next year," and they faithfully attend as many games as they can. *(2)*

6. Some of them openly complain that the Cubs will never win a World Series again. *(3)*

7. Although the Cubs may be a very poor team in some critics' opinions, their fans love them deeply. *(2)*

8. The fans eagerly purchase Cubs T-shirts and caps. *(1)*

9. They support their team enthusiastically. *(1)*

Learning Language With a partner, have a conversation about a topic you like, such as a favorite movie. Take turns asking questions with *when, how often, how long, where, how much* or *how little* about the topic. Explain your answers using adverbs of time, place, manner, and degree in sentences. Make a chart listing the adverbs from your conversation. Discuss any words that have you questions about.

PARTS OF SPEECH

Adverbs

Special Kinds of Adverbs

772.1
Conjunctive Adverbs

A conjunctive adverb can be used as a conjunction and shows a connection or a transition between two independent clauses. Most often, a conjunctive adverb follows a semicolon in a compound sentence; however, it can also appear at the beginning or end of a sentence. (Note that the previous sentence has an example of a conjunctive adverb.)

also	besides	however	instead
meanwhile	nevertheless	therefore	

Forms of Adverbs

Many adverbs—especially adverbs of manner—have three forms: *positive, comparative,* and *superlative.*

772.2
Positive Adverbs

The positive form describes but does not make a comparison.

> Juan woke up late.

> He quickly ate some breakfast.

772.3
Comparative Adverbs

The comparative form of an adverb *(er)* compares two things.

> Juan woke up later than he usually did. (See page 537.)

Some adverbs that have more than one syllable show comparisons by their *er* suffix, but many of them use the modifiers *more* or *less.*

> He ate his breakfast more quickly than usual.

772.4
Superlative Adverbs

The superlative form *(est* or *most* or *least)* compares three or more things. (See page 537.)

> Of the past three days, Juan woke up latest on Saturday.

> Of the past three days, he ate his breakfast least quickly on Saturday.

772.5
Irregular Forms

Some adverbs use completely different words to express comparison.

Positive	Comparative	Superlative
well	better	best
badly	worse	worst

TEKS 6.19A(iv)

Grammar Practice

Adverbs 2

■ **Conjunctive Adverbs**

Number your paper from 1 to 3 and write the three conjunctive adverbs that appear in the following paragraph. Read aloud with a partner.

Example: When money was invented, it made buying and selling easier. Thus, one coin could replace a basketful of vegetables.

Thus

Many people like to pay with cash; others, however, prefer to barter for goods. Buying from these people may be more difficult. A lot of shoppers today prefer to buy what they want at a mall instead. Meanwhile, the computer age and its electronic money are steering us toward a cashless economy. Electronic credit may eventually be all that people use to buy and sell.

■ **Comparative Adverbs**

For each sentence below, write the correct comparative form of the underlined adverb.

Example: A computer can solve a difficult arithmetic problem fast than a human can.

faster

1. Some students think the computer in Ms. Stowe's room works well than the one in the library.

2. The new word processor program actually runs slowly than the old one.

3. This green mouse moves smoothly than that red one.

4. The keys on Kayla's keyboard stick badly than mine do.

Prepositions

Prepositions are words that show location, time, or direction. They also provide details. Specifically, a preposition shows the relationship between its object and some other word in the sentence.

> **Raul hid** under **the stairs.** (*Under* shows the relationship between *hid* and *stairs.*)

774.1
Prepositional Phrases

A preposition never appears alone; it is always part of a prepositional phrase. A prepositional phrase includes the preposition, the object of the preposition, and the modifiers of the object. (See pages **540–541**.)

> **Raul's friends looked** in the clothes hamper. (preposition: *in*; object: *hamper*; modifiers: *the, clothes*)

A prepositional phrase functions as an adjective or as an adverb.

> **They checked the closet** with all the winter coats. (*With all the winter coats* functions as an adjective modifying *closet.*)

> **They wandered** around the house **looking for him.** (*Around the house* functions as an adverb modifying *wandered.*)

NOTE If a word found in the list of prepositions has no object, it is not a preposition. It is probably an adverb.

> **Raul had never won at hide 'n' seek** before. (*Before* is an adverb that modifies *had won.*)

Prepositions

aboard	apart from	beyond	from	like	outside	under
about	around	but	from among	near	outside of	underneath
above	aside from	by	from between	near to	over	until
according to	at	by means of	from under	next	over to	unto
across	away from	concerning	in	of	owing to	up
across from	back of	considering	in addition to	off	past	up to
after	because of	despite	in front of	on	prior to	upon
against	before	down	in place of	on account of	regarding	with
along	behind	down from	in regard to	on behalf of	since	within
along with	below	during	in spite of	on top of	through	without
alongside	beneath	except	inside	onto	throughout	
alongside of	beside	except for	inside of	opposite	to	
amid	besides	excepting	instead of	out	together with	
among	between	for	into	out of	toward	

TEKS 6.19A(v)

ELPS 3E

Grammar Practice

Prepositions

For each sentence below, write the prepositional phrase or phrases. (The number of phrases in each sentence is in parentheses.) Circle the prepositions.

Example: The first issue of the *Cherokee Phoenix* newspaper was printed in English and in Cherokee. *(3)*

⟨of⟩ the Cherokee Phoenix newspaper, ⟨in⟩ English, ⟨in⟩ Cherokee

1. For many years, Cherokee history was told from memory. *(2)*

2. No written form of their language existed at the time. *(2)*

3. A Native American named Sequoya was a silversmith and a trader in Georgia. *(1)*

4. His name was given to him by missionaries. *(2)*

5. Until his creation of a symbol for each sound in Cherokee, none of the Cherokee could read or write. *(5)*

6. Sequoya wrote a story in Cherokee on some paper, and his daughter read it. *(2)*

7. He traveled throughout Arkansas so he could teach other Cherokee. *(1)*

8. Then he moved with the whole tribe to Oklahoma. *(2)*

9. Without his assistance, the Cherokee might not have become such a strong, united people. *(1)*

10. On account of Sequoya's achievement, the Cherokee people became leaders among Native Americans. *(2)*

11. The giant California trees called *sequoias* are named after him. *(1)*

12. He is remembered, along with other great Americans, for his contributions. *(2)*

Next Step: Pick five prepositions from the list on the facing page. Write several sentences using those prepositions correctly. Exchange papers with a classmate and circle each other's prepositional phrases. Discuss your findings.

PARTS OF SPEECH

Conjunctions . . .

A **conjunction** connects individual words or groups of words. There are three kinds of conjunctions: *coordinating, correlative,* and *subordinating.* (See pages **542–544.**)

776.1

Coordinating Conjunctions

A coordinating conjunction connects a word to a word, a phrase to a phrase, or a clause to a clause. The words, phrases, or clauses joined by a coordinating conjunction must be equal, or of the same type.

Polluted rivers and streams can be cleaned up. (Two nouns are connected by *and.*)

Ride a bike or plant a tree to reduce pollution. (Two verb phrases are connected by *or.*)

Maybe you can't invent a pollution-free engine, but you can cut down on the amount of energy you use. (Two equal independent clauses are connected by *but.*)

NOTE When a coordinating conjunction is used to make a compound sentence, a comma always comes before it.

776.2

Correlative Conjunctions

Correlative conjunctions are conjunctions used in pairs.

We must reduce not only pollution but also excess energy use.

Either you're part of the solution, or you're part of the problem.

Conjunctions

Coordinating Conjunctions
and, but, or, nor, for, so, yet

Correlative Conjunctions
either, or   neither, nor   not only, but also   both, and   whether, or   as, so

Subordinating Conjunctions
after, although, as, as if, as long as, as though, because, before, if, in order that, provided that, since, so, so that, that, though, till, unless, until, when, where, whereas, while

Grammar Practice

Conjunctions

■ **Coordinating Conjunctions**

Combine the following pairs of sentences by using a coordinating conjunction to connect the sentence parts given in parentheses.

Example: Every country has a flag. Each flag is different. *(clauses)*

Every country has a flag, but each flag is different.

1. Sonja likes the Canadian flag. Sanjeev likes the Canadian flag. *(words)*

2. Displaying a flag can be patriotic. Carrying a flag can be patriotic. *(words)*

3. You can buy a cotton flag. You can buy a nylon flag. *(phrases)*

4. The school flag got very wet. The janitor dried it. *(clauses)*

5. Does this flag belong to Sweden? Does this flag belong to Denmark? *(words)*

6. Citizens honor their flag. A flag represents the country. *(clauses)*

■ **Correlative Conjunctions**

Use a different set of correlative conjunctions to combine each sentence pair below. Underline the conjunctions.

Example: Jaguars live in rain forests. Tapirs live in rain forests.

Both jaguars and tapirs live in rain forests.

1. Elephants do not live in South America. Tigers do not live in South America.

2. In a rain forest, people walk. They also ride in boats.

3. The Amazon is one of the longest rivers in the world. It flows through one of the largest rain forests in the world.

4. If we want to use rain-forest plants for medicines, we must save the rain forests. If we want to use rain-forest plants for food, we must save the rain forests.

Conjunctions

778.1
Subordinating
Conjunctions

A subordinating conjunction is a word or group of words that connects two clauses that are not equally important. A subordinating conjunction begins a dependent clause and connects it to an independent clause to make a complex sentence. (See page **565** and the chart on page **776**.)

> **Fuel-cell engines are unusual** because **they don't have moving parts.**

> Since **fuel-cell cars run on hydrogen, the only waste products are water and heat.**

As you can see in the sentences above, a comma sets off the dependent clause only when it begins the sentence. A comma is usually not used when the dependent clause follows the independent clause.

NOTE Relative pronouns and conjunctive adverbs can also connect clauses.

Interjections

An **interjection** is a word or phrase used to express strong emotion or surprise. Punctuation (a comma or an exclamation point) is used to separate an interjection from the rest of the sentence.

> Wow, **would you look at that!** Oh no! **He's falling!**

Forget it! We aren't using activity money for that.

Yikes, I've told everyone that we could buy a plasma-screen TV for our classroom!

TEKS 6.19A(vii)
ELPS 3E

Grammar Practice

Conjunctions and Interjections

■ Subordinating Conjunctions
■ Interjections

 Write the subordinating conjunction that connects the clauses in each of the sentences below. (The chart on page 776 will help.)

Example: The buffalo became a symbol of the Native
Americans because it was vital to their survival.

because

1. After the Native Americans killed the huge animals they needed, they used every part of the buffalo, from horns to tail hairs. Wow!

2. Before the settlers moved into Native American areas, millions of buffalo roamed through the prairies.

3. Because buffalo herds were deliberately overhunted during the 1800s, the herds declined in the United States.

4. Oh dear, the buffalo was almost extinct when President Ulysses S. Grant created Yellowstone National Park.

5. Although the buffalo no longer rules the prairies, many tribes of Native Americans are working to increase the herd numbers.

6. Gee, more than 55 tribes have joined together to help restore the buffalo herds since the Intertribal Bison Cooperative was formed in 1990.

7. While Native Americans no longer need food from the buffalo to survive, selling buffalo meat has become a huge industry.

8. Whereas the buffalo once meant food and clothing to the Native Americans, today the meat can be sold to help support the tribes.

9. Well, the Native Americans can still make use of the majestic animal as long as the buffalo herds continue to grow.

Next Step: Find the four interjections in the sentences above and write them on your paper. Read them to a partner.

Quick Guide: Parts of Speech

In the English language, there are eight parts of speech. Understanding them will help you improve your writing skills. Every word you write is a part of speech—a noun, a verb, an adjective, and so on. The chart below lists the eight parts of speech.

Noun

A word that names a person, a place, a thing, or an idea

Alex Moya   Belize   ladder   courage

Pronoun

A word used in place of a noun

I   he   it   they   you   anybody   some

Verb

A word that shows action or links a subject to another word in the sentence

sing   shake   catch   is   are

Adjective

A word that describes a noun or a pronoun

stormy   red   rough   seven   grand

Adverb

A word that describes a verb, an adjective, or another adverb

quickly   today   now   bravely   softer

Preposition

A word that shows position or direction and introduces a prepositional phrase

around   up   under   over   between   to

Conjunction

A word that connects other words or groups of words

and   but   or   so   because   when

Interjection

A word (set off by commas or an exclamation point) that shows strong emotion

Stop! Hey, how are you?

punctuate *edit* capitalize
improve SPELL
781
ELPS 3E
Using the Parts of Speech

Grammar Practice

Parts of Speech Review

For each numbered sentence below, write whether the underlined word is a noun, a pronoun, a verb, an adjective, an adverb, a preposition, a conjunction, or an interjection.

Example: <u>Wow</u>, it took months for an immigrant to travel across the ocean in the 1800s.

interjection

(1) Ellis Island was the first <u>stop</u> for many immigrants seeking a better life in the United States. **(2)** Between 1892 and 1954, the island was the country's <u>main</u> immigration center. **(3)** More than 12 million immigrants <u>passed</u> through its gates during that time.

(4) In its first year of operation, nearly 450,000 people stepped <u>on</u> American soil for the first time at Ellis Island. **(5)** <u>It</u> welcomed 11,747 immigrants, the most in a single day, on April 17, 1907. **(6)** About 40 percent of all Americans have an ancestor who arrived at Ellis Island, <u>but</u> it accepted its last immigrant in November 1954.

(7) After the center closed, the great limestone walls of the Main Arrival Building <u>slowly</u> began to crumble. **(8)** Then, in 1965, Ellis Island <u>became</u> part of the Statue of Liberty National Monument. **(9)** Through <u>generous</u> private donations, the building was restored to its original state. **(10)** The <u>cost</u> was more than $156 million. **(11)** <u>Wow!</u> **(12)** In 1990, the doors of the old building, now a museum, <u>finally</u> reopened.

(13) Today, museum visitors research <u>their</u> ancestors. **(14)** Exhibits <u>and</u> hundreds of photographs honor this country's immigrant heritage. **(15)** Every U.S. citizen should make a trip <u>to</u> Ellis Island.

Next Step: Write a two-word sentence (noun and verb). Exchange papers with a classmate and keep adding words to each other's sentences until they have all eight parts of speech.

Credits

Photos: P. cover (astronaut), x (fire), 204, 353, 366, 368, 496, 499, 603 ©Corbis; cover (headset), v, vi, ix, xi (satelitte, antenna), xii, 1, 5 (doorknob), 9, 29, 32, 57, 93, 97 (flashlight), 101, 105, 107, 113, 115, 123, 129, 137, 142, 145 (scale), 161 (eggs, can), 165, 169, 175, 181, 191, 192, 197 (remote, headset), 231, 235, 241, 243, 247, 263, 271 (fishbowl), 274, 276, 284, 286, 305, 309, 315, 327, 339, 349, 375, 380, 391 (fish, mic), 417, 425, 435, 452, 455, 473, 475, 477, 479, 483, 485, 489, 491, 503, 507, 509, 545 (all), 571, 782 ©Comstock/Getty Images; cover (moon) Courtesy of NASA; cover (saturn,star), cover (windows), back cover, endsheet, x (rock, coffee pot), xi (periscope, flashlight), xvii, xviii, 10, 33, 44, 45, 71, 75, 97 (turtle shell), 129, 145 (pencil, clipboard, donut), 161 (chicken), 173, 205 (pencil), 211, 227 (mouse, cheese), 271 (computer, kitten), 276, 277, 301, 331, 353, 361, 371 (monkey, duck), 375, 382, 467, 469, 471, 477, 487, 489, 495, 499, 505, 595, 603 ©Photodisc/Getty Images; cover (solar panel) ©Digital Vision/Getty Images; 5 (key), 9 ©Thinkstock/Jupiter Images; 11 ©Blend Images/Alamy; 65, 68, 83 ©Stockbyte/Getty Images; 197 (cardboard) Harcourt; 205 ©Comstock/Jupiter Images; 227 (branch) ©Getty Images; 297 ©Artville/Getty Images; 365 Sam Dudgeon/HRW; 371 (cat) John Langford/HRW; 373 ©Eyewire/Getty Images; 391 (mask), 507 HMH Collection; 414 ©Alamy; 472 ©Sami Sarkis/Photographer's Choice RF/Getty Images; 478 ©Roger Weber/Digital Vision/Getty Images; 484 ©Steve Skjold/Alamy; 490 ©Jose Luis Pelaez, Inc/Blend Images/Getty Images; 502 ©Toby Burrows/Digital Vision/Getty Images; 508 ©SuperStock RF/SuperStock; 510 ©Ablestock.com/Jupiter; 515, 569, 581 ©Artville/Getty Images.

Texas Essential Knowledge and Skills (TEKS) for English Language Arts

The TEKS for English Language Arts are the skills you need to master by the end of Grade 6. The first column in the chart below lists the English Language Arts TEKS. The second column shows where these TEKS are taught in *Texas Write Source*.

⭐ (TEKS) 6.14 Writing/Writing Process

Students use elements of the writing process (planning, drafting, revising, editing, and publishing) to compose text. Students are expected to:

A plan a first draft by selecting a genre appropriate for conveying the intended meaning to an audience, determining appropriate topics through a range of strategies (e.g., discussion, background reading, personal interests, interviews); and developing a thesis or controlling idea;	pages 7, 8, 13, 73, 78, 85, 87, 89, 95, 102, 103,140, 155, 158, 163, 170–172, 177, 208, 221, 224, 229, 236, 274, 291, 294, 299, 306, 308, 316, 342, 356, 367, 392, 408, 410, 444, 573, 578, 592–595, 600, 601
B develop drafts by choosing an appropriate organizational strategy (e.g., sequence of events, cause-effect, compare-contrast) and building on ideas to create a focused, organized, and coherent piece of writing;	pages 8, 13, 76, 77, 79–82, 85, 87, 89, 96, 108–109, 111, 114–116, 141, 172–174, 179, 182–184, 229, 237, 240, 275, 307, 308, 311–314, 343, 358, 367, 418, 421, 445, 578, 582–588, 596–599
C revise drafts to clarify meaning, enhance style, include simple and compound sentences, and improve transitions by adding, deleting, combining, and rearranging sentences or larger units of text after rethinking how well questions of purpose, audience, and genre have been addressed;	pages 7–9, 17–21, 42, 43, 96, 107, 112, 114, 115, 117, 126, 143, 175, 180, 185–189, 194, 241, 246, 248, 249, 254, 309, 314, 317, 319–321, 360, 417, 418–421, 559–561, 563, 564, 578 pages 104, 116
D edit drafts for grammar, mechanics, and spelling; and	pages 9, 22, 23, 44, 74, 82, 85, 87, 89, 124, 128, 144, 164, 191, 196, 210, 230, 257, 281, 300, 330, 361, 369, 432, 578
E revise final draft in response to feedback from peers and teacher and publish written work for appropriate audiences.	pages 9, 18, 19, 29, 30, 59, 63, 64, 66, 67, 122, 143, 144, 164, 190, 197, 210, 252, 256, 276, 324, 344, 361, 369, 419, 426, 433, 445

*Page References in *Student Edition*
*Page References in *SkillsBook*

⭐ TEKS 6.15 Writing/Literary Texts

Students write literary texts to express their ideas and feelings about real or imagined people, events, and ideas. Students are expected to:

A write imaginative stories that include:

pages 150, 151, 354–360, 362–364, 604–607

(i)   a clearly defined focus, plot, and point of view;

(ii) a specific, believable setting created through the use of sensory details; and

(iii) dialogue that develops the story;

B write poems using:

pages 366, 368, 370–373

page 172

(i)   poetic techniques (e.g., alliteration, onomatopoeia);

(ii) figurative language (e.g., similes, metaphors); and

(iii) graphic elements (e.g., capital letters, line length).

⭐ TEKS 6.16 Writing/Narrative Texts

Students write about their own experiences. Students are expected to write a personal narrative that has a clearly defined focus and communicates the importance of or reasons for actions and/or consequences.

pages 99, 100, 103, 108–112, 138, 139, 141, 142

⭐ TEKS 6.17 Writing/Expository and Procedural Texts

Students write expository and procedural or work-related texts to communicate ideas and information to specific audiences for specific purposes. Students are expected to:

A create multi-paragraph essays to convey information about a topic that:

pages 162, 167, 168, 170, 173, 176–180, 182–185, 205–207, 209, 210, 212, 214, 215, 409, 414, 419, 620, 621

(i)   present effective introductions and concluding paragraphs;

(ii) guide and inform the reader's understanding of key ideas and evidence;

(iii) include specific facts, details, and examples in an appropriately organized structure; and

(iv) use a variety of sentence structures and transitions to link paragraphs;

*Page References in *Student Edition*
*Page References in *SkillsBook*

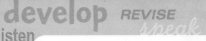
B write informal letters that convey ideas, include important information, demonstrate a sense of closure, and use appropriate conventions (e.g., date, salutation, closing):

(1) write informal letters that convey ideas;

(2) write informal letters that include important information;

(3) write informal letters that demonstrate a sense of closure; and

(4) write informal letters that use appropriate conventions;

pages 90, 91, 218, 219, 284–289

C write responses to literary or expository texts and provide evidence from the text to demonstrate understanding;

(1) write responses to literary or expository texts; and

(2) provide evidence from the text to demonstrate understanding;

pages 148, 149, 217, 303, 304, 306–308, 310–314, 320, 340–343, 346–351, 448

D produce a multimedia presentation involving text and graphics using available technology:

(1) produce a multimedia presentation involving text using available technology; and

(2) produce a multimedia presentation involving graphics using available technology.

pages 60, 63, 64, 197, 263, 433, 444–447, 449–451, 622, 623

⭐ (TEKS) 6.18 Writing/Persuasive Texts

Students write persuasive texts to influence the attitudes or actions of a specific audience on specific issues. Students are expected to write persuasive essays for appropriate audiences that establish a position and include sound reasoning, detailed and relevant evidence, and consideration of alternatives.

pages 233, 234, 237–240, 242–246, 249, 252, 253, 272–275, 279, 282, 283, 285, 294

*Page References in *Student Edition*
*Page References in *SkillsBook*

⬥ TEKS 6.19 Oral and Written Conventions/Conventions

Students understand the function of and use the conventions of academic language when speaking and writing. Students will continue to apply earlier standards with greater complexity. Students are expected to:

A use and understand the function of the following parts of speech in the context of reading, writing, and speaking:
  - (i)   verbs (irregular verbs and active and passive voice);
  - (ii) non-count nouns (e.g., rice, paper);
  - (iii) predicate adjectives (She is intelligent) and their comparative and superlative forms (e.g., many, more, most);
  - (iv) conjunctive adverbs (e.g. conjunctive adverbs (e.g., consequently, furthermore, indeed);
  - (v)   prepositions and prepositional phrases to convey location, time, direction, or to provide details;
  - (vi) indefinite pronouns (e.g., all, both, nothing, anything);
  - (vii) subordinating conjunctions (e.g., while, because, although, if);
  - (viii) transitional words and phrases that demonstrate an understanding of the function of the transition related to the organization of the writing (e.g., on the contrary, in addition to);

pages 16, 21, 104, 106, 116, 117, 125, 185, 192, 193, 250, 251, 258, 259, 312, 313, 319, 326, 428, 517, 521, 526–528, 533, 540–542, 544, 567, 576, 588, 620, 621, 640, 641, 652, 653, 738, 739, 746, 747, 756, 757, 760, 761, 768, 769, 772–774, 776, 778, 779

pages 79–82, 139, 140, 145, 146, 161–164, 167, 168, 173–176, 181, 182, 187, 188, 193, 194, 201, 202

B differentiate between the active and passive voice and know how to use them both; and

pages 326, 528, 760, 761
pages 167, 168, 201, 202,

C use complete simple and compound sentences with correct subject-verb agreement.

pages 194, 260, 429, 554–557, 563, 564
pages 93–98

*Page References in *Student Edition*
*Page References in *SkillsBook*

⭐ (TEKS) 6.20 Oral/Written Conventions/Handwriting, Capitalization, and Punctuation

Students write legibly and use appropriate capitalization and punctuation conventions in their compositions. Students are expected to:

A use capitalization for:
  (i)   abbreviations;
  (ii)   initials and acronyms; and
  (iii) organizations;

pages 195, 261, 662, 663, 670, 671, 676–679
pages 45, 46, 49–52, 57, 58

B recognize and use punctuation marks including:
  (i)   commas in compound sentences;
  (ii)   proper punctuation and spacing for quotations; and
  (iii) parentheses, brackets, and ellipses (to indicate omissions and interruptions or incomplete statements);

pages 111, 121, 127, 128, 328, 394, 411, 413, 430, 431, 604, 636–639, 644–647 658–661
pages 15, 16, 19, 20, 23, 24, 33, 34, 41, 49, 50, 57, 58

C use proper mechanics including italics and underlining of titles of books.

pages 329, 344, 415, 416, 648, 649
pages 25, 26

⭐ (TEKS) 6.22 Research/Research Plan

Students ask open-ended research questions and develop a plan for answering them. Students are expected to:

A brainstorm, consult with others, decide upon a topic, and formulate open-ended questions to address the major research topic; and

pages 208, 213, 376, 396–398, 434

B generate a research plan for gathering relevant information about the major research question.

pages 213, 376, 399, 434

*Page References in *Student Edition*
*Page References in *SkillsBook*

⭐ (TEKS) 6.23 Research/Gathering Sources

Students determine, locate, and explore the full range of relevant sources addressing a research question and systematically record the information they gather. Students are expected to:

A follow the research plan to collect data from a range of print and electronic resources (e.g., reference texts, periodicals, web pages, online sources) and data from experts;	pages 213, 376, 378, 380–382, 385, 386, 400, 401, 434
B differentiate between primary and secondary sources;	pages 376, 378, 379, 390, 402, 434
C record data, utilizing available technology (e.g., word processors) in order to see the relationships between ideas, and convert graphic/visual data (e.g., charts, diagrams, timelines) into written notes;	pages 376, 403, 404, 434
D identify the source of notes (e.g., author, title, page number) and record bibliographic information concerning those sources according to a standard format; and	pages 213, 376, 389, 403, 404, 406, 415, 416, 434
E differentiate between paraphrasing and plagiarism and identify the importance of citing valid and reliable sources; (1) differentiate between paraphrasing and plagiarism; and (2) identify the importance of citing valid and reliable sources.	pages 213, 376, 387, 388, 390, 405, 412, 413, 434

⭐ (TEKS) 6.24 Research/Synthesizing Information

Students clarify research questions and evaluate and synthesize collected information. Students are expected to:

A refine the major research question, if necessary, guided by the answers to a secondary set of questions; and	pages 377, 397, 398, 407, 434
B evaluate the relevance and reliability of sources for the research.	pages 377, 390, 400, 402, 403, 434

⭐ (TEKS) 6.25 Research/Organizing and Presenting Ideas

Students organize and present their ideas and information according to the purpose of the research and their audience. Students are expected to synthesize the research into a written or an oral presentation that:

A compiles important information from multiple sources;	pages 213, 377, 392, 394, 395, 399, 409, 410, 434, 436, 439, 448
B develops a topic sentence, summarizes findings, and uses evidence to support conclusions;	pages 213, 377, 392–395, 404, 408, 409, 412–414, 420, 422, 437, 439, 448, 449, 451
C presents the findings in a consistent format; and	pages 212, 213, 377, 410, 411, 413, 427, 434, 438, 439, 451
D uses quotations to support ideas and an appropriate form of documentation to acknowledge sources (e.g., bibliography, works cited).	pages 377, 388, 393, 395, 404, 405, 411–413, 415, 416, 423, 434, 436, 448, 449, 451

*Page References in *Student Edition*
*Page References in *SkillsBook*

English Language Proficiency Standards (ELPS)

The English Language Proficiency Standards (ELPS) outline expectations for students who are learning English. The first column in the chart below lists selected ELPS. The second column shows where these ELPS are taught in *Texas Write Source*.

⭐ ELPS 2 Cross-curricular second language acquisition/listening

The ELL listens to a variety of speakers including teachers, peers, and electronic media to gain an increasing level of comprehension of newly acquired language in all content areas. ELLs may be at the beginning, intermediate, advanced, or advanced high stage of English language acquisition in listening. In order for the ELL to meet grade-level learning expectations across the foundation and enrichment curriculum, all instruction delivered in English must be linguistically accommodated (communicated, sequenced, and scaffolded) commensurate with the student's level of English language proficiency. The student is expected to:

D monitor understanding of spoken language during classroom instruction and interactions and seek clarification as needed.

pages 454, 457, 460, 467

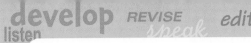
⭐ ELPS 3 Cross-curricular second language acquisition/speaking

The ELL speaks in a variety of modes for a variety of purposes with an awareness of different language registers (formal/informal) using vocabulary with increasing fluency and accuracy in language arts and all content areas. ELLs may be at the beginning, intermediate, advanced, or advanced high stage of English language acquisition in speaking. In order for the ELL to meet grade-level learning expectations across the foundation and enrichment curriculum, all instruction delivered in English must be linguistically accommodated (communicated, sequenced, and scaffolded) commensurate with the student's level of English language proficiency. The student is expected to:

A practice producing sounds of newly acquired vocabulary such as long and short vowels, silent letters, and consonant clusters to pronounce English words in a manner that is increasingly comprehensible;

pages 463, 487, 505

G express opinions, ideas, and feelings ranging from communicating single words and short phrases to participating in extended discussions on a variety of social and grade-appropriate academic topics; and

pages 6, 12, 15, 16, 18–23, 27, 32, 47, 56, 58, 70, 72, 77, 92, 94, 100, 110, 160, 168, 180, 182, 185, 188, 207, 219, 223, 234, 254, 299, 304, 326, 327, 351, 352, 355, 364, 369, 376, 382, 387, 390, 395, 397, 400, 441, 442, 452, 457, 458, 465, 467–469, 472, 473, 474, 478–481, 484–487, 490–494, 496–500, 502–505, 508, 509, 514, 528, 535, 541, 560, 561, 564, 590, 629, 771

pages 44, 91

H narrate, describe, and explain with increasing specificity and detail as more English is acquired.

pages 12, 15, 19, 27, 31, 32, 36, 47, 58, 60, 66, 74, 78–82, 92, 94–96, 103–106, 108–112, 114–116, 118, 121, 122, 140, 141, 143, 180, 188, 223, 226, 228, 255, 296, 327, 343, 351, 357, 368, 424, 431, 440–442, 449, 455, 458, 460, 461, 465, 468, 472–474, 478–480, 484–486, 490–492, 496, 497, 500, 502–504, 508, 509, 541, 590, 755

pages 34, 44, 148, 172

*Page References in *Student Edition*
*Page References in *SkillsBook*

⭐ ELPS 4 Cross-curricular second language acquisition/reading

The ELL reads a variety of texts for a variety of purposes with an increasing level of comprehension in all content areas. ELLs may be at the beginning, intermediate, advanced, or advanced high stage of English language acquisition in reading. In order for the ELL to meet grade-level learning expectations across the foundation and enrichment curriculum, all instruction delivered in English must be linguistically accommodated (communicated, sequenced, and scaffolded) commensurate with the student's level of English language proficiency. The student is expected to:

C develop basic sight vocabulary, derive meaning of environmental print, and comprehend English vocabulary and language structures used routinely in written classroom materials.

pages 12, 16, 17, 31, 34, 35, 37, 46–48, 92, 160, 162, 193, 299, 361, 374, 382, 452, 459, 462, 463–466, 468, 469, 471, 472, 475, 476, 479, 482, 487–490, 493–496, 499, 500–502, 504, 506–508, 511–514, 542, 544, 558, 590, 626, 627–628, 630,632, 634, 636, 640, 642, 644, 646, 648, 650, 654, 656, 658, 660, 662, 664, 666, 668, 670, 672, 674, 676, 678, 694, 696, 698, 700, 702, 704, 706, 708, 710, 712, 714, 716, 718, 720, 722, 724, 726, 728, 730, 732, 734, 736

⭐ ELPS 5 Cross-curricular second language acquisition/writing

The ELL writes in a variety of forms with increasing accuracy to effectively address a specific purpose and audience in all content areas. ELLs may be at the beginning, intermediate, advanced, or advanced high stage of English language acquisition in writing. In order for the ELL to meet grade-level learning expectations across foundation and enrichment curriculum, all instruction delivered in English must be linguistically accommodated (communicated, sequenced, and scaffolded) commensurate with the student's level of English language proficiency. The student is expected to:

B write using newly acquired basic vocabulary and content-based grade-level vocabulary; and

pages 3, 163, 164, 173, 176–179, 193, 436, 437, 449, 458, 463, 467, 469, 470, 479, 481–483, 487, 488, 493, 499, 501, 505, 506, 511, 513, 517, 694–727, 757, 759, 771

pages 162, 168, 190, 192

G narrate, describe, and explain with increasing specificity and detail to fulfill content area writing needs as more English is acquired.

pages 35, 41, 78–82, 95, 96, 103–106, 108–112, 114, 115, 118, 122, 140, 141, 143, 156, 157, 164, 176, 177, 178–180, 219, 224, 242–246, 299, 300, 306, 308, 311–313, 343, 368, 410, 414, 415, 436–437, 449, 454, 456, 458, 461, 473, 476, 485, 489, 491, 497, 500, 503, 509, 531, 540, 558, 755, 759, 771

pages 45, 50, 62, 98, 154, 158, 160, 164, 176, 182, 188, 195

*Page References in *Student Edition*
*Page References in *SkillsBook*

Index

This **index** will help you find specific information in the handbook. Entries in italic are words from the "Using the Right Word" section. The colored boxes contain information you will use often.

process BASICS resource
forms proofreader's guide
795
Index

brainstorm chart, 102
brainstorming, 377, 397, 608
brainstorm list, 162
brake/break, 700.3
bring/take, 700.4
build background, *see* background, building.
bulleted list, 61–62
business letter, 284, 285, 625, 642.3
business names, 664.2
buy/by/bye, 700.5
by/bye/buy, 700.5

C

call numbers, 383
call to action, 246, 486
camera view, 364
can/may, 700.6
canvas/canvass, 702.1
capital/capitol, 702.2

capitalization, 511–512, 662–671
abbreviations, 670.1
acronyms, 194
checklists, 44
days of the week, 664.3
editing for, 74
first words, 194, 668.1
historical events, 664.5
holidays, 664.3
initials, 194, 662.2
letters (alphabet), 670.3
months, 664.3
names, 261, 662.2–662.4, 664.2, 666.1, 666.2, 670.2
nationalities/races/languages/religions, 664.3
proper adjectives/nouns, 662.1, 738.2, 766.2
seasons, 664.3

subjects in school, 664.1
titles, 668.2, 668.3

captions, 279
cartoons, 278, 279
categories, 38
cause-effect organizer, 596
cause-effect relationship, 611
cell/sell, 702.3
cent/sent/scent, 702.4
characterization, 363
characters, 354–355, 363, 498
character sketch, 602
charts, 172, 376, 394, 437, 448

checklists,
editing for conventions, 22, 44, 128, 196, 262, 330, 432
expository writing, 196
multimedia presentation, 447, 451
narrative writing, 144
paragraph, 589
persuasive writing, 256, 262
in portfolio, 67
practicing speeches, 441
research writing, 426, 432, 434, 441, 447, 451
responding to texts, 324
revising, 122, 190, 256, 324, 426
videos, 451

chord/cord, 702.5
chose/choose, 702.6
chronological order, 14, 38, 104, 116–117, 476, 582, 599, 620, 770.1
circle graphs, 622
cite/site/sight, 720.4
citing sources, *see* sources, citing.
clarification, 457, 621

classification essay, 205–210
class minutes, 152, 153
classroom journals, 146–147
classroom skills, 454–458
clauses, 734
dependent, 544, 565, 734.3
independent, 544, 563–564, 640.1, 734.2
punctuation of, 632, 638.1, 640.1
restrictive/nonrestrictive, 632.1
closing of a letter, 284, 286, 288
closing sentences, 608
descriptive writing, 72, 575
expository writing, 162, 176, 184, 576
MODELS, 72, 94, 162, 228, 298, 346, 572, 574–576, 577, 582, 583, 584, 585
narrative writing, 94, 96, 107, 574
organization methods and, 582–585
paragraphs, 572–573
persuasive writing, 242, 244, 245, 577
responding to texts, 298, 310
cluster, 13, 85, 95, 170, 224, 299, 347, 367, 396, 592
coarse/course, 702.7

coherence, focus and (writing trait), *see* focus and coherence.

collective nouns, 516, 738.5
colons, 642–643
combining sentences, 42–43, 126, 194, 559, 560–562, 564, 601
commands, 566
commas, 630–639
in addresses, 630.3
appositives, 568, 634.1

D

process BASICS resource
forms proofreader's guide **803**
Index

process BASICS resource
forms proofreader's guide 813
Index